THE CITY

ROSE HUM LEE

Department of Sociology, Roosevelt University

THE CITY

URBANISM AND URBANIZATION

IN MAJOR WORLD REGIONS

J. B. LIPPINCOTT COMPANY

Chicago   *Philadelphia*   *New York*

TO

GLENN

Preface

THIS TEXTBOOK stresses the dominant role cities have played in initiating and perpetuating changes in behavior patterns and institutional organizations. It points out the methods devised for coping with diverse and large populations in a relatively small land area and the manner in which man's ingenuity has met the challenge of dovetailing his complex needs within an ever-changing physical and social environment.

The changes taking place in cities have long been associated with many complex factors, of which commerce and trade, technology, industrialization, and innovations are a few. Studying the impact of these factors upon society has necessarily made us focus our attention on the growth and development of Western cities. We have failed to take into account the non-industrial factors promoting and furthering urban growth. This textbook tries to overcome this deficiency by tracing the growth and development of Western and non-Western cities and by identifying specific kinds of centers with the social organizations of society.

This approach enables us to see how cities differ in their physical layout, population composition, social and occupational structures, state of industrial development, and so on. At the same time, it gives us some basis for selecting out the elements common to all cities: heterogeneity of population, limited land area and high density of population, a complex system of social differentiation, the pervasiveness of fads and fashions, the emergence of new values and social types, and the manifestations of various social problems.

The organization of the book provides a logical scheme for studying the changes affecting social life as cities grew and multiplied.

Parts One and Two set forth the natural growth of cities in selected world regions and compares the urban growth between and within these regions. Cities may be of a highly industrialized type or they may exhibit pre-Industrial Revolution characteristics.

The third Part deals with the physical and population structures. Most urban texts stress the diversity of population but fail to point out the significant effect of "steel and concrete" on population distribution, social interaction, and individual behavior patterns. The formation of ghettos according to religion, language, territorial ties, and culture has been previously ignored.

Part Four stresses the distinction between the organization forms of institutions, on the one hand, and their role in patterning formal social relations, on the other. The role of associations in integrating society is accorded its proper place.

v

The major changes in individual and group behavior patterns as well as the emergence of social types according to given localities and class membership are found in Part Five. Up to the present time, there has been scant attention paid to the role of mass media in formulating and disseminating mass and traditional culture patterns.

While no attempt is made to "play down" urban problems, only the most important ones are included in Part Six. The emphasis in this volume is on the multi-dimensional aspects of social problems.

The study of the city brings with it certain prerequisites: predicting the foreseeable changes and their impact on social life and behavior patterns, and setting forth the objectives many urbanites believe desirable to cope with a constantly changing physical and social environment. Thus, the last part of the book summarizes the hope for controls and embryonic programs without attempting to place them in ordinal importance.

Words are inadequate in expressing the author's thanks and appreciation to the many people who believed in and helped make this book a reality but they know her deep obligation and gratefulness. Any mistakes are, of course, her own.

The author is greatly indebted to the late Dr. Frederick Juchhoff for his unfailing encouragement and help, even during his illness, and for the many ideas which found their way into the pages. His wide range of knowledge in the social sciences, law, medicine, accounting, education, and history was unsurpassed.

To the late Professor Louis Wirth she expresses deep appreciation for his guidance and advice in formulating the contents of several chapters.

The author is particularly grateful to Professor R. A. Schermerhorn of Cleveland College, Professor Richard E. Dewey of the University of Illinois, and Professor Mozell C. Hill of Atlanta University for their continued interest and constructive criticisms of the manuscript.

To her colleagues of the Sociology Department of Roosevelt University she is indebted for their encouragement and for materials of the cities they visited and studied.

She gives special acknowledgment and gratitude to Eva Curless for the many hours she spent poring over the manuscript, and to Yuan Liang for his translation of primary sources of Asian and other materials. Yvonne Welling Priest, Dora Seu, and Walter Kaufman, too, have been equally helpful with the many technical details.

The members of her family have her everlasting appreciation and gratitude for their patience, understanding, and encouragement.

R. H. LEE

Roosevelt University
Chicago, Illinois

Contents

Preface . . . . **v**

Part One   An Orientation

1 INTRODUCTION 3
2 THE CITY IN TIME AND SPACE 7

Part Two   The Growth of Cities in Major World Regions

3 WESTERN EUROPEAN CITIES 20
4 NORTHERN ASIAN CITIES 41
5 THE CITIES OF SOUTH ASIA AND OCEANIA 93
6 AFRICAN CITIES 133
7 THE CITIES OF THE UNITED STATES 177

Part Three   The Physical and Population Structure

8   URBAN POPULATION COMPOSITION 205
9   ECOLOGICAL ORGANIZATION 231
10 THE WORLD OF ARTIFACTS 263
11 URBAN GHETTOS 287

Part Four   Urban Social Institutions

12 ECONOMIC ORGANIZATION 305
13 POLITICAL ORGANIZATION 318
14 RELIGIOUS ORGANIZATION 341
15 THE URBAN FAMILY 364
16 VOLUNTARY ASSOCIATIONS 380

Part Five   Urban Ways of Life

17 URBAN STRATIFICATION 397
18 MEDIA OF COMMUNICATION 413
19 LEISURE-TIME ACTIVITIES 435
20 URBAN PERSONALITY AND SOCIAL TYPES 453

Part Six   Urban Social Problems

21   Interstitial or Blighted Areas 473

22   Housing Problems 488

23   Personal and Social Disorganization 503

Part Seven   Urban Planning and Social Trends

24   Planning and Model Communities 523

25   Future Trends and Objectives 540

Index 551

Part One

An Orientation

Chapter One

Introduction

WHENEVER WE speak of cities we associate their existence with a way of life which began with the development of modern civilization and the subsequent man-made changes in his physical and social environment. The growth of cities as we know them is closely related to industrialism, commerce and trade, the technological revolution, mass transportation and communication, and widespread population movements. These factors have extended urbanization and industrialization, and in turn produced changes in the city's physical, ecological, and social structures. We can recognize urbanites—whether they live in Kampala, Uganda, Unobad, Pakistan, Belle Horizonte, Brazil, or Amarillo, Texas—by their general life organization and behavior patterns. The phenomena of urbanism and urbanization are world-wide, although cities differ according to their cultural settings in the same manner as urbanites do.

Since cities made their first appearance in the Near East some five millennia ago, there have been two main streams of urban development. One, familiar to us, moved westward and gradually urbanized much of the Western world. The other, encompassing Asia and Africa, has received scant attention, and the existence of cities there is directly attributed to the impact of Westernization and industrialization. Thus, urbanism and urbanization are seldom studied as world-wide phenomena, much less with a cross-cultural evolutionary approach, since the general impression is that few cities existed in the non-Western world until the era of European colonialism.

Most cities, or parts thereof, built by Europeans throughout the world, date far back into history, but many non-Western ones antedate even some of the European and most of the cities of the American continent. In 1950 the Asian continent had more cities of over a million population than had Europe. The primary reason for the usual omission of non-Western cities in the study of urbanism and urbanization is that they do not exhibit one of the chief characteristics associated with Western urbanization: industrialism. But different as these cities are because they have retained some of the characteristics of the pre-Industrial Revolution era, they are nevertheless cities.

Insofar as we are able to trace the growth of Western cities from past to present, cities evolved slowly, beginning with the transformation of a group of villages into religious, tribal, and administrative centers. The rise of city-states followed, and defense and commercial cities gained importance. After the Industrial Revolution, industrial cities grew in large numbers. The development of cities in the other half of the globe followed the same early course as Western centers, but they remained primarily administrative capitals, religious centers, or commercial cities. Industrial cities are few and far between. Moreover, the city-state as an urban form does not appear to have existed.

Therefore, in studying non-Western societies, the customary indexes used to measure the urbanism and urbanization of Western societies are frequently inapplicable and, where applied, have not given satisfactory results. The non-industrial factors contributing to urban growth and development have been neglected, and the role that Western urbanized societies have played in furthering them is frequently overlooked.

It is fairly obvious that no single frame of reference can be used in conceptualizing either the component and significant changes resulting from urbanization and urbanism or the type of social organization a given society has and its relationship to urban growth. A frame of reference applicable to African cities may be unsuited for the Far East, and what is valid there may not be so for the Western societies. Where we find similarities between cities which are geographically and culturally different, we may gain some knowledge of the factors that contribute to urban growth. On the other hand, these factors may be the result of culture contacts, serving as links between cities of one region and cities of the next.

In studying cities, we are frequently handicapped by the varying terms used to define them. The size of population is an official index generally in use. But size of population must be considered with two other variables: land area and density of population. By relating the ratio between absolute population and absolute land area to the degree of density exhibited in and around the city's confines, other characteristics are found, such as heterogeneity of population, division of labor, and diversified behavior patterns.

While the number of cities and the percentage of urban population are some of the valid indexes of urbanism and urbanization, they frequently do not encompass the multi-dimensional aspects of the city as a social entity. Cities not only vary in demographic characteristics, but exhibit a diversity of racial and social classes, as well as occupational, religious, educational, and other divisions. Older cities are located on strategic sites, determined by geographical features, while cities built after the Industrial Revolution are functionally related to the sources of raw materials, distributing facilities, efficient transportation and communication, capital, and the required kind of labor force.

It is easier to conceptualize in studying cities if one relates the cities to the type of social structure a given society has—whether folk, feudal, semi-feudal, or secular—and to the nature of the social organization—kinship, tribal, elite ruling class, caste, or complex industrialism. Many social scientists have contributed to our knowledge of the particular distinguishing attributes one type of society retains, and what has been altered or lost in the process of transformation. Toennies' *Gemeinschaft-Gesellschaft*, Durkheim's *mechanical-organic solidarity*, Toynbee's *primitive culture-civilization*, and Redfield's *folk-secular* schemes are descriptive concepts pointing to the progressive transformation of human society from the simple, preliterate sacred-folk to the complex, secular, urban-industrial type. In our typology, we shall use the terms *rural-folk, feudal, semi-feudal*, and *urban-industrial*.

As societies progressed from the rural-folk stage, each type of society created its special urban form. By establishing the interrelationships of the social structure and social organization to the development and growth of cities, we can compare satisfactorily the urban growth of one region of the world with that of the next as well as the cities within one region. The factors contributing to the growth of cities in areas where industry is relatively light may become known. These areas may have large and numerous cities, but they have retained many of the folk-prescribed-sacred and feudal characteristics.

By selecting several major world regions, illustrating the three major types of social structures and social organization—the rural-folk (tribal); feudal (elite ruling class or nobility); and urban-industrial—as well as their variations, we may see how the processes of transformation operate. At the same time, we can see the changes resulting from the impact of Westernization on rural-folk and feudal societies.

Cities do not appear in small, isolated, fishing, nomadic, or agricultural societies. They arise when several large villages in an area combine into a larger social unit, provided there is an agricultural surplus to support a non-agricultural population. The sacred-orientation of such a society is symbolized by the creation of tribal and religious centers, which often function as administrative capitals which control their population and institutional organizations as well as those of the surrounding countryside. These cities have a simple division of labor, and there is no elaborate social stratification system. Kinship ties and traditional norms unify the various subgroups within the society. Africa today is the region of the world which has perhaps the greatest retention of tribal affiliations. However, Africa is becoming urbanized and Westernized at a rapid rate. The course of urban development there enables us to see the social effects of rapid urbanization, industrialization, and detribalization.

The countries of the Far East have primarily feudal or semi-feudal social structures, and the social system is rigid and more elaborately stratified than is the African tribal system. A more complex division of labor and a greater development of commerce and trade are found along with an agricultural economy. Cities are the habitats of the small ruling class, composed of the nobility, officials, landlords, militarists, priests, scholars and their retinues, and functionaries, all of whom set the cultural standards for the masses. However, this elite group frequently is most resistant to Western influence. Towns and cities are the focal points of concentration of agricultural surpluses, goods, and services. Transportation and communication systems, though slow and often inefficient, link towns and cities together. After Westernization made its impact on these countries, new social classes developed which exhibited Western values and behavior patterns. The new social classes have driven a wedge between the upper class and the masses. They are composed of persons who could not effect social and occupational mobility through the traditional social system. To this extent, the rural and urban differentiations are not only clearly distinct among countrysides, towns, and cities, but between the old and new urbanites.

With the ascendancy of the urban-industrial society, great changes have occurred. These changes are more clearly evident in a new society such as that of the United States than they are in Europe, where modern urban communities grew out of a feudal social structure, and where mass culture—so frequently associated with a rapidly changing urban society, knit together by mass media—is less pronounced. The continuous development of cities over a longer span of time tends to produce fewer incidents of social and personal disorganization.

If we study urbanism and urbanization by comparing Western and non-Western aspects of various cultures, we may gain a clearer perspective of what has transpired and is transpiring in other societies. An analysis of urbanism in different world areas is more likely to show which are the common elements of city life, for many of these changes of urbanization —while still underway in Western societies—are very advanced, and we do not always have a clear conception of the various factors in operation.

The City in Time and Space

Tㅐㅌ sᴏᴄɪᴀʟ complexity of the city has brought about a unique way of life, characterized by the term urbanism. This way of life is constantly being modified by further alterations in the urban environment. Urbanization, defined as the extension of urban patterns to new areas and populations, is one of the major contemporary social changes. The most pronounced changes in urban living and environment followed the Industrial Revolution. In Western societies, urbanization annd industrialization are generally associated with each other.

In order to understand the complex nature of the city, it is necessary to distinguish among several major aspects of urban existence: the physical and population structure, the major social institutions, the behavior pattern of urbanites, the problems following urban growth and expansion, and the role of social planning in gaining still greater control of the environment. The nature of all of these attributes is largely determined by the size, heterogeneity, and density of the population.

Cities are basically population aggregates which are large, heterogeneous, and densely settled within a limited land area.[1] The phenomenon of high density and low net land area per urbanite influences the nature of the interaction between individuals and groups. Typical urbanites may live in physical proximity, but they have such diverse interests, occupations, socio-economic backgrounds, and ethnic or racial origins that social distance and impersonality are major characteristics of urban life. These social characteristics, in turn, impinge upon the values, norms, and behavior patterns of the population and the social organization of the economic, political and social systems.

Large aggregates of people give rise to varied pursuits which interest and attract people from various geographical locations. This leads to greater opportunities for anonymity, mobility, and gives a utilitarian

[1] Louis Wirth, "Urbanism as a Way of Life," *American Journal of Sociology,* 44 (July, 1938), 1–25.

purpose to human associations. Persons are more often cultivated for specific gains and objectives rather than on an intimate face-to-face basis.

Diversity gives rise to segregation as well as concentration, and the city's ecological and social order is reflected in the various natural areas, or local communities, which exhibit the socio-economic and other characteristics of their inhabitants. As one travels from one end of the city to the other, these areas stand out in sharp contrast, with well-kept residential neighborhoods next to the slum or an area of middle-income rowhouses with small lawn-patches surrounded by towering, glass-fronted, efficiency apartments.

There is a need for each other's goods and services, but this dynamic equilibrium of the city is constantly undergoing change as the result of the mobility and relocation of population and institutional organizations. The internal spatial patterns of cities are likewise altered, while the inhabitants of these natural areas are continually realigning their social relations both within and without the area.

The unique character of urban populations has altered the nature of and in turn has been affected by the physical structure and equipment of cities. Perhaps the most tangible evidence that urbanization has altered the physical environment is the manner in which modern technology has created distinct working, living, and recreation space within a limited total land area. Moreover, the city's relationship to its hinterland and distant lands and cities, is determined by the amount and kind of technological equipment devised and installed for facilitating the exchange of goods and services.

Since the Industrial Revolution the growth and increase of metropolitan cities and their outlying fringe areas has modified the configuration of cities, but the center of dominance remains in the heart of the metropolis. The extension of urban dominance proceeds along well channelized routes of transportation and communication integrating the central city and the adjacent territories as a socio-economic unit which transcends political boundaries and local loyalties and sentiments.

In ancient cities of the Western World the temple was the center of dominance until the heavily guarded medieval castle replaced it. In the Middle Ages it was the invention of gunpowder and cannon that made the city walls useless. Now, new modes of transportation and communication have rendered the political boundaries of modern cities ineffective. Modern cities are built around the market place, the downtown business district, where the major financial, corporate, and political institutional organizations are centralized.

One of the consequences of large-scale economic enterprises is the establishment of far-flung branch offices and the removal of men from the main centers of administrative control. The other is the specialization of labor. Industrial organizations select personnel on the basis of ability to conform to directives and routines. Speed, precision, and output often take precedence over human relations and intergroup contacts, thus heightening feelings of insecurity and anxiety. In modern urban society, industry picks man; man does not pick industry. He must fit into the organization pattern or be discharged.

The typical modern urbanite depends upon a wage economy. This fact, in combination with periodic economic fluctuations and technological changes, has caused the economic system to supersede others in influencing and modifying behavior patterns and values. The economic institutions assume an important role in determining the status, roles, and life chances of occupational groups. The occupational differentiation of urbanites is one of the most crucial and yet complex institutional matrices affecting urban social stratification. As the division of labor becomes more and more specialized, and because new occupations are constantly being created, it becomes exceedingly difficult to discern definite and simple hierarchical arrangements within the general social system.

The heterogeneity of urban population is at once the cause of greater industrialization and urbanization and the result of it. The most disruptive influence of the impact of Westernization and urbanization on underdeveloped areas (now commonly defined as areas without great urbanization) is the uprooting of millions from their homelands and their removal to areas where urbanism is well advanced. This transplantation of peoples has contributed to the heterogeneity, size, and density of populations of many modern cities and has been partly responsible for greater industrialization. The heterogeneity is further reflected by the mosaic pattern of cultures found in the world's large metropolises. Modern industrial man —the Western urbanite—although a small part of the world's population, has made his power and influence felt around the globe.

At one time, the vast reservoir of labor in underdeveloped areas was frequently tapped by means of enslavement. Since the Industrial Revolution two other methods of recruitment have been adopted: indentured labor and the contracting of labor on a long or short term basis. Within the last two decades, indentured labor has been abolished, but large groups of unskilled laborers are still being recruited and brought into industrialized areas. The continuous need for cheap labor has urbanized more of the world's population than is generally known.

It is generally acknowledged that rapid urbanization and industrialization may produce a higher incidence of social and personal disorganization. Yet, our attention has been confined mainly to urbanization in the Western world. We have not probed very deeply into the effects that Westernization and industrialization have had in less urbanized areas. These effects include the weakening of traditional familial, political, and social organizations; the lowering of the birth rate (but the increase of population in industrialized areas); and the spread of disease. Were all the facts known, the social problems of Western urbanized areas may be less pronounced, since underdeveloped areas lack the means and methods to resolve such social problems. Moreover, social, economic, educational, familial, political, and other changes are occurring so rapidly that they affect every aspect of the society before new forms of social organization and social control can be adopted.

Two other factors which initiated population mobility and social change were the global wars and the accompanying acceleration of industrialization. After each war, more and more of the world's people in underdeveloped areas have become urbanized. It would not be untoward to say that modern wars are the results as well as causes of modern urbanization, as to their origin, planning, and execution. It is ironical that many people of underdeveloped countries should have their first encounter with Westernization and urbanization through firearms and other weapons of destruction. It is equally ironical that among all the artifacts produced by modern technology, these countries frequently select not those which promote greater industrialization, but those which protect them from, or are useful in, promoting modern warfare.

When Western societies initiate contacts with others, it is primarily through the cities, the points of cultural contacts. To this extent a "cake" of urban customs, values, and behavior patterns has developed, transcending national boundaries and obscuring racial, religious, and ethnic lines. The "feelings of belongingness" and "consciousness of kind" experienced by modern man are not always associated with the members of his immediate local community, but with members of urban communities elsewhere.

Moreover, communication between urbanites of advanced and less advanced technological societies is accomplished through sharing of common understandings and attainment of common objectives. For example: when planning measures are undertaken to raise the standard of living of underdeveloped areas, Western methods and implements are frequently employed by common consent. In regard to plans and their execution, there is often more understanding between Western and non-Western urbanites than there is between the rural and urban populations of the country concerned.

The role of mass media in disseminating ideas, attitudes, ideologies, values, and other traits has helped develop a uniform set of behavior patterns not only within urbanized countries, but in the cities of less developed areas as well. The growth of a mass culture in our society and modification of the traditional culture are generally recognized, but the extent of these phenomena is often overlooked. Where new social classes are created in less urbanized countries, their behavior patterns may actually be more exacting than those of Western urbanites, who have a longer history of urban settlement. When these classes are enlarged, urbanism and urbanization make greater headway. Traditional culture is transmitted through the social, familial, political, and other age-old organizations, while the mass media induce collective behavior patterns.

In our society, mass culture has permeated the behavior patterns of both the urban and rural populations to the point where it is often difficult to distinguish between these two ways of life. The reciprocality between mass media and economic institutions constitutes another source of impact on urban behavior, influencing the consumption habits, styles, home decorations, and merchandising. The mental and emotional patterns of individuals are constantly being exposed to their stimuli. However, a portion of the lower socio-economic group, whose participation in the more traditional institutional organizations and associations are restricted by monetary and status considerations, places more reliance upon the direction and instruction of mass media than does the upper socio-economic strata. In non-Western societies mass media are frequently both the source and the result of new behavior patterns.

Personal behavior patterns, as distinguished from mass behavior patterns, have likewise felt the impact of urbanization. The tyranny of the clock has caused urbanites to rush from one place to another despite the greater amount of leisure—an advantage supposedly associated with urban living and the mechanization of industry. Persons, regardless of frequency of contact, seldom see each other in all social situations. They know only segments of each other's personalities. Limited observance of the other as he performs his role in occupational and social situations is a determining factor in intra- and intergroup relations.[1] A high value is placed on fleeting impressions and mannerisms.

Cities tend to attract persons whose behavior patterns may be different from those of their immediate associates. At the same time persons whose life organizations differ from those of the prevailing members of the society, go to cities to find others who accept them as social equals. The roles social deviants play frequently have value to a segment of the society, if not to the whole, through the performance of specific activities. Thus, the social pariahs, professional gamblers, criminals, political agitators and bosses, promoters, prostitutes, and bohemians find their habitats in cities. Conversely, aspiring artists, actors, writers, musicians, poets, and

[1] *Ibid.*

critics must go to cities to find success. Cities are organized around economic organizations as well as several social systems. The business tycoons, debutantes, philanthropists, and reformers are other social types, and some of them occupy the highest prestige positions.

Although cities are frequently identified with new behavior patterns and with technical innovations, survivals of rural practices and beliefs are not uncommon and provide the bases for many of the contemporary social problems and personal conflicts. Since the city draws upon rural areas for its population replacement, and many immigrants from foreign lands have rural backgrounds, the schemes of city life exhibit many traditional patterns. The more rapidly people adapt to the urban milieu, the less they rely upon these traditions, and the more readily they incorporate urban behavior patterns. While undergoing the assimiliation process, which may not be completed in one generation but continue into the second and third, feelings of conflict are expressed by many urbanites. Indirectly, the assimilation process not only produces more marginal people—the cultural hybrids—but often contributes to the rising rate of personal disorganization.

Institutional organizations also may retain rural characteristics that are unsuited to a rapidly changing society. The religious organizations of modern society, together with their rituals, ceremonies, and beliefs, are the best illustrations. The secularization of modern urban society has caused many changes in the traditional forms of religious beliefs, practices, and functions, thus weakening their effectiveness as methods of social control. On the other hand, religious affiliations and the adherence to them assume a utilitarian character, as the support of the institutions that symbolize stability and morality brings status and praise.

It is interesting to note that the transplanting to underdeveloped areas of Western religious institutions, often in their traditional forms and with their traditional content, helps initiate the process of urbanization. This process often begins with academic education in addition to religious teaching and plays an important role in effecting the social and occupational mobility of the masses who have had few opportunities to rise within the traditional social system. Missionaries and educators (and medical personnel) frequently are the innovators of Western ways of life in the remotest regions of the world. They convert rural dwellers into urbanites by "sending them out of the darkness." These urban converts become the perpetuators of urbanism and urbanization when a new social structure is created. They re-create Western institutional organizations that transmit stable culture, but if an industrial organization or business enterprise is withdrawn or collapses, it may not be reorganized. The process of urbanism and urbanization finds continuance through these indigenous leaders who, when permitted, in time replace the elite ruling class. To bolster the new social structure they draw others into the influence of Westernization and urbanization. This partially explains how urban behavior patterns and organizations continue and multiply, and how a type of superculture draws non-Western groups into the orbit of Westernization.

No consideration of the city in time and space can omit the political institutions. The size, heterogeneity, and density of population and the weakening of traditional mores render informal means of social control ineffective. Diverse behavior patterns are controlled by formal methods, and the city's political organization—the symbol of power and enforce-ment—grows as large and complex as the population coming under its jurisdiction. Political patterns are often resistant to social change. Despite the criticisms that political institutions are rural survivals in form and practice, they attempt to provide the protective and welfare services needed by the citizenry. The more interconnections there are among insti-tutional organizations, particularly the political machine, the greater their power and social control. Historically, it is the emergence and develop-ment of municipal government that weaken the tenacity of familial, tribal, or religious forms of social organization and mark the trans-ference of local loyalties to the promotion of common interests. In societies where the political organization is closely interwoven with that of the economic in promoting modern industrialization, the process of ur-banization is frequently accelerated.

The growth of cities and the increase of industrialization have produced a series of interrelated conditions that contribute to the development of social and personal disorganization, and consequently, of social problems. Social problems may be related to the rapid areal expansion of the city, changing land use and land patterns, or the inadequacy of the subsocial base in coping with a large number of persons crowded into a small land area. On the other hand, the composition of urban population is often deficient in growth trends or sex ratio, which, in turn, causes problems to develop. The heterogeneity of population gives rise to divergent be-havior patterns and the changing environment alters existing values, thus creating conflicts and tensions between the supporters and the deviants.

Social disorganization occurs more frequently because one or more of the social systems functions badly, while the breakdown of consensus and social controls contributes to the increase of personal disorganization. The outward manifestations of these disruptive influences on individuals and groups are sufficiently widespread for them to be categorized and recognized as social problems confronting the society. Concerted efforts are made to gain greater control of the environment. Remedial measures are devised to re-establish the social system or correct existing maladjustments. These steps may, in turn, reduce personal tensions and conflicts and the incidents of personal disorganization.

The growth of cities and the increase of industrialization have produced a series of social characteristics that distinguish one type of city from another. Cities differ according to economic activities, size of labor force, the number of persons employed by local industries, and by others located outside of the city's confines (especially cities close to metropolises), income level of inhabitants, composition of population, and the type of services performed for its residents. Cities may be independent and not satellites or suburbs within a metropolitan district, or they may be central cities connected with a series of smaller cities.

One way to differentiate types of cities is by noting the dominant functions of their industries and relating these to the numbers employed by various industrial organizations.[1] For instance, cities may be classified as primary extraction, resort, cultural, political, historical, manufacturing, commercial, religious, residential, or diversified. The diversification of functions is greatest for large cities, but the predominance of one major function can influence the social structure and social organization of the city as well as the activities and social relations of its inhabitants.

Cities have varying spatial patterns, influenced by topographical features, size of land area, location, and age. Since cities are products of growth and expansion, their shapes vary as to population, institutional structures, and residential increase or decrease. Furthermore, the social and cultural emphasis of the society imparts a distinct tone to the general style of architecture, street layout, physical equipment, and institutional organizations. In this respect, cities may be said to have "distinct personalities," the physical, social, and cultural characteristics of which set them apart from each other.

Insofar as two separate classificatory schemes related to functions can be formulated, cities of highly industrialized areas reflect the diversification and specialization of industrialism; and in contrast, cities of non-industrialized areas would appear rudimentary and simple, classified under commerce, administrative capitals, centers of worship, and perhaps, primary extraction and light manufacturing.

The study of cities in major world regions is timely, since the beginning of a new era of urbanism and urbanization is at hand. Since World War II, underdeveloped areas have shown a growing tendency to accept and adopt Western patterns of urbanism and urbanization. Our industrial methods are being emulated on a wider scale. It is not within the prov-

---

[1] G. M. Kneedler, "Functional Types of Cities," *Public Management,* 27 (July, 1945), 197–203.

ince of sociology to indicate what aspects should be diffused, what omitted, and what ignored; but a general understanding of the complexity of cities and the nature, extent, and impact of former eras of Westernization and urbanization is essential for the study of societies and human nature and conduct.

Finally, a comparative study of highly industrialized cities and those retaining the characteristics of cities of the pre-Industrial Revolution eras contributes to our understanding of the historical role which cities played in the development of civilization. The phenomena of urbanism and urbanization and their modification of society and human behavior are seen in their totality.

Part Two

The Growth of Cities in Major World Regions

PROLOGUE *Cities, found in varying numbers throughout the world, are not recent phenomena. Ancient Near Eastern and Egyptian civilizations created this form of social organization some five millennia ago. Some cities arose where topographical features interrupted the continuous flow of population and goods. Others became administrative centers controlling wide hinterlands ruled by priestly kings and leaders of tribal kingdoms. Many had already developed into commerce and trade cities before the Industrial Revolution. From the beginning of the modern period to the present, urban growth has become synonymous with industrialization and westernization, for cities are the workshops of industrialized Western societies. But cities of other societies did not exhibit as profound a transformation in social organization, behavior patterns, and social relations until the turn of this century.*

In studying the natural history of cities, we come to understand the evolutionary processes connected with urban growth and development. From a sociological point of view, urbanism and urbanization result from, and are concomitant with, various aspects of social change. The major factors associated with the processes of urbanization have not only in-fluenced the increase of cities of the Western Hemisphere, but have also contributed to the spread of urbanism outside of these regions. The degree to which urbanism and urbanization have changed non-Western societies depends upon such factors as which country controls them politically and economically, whether the local population desires to steer its own course of urban development in the future, and the extent of Western impact on social life and behavior patterns.

In the chapters that follow several evolutionary aspects are emphasized. Western European cities show the genesis and development of several major types of cities as they coincide with the economic, social, and cul-tural development of the continent. On the other hand, Asian and African cities show significant differences in the course of their development, and the non-industrial factors contributing to the growth of these cities must be taken into account. Depending upon the society selected for analysis, social phenomena can be found, such as divergent patterns of internal city layout, population composition, division of labor, and others. These dif-ferences are related to the type of social structure a given society possesses and the extent of the impact of Western urbanism. To a high degree, the urban development of Asia and Africa can be divided into two main periods: pre-Western and post-Western.

American urbanism, in contrast, developed in a very brief span of time, but many American cities were able to develop from a pre-industrial era and without predetermined patterns, thus offering some of the best exam-ples of modern industrial urbanism. The only other society which has changed from an agrarian to an industrial social order in a comparable period of time is Japan. Japan, however, had major pre-existing urban centers, which affected later development. Whereas American cities de-

veloped largely without planning, Japanese cities reflect the revolutionary changes under Western influence made by the Meiji emperors.

We can see from the foregoing that no single set of criteria can be regarded as universally applicable in our study of urban growth, although certain indexes, such as size and composition of urban population, state of industrialization, occupational and social structure, and major social institutions may be profitably utilized when comparing one region of the world to another. When these indexes are used, we must bear in mind that some of the available sources given for non-Western societies are not as reliable and accurate as those of Western countries.

Western European Cities

T HERE IS parallel historical and sociological significance in the growth and development of major types of cities as they spread from the Near East throughout Europe. As a part of the general process of social evolution, cities have fulfilled specific functions in the era with which they are identified. Ancient cities were primarily tribal capitals or centers of religious worship and administrative control. City-states represented a more advanced form of social organization and a change in man's familial and tribal relationships. Feudal cities of the Middle Ages were built for defense, and some were later transformed into centers for commerce and trade. The Industrial Revolution initiated the rise of industrial cities and completed the transformation of agrarian societies into a world-wide industrial-urban civilization.

With each type of city have come changes in social organization, social structure, occupational hierarchy, and social behavior, as well as the modification of physical urban features. The composition of urban population has grown increasingly heterogeneous, and social relations have become more diversified, thus introducing new problems of social adjustment.

A brief treatment of each type of city, together with the economic, social, and cultural processes which influenced its formation and survival, will give us a basis for comparing the urban growth and development of other societies. Similarities and differences will become meaningful as the contents of the remaining chapters of this section are read.

Ancient Cities

Two of the earliest cities of the world were Memphis and Thebes, both located in the valley of the Nile River.[1] As one of the most remarkable rivers, geographically and historically, the Nile has from time immemorial

[1] *Encyclopedia of the Social Sciences,* "The City," 2, 474–482.

Joint expedition of University of Pennsylvania and Oriental Institute, University of Chicago

Nippur, Iraq. Scribal quarter, level 5, showing houses where many tablets dating back to the 20th century, B.C. were found. Note depth of excavation; cities were superimposed one upon the other on this site.

served as the principal means of communication and cultural contact among the Near East, North Africa, Asia, and the European countries rimming the Mediterranean Sea.[1]

Ancient centers of civilization arose in fertile river valleys, where agricultural production reached a stage of development that insured a surplus of food. This led to the growth of a non-agricultural group of people who could be freed from toiling in the fields in order to devote time to devising a language and system of writing, perfecting art objects, and making consumers' goods.

Memphis and Thebes existed about five thousand years ago. As ancient shrine cities they were among the first urban centers to develop. This happened when a group of surrounding villages organized and established control over a hinterland. From this hinterland came an agricultural surplus, while reciprocal goods and services of the cities found outlets in all the various villages. In time other urban formations grew and spread

[1] C. Issawi, *Egypt: An Economic and Social Analysis* (London: Oxford University Press, 1947), 1–3.

throughout the Nile and Tigris-Euphrates valleys. The names of other ancient cities—Nippur, Ur, Ninevah, Babylon, and Sumer—bring to mind the decline and pillage of famous cities of the Mesopotamian Empire.[1]

What further distinguished these cities from their surrounding areas was that their leaders learned to exercise control over man, goods, services, and institutional organizations. They were able to teach or discipline others to cooperate in larger units and forsake the rural environment. Through concerted efforts they increased the productive powers of those who served them.

Cities became centers of trade, commerce, wealth, power, and education. As a higher degree of urban concentration of population resulted, more persons were available for the various occupations found within the city, such as erecting huge and splendid structures, building roads, and other construction. Others promoted intellectual pursuits or business enterprises. When necessary, slaves were imported to perform the more tedious and monotonous tasks.

The privileged classes, with more leisure, devoted increasing attention to satisfying their new economic and social wants. They devised means of collecting taxes from the countryside and were instrumental in creating new occupations and industries to supply the goods and services needed by the agricultural portion of the population. The urban setting provided opportunity for exchange of ideas and furnished the incentive for transforming the ideas into actualities. Acquisition and retention of wealth were easier and safer. This ease and safety induced men to seek means of accumulating still more. The riches they acquired were bequeathed to their descendants, so that in time an hereditary elite was established. It became right and proper that persons with wealth and influence should have more rights and privileges.

Because waterways were the main arteries of transportation, earlier cities were located either at the heads of rivers or near to their banks or tributaries. Before the invention of modern water distribution plants and sewerage systems, urban populations congregated where water was plentiful. Moreover, waterways were vital in transporting the agricultural surplus to cities and goods produced in them were shipped to the surrounding villages. The seat of administrative control had to be near the main thoroughfare of trade and communication. The city attracted the adventurous, the ambitious, the industrious, and the social deviate. As more people settled in cities, services were created to meet their needs. The result was a higher division of labor.

[1] Lydia Braidwood, *Diggings Beyond the Tigris* (New York: Schuman, Inc., 1953), describes the Nippur excavations. See especially Chs. 7 and 9.

Many ancient cities served as tribal capitals.[1] Located around the Mediterranean, they were also the marketing centers for the Mediterranean countries before and after the Roman conquest of Egypt. In time, smaller satellite cities arose, each clustered around a major city, thus aiding the larger center in its domination of surrounding territories. Cities formed alliances so that the position of each would be reinforced by the other. Roads were extended to link cities by a transportation network. Along these arteries of communication and transportation arose more cities, so that a series of interrelated and interdependent municipalities developed. The major city, the nucleus of this development, was the seat of political power.

Cities lost their identity or declined in importance when tribes were conquered or when they fused with others. Babylon, for example, was destroyed by the Assyrians about 700 B.C. Conquerors built new cities that served as forts and military posts after sacking and pillaging of the old cities. This practice was adopted by the Phoenicians, who for several centuries were unrivaled in their maritime power. They dominated the entire North African seacoast and controlled regions as far as the present shores of England. Tyre and Sidon, seaports of Phoenicia, were among the earliest great commercial centers. Like Carthage, they were built for the purpose of conducting extensive commerce among their own trading posts and colonies situated along the north and south shores of the Mediterranean. Carthage, exceeding both Tyre and Sidon in importance, attested to the Phoenicians' ingenuity as traders and exchangers. At her zenith, Carthage was said to have had almost a million persons living within or near her boundaries.[2] In 146 B.C. she was completely destroyed, but was restored a hundred years later. She regained importance during the second and third centuries of the Christian era at a time when another type of urban development—the city-state—emerged.

City-States

One important consequence of the city-states was their initiation of new forms of municipal government.[3] The Greeks developed a system of independent, self-governed cities, each the center of vigorous political life. Miletus, Athens, Corinth, Sparta, Syracuse, Chalcis, Samos, Aegina, and

[1] A. H. M. Jones, *The Cities of the Eastern Roman Provinces* (Oxford: Clarendon Press, 1937). A detailed description of early cities.

[2] H. G. Wells, *The Outline of History* (New York: Garden City Publishing Co., 1930), 157–158, 162–164.

[3] W. B. Munro, *Municipal Government and Administration* (New York: The Macmillan Co., 1923), Ch. 1.

Eretria were among the better-known. It appears that agricultural and urban life were intermixed in the ancient Greek cities, for olive groves and vineyards were found within the city walls. Cities were located at the bases of mountains, in valleys, or near the water routes. Often a wooden or stone wall divided one city from the next. This wall prescribed the extent of the city's protection for its citizens during times of invasion or threatened unrest.

Inside the city wall were the homes of the citizens. The ruling nobles and their families and the political dignitaries lived in the better sections close to the center of the city. Nearer the wall were the huts of artisans, merchants, traders, and farmers. Slaves and plebeians lived outside the city's confines, for they had no citizenship status. Many villages were clustered around the main city so as to be protected during times of invasions.

As a new type of social organization, the *polis* or city-state, was quickly formed as soon as tribes decided to federate.[1] Tribes were composed of several phratries, the next lower grouping in the hierarchy. Phratries consisted of families who worshiped the same gods and who had organized into a larger unit for mutual aid and protection. After the formation of the city-state, citizenship was acknowledged through a public religious worship. A man who possessed this privilege was declared a citizen of his local municipality—Athens or Sparta, for example. A male resident of Athens was simultaneously a member of a family, a phratry, a tribe, and city-state. This status was reached at the age of sixteen after participation in a public worship ceremony before a set of idols belonging to the whole city. This marked the supersedence of citizenship status over that of the family, phratry, or tribe.

One of the significant outgrowths of the formation of the city-state was the transition from a kinship to citizenship status. Public service superseded kinship responsibilities when change in the social structure followed the federation of tribes into a city-state. The family head, who formerly had an important position and acted for his immediate group, surrendered a part of his authority to the leaders selected to head the union of families, or phratries. These leaders, in turn, were subordinate to tribal leaders. The latter rose to the top of the political structure and became leaders of the city-state.

The municipality was the center of social and cultural life. The wealthier classes had leisure to enjoy and promote cultural activities. They had legal rights and privileges, owned land, constructed highways, enacted laws, and dispensed welfare. In times of war they levied taxes, conscripted

[1] Numa Denis Fustel de Coulanges, *The Ancient City* (Boston: Lee and Shepard Co., 1889), 111–178.

soldiers, and led armies. The power to end wars and ratify treaties also belonged to them. In effect, they controlled the welfare of the plebeians and slaves.

To almost all Greeks, the city-state appeared to be the largest feasible political unit. The ideal city-state, as envisioned by Plato, should contain no more citizens than could gather together in the assembly. This belief extended even into the period of domination by Athens and Sparta. Aristotle's *Politics,* written at a time when the Macedonian Alexander was already building an empire, still dealt only with the problems of individual city-states, ignoring the fact that the self-contained city-state had already begun to decline.

When war was declared by one city-state against another, the plebeians and slaves were mobilized. In order to enlist their support, city-state leaders had to promise them more rights and privileges. Some were admitted to political power after becoming citizens, a reward for military service. In time the slaves and plebeians wrested more and more power from their masters and imitated them in their social activities. Gradually they acquired the land once owned by their masters and became powerful. This was one of the major reasons for the weakening of the Roman and Greek city-states.

Rome. At this point it is of interest to view the life and culture of Rome as a city-state. Rome was situated on the Seven Hills overlooking the Tiber River. Direct access to the sea was twenty miles away. As her population increased, the city walls were torn down and rebuilt to enclose the "clingers" who lived at the outer fringes at the foot of the wall, where protection by the local guard was available. By limiting the expansion and direction of city and population growth, older cities grew in an orderly fashion. All roads led from the center to the outer walls. Passage in and out of the city was through huge gates that were barred at the end of the day.

The dominant point was the seat of public worship located at the center of the municipality. Inner lanes, narrow and crooked, branched off from the main thoroughfares leading to the city's gates. Transportation was poor, scarce, and unsatisfactory within the city, and many residences and shops were crowded near the center. Considerable congestion resulted and sanitation was a severe problem.

Although Rome had a system of viaducts that transported water into the city, no organized sanitary control was exerted. Her population of 800,000 was crowded either into tenement-like quarters or palatial estates. Altogether, some 50,000 homes accommodated the population, but the poorer classes were confined to a very small section of Rome. Housing conditions became even more acute when many buildings were demolished for the construction of public works, highways, temples, arenas, and public squares. As a result, the Romans spent a good portion of their waking hours out of doors. Public squares and public baths became favorite meeting places for social and commercial activities. To support and construct public projects, Rome exacted tribute from surrounding territories. Citizens and non-citizens alike were taxed.

The Romans were the first to develop the legal idea that a body of persons might be clothed with a corporate personality, thus becoming a corporation or artificial person in law.[1] The concept of a city as a municipal corporation, able to sue and be sued, has continued to the present.

Where Greece had failed, Rome succeeded. The city-state was enlarged into an empire, and with it arose an adaptation in political and social organization which went far beyond that of the city-state. The masses, alternately oppressed and in revolt, no longer had any representation in government so successful government had to appease by furnishing "bread and circuses." At the same time it was the urban masses who increasingly adhered to the new Christian religion, eventually assuring its spread throughout the Western world.

However, the increased schisms among Romans, together with foreign "barbarian" invasions, brought about the downfall of the empire, and what was left of Rome was significant largely because it was the seat of Christendom and classical learning. Italy again saw an era of city-states: Venice, Florence, Naples, Milan, and Genoa were to become the first cities in the urban revival following the Middle Ages.[2] Venice, founded by fugitives from the invaders, had indeed never been conquered and remained with the influence of the Byzantine Empire while the Dark Ages descended upon most of Europe.

Urban decline. Urban growth was considerably retarded between the fourth and ninth centuries because of the fierce Norse and Moslem attacks. The lack of federation between city-states made them vulnerable. The city people fled to villages and tilled the soil. The Dark Ages blotted out the gains which had been so painstakingly made by the earlier founders of Mediterranean cities. During these five centuries of prolonged warfare, the Moslems dominated the seas and restricted trade and commerce between the Near and Far East and parts of Europe. There was insufficient food to support a non-agricultural population. At the same time, the Norse invasions swept southward throughout Europe, causing further unrest and warfare. Despite these adversities some cities in Central Europe survived and were transformed into medieval cities.

[1] Munro, *op. cit.,* 33 and *Commonwealth* vs. *Moir,* 1901, 199 Pa., 534.

[2] H. B. Cotterill, *Italy from Dante to Tasso* (New York: F. A. Stokes Co., 1919). A volume devoted to the city-states through the sixteenth century.

Medieval Cities

Although urban growth was retarded in and around the Mediterranean Sea during the Dark Ages, cities in southern France and in southern and western Germany survived the Norse and Moslem invasions. Piracy had further reduced commerce and trade conducted by cities located on the southern, eastern, and western shores of the Mediterranean Sea. Urban population dwindled as the hazards of warfare increased. City finances were undermined by the shrinkage of revenues from taxes and tributes exacted from the hinterland and the neighboring cities over which larger cities had dominance. Three major types of cities are attributed to this era: the "episcopal," the bourg, and commerce and trade.

Episcopal city. German and French cities were saved from destruction because of the Church's influence over tribal invaders.[1] Church dignitaries were permitted to assume and retain political administrative positions. Thus Tours, Amiens, Cologne, Treves, and Laon escaped pillage and were transformed into "episcopal cities," functioning as administrative seats for the international organization of the Christian clergy. Moreover, some of the invaders preferred to live in cities and thus insured their survival.

The bourg. Another type of city, the bourg, existed in large numbers during this era. Primarily built for defense, bourgs were located on islands, at the foot of mountains, in low valleys, or on high mountain ridges which afforded strategic commands over wide hinterlands. These cities served as havens of shelter for the rural population of the surrounding territories during raids or invasions. Thick walls which followed the contour of the terrain enclosed the city proper. Watchtowers were constructed at intervals, and a wide moat for added protection extended beyond the city's confines. Weapons were manufactured and stored in the main feudal lord's castle, whereas in the "episcopal city" the towering cathedral's recesses were used for this purpose. A small resident guard protected the weapons and garrisoned the gates of the wall.

Insofar as these cities were dominated by either defense or religious activities, the internal spatial arrangement reflected the major emphasis associated with its respective type. The main thoroughfare led directly from the cathedral or feudal castle to the outer gates, thus enabling quick access to the source of protection and power. Lesser roads were often crooked, narrow, and unpaved; but, nevertheless, they were directly connected to the major thoroughfares. A portion of the land was reserved

[1] Henri Pirenne, *A History of Europe from the Invasion to the 16th Century* (New York: W. W. Norton, 1948), Ch. 2.

for expansion. When the population increased to the point where the internal city area was insufficient to accommodate them, the older fortifications were torn down and new walls built.

Thus, medieval cities which have survived are famous for their concentric, ring-like boulevards. The former site of city walls not only constricted population and areal growth in an orderly fashion, but were later transformed into wide boulevards and became a part of the modern street system. The famous boulevard ring of Paris, for example, is a reminder of its medieval origin and the fact that wide roads were a military necessity.[1] Moreover, six or seven walls may have been erected—their former sites now used as boulevards—separating the "old" and new city, as exemplified by Venice, London, and Rome. Of interest is the recent excavation of as many as six walls around ancient sites of buried cities (Troy, Cnossos, Jericho), dating back to the pre-Christian era and testifying to the role which cities played as centers of defense and protection.[2]

Commerce and trade city. A third type, the commerce and trade cities, developed after the eleventh century, following the return of stable social and economic conditions.[3] Although a limited amount of trade and commerce extended into the hinterland from the "episcopal" and defense cities, sponsored by either the Church officials or the feudal nobility, the large-scale revival of commercial and industrial enterprises did not resume until this period. Trade flourished between the Near and Far East and Italian and Sicilian cities.

Another trade route connected Mediterranean cities with cities located on the Flemish coast so that interurban and intercontinental maritime and commercial relations embraced a wider scope than ever before known. Ships sailed as far north as the Baltic Sea and the British Isles. Industries were stimulated by trade. Woolen products were manufactured in Flemish cities; wines were produced in Italian and Sicilian centers; and metalcraft flourished in French and German ones. The Orient exchanged these products for spices, silks, and luxury art goods. City fairs and city markets were held periodically to facilitate the exchange of goods.

The abolition of market-tolls (*teloneum*), which had previously hindered free circulation of goods, also contributed to the growth and expansion of commerce and industry. This, together with the invention of gunpowder, was responsible for limitless exchange of goods, services, and credit. Through the invention of navigational instruments and newer types of firearms, the trading area was widened. New routes across the

[1] Harold M. Lewis, *Planning the Modern City* (New York: John Wiley & Sons, Inc., 1949), 1, 24–26.

[2] Anne T. White, *Lost Worlds* (New York: Random House, 1941), 31–35 and 77–90.

[3] Henri Pirenne, *Economic and Social History of Medieval Europe* (London: Kegan Paul, Trench, Trubner & Co., Ltd., 1936), 14–46.

Pacific, Indian, and Atlantic oceans were being explored as Europe entered the Commercial Revolution during the eleventh century.

At the same time, a host of small towns became connected with large commercial cities so that goods could be shipped further inland.[1] Raw materials were transported to processing centers, and the finished products were distributed to other cities. In order to protect trade and commerce, cities joined into federations known as *hanses*. Merchants within cities were able to ally with those of other countries. They organized for mutual protection, concerted action against piracy, promoting fairs, and maintaining monopolies on raw materials and markets. The merchants of the London and German hanses monopolized the wool and grain trades, for example.

As a result of the hanses' activities, cities grew and spread eastward, northward, and westward throughout Europe. This acceleration of urban growth was in no small measure due to the maintenance of a large navy and army by the German Hanseatic League, which controlled trade and commerce as far north as the Baltic and as far south as the Mediterranean Sea. It gained considerable political strength. By the end of the fourteenth century, European commerce and trade flourished on a scale comparable to that at the height of the Roman Empire.

Factors of growth. Several other economic, social and cultural factors were instrumental in the growth and perpetuation of medieval cities. Primary was the creation and promotion of a new social structure.[2] By the eleventh century the inhabitants of bourgs became known as bourgeoisie, embracing such groups as innkeepers, bakers, brewers, shoemakers, artisans, weavers, merchants, money changers, gold and silver smiths, and freed serfs. Yet others were the municipal administrators, military personnel, scribes, schoolmasters, lay vassals, and clergy of the Church. A more complex division of labor had become firmly entrenched, and a larger non-agricultural population became permanent residents of the city. As the members of the rising middle class they banded together and consolidated their power in an effort to guarantee themselves more economic and political opportunities. Moreover, they had succeeded in wresting more and more power from their former leaders—the Church officials and feudal nobility. They demanded and received more participation and control in municipal affairs.

The new middle class effected the enactment of laws which protected their interests and personal liberty. As a sizable group who contributed

---

[1] Henri Pirenne, *Medieval Cities: Their Origins and the Revival of Trade* (Princeton: Princeton University Press, 1925). The best account of the association of local merchants and those of distant cities.

[2] *Ibid.;* see also Franklin C. Palm, *The Middle Classes: Then and Now* (New York: The Macmillan Co., 1936).

revenue toward the upkeep of the city's services they affected a permanent change in attitudes toward economic acquisition. Whereas the older feudal social structure had a system of values and behavior pattern based upon the ownership of large agricultural estates and the subordination of a subservient group of serfs or lay clergy, the new status symbols centered around commerce.

The merchants became powerful and were directly responsible for initiating and directing new trade and industrial changes as well as mobilizing the new middle class toward breaking the opposition offered by the feudal nobility and Church authorities. Composing the wealthiest and most enterprising segment of the new social structure for some centuries, they spearheaded the movement toward creating a system of municipal taxation, which provided the various services needed by a growing urban population. Street lighting was installed, and this reduced the number of robberies and crimes. The organization of the fire brigade followed. More streets were paved and public sanitary facilities installed. Ordinance required removal and disposal of waste products. Medieval cities became more habitable and functional.[1]

Another contribution to the growth and expansion of medieval cities was the steady increase in population and the migration of the surplus to cities. The larger agricultural surplus, as well as the importation of food from other areas, reduced the deaths formerly caused by famines and crop failures. Moreover, better agricultural methods were directly responsible for the increased crop yields. The multiple yoke was harnessed to oxen. After innovations in shoeing and harnessing, horses were used for transporting food to cities. The invention of watermills and windmills lightened the labor of many farmers and freed others for industry, commerce, and arts and crafts. Irrigation made new agricultural areas available for the support of a greater non-agricultural population. Meanwhile, serfdom was declining and many freemen sought work in cities.

As important as the increase in population was the transformation of "episcopal cities" and bourgs into important financial and political centers, free from control of the Church or feudal nobility. This was brought about by the enactment of new ordinances requiring the election rather than the appointment of civil servants. The Church's influence over civil administration waned as schools were established to teach the rudiments of a new type of education adapted to the conduct of growing muncipal government.[2] Thus clerks, notaries, advocates, and other public servants

[1] Svend Riemer, "Functional Housing in the Middle Ages," in *Proceedings, Wisconsin Academy of Science and Letters,* 1949 (published in 1951) 77–91. Also see Riemer's *The Modern City* (New York: Prentice-Hall, Inc., 1952), 23–25.

[2] J. Giese, *Man and the Western World* (New York: Harcourt, Brace & Co., 1940), Ch. 12.

replaced the theocratic hierarchy in governmental posts. Feudal control over the bourgs was also weakened. Furthermore, the growth of important voluntary associations and guilds caused other historical functions of the Church to be transferred from its jurisdiction. The care of the aged, ill, indigent, widowed, and orphaned was undertaken by the guilds.

The greatest single factor leading to the permanent growth of urban population in medieval cities was the enactment of municipal laws guaranteeing the status of the individual. Regardless of the wealth or occupation of an urbanite, he had equal status in law. Freedom was a right and privilege guaranteed to everyone who had lived for a year and a day within the city limits, a right conferred as a matter of course. This freedom attracted many a serf, held by hereditary bondage to a noble, to seek safety in the city and take advantage of the statute of limitations. All rights which a former owner had exercised over person and chattel were abolished, and a serf became a bourgher in the same manner as other residents. Moreover, all citizens could own, sell, or transfer land and could accumulate wealth in accordance with their capabilities.

On the other hand, legal tribunals for the enforcement of newly created ordinances were established. These legal reforms further weakened the control of the Church and feudal nobility over municipal affairs, and the emphasis of personal allegiance previously directed to a small select hierarchy was shifted to a duly constituted authority based upon law enacted by a free citizenry. Thus the city became equated with the rise of individualism and personal achievement. Upon these foundations rose the modern cities of the era dating from the Industrial Revolution to the present.

Modern Cities

The cities of today had their roots in the Industrial Revolution, which initiated the factory system on an extensive scale, revolutionized the processes of production and distribution, and complicated the occupational structure of Western societies. The term modern cities has thus become associated with the growth and development of the Industrial Revolution and is symbolic of the technological progress and inventions following therefrom. On the other hand, the less urbanized areas have barely reached a stage of urban development comparable to that found in the ancient Roman and Greek empires. Others have some of the characteristics found in medieval Europe.

The cities of Europe during the early years of the Industrial Revolution were of two main types: primary extraction and secondary production centers. Since raw materials, such as coal, iron ore, copper, gold, silver,

Ewing Galloway

Paris, France, aerial view. The Arc de Triomphe is in the center and major streets radiate therefrom. The most beautiful street is Champs Elysees (lower right).

tin, zinc, and timber, were needed in large quantities for large-scale manufacturing operations, many new cities were built for the extraction of natural resources. These were used locally (as for example, coal and clay for pottery manufacturing at Hanley and Preston) or they were shipped to other cities where the processing into finished products was completed. Thus English coal-mining industries flourished only as long as the textile and dye factories produced at Manchester, Leeds, and Birmingham.

Some cities functioned as both primary extraction and secondary production centers. As markets widened and a growing group of urbanites required more goods and services, cities became important reshipping centers of finished products as well as in the transshipment of raw materials. Others, like London, Paris, Liverpool, Hamburg, and Bilboa, combined domestic and foreign commercial activities and industrial activities.[1] When local raw materials and markets became insufficient to maintain the growing manufacturing enterprises, foreign sources were actively sought and cultivated. Beginning with the seventeenth century, the Euro-

[1] Witt Bowden, Michael Karpovich, and Abbot P. Usher, *An Economic History of Europe since 1750* (New York: American Book Co., 1937), Chs. 4–8, 20, 31.

pean models of modern cities were transplanted to the Near and Far Eastern, African, and American continents. This competition for overseas expansion was intensified during the nineteenth century, stimulated by the needs of a rapidly expanding industrialism experienced by England, Germany, France, Italy, Belgium, The Netherlands, and others.

Accompanying the overseas expansion of European countries was the practice of superimposing a Western form of social organization upon the strategic areas of the Near and Far East and Africa. Furthermore, Western officials and agents of the respective countries as well as private individuals seeking occupational and social mobility settled in the cities they helped to create *en toto* or in the areas segregated for their residence. The middle-class migration from European countries to less urbanized areas was composed of civil servants, merchants, engineers, white-collar workers, sailors, and soldiers. Likewise, teachers, missionaries, doctors, nurses, and public health personnel found overseas opportunities. On the whole, the persons who spent years abroad were rewarded with more rapid social mobility and wealth than those who remained at home.[1]

There was a sharp contrast between the areas inhabited by the European and local populations. Two distinct and different modes of urban life may exist within one city. Shanghai, Tunis, Calcutta, Rangoon, Singapore, Johannesburg, and Bangkok are regarded as modern because their growth and prosperity are closely linked to European overseas enterprises.

As modern cities passed through the various technological changes following the Industrial Revolution and as diversified industries developed, a trend toward specialization resulted. Cities may be noted for specific functions: manufacturing (Birmingham), recreation (Cannes, Nice), transportation (Le Havre), religion (Vatican City, or political activities (capitals). This tendency has affected their economic organization as well as the occupations and living habits of urbanites.

Other changes. The Industrial Revolution brought many more changes to European cities. The more important of them will be considered.

Primary is the increase in large metropolitan cities—of 100,000 and more population—and their dominance over surrounding areas. There were few big cities in Europe during the early part of the seventeenth century. Paris and London each had over 750,000 inhabitants in 1750.[2] The redistribution of population and its settlement in and around the metropolises followed as industries attracted more and more workers and their families. Today Europe has the greatest number of metropolitan cities in the world, or 364 out of a total of 858 (Table 1), including sixteen of cities with more than a million population.

[1] Report of London Colonial Office, "Conditions in Singapore in 1951."
[2] Bowden, Karpovich, and Usher, *op. cit.,* Ch. 1.

TABLE 1. CITIES OVER 100,000 POPULATION IN MAJOR REGIONS OF THE WORLD, 1945 AND 1950 [1]

Area	1,000,000 and over		500,000 to 1,000,000		250,000 to 500,000		100,000 to 250,000		Total Cities		Increase [‡]
	1945	1950	1945	1950	1945	1950	1945	1950	1945	1950	
Africa	1	1	1	3	5	6	17	27	24	37	13
Asia (excludes USSR) * (includes Near East)	13	20	23	22	33	43	141	178	210	263	53
Europe (includes USSR, 1945)	15	14	36	28	65	46	211	187	327	364	37
USSR †		2		9		20		58			
North America	6	7	12	15	24	27	77	91	119	140	21
Oceania	2	2	—	—	2	3	5	5	9	10	1
South America	3	3	6	4	5	11	18	26	32	44	12
Total	40	49	78	81	134	156	459	572	721	858	137

* China's list of cities was incomplete for 1950 and based upon estimates.
† Russia's figures for 1939 were used for 1950.
‡ *Note* that Mark Jefferson in "Distribution of the World's City Folks: A Study in Comparative Civilization," *Geographical Review* (1931), 446–465, reported 537 "great cities" in 1930.

[1] *Source:* Adapted by permission from Noel P. Gist and L. A. Halbert, *Urban Society* (3rd edition, Thomas Y. Crowell, 1948), p. 21; and United Nations Demographic Yearbook, 1952, Table 8, 202–214. The 1945 figures represent the "latest available census data or population estimates up to 1945; Russia's figures were for 1939; England's, 1941; and The United States, 1940," as footnoted for Gist and Halbert, 21.

Density of urban population has likewise increased. For example, London had less than a million inhabitants two centuries ago. The present number of persons living within the metropolitan area, of which London is the center, is almost ten million, a tenfold increase. Dispersion to the suburban areas has proceeded, assuming a pattern similar to that of the United States. At the same time, the city proper of London has not grown in land area and is but one square mile. To accommodate the clustering of population and to facilitate the administration of the metropolitan area, 41 surrounding boroughs were created in 1885 by the British parliament. These boroughs and London make up the metropolitan area. The area is governed by a metropolitan board composed of 129 elected men and women forming the London county council. This board and the respective borough councils work together in providing the services needed by the metropolitan residents.

Before the Industrial Revolution, and the concomitant large-scale urbanization of the Western world, Asian populations tended to increase more rapidly (Table 2). One of the first consequences of the Industrial

TABLE 2. WORLD POPULATION FOR MAJOR CONTINENTS
1900 AND 1950 [1]

Continent	Total Population		Total Increase	
	1900	*1950*	*Number*	*Per Cent*
Africa	140,700,000	197,900,000	57,200,000	29
America	151,000,000	320,800,000	169,800,000	105
Asia	838,900,000	1,253,500,000	414,600,000	33
Europe	352,100,000	592,000,000	239,900,000	40
Oceania	6,200,000	12,400,000	6,200,000	100
Total	1,461,900,000	2,376,600,000	887,700,000	61

[1] *Source:* Adapted from Statistical Studies Section, World Health Organization, June 29, 1950.

Revolution was reduction in mortality and an improvement in the food supply, which brought about a large increase in the proportion of Europeans, more and more of whom were urban. As transportation improved, ever greater numbers moved to cities, and others in turn emigrated to less urbanized regions of the world. Some of these emigrants, although many of them had to revert to rural ways of life, were largely displaced urbanites. Others settled in foreign cities or helped to build new ones.

Europe's population increased from approximately 18 per cent to 23 per cent of the world's total between 1650 and 1947. If those of European stock residing outside of Europe are included, the total rises to 30 per cent of the world's total population.[1]

At the beginning of the seventeenth century, England, France, and Italy had the largest number of urbanites. France had approximately 8 per cent of her total population living in cities of more than 100,000 and 12.9, in cities of more than 20,000 inhabitants.[2] For the same period Italy had 28 per cent of her population in urban centers with more than 10,000 inhabitants. England exceeded both by approximately 2 per cent. Switzerland, as an illustration of a country which did not experience a high degree of urbanization and industrialization until the nineteenth century, had a total urban population of approximately 100,000 in ten of her largest cities in 1798.[3]

The period before the Second World War showed great gains in European urban population. Great Britain, Denmark, and France had 80, 65.1, and 52.9 per cent of their total population in cities. Belgium, Sweden, and Ireland had 60.5, 42.3, and 37.6 per cent, respectively (Table 3). After the war, Great Britain showed a negligible increase, and no recent figures are given for France, but urban population losses due to war casualties are probably more than offset by large numbers of refugees. Countries that showed gains in urban population included Denmark, Belgium, Sweden, and Ireland—countries which did not experience as much direct aerial bombardment and ground warfare. It is well to bear in mind that the definition of urban places varies according to local practice: 1,500 and over for Ireland, 2,000 for France, and 5,000 for Belgium, and so on (see Table 3).

The density of population for Europe as a whole has steadily increased with greater urbanization. The areas of high density are localized in northern and central Italy, southern Germany, and the coastal and river areas of France, Spain, Portugal, and Sicily. Other concentrations have formed around the industrial cities of the Low Countries, Scandinavia, and the Balkan States. The most congested European countries are also among the most industrialized, as, for example, 272.1 persons per square kilometer in Belgium; 270.2 in England; and 260.3 in The Netherlands.[4]

The growth of urban population is attributable to several other factors. There is more complete utilization of heretofore uncultivated land, thus insuring a larger surplus of food for support of the non-agricultural portion of the population. Introduction and wide-scale adoption of advanced

[1] A. M. Carr-Saunders, *World Population* (Oxford: Clarendon Press, 1936), 42; and United Nations Statistical Office, *Statistical Papers,* Ser. A, 6 (June, 1949), "Population and Vital Statistics Reports."

[2] Bowden, Karpovich, and Usher, *op. cit.,* 13–22.

[3] K. B. Mayer, *The Population of Switzerland* (New York: Columbia University Press, 1952), Ch. 11 and especially pages 244–245 and 248.

[4] Ta Chen, "Population in Modern China," *American Journal of Sociology,* 52 (July, 1946), 24.

TABLE 3. PER CENT URBAN POPULATION, 1930 TO 1951, AND DEFINITION OF URBAN AREAS FOR SELECTED COUNTRIES OF THE WORLD [1]

Country	Per Cent Classified As Urban and Date 1930–1946	Date	Per Cent Classified As Urban and Date 1947–1951	Date	Rank 1930–1946	Rank 1947–1951	Definition of Urban
United Kingdom	80.0	1931	80.7	1951	1	1	County boroughs, municipal boroughs, urban districts, London Administrative County.
Denmark	65.1	1945	67.3	1950	2	2	Towns and agglomerations, including suburbs of the capital and of provincial cities.
United States	56.5	1940	64.0	1950	5	3	Incorporated places of 2,500 or more, and certain additional thickly settled areas designated as urban for census purposes.
Belgium	60.5	1930	62.7	1947	3	4	Administrative subdivisions of 5,000 or more.
Canada	54.3	1941	62.1	1951	6	5	Incorporated cities towns and villages of all sizes.
New Zealand	60.5	1945	61.3	1951	3	6	Cities, boroughs, and town districts of 1,000 or more.
Sweden	42.3	1945	56.3	1950	8	7	Cities or towns with an urban administration.
France	52.9	1946	—	—	7	8	Communes having more than 2,000 inhabitants in the chief town.
Union of South Africa	36.4	1946	42.4	1951	11	9	All towns and villages having some form of local government.
Ireland	37.6	1946	40.5	1951	9	10	Towns of 1,500 or more inhabitants.
Panama	37.2	1940	35.9	1950	10	11	Populated centers of 1,500 or more inhabitants which have essentially urban living conditions.
Mexico	35.1	1940	—	—	12	12	Populated centers of more than 2,500.
Portugal	31.1	1940	—	—	13	13	Places of 2,000 or more inhabitants.
Egypt	25.1	1937	30.1	1947	15	14	Governorates and chief towns of provinces and districts.
Colombia	29.1	1938	—	—	14	15	Centers of more than 1,500 inhabitants which are seats of municipalities or districts.
India	12.8	1941	17.3	1951	16	16	Towns of 5,000 or more inhabitants possessing definite urban characteristics.

[1] *Source:* By permission from *United Nations Demographic Yearbook,* 1948 and 1952.

technology in various industries has been responsible for increased employment of urban workers as well as contributing to greater division of labor. Moreover, the extensive exploitation and utilization of new raw materials has stimulated industrial growth. Increased purchasing power of consumers has aided the growth of more urban goods and services, so that today a ready-made consumer base is available for new industries. Expansion of commerce and industries and creation of capital wealth have been furthered by the policies which some European nations have adopted to enlarge their power and prestige. When necessary, political and military pressures have been employed in the domination of foreign lands for raw materials and markets.[1]

The revolution in communication and transportation should not be overlooked. The major arteries of transportation either begin or end in cities. The same is true of the modern media of communication. Both these factors are vital for the maintenance of an intricate and complex urban culture. Without a doubt they have greatly influenced the change in values, attitudes, behavior patterns, and social relations between persons and groups whether they be urban or rural dwellers.

Summary

Ancient cities served as religious, tribal, or political centers dominating and controlling a series of adjacent villages. The principal city was located near waterways. A series of satellite cities was often connected to it by routes which permitted the agricultural surplus, labor supply, and tribute from the hinterland to centralize at one major point. The city, in turn, sent its goods and services inland to the territories it controlled. Cities declined when tribes were conquered or absorbed by others.

The next type of urban development was the city-state, which became organized after families formed phratries, phratries enlarged into tribes, and several tribes merged into a larger social organization. There was a shift from familial and religious affiliation to civic status. The first attempt to create the concept of the city as a municipal corporation was made by leaders of the city-state. The enhancement of citizenship status came about when those who controlled the bureaucratic structure were forced to grant rights and privileges to the plebeians and slaves in return for military protection against outside invasion.

The fierce Norse and Moslem attacks between the fourth and ninth centuries caused a decline in urban growth. Cities which survived in Germany and France were transformed into "episcopal cities." Bourgs, built for defense purposes, grew in sufficient numbers to constitute a

---

[1] Bowden, Karpovich, and Usher, *op. cit.,* Ch. 31.

second type of medieval city, while the revival of trade and commerce beginning with the eleventh century contributed to the increase of commerce and trade cities. The power of the Church and the feudal lords declined with the growth of commerce and trade centers. A new social structure emerged, and a higher division of labor developed. A new middle class evolved whose success in enlarging and developing new goods and services supported a growing group of non-agricultural, non-ecclesiastical, and non-feudal residents.

Modern cities are associated with the advent of the Industrial Revolution. Henceforth, Western societies experienced a greater impact and change in social life, values, attitudes, behavior patterns, and social organizations than did those areas where urbanism first developed. Western forms of urbanism became diffused to less urbanized areas and are today instrumental in furthering the trend toward greater urbanization throughout the globe.

DISCUSSION QUESTIONS

1. How may we explain the fact that so little attention has been paid to cities in non-Western areas?
2. How did ancient cities differ in their social organization from the city-states? The city-states from the medieval cities? The "episcopal" cities from the bourgs?
3. Which cities existed before the Industrial Revolution and have remained important up to the present? In what way have they adapted to new social and economic conditions?
4. What were the major causes for the disappearance of ancient cities? Of medieval cities?
5. Discuss how industrialism and commerce are interdependent variables in stimulating urban growth.
6. Discuss how the cities of the less urbanized areas are influenced by Western urbanism.

SUGGESTED PROJECTS

1. Determine why countries which use water transportation and a large amount of human and animal carriers are slow in urban growth.
2. Is there any basis for assuming that Far Eastern cities grew during the Dark Ages in Europe because they supplied many of the needs of the European population?
3. Study the growth of the non-agricultural portion of the population as urbanism has advanced for one of the major European countries.
4. Trace the development of the medieval middle class and show how this stratum has influenced the division of labor and social gains.

READINGS

Encyclopedia of the Social Sciences, "The City," 2, 474–82.

A comprehensive article on the rise and development of the city.

John Frost, *Great Cities of the World.* Buffalo: John E. Beardsley, 1852.

A study of the prosperity and decline of European, Asiatic, African and American cities.

Gordon Ericksen, *Urban Behavior.* New York: The Macmillan Co., 1954.

A textbook designed for the undergraduate student and teacher.

Patrick Geddes, *Cities in Evolution.* New York: Oxford University Press, 1950.

The section, "Cities Exhibition," includes photographs and diagrams of the physical layout of medieval, renaissance, capital, and garden cities. Appropriate written material to explain the differences in configuration and functions of various types.

N. S. B. Gras, *Industrial Evolution.* Cambridge: Harvard University Press, 1930.

A scholarly presentation of the various phases of economic development from pastoral to industrial economy.

Louis Mumford, *The Culture of Cities.* New York: Harcourt, Brace & Co., Inc., 1938, Ch. 2.

A graphic description of the insensate industrial town.

Henri Pirenne, *A History of Europe from the Invasion to the 16th Century.* New York: W. W. Norton, 1948.

Chapter Two in particular discusses the effect of the Norse and Moslem invasions on European cities.

Henri Pirenne, *Medieval Cities: Their Origins and the Revival of Trade.* Princeton: Princeton University Press, 1925.

Discusses the rise of medieval cities and the effect of trade in assuring their survival.

Chapter Four

Northern Asian Cities

S INCE we are not accustomed to thinking of Asia as industrialized and urbanized, we do not realize that roughly one-fourth of the world's cities with metropolitan status were located there in 1950 (see Table 1). Nor do we often associate the existence of ancient urban centers with Asia. As a fact of historical significance, some of the world's oldest cities have been excavated in India and China.

The Indian Harrappa and Mohen-jo-daro excavations revealed the ruins of half a dozen cities belonging to the Neolithic period. Cities were built in the Indus Valley and the Punjab and Ganges plains.[1] The site of a Shang dynasty capital, existing around the fourteenth century B.C., was discovered in China at the turn of this century but not thoroughly explored until 1928.[2]

This chapter deals with the urban development of China, Japan, Korea, and Formosa. These four countries constitute a cultural unit, with China's influence upon all of them being uppermost until the impact of westernization caused Japan to pursue a different course. Japan's urbanization and industrialization became accelerated from the middle of the nineteenth century and has exceeded China's since then. However, Japan's power to control the urban development in Korea and Formosa within the last half century has ended. In the future, urban growth in these two areas may increase as each charts its own economic, political, and social development.

---

[1] Kingsley Davis, *The Population of India and Pakistan* (Princeton: Princeton University Press, 1951), Ch. 4; *International Social Science Bulletin,* "Documents on South Asia," 3 (Win., 1951), 771–775; and *UNESCO Courier,* June, 1952, 10; Henry S. Churchill, *The City Is the People* (New York: Reynal & Hitchcock, 1945), 2–4.

[2] Herrlee G. Creel, *Birth of China: A Story of the Formative Period of Chinese Civilization* (New York: Reynal and Hitchcock, 1937), Chs. 1–5; *China Handbook,* 1950, 45 and 85–86.

China

Certain Chinese cities existed for more than two thousand years before any others appeared on the Asian continent. The evolution of cities corresponds to the historical development of the nation itself, for cities grew as territory and population expanded. Six major periods of city growth are presented in one of the few studies available.[1] A seventh period has just begun.[2] They are as follows:

1. From 2205 B.C. to 1120 B.C.: tribal capitals; administrative and religious centers.
2. From 1121 B.C. to 221 B.C.: feudal cities.
3. From 222 B.C. to 220 A.D.: inland commerce and trade cities.
4. From 221 A.D. to 959 A.D.: inland cities spreading toward Korea, southern China, Near East, and Europe.
5. From 960 A.D. to 1644 A.D.: southern cities, riverports, lakeports, and provincial capitals.
6. From 1644 A.D. to 1950 A.D.: coastal cities and modern cities along the Pacific Ocean for commerce and trade with Western societies after 1850.
7. 1950—: growth of inland and northern cities.

Each period reflected the relationship of cities to the culture of the dynasties of which they were an integral part. The modern period has the greatest interest to us, because the rise and growth of coastal cities fronting the Pacific Ocean was largely due to the impact of Western culture.

First period. The first period of city development coincided with the founding of the original home of the Chinese in the Wei Ho Valley of the southwestern portion of the Loess Plateau. From approximately 2205 B.C. until 1120 B.C.—the Hsia and Shang dynasties—historians recorded the concentration of tribal communities and later feudal states in the central part of China. This period corresponded to the era of the Egyptian Thebes' and Memphis. Archaeological diggings testify that there existed at Anyang a culture comparable to the last phase of the Stone Age.[3] Moreover, a Shang capital has been excavated at the "Waste of Yin," in Northern Honam in the banks of the Yellow River. The land

[1] Pak Si Wu, "Urbanization in China: A Study of Shanghai and Peiping" (unpublished Master's thesis, University of Chicago Libraries, Dec., 1940).

[2] Lawrence K. Rosinger and associates, *The State of Asia* (New York: Alfred A. Knopf, Inc., 1951), 50–82.

[3] Harley F. MacNair (ed.), *China* (Berkeley: University of California Press, 1946), Chs. 4 and 5.

Urban development in Asia (see facing page) is more concentrated in the north than the south or along coastal and river areas. Industrialization is generally greater where cities reach over half a million population.

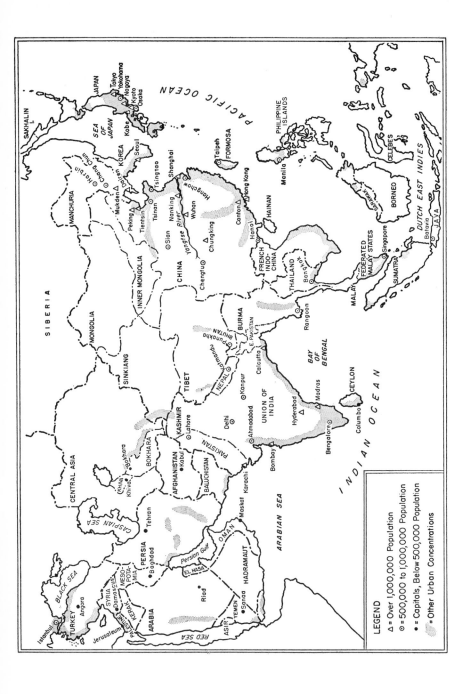

LEGEND
△ = Over 1,000,000 Population
⊙ = 500,000 to 1,000,000 Population
• = Capitals, Below 500,000 Population
░ = Other Urban Concentrations

in that area has always been very fertile and is densely settled at the present time.

Ancient Chinese cities were ruled by farmer-kings. Inside the city were centers of worship, erected by command of the Emperor, where elaborate religious rituals were directed to supernatural powers. Many of these early cities functioned as religious, administrative, and tribal capitals. For example: during the fourteenth century B.C. (Shang dynasty), Pin grew to be one of the largest capitals in the world, having over 100,000 inhabitants. Presumably, like other ancient cities, it resulted from the consolidation of various small villages and gradually evolved into a new form of social organization.[1]

Dynasties revolved around a succession of family rulers, each of whom had followers and administrators living within a walled city. For defense purposes 163 walled cities were built during these early dynasties.[2] The surrounding population sought refuge there during tribal invasions or, in case of some natural catastrophe such as flood, famine, or epidemic. As population expanded and warring tribes were subjugated, more cities were built for administrative purposes. As dynasties succeeded to power, they built more cities. The capital city exerted undisputed authority in dominating the entire country. Lesser cities were joined to the larger but were controlled by the king's family members or kinsmen. Persons selected to serve the emperor were "rewarded" with residence in cities. This change of status and residence provided an incentive for ambitious persons seeking social and occupational mobility to obtain posts connected with the royal administration. Civil service became the socially sanctioned avenue of mobility and individualism. Luxuries which were unknown in rural areas were enjoyed by the civil servants.

Often cities were built at a site which a dynastic ruler fancied, as, for example, Hangchow, the "lake city." Often vanity and the struggle for power between two kings determined the location, plan and elaborateness of the city erected. The time consumed in building the cities had little bearing, since citizens were conscripted to help with the task. When a king lost his power, the city he favored would be abandoned, permitted to decline, and a new one founded. Thus, many ancient cities have served as dynastic capitals or as resort centers for emperors and their retinue.

This practice of selecting capitals when a new group rose to power is retained to the present day. When the Manchu dynasty was overthrown by Dr. Sun Yat-sen and his fellow revolutionists, they selected Nanking

---

[1] Creel, *op. cit.,* Ch. 4.

[2] Data is contained in an unpublished manuscript, "Urbanization in the Far East," by Yuan Liang, 1949.

as the capital. It was completely modernized with the help of American architects, engineers, and planners after the Central Government (Kuomintang) moved northward from Canton in 1927.[1] Nanking was considered more strategically located for the national seat of government than Peking to the north. Furthermore, Nanking symbolized a return to Chinese, rather than Manchurian, control of the nation.

When the "People's Government" came into control in October, 1949, they readopted Peking and abandoned Nanking. This move was based upon the subtle claim that about a thousand years ago a modified form of socialism was practiced there at one point during the Sung era (1068–1085 A.D.).[2] As one can see, any serious student of Chinese history is confronted with the task of remembering when a given ruler built or readopted a city as a capital, and when it was forsaken or lost popularity.

Second period. The second period of urban growth lasted from 1121 B.C. to 221 B.C., known as the Period of Spring and Autumn and the Period of War. The country was divided into several feudal states and expanded as far north as the present boundaries touching Manchuria, Mongolia, and Sinkiang. Some 585 fortress-like cities (bourgs) were built for defense and control of the areas adjacent to the state's principalities.[3] Famous cities of the era were Hsianfu, Loyang, Honanfu, and Lanchow, situated on the Yellow and Wei rivers. Trade was conducted among cities within the state. Recurrent periods of war against "barbarians" seeking to conquer the feudal states caused considerable population mobility. Young men were drafted into the armed forces and brought to cities, thereby enlarging the urban aggregation. From the eighth century B.C. until the middle of the third century B.C., China may be said to resemble, roughly, the Europe of the Middle Ages.[4] The local princes owed homage, tribute, counsel, and military service to their king. Silk, wheat, and metal nuggets were used as mediums of exchange or as tribute to rulers. In fact, payment in kind is still acceptable in many urban and rural areas.

The most momentous occurrence affecting Chinese social and ethical development occurred under the Chou dynasty; both Confucius and Lao-tze lived during this time. Many young men became Confucian scholars as this mode of life paved the way for social and occupational mobility. Gradually, a rigid social structure emerged, with the scholars at the top of the hierarchy, the farmers next, the artisans below them, and

[1] Edward Y. K. Kwong, "Planning a New Nanking," *China Critic,* 2 (1929), 729–732; see also his "Nanking Eight Years After," same periodical, 16 (1937), 224–226.

[2] MacNair, *op. cit.,* 93–95.

[3] Liang, *op. cit.*

[4] K. Latourette, *The Chinese: Their History and Culture* (3rd ed.; New York: The Macmillan Co., 1947), 46–47.

the merchants before the common laborers. It was not until the impact of Western influence that this class structure changed. More will be said later about the new socio-economic groupings developed during the last half-century.

In European cities the merchant class grew very powerful, whereas in China their status was deliberately relegated to a rank beneath that of rulers, educators, farmers, and artisans. To what extent the absence of a national monetary system and the minimizing of the merchant's role in the social structure affected urban growth would be an interesting topic for further study. In Europe the rising merchant class helped bring about the collapse of feudalism. In China the feudal system of granting titles to members of the nobility ended with the Chou dynasty, but in its place was substituted landlordism mixed with Confucian ethics, Taoism, and later, Buddhism. These systems fostered ideas of self-denial, meditation, and reverence for the preservation of an ancient heritage.

A major event occurring during the early Christian era was the diffusion of Buddhism into China. Confucianism and Taoism, the two philosophical and ethical systems founded by Confucius and Lao-tze, preceded Buddhism by five hundred years. Neither originated as a religious system, although the performance of elaborate rituals and ceremonies give both some of the characteristic features of older religions.[1] These rites and observances were more strictly observed by the followers of Confucianism or Taoism when Buddhism gained adherents. It should be noted that the two philosophical and ethical systems have always had more support from the male segment of the population. Women took to Buddhism in greater numbers. To offset this challenge, Confucian and Taoist temples were erected throughout the land to match the elaborateness of those of the Buddhist faith. Their respective influences upon the internal spatial aspects of cities will be discussed later. Suffice it to say now that Taoism later became both a philosophical and religious system because Taoism is more mystical in its conception than Confucianism and could be more easily converted into formal religious patterns. Until the inroad made by Christianity a millennium later, no significant change in the value system of the Chinese was evident.

Although walled cities continued to be built after the Chou dynasty, they were oriented toward trade and commerce. The reason for the retention of the outer fortifications was the absence of a unified defense system and the fact that local police, the militia, and the armies of the provincial military leaders found walls to be effective barriers against

---

[1] J. K. Shryock, *The Origin and Development of the State Cult of Confucius* (New York: Century Publishing Co., 1932); Herrlee G. Creel, *Confucius: The Man and Myth* (New York: John Day Co., 1949); and MacNair, *op. cit.*, Pt. 3.

banditry and wandering ne'er-do-wells. Many cities have retained their walls through the centuries. When martial law had to be enforced, local residents stayed inside the city's walls. But when countryside and cities were both overcrowded, residents outside the city wall could be denied admittance into the city during periods of unrest.

A high population density is at times found in other than urban areas.[1] The urban and surrounding rural areas in many parts of China tend to form relatively self-contained units, depending on each other for most needs, since remote areas are isolated by the lack of an adequate national transportation network. Urbanites become an essential part of the food sustenance chain, since farmers depend on human waste from the cities in order to fertilize the land. The "honey bucket," familiar to Americans in Korea, is crucial to subsistence economies in many parts of the world.

Professor King has estimated that a million urban dwellers congregated in cities accounted for approximately 13,000 pounds of nitrogen, 2,700 pounds of phosphorous, and almost 4,500 pounds of potassium in the daily night soil content, which is systematically collected and distributed throughout the surrounding countryside.[2] Therefore, if the city's population declines, less food is produced to support the remaining residents. This condition may have existed in earlier Western cities, for whenever invasion or unrest disturbed the equilibrium maintained between the food-growing and non-agricultural portion of the population, the process of urban growth was interrupted. A new balance had to be achieved before urban growth proceeded.

At the end of this era, some of the southern territories had been annexed. Cities began to develop below the south banks of the Yangtze River, and no other country in Asia had cities comparable in size to those in China. For example: Loyang, an important city located in the center of several feudal states, subsequently became a large commercial city. Tseng, the capital of a feudal state, was also a military and commercial center. The beautiful courtesans who lived there were extolled in literature and poetry. The city of Liang was pictured as having an unbroken line of chariots and horses traversing her busy streets all through the day and night. Hancheng was already famous for its iron factories. Linchu, the first important coastal city, founded along the coastline of the Pacific Ocean, had salt and iron industries. Her population totaled more than 300,000. Wu, the second largest municipality in size, had more than

[1] F. Keyes, "Urbanism and Population Distribution in China," *American Journal of Sociology*, 57 (May, 1951), 519–527.

[2] See F. H. King, *Farmers of Forty Centuries* (New York: Harcourt, Brace & Co., 1926), 75, 171–176; G. F. Winfield, *China: The Land and the People* (New York: Wm. Sloane Associates, Inc., 1948), 45–46; and J. L. Buck, *Land Utilization in China* (Nanking: The University of Nanking, 1937), 132, 143–144.

100,000 of her inhabitants living on the banks of the Yangtze River. Her city walls measured nearly fifty miles in circumference. Tao and Yangjer were other large commercial cities.[1]

Third period. The third period of municipal growth extended from the Chin through the Han dynasties (222 B.C.—220 A.D.), when 540 and 469 new cities, respectively, were built. The Chin period is noted for the erection of the Great Wall, which prevented the Tartars from disrupting the internal security of the empire. Commerce and trade cities appeared as far north as the present boundaries of Siberia and as far south as Indochina.[2] Hsiengyang, the national capital, was one of the largest cities and had a population of approximately half a million. Only Changan, the city designated by the throne for foreign trade, exceeded the former city in size and importance.

At the head of the Yangtze River was Chengtu, a new city founded for the purpose of conducting overland trade with India. It has remained one of the important cities of West Central China. Today airplanes connect it with coastal and foreign cities. During the Second World War, many air flights over the "hump" began and ended here. Other present-day cities founded during this period include Canton, Wuchang, Changsha, Kaifeng, and Taiyuan.

Fourth period. Many cities were destroyed during the Period of the Three Kingdoms, as this epoch is known, extending from 221 A.D. to 617 A.D. Internal warfare divided the country, and it was not until the rise of the Tang dynasty (618 to 959 A.D.) that prosperity and trade was resumed. Over 350 new cities were built as the country expanded in land area, encompassing Korea to the east and a part of West Asia. Trade was conducted between the Near East, India, and Siam because of the demand for Chinese porcelains, silks, and embroideries. A higher standard of living resulted, and many Chinese historians claim this dynasty to be one of the most prosperous. The annual exports from the capital, Changan, amounted to more than ten million dollars.[3] The famous "Silk Road" leading to the Near East was constructed during this period and Arab merchants came during the second century to trade in China.

Fifth period. The fifth period covered the Sung dynasty (960–1279 A.D.), the Yuan or Mongol dynasty (1280–1367 A.D.), and the Ming dynasty (1368–1644 A.D.). Southern cities increased in number and importance as the population was expanding toward Indochina and Burma, resulting in 315 more cities being established before the conquest by the Mongols

[1] Liang, *op. cit.*

[2] "Trade Routes to China from Ancient Times to the Age of European Expansion" by L. Carrington Goodrich, in *Highways in Our National Life,* Jean Labatut and Wheaton J. Lane (eds.), Princeton University Press, 1950, Ch. 3.

[3] Liang, *op. cit.*

invading from the north. The Mongol kings built 96 more cities and occupied all of those existing before their conquest. Former leaders were
retained for administrative posts, and placed under the supervision of
Mongolian tribal leaders. The cities founded during their reign served as
points of control over their extensive empire, conveniently divided into
regions for effective administration. Canals built at strategic points stimulated trade.

The Mongol invasion of Europe caused the building of many military
roads, thereafter facilitating trade and travel between the two continents.
Marco Polo visited Genghis Khan's court and returned to Italy with
accounts of the high state of culture in China. He was particularly impressed by Hangchow, a capital city built before the Mongol invasion
and beautified by the invaders. Situated on West Lake, with many beautiful pavilions and the finest tea orchards, it is now a famous resort, silk,
and cultural center. Marco Polo described it as the "largest city in the
world" because its population was almost two million.[1] Suchow was second in size, having half Hangchow's total.

After the downfall of the Mongol dynasty, the capital was moved back
to Nanking where the seat of the Sung government had been. More cities
were built along the Yangtze River basin, such as Wuchang, Hukou,
and Nanchang.

Southern cities were also becoming important. The city which has enjoyed the greatest international fame is Macao. In 1557 Portuguese traders
founded their colony in Macao and placed it under Portugal's jurisdiction.
Its political status has never been changed, and today it is one of the few
places where entry into China proper is possible and not too difficult.[2]
During the Second World War, Macao was the haven for refugee, missionary, business, and intellectual groups. Its gambling establishments are
world renowned.

Another southern city which rose to importance is Canton, located on
the Pearl River some 90 miles from Hong Kong. As the chief southern
seaport, its contact with foreign influence came as early as the second
century of the Christian era. Arab, French, Dutch, and Portuguese traders
came to the Canton shores but were not permitted to remain. When the
British merchants came to the city in 1637, they were required to transact business with Chinese merchants who had been especially designated
by the Ming throne. As seen from the preceding paragraphs, foreign merchants were not free to travel throughout the country, but were required
to conduct trade through specially designated cities.

The British merchants were extremely frustrated by this limitation of

[1] *Ibid.*
[2] *Time,* June 29, 1953, 25–26.

freedom, because their objective was to expand trade from the Indian Ocean to the north China seacoast and eventually to Peking. They conceived of a three-way trade between Europe, the Near East, and Asia. What was more irksome to them was the imperial edict segregating them in quarters known as the "factories," located on the south river bank opposite the main city.[1] They could not live nor trade elsewhere.

It was not until a valuable cargo of opium belonging to the East Indian Company was destroyed that a pretext for landing British troops at Canton was possible. China was defeated in the Opium War of 1839–1842. After signing the Treaty of Nanking in 1842 (Manchu dynasty), China agreed to open Canton and four other river ports for unrestricted foreign trade and to permit foreign concessions—or segregated areas—to be reserved for the political, economic, and social activities of nationals from Western societies.

The "factories" were abandoned in 1861, when the island of Shameen (Sha Min) was built and restricted to the residential and trade activities of foreign nations in Canton.[2] (See maps of Canton.) The island is one mile in circumference surrounded by a wide moat and enclosed by barbedwire fortifications. The banks, commercial firms, stores, consulates, private residences, clubs, and recreational facilities belonging to countries enjoying extraterritoriality or concession rights were located there until recently. Extraterritoriality was the right and privilege of a foreign country—or countries—to maintain an autonomous political, economic, and social system on Chinese soil. Although the main portion of the island's population is Caucasoid, some firms and households provide living quarters for their local domestics. On the whole, Chinese employees are expected to leave the island by nightfall, at which time the gates facing the main city are locked.

One significant consequence of extraterritoriality was alteration of the city's spatial pattern and the location of institutional organizations in Chinese cities wherever the extraterritorial practice was enforced along the Pacific seacoast, the Yangtze and Pearl rivers, and eastern Manchuria. The foreign concessions became the model and standard by which China's urban development, social values, and behavior patterns were measured.

[1] A. C. Hunter, *The Fan Kwae in Canton* (Shanghai: Kelly & Walsh, Ltd., 1911), 25; and Hwei-shung Gao, *Police Administration in Canton* (Peking: Peking Express Press, 1926), 1.

[2] E. T. C. Werner, *History of Chinese Civilization* (Shanghai: Shanghai Times, 1940), 310 and Gao, *op. cit.,* 3 and 17.

Within the old-city walls of Canton (see facing page) are many historical sites of the clan-family, Confucian, Taoist, Buddhist, and Moslem temples. Main streets leading to the point of dominance join with the ribbon-like development of the Bund, or central business district. The foreign concession, Shameen, is separated from the rest of the city. Modern educational, welfare, and religious organizations are located in the new section of Canton.

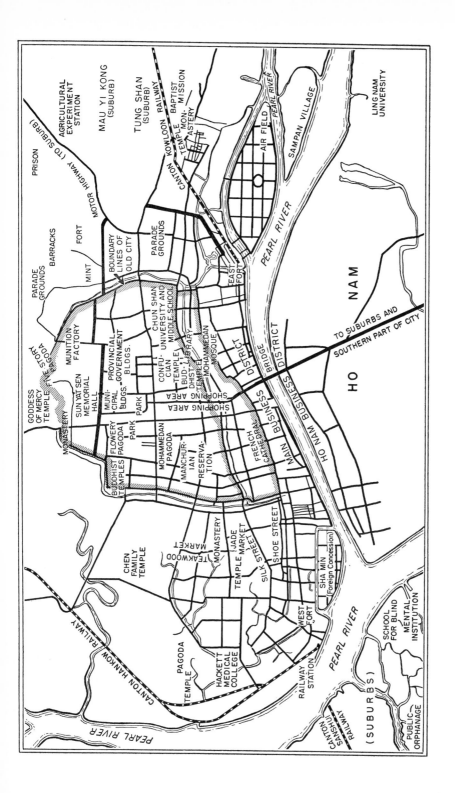

Chinese urbanites imitated and adopted Western habits according to their leanings and financial ability. Also, some of the urban traits were diffused to rural areas as contacts were made between westernized coastal cities and the hinterland.

Modern period. Although the opening of seaports to foreign trade began during the Ming dynasty, more cities were included in the extraterritoriality arrangements after the Manchu or Ching dynasty came into power.[1] Two major phases of the period of modern cities lasted from 1644 to 1911 A.D. (Ching or Manchu dynasty) and from 1911 to 1949 (beginning of Republic of China to end of Kuomingtang regime). Many cities of this period were modernized by Western nations. For example: Shanghai was founded in 1557 and was a leading silk and tea center dominating the entire Yangtze River basin and all of the south and north hinterlands from Manchuria to Canton.[2] Its fame did not reach the Western world until 1845, when the International Settlement and French Concession were created. Westerners referred to the Native City, where the local population lived and worked, as the "mud flats." They contrasted its medieval squalor with the tall skyscrapers, modern hotels and department stores built in the westernized portion. At the height of Shanghai's development, two-thirds of the country's industrial development and 60 per cent of the foreign trade was concentrated here. Shanghai's importance began to dim when extraterritoriality ended in 1942.[3]

There were also cities like Tientsin, Dairen, Swatow, Amoy, Tsingtao, Hankow, Foochow, Port Arthur, and others which grew into important commercial seaports due to the impact of westernization.[4] To a lesser degree they are known for their industrial activities, many of which are of the cottage type.

Realizing the need to encourage exploitation of natural resources and the development of factories to provide for local consumption, the Central Government undertook to establish "model factories" in cities selected for this purpose after 1928. Hankow, an inland Yangtze riverport, became the leading steel manufacturing city and is often referred to as the "Pittsburgh of China." Canton had textile, cement, sugar refining, and chemical factories. The silk filatures at Hangchow, Wusih, Wuhu, and Soochow were encouraged to perfect their silk growing and winding processes in order to compete with the Japanese silk market abroad. These plans were abandoned when the Sino-Japanese War began on July 7, 1937.

---

[1] *China Handbook,* 1950, 71.

[2] Harrison Forman, *Changing China* (New York: Crown Publishers, 1948), 223–228.

[3] *China Handbook,* 1950, 71; and Ernest O. Hauser, *Shanghai: City For Sale* (New York: Harcourt, Brace & Co., 1940).

[4] W. W. Willoughby, *Foreign Rights and Interests in China* (Baltimore: Johns Hopkins Press, 1927).

At the same time, repeated attempts were made by the Central Government to connect various coastal and inland areas by a more effective system of transportation.[1] This was difficult because the construction and financing of the various independent railway systems existing from the middle of the nineteenth century were under the control of various European governments. The respective systems began and ended where foreign spheres of interest predominated. For example, the French-owned and operated lines covered the southwestern provinces leading into Indochina and the leased territories of Hainan. British lines ran from Hong Kong through Canton to Changsha, northward to Hankow on the south banks of the Yangtze River, and thence to Shanghai, where British control was centered in the International Settlement. This same situation applied to north China where Russian and Japanese interests conflicted with those of Germany. Thus a network of transportation connecting coastal and inland cities was slow in developing. The east-west transportation system consisted mainly of rivercraft, buses, wheelbarrows, and manpower. It should be noted that China is geographically bisected east and west by three major rivers, the Yellow, Yangtze, and Pearl.

It has been estimated that in some sections of China, one-third of the population are employed as "human carriers" or coolies who cover approximately 20 miles a day.[2] As a point of contrast, China has 27 miles of rails per million population, while the United States has nearly 2,000 miles per million. What has contributed more to the growth of inland cities is highway construction. Much of the mileage was completed because of military necessity, and about 80,000 miles of highway connect rural areas, market towns, and county seats with large municipalities.[3] The more inaccessible southwestern and mid-central and northwestern cities of Szechuan, Kweichow, Yunnan, and Sian are linked to the coastal cities by airplane.

In summary: until the sixteenth century, China's front door faced Europe through the overland routes leading to the Near East. Cities and trade entrepôts linked the two areas, while other municipalities grew along the overland routes. After the Opium War the country's front door changed to face the Pacific Ocean. The ancient trade routes were closed until the present "People's Government" made concerted efforts to revitalize it by occupying Tibet.[4] For a few years during the height of

[1] Chang Kia-Ngau, *China's Struggle for Railroad Development* (New York: John Day, 1945) and Forman, *op. cit.,* Ch. 20.

[2] Richard J. Russell and Fred B. Kniffen, *Culture Worlds* (New York: The Macmillan Co., 1951), 420.

[3] *China Journal*, 1935, 373; and Forman, *op. cit.,* Ch. 21.

[4] Ekvall Farrar, *Tibetan Skylines* (New York: Strauss and Young, 1952); Amaury de Riencourt, *Lost World: Tibet, Key to Asia* (London: Victor Gollanc, Ltd., 1950); and Lowell Thomas, Jr., *Out of This World* (New York: American Book Co., 1950).

the Second World War, the "back door" was revived through the construction of the Burma Road. As a result, Chungking, Kunming, Chengtu, and cities located along the famous "Silk Road" (over which Marco Polo traveled) prospered.[1]

Seventh period. Beginning in 1950 the present "People's Government" has initiated what appears to be the seventh period of urban development.[2] The world's attention has been drawn to the systematic dismantling of factories and the large-scale evacuation of population from seaboard cities.[3] The abandonment of these cities is based upon the premise that if the natural resources found in the various areas within the nation are to be utilized effectively, cities and industries must be located there and not on the Pacific seaboard, and that the coastal cities have grown in importance and wealth because of Western influence, not local conditions. Therefore, inland cities are being encouraged to manufacture consumer goods and to trade with each other. Only by so doing can all traces of "foreign imperialism" be removed, the present regime believes. It should be noted that Hong Kong, Macao, and Harbin retain extraterritoriality status, in that they are yet under the jurisdiction of foreign powers.

An added reason for adopting this policy is linked with the system of municipal administration which the former government accorded large municipalities, giving them special or "first class" status.[4] Twelve cities came under the direct jurisdiction of the Executive Yuan and were considered separate political entities, enjoying complete autonomy from the provincial government. Governors of these provinces could not exercise jurisdiction over Canton, Chungking, Dairen, Hankow, Harbin, Mukden, Nanking, Shanghai, Peiking, Tientsin, Tsingtao, and Sian.[5] The Central Government appointed the mayors for these cities, and the cities had their own elected delegates to the National Assembly which could deal directly with the Central Government on matters of importance. The present regime has not changed this system, but has removed Hankow, Harbin, Tsingtao, and Sian from the special or "first class" list and has substituted several northern cities (Anshan, Fushun, Penki, and Wuhan) as leading cities.[6]

[1] *China at War,* 2 (Jan., 1939), 1–5; 71–72; and 74–75; also see Hollington K. Tong (ed.), *China After Seven Years of War* (New York: The Macmillan Co., 1945) 31–64.

[2] Benjamin I. Schwartz, *Chinese Communism and the Rise of Mao* (Cambridge: Harvard University Press, 1951).

[3] John Blofeld, *Red China In Perspective* (London: Allan Wingate, 1952), Ch. 28 and esp. pages 235–239.

[4] *China Handbook, op. cit.,* 33.

[5] Randall Gould, "Shanghai During the Takeover," 1949, *Annals of the American Academy of Political and Social Science* 277 (Sept., 1951), 182–192. Also see E. Stuart Kirby's article, "Hong Kong and the British Position in China," same issue, 193–202.

[6] *Statesman's Yearbook,* 1952, 850.

On the other hand, the former front door leading to the Near East, parts of Eastern Europe, and Russia, is being reopened. Cities which once were thriving municipalities in former eras may regain their status. Thus, Mongolian, Manchurian, Sinkianese, and Tibetan cities will link the territories between Russia and China as well as some of the countries of Europe.[1] Under the proposed Five-Year Plan for industrialization, the coal and iron regions near Anshan, Manchuria will be developed and integrated with the Siberian Lake Baikal and the Khabarovski-Komsomolsk projects. Tangshan, Peiping, Taiyuan, Hankow, Wuhan and Chungking are likewise being designated as heavy industrial areas.

Number of cities. By using the Ministry of Interior's report showing the geographical distribution of major Chinese cities up to 1948, a fairly comprehensive summary of cities based upon size of population is possible (Table 4). There were 177 cities having more than 50,000 population. Seven cities had over a million inhabitants; ten between 500,000 to one million; 25 between 200,000 and 500,000; 49 between 100,000 to 200,000; and 86 between 50,000 to 100,000.[2] Cities below 50,000 are frequently omitted in the official census, and it is doubtful if a systematic recording of cities by size or number has ever been taken. It should be noted that most cities existed before Western influence gained headway.

The United Nations' report of cities in 1950 showed a larger population total for most of the leading cities.[3] Although these figures are estimates, it is probable that the 1950 totals show a better picture of the distribution of urban population after V-J Day. Whereas in 1948 seven cities had over a million inhabitants, two more reached this status in 1950. It should be noted that Hong Kong was listed as a supercity in the 1948 report and omitted in 1950, so that there was an actual increase of three of these cities in China proper.

Various authorities have attempted to estimate the size of the urban population. Estimates vary between 65–100 million, or roughly 16–20 per cent of the population.[4] On the basis of 1952 figures, 394,498,491 persons out of 486,571,237 were rural dwellers (Table 5). Thus, 19 per cent of the total population was considered urban. At the present writing no further statistics are available. Although percentagewise China's urban population is lower than Great Britain's (the country having the highest urban total in 1951), the absolute number of urbanites in Chinese cities is almost twice the latter's total population.

[1] Martin N. Norins, *Gateway to Asia: Sinkiang* (New York: John Day Co., 1945), 117–122 and Chs. 10 and 11.
[2] Ministry of Interior, *Cities of China* (Shanghai: Great China Press, 1948), 11 (in Chinese).
[3] *United Nations Demographic Yearbook, 1952*, Table 8, 202–214.
[4] Keyes, *op. cit.*, 522–525.

TABLE 4. GEOGRAPHICAL DISTRIBUTION OF MAJOR CITIES
IN CHINA WITH POPULATION 50,000 OR OVER [1]

	Number of Cities with Population					
Region	*Over* 1,000,000	*500,000 to* 1,000,000	*200,000 to* 500,000	*100,000 to* 200,000	*50,000 to* 100,000	*Total*
Manchuria *	1	3	5	10	12	31
Sinkiang-Mongolia	—	—	—	—	3	3
Tsinghai-Tibet	—	—	—	—	1	1
Upper Yellow River Region	—	1	1	2	7	11
Northern China	2	2	3	6	20	33
Central China	—	—	—	3	3	6
Yangtze River and Great Lakes Region	—	1	3	5	9	18
Szechwan Region	1	1	—	—	5	7
Yünnan-Kweichow	—	—	2	—	5	7
Pearl River Region	1	1	4	3	4	13
Southeast Coastal Region	—	—	3	11	7	21
Nanking-Shanghai Region	2	1	4	9	10	26
Total	7	10	25	49	86	177

* Nine provinces in Manchuria and three neighboring provinces.

[1] *Source: Cities of China* (in Chinese), Ministry of Interior of China (Shanghai: Great China Press, 1948), 11. Translated into English by Yuan Liang.

As far as the geographic distribution of the 177 cities mentioned above is concerned, 62 per cent of them, or 111, are located within 155 miles of the Pacific seaboard. The rest of the country, comprising 88 per cent of the total area, had 38 per cent of these cities. Only one city with a million population was situated in this vast terrain up to 1948.[1] A redistribution of population has taken place, and cities in Manchuria and the outlying northern provinces are increasing in population. The redistribution of population is made possible by combining the railroads constructed by foreign powers. According to proposed plans, new rail systems will connect Chinese cities with those in Russia.

Other political units. In addition to the municipalities of the "special or first class" category and others of lesser political importance, several other types, hsiens or county seats, towns, and market centers have existed for about two thousand years and are closely linked with cities. The country has 2,023 hsiens, each with a county seat functioning as the health, educa-

TABLE 5. POPULATION OF CHINA, 1950 [1]

Region	Total Population	Agricultural Population
Total	486,571,237	394,498,491
North	67,068,386	54,372,349
Northwest	23,471,480	21,264,365
Northeast (Manchuria)	41,570,678	33,774,063
East	140,928,712	121,317,365
Mid-South	136,775,290	106,414,718
Southwest	70,634,691	57,355,631
Inner Mongolia	2,400,000	*
Tibet	3,722,000	*

* Information not available.

[1] *Source: People's Handbook*, Shanghai, Tai Kung Pao, 1952, 153 (in Chinese). Translated into English by Yuan Liang.

tional, and welfare center for the area over which it has jurisdiction. These county seats exhibit degrees of urbanization commensurate with their size. The next type of population concentrations are towns and market centers, where the residents from several villages or towns gather every five days (or as prescribed by local custom) for the exchange of goods and services. The number of residents exceed what is considered an "urban place" in this country.

A striking illustration of a number of cities connected into one functional unit is offered by cities in the outlying provinces of Mongolia and Sinkiang.[2] A given area is dominated by one large city. Within this area is a series of small cities whose arrangement and size is the result of trade routes. It must be kept in mind that transportation of goods is largely a matter of human and animal carriers. The cities away from the central

[1] Liang, *op. cit.*
[2] Keyes, *op. cit.*

city are significant as supply centers for travelers and are spaced in terms of days of travel. The cities nearest to the central city tend to be the smallest, since there is less demand for the replenishing of supplies; and the cities farther along this chain are larger. This is in marked contrast to satellites around American cities, which tend to get smaller as the distance away from the central city increases.

Modern, feudal, and primitive cities. Chinese cities may in general be classified as predominantly modern, medieval or feudal, or "primitive," depending on their major characteristics. The modern cities are similar in many respects to cities in the West. Cities such as Shanghai, Hong Kong, Nanking, Dairen, and Tsingtao have many facilities constructed for the accommodation of resident foreigners and westernized Chinese.

The second type is often called the "medieval city" because it has some of the characteristics found during the Middle Ages in Europe—the guild system, a local militia, a city wall, and a closer interrelationship to the surrounding agricultural area. Many have survived to the present and have been clothed with some modern changes, as exemplified by Peking, Canton, Tientsin, and Amoy. Both medieval and modern characteristics may be found in these cities.

When this is the case, the westernized portion has been grafted on the old. In Canton, for example, a modernization program took place after 1920. The thick city wall which formerly girdled and constricted population and areal expansion has been leveled off and used as one of the main arteries of transportation for motor vehicles, buses, and rickshaws. Suburbs form a portion of the new city where urbanites who have acquired Western ideas and tastes prefer to live. The traditional families live in the older section, in homes which have housed several generations.

The third type are "primitive" inland cities which retain much of their ancient squalor, but are vital for trade and commerce. Many are located where topographical breaks between land and water occur, or where small bodies of water flow into larger ones. As transfer points for goods, services, or passengers, they have remained important.

Ecological organization. The ecological organization of a given city is affected by its age, location, and the composition of the population. Briefly, the ecological organization of a city is concerned with the manner in which various groups distribute themselves within a limited land area, and how this arrangement influences their relationships with each other. Moreover, the extent to which Western influences have left their impact upon the spatial distribution of population and institutional organizations is a contributing factor. It is therefore difficult to generalize that any one city pattern is representative of the many different cities found in China today. At best, a few comparisons can be made.

Modern coastal cities are extremely heterogeneous in population and culture. The "native city," so designated by the Western nationals, is always teeming with people. A food famine, drought, civil war, or quarrel with family members has caused many rural migrants to go to cities in search of economic or social betterment. Many come to find a solution to personal problems. Once there, citizens from various villages, districts, provinces, or regions form their respective "local areas," so that a given dialect and a special set of organizations are perpetuated. Shanghai and Peking have their Cantonese, Ningpo, Szechuan, or Kiangsi areas. Canton has Mongolian and Manchurian reservations. (See map of Canton.) The latter are reserved for the descendants of former Mongolian and Manchurian officials who settled during the Yuan and Ching dynasties. Although their members are rapidly disappearing through marriage with local inhabitants, many cultural ties bind them together.

Ghetto-like formations, therefore, are based on territorial, ethnic, or linguistic relationships. The residents of such areas are bound together in mutual-aid and protective associations which had to be created in cities to care for the ill, infirm, indigent, widowed, or orphaned. This type of association is necessary in a society where a national welfare system is relatively new and where the population's earning power is irregular and insufficient for the establishment of a tax supported welfare system.

The longer some families settle in cities and the more westernized they become, the more they are apt to resettle in or near the areas reserved for foreign nationals or to create communities based on economic differentiation. Still, many retain ties with their home villages, districts, or native provinces. A story is told of two strangers meeting in an air-raid shelter in Chungking, the Mecca for refugees from many parts of China during World War II. There was the usual polite exchange of "What is your honorable surname?" and "What is the name of your distinguished village?" between the two. The first then asked, "Are you a native of Chungking?" whereupon the second replied with haste, "Most assuredly not. My family has lived here only 400 years!"

Where a sizable group of foreign nationals live in cities, the areas they occupy are differentiated by racial origin, religious differences, or social status. Thus in Hong Kong the Sikh, Parsi, Hindu, and Moslem groups each maintain their own small settlements and remain aloof from neighboring residents, regardless of their racial or social background. The Eurasians, offspring of Mongoloid-Caucasoid unions, occupy the "in-between" areas, midway between the section reserved for the Caucasoids and the local population. They live as far as possible from the local population and as close to the Peak as possible, where Europeans have preferential residence (before Pearl Harbor, only Europeans lived here). In Shanghai,

American Steamship Line

Hong Kong, outpost of Great Britain's influence in South China. Race course to the right. Thatch-covered roofs to the left ward off the summer heat in homes and office buildings. Note the cosmopolitan nature of advertising signs and architectural design in this coastal city.

Harbin, Macao, Tsingtao, and other large port cities where some miscegenation has taken place, the Eurasians occupy a marginal position that is reflected in their selection of residence and in their social intercourse with others. They strive to identify themselves with the Caucasoid group but are not totally accepted by them. They avoid intimate contacts with the Chinese because they feel this may lead to misidentification.

Residents from European countries, The United States, and Japan settled in the concessions reserved for them. In cities where the Germans formerly held such areas, the Japanese have taken over after World War I. The influx of White Russian and other European refugees after World War I resulted in considerable congestion in the concessions, but there was no great tendency to invade the areas occupied by the Chinese. The boundary lines between one concession and the next are narrow. The Chinese section often is so close that physical nearness is inevitable; yet the maintenance of social distance is so great that the acculturation and assimilation of Westerners into Chinese culture is rare. For many members of the Caucasoid group, urban residence in China is regarded as "temporary." However, the

Ewing Galloway

Washien, China, an inland city of 220,000 population on the Yangtze River, Szechuan Province. The city is reached by junks and sampans. Bamboo poles are the foundations for buildings above the water table. In the center, a vendor and his customers stand between concrete step streets leading to shops with canopy-like awnings. To the left are matsheds; one at right has smoke seeping through.

institutions which perpetuate the Western way of life are numerous, as, for example, the cinema, English press, schools, restaurants, food shops, dairies, dancing schools, and bakeries. Both Shanghai and Hong Kong feature "famous American steaks," "real American chop suey," and "stateside ice cream."

Cities which have medieval characteristics are different in their spatial pattern. Founded centuries before the impact of Western urbanism, the physical lay-outs were too well established to permit extensive alteration. Many have an old and new section. The older sections of these cities are unbelievably congested and located near the waterfronts. Many crooked and winding streets lead to the residential areas, retail shops, and temples. The main business districts face the waterfronts and stretch in ribbon-like developments from one section of the city to the other. It is as if Fifth Avenue, New York, were built along the waterfront. The land values are highest at the waterfront or Bund.

Vice areas may be near or inside the central business district, or at the edge of the waterfront where the sampans and junks crowd together. Sampans and junks are frequently used for prostitution and as gambling dens or thieves' hideouts. They are floating places of recreation, frequented as theatres and restaurants by the wealthier urbanites. Single persons live close to the downtown section or at the city's periphery where the newer industries are located.

The domination of many areas by ancestral dwellings of the more powerful families made it difficult for industrial and commercial establishments to invade these areas and change the pattern of land use. Large and spacious homes with courtyards are often hidden behind inconspicuous outer gates near to the main business district, while industries are found in some of the newer residential sections. Specific areas throughout have been set aside for one type of merchandise, so that comparison shopping is made easier. "Shoe Street," "Jade Street," "Silk Street," "Teakwood Row," and "Antique Section" have store after store selling but one type of goods.

The slum location differs from American cities. Since many Asian cities cannot expand outward from the center, slums are either near factories at the city's outskirts or at the outer edge of the waterfront. The Canton "floating population" was estimated in 1934 at 200,000 living on 40,000 sampans at one time, and that of Shanghai, at close to a million.[1] The "waterfront" slums are the largest of such areas in the city.

As it developed, the city attracted a new group of inhabitants, the human carriers and unskilled laborers for the transport of goods from steamships, railroad cars, and big junks. The next large group attracted was the factory employees. Having no place to live, a large portion is found in floating homes in sampans, mud huts, straw-thatched sheds, or crowded tenements. Many live at the lower end of the long waterfront in poorly constructed wooden shacks raised on wooden stilts. These communities are called "pile villages" and also exist in South Asia. Others live in make-shift huts near factories or warehouses. Thousands upon thousands of small watercraft serve as homes, stores, temples, churches, freight trucks, ferries or taxis. Indeed, one sampan may fulfill all of these functions.

Sampan dwellers are born, grow up, and die on their small craft, maintaining with the land residents a minimum of social contacts limited to the business at hand—freighting a cargo across the river or ferrying passengers. Where means of transportation are limited, the sampan groups compose a necessary part of the social and occupational structure. Social mobility is difficult to achieve because many of the rights and privileges enjoyed by

[1] Lingnan Social Research Institute, *Shanam Boat People: A Social Survey* (Canton, China: Lingnan University, 1934), 2.

the land residents are not offered to them. Illiteracy is high because educational facilities are almost totally lacking. Opportunities for occupational mobility are few. Health measures are not enforced, and a high death rate from epidemics and communicable diseases is a part of the people's lot.

In contrast, the *nouveaux riches* (consisting of the families of the middlemen or compradores, the professionals, some white-collar workers, and those having acquired Western standards) live in surroundings which approximate the suburbs or exclusive residential districts of Western cities. Whereas older families living near the business districts prefer rickshaws manned by liveried pullers, the "newer social classes" sport imported automobiles, if circumstances permit, or they ride street cars and buses.

Inland cities, far removed from the seacoast, but frequently located near rivers, are still walled and guarded by local militia. City walls have not been torn down to make way for automobile or bus traffic. Rickshaws and bicycles provide the major means of transportation. Streets are short, narrow, and crooked. Merchandise is openly displayed in front of shops or spread out on the thoroughfare and taken in at night. Modern sewerage, water, or utility systems have not been installed. Electric voltage is weak, and individual wells supply the water required by homes and businesses. Buildings are seldom taller than two stories. The roof-top open-air dining room, dance halls, and theatres of large coastal cities are absent. Few institutions of higher learning are located in the more remote inland cities, and what ones there are usually are operated by the provincial government as two-year normal colleges and four-year high schools.

The majority of the cities have one main street leading from the waterfront or main gate to a dominant point within the city, often the seat of local government. If the city is a provincial capital or a special municipality under the jurisdiction of the national government, administrative control is the center of dominance (see map of Canton). Important business and commercial houses are located on the streets leading to this center.

Because of the high cost of transportation and the time consumed in going from one section of the city to another in rickshaws or on foot, many retail subcenters are found. Department stores are for the wealthy, as are luxuries such as silk, jade, and teakwood products. Only on rare occasions, like shopping for a wedding, would the lower economic groups buy at these areas.

Within any city are found Confucian, Taoist, or Buddhist temples that attract settlers and visitors. (See map of Canton.) As stated earlier, Confucian followers are primarily males because the rites and observances are designed for the educated. Moreover, Confucianism supports the patriarchal family system, and women are considered outside of the system and have to rely upon the male members of the family to give them status.

Wherever a Confucian temple is erected, there are shops dealing in hand-carved seals, brush pens, rice paper for calligraphy, antique porcelains, jades and vases, sacred books and scrolls appealing to collectors.

Buddhism has more female followers, and the Goddess of Mercy is the saint to whom women pray for offspring to support the Confucian system. The important reason why fewer males embrace Buddhism is because of the strong patriarchal Chinese family system, and families do not wish their sons to enter the priesthood, which requires the maintenance of celibacy. Therefore, a part of the family may practice Buddhism as an assurance that there will be many sons to continue the family. All the necessary articles for religious offerings, such as paper effigies, incense, candles, fruit, and meat, are found in the shops close to the Buddhist temples. Professional letter-writers, fortune-tellers, and herbalists operate stalls nearby. In some of these stalls and shops merchandise for small children is sold, since mothers often bring their offspring to pray before and be blessed by the Goddess of Mercy. This same arrangement holds true for Taoist temples, since these were erected to counteract the influence of Buddhism. Teahouses, restaurants, and sedan chair stations are other establishments located near these places of worship. Until the building of Christian churches in cities, temples constituted important minor subcenters.

Social and occupational structure. As pointed out earlier, the social structure of the country remained fairly stable for many centuries following the Confucian era of the Chou dynasty. That is, the system of established patterns of ideals and actions within which individuals acted according to certain social positions began to crumble under the impact of Westernization. The rise of new occupations and industries, although of the cottage-type, following the establishments of British influence in South China, caused a gradual weakening of the Confucian or pre-Republican social structure. The scholar, farmer, and artisan groups of the Confucian social structure lost status as a new group of persons found greater social mobility and status by identifying themselves with Western practices in conducting business, but a considerable period of time had to elapse before the new social structure of the Republic crystallized.

The development of a middle class, so frequently associated with urban growth in Western societies, came slowly. Knowledge of English was requisite, and it was not until after the downfall of the Manchu dynasty and the abolition of the Confucian classical educational system that a new educational system was adopted. The new educational system, from elementary school through the university level, was patterned after the American system, because a large number of Chinese students and educators were selecting institutions of higher learning in America as their bases of training. The influence of American missionaries should not be overlooked, because it was they who introduced coeducation at the turn of this century. Later, they started medical, nursing, and social service training in the schools they established or supported financially. Only then could a middle class develop. Many recruits were drawn from the families who were used as intermediaries (or *compradores*) between foreign and local merchants. Others came from the gentry and landowning group.[1] To the extent that a middle class could be said to exist before the downfall of the Central Government of China, approximately 15 per cent of the population was assigned to this rank. About 80 per cent of the population comprised the lower class, and roughly 5 per cent belonged to the upper class.[2]

Republican social structure. The Republican social hierarchy consisted of the following groups:[3]
1) official (military and civil)
2) educator
3) liberal professions (physician, engineer, lawyer, etc.)
4) manufacturer
5) merchant (also included money changers, bankers, etc.)
6) factory worker
7) artisan
8) farmer
9) laborer (agricultural and other).

The increase of urban occupations following the rise of modern cities added the classifications of liberal professions, manufacturer, merchant, and factory worker. There was not a clear-cut distinction between some of the classifications; *e.g.,* educator, manufacturer, merchant often overlapped with the official. Since the latter had the highest rank, an official probably desired to be so known, although his activities in the other fields may have been greater. Or an absentee landowner, while technically a farmer, could have become either an official, merchant, manufacturer, or indeed all three. Prestige overshadowed monetary considerations.[4] Although many of the upper-class members lived in cities, they retained through the centuries their power and landholdings in rural areas by giving employment to poor relatives and continued to increase their wealth and status by alliances with other families.

In 1947 a study of the occupations pursued by residents over 12 years of

[1] Ta Chen, *op. cit.,* 43–44.
[2] *Annals of the Academy of Political and Social Science,* 277 (Sept., 1951), 13–16, 19–20.
[3] Ta Chen, *op. cit.,* Ch. 5.
[4] Hsiao-tung Fei, "Peasantry and Gentry: An Interpretation of Chinese Social Structure and Its Changes," *American Journal of Sociology,* 52 (July, 1946), 17; and his *China's Gentry* (Chicago: University of Chicago Press, 1953).

age in 12 cities and provinces was conducted by the Ministry of Interior of China to determine the distribution of the labor force.[1] In Shanghai, out of a total of 2,925,247 persons over 12 years of age, 121,017 were engaged in agricultural enterprises as against 578,160 in commerce; 546,730 in industries; 176,217 in communication and transportation; 61,024 in civil service; 151,350 in social service; and 132,424 in other professions. Unfortunately, data for the other eleven cities were not given.

During the same year, 15,049 factories having a paid personnel of over 30 and paid-up capital investment of more than $10,000 were reported for the entire country.[2] The large majority were privately owned and managed industries, a condition which is probably not true at the present time. The textile, chemical, and food and beverage industries employed the greatest number of administrative and manual workers, although those engaged in the manufacture of metallurgical, machine, metal, and electrical equipment, clothing, and printing products employed around a million workers in all classifications. The total number of industrial workers before World War II was listed at approximately 3 million.[3] Another 10 million persons were employed as industrial administrative personnel, government employees, teachers, and as commercial and handicraft workers.

Added evidence that urban occupations were growing in importance was pointed up by the growth of labor union membership. At the end of 1947, 5,003,598 workers had membership in 11,522 registered labor unions, the majority of which were quartered in big cities.[4] The rise of war industries undoubtedly caused an increase in the gainfully employed as well as strengthening the role of labor unions, but the prestige and status of factory personnel was not as firmly entrenched as that of the artisan groups.[5]

On the other hand, artisans have experienced a considerable decline in status and number since 1850. Artisan-made goods are unable to compete with foreign imports and to meet the changing tastes of the population. They often cost more than machine-made goods, which were and are permitted to enter the country through the duty-free ports of Hong Kong, Macao, and Harbin. Moreover, the older generation, which prefers handmade articles to foreign imports, is declining in number. An added drawback to guild growth is that a national guild organization has never existed, although the same kind of goods may be made in different cities.

[1] *China Handbook, op. cit.,* 20.

[2] *Ibid.,* 381–383.

[3] *Annals of the American Academy of Political and Social Science,* 277 (Sept., 1951), 126; "Labor Policy and Factory Management in Communist China" by W. Ayers.

[4] *China Handbook, op. cit.,* 432.

[5] Ta Chen, "Basic Problems of the Chinese Working Classes," *American Journal of Sociology,* 53 (Nov. 1947), 184–191, and Nym Wales, *The Chinese Labor Movement* (New York: John Day Co., 1945).

The relatively slow rate of industrialization has resulted in fewer opportunities for social and occupational mobility for the growing group of landless farmers, laborers, entrepreneurs, white-collar workers, and professionals. Since 1850 there has been a steady emigration of Chinese nationals desiring social and occupational mobility. In June, 1948, the Chinese Overseas Commission reported 9,115,357 persons of Chinese extraction abroad, of whom the great majority are in South Asian countries.[1] The Americas have 209,039, as compared to 53,622 in Europe, 57,274 in Oceania and 14,851 in Africa.[2] Where the Overseas Chinese have settled in large numbers they have contributed to the heterogeneity of population and have influenced the occupational and social structure. These influences will be discussed in the following chapter.

It is now apparent that changes are taking place in the Republican social structure as a result of the ascendency of the "People's Government."

"People's Government" social structure. Insofar as some tentative observations can be made concerning the fluctuating socio-economic status of groups found within the "People's Government" social structure, it is apparent that the groups subordinate to official status are undergoing a period of instability. Efforts are being directed toward remolding the Chinese society.[3] A new system of rewards and privileges for both sexes seems to be taking shape in order of rank as follows:[4]

1. Official
   a. party leaders
   b. party cadres
   c. peasant organizers
   d. military personnel
2. Farmers
   a. owners-tillers
   b. renters
   c. laborers
3. Workers (primarily state employed)
   a. technicians
   b. administrators
   c. industrial workers (all types)
   d. common laborers
4. Educators
   a. vocational emphasis

---

[1] *China Handbook, op. cit.,* 20–44.

[2] *Ibid.,* Tables 11 and 22.

[3] Theodore H. E. Chen "The Marxist Remolding of Chinese Society," *American Journal of Sociology,* 58 (Jan., 1953), 340–346.

[4] *Annals of the American Academy of Political and Social Science,* 277, 113–134.

  b. theoretical emphasis
  c. propagandist
  d. recreation leaders (theatricals, folk dancing,
      story tellers, writers, etc.)

Although the educator group had once enjoyed the highest status but is now relegated to a position of less social power, its prestige remains high so long as it fulfills its role in (1) combating illiteracy, and (2) participating whole-heartedly in the training of the technicians and administrators needed by the state's industrial and agricultural enterprises. There is a concerted effort to enlarge these groups as rapidly as possible by de-emphasizing theoretical subjects. All social science subjects are receiving careful scrutiny as to content and theory and in many instances are being omitted from the college curriculum. Educators who have successfully demonstrated a reorientation of attitudes through "brain washing" and have become committed to the political, economic, and social policies of the present government, have a reasonable expectation to hold a place in the social structure.[1] Because most institutions of higher learning are in cities, the urban professional groups—of which the educators are a large segment—are facing the threat of being declassed.

Undeniably, the farming and working groups are being upgraded because the success of the "revolution" is correlated with their acceptance of mass reforms in connection with the land redistribution and industrial expansion programs. The cooperation of these groups is needed to insure the permanence of the present government.[2]

At the top of the social ladder are the Party leaders and cadres, followed by the peasant organizers and military personnel. The Party officials establish the policies for the groups within the upper class to execute and extend to the ranks below.[3]

It should be noted that in the Confucian and Republican social structure, the military groups were accorded a low social rating. Many urban migrants, however, saw military service as a road to urban living and a means of both spatial and social mobility. The higher ranks of the armed and aeronautical forces were often held by persons listed as "officials" during the Republican era. A common soldier was popularly equated with the common urban or rural laborer, but in practice the military personnel had a great opportunity at social mobility by cooperating with the official class.[4]

[1] *Ibid.,* 135–145.
[2] *Ibid.,* 24.
[3] *Ibid.,* 113 and 124–125.
[4] Lt. Col. Robert B. Riggs, *Red China's Fighting Hordes* (Harrisburg, Pa.: Military Service Publishing Co., 1951), Ch. 5, and Morton H. Fried, "Military Status in Chinese Society," *American Journal of Sociology,* 57 (Jan. 1952), 347–357.

Ewing Galloway

In Shanghai a coolie and helper—the human transportation system—deliver a wheelbarrow-load of imported sanitary facilities. Behind the wheelbarrow are rickshaws.

It should be noted that the present government is attempting to break the Confucian family system by granting women equal places in the social hierarchy. Should the present government succeed in its aims—(1) industrialization of China, and (2) mobilization of the masses by promising an equalization of wealth—urbanization may increase if foreign trade continues.

Non-industrial factors promoting urban growth. A summary of the various factors promoting urban growth will show these to be mainly of a non-industrial nature. Most Chinese cities are noted for their commerce and trade, rather than for their industrial activities. The exception is Shanghai. Natural resources have not been sufficiently developed, or if developed, are not fully utilized by local industries for the manufacturing of consumers' products. Before the Korean conflict raw materials were shipped abroad to other cities in Europe, North America, or Japan for processing, and the finished products were reshipped as "foreign merchandise." The chief exports were wheat and wheat flour, cotton, timber, leaf tobacco, tung oil, soybeans, vegetable seeds and oils, silk, hog bristles, tea, hides, skins, wool, eggs and egg products. Ramie, mattings, and bamboo constituted other items.[1]

In return China imported a vast quantity of goods and clothing for her large population. This unfavorable foreign trade balance has hindered the development of local industries.[2] Yet China's raw materials and their processing have contributed to the industrial, financial, and commercial importance of Western cities.

There has been an influx of human carriers to cities where commerce and trade flourishes. As seen earlier in this chapter, the sampan dwellers along the riverfront may constitute as much as a sixth of the city's total population. In Canton, they were reported in 1934 as 200,000 out of a total of a million and a quarter persons. The exact number who are migratory "human carriers" is unknown, although it is estimated that some 33 per cent of the population of some sections of the country is so employed at all times.[3] Although there is a change in the actual personnel involved, a like number would in all probability enter the city to replace them.

A third factor is that urban conveniences and the privilege to enjoy them draw the upper class and the rising middle class to cities.[4] Urban living is expensive, since foreign goods and services must be paid for in the Chinese dollar, which, in normal times, is worth approximately one-sixth of a United States dollar. Whereas at one time the civil servants through holding a Hanlin degree by passing the Confucian-imperial examinations won the privilege of urban residence, money and a place in the Republican social structure have since replaced it as a prestige steppingstone. Many persons within the higher classes shun manual labor or any efforts associated with it. As absentee landlords or as dependents of landlords living on rents, interests, or other investments, they are able to meet the new urban standards.

The upper classes attract and give homes to many poor relations, unemployed family friends, and displaced farm workers who otherwise would have difficulty in finding subsistence. "Unpaid family workers" and relatives make up another group whose size is greater than that of the upper classes. The practice of nepotism (or, according to relatives and close friends, "preferential employment") as a method of spreading the cost of a non-organized nation-wide relief system has aroused considerable criticism within and without China.[5] Despite the fact that persons holding

[1] T. H. Shen, *Agricultural Resources of China* (Ithaca: Cornell University Press, 1951), Ch. 41.

[2] Kuo-Heng Shih, *China Enters the Machine Age* (Cambridge: Harvard University Press, 1944).

[3] Russell and Kniffen, *op. cit.*, 240.

[4] Fei, *op. cit.*, 17.

[5] Rose Hum Lee, "Research on the Chinese Family," *American Journal of Sociology,* 54 (May, 1949), 503.

Ewing Galloway

Chungking, China: step-like streets leading from waterfront to the city proper. Wealthier persons used four-manpower sedan chairs. Water carriers with wooden buckets beside them are resting on steps.

positions of power and status can alleviate their own burdens by supporting nepotism, many others find no opportunities for employment and become unpaid workers in the immediate family or family-owned and operated enterprises. Even in Japan this situation exists, and as late as 1940 almost one-third of the total number of gainfully employed persons were in family enterprises. In most instances they worked for no specific wage.[1]

Another factor promoting urban growth is the desire for higher education and, especially, Western education, which is found only in cities where missionary, public, or private-endowed universities were established. The extent to which the missionaries contributed to urbanization would be an interesting topic for further study. At least, the persons having the means to study in Westernized institutions are the social climbers and persons seeking to identify themselves with the system of Western urban values.

Other factors can be briefly mentioned. The greater safety of cities has attracted settlers. Fear of civil war, banditry, kidnaping, robbery, and personal injury has caused many families to send their sons or husbands to

[1] Irene B. Tauber, "Family, Migration and Industrialization in Japan," *American Sociological Review*, 16 (Apr., 1951), 153.

cities. The growing independence of women, although relatively unad-
vanced as compared to Western societies, has enlarged the urban population by women taking jobs in industry or as domestic helpers. Famine,
drought, and population pressure on land have likewise caused cityward
migration.[1]

Japan

As the most industrialized nation in the Orient, Japan has a higher per-
centage of urban dwellers than any other Asiatic country. Ever since she
began to develop a modern economy a century ago, the rate of urban
growth has increased steadily. This fact is all the more remarkable because
Japanese culture had its earliest recordings about the fifth century of the
Christian era and developed more than two thousand years later than
China's or India's. By 1950, within less than a century of the opening of
Japan to the West, 37.5 per cent of her total population resided in cities.[2]

The total area of Japan is divided into 46 prefectures. Each prefecture
is divided into *shi* (city areas) and *gun* (rural counties). A "shi" city is an
incorporated area usually having a clustered population of more than
30,000.[3] The 1950 urban total was double that of 1920, when 18.1 per cent
was urban. This census definition of an urban population is a conservative
estimate. Should a different numerical base, say 2,500 (United States) or
5,000 (India) be used, the urban total would be higher. However, the
larger population base is perhaps more realistic when one attempts to show
the distinctions between the urban and rural characteristics of the country's
people. In spite of rapid urbanization, Japan's cultural pattern has many
"feudal survivals."[4] In spite of the fact that governmental agencies use a
different numerical basis for defining an area as a city, Japan's urbanization has paralleled that of Western societies within the last hundred years.

Periods of urban growth. Five major periods of urban growth have
taken place from the beginning of cities to the present:

1) Ancient (660 B.C. to 1185 A.D.)
2) Pre-Togukawa (1185 A.D. to 1603 A.D.)
3) Togukawa (1603 A.D. to 1868 A.D.)

---

[1] Shu-Ching Lee, "Agrarianism and Social Upheaval in China," *American Journal of Sociology,* 56 (May, 1951), 518.

[2] Except where indicated, statistics for Japanese cities were secured from the Bureau of Statistics, Office of the Prime Minister, Tokyo, Japan.

[3] Bureau of Statistics, Office of the Prime Minister, *Official Count of Census of Population,* Oct. 1, 1950.

[4] See John F. Embree, *The Japanese Nation: A Social Survey* (New York: Farrar and Rinehart, Inc., 1945) and Ruth Benedict, *The Chrysanthemum and the Sword* (Boston: Houghton, Mifflin Co., 1946).

4) Meiji Restoration (1868 to 1941)
5) War and Postwar (1941–)

The last two periods are the most significant insofar as the acceleration of urbanism is concerned.

Ancient period. The founding of cities during the ancient period dates back to 660 B.C. when the unification of tribal villages in and around the province of Yamato resulted in the establishment of the capital city of Kashiwabara. This ancient city remained the seat of political power until Nara was selected in 710 A.D. for this purpose because this city was accessible to China, where Japan had close ties with the Tang dynasty.[1]

Nara, the newly selected capital, was modeled after Changan, China's Tang dynasty capital. It was also a cultural center of the 200,000 persons living there, where approximately 10 per cent of the population studied Chinese art, literature, philosophy, and architecture. With the diffusion of Buddhism into Japan, through China and Korea, the erection of large Buddhist temples and shrines followed. Thereafter, many Japanese cities became religious centers, adopting the Buddhistic style of architecture.

In 794 A.D. Heian-Kyo (modern Kyoto) was chosen as the capital by the Emperor Kwammu when Nara's territorial confines became too small to accommodate the growth of population. The seat of political power remained at Kyoto until Yedo, or modern Tokyo, was selected for this purpose in 1603. Other cities which grew to importance during the ancient period are Kobe, to the west, and Kaka and Sakai, in mid-central Japan. Thus, only half a dozen important cities were established and created for administrative, religious, and trade purposes during the ancient period. They enjoyed national status and superseded the provincial cities of Naniwa and Hakata in size, population, and trade activities. The cities of this period showed strong Chinese influence in physical layout and architecture and the behavior patterns of the urbanites were governed by Confucian ethics and thought.

Pre-Tokugawa period. The Pre-Tokugawa period (1185–1603 A.D.) is considered to be the age of feudalism in Japan.[2] In 1192 Minamoto Yoritomo became the *shogun* (feudal military dictator of the country) by creating the system of shogunates, or feudal military lords, who superseded the emperors in ruling the country. This practice continued until the Meiji Restoration in 1868. Many fortified cities were built during this period, when each military lord controlled a province and maintained a retinue of followers. At the same time, the shogunates promoted merchandise fairs and encouraged commerce and trade.

After a time, the growth of commerce and trade resulted in the develop-

[1] Liang, *op. cit.*
[2] Russell and Kniffen, *op. cit.*, 439.

ment of the merchant group who succeeded in acquiring more wealth and power than the shogunates. The shogunates were forced to borrow from the merchants when they were unable to pay their followers or when starting new enterprises.

As the merchants grew stronger, they became more enterprising. Textile arts of spinning and weaving were brought from China, and the manufacture of firearms followed the visits of Portuguese traders to Sakai in 1541. Expanding commercial and industrial activities caused other cities to be founded during this period: Tokyo (1457); Osaka (end of fifteenth century); Nagoya (1610); Kamakura (thirteenth century); Nagasaki, a port earmarked for foreign trade when the rest of Japan was closed to outside contacts for two and a quarter centuries. Fukuoka, Hiroshima, Gifu, and Kawasaki were other trade cities of this period.

Tokugawa period. In 1603 Iyemitsu Tokugawa made himself the supreme shogun by defeating the other feudal lords whose struggle for power disturbed the economic, political, and cultural growth of Japan. Thereafter, more than two centuries of peace and prosperity followed during which considerable attention was devoted to the promotion of trade and commerce and the development of the arts.

Cities grew in importance during that time. Tokyo was selected as the seat of the shogun government, but it was equally renowned as a center of culture and art. Osaka, on the other hand, enjoyed unrivaled prestige as the trade and commercial center. Nagasaki was her chief rival in the volume of foreign trade conducted between China and Europe.

After the second decade of the seventeenth century a wave of isolationism swept Japan, and her ports were closed to foreign influence. Although this move was primarily aimed at rooting out Christianity, cultural contacts between the Japanese and the Chinese, Dutch, Portuguese, and others were strictly prohibited so that Japanese culture would not be contaminated. Only the port of Nagasaki was open for trade with the rest of Japan and a trickle of export trade. This policy was abandoned in 1853 when Commodore Perry of the United States succeeded in establishing the "open door" policy with Japan.[1] Kobe, Yokohama, Hakodate, and Nagasaki became important trading centers as a result.

The most significant result of more than two centuries of enforced isolation was the unification of Japanese culture and the promotion of ethnocentrism. Another result was the decline of Chinese influence, terminating the amicable relations which had characterized the cultural contacts between Japan and China for several centuries. After the reopening of Japan to outside contacts, she turned her face to the West. Thus, the era of modern cities is directly related to the influence of Western urbanism.

[1] Francis J. Horner, *Case History of Japan* (New York: Sheed and Ward, 1948), Chs. 7 and 8.

Meiji restoration. The Emperor's resumption of direct rule of the nation after 1868 following the "open door" policy, ushered in an era of modernization and urban growth comparable to that of Western societies of the same period. A series of measures was systematically taken by the Japanese government and a combine of feudal lords and high military officials to promote the growth of commerce and industries.[1]

Some of the measures taken during the next 75 years toward modernizing Japan included (1) government sponsorship and financing of industries, utilities, mineral extractions, and transportation systems; (2) the alliance between eight large family groups (the Zaibatsu) and the government to control commercial, financial, industrial, transportational and metal combines throughout Japan and the auxiliary territories she controlled (Formosa, Korea, Manchuria, Sakhalin, etc.);[2] (3) the training and enlargement of professional, managerial, and administrative groups for various enterprises established by the Zaibatsu and the government, to be utilized in Japan and auxiliary territories; (4) the annexation and control of territories through military "expeditions" in other Far Eastern countries to insure a continuous supply of raw materials which Japan lacked, so that industrial expansion was not hampered;[3] (5) a systematic recruiting and allocating of the young adult population for civil, military, managerial, professional, and white-collar positions in auxiliary territories, in order to relieve the population pressure at home and to promote greater occupational and social mobility for the ambitious;[4] (6) permitting the military cliques and navy personnel to enforce administrative and political control where necessary;[5] (7) dominating the world market in raw silk, toys, novelties, porcelains, and cotton goods; (8) cornering the Far Eastern market for consumer goods by underselling Western competitors; (9) raising the standard of living and the educational level of the populace; (10) creating a network of internal transportation enabling raw materials to be shipped to production centers and the maintaining of a merchant marine for foreign trade; and (11) consciously borrowing, adapting, and integrating into her political and economic order the complex traits that made Western countries develop a high degree of urbanism.

The most important factor contributing to Japan's rapid urbanization was the dovetailing of national economic, political, and military policies

[1] Inazo Nitobe (ed.), *Western Influences in Modern Japan* (Chicago: University of Chicago Press, 1931), 271–306; and Russell and Kniffen, *op. cit.,* 444.

[2] The Mitsui, Mitsubishi, and Sumitomo monopolies of the Zaibatsu controlled shipping, banking, textile, mining, and other enterprises.

[3] Nitobe, *op. cit.,* 399–407.

[4] W. S. Thompson, *Danger Spots in World Population* (New York: Alfred A. Knopf, 1929); and his *Population and Peace in the Pacific* (Chicago: University of Chicago Press, 1946), Chs. 6–12.

[5] Nitobe, *op. cit.,* 408–443 and E. C. N. Cuaston, *Militarism and Foreign Policy in Japan* (London: G. Allen & Unwin, Ltd., 1936).

by the end of the nineteenth century, when the Sino-Japanese War was fought and a foothold gained in Korea after China was defeated. To insure against a possible counterattack as well as to insure more food for her growing population, Japan annexed Formosa during the first decade of the twentieth century. By securing a vantage point in Korea, Japan gradually gained control of Manchuria by 1931, on the pretext of suppressing the recurring "incidents" of civil war, banditry, and warlordism and of protecting Japanese investments in coal and iron ore mines, railroads, and heavy industries.[1] Soya bean farming and the processing of the bean for sauces, bean curd, and fertilizer were other lucrative enterprises operated by Japanese capital, although the Russians who settled there offered keen competition in these undertakings. The story is now history of how Japan later began the invasion of China and other Asian countries to insure a continuous supply of rubber, copra, cotton, rice, tin, manganese, and tungsten.

The combine of noble feudal families, known as the Zaibatsu, who cooperated with the Imperial Government in promoting industrialization and urbanization was an added force. The government gave legal protection to cartels owned and operated by the "big three"—Mitsui, Mitsubishi, and Sumitomo—and other monopolies so that they controlled the shipping, raw materials, banks, export-import firms, and the major steel, silk, and chemical industries. Although Japan had succeeded in raising the standard of living of the general population to the point where it was higher than the rest of Asia, most of the wealth and benefits went to the Zaibatsu and their relatives, employees, and affiliates.

The Zaibatsu was dissolved after V-J Day through the enactment of an anti-monopoly law; but this was amended on July 25, 1953, and the big firms are again permitted to unite, subject to government controls.[2] The return to the former practice is regarded as necessary for the revival of foreign trade and the creation of capital for new enterprises. The first passenger and freight steamship sailing between the United States and Japan left Yokohama at about the same time, thus resuming another of the operations temporarily halted by war.

In order to give her growing population opportunities for achieving occupational and social mobility, a large number of young adults were sent to Korea, Formosa, Manchuria, and other countries to work and create new industries. Japan is a good illustration of a country which has reduced her death rate with the adoption of Western science and medicine—but not her birth rate. Population has continued to outrun subsistence. A concerted

[1] Gustave Eckstein, *In Peace Japan Breeds War* (New York: Harper & Bros., 1943) and Hillis Lory, *Japan's Military Masters* (New York: Viking Press, 1943).
[2] *Chicago Tribune*, July 26 and 29, 1953.

attempt to alleviate the population pressure by emigration was one of the solutions.

War and postwar. Although the entrance of Japan into World War II caused a temporary setback in urban growth and population, her recovery is well underway. Her industrial, commercial and financial strength is gaining. The midcentury census listed 248 "shi"—cities with a total population of 31,203,191 (Table 6). Sixty-four cities each having more than 100,000 inhabitants had a total population of 21,326,215. The total urban population, as previously defined, was 37.5 per cent and 25 per cent of the country's population lived in 64 metropolitan cities.

The increase in the number of urban centers for four consecutive decades was from 81 in 1920, to 107 in 1930, to 166 in 1940, and to 248 in 1950. The urban population rose from 18.1 per cent in 1920 to 24.1 in 1930, to 37.9 in 1940, but it dropped to 14.1 in 1944. Between 1944 and 1950 an added decline of 3.6 per cent was caused by the bombing and destruction of cities, the migration of urbanites to rural areas, and by unemployment. The greatest reduction in urban population occurred between 1944 and 1945, the period of severe aerial bombardment, when the percentage fell from 41.1 to 27.8. The upswing was resumed after V-J Day so that the 1950 census returns revealed a partial reversal of the downward trend, but the present urban population percentage has not reached that of 1940.[1]

Although the 1950 urban population was 37.5 per cent, the absolute gain in urbanites was 3.7 million within the decade 1940–1950. The greatest influx has been toward cities with a population of between 100,000 and 500,000.[2] One-fourth of the country's total population lives in these large centers, and slightly less than a third of all urbanites cluster around the "big four"—Tokyo, Osaka, Kyoto, and Nagoya. The repatriation of Japanese nationals from Korea, Manchuria, Formosa, Sakhalin Island, Pescadores, and elsewhere, as well as the natural rate of increase, swelled the country's total population by 11.2 million between 1945–1950. Despite the emigrations from Japan of half a million Koreans, Formosans, and Chinese after V-J Day, there was a net gain of 10.7 million.[3] This increase resulted in 82 more incorporated areas attaining "shi" status within the decade 1940–1950.[4] The 1950 census recorded the population of Japan at 83,199,637. Of the inhabitants, 31,203,191 were urban, and 51,996,446 were "gun," or rural.

The "gun" counties remained almost stable. A "gun" area is subdivided

[1] Bureau of Statistics, Office of the Prime Minister, "Preliminary Results of the 1950 Population Census and Selected Historical Statistics," contained in *The Japanese Economic Bulletin,* 52 Sec. 3 (Dec., 1950), 3.

[2] *Ibid.,* 4

[3] *Ibid.,* 2

[4] *Ibid.,* 4

TABLE 6. NUMBER OF CITIES BY POPULATION SIZE AND PER CENT DISTRIBUTION, JAPAN, OCT. 1, 1950 [1]

Size of City *	Number of Cities	Total Population	Per Cent
Total	248	31,203,191	37.5
1,000,000 or more	4	9,473,191	11.0
500,000–999,999	2	1,716,624	2.0
100,000–499,999	58	10,135,895	12.0
50,000–99,999	86	6,019,743	7.0
40,000–49,999	46	2,057,376	
30,000–39,999	51	1,772,329	5.0
20,000–29,999	1	27,528	

* "Shi" are incorporated urban places, usually having a cluster of 30,000 or more population.

[1] Source: Bureau of Statistics, Office of the Prime Minister, Population Census of 1950, 1, Nov. 1951, and Japanese Economic Statistics, 52, Sec. 3 (Dec., 1950), 4.

into "machi" and "mura" for census purposes. When the population in these two types of areas increases to the point where either singly or in combination they bring the total to 30,000 inhabitants or more, a redesignation of their status to "shi" follows. In this fashion, 40 places acquired "shi" status between 1940–1945 and 42 others between 1945–1950. In other words, the emigration of population from the "gun" areas elevated these places to "shi" status more rapidly than if the redistribution of population had not occurred.

Sex ratio. When the midcentury Japanese census returns were released, the sex ratio favored the females. There were 96.3 males to females in 1950, a considerably higher ratio than at the end of World War II when it stood at 87. Thereafter, the sex ratio rose and has been more normal than at any time since 1940. This is largely due to the repatriation of males to Japan. The urban sex ratio was also better balanced.

Type of cities. Japanese cities have reached such a stage of specialization that several types of cities can be described. Their diverse industrial and commercial activities contrast sharply with other Asian cities, which by comparison appear undeveloped.

Tokyo, the capital city, became the world's third largest city at the time of World War II. Its present population is 5,385,071. Because it is the site of the Imperial Palace, the Imperial University, and historic shrines and temples, it is the main cultural center. Many modern hospitals, schools, hotels, department stores, and other establishments are located in Tokyo. Its industrial enterprises produce electrical equipment, airplane parts, and machine tools and many other items. Although partially destroyed by a devastating earthquake in 1923, followed by a tidal wave and fire, the city was completely rebuilt and modernized by 1930. Situated on the northwest shores of Tokyo Bay, harbor facilities are inadequate. Its outlet to the sea is through Yokohama to the south. The Sumida River flows through the city, and many picturesque canals span the river banks.

Tokyo's suburban center is Kawasaki, with a population of approximately 319,226. A municipality in its own right, Kawasaki is noted for the ancient shrines built during the twelfth century. Many worshippers make annual pilgrimages to the shrines. In recent years it has grown into a manufacturing center, producing heavy electrical and aircraft equipment and chemicals.

Yokohama, Japan's chief port city, has a population which is nearing the million mark. Yokohama was the world's foremost silk exporting city before nylon replaced silk in many industrial processes. Her industries include shipbuilding, automobile manufacturing and heavy electrical equipment. An insignificant fishing village until after Commodore Perry's visit, she is Tokyo's chief outlet to the sea because of the modernization of harbor facilities. An electric interurban transit system connects Tokyo to Yokohama.

Yokohama, Tokyo, and some other major seaport cities, boast modern conveniences that distinguish them from other Far Eastern cities. Tokyo's modern department stores display the merchandise of many foreign countries. The bazaars and tea houses, frequented by many people still clad in kimonos, afford a contrast to ice cream parlors and department stores.

Seaport cities. Other major seaport cities include Nagasaki, Osaka, Kobe, Fukuoka, Sasebo, Kure, and Yawata. Nagasaki, with one of the most beautiful harbors in the world, was the only port opened to trade and foreign contacts during the two and a half centuries when Japan's enforced isolation was in operation. Reopened for active trade in 1859, it became Japan's leading coal station. It has major shipbuilding industries and many thriving commercial enterprises. During World War II almost half the city was destroyed by an atomic bomb. Considerable rebuilding has taken place, and trade has been resumed with some Western and South Asian cities.

Osaka is Japan's second largest city. It was the capital of the country toward the end of the sixteenth century; and the Toyotome castle, the mint, and arsenal still stand. Today it is a diversified manufacturing city specializing in production of chemicals. Kobe, another seaport and commercial city, is closely connected to Osaka. There are fine harbor facilities in Kobe. One part of the city is built along the north shores of Osaka Bay and the other part on a hillside. Although second to Yokohama in port activities, shipbuilding and the manufacture of heavy electrical equipment and aircraft, nevertheless, its commercial importance is attested to by branch offices of many foreign business firms. Consulates are also located in Kobe. Its rubber industries are among the largest in the Far East. Kobe, Osaka, and Amagasaki (a suburb of Osaka) form a triad of centers producing steel and pig iron.

Fukuoka is another center manufacturing iron and steel. Sasebo is one of the larger naval bases. The latter's dockyards and arsenals are located along the large inlet of outer Omura Bay. Kure is the seat of the naval academy and has a fine, spacious harbor. Its steel factories and shipyards are numerous. Yawata, sometimes called the "Pittsburgh of Japan," has developed large iron industries since 1897.

Other cities. Other large cities include Hiroshima, Nagoya, Kyoto and Sapporo. Senai is a renowned cultural center; one of the Imperial Universities is located there, as are famous castles belonging to feudal lords of the sixteenth century. Nagoya is the seat of fine Buddhist temples and castles, preserved and retained for the Imperial family. Kyoto is the center of Japanese art.

Fukui, Kanazawa and Fukushima are important textile-producing cities, especially habutai (a thin soft silk). Lacquer ware, pottery, and bronze made Takaoka and Wakayama famous. Other cities are engaged in the production of patent medicines, religious paraphernalia, the distilling of sake, or the packaging of tea.

In contrast to southern Japan, there are but few cities located in the northern part. Among the most outstanding is Muroran, a naval base, coal port, and iron and steel center. On the west lies Otaru, situated on Otaru Bay in an inlet of the Sea of Japan, where trade is handled between Japan and Soviet Russian ports. Joji is the seaport closest to Korea. During the nineteenth century this port was used as a military base for wars against China and Russia. A city with a large artificial harbor is Omuda. The harbor was built and owned by the Mitsui family to facilitate the extraction of coal and ore in this region. The Mitsui also owned and operated many of the steamers and railroads leading from the North to the South.

Industrial and occupational structure. Table 7 shows the male and female segments of the Japanese labor force. The category of "craftsmen, production process workers, and laborers" exceeded all others. This corresponded roughly to more than a third of the gainfully employed, while sales, clerical, and other similar types of workers constituted less than a third of the total. Approximately 10 per cent belonged to the professional, technical, managerial, and official classifications. The remainder belonged to the semi-skilled working in mines, quarries, lumbering, fishing, farming, and service industries. About a third of the labor force was made up of women, with the largest number engaged as artisans, production-process workers, and laborers. The rest were employed at farming, lumbering, fishing, sales, and clerical duties. Relatively few women were in transport activities.

The size of a country's labor force is related to the type of industrial structure it has developed [1] (Table 8). Of the total gainfully employed, the largest number of males were engaged in industries manufacturing such items as food, tobacco, textiles, apparel, furniture and fixtures, wood products, paper products, printing, chemicals, leather, metals, machinery, transportation equipment, and precision instruments. The wholesale and retail trade industries employed more females than did manufacturing and service enterprises. In no instance did women outnumber men in urban industries.

[1] An enterprise is considered an industry if employing over 30 persons.

TABLE 7. LABOR FORCE BY MAJOR URBAN OCCUPATIONS, MALE AND FEMALE, JAPAN, OCT. 1, 1950 (IN THOUSANDS) [1]

Occupations	Total *	Male	Female
Total population, 14 years old and over	21,407	10,376	11,031
In labor force	12,169	8,391	3,769
Total employed	11,715	8,079	3,636
Professional and technical workers	802	560	242
Managers and officials	440	422	18
Clerical and related workers	1,784	1,224	560
Sales workers	1,732	1,124	608
Farmers, lumbermen, fishermen, and related workers	1,605	862	743
Workers in mine and quarry occupations	89	82	7
Workers in operating transport occupations	226	223	3
Craftsmen, production process workers and laborers	4,100	3,202	898
Craftsmen and production process workers	3,386	2,602	785
Laborers (except farm, mine, and service)	715	600	115
Service workers	910	362	548
Not classified and not reported	31	20	11
Unemployed	454	312	142
Not in labor force	9,228	1,981	7,247
Labor force status not reported	9	5	4

* Based upon 10 per cent sample tabulation of 1950 census.

[1] *Source:* Bureau of Statistics, Office of Prime Minister, *Labor Force Status*, Dec., 1951, and *Employed Persons by Occupation*, March, 1952.

Japan, like many other Asian countries, maintains in many industries the practice of utilizing "family workers," who are not paid a specific sum for their services but may be included in the official census enumeration as being difficult to classify.[1] However, women may work in family enterprises and be omitted in the count, although their labor is a decisive factor in making the business a success. This practice partially accounts for the smaller number of women "gainfully employed." During periods of economic adjustment—for example: postwar recovery and return to normalcy —the proportion of male and female "family workers" could increase.

TABLE 8. POPULATION BY MAJOR URBAN INDUSTRIES, MALE AND FEMALE, JAPAN, OCT. 1, 1950 (IN THOUSANDS) [1]

Industry *	Total	Male	Female
Total Employed	11,715	8,079	3,636
Agriculture	1,499	762	737
Forestry and logging	24	20	4
Fisheries and aquaculture	117	106	11
Mining	137	123	14
Construction	610	580	30
Manufacturing	3,240	2,426	814
Wholesale and retail trade	2,302	1,449	853
Finance, insurance, and real estate	257	169	88
Transportation, communication and other public utilities	946	834	112
Services	1,690	887	803
Government	856	697	159
Not classified and not reported	37	26	11

* Based upon 10 per cent sample tabulation of 1950 census.

[1] *Source:* Bureau of Statistics, Office of the Prime Minister, *Employed Persons by Industry* (Feb. 1952).

Although these workers do not receive a stipulated salary, their food, board, clothing, and incidental expenses are provided by the person or firm using their services.

The repatriation of five million Japanese nationals from outside Japan after V-J Day has created an added strain on local industries which had difficulty in absorbing the ever-growing labor force during prosperous times.[2] In the main, the repatriated had lived in cities while abroad and were engaged in urban occupations. They had shunned the menial tasks and agricultural pursuits where they settled because native laborers had a

[1] Included in the "Monthly Labor Force Survey" conducted by the Bureau of Statistics, Office of the Prime Minister, Jan.–Dec., 1950.

[2] Japanese Economic Statistics, *op. cit.,* 2.

lower standard of living and could work for wages which the Japanese nationals found to be inadequate.[1]

Korea

Korea's urban development has been relatively retarded, although her known history antedates Japan's by almost five centuries (1122 B.C.).[2] The invasion of Korea by groups who were a mixture of Tungusic and proto-Caucasoid origins, resulted in the Koreans and the invaders joining to-gether and forming the ancient Kingdom of Chosen. They had consider-able control of territory which is a portion of present day Manchuria. When these tribes were overcome by Chinese invaders in 108 B.C., Pyong-yang near the 38th parallel was selected as the capital.[3] By 668 A.D. Korean leaders succeeded in unifying the country and moved the capital to Kyonju, where it remained until 1392 A.D. Thereafter, Seoul in central Korea was designated as the seat of political administration. As the only Korean city with more than a million population, Seoul has been the center of art and learning as well as an important commercial and industrial center.

Urban development. Korea's early urban development was influenced by China. Korea came under China's political jurisdiction until after the Sino-Japanese War of 1895. Urban growth was slow, however, as only 11 cities with more than 14,000 inhabitants were reported in 1910, and 4 per cent of the total population resided in them.[4] By 1940 the urban population rose to about 15 per cent of the total population, while these same large cities had 8.4 per cent of the total urbanites. At this time, 50 cities of vary-ing sizes were scattered throughout the country.

The growth of urban population was due primarily to the influx of Japanese who concentrated at Seoul, Fusan, and other large commercial and industrial cities. The Koreans represented 11.5 per cent, and the Japanese 71 per cent of the total urban population.[5]

A more recent report showed that 19 large cities and 1,524 towns and townships had developed, but that the "Korean incident" had reduced the urban population to 7.5 per cent.[6] Table 9 gives a partial list of principal southern Korean cities.

Major northern cities included Sishu, Samsuo, Bakdusan, and Kwainei along the banks of the Yalu River adjacent to the Manchurian boundary

[1] Warren S. Thompson, *Population Problem* (New York: McGraw-Hill Book Co., Inc., 1942), 266–268.

[2] M. Frederick Nelson, *Korea and the Old Orders in Eastern Asia* (Baton Rouge, La.: Louisiana State University Press, 1945), Pt. 1.

[3] George M. McCune, *Korea Today* (Cambridge: Harvard University Press, 1950), Ch. 1.

[4] Andrew J. Grajdanzev, *Modern Korea* (New York: John Day Co., 1944), 80–81.

[5] *Ibid.*

[6] Korean Pacific Press, "Korean Report, 1948–1952," 5.

line. Pyongyang is another important northern city with 286,000 inhabitants. Heavy industrial development was mainly found in the northern half of the country where Japan had established facilities for the extraction of coal, iron ore, gold, graphite, tungsten and alunite. Lesser minerals, such as zinc, copper, lead, magnesite and silver, were mined in varying quantities, exported to Japan, or sold to other countries.

The southern portion of the country is mainly agricultural. Some textile industries, specializing in cotton and silk weaving and spinning, are lo-

TABLE 9. POPULATION OF THE PRINCIPAL CITIES
OF SOUTH KOREA, AUGUST 25, 1946 [1]

Name	Population	Name	Population
Seoul	1,141,766	Kaesong	87,962
Punsan	400,156	Chinju	86,852
Taegu	269,113	Chonju	83,333
Inchon	215,784	Musan	82,175
Mopko	103,081	Gunsan	66,715
Kwangju	100,451	Chungju	51,522
Taejon	96,207	Chunchon	46,089

Source: Vital Statistics Section, Department of Public Health and Welfare, USAMGIK, *Population of South Korea by Geographic Divisions and Sex*, Seoul, September, 1946.

[1] Adapted by permission of the publishers from George M. McCunes's *Korea Today* (Cambridge, Mass.: Harvard University Press, 1950).

cated there. In both north and south Korea, cities are located along the seacoast on banks of rivers. Pusan, a shipbuilding and repair center, is also a major seaport. This is also true of Taegu, Mokp, Kunsan, Inchon and Haeju to the south. Northern seaports include Chinnam, Wonsan, Hamhung, Songlin, Chongjin, Najin and Ungai. Chemicals and explosives are manufactured in cities bordering the Yellow Sea because of proximity to the sources of raw materials. The finished products are transhipped from Ch'ungch'ong-mando, Taejon, Sochon, and other cities. Other urban industries manufacture cement, textiles, and metalware, or are engaged in the refining of ores and metals.[1]

Factors affecting urbanization. The relative absence of industrialization and urbanization is due to several factors.

Primary was the effort made by Japan between 1905 and 1945 to utilize the raw materials extracted from Korea for the bolstering of Japanese industrialization or for commerce and trade with other countries.[2] The

[1] The Department of State, *Korea: 1945 to 1948* (Washington, D. C.: United States Government Printing Office, Far Eastern Series 28, Oct., 1948). See map for location of various industries and natural resources.

[2] Thompson, *Population Problems, op. cit.,* 266–267.

Korean economy suffered because more material was taken out of the country than was returned. At the same time Japan constructed railroads, highways, heavy and light manufacturing industries, public utilities and hydro-electric resources to bring this about, but these modern improvements were not intended to benefit the Koreans. A part of Japan's policy toward Korea was to keep the Korean farmers on the land as food-growers and to deny them the benefits of industrialization and urbanization. The surplus food grown was sent to Japan.[1] Most Japanese lived in cities and did not engage in farming. Only 5.4 per cent of the Japanese farmed in Korea.

Table 10 gives some indications of the differences between Koreans and Japanese in regard to their various occupations. Although the Koreans are more numerous in most categories, there were proportionately more Japanese than Koreans in managerial, clerical, white collar, professional, technical, civil service, and private enterprises. Koreans had few opportunities to hold positions of responsibility.

Another factor retarding urbanization was that Japan found it expedient to retain the ancient agrarian economy. They permitted landowners to retain ownership of their land so long as they did not interfere with Japanese interests. Landowners, in return, were expected to discourage rural-urban migrations. What industries were permitted to develop were of the cottage type and located in rural areas as a conscious attempt to restrict the development of Korean industrialization.[2]

Since the end of World War II, the desire to modernize and industrialize has already been shown by young Koreans. It is probable that when conditions return to normal, urbanization will proceed.

Some South Korean cities, particularly Pusan, have been important as ports for United Nations forces, as well as sanctuaries for the major part of the displaced millions of Koreans. After a peace settlement has been reached, many of these displaced persons may remain and form the nucleus of an urban unskilled labor force.

Taiwan (Formosa)

Formosa, like Korea, was ceded to Japan by China after the Sino-Japanese War of 1894–95. At the end of World War II, Formosa—or Taiwan, as she is officially known—became the thirty-fifth province of China (October 25, 1945). The provincial capital Taipeh was later designated as the seat of the Central Government of China. Until December 8, 1949, the Central Government offices had been located in Nanking.[3]

[1] Russell and Kniffen, *op. cit.*, 435.
[2] McCune, *op. cit.*, 29–37.
[3] *China Handbook*, *op. cit.*, 33–39.

TABLE 10. POPULATION AND EMPLOYMENT OF KOREANS AND JAPANESE, KOREA, 1944 [1]

Name	Managerial		Clerks and White Collar Workers		Professional and Technical		Laborers		Public Servants and Small Businessmen		Unemployed		Total
	Male	Female	Male	Female	Male	Female	Male	Female	Male	Female	Male	Female	
Koreans	7,151	365	172,422	10,166	27,901	366	6,292,704	3,626,909	122,130	11,273	5,898,865	8,949,923	25,120,174
Japanese	3,412	253	53,357	14,344	14,486	352	74,564	34,623	38,240	7,066	159,116	308,635	708,448

[1] Source: Condensed by permission from Tables 6A and 6B, Appendix B, 330–331 in *Korea Today* by George M. McCune (Cambridge: Harvard University Press, 1950). Figures for these tables were taken from *Results of 1944 Census* (in Japanese), Chosen Government-General, May, 1944.

Although Taiwan has a long coastline, only two cities—Keelung in the north and Kaohsiung in the south—are suitable for ocean steamers.[1] The remainder are small port or inland cities for trade (Table 11). The largest industrial enterprises are concentrated in the five major cities, and these cities were treated in the same manner as "mainland" ones until after 1949.

It is difficult to determine what percentage of the 7,617,753 Taiwanians are urbanites.[2] The five major cities have within their confines a total pop-

TABLE 11. MAJOR CITIES OF TAIWAN (FORMOSA), 1950 [1]

City	Type of City	Number of Households	Population Male	Female	Total
Taipeh	Capital of Taiwan; transportation, industrial, commerce and trade	108,775	217,640	233,137	450,777
Keelung	Chief harbor; railway, shipbuilding, financial, airport	35,681	78,234	67,006	145,240
Taichung	Jute processing; fruit and tobacco production and export	41,008	107,044	99,965	207,009
Tainan	Airport, jute and sugar processing, commerce and trade	45,308	117,200	122,252	229,452
Kaoshiung	Commerce and trade, coastal city; railroad center, financial enterprises	62,708	149,578	125,985	273,563
Hsincho	Railway	—	—	—	125,120 *
Hualien	Airport, manufacturing	—	—	—	— †
Taitung	Airport, shipping	—	—	—	—
Makung	Airport, shipping	—	—	—	—
Anping	Commerce and trade	—	—	—	—
Tamsui	Commerce and trade	—	—	—	23,000

* 1948 figure.
† Not available.

[1] Source: *Directory of Taiwan*, 1951, 6–18, and *Webster's International Dictionary*, 2nd Ed., 1945.

ulation of 1,308,041, or slightly more than 17 per cent. A more recent report showed, however, that 1,600,000 persons belonging to "11 cities and counties" voted at the last municipal election for new mayors and 814 councilors, officials for their respective legislative chambers.[3] This would indicate that the five major urban areas contain a portion of the county wherein they are located, and that both urban and county residents are regarded as "urban." If this is the case, the urban total is raised to 21 per cent.

In comparison to Korea, Taiwan is more urban and is second to Japan in urbanization among the North Asian countries. In reverse of their activities in Korea, the Japanese exerted effort in modernizing Taiwan and

[1] *Directory of Taiwan*, 1951, 28 and 49–50.
[2] *Ibid.*, 5.
[3] *Chinese News Service*, Dec. 30, 1952.

gave more to the local population in terms of wealth and education.

Taiwan has a greater degree of industrial development than Korea. The manufacturing of paper, chemicals, cement, ceramics, textiles, and metal products is scattered throughout the island's industrial plants. The extensive exports of rice, sugar, tea, fruits, nuts, jute, tobacco, and minerals spurred the Japanese government to construct highways, build railroads, and widen harbors. Since the end of 1949, air transportation has connected the island's cities into a network.

The 1950 census enumeration disclosed that 200,000 gainfully employed persons were industrial and mine workers, 235,399 in fishing industries, and 100,000 craftsmen and transport operators. There were 6,484 doctors, nurses, and midwives.[1] A large majority of the skilled personnel had been trained by the Japanese, although in recent years Chinese from the mainland and South Pacific countries have settled there. Between 1952 and 1953, 34 factories from Hong Kong, Japan, the Philippines, Indonesia, and Singapore have moved to Taiwan.[2] At the same time, the armed forces utilize a large segment of young male adults and some 4,000 persons are employed by the Central Government to assist farmers in agricultural reform and the adoption of new techniques. Approximately 60 per cent of the total rural population are farmers.

Since Taiwan's return to Chinese administrative control, concerted efforts have been made to increase her economic stability by promoting industrial expansion, greater exploitation of resources, increasing export trade, and enlarging transportation and communication facilities. The United States has had a large share in spearheading better work and wage conditions for urban workers as well as providing the financial backing for industrial and commercial expansion.

Summary

China has had seven major periods of urban growth since the founding of ancient tribal capitals. Cities are mainly located near rivers or seacoasts. Some are railway, bus, or airplane terminals. Their primary function is commerce, with the export and transshipment of raw materials exceeding that of manufactured products. Non-industrial factors contributed more to stimulate the growth of cities than industrialization.

Since 1850 the cities bordering the Pacific Ocean have grown in size and importance, but it is probable that in the future those which lead to Eastern Europe and the Near East will regain status as trade centers. China's front door is again facing Europe and the Near East. Approximately 19 per cent of the population is urban.

[1] *Ibid.,* 18, 19 and 24.
[2] *Chinese News Service,* June 30, 1953.

Japan's urban development has exceeded that of other Asian countries, and 37.5 per cent of her population are residents of centers that have more than 30,000 inhabitants. Since 1868 a concerted effort has been made by industrialists, bankers, exporters, and military officials to cooperate with the Japanese government in promoting greater urbanization. Approximately five million Japanese nationals were resident in Far Eastern countries where they controlled the extraction of raw materials, trade, commerce, and industrial development to insure the success of Japan's modernization and industrialization. The repatriation of these overseas urbanites as well as the natural rate of increase has swelled the urban aggregation. Between 1940 and 1950, 82 more "shi" areas were reported by the midcentury census. Japanese cities show a high degree of specialization and produce a large share of the goods and services needed by the lesser industrialized countries of the Far East.

Both Taiwan and Korea had few urban centers, although they came under the direct influence of Japan for half a century. Most of their cities are commerce centers, although by comparison Taiwan's industrialization exceeded Korea's. In 1948, 7.5 per cent of the Korean population lived in cities, as compared to about 21 per cent for Taiwan in 1952. A greater degree of industrial and commercial diversification existed in Taiwan's cities than in Korean cities. Both countries are likely to experience greater industrialization and urbanization in the future.

DISCUSSION QUESTIONS

1. Discuss the impact of Western urbanism upon Chinese cities after 1850.
2. In what way may Chinese cities differ from Western cities in internal spatial pattern?
3. Explain the various factors which have contributed to the growth of urbanism and urbanization in Japan since 1857.
4. In what ways have these factors hindered or promoted the development of urbanism in Korea? In Formosa?
5. To what extent has the concentration of commercial and trade activities retarded industrial development in North Asian cities (with the exception of Japan)?
6. What role will Japan play in the postwar period in Asian industrialization?
7. What role will Mongolian, Manchurian, Tibetan, and Sinkiangian cities play in China's postwar commercial and industrial expansion?

SUGGESTED PROJECTS

1. Trace the growth and development of any major city in North Asia: Tokyo, Kobe, Shanghai, Hong Kong, Seoul, Taipeh, etc.

2. Study the growth of the Japanese "middle class" who settled in other countries in order to rise occupationally and socially.
3. Compare the industrialization of Formosa before and after Japanese occupation.
4. Study the growth and development of the Chinese treaty port cities.
5. Study the role of the Zaibatsu combine in Japan before and after World War II.

READINGS

Ruth Benedict, *The Chrysanthemum and the Sword: Patterns of Japanese Culture*. Boston: Houghton Mifflin Co., 1946.

An eminent anthropologist's analysis of national character and culture patterns.

Clarence Decker, "Formosa—Main Road to Free China," *New Republic,* Jan. 12, 1953.

A report by the Assistant Director of the Mutual Security Agency in charge of the Point Four Program for the Far East indicates a restoration of prewar economy and industrial expansion since 1950.

John F. Embree, *The Japanese Nation: A Social Survey*. New York: Farrar and Rinehart, Inc., 1945.

A comprehensive survey of Japan, with emphasis upon the social, economic, and political changes before the end of World War II.

Harley F. MacNair (ed.), *China*. Berkeley: University of California Press, 1946.

A volume of the United Nations series on China, containing chapters written by experts in economic, social, political, educational, and welfare institutions. The topics of philosophy, art, ethics and music are not overlooked.

Edwin M. Martin, *The Allied Occupation of Japan*. Stanford: Stanford University Press, 1948.

A résumé of the changes found in Japan under Allied occupation with special emphasis upon the postwar role of Japan in relation to her Far Eastern neighbors in the spheres of trade and politics.

George M. McCune, *Korea Today*. Cambridge: Harvard University Press, 1950.

A brief treatment of ancient Korea. Greater emphasis is paid to the country's changing conditions within the last half century.

Edwin O. Reischauer, *Japan: Past and Present*. Second ed., New York: Alfred A. Knopf, 1953.

Said to be "the most lucid and authoritative short history of Japan" in an enlarged and revised edition.

Laurence K. Rosinger, ed., *The State of Asia*. New York: Alfred A. Knopf, Inc., 1950, 3–220.

A survey of conditions in China, Mongolia, Sinkiang, Tibet, Korea, and Japan since the end of World War II; written by authors who have a thorough knowledge of these countries and their course of development.

Kuo-Heng Shih, *China Enters the Machine Age*. Cambridge: Harvard University Press, 1944.

One of the few studies of urban labor problems confronting an Asian country which is industrializing. Emphasis is upon the period from 1937 to 1943.

Other sources for information on Asian cities, their population, spatial layout, and chief functions:

Chinese Year Book; Encyclopedia Britannica World Atlas; Handbook for China by Carl Crow (New York: Dodd, Mead & Co., 1926); *Statesman's Yearbook.*

Chapter Five

The Cities of South Asia and Oceania

T HE HETEROGENEITY of the cities of South Asia and "down under" reflects the wide differences in the culture of the countries in which they are
located. There are cities of countries which have gained autonomy since
the end of the Second World War: The Union of India, Pakistan, Burma,
and the Philippines. Indochina and the Malay States are still under
some measure of colonial control, complicated by civil war. Of all the
South Asian countries, only Thailand (Siam) has always been at least
nominally independent, and urban development reflects the influence
both of the indigenous cultures and the cultures and interests of the colonial powers. Australia and New Zealand, both of which are members of
the British Commonwealth, offer a marked contrast to the rest of South
Asia. This is largely the result of the actual colonization of these areas by
British settlers, whereas European influence in South Asia was primarily
a matter of political and economic control rather than permanent settlement.

The differences among the various countries in this area are clearly
shown by the varying proportions of urban population in each country,
which range from 3.8 to 61.3 per cent. The population of the area includes
the three major races and their subgroups, who together constitute one of
the largest aggregations of population found in one major continent.
The representatives of most of the major religions of the world are found
here. The heterogeneity of population has become more pronounced after
the impact of Western powers because of the practice of importing cheap
labor from neighboring countries within the continent to develop mineral
resources and promote commerce and trade. Although some of the cities
in the area antedate cities of the Western world, the impact of the West
has accelerated urban expansion and many phenomena which are usually
associated with modern urbanization have appeared.

The urbanization of South Asia, at present under way and influenced by
the West, provides an interesting example of the consequence of social

change in what may best be described as feudal societies. It is yet too early to tell whether such factors as industrialization and urbanization will ultimately bring about a general reorganization of the social order, and whether the changes which these factors made in the West will be analogous in South Asia. The varying aspects of social change can be seen in situations such as the interrelationship between religion and the distribution of urban population, the occupational structure, and education in the Union of India and Pakistan. In the same manner, the "Chinese problem" facing many South Asian countries resulted from the era of free immigration, following the restriction of indentured labor, when a large labor supply and a small number of entrepreneurs were needed, is best illustrated by the Malay States and Thailand. In the Malay States the Chinese and Malaysians are almost equal in numerical strength, thus heightening the interethnic competition for the control of the economic, social, and political systems which were once held by Western powers.

In order to provide some basis for comparison between the various South Asian countries, a few items may be selected for analysis. These include the percentage of urban population, major cities and their functions, the composition of the labor force, and the influence of westernization upon a given area. More attention is devoted to the Union of India, Pakistan, and the Malay States because of the special factors obtaining there as well as the availability of data.

Burma

Burma, one of the new nations created after the end of the Second World War, was settled by people of Mongolian stock during the third century A.D. These people resemble their Tibetan neighbors in physical characteristics and adherence to Buddhism. The early communities were on the coast and river banks near the Indian border. During the eleventh century A.D. Burma was unified, and Pagan was selected as the first capital. A monarchical form of government continued until the eighteenth century, when a modern Burmese state was formed as a part of the British Empire. Burma gained her independence in 1948.

Major cities. Burma's largest cities are Rangoon and Mandalay, located on the Rangoon and Irrawaddy rivers. Rangoon—the present capital—is a railway terminus and seaport. It is a well laid-out city with an abundance of gardens, parks, and public buildings. Mandalay is a colorful city with 450 Buddhist temples, 750 pagodas, and 34 monasteries, some of which form a solid compound on Mandalay Hill within the city limits. Pegu, another large city and former ancient capital, is an important railroad center as well as the site of the famous Shew-maw-dew Pagoda.

Prome, Moulmein, Myingyan, Bassein, and Pakokku are important commercial centers for teakwood, rice, and tea.[1] Rice is the major export, however, with teakwood next, followed by lead, silver, tungsten, tin, and precious stones. Mergui, another commercial center, exports tin, ore, and rubber. Located in the heart of the rice and tobacco field is Hengada, the rail junction city at the head of the Irrawaddy River. Akyab is the chief seaport and airport situated at the Bay of Bengal and at the mouth of the Kaladan River.

Burma's total population was estimated at 17 million, of which 10.4 million were urban.[2] The rural population consisted of the Burmese and the non-indigenous Kachins, Chins, and other tribes living in the Karenni States, Tenasserim, and the Irrawaddy and Sittang deltas. Two other non-Burmese groups, the Indian and Chinese, were mainly urban and were engaged in urban occupations to a larger extent than the Burmese or any other of the tribal groups mentioned above.

The labor force. Until Japan occupied Burma from 1942 to 1946, over a million migrant Indian laborers entered Burma annually for industrial employment. About 60 per cent of the 90,000 workers in the following industries were Indian: rice, lumber, mining, oil refining and extraction, transportation, shipbuilding, textiles, and cement industries.[3] No figures are available as to how many of the remainder were Chinese or Burmese, save the statement that "some 200,000 Chinese were engaged in small businesses or worked as laborers in mines."[4] Most of the governmental, managerial, executive, and professional occupations were filled by the British nationals resident in Burma. The Burmese were used as minor civil servants, in the lower clerical and sales occupations, and as laborers.

Because they worked for lower wages, the Indian laborers were preferred to the Burmese rural migrants seeking employment in cities. This competitive condition was permitted and often promoted because Burma's industrial and agrarian development was controlled or owned by Indians, Chinese, or Europeans. During Japanese occupation some enterprises and farms were returned to the Burmese.

The Chinese have intermarried more frequently with the local inhabitants and were regarded with less hostility than the Indians until a large group of Chinese refugees and soldiers of the defeated Central Government's army entered North Burma and became a problem. Although the prewar Indian and Chinese population was but 4 per cent of the country's total, these two groups were proportionately more urban because of the nature of their occupations and enterprises.[5]

The industrial and occupational structure has changed since Burma won

[1] Rosinger, *op. cit.*, 294.
[2] *United Nations Demographic Yearbook*, 1952; a 1930 estimate.
[3] Rosinger, *op. cit.*, 294.
[4] *Ibid.*, 293; *The China Handbook, op. cit.*, 22 listed 193, 594 Chinese in Burma in 1937.
[5] Bruno Lasker, *Asia on the Move* (New York: Henry Holt & Co., 1945), 14 and 30.

Government of India Information Service

A street scene in the Union of India. A bangle seller and his wares. His customer wears caste-marks on her forehead and the left side of her nose.

her independence in 1948. Many industrial, financial, and commercial enterprises are now owned and operated by Burmese citizens or the Burmese government. For example: the financial corporations once belonging to the Chettyars—an Indian banking caste from Madras—were dissolved. The British and Indian plantations and mines producing rubber, tin, teakwood, and other products for export have been nationalized. The country's major transportation and communication systems, constructed by foreign capital, now are also operated by the government.[1] Efforts are being made to train competent civil servants, enlarge the various occupational groupings, and attain a higher level of industrial and commercial expansion. A wider system of transportation is being undertaken so that the rural areas will be linked with urban centers.

India and Pakistan

Some of the world's oldest cities originated in what is now the Union of India and Pakistan, as is revealed by the Mohenjo-daro excavations. Yet, these two countries—especially India—until this past decade showed no

[1] Woodrow Wyatt, *Southwards from China* (London: Hodder and Stoughton, 1952), 108–112.

Government of India Information Service

New Delhi, Union of India: a street scene in the capital of the Union of India. Note the verandah-type buildings. The streetcar, rickshaw, and bicycle are used as transportation within the city.

strong tendencies toward abandoning their compact village communities, and made few advances in urbanism. The inhabitants of these small and nearly self-sufficient agricultural villages were reluctant to migrate to cities and adopt new modes of life. Therefore, cities have grown slowly and many have retained their ancient characteristics. In general, urban growth in India and Pakistan can be divided into two broad periods: pre-British and post-British.[1]

Pre-British. The Neolithic period of urban development paralleled the Egyptian Memphis and Thebes, and it is believed that the diffusion of urban culture throughout the Near East into Pakistan resulted in the growth of cities in the Indus Valley and the Punjab and Ganges plains.[2] These ancient Indian cities were said to be the only ones in this era without city walls and temples. The inhabitants were primarily engaged in mercantile activities.[3] The cities disappeared when the climate changed

[1] Davis, *op. cit.*, Ch. 13.

[2] *Ibid.;* and Gilbert Slater, *The Dravidian Elements in Indian Culture* (London: Ernest Benn, Ltd., 1924).

[3] Churchill, *op. cit.*, 3–4.

and the river beds became dry. These cities were symmetrically designed to accommodate the various socio-economic groupings. Their physical layouts could serve as models for modern municipalities. Brick houses, granaries, and imposing public buildings of varying heights governed the streets—their width and intersection with other avenues of transportation.

The buried remains of these structures have escaped the ravages of decay well enough that it is possible to piece together a comprehensive picture of ancient urban life. Wood, metal, and leather articles were unearthed in what had been an industrial area where artisans lived in two room houses, which were all of similar design. The tools of textile weavers and millers were found in this same sector. These implements are testimony that the workers had attained a high degree of advancement in the arts and crafts. In another part of the city were the residential quarters occupied by rulers, priests, and the wealthy classes. The residential quarters boasted of large public baths, wells, and an underground sewerage system. These conveniences were not shared by the soldiers, scribes, and slaves who lived near to their superiors.

Since the end of World War II, more excavations have been conducted and another ancient buried city discovered at Amballa, 120 miles north of New Delhi, in the Union of India. Others probably remain for the archaeologist to uncover.

From the Neolithic period to the beginning of the first decade of the seventeenth century A.D., three major types of cities had been established. Many of these have survived to the present.

Primary are the religious centers, renowned for their shrines and temples, to which worshippers make pilgrimages at designated times. Religious functions are foremost and their commercial and handicraft industries are secondary. Sentiment and tradition have favored their continuance and the retention of their archaic layout and mode of life. Cities bordering the Ganges River, for example, fall into this category.

Benares is a renowned religious city containing thousands of Hindu and Buddhists temples, to which devout worshippers make pilgrimages. It is easily accessible by both railway and water transportation. Allahabad, on the Jumna and Ganges rivers, shares religious honors with Benares. Every Hindu hopes either to die or be cremated on the banks of the Ganges. Both cities manufacture large quantities of brass cooking utensils as many Hindu castes can use no other kind.

The next type embraces capital cities which served as seats of political administration favored by rulers in former times. Moslem rulers were noted for their whimsical selection and abandonment of capital cities in much the same manner as former Chinese dynastic kings. The old capitals lost importance while the newly selected sites flourished as population and

Government of India Information Services

Bombay, Union of India. Street scene showing British influence competing with the local, especially in architectural style.

organizations moved and were re-established. Many became the provincial capitals of the country, such as, Agra, Delhi, and Dacca, and have retained this role to the present.

The breaks in physical features of the land—between water and land, mountain passes or jungles—caused other cities to rise in what is now Pakistan. These cities grew wherever there was a topographical interruption of the continuous movement of goods and travellers. Some cities were built for defense against invaders from Europe, while others grew into important industrial, commercial, and trade centers. The latter type grew in importance after the early part of the seventeenth century in what is now the Union of India, due to the impact of Western urbanism, largely of British origin. Such cities include Bombay, Sakchi, and Calcutta.

Post-British. Two of the consequences of British influences were the growth of population in cities catering to import-export trade and the production of consumer goods. This second phase came much later, however. Another aspect of this influence was the change in architectural design of buildings and the introduction of modern utilities. By far the greatest change came in the alteration of the economic and political organization of the society. Available statistics showed that India's urban population increased slowly until 1931 [1] (Table 12). The slight decrease between 1901 and 1911, from 10 to 9.4 per cent, is attributed to a plague epidemic which temporarily depopulated some Indian cities. Although the percentage of increase for six decades is small, the absolute number of urbanites has risen steadily. The growth of India's urban and rural population has continued, so that the proportion of rural-urban population has remained more or less stationary until 1931. Davis indicates that between 1881 and 1941, India's

TABLE 12. GROWTH OF INDIA'S URBAN AND
TOTAL POPULATION, 1871 TO 1951 [1]

Year	Total	Per Cent Urban
1871	203,415,000	—
1881	250,160,000	9.3
1891	279,593,000	9.4
1901	283,870,000	10.0
1911	303,041,000	9.4
1921	305,730,000	10.2
1931	338,171,000	11.1
1941	388,998,000	12.3
1951	356,829,485	17.3

Note: Total population of India, excluding Pakistan, was 314,766,380 in 1941.

[1] *Source:* Adapted with permission from Kingsley Davis, *The Population of India and Pakistan* (Princeton: Princeton University Press, 1951), 27 and 127; *Census of India*, 1952, No. 1, Table 4, 16.

urban population gained 41 per cent, while that of the United States for the same period increased by 111 per cent.[2]

The greatest gains in urban population occurred after 1931, and this trend is expected to continue. Greater attention is being paid to industrialization and better labor conditions. Labor organizations are aiming at long range improvements in housing, education, health facilities, and at better pay. Moreover, the uprooting of Hindu and Moslem communities during the partition of India and Pakistan in 1947 disrupted many agricultural villages and stimulated the migration of displaced persons to cities. A final factor has added to the increase in urban population: the growth of the country's population by 13 per cent since 1941. The total population of

[1] Davis, *op. cit.*, 127, "the definition of urban includes places of 5,000 or larger but makes numerous special exceptions. So far as possible the figures for the various census have been made comparable by us. See Appendix H."

[2] *Ibid.*, 128.

India was estimated at 388,998,000 in 1941 (Table 12). The population of the Union of India, without Pakistan, was 356,829,485 in 1951.[1] Pakistan's population was 75,687,000 in 1951.[2]

This rapid increase in population is a sign that some of the social effects of westernization are being felt. The increase is the consequence of reduction of the death rate through improved medical and sanitation facilities. The toll of famine which has historically plagued India has been cut down since food from other sources can now be distributed in famine areas by use of the new systems of transportation. However, such an expanding population may in the long run be self-defeating. If industrialization of under-developed areas is undertaken in order to raise levels of living, it must be noted again that rapidly expanding populations are also young populations. Even without the severe restrictions on child labor which are found in more developed areas, a large part of the population is not economically productive.

But this sort of a population does need many consumer goods. If the limited industrial production spends itself satisfying these needs, then there is that much less capital and equipment to produce goods for the further development of industry. An increasingly urban population could further outgrow the industrial base on which it depends. In such an eventuality there would be a decrease rather than an increase in levels of living.

At present there are few signs that any large segment of the population, even the urban population, is consciously attempting to control family size, and it is probable that the population of India and of Pakistan will increase for some time to come.

Number and location of cities. In 1941 India had 155 cities with more than 50,000 inhabitants each, and 58 of this total were of metropolitan size. The total urban population in 1941 was 12.3 per cent. The fifteen largest cities have more or less consistently ranked as important centers of population growth for the last six decades. Most cities are located near seacoasts, rivers, or at junction points which are accessible by railway, water, or air. Many are provincial capitals as well as industrial and trade centers and command a wide hinterland. Often one of these is the only city within a district, but it is vital to the area for the services it provides.

Cities after partition. After the partition of India in August 1947 into the Union of India and Pakistan (excluding Kashmir, whose status was indefinite until 1954, when the local population voted to join the Union of India), each country received its share of population according to Hindu

[1] Census of India, 1952, No. 1 Table 4, 16.

[2] Census of Pakistan, 1951, "Provisional Tables of Population" office of the Census Commissioner, Government of Pakistan, Ministry of the Interior, Karachi. The *Statesman's Yearbook, 1952,* gives the total as 75,842,165.

Left, a coconut seller of East
Pakistan. He will husk the coconut while the customer waits,
or sell what he has already
husked.

Below, the noted Merewether
Tower, Karachi, is located on a
busy intersection.

Embassy of Pakistan

or Moslem affiliations.[1] Some 40 million persons were uprooted. The areas allotted to and now comprising East and West Pakistan had few cities, and therefore Pakistan has a lower urban ratio. That is, when India as a whole was considered, 12.3 per cent of the population was urban and there were 155 cities with more than 50,000 inhabitants. But the Pakistanian areas had about 6.5 per cent of the population in urban centers after the partition.[2] The 1951 preliminary census revealed that approximately 3.5 per cent of the Pakistanians lived in twelve major cities, and the remaining 3 per cent were perhaps in smaller centers (Table 13). It should be noted that Paki-

TABLE 13. MAJOR CITIES, PAKISTAN, 1941 AND 1951 [1]

	Population	
City	1941	1951
Karachi	358,492	1,005,000
Lahore	671,659	849,000
Dacca	213,000	401,000
Rawalpindi	181,000	243,000
Hyderabad	75,767	229,000
Multan	108,351	190,000
Lyallpur	43,000	180,000
Sailkot	85,093	152,000
Gujranwala	38,716	124,000
Chittagong	53,156	126,000
Peshawar	87,440	114,000
Quetta	60,272	82,000

Note: The United Nations Demographic Yearbook, 1952, Table 8, 202–214, shows population total of 1,126,417 for Karachi.

[1] *Source:* 1951 census preliminary count from *Statesman's Yearbook*, 1952, 199. 1941 figures from Davis, *op. cit.*, 132–134 and 200–201 and Rand McNally *World Atlas*, 1945.

stan is one of the rare illustrations of a country reversing an urban ratio. In general, the opposite is true—an increased urban ratio.

On the other hand, the Union of India gained urban population. A redistribution of population between the two countries has resulted in the reversal of the Moslem-Hindu rural-urban ratio. Moslems who had shown greater tendency than the Hindus toward settlement in cities in what is now the Union of India had to make a readjustment in Pakistan where relatively few cities existed. Conversely, the Hindus who were predominantly rural migrated from village communities in Pakistan to cities

[1] Joseph B. Schechtman, *Population Transfer in Asia* (New York: Halesby Press, 1949), Ch. 1, "The Hindu-Moslem Exchange of Population."

[2] Davis, *op. cit.*, 200–201.

within the Union of India. The 1951 urban population of the latter was 17.3 per cent.[1]

This increase to 17.3 per cent has meant that the mean decennial growth rate for the entire population of the Union of India between 1941–1951 was 12.5 per cent. This figure represented the net increase in urban population. The growth of urban population was greatest for 73 metropolitan cities, whose mean decennial growth rate was 36.2 per cent. In 1941, 16,-733,088 persons lived in 46 metropolises as compared to 24,126,592 in 73 of these cities a decade later.[2] Almost 300 districts had urban concentrations of more than 5,000 people.[3] The total urban population for the Union of India was 61,825,214 in 1951. Of the 25 major municipalities having absolute gains in their inhabitants between 1941 and 1951, only Bareilly showed a decline during this period.

Lahore and Karachi were the only two super-cities among the 25 major ones in 1941 which were within the Pakistan area before partition took place. Dacca, Rawalpindi, and Multan were other metropolises allocated to Pakistan along with eight others below metropolitan status. It is evident that the growth of cities in the Pakistan area has not paralleled that of the Union of India. The "new" cities, however, showed gains in population between 1941 and 1951 (Table 13). Karachi, the nation's capital, and Hyderabad each had a threefold increase. Five others gained metropolitan status by 1951.

A similar change, although of a lesser degree, has taken place in the Union of India. Bombay gained over a million inhabitants within a decade, and Madras almost doubled her population.[4] These increases were due largely to the redistribution of population between the two countries and the uprooting of former rural dwellers. The growth of population may have had a bearing as combined populations of the two countries totaled almost 430,000,000 at the last census.[5] India gained over 42 million in a decade and Pakistan, one and one-half million.

Future urbanization. Although the exact facts and statistics are not available as to how rapidly either part of "old India" is proceeding with industrialization and urbanization, there are several indications that there is a possibility of the Union of India becoming more urban than Pakistan.

One important factor is related to the extent of natural resources that each part received after partition. Pakistan has a lower population density and fewer natural resources with which to build the essential base needed

---

[1] Census of India, 1951, Nos. 1, 16 and 24.

[2] *Ibid.;* including the Pakistan area, there were 58 metropolitan cities in 1941 according to this report.

[3] *Ibid.,* 20–21, footnotes.

[4] *Ibid.,* 24–25.

[5] *Ibid.,* 16, and Census of Pakistan, 1951, *op. cit.*

by large scale industrialization. East Pakistan is almost devoid of coal and iron ore, the essential primary minerals related to modern industrial development. West Pakistan has an abundance of oil and potential water power but lacks secondary minerals such as copper and manganese. At the time of partition, India received the major share of the natural resources because of their location in Hindu territory.

Large coal and iron deposits are situated in the Bihar-Irissa-Bengal region within the Union of India. The Tata Iron Works in Jamshedpur is the largest producer of low cost pig iron in the world. There are further iron ore and limestone deposits in Mysore province. Large timber tracts and an abundance of oil add to the country's natural wealth. Other minerals found in sizable quantities are manganese, bauxite, aluminum, tungsten, salt, and mica. These are rated as secondary minerals and are required in industrial processes and in the manufacture of heavy machinery and tools. With the exception of the United States and Soviet Russia, the Union of India has the largest reserves of primary and secondary minerals.[1] Because of the above facts, the Union of India is regarded as having a higher industrial and urban potential than Pakistan.

A second factor influencing industrialization and urbanization of the two countries was the allocation of established industrial plants at the time of partition.[2] The Union of India received 97 per cent of the industries (or 771), and Pakistan received 3 per cent (or 24).[3] A comparison of a few industries will further clarify the picture.

The Union of India received 380 cotton mills, while Pakistan received nine. All the 18 iron and steel mills and the 108 jute plants were in the Union of India. Pakistan's share of sugar mills was ten out of the total of 156. She supported two glass factories as compared to the 77 of the Union of India. In addition, the greater amount of developed transportation and communication facilities were outside Pakistan. Although both countries need more railroads, the Union of India's railway mileage is twice that of Pakistan's, and the highway mileage is six times greater.

Commerce as well as industry shows great differences between the two countries.[4] The Union of India's five major seaports—Bombay, Calcutta, Cochin, Madras, and Vizagapatam—handle six times the volume of imports and exports of the two seaports in Pakistan. Moreover, a distance of

[1] Thompson, Population and Peace in the Pacific, *op. cit.,* Ch. 14, and Rosinger, *op. cit.,* 443.

[2] Tulsi R. Sharma, *Location of Industries in India* (Bombay: Hind Kitabs, 1946), Ch. 5; and Maneck B. Pithawalla, *An Introduction to Pakistan: Its Resources and Potentialities* (Karachi: 1948).

[3] From pamphlet prepared by G. O. Birla, leading Indian industrialist and publisher of *Hindustan Times,* June, 1947.

[4] N. V. Sovani, *Economic Relations of India with South East Asia and the Far East* (New Delhi: Indian Council of World Affairs, 1949).

1,500 miles separates Pakistan's important seaports. Karachi, the capital is on the west coast, while Chittagong is on the east, separated by the Union of India. These two annually handled less than 3 million tons of exports before the partition.

A final factor favoring the Union of India's more rapid industrialization was that about 90 per cent of the trained industrial personnel was apportioned to her by virtue of religious affiliation at the time of partition.

Pakistan is making efforts to overcome these social and economic difficulties by providing employment for the uprooted professionals, merchants, craftsmen, traders, and artisans; and by building cities and creating industries.[1] A modern city, Unobad, is being constructed between Kotri and Hyderabad and will accommodate 100,000 persons. The greatest problem is how to use efficiently the resources and personnel in East and West Pakistan in the face of the expanse of India separating the two areas.

A problem of even greater importance is how to cooperate with the Union of India in the exchange and sale of natural resources, finished products, and food. For example: the Union of India is dependent upon Pakistan for much of its food, cotton, and jute. On the other hand, Pakistan needs the textile and jute mills located in the Union of India. As a result, the production of textile fabrics and jute bags has dropped since partition took place.[2]

The dispute between India and Pakistan over the control of Kashmir Province, though nominally settled, has explosive tendencies, and has caused each of the countries to maintain a large standing army. Since each country devotes over one-half of its budget to the support of these armies, there is a substantial reduction in capital available for industrial and urban expansion.

Some important projects have been completed in Pakistan with outside financial and technical assistance. The projects include the Ford Assembly plant, the Mardan sugar factory, and the Chittagong port improvement scheme.[3] Four new jute factories, six textile mills, a paper factory, and a hydroelectric plant were constructed in 1949. A major share of the small enterprises manufacturing cement, glass, chemicals, dyestuff, and tanning products were financed by wealthy Moslems who believed in the industrial future of new Pakistan.

Urban residence and religious affiliation. Religious beliefs, practices, and rituals permeate the whole social, economic, and political life of the Union of India and Pakistan. Religious observances and their restrictions regulate

[1] *UNESCO Courier*, 5, No. 7 (July, 1952), 5–6.
[2] Rosinger, *op. cit.*, 463–469 and 507–511.
[3] *Ibid.*, 510.

the type of work and therefore determine the extent of urban residence of the Hindu, Moslem, Jain, Sikh, Christian, Buddhist, Parsi, Jewish, tribal, and other groups.

According to the latest figures, the Hindus constituted the largest religious group, followed by the Moslem and the tribal, who together constituted 97 per cent of the total population of the two countries.[1] Hindus made up 69.46 per cent of the total population before partition, while 24.28 per cent were Moslems, and 2.26 tribal. About 2 per cent were Christians, one and one-half per cent were Sikhs. The Jain, Buddhist, Parsi, Jewish, and other religious groups together accounted for less than 1 per cent of the total. Since partition, there has been a resettlement of the Hindu and Moslem groups, with the followers of each faith migrating to the Union of India or to Pakistan, depending upon religious affiliation. The lesser religious groups thus found themselves within the Union of India, although we should not overlook the fact that there is a Hindu minority within Pakistan, and some Moslems yet live outside the "new homeland." For example: 12.9 per cent of Pakistan's total population is Hindu, .07 per cent is Christian, and 85.9 per cent is Moslem.[2]

The Hindu, tribal, and Sikh groups have traditionally had a higher proportion of rural dwellers than other religious faiths. Moslems showed a tendency toward living in cities with less than 500,000 inhabitants and before partition were mainly concentrated in small centers throughout the nation.[3] As indicated earlier, many have now moved to Pakistan where fewer cities are located.

The Sikhs lived primarily in West Pakistan before partition, and only 7.8 per cent were urbanites in 1931.[4] Their resettlement in the Union of India since 1947 did not change their major occupation. Most of the Sikhs are soldiers—and excellent ones. They are in great demand in the Indian army, which is composed largely of Sikhs. Their longtime affiliation with the army has made the Sikhs prosperous and literate. Many civilian Sikhs are engaged as carpenters, masons, and goldsmiths.

The smaller religious groups have shown greater inclination toward urban settlement and urban occupations and enterprises than the groups mentioned above.

The Jains, constituting 3.7 per cent of the total population in 1941, were among the first to take advantage of Western education. They are mainly urban and have prospered in business enterprises.[5] The Jews, numbering

[1] Davis, *op. cit.*, Ch. 19.
[2] *Statesman's Yearbook*, 1952, 199.
[3] Davis, *op. cit.*, 193.
[4] *Ibid.*, 183.
[5] *Ibid.*, 183.

23,000, have always been predominantly urban. More than a third of them live in Bombay City, and the next largest concentration is at Cochin. The remainder live in smaller cities within Bombay province, the most urban province in the Union of India. The members of the Jewish group have the second highest literacy rate in India. Only the Parsis have a higher proportion of literate members. Of the Parsis 79.1 per cent are literate, as compared to 41.6 per cent of the Jews. However, both are equally literate in regard to English.[1]

The Parsis have been an outstanding urban group whose wealth and success in commerce have placed them at the top of the economic hierarchy.[2] Around 90 per cent of them lived in India's principal cities in 1941. A major concentration was, and is, at Bombay City, where they represented 5 per cent of the city's total population in 1941.

The Christians are more urban than the Moslem, Hindu, or tribal groups. Twenty per cent of the Christian group have been living in cities since 1931.[3] They have shown the impact of westernization in several areas. Their educations and command of English are better than the average, and they marry at a later age than do members of other religious groups. The group has a higher percentage of single females than the other religious faiths due to the later age at marriage and emphasis upon education.

It should be noted that despite the settlement in cities of the lesser religious faiths, their birth rates have not declined, indicating that one phase of urbanism has not touched the general population of the two countries. As pointed out earlier, the rural and urban birth rates have not changed noticeably for the past half century.

Male-female urban residence. All groups in the population, however, have had a greater number of males than females settling in cities. There are several reasons for this. The primary reason is that more types of occupations offered in cities are open to the males. The ten major occupations include (1) exploitation of animals and vegetation, (2) exploitation of minerals, (3) industry, (4) trade, (5) transport, (6) public force, (7) public administration, (8) professions and liberal arts, (9) living on income, and (10) domestic service.[4]

Percentagewise, cities with 500,000 or more inhabitants had more workers in industry, transport, domestic service, and trade (in order of rank) than smaller centers. Those cities of less than 50,000 offered more work opportunities in industry, transport, exploitation of animals and vegetation and domestic service. The more industry, trade and transport activities

[1] *Ibid.*, 159.
[2] *Ibid.*, 185.
[3] *Ibid.*, 186–188.
[4] *Ibid.*, 138–139.

a city had in 1931, the faster it grew in population. Males rather than females were attracted to cities that offered employment in these industries. Domestic service is not solely confined to women workers.

The second factor influencing the migration of males to cities is that females have had less education, and have therefore acquired fewer skills. Also, custom forbade the emigration of women from the village community. Furthermore, the cities had fewer services and conveniences to accommodate women and children during periods of illness, unemployment, or other crises. By comparison, the self-contained village offered more social life, better housing, and mutual aid. Therefore, the urban sex ratio reflected the composition of the occupational structure, and for every 100 women there were 123 men.[1] There are some indications, however, that the status of women is slowly changing. The manifestations of unrest are expressed more freely and openly in cities than in villages, although both units are producing some social changes.[2]

More women are seeking employment in cities. The lesser educated and unskilled turn to domestic service or work in factories. Those seeking greater prestige become nurses, teachers, or typists. The professions of medicine, journalism, public relations, instruction in music and dance, and politics offer greater avenues of occupational mobility. Not a few are found in the film industry where high incomes combined with glamour have provided rapid occupational and social mobility. Others become social workers, specializing in child and maternal welfare.[3] All are deeply interested in politics and the promotion of women's rights.

Some women prefer to remain single and pursue careers. The single status carried social condemnation a generation ago. Those who pursue the middle course, bowing to the custom of marriage and child-rearing and yet desire higher education and careers, are delaying marriage until their educations and careers are within reach. In a survey made by the Statistical Laboratory of Lucknow University between 1947 and 1948, the average age of marriage for some of the members of the new middle class (university teachers, lawyers, editors, and government officials) was revealed to be 23.5 years for the males and 18 years for the females.[4] The traditional age at marriage had been between 12 and 13 years, although marriage at nine years of age was not uncommon. In the future the higher age of marrying may become more widespread.

Two of the most significant signs of increasing urbanism in a society are, first, the settlement of families in cities and, second, the increase in the number of occupations and professions open to women. The migra-

[1] *Ibid.,* 139, Table 55.
[2] International Social Science Bulletin, *op. cit.,* 793–801.
[3] *Ibid.,* 796–797.
[4] *Ibid.,* 799–800.

A picturesque street in Hyderabad, Sind, Pakistan.

This semi-circular building, situated near the Keamari Docks, houses the Offices of the Karachi Port Trust at Karachi, the capital of Pakistan.

tion and settlement of families in cities accelerate the break with rural ties and tradition and hasten the creation of better and greater services and conveniences for men, women, and children. The gradual emancipation of women symbolizes (1) the breakdown of traditional controls and norms, (2) the state of transition reached by a society undergoing change from the rural-folk to urban type, (3) the subsequent lowering of birth rates, and the reduction in size of the family, and (4) the adoption, perpetuation, and diffusion of urban traits and behavior patterns at a more rapid rate. Before the settlement of families and increase in the number of single women in cities, the urban society was primarily "male-oriented" and exhibited some of the social characteristics of a frontier society.

The change in the sex composition of the urban population in the Union of India and Pakistan is correlated with the strength and pervasiveness of the various caste systems carried to and maintained in cities.[1] The maintenance or disregard of traditional caste restrictions and taboos can further retard or accelerate urbanism.

Caste and the urban environment. Although a large majority of the inhabitants of the Union of India and Pakistan maintains and practices the respective caste observances and restrictions, the urban environment has created conditions which have modified the strict adherence to regulations.[2] Several reasons may be advanced for this.

In cities it is not always possible to learn and pursue the traditional occupations of each caste. For example: persons who belong to a caste specifying agriculture as the main means of livelihood may find work of this nature in cities, but as the city grows his children will find less opportunity to till the soil. This also happens to domestic service and unskilled labor classifications as industrialization gains headway, as exemplified by the change in the industrial and occupational structure of Western cities.

The urban environment also modifies caste regulations and practices because of the difficulty in fitting these into the hours of work. Hindu caste members are forced to eat food prepared by other castes as a matter of necessity, as likewise are the Moslems, Christians, and Jews. Although each caste segregates itself geographically within the city, greater effort must be exerted to maintain the strength and consistency of caste practices. Moreover, urban-born children are apt to experience the caste regulations and restrictions to a lesser degree than their parents. Thus, the

---

[1] *Ibid.,* 801. For a thorough study and analysis of the caste system see J. H. Hutton, *Caste in India* (Cambridge: Cambridge University Press, 1946); and E. A. H. Blunt, *The Caste System in Northern India* (London: Oxford University Press, 1931); and L. S. S. O'Malley, *Indian Caste Customs* (Cambridge: Cambridge University Press, 1932).

[2] Davis, *op. cit.,* Ch. 18.

process of assimilation occurring within the urban environment modifies caste systems.

The spread of education as well as the training for specific urban occupations such as nursing, medicine, social work, government service, and skilled factory techniques, provide caste members with the opportunities to overcome caste practices. In fact, no caste has been created for these new urban occupations where training and skill determine fitness to undertake the work.

Perhaps the greatest evidence that caste has less meaning and control over urbanites in the Union of India and Pakistan is that many do not report caste membership to the census. This was revealed in the Census of India for Bombay Cities in 1931. This tendency is expected to become more pronounced because a greater portion of the population has become more mobile through partition and settlement in cities.

A final reason for the modification of caste can be mentioned. Membership was relinquished in the castes which offered few opportunities for occupational and social mobility, and newer castes were adopted by religious conversion. In Madras the membership in Christian churches increased by 275,000 within a decade (1921-1931) because the depressed caste members believed that conversions would raise occupational and social status. It is entirely possible that more of the untouchables, now legally free to rise on the occupational and social ladder, may join religious groups which will permit them to shed their former undesirable status.

Davis predicts that the caste system will be transmuted into a class system, and that such a possibility is dependent upon the degree of industrialization the two countries will be able to effect. As the Union of India is demonstrating greater possibilities for rapid urbanization due to the advantages she obtained through partition, it is probable that the caste system will grow weaker by the end of this century.[1] Pakistan, with its more or less homogeneous population of Moslems, can relax some of the caste practices and bring about the same results. However, the caste systems of both countries will disappear more rapidly if urbanism and urbanization proceeds along with industrialization.

Indochina

Indochina has a population of 27 million. Of this total number, 43,000 are of Caucasoid origin, and 600,000 are immigrants of Mongoloid origin. Indochina has about a dozen sizable cities, but none of them exceeds 150,000 inhabitants. It is estimated that over 90 per cent of the population is rural.

[1] *Ibid.,* 175-176

Hanoi, the capital, has the largest population, numbering 149,000.[1] As an important railway terminus and a leading cultural center, it is located on the Coi and Mekong rivers about 40 miles from the sea. Its population composition is heterogeneous. The Europeans, mainly French, live along the lake and occupy the better residential sections. The native groups from Cambodia, Annam, Tonkin, Lao, and Cochin China occupy their own quarters and pursue a way of life distinctive from that of the European areas. The Chinese, who have for many generations settled here for business and trade purposes, form the third largest settlement. Lesser groups include the migrants from the Union of India and Pakistan, and the ethnic minorities, the Thai peoples from the mountains of northern Tonkin, and the Moi from southern Annam. Cholon (134,060 population) is an industrial city close to Hanoi on the Mekong River.

The most oustanding commercial city is Saigon. Its population is as heterogeneous as that of Hanoi but numbers only 123,298, of whom 11,115 are Europeans. Located on the Saigon River, it has access to the sea and commands one of the best harbors in the Far East. It is a well constructed modern city, and many importing-exporting firms are located there.

Pnom Penh (103,000) is at the juncture of the Mekong and Toule Sap rivers.[2] It is the marketing center for products from Cambodia, Laos, and East Siam. In this city are found some of the elaborate temples and palaces of the old Cambodian kings. Haiphong, the foremost northern seaport, has 80,000 residents, many of whom are Chinese. It is close to the southern border states of China, and many Chinese have crossed the border to become residents of Haiphong.

Angkor, the old capital of the Khmers, is located in the great lake regions of northwestern Cambodia. It is regarded as the historical and cultural center of Indochina, although the city was destroyed and buried in the jungles during the fourteenth century. The ruins of palaces, temples, and the Bayon tower (richly carved with the four faces of Siva), have attracted considerable attention and reverence since their rediscovery in 1858.[3]

Other cities are primarily located near rivers or seacoasts and function as commercial centers. Although Indochina had cities before other countries in this region, urban growth has been slow and did not assume any sizable proportions until the impact of French influence.

Industrial development. The relatively slow growth of cities is due to the fact that the majority of the Indochinese are primarily engaged in

[1] Virginia Thompson, *French Indo-China* (New York: The Macmillan Co., 1942), 143.

[2] Rand McNally, *World Atlas,* 248.

[3] George B. Cressey, *Asia's Lands and Her Peoples* (New York: McGraw-Hill Book Company, Inc., 1944), 519–520.

rice cultivation and have shown little interest in commercial and industrial activities. Approximately 90 per cent of the population are rural, and 56 per cent of this total form the active laboring class.[1] Many of the rice plantations are French-owned, as is true of the rubber plantations in the south and the mines in the north.

Industrialization is on a small scale and is mainly confined to the refining of sugar, milling of rice, the making of alcohol and wine from rice. Other industrial plants manufacture glass, paper, cotton, and cement products for local use. In the main, the raw materials extracted from the mines, such as coal, iron ore, tin, zinc, phosphates, tungsten, are exported to France and her territories for processing and returned as finished products. This practice has retarded the growth and expansion of local industries.

Social and occupational structure. At the time of the Second World War, around 40,000 nationals from France resided in Indochina. They held the leading civil and military posts and the higher white-collar positions; owned and managed rice and rubber plantations and mines; or were merchants, bankers, or technicians. Although the wartime conditions reduced the number of French nationals, a large group of military personnel has entered the country since the end of World War II in order to cope with the internal disturbances.[2] The remainder of the Caucasoid group were officials, businessmen, and professionals.

The largest group is the Vietnamese, whose 18 million comprises roughly three-fourths of the country's total population. Most of the inhabitants are rice and cotton growers, laborers in mines, fishermen, or unskilled seasonal workers. Ethnically they are closer to the Chinese than the inhabitants of Thailand, because this area was once a part of China and intercommunication has continued for many centuries. The two groups have intermarried to a considerable degree, and over 100,000 Indochinese in Cambodia alone have Chinese ancestry.

There were 538,531 of Chinese ancestry in Indochina in 1940, according to the estimate of the Overseas Commission of the Central Government of China.[3] In all probability this figure did not include those who had become assimilated into the social structure. Such persons regard themselves as belonging to Indochina and did not register as Chinese. Moreover, a head tax is levied upon those who retain Chinese citizenship and persons registering as aliens come under the jurisdiction of the various Chinese consulates at Saigon, Hanoi, Haiphong, Pnom Penh, and Cholon. The reason for this is that regardless of length of residence in Indochina,

---

[1] Thompson, *op. cit.,* 143.

[2] Rosinger, *op. cit.,* 221–267 and Wyatt, *op. cit.,* 113–127.

[3] *China Handbook, op. cit.,* 22.

a Chinese is considered a citizen of China, unless he desires to ignore this status. He is, at the same time, a subject of France. These dual citizenships, with neither country giving suitable legal and political protection, have caused many Chinese in Indochina and other parts of South Asia to be caught in the middle of political rivalries and guerrilla wars that did not directly concern them.[1]

The Chinese in Indochina are divided into five distinct groups: the Teochiu, Cantonese, Hokien, Hakka, and Hainanese. These divisions, based upon dialect and origin in China, have been recognized by the French government since 1891.[2] Where the Chinese reside in cities—for example: in Pnom Penh and Cholon—each group or *congrégation* is represented by a chief elected by all members of the *congrégation* who are over 18 years of age. The chief acts as the official intermediary between the Cambodian or Vietnam administration and the *congrégation*. Each chief is responsible for seeing to the upkeep of community schools, hospitals, pagodas, and the collection of taxes and hospital and deportation fees. The French government does not interfere with the internal affairs or politics of the *congrégations*. Although an observer may see the Chinese section of a city in Cambodia, he may not be aware of the distinct divisions of the section according to dialect and origin in China. Nor is it apparent from casual observation that many Sino-Cambodian or Sino-Vietnamese Métis, or offspring of Chinese and Indochinese unions, live in this area because they consider themselves culturally Chinese rather than Cambodian or Vietnamese.[3]

This form of social organization is reflected in vocational activities. The Teochius are predominantly businessmen, but many are boatmen and farmers. The Cantonese engage in commerce, and a large number of them are artisans. The Hokiens concentrate upon trade and business, while the Hainanese are mostly pepper planters and domestic servants. The Hakkas tend to be workmen and agricultural laborers.

The various groups control the internal marketing of local products and the retail trade. The Chinese buy up most of the rice, transport it to mills owned and operated by the members of the group, and export it to Chinese firms in the major seacoast cities of Southeast Asia. The Chinese have a virtual monopoly on fishing, market vegetables, pepper, and animal husbandry. The sugar, cotton, and lumber businesses are also in their hands. Many are large holders of urban property since they are excluded by law from purchasing the best rubber and ricelands and mines. However, the rice growers must sell their paddies to the Chinese

[1] G. William Skinner, *Report on the Chinese in Southeast Asia,* Cornell University, Department of Far Eastern Studies, Dec., 1950, 17 and 22.
[2] *Ibid.,* 16.
[3] *Ibid.,* 15.

as the latter have built up a comprehensive rice purchasing system that covers the entire country. The rice must be milled at the Chinese-owned and operated rice mills.

The economic strength of the Chinese in Indochina has caused the government to take steps to curb its expansion.[1] Since the beginning of World War II, restrictions have been placed on their operations by granting new licenses for certain businesses to Cambodians and Vietnamese. The same situation applies to certain trades. However, a Chinese is often hired to run the business because the Indochinese does not know how, or the business is sold to a Chinese when the Indochinese is faced with financial difficulty.

The situation as described above is fairly typical of the position which the Chinese occupy in Southeast Asia. Some years may pass before the indigenous population can wrest the control of the economic system from the outsiders. In the meantime the Chinese are caught in the anomalous situation of being needed but feared on two counts: their economic power and their dual citizenship status (as nationals of China and subjects of France).

Thailand (Siam)

Thailand's total population was reported at 17,316,951 in 1947, and approximately 18,836,000 by 1951.[2] Of this total, the Chinese constitute 3,000,000; the Malaysian-Moslems, 700,000; and the Indians, 150,000. Eight per cent of the country's population live in a few large cities.

Until 1932 self-government in municipal areas was unknown because it had been the custom for the central government to appoint officials to administer the townships in which cities were located.[3] The Law on Municipalities was introduced and adopted when young progressive-minded officials gained power in the government. This law authorized the establishment of three types of self-governing municipalities: the commune (*tabol*); town (*muang*); and city (*nakorn*).

Thickly populated groups of villages could initiate the commune type of municipal government, but since the enactment of the law, comparatively few village communities have adopted this form of local government. On the other hand, there have been municipal governments formed in 114 towns, the population of which exceeded 5,000 inhabitants and with a population density of not less than 2,000 persons per square kilometer.

Only Bangkok, Dhohburi, and Chiengmai have the *nakorn* or city

[1] *Ibid.*, 16 and 20.

[2] *United Nations Demographic Yearbook*, 1948, 127; *Statesman's Yearbook*, 1952.

[3] W. D. Reever, *Public Administration in Siam* (London: Royal Institute of International Affairs, 1951), 43–45.

Ewing Galloway

Bangkok, Thailand (Siam), airview of the Wat Aran Temple of the only large city in Thailand. The country is noted for its picturesque architecture, consisting mainly of elaborate temples.

type of government because the law stipulates that the urban population must exceed 30,000 before this form of municipal incorporation is permitted.

Since less than five per cent of the eligible voters trouble to exercise their franchise—largely because of inexperience—a proposal has been made to place the management of each municipality under a competently trained city manager. This would reduce the size of unwieldy municipal assemblies, prevent the misappropriation of funds and abuse of authority, and insure greater efficiency in local self-government. At the present time, the governor of a province has the power to advise the Ministry of Interior to withdraw a city's charter, terminate self-government if any city is mismanaged, or challenge the status of any or all of the municipal councilor's status and his right to be appointed to the municipal assembly.[1]

Major cities. Bangkok, the capital since 1782, is Thailand's only port of any size, and it is through this city that three-fourths of the country's foreign trade passes. Cargoes designated for inland areas are transshipped by rivercraft up the Menam Chao Phraya River. Within the past decade, Bangkok has become an important international airport. Some sixteen airlines connect her with various parts of the globe, the Far East, and most of Thailand.

Bangkok did not lose its picturesqueness even when the modern section was added after French influence made its impact in 1851. The old city is built on pontoons and piles and is interspersed with many canals.[2] Pile villages are found in large numbers in Southeast Asia, and this style of construction was retained when building cities. Piles are driven into the shallow waters, and on them platforms are laid which serve as floors of houses. Streets are narrow and crowded because progress between houses and stores is made by means of boards, or "streets." The importance of the house or street determines the width of the boards. A small side street may be one board wide; a main street, several boards.

In contrast, the modern section has finely paved streets, Western style buildings, and innumerable Buddhist temples. In proportion to the population, Bangkok has more inhabitants than almost any other capital in the world.[3] Moreover, the inhabitants are extremely reluctant to leave and settle elsewhere. Bangkok is far more advanced than the rest of Thailand in terms of Western influence and has attracted many tourists from other lands. Many come to admire the beautiful architecture of the royal palaces and courtyards.

Chieng Rai developed as an urban center because of its command over the Mekong River and is located where several highways converge. Near the Burma border on the upper course of the Ping River is Chiengmai, famous for its teakwood industries. Thailand exports considerable quantities of teakwood and is second to Burma in this undertaking.

The city of Ayudhya resembles Venice because of its many canals. A large portion of its population lives on boats. Ayudhya lies within a very fertile agricultural section of Thailand and is a marketing and trade center. Phuket, located in the south, is one of the main seaports bordering the Indian Ocean. Phitsanulok, a city of 250,000, built near the banks of the Nan River, functions as a railroad center, but it is equally famous

[1] *Ibid.,* 45.

[2] Fay Cooper-Cole, *The Peoples of Malaysia* (New York: D. Van Nostrand Co., Inc., 1945), 124–125. Pile villages are found near the waterfront areas of Chinese cities.

[3] Virginia Thompson, *Thailand: The New Siam* (New York: The Macmillan Co., 1941), 324–325.

for its many temples and shrines to which pilgrimages are made. Other cities include Korat, Chantabun, Singora, and Lampang.

A major reason that Thailand has been relatively retarded in urban growth is the fact that her resources and economy have not been developed by foreign investors nor governments to the same extent as was the case in Burma, Indochina, India, Pakistan, or the Malay States.[1]

Social and occupational structure. Thailand's monarchical system is one of the few remaining in the Far East. The small upper class consists of numerous members of the royal family, a few old aristocratic families, and high officials. Should a royal family lose its right of succession, the members may retain royal titles until the fifth generation.[2]

The middle class is composed of civil servants, military and naval officers, a few professionals, and merchants. The latter group is composed mainly of Chinese and Indians. A merchant group of Thailanders hardly exists. Most of the import trade and banking, and all the export and internal trade are in Chinese hands.[3] The only exceptions to this monopolistic tendency are the tin-mining and teak forestry enterprises. The fifty-odd large tin mines in southern Thailand are owned and managed mostly by Britishers or Australians employing Malay workers. The Thailanders own and operate teak forests and small rubber plantations and a few factories manufacturing and processing textiles, tobacco, and soap for local use. The Chinese provide nearly all the heavy labor and produce most of the handicraft.

The lower class is engaged in farming, fishing, and manual work in mines and forests. A pre-World War II census showed that 88 per cent of the gainfully employed Thailanders were found in these occupations. Some are employed in handicraft, making silver objects, baskets, fishnets, embroideries, pottery, weaving, and lacquerware.

Since World War II, Thailanders have become increasingly aware of the role which the Chinese have played in various business operations. The government is encouraging more Thai merchants to become interested in various enterprises to counteract the Chinese monopolistic control over commerce, banking, and arts and crafts. Another fact causing the government to adopt this policy is that the Chinese segregate themselves in ghettos (in the same manner that Europeans do) and maintain their own social organization and institutions despite many generations of residence. For example: teachers are brought from China to staff the schools where Chinese is taught. Disputes within the community are settled by Chinese societies interested in arbitration, rather than by Thai

[1] Wyatt, *op. cit.*, 135–137.
[2] Reever, *op. cit.*, 7.
[3] *Ibid.*, 9–10.

courts. Although considerable intermarriage has taken place, and many of the 3,000,000 Chinese have mixed origins, a large number, especially the recent immigrants and their families, maintain allegiance to the "homeland." As can be expected, the allegiance to the homeland on the Asiatic mainland is having the most disturbing repercussions. In order to reduce the probabilities of greater infiltration of undesirable political influence, the annual immigration quota for the Chinese has been reduced from 10,000 in 1947 to 200 by 1949.

It should be noted that the impact of westernization upon Thai culture and habit patterns is greatest in the area of education. Since the early part of the seventeenth century, French Catholic missionaries have introduced a modern educational system which the upper class and groups dealing with commerce and trade have accepted. On the other hand, Protestantism has exerted lasting influence in the fields of social service, medicine, teaching, and public health.[1]

The Malay States

The northern portion of the Malay States border upon Thailand. The Malay States consist of nine states making up the Federation of the Malay States and the three Strait Settlements of Singapore, Penang, and Malacca. The Federation is directly administered by the nine respective sultans, while the Strait Settlements are British Colonies.[2]

The Malay States are more advanced industrially and economically than the other South Asian countries so far discussed because they are at the crossroads of trade. The major industries, rubber and tin, have bolstered the economy. Malaya is an important military outpost and guards the entrances to Oceania, the Indian Ocean and the Suez Canal.

Out of a total population of 5,900,000 reported by the 1947 census, 35.1 per cent was urban. This was a 5.6 per cent increase over 1931 when the urban total stood at 29.5.[3] The term "urban" as defined in the 1947 census included "towns and villages with populations of 1,000 and upwards."[4] Although between 1931 and 1947, urban population gained by 5.6 per cent and the distribution of urban Malaysians, Chinese, Indians, and others was fairly stable, the total urban population increased 60 per cent during the sixteen-and-a-half-year period. In other words, despite the fact that the urban population gained in absolute numbers, it was not apparent per-

[1] V. Thompson, *op. cit.*, Chs. 20 and 21.
[2] Roslinger, *op. cit.*, 332–362 and Wyatt, *op. cit.*, Ch. 7.
[3] T. E. Smith, *Population Growth in Malaya* (London: Royal Institute of International Affairs, 1952), 5.
[4] *Ibid.*

centagewise because of the growth of the total population of the various states and settlements.

Urban population and occupations. The types of occupations pursued by a group of people often provide the clues as to whether the residence is rural or urban. At the same time, they afford some basis for evaluating the occupational mobility and indirectly, social mobility. It could be assumed that immigrants in the Malay States entered the unskilled and agricultural occupations during the first years of settlement and later were able to effect a change. By comparing the occupational mobility and residence of the immigrants, Chinese and Indians, with the local groups, or Malaysians, the degree to which the aspirations of the immigrant groups were realized can be measured.[1] This assumption is based upon the fact that most immigrants are seeking economic betterment and social mobility. They also hope that their descendants may climb higher than they.

The Chinese. The Chinese outnumber all other groups in urban residence because of their extreme concentrations in the tin-mining areas and large cities. Over 40 per cent of them lived in cities having 10,000 or more inhabitants, although as a group their urban residence was reported as 53.7 per cent in 1947. About half a million were within the municipal confines of Singapore, said to be the biggest "Chinese city" outside China, while Penang and Kuala Lumpur both reported more than 100,000 Chinese (Table 14).[2] Four other cities, Taiping, Ipoh, Seremban and Malacca, each had more than 20,000 Chinese. Although the urban Chinese population was predominantly male, especially during the early years of settlement (until the 1930's), the subsequent entry and settlement of women had narrowed the sex ratio to a considerable degree by 1947.[3] The number of Chinese almost equals the number of Malaysians, a fact which augments the competition and hostility between the two groups. This problem and an attempt to suppress Communist guerilla activities led to the policy of restricting the "free immigration" of Chinese into the Malay States.[4]

The Chinese have left the rice planting, fishing, and mining occupations. The men were predominant in the "manufacturing, repairing, construction, commercial, and financial occupations" (Table 15). The "transport and communication" classifications have the next highest proportion

[1] Victor Purcell, *The Chinese in Malaya* (London: Oxford University Press, 1948); Richard Winstedt, *Malaya and Its History* (London: Hutchinson, 1948); and Virginia Thompson, *Post Mortem on Malaya* (New York: The Macmillan Co., 1943), Ch. 8.

[2] Smith, *op. cit.*, 5, 66, 74.

[3] *Ibid.*, 63–72 and Wyatt, *op. cit.*, 140–141.

[4] Skinner, *op. cit.*, 38 and 52.

TABLE 14. PERCENTAGE OF URBAN DWELLERS IN
TOTAL MALAYSIAN AND CHINESE POPULATION,
MALAYA, 1947 [1]

State or Settlement	Urban Population Malaysian	Chinese *
Singapore	72.0	81.1
Penang	25.5	70.9
Malacca	8.1	47.8
Perak	10.5	42.7
Selangor	18.1	48.7
Negri Sembilan	7.4	32.9
Pahang	6.3	22.6
Johore	14.6	28.9
Kedah	6.7	34.7
Kelantan	5.7	—
Trengganu	21.0	—
Perlis	3.8	—

* *Note:* Seven cities have 20,000 or more Chinese: Singapore, Penang, Kuala Lampur, Ipoh, Malacca, Taiping, Seremban.

[1] *Source:* Reproduced by permission from T. E. Smith, *Population Growth in Malaya* (London and New York: Royal Institute of International Affairs, 1952), 76.

of the gainfully employed males, followed by "entertainment, sport, and personal services, and clerical occupations."

The gainfully employed Chinese women had the highest concentration in the "rice growers and other agriculture" and "entertainment, sport, and personal services," followed by "manufacturing, repairing, construction, commercial, and financial" occupations. Since no adequate definition of what type of work may be included in "other and indeterminate occupations" for men and women workers, even tentative conclusions are difficult to make.

In the territories where the Chinese have gained a foothold, they own and operate plantations and mines, clothing shops, food stores, and repair shops. They process rubber, oil, copra, and cotton for export. Spices are among their leading businesses. Moreover, they control the banking operations, and lend money to Malaysian farmers and laborers. Others are actively engaged in wholesale trade, over which they hold a monopoly. As the "middlemen" of the society, many have become well-to-do, and some are very wealthy.[1] The Chinese men are seven times more numerous in commercial and financial occupations than the Malaysians, and they exceed the Indian group by 6.5 per cent. The same situation applies whether considering Chinese men or women.

[1] V. Thompson, *op. cit.*, 124.

The Chinese living in large municipalities are conversant with English as well as Malaysian and Chinese. By no means are the members of this group homogeneous, since twelve different dialects and geographical areas of southern China are represented. The majority migrated from the southern Chinese maritime provinces having a direct and easy access to the Malay States. Approximately half of the group are young native-borns who have no strong ties to China and intend to remain in Malaya.[1] It is fortunate for them that their former protectorate status was abolished on September 15, 1952, and citizenship status was substituted. Thus, 60 per cent automatically received citizenship as did 180,000 Indians. This ment that any former reservations about their status as Malaysian residents has been abolished, and their efforts can be directed toward the wholehearted development of the Malay States' economic, political and social welfare.[2]

The Indians. The majority of the Indians now remaining in the Malay States are descendants of earlier immigrants who, like the Chinese, were recruited as indentured laborers. When their contracts expired, many males returned to India, to join their families. The Indian governmental restriction on the emigration of its subjects after 1938 to territories controlled by Great Britain, and more especially the South Asian countries, has further reduced the size of the Indian population in Malay States.

The 1947 census reported 600,000 persons of Indian extraction as against 620,000 in 1941.[3] Their primary occupations are labor on rubber plantations, road construction, and railway building. Many second generation Indians are teachers, clerks, railway officials, money lenders, retail merchants, importers, and exporters. The educational level of the younger groups has risen, and during the past several decades, the members of this group have demonstrated occupational and social mobility.

The Malaysians. The native group, or Malaysians, is the largest of the three mentioned. Its members are predominantly rural and are engaged in fishing, rubber growing, rice planting, and other agricultural pursuits.[4] A large number are clustered around the upper part of the Malay States where large plantations and mines, whether European or Chinese-owned and operated, employ them in large numbers. Their urban occupations showed a concentration in the "transport and communication, manufacturing, repairing and construction, and public administration and defense" categories (Table 15). Save for the "entertainment, sport and personal service" occupations, female employment did not show the same tendency as that of the Chinese or Indians.

[1] Smith, *op. cit.*, 64–65 and V. Thompson, *op. cit.*, 125.
[2] Smith, *op. cit.*, Ch. 6.
[3] *Ibid.*, 82–84 and V. Thompson, *op. cit.*, Ch. 1.
[4] Smith, *op. cit.*, Ch. 2.

TABLE 15. PERCENTAGE DISTRIBUTION BY OCCUPATION GROUP OF THE GAINFULLY EMPLOYED MEMBERS OF THE MALAYSIAN, CHINESE, AND INDIAN COMMUNITIES, FEDERATION OF MALAYA ONLY, 1947 [1]

Occupation	Malaysians		Chinese		Indians	
	Male	Female	Male	Female	Male	Female
Fishing	6.3	0.4	3.0	0.1	0.2	0.0
Agriculture {Rubber growers	18.8	22.7	20.0	36.0	36.4	78.5
Rice planters	45.5	56.9	5.8	7.7	0.4	0.3
Other	7.8	3.3	16.2	19.3	8.2	9.5
Mining and quarrying	0.7	0.1	4.1	5.3	1.7	0.8
Manufacturing, repairing, and construction	3.8	9.6	15.1	5.3	8.1	1.7
Transport and communications	4.0	0.1	4.1	0.2	7.6	0.4
Commercial and financial occupations	2.8	3.6	16.5	5.7	10.0	0.7
Public administration and defense (not elsewhere classified)	2.4	0.0	0.2	0.0	1.1	0.0
Professional occupations	1.6	1.3	1.5	2.9	2.1	0.9
Entertainment, sport, and personal service	1.2	1.6	6.1	15.2	7.2	2.6
Clerical, etc., occupations	1.1	0.0	3.5	0.6	2.7	0.0
Other and indeterminate occupations	4.0	0.4	3.9	1.7	14.3	4.6
Total	100.0	100.0	100.0	100.0	100.0	100.0
Numbers gainfully occupied (in thousands)	644	218	580	137	220	81
Gainfully occupied as percentage of total population	54.0	18.1	55.8	16.2	69.8	37.7

[1] Source: By permission from T. E. Smith, Population Growth in Malaya (London and New York: Royal Institute of International Affairs, 1952), Appendix A, Table 55, 121.

Since 1931, the Malaysians have gradually replaced the Indian and Chinese laborers in rural occupations, but they have not made the same headway in urban vocations. Many young Malaysians are awakening to the greater opportunities for effecting occupational and social mobility in cities. Where they have established themselves, they are competing with Indian and Chinese workers for available employment. The percentage of Malaysian urban dwellers rose from 10.6 per cent to 14.1 per cent between 1931 and 1947.[1]

Another indication of the wider participation of Malaysians in civil service and skilled occupations is the changing literacy rate. Literacy is greater for the younger males between 15 and 29 than it is for males of between 35–39 years of age. Moreover, the longer the urbanite maintains residence in a city, the higher the literacy rate. The female literacy rate is also rising.

Others. The European population has always been numerically the smallest but the most urban.[2] "Others" it is assumed would include persons of mixed origin (Eurasians) who likewise have been predominantly urban dwellers. The members of these groups have the greatest knowledge of the English language, a primary requisite in the conduct of commerce. The occupations pursued by the Europeans have fallen into the "sheltered" categories, *i.e.,* owners, managers, or operators of plantations and mines, or technicians connected with mining or agriculture; government officials and military personnel; and exporters, importers, and higher white-collar positions. In contrast, the Eurasians worked as clerks, bookkeepers, typists, and minor executives, or civil servants.

It should not be overlooked that many Europeans came to Malaya, as they did to other Asian countries, to effect social and occupational mobility. Many won their reward by retiring and returning to Europe to enjoy their hard-earned status. In order to maintain their prestige and dominance, many resorted to keeping social distance between themselves and the local groups, whether these groups were indigenous or immigrant. Many did not learn the language, customs or psychology of the peoples.

Wyatt declared that many Europeans had had limited linguistic and foreign experience before leaving the home country for the Far East or Malay States. While abroad, their attention was confined to one area. Mainly drawn from a middle-class background of the "narrower sort," they believed in an "unintelligent imperialism."[3] So long as the home country dominated these backward countries, their opportunities for rising in the occupational and social scale were assured. Believing them-

[1] *Ibid.,* 22.
[2] V. Thompson, *op. cit.,* Ch. 1.
[3] Wyatt, *op. cit.,* 154–155.

selves to have become members of some "superior aristocracy," they be-
haved as they imagined the upper classes did in the home country.

Another example of how social distance was maintained between the
European and local population is the role the former forced the Chinese
and Indians to play. The latter were imported in large numbers as indentured laborers and in time permitted to rise occupationally and socially
by becoming the small middlemen, supplying the goods and services
needed by the local population as the economy expanded under European
control. The Europeans could thus concentrate upon the larger enterprises. The local population was relegated to the bottom of the social scale
and held down.

As the local population became aware of the conscious manipulation of
the economic and social order, they vented their hostilities upon the
Chinese and Indians, who, like the local population, desire to improve the
social order and make Malaya their homeland. As more and more Europeans are leaving Malaya, hostility toward the Chinese and Indians has
increased because the local inhabitants believe the places vacated by the
Europeans belong to them, not the outsiders. On the other hand, many
Malaya-born Chinese and Indians have no desire to leave the country and
resettle elsewhere.

Factors retarding industrialization. Although the Malay States have
been especially favored from the economic standpoint because of trade
in rubber, tin, palm oil, spices, and copra; large-scale industrialization has
been retarded. Four major factors have contributed to this condition.[1]

Primary is the lack of the type of enterprises required to promote greater
industrialization. Industries are either of the cottage or light manufacturing type, engaged in the processing of raw materials for export. The ultimate objective has not been to promote or stimulate local manufacturing.
Hence, commerce rather than industrialization has caused the growth of
cities.

A second factor is the persistence of the traditional conception of property and wealth and the inability to develop a working monetary system.
New methods for the creation of wealth are nearly unknown, and wealthy
persons compete for the ownership of plantations and mines, farmlands,
or commercial and residential properties. Corporate enterprises, requiring a knowledge of modern business techniques, have not been enthusi-
astically received because of the general fear of new ventures. At the same
time, the country's monetary system cannot expand on its own strength
because it is too closely tied to the world market's demand for rubber and
tin. Two measures should be taken for greater industrialization: the de-

[1] Smith, *op. cit.,* Ch. 5.

velopment of ways and means to exploit other avenues of investments, and the creation of other forms of wealth.

The lack of intimate knowledge of modern productive techniques and methods of organization is a third factor. That is, the majority of the population—save the Europeans—has not been trained for modern, efficient business organization and management. Corporate enterprises are rare, and there is an insufficient number of managers, executives, researchers, and specialists in all fields of production and business.

The lack of skilled labor is another great drawback. This condition is not unusual for a country whose economy leans heavily toward extractive and export industries. Since a major portion of the raw materials is exported rather than processed within the country, less attention has been paid to enlarging the skilled labor force.[1]

For some years there will be a discrepancy between the demands for more local industries and the ability of the people to undertake such enterprises. This condition is true of most underdeveloped countries, moreover. These enterprises will absorb an increasingly large portion of the population who in time will become more urbanized.

Indonesia

As a new nation, Indonesia ended 350 years of Dutch control and rule on December 27, 1949.[2] Having had continuous trade relations with European nations for more than four centuries, she had experienced the impact of westernization for a longer period than many other Asian countries. The relationship with Europe began even before the Dutch merchants and their government assumed such an important role in developing the country.

The 1930 estimate of Indonesian population was 60,727,233.[3] Another source states this to be 75,000,000, while a later estimate gives 78,000,000.[4] In addition to the large native population (mainly Malaysian stock) there were some 1,250,000 Chinese, 250,000 Europeans and Eurasians, and a negligible number of Japanese and Indians. These various latter groups constitute only 2 per cent of the total population, but they control the larger portion of the national income. The bulk of the Europeans are the Dutch and their descendants, and the Eurasians. These groups enjoy the upper class status. They are engaged in business enterprises, own and

[1] *Ibid.*, 106.

[2] Rosinger, *op. cit.*, 405–442.

[3] *United Nations Demographic Yearbook*, 1948, 81.

[4] Otis W. Freeman (ed.), *Geography of the Pacific* (New York: John Wiley and Sons, Inc., 1951), 461, and *Statesman's Yearbook*, 1952.

Soengei Gerong, Sumatra. The Standard Vacuum Petroleum Maatschappij refinery seen from across the Moesi River offers a sharp contrast to river sampans and the underdeveloped area in foreground.

operate large plantations, or are employed as technicians, governmental officials, or professionals. The majority are concentrated in Java, the most urban island. The Chinese, Japanese, and Indians are mainly retail merchants, craftsmen, and money lenders. Some are laborers in mines and on plantations.

There are 23 cities ranging in population from 7,500 to 600,000 population (Table 16).[1] Almost half of them are in Java and the remainder in the outer islands. On the basis of these figures Java has 2,300,000 urban persons, while the outer islands had 617,500. The urban population is roughly 3.8 per cent of the total.

The relatively slow rate of urban growth is due to the fact that many of the exploited raw materials, *i.e.,* rubber, tea, quinine, sugar, palm oil, phosphate, sulphur, coal, petroleum, bauxite, and agricultural products, were exported and not processed locally. A large share of these, as well as the profits derived from them, was used toward maintaining and bolster-

[1] Freeman, *op. cit.,* 493.

TABLE 16. MAJOR CITIES OF INDONESIA, FOR JAVA AND
OUTER ISLANDS [1]

City (Java)	Population	City (Outer Islands)	Population
Batavia	600,000 *	Palembang, Sumatra	125,000
Surabaya	450,000	Medan, Sumatra	90,000
Semarang	250,000	Padang, Sumatra	60,000
Bandung	200,000	Macassar, Celebes	100,000
Surakarta	200,000	Menado, Celebes	35,000
Jokyakarta	150,000	Benjermasin, Borneo	80,000
Malang	100,000	Balikpapan, Borneo	35,000
Pekalongan	80,000	Pontianak, Borneo	50,000
Buitenzorg	80,000	Ambon, Moluccas	20,000
Kudus	65,000	Singaraja, Bali	15,000
Cheribon	65,000	Ternate, Halmahera	7,500
Megelang	60,000		
Total	2,300,000	Total	617,500

* *Note:* Figures are estimates based upon 1930 census. New Guinea urban totals excluded.

[1] *Source:* Reprinted with permission from Otis W. Freeman (ed.), *Geography of the Pacific* (New York: John Wiley & Sons, Inc., 1951), 493.

ing the economy of The Netherlands. It was estimated that the Dutch standard of living was raised 25 per cent, so long as Indonesia remained under her control.[1] Up to the present time, heavy manufacturing industries have not been established.

Up to the time of Indonesia's independence, the skilled and professional groups were largely European and Eurasian. Eurasians are in a difficult position in most of Asia, since they are usually not fully accepted by either Europeans or Asians. They are westernized, urban, and mainly middle class, concentrated in the white-collar occupations. The Dutch in Indonesia, unlike many other Europeans elsewhere in Asia, accept the Europeanized lighter-skinned Eurasians, who in turn identify themselves with the Dutch. Thus the end of Dutch control brought about an exodus of both Europeans and Eurasians, leaving a serious deficiency of skilled and professional workers.[2] Those that remained have lost most of their power and status. Some 300,000 persons belonged to the Eurasian group. It should be noted that the official count is lower than the actual number of Eura-

[1] Wyatt, *op. cit.,* 164–165.

[2] Chicago *Tribune,* April 14, 1953. More than 100,000 of the Eurasians migrated to Holland. About 5,000 of them resettled in New Guinea along the coast on farms and plantations but found conditions too difficult and about 2,000 returned to The Netherlands. For a thorough treatment of "The Eurasian Minority in Indonesia," see J. M. van der Kroef, *American Sociological Review,* 18 (Oct., 1953), 484–493.

Standard Oil Co., New Jersey

North Klamono, New Guinea. Workmen cutting a path through the jungles.

sians because the official count is based on the predominance of Caucesoid physical characteristics.

The Philippines

Like Indonesia, the Philippines consist of a series of islands. This country gained its independence on July 4, 1946, and has many of the problems of a young republic.

The 1948 census reported 19,234,182 persons living on the eleven islands making up the total area of the Philippines.[1] The foreign population was estimated in 1947 at 325,000 of whom 300,000 are Chinese; 20,000, Ameri-

[1] *Statesman's Yearbook,* 1952, 1289.

cans with non-military and governmental status; several thousand Spaniards; and other Asiatics.[1] The urban population was 24.1 per cent in 1948, according to the United Nations Demographic Year Book, 1952.

Urban incorporation and population have a combination of Spanish and American influences. Territorially, the municipalities and municipal districts resemble the New England American town.[2] Within each municipal district is the principal city and perhaps a quasi-urban area, while the city hall is located at a strategic central point as the symbol of control over both territories. The *barrios,* or townships, have semi-urban and rural populations. Many barrios may have several centers of population which *en toto* make up a municipal district.

Three types of urban formations are found: the municipality, municipal districts, and chartered cities. By 1939, there were 936 municipalities, 261 municipal districts, and 9 chartered cities. Three more chartered cities have been added since that time. Most municipalities and chartered cities have about the same status and powers as American cities, although their populations may range from less than 2,000 to 150,000.[3] Many cities in the Philippines have histories which antedate our own and the retention of Spanish influence is noticeable.

Major cities. The largest and oldest cities have more Spanish than American influences in their physical design and architecture. Whenever a new portion has been added to a city, it has been haphazardly built around the old and formally arranged Spanish section. Philippine cities differ from the American in that there are few clearly defined areas. Heavy and light manufacturing industries are grouped together and some cities do not have a major central business district.

Some pre-Spanish important cities are Manila (983,906); Cebu (167,503); Iloilo (110,102); Samboanga (103,317); and Davao (111,263).[4] Other cities having metropolitan status include Quezon—on Luzon—and Bacolod. About twenty others had more than 10,000 population.[5] Manila has been both the Spanish and American capital of the island, but plans are underway to build a new capital, Quezon City, at the northeastern fringe of the city.

Although urban population has steadily increased, industrial growth has not kept abreast to absorb the available labor force. Some time will elapse before this condition is corrected. Concerted efforts are being made to reduce substantially the 15,000 Chinese-owned and operated mercantile and

---

[1] Department of State, "The Philippines Today," Washington, D. C., Nov., 1951, 2.

[2] Joseph R. Hayden, *The Philippines: A Study in National Development* (New York: Macmillan Co., 1947), 262–263.

[3] *Ibid.,* 263–265.

[4] *Statesman's Yearbook,* 1952, 1289 and 1290.

[5] Freeman, *op. cit.,* 323–324.

industrial firms and to encourage more Philippinos to be interested in developing their own economy.[1]

Ceylon

Ceylon, the small area enjoying Commonwealth status south of The Union of India, has an urban population totaling 15.4 per cent in 1950.[2] Among the large cities are Colombo (362,000), Jaffna (63,000), Dehiwala (56,900), Kandy (51,200), Moratuwa (50,700), and Galle (49,000).

Urban industries are well developed. They manufacture steel bars, chemicals, ceramics, textile and paper products, and sole crepe. Many firms process plywood and cocoanut oil for export. Silk weaving is a major industry. Exporters handle copra, raw rubber, graphite, spices, and black tea.

A greater degree of literacy is found among the inhabitants of Ceylon than they are generally thought to have. The local population has overcome many of the caste barriers which retarded urbanization in the Union of India. The University of Ceylon and Technical College have trained many professionals, technicians, managers, and white-collar workers. Educators from the United States have influenced and directed many of the recent changes. Researchers are engaged in all phases of industrial development. Greater urban growth is foreseen for Ceylon.

Australia

Australia, a highly industrialized Western country, has a larger proportion of urban dwellers than many of the South Asian countries mentioned above. The 1947 census listed 2,984,838 urbanites from among 7,794,880 persons, or 26 per cent of the total population. The urban male and female sex ratio was about equal, as the females exceeded the males by only 415 persons.[3] These figures apply to the Europeans for the aboriginal and mixed genetic groups are regarded as outside of the social system.

An urban area in Australia is defined as a "city or town with 2,000 or more persons, whether incorporated or not."[4] By this definition, Australia had 247 cities. Using 3,000 or more as a basis for computation, there were 150 cities. The urban population has increased by 14.76 per cent since 1933. The greatest gains were found in metropolitan areas which had an increase of 20.14 per cent.[5] The population in these areas rose from 46.87 per cent in

---

[1] Hayden, *op. cit.*, 698–699.

[2] *Statesman's Yearbook*, 1952, 213.

[3] Commonwealth Bureau of Census and Statistics, 1951, as contained in *Statesman's Yearbook*, 1952, 525.

[4] *Ibid.*, 522.

[5] *Ibid.*, 525.

1933 to 50.72 per cent in 1947.[1] This tendency of urbanites to cluster around metropolises is found in many other Western societies.

Sydney and Melbourne, together with their respective suburbs, are two super-cities each with over a million population. In addition to four others of metropolitan size, there were 33 having between 10,000 to 50,000 inhabitants (Table 17). The remainder had varying population aggregations between 2,000 to 10,000.

TABLE 17. POPULATION OF SELECTED
URBAN INCORPORATED AREAS,
AUSTRALIA (EXCLUDES FULL-
BLOOD ABORIGINALS) 1947
CENSUS, FINAL COUNT [1]

City	Population
Sydney and suburbs	1,484,004
Melbourne and suburbs	1,226,409
Brisbane and suburbs	402,030
Adelaide and suburbs	382,454
Perth and suburbs	272,528
Newcastle and suburbs	127,138
Hobart and suburbs	76,534
Geelong	44,561
Launceston	40,449
Ballard	40,181
Bendigo	30,779
Broken Hill	27,054
Kalgoorlie	22,376
Maitland	19,151
Wollongong	18,116
Canberra	15,156
Port Pirie	12,019
Cabramatta	10,966
Whyalla	7,845

[1] *Source: Statesman's Yearbook*, 1952, 529.

The major seaboard cities are diversified in function, modern in physical layout and institutional development, and have many characteristics of Western cities. Cities will continue to expand in land area and population as the result of the greater mechanization of farms, the continued expansion of manufacturing, and the growth of service industries. The immigration of displaced persons after World War II has accelerated industrial and urban growth. Between 1947–1948 a net migration of 55,115 persons was reported.[2]

[1] *Ibid.*, 528.
[2] *Ibid.*, 520.

Already some of the larger cities are experiencing the consequences of their previous lack of foresight in establishment of municipal boundaries and failure to take steps toward accommodating future population growth. Traffic congestion and housing shortages are pressing problems.[1] The removal of population and institutions from crowded cities to suburbs is well underway, despite the fact that the transportation system has failed to keep abreast with new trends. Australian cities in many ways resemble Western cities, and it is not necessary to describe them at length here.

New Zealand

With a population of less than two million, New Zealand has 1,184,672 urbanites in cities and boroughs. Her urban population percentage of 61.3 per cent in 1951 was more than twice that of Australia. New Zealand is the most urbanized of all the countries mentioned so far. However, her cities do not reach the population aggregation of Australia's. The two metropolitan cities, Auckland and Christ Church, had 329,123 and 174,221, respectively in 1951, and Wellington and Dunedin had between 50,000 to 100,000 inhabitants.[2] The remaining ten large cities had between 10,000 to 50,000 (Table 18). It should be noted that the major reason for New Zealand's urban population being larger than Australia's is due to classifying all places as urban if 1,000 and more inhabitants are there.

Most of the cities are located along the coastal regions. For example, Auckland, the commercial capital and largest city, is situated on the most spacious harbor of the country. It is also accessible by airplane and railroad. Christ Church and Dunedin are two other large port cities. New Plymouth, Wanganui, Wellington, are modern inland gold-mining cities. The remaining cities are well scattered throughout New Zealand. A well planned transportation system has facilitated the exchange of raw materials obtained from agriculture and mining areas and carried them to cities for processing into finished products. A large portion of the goods is sold abroad. Before the Second World War there were 17,500 factories employing 123,500 workers, engaged in manufacturing chemicals, paper, and tobacco products. Others made home furnishings, radio, and munitions, and there were some which assembled automobiles.[3]

Unlike Australia, the aboriginal (Maori) population is encouraged to settle in cities, enter urban occupations, participate in political affairs, and effect social mobility. Some 115,000 Maoris are not included in the population figures shown above.

[1] Freeman, *op. cit.*, 153–154.
[2] *Statesman's Yearbook*, 1953, 505.
[3] Freeman, *op. cit.*, 446–448 and 455–456.

TABLE 18. MAJOR CITIES,
NEW ZEALAND, 1951 [1]

Name	Population
Auckland	329,123
Christ Church	174,221
Wellington	133,414
Dunedin	95,457
Hutt	74,878
Hamilton	33,137
Palmerston North	32,908
Invercargill	31,613
Wanganui	29,717
New Plymouth	24,923
Napier	24,538
Hastings	23,797
Timaru	22,851
Nelson	20,497
Gisborne	19,774

[1] *Source: Statesman's Yearbook*, 1952, 505.

Summary

The various countries under consideration vary greatly in urban population and the degree of industrialization. From about 4 per cent of the total population in urban areas for Indonesia to 61.3 per cent for New Zealand, there are wide gaps among the urban conditions found in the various South Asian and Oceanic countries. Those with a small urban population in South Asia are likewise retarded in industrialization. Commerce is the major factor influencing urban concentrations and their occupational structures. The raw materials extracted are processed mainly in European centers.

Other factors which retard industrialization can be regarded as applying to all South Asian countries with the exception of Australia and New Zealand. They are: (1) low productivity of native labor, (2) immigrants from Asia to areas with greater economic opportunity encounter a ceiling in occupational and social mobility because of either local prejudice or a colonial system, (3) lack of capital of indigenous and immigrant Asiatic groups, (4) lack of vocational training and higher education for skilled urban occupations, (5) overemphasis upon commerce, (6) lack of heavy manufacturing industries, (7) limited occupational opportunities for women, (8) interethnic competition and hostility, especially between the local and Chinese populations, and (9) problem of meeting needs for consumer goods.

The factors favoring greater industrialization and urbanization in the future include: (1) growing awareness and attainment of independent political and economic status, (2) higher literacy rate for male and female, (3) settlement of families in cities, (4) closer interrelationship between rural and urban areas in industrial development, and (5) the beginnings of large scale manufacturing enterprises.

DISCUSSION QUESTIONS

1. In what ways is India's caste system affected by urban residence? By new occupations?
2. Explain why the native populations of Burma, Indochina, and the Malay States have been reluctant to settle in cities and to engage in urban occupations.
3. Compare the occupational and social status of the Europeans and the Chinese or Indians in Indochina or the Malay States.
4. Explain why commerce stimulates urban concentration of population but not the growth of local manufacturing.
5. Why is the increase of employment of women in cities regarded as an indication of greater industrialization and urbanization?
6. Why is the sudden increase of population often associated with industrialization and urbanization?
7. Discuss the Chinese problem in Thailand and the Malay States.

SUGGESTED PROJECTS

1. Study the role of nationalism in promoting industrialization for any of the Asiatic countries.
2. Compare the occupational distribution of India with that of the United States over a period of 50 years.
3. Compare the growth of cities and urban population of Australia and New Zealand for the last 50 years.
4. Compare the traditional and urban occupations of gainfully employed females of one of the South Asian countries.

READINGS

Annals of the American Academy of Political and Social Science, "America and the New Asia," 294 (July, 1954).

A volume devoted to the realignment of our social, economic, and political relationships with Asian countries, especially the "new republics."

George B. Cressey, *Asia's Lands and Peoples*. New York: McGraw-Hill Book Co., Inc., 1944, Ch. 29–40.

A revised edition with first-hand material and excellent bibliography on South Asian countries.

Cora DuBois, *Social Forces in Southeast Asia*. Minneapolis: University of Minnesota Press, 1949.

A small volume explaining the status hierarchy of the Asiatics and Europeans.

Otis W. Freeman, ed., *Geography of the Pacific*. New York: John Wiley & Sons, Inc., 1951, Ch. 5, 11, 15 and 16.

A treatment of Australia, New Zealand, Philippine Islands, and Indonesia as to population, natural resources and leading industries.

Hardey C. Grattan, *Australia*. Berkeley: University of California Press, 1946.

A volume within the United Nations series describing Australia's economic, social, political, and cultural growth.

A. R. T. Janse, *The Peoples of French Indochina*. Washington, D. C.: Smithsonian Institute, 1944.

Ethnology and description of Indochina, together with the social effects of recent changes.

Dhurjate Mukerji, *Modern Indian Culture: A Sociological Study*. Second ed., Bombay: Hind Kitabs, 1948.

An enlarged edition of the social conditions of India and her cultural development.

Report of the Director-General, Asian Regional Conference, 1950. Geneva: International Labour Organization.

A terse and pertinent summary of the necessary steps to be realized before greater industrialization and urbanization can proceed.

G. William Skinner, *Report on the Chinese in Southeast Asia*. Ithaca: Cornell University, 1950.

A survey of the Chinese population, its role in the economic, social and political structure, and future influence in the Southeastern countries of Asia.

Virginia Thompson, *Labor Problems in Southeast Asia*. New York: The Macmillan Co., 1949.

A treatment of the indenture and farmholding systems confronting native and migrant laborers.

Chapter Six

African Cities

THE AFRICAN continent has cities dating back to the beginnings of recorded history. The rise and development of Egyptian cities paralleled that of cities near modern Baghdad in Iraq some five millennia ago. The archaeological excavations of ancient Nippur and Egypt show that the fertile valleys of the Nile and the Tigris-Euphrates Rivers gave birth to the urban culture which was subsequently diffused through India and Europe.[1]

Despite the antiquity of cities in this region, urban growth has been slow when measured by Western standards. Little attention was paid to Africa south of the Sahara Desert until the discovery of gold, copper, diamonds, and other resources. The influx of new settlers into the territories south of the equator initiated an era of "boom town" developments which resemble the decades of rapid urbanization experienced by the United States. The full significance of westernization and industrialization upon the various parts of Africa—none of which are totally similar in geography, social organization, and population composition—is becoming more and more recognized. For this reason it is difficult to treat the urban growth and development of African cities within any single frame-of-reference. The growth and development of African cities differ in several respects from other areas.

On this continent, many of the rural-folk characteristics associated with a tribal organization remain. By studying the impact of westernization and industrialization upon this form of social organization, some insight into the processes underlying the transformation of the rural-folk to the urban-industrial type is possible. At the same time, the social effects resulting from this impact can be contrasted with those experienced by the

---

[1] William A. Albright, "The Rediscovery of Civilization: Digging for Buried History," *Commentary* (Dec., 1948), 570–577; D. E. McCown, "Recent Finds at Nippur, a Great City of Ancient Mesopotamia," *Archaeology*, 5 (Sum., 1952), 70–75.

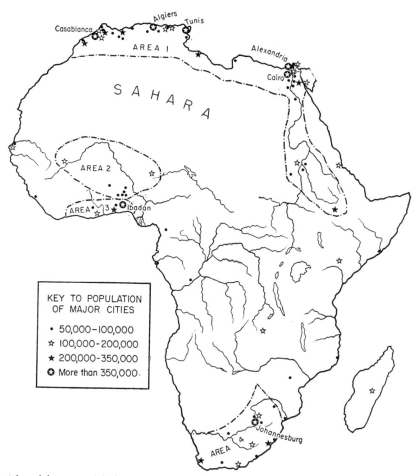

Adapted from an original map by Robert E. T. Roberts.

Areas 1, 2, and 3 contain cities built by the local population, with European sections added after the era of European expansion. Cities of Area 4 are primarily built by Europeans but have sections reserved for the Coloured, Native, and Asiatic populations. In the other three areas, population is segregated by religious affiliations.

feudal-like societies of the Far East. On the other hand, urban growth and development are not uniform when comparing North and South Africa, so that another set of consequences is present.

Africa is one of the few areas today where European powers retain their colonial policies. When the various European nations divided Africa among themselves and set up discreet political units, little regard was given to geographic features; cultural, linguistic, and tribal ties; and local sentiments. In the words of one writer, "there is scarcely an international boundary throughout the length and breadth of Africa that does not cut a tribe in half."[1] In many instances tribes are separated into several isolated units, each under a different political administration. For example, the Ewe tribe of one million members was divided between French Togoland, British Togoland, and the Gold Coast.

Each European nation's colonial policy toward the indigenous population differs, so that the five universal traits of colonialism—racial division; political control; economic dependence upon, and control by, the mother country; low stage of development of social services, especially education; and rigid social barriers between the ruling class and the subject people—show corresponding variations.[2] These divergent policies have their greatest implications in urban areas where the contacts between groups are intensified by competition for available goods, services, occupations, and status. At the same time, these policies affect the settlement of population and the spatial pattern of cities. The size of the non-European urban groups and the rate of their influx in cities, in turn, influence the degree to which colonial policies are enforced and their social implications highlighted.

Another point for consideration is that many Europeans came to settle permanently in Africa and regard it as their homeland. Many have severed ties with the "home country" and are attempting to set up national and administrative machinery which will permit a multi-racial and rapidly changing society to function according to locally established policies. Many of these policies, however, have their antecedents in European countries and represent a shift in the center of control rather than a departure from tradition. On the other hand, where the non-European population controls the administrative machinery or is being prepared by degrees to assume control—as in the Gold Coast and Anglo-Egyptian Sudan—interracial contacts have fewer tensions and conflicts.

A final point for consideration is to see how the cities built by tribal empires have met the needs of the local population. Many have persisted to the present and reflect the cultural development of the society. As has been the case in other areas of the world, former cities are known to have existed, but data concerning their existence have been treated as unimportant until the era of European expansion. When cities in Africa or Asia are mentioned, the so-called native cities are either ignored or treated as insignificant because they do not show a high degree of industrialization.

[1] E. S. Munger, *Relational Patterns of Kampala, Uganda* (Chicago: University of Chicago Press, Sept., 1951), 1–2.

[2] Raymond Kennedy, "The Colonial Crisis and the Future," in Ralph Linton (ed.), *The Science of Man in the World Crisis* (New York: Columbia University Press, 1945), 306–346, and especially 308–311; see also H. A. Wieschhoff, *Colonial Policies in Africa* (Philadelphia: University of Pennsylvania Press, 1944).

Since one of our primary purposes is to study different kinds of cities as well as correct misimpressions concerning cities about which we have little knowledge, a more detailed treatment of the non-European African cities will be included.

The above-mentioned aspects and others provide a basis for making comparisons between the growth and development of African cities and other regions as well as between the four major urban areas within the continent.

Major Urban Areas

There are four major urban areas, three above and one below the Equator which show the influence of geographic features and historical factors upon the growth and development of cities. The three urban areas above the Equator existed before European expansion, while the cities of Area Four are primarily due to European efforts (see Map of African Cities). The majority of the leading cities are located near the long, winding coastline or near large rivers, for no great gulf or sea penetrates the heart of Africa.[1] Furthermore, the Sahara Desert and the tropics make human settlement difficult and interfere with intercommunication. Railroad and highway development take on many of the same characteristics of South Asia. Colonial powers have constructed arteries which connect territories under their control or through areas to which they must have access. But there has been little interest in establishing a unified transcontinental system.

Despite the antiquity of urban development, Cairo is the only city with more than a million population, although Johannesburg—a new city—in South Africa is rapidly approaching this figure (Table 19). Africa has 36 metropolitan cities and has fewer large cities than any major continent. In 1930 there were 12 "great cities" in "European Africa," and by 1950, the increase of large cities was threefold.[2] Urban growth was greatest in South Africa.

The extraction of raw materials and the development of new industries have attracted an influx of urban settlers,[3] and three streams of population influx into South African cities have occurred simultaneously: settlers and refugees from Europe between the two world wars, the descendants of earlier European settlers, and the non-European. The latter include the

[1] L. Dudley Stamp, *Africa: A Study in Tropical Development* (New York: John Wiley & Sons, Inc., 1953), 3–4.

[2] Mark Jefferson, "Distribution of the World's City Folks: A Study in Comparative Civilization," *Geographical Review*, 1931, 446–465.

[3] Roderick Peattie, *Struggle on the Veld* (New York: Vanguard Press, Inc., 1947), 238–242.

TABLE 19. CITIES OF AFRICA: 50,000 TO 100,000
AND ABOVE POPULATION [1]

Algeria		*Angolo*	
Algiers	315,210	Loanda	77,130
Oran	256,661		
Constantine	118,774	*Mocambique*	
Bone	102,823	Lourence Marques	69,861
Tlemoen	69,668		
Belda	61,607	*Bechuanaland*	
Sidi-Bel-Abbes	61,355	Salisburg	62,000
Philippeville	57,091		
Mostaganem	53,464	*Gold Coast*	
Setif	51,464	Accra	135,926
		Kumasi	78,483
Belgian Congo			
Elizabethville	104,829	*Sierra Leone*	
		Freetown	86,000
Anglo-Egyptian Sudan			
Omdurman	117,650	*Morocco*	
Khartoum	75,000	Casablanca	569,500
Il Obeid	70,000	Marrakech	239,200
Wad Mendani, Blue Nile	57,300	Fez	202,000
		Meknes	162,400
Nigeria & Br. Cameroons		Rabat	161,000
Ibadan	500,000	Teutan	93,658
Lagos	230,000	Oujda	90,100
Kano	107,000	Sale	58,200
Iwo	86,000	Pt. Lyantey	57,800
Oyo	79,000	Safi	51,600
Ogbomosho	79,000		
Kumasi	70,705	*Tunisia*	
Oshogbo	64,000	Tunis	364,593
Onitsha	60,000	Sfax	54,637
Abeokuta	54,000		
Ilorin	53,000	*Kenya*	
Ede	51,000	Nairobi	161,500
Union of South Africa		*Tanganyika*	
Johannesburg	880,012	Dar-es-Salaam	74,000
Durban	463,120		
Cape Town	239,785	*Egypt*	
Pretoria	284,182	Cairo	2,100,056
Port Elizabeth	199,287	Alexandria	925,081
Germiston	169,748	Port Said	178,432
Bloemfontein	109,130	Tanta	139,965
Vereeniging	96,391	Mahalla	115,509
Pietermaritzburg	92,555	Suez	108,250
East London	92,715	Mansura	102,709
Brakpan	83,242	Asyut	90,378
Krugersdorp	74,138	Zagazig	89,912
Benoni	72,034	Damanbar	84,983
Roodepoort	71,631	Taiyum	74,314
Kimberley	64,699	Minya	69,667
Maritzburg	63,162	Giza	68,520
Boksburg	53,419	Beni Suef	57,464
		Damielta	53,620
French Cameroons		*Libya*	
Yaounde	50,000	Tripoli	140,000
		Benghazi	62,300
Eritrea			
Asmara	117,000	*French Equatorial Africa*	
		Brazzaville	50,000
Ethiopia		*French West Africa*	
Addis Ababa	300,000	Dakar	140,000
		Bamako	101,650
Italian Somaliland		St. Louis	63,000
Mogadiscio	70,000	Bobo-Dibulasso	52,000

[1] *Sources:* Reproduced with permission from E. Dudley Stamp, *Africa: A Study of Tropical Development* (New York: John Wiley & Sons, Inc., 1953); United Nations, *Non-Self-Governing Territories,* 2, 1950; Union of South Africa Government Information Office statistics; *Statesman's Yearbook,* 1952.

Asiatic, Coloured, and various Negroid groups. The European, Asiatic, and Coloured groups within the Union of South Africa were attracted to cities because of the growing economy. The Negroid groups came there primarily as recruited labor for the mines.

North Africa. The countries comprising North Africa include Egypt, Libya, Tunisia, Algeria, Morocco, Eritrea, and Ethiopia. These areas bordering the Mediterranean Sea compose what has sometimes been treated by historians and political scientists as an extension of the Near or Middle East or as a part of Mediterranean Europe because of the geographical proximity of northwestern Africa to southern Europe. The alternate waves of domination and conquest by Berbers, Phoenicians, Romans, Arabs, Turks, and modern European powers, from 1200 B.C. to the present, have introduced both Western and Islamic cultures. Both cultures have had good effects, depending upon the era under study. What is generally known as Islamic culture has persisted and united the population into a religious and cultural unity which supercedes all other social attributes. For our purposes this area is treated as a part of North Africa, rather than the Near or Middle East, although many of the urban characteristics of the latter are found here.

The population of the area is divided into indigenous and European, to distinguish between the settlement of Berbers, Turks, Arabs, Jews, Negroes, and other subgroups here before the pervasion of modern European influence dating from the fifteenth century.[1] The Europeans have not generally followed the practice of crossing racial and religious lines, and less intermingling has resulted, as distinguished from earlier eras. Race-consciousness is not as prevalent, and genetic heterogeneity of population resulting from intermarriage among groups and persons of the same religion and economic status is secondary to religious affiliation.

It should be noted that the Portuguese and French in Africa do not hold rigidly to the color line as a matter of official policy.[2] Non-Europeans who have become assimilated into European culture are frequently classified as "Europeans."[3] The indigenous population regards groups believing in other than the Moslem faith as minorities. These minorities include the Copts, Jews who have become Christians, Lebanese, Syrians, and others. They are minorities in the same manner that such subgroups set themselves apart in the United States by retention of religions, family patterns,

[1] Sylvia Pankhurst, *Ex-Italian Somaliland* (London: Watts & Co., 1951), 380, writes that "indigenous persons are those who are born in the Territory, permanently reside therein, and accept citizenship of the Territory."

[2] Kennedy, *op. cit.*, 334, "Portugal . . . has followed a weak imitation of the French policy . . . may be described as assimilationists. . . . Although race prejudice is less prevalent . . . and intermarriage quite common, little positive effort has been made to improve the status of the subject peoples."

[3] However, those so classified are a small group of European-educated persons who are frequently used to uphold colonial policies.

languages, or combinations of these factors.[1] These group distinctions are based upon religious and ethnic differentiations rather than race.

The penetration of modern European influence began with the establishment of trading posts and slave-trading by the Portuguese and Spaniards. Large permanent settlements of Europeans did not follow until the turn of the nineteenth century, when France invaded Morocco and Tunis in 1930 and created protectorates. The Italians conquered Tripolitania and later Ethiopia. The Spaniards acquired Ifni, Rio de Oro, and a part of Morocco. The British took control of Egypt, the Anglo-Egyptian Sudan, and parts of the Near East. The last wave of outside influence has encountered the tide of rising nationalism and revolt. The uprisings of recent years, attracting considerable journalistic and diplomatic attention, reveal the strength of the religious and cultural unity of the Islamic world.

North Africa has more than half of the large cities of the continent. Egypt has the greatest percentage of urban population, or 30.1, and cities of varying sizes: seven metropolises; eight other cities with populations of between 50,000 and 100,000; and six of between 25,000 and 50,000.[2] Algeria and Morocco have four and five metropolitan cities respectively, and a similar number of others with populations ranging between 50,000 and 100,000. Cities are few in the countries distant from the Mediterranean coastline, as can be seen in Ethiopia, Eritrea, and ex-Italian and British Somaliland (Table 19).

A primary reason for the small number of large cities is the lack of a continuous supply of water. Cairo, Alexandria, Fez, Tunis, and Casablanca have survived the downfall of empires and kingdoms because of their proximity to the seacoast. Many of the buried cities now being excavated declined because the water supplies dried up or rivers changed their courses. This is the same thing that happened to the ancient Mohenjo-daro cities.

The rigidity of the social structure and the division of labor has some influence on urban growth. In North Africa, the division of labor has historical, political, and religious implications. According to Professor Coon, "other incidents in the past, less simple to trace, will explain the special role of the Armenians or tell us why all the well-diggers in Morocco come from the land of the Dra'a, or why until most recently most clerks in Egypt are Copts. However it happened, the peoples of the Middle East are organized into a complicated social system based on an ethnic division of labor."[3]

[1] R. A. Schermerhorn, *These Our People* (New York: D. C. Heath & Co., 1949), 5–7.

[2] *United Nations Demographic Yearbook, 1952,* Table 8, 202–214 and *Statesman's Yearbook, 1952,* 920–921.

[3] Carleton S. Coon, *Caravan: The Story of the Middle East* (New York: Henry Holt & Co., 1951), 3.

But the pattern of ethnic division of labor is not due to a rigid caste system with hereditary occupational status. It owes its continuance to the lack of raw materials for industrialization and knowledge of how to enlarge existing enterprises. Skills once learned are retained and transmitted to descendants. For instance, Armenians and Syrians in settling in North Africa saw the need for textile merchandising and took steps to monopolize it. Succeeding generations of Armenians and Syrians became identified with this business. In the same manner, the Jews of Yemen have a virtual monopoly on import-export trade, financial transactions, stone masonry, and ironwork. Those groups cultivating the land or herding sheep have done the same work for centuries. A high degree of localism has resulted. Many groups live their own lives, perpetuate their own communities, and recognize the authority of local religious leaders.[1] The complications attending this system are found in Fez, Rabat, and Tunis, where each religious group is governed by its particular head, rather than by municipal authorities, and each group occupies a separate section of the city. The effect this system has upon the spatial pattern of cities will be illustrated by Fez in the pages that follow.

Town and city differentiation. Large cities, as we have seen, are few, but towns are numerous. One of the more accurate methods for distinguishing between a town and city has been described by Professor Coon.[2] Cities represent the largest aggregation of population, while a town may have, at the utmost, several thousand inhabitants. Below the town are the village and nomad camp, two other units of community life, which utilize the town and city for the sale or procuring of goods and services.

A major difference between town and city is in the division of labor and religious homogeneity or heterogeneity. A town is a community of traders, merchants, and a few specialists who serve not only the local population, but that of surrounding camps and villages. Save for the highly skilled specialists, like mechanics and truck drivers whose skills are not learned locally, the majority are residents of the town and there are few strangers. Much of the business is transacted around outdoor markets where everyday necessities and a few luxuries are sold. Candles, needles, thread, cloth, hardware, and food are common items for purchase. Services are furnished

---

[1] A. H. Hourani, *Minorities in the Arab World* (New York: Oxford University Press, 1947), 20–21. "The *millet* system made it possible for the Christians and Jews to maintain something of their communal life and social position. . . . The autonomy of the millets are based . . . on ancient custom which was reinforced in the nineteenth century by specific edicts . . . The millets were autonomous in spiritual and in certain administrative and judicial matters. Their jurisdiction embraced, in the . . . administrative sphere, properties, including cemeteries, education, and churches; in the judicial sphere, marriage, dowries, divorce, and alimony."

[2] *Op. cit.,* Ch. 14, 226.

by the blacksmiths, tailors, shoemakers, and the like. Political control of the town is in the hands of a minor official.

The city is the seat of important administrative and religious control. The large cities of Morocco are excellent illustrations. Morocco was divided in 1912 into three parts: the French zone, Spanish zone, and international zone at Tangier.[1] The Sultan's religious and administrative powers and the safety of his person are guaranteed by a treaty. He remains in name the supreme civil and religious authority as Commander of the Faithful. In practice, his civil powers are superseded by the French Resident General— or a Commissioner, if a civil official—at Rabat. His powers in the Spanish zone are delegated to the Caliph.

The Sultan normally resides at Rabat, although he has residences at Fez, Marrakesh, and Meknes. The Caliph and Spanish High Commissioner are at Tetuan. All these cities have larger populations than those without administrative and religious significance. The only exception is Casablanca, a modern French city, where roughly a fourth of the population is European.

Another difference between a town and city is that the latter has several Moslem, Jewish, and Christian sects, while a town is more homogeneous in religious affiliation. A greater degree of segregation is found in large cities antedating the era of European expansion because each religious group withdraws into its own quarters, often separated by walls, at the close of the business day.

The volume of trade in cities is larger. The craftsmen are very skilled, making one or more kinds of luxury objects which have a national, if not international, market. The type of luxury item manufactured is dependent upon the quantity of some special raw material, which, in turn, has stimulated the development of special craftsmen handling and perfecting the material. Fez is noted for superb leather articles, for example. Wholesale export-import merchants handling a variety of merchandise are city dwellers, while in towns merchants concentrate upon one or two necessities, like cloth or cereal. In towns the retail merchants are numerous and constitute a recognized class. In cities the retail and wholesale merchants are more powerful and wealthy.

The town becomes a city when the number of individuals engaged in a given craft or trade increases to the point where the market provost and his deputies are unable to cope with the problems or situations arising between the members of a single craft or between crafts. At this stage, each craft organizes separately and elects its own officials. The town becomes a city.

Fez: the Moslem city. Fez ranks with Tunis, Cairo, and Alexandria as

[1] Stamp, *op. cit.*, 237–242.

a key city of the old Moslem World and has an internal spatial pattern which is different from any found in the Western world. Fez is the crossroad "between the north-south caravan road from Tangier, and thence Europe, to the Sudan, and the east-west Sultan's Road, which ties the fertile Atlantic plain of Morocco to the rest of the world of Islam." [1] Moreover, Fez, one of the few cities with an adequate and constant water supply, was founded in 808 A.D. by a sharif, a holy descendant of the Prophet. That is, it became a city instead of remaining a town, for its present site was once inhabited by Christians and Jews who used it as a market center for the surrounding tribes.

The city is divided into separate quarters. Soon after Fez was founded Cordova craftsmen settled on the south bank of the Wed Fas River in what is now known as the Andulusian Quarter. Merchants from Quairawan in Tunisia settled on the north bank and formed another quarter, in which a small Jewish section, or hostel, is included. These two quarters functioned as separate cities for more than two centuries, with a wall dividing them. In 1070 A.D., the wall was torn down and a third quarter was added to the west.

This new quarter contained the royal palace, its grounds, a quarter for Moslems who were not of local descent, a Jewish quarter for those wishing to move from the older Jewish hostel, and a fortified stronghold to provide protection for the city. This addition is still called the new city, and when the French took control of Fez in 1911, a modern or European "quarter" was built three miles westward. Four cities actually constitute what is known as Fez, with many subdivisions within the various quarters, based upon religious affiliation. For example: the Jews who moved from their hostel to the new city are the orthodox believers. Those who remained in the hostel became Moslem converts.

The entire city is walled with each quarter separated by inner walls, and gateways lead from one quarter to the next. The doors of gates may be locked during times of unrest. In addition, more walls separate the city into wards, and reflect the land use pattern or socio-economic status of the inhabitants. For example: the Gate of Peaches on the east side of Fez opens into a sprawling section reserved for wealthy residences where each home is set in spacious gardens. The area near the Tangier gate is mainly used by Riffs who sit on benches or work in the shade of the wall. Others work in the shops within this enclosure.

Most Moorish walled cities, of which Fez is an example, have, inside one of the principal gates, a large open space serving as the major business center. At the end of the road leading from the main gateway of Fez is the heart of the city's business section where merchants display their wares.

[1] Coon, *op. cit.,* 231–259.

Ewing Galloway

Tunis, Tunisia. A typical street scene in the native quarter. Sidewalk cafe is to the right. The white domes of the mosque are not far away.

Here the members of the principal trades have their guild halls. Some of these halls may have a hundred rooms in which to accommodate the transient customers and their exchange of social amenities. Other leading institutions of city-wide or regional importance, such as the university, mosque, shrines, and schools are located here also. Lesser mosques, schools, and so on, are found in each quarter.

The business section wherein the wares are sold is laid out according to the type of commodity sold. The displays of costly wearing apparel and luxury items are grouped together in the most desirable and centralized location. Around these displays are the less fashionable merchandise and utilitarian items and so on. Once a week a special market is held outside the city's walls for the sale of livestock and rugs. Industry is located along the river, if the processing of materials requires water. Other industries are scattered throughout the city according to space and rent considerations.

Residences are located away from the center of the city, and within each residential area is a bazaar. The poorer families often live where single rooms are abundant. Each family's room is separated from the other's by a cloth. Families of higher economic status occupy several rooms, but westernized families live in houses with two to three stories. Wealthy families live in detached homes built around courtyards, surrounded by blank brick or plaster walls. The main rooms of these homes face the garden which is the spot farthest from the street.

Cairo is another interesting example of a city divided into quarters. The eastern half of the city was formerly walled and closed at night by massive gates. A few of these gates remain at the present time. In addition to the Mohammedan quarters, usually called after the trade of the inhabitants or some notable building, there are the Copt or Christian quarter, the Jewish quarter, and the old "Frank" quarter. The last is the Muski district where the Frank merchants are permitted to live and trade. Some of the principal European shops are found here. In the Copt quarter are also Armenian, Syrian, Maronite, Greek, and Roman Catholic churches. In the Copt, Jewish, and Arab quarters, the streets, are winding and narrow. They are so narrow that the projecting upper stories of the houses nearly meet.

The separation of population in cities according to religious affiliations and occupations has other interesting features. Each quarter has a sufficiently large population to satisfy most of its needs, so that social and work life do not necessarily coincide, a phenomenon found in most "ghetto" situations. That is, a shoemaker with a shop in the center of Fez will retire at the end of the work day to his home in a given quarter where social contacts are mainly confined to members of his own group. This has preserved the status of groups desiring to retain their identity despite centuries of residence. This is true of the Copts in Egypt, Ethiopia, and Morocco. For example, in-marriage has perpetuated the group while language and customs are transmitted. In large cities where several Moslem, Jewish, and Christian sects exist, three different Sundays are observed: with the Moslems celebrating Friday; the Jews, Saturday; and the Christians, Sunday.[1]

What makes the city function as a unit is the people's need for each other's goods and services. The division of labor often cuts across religious lines and a degree of mutual interdependence results, a situation well illustrated by Cairo. The Coptic Christians who desire professional status often study under British, French, or Arab teachers. The majority of the literate persons depend for news upon the Syrian-operated press. Customers buy foreign goods from either Syrian, Armenian, Greek, Jewish, and

[1] Issawi, *op. cit.,* Ch. 11.

British merchants. Factories employ Greek workers who comprise a major portion of the urban labor force, and so on.[1]

In summary, the cities of North Africa have many characteristic features dating back to former empires. Many walled cities have resisted the impact of westernization—in appearance, at least—and the various quarters have retained much of their colorfulness. The Europeanized sections offer a sharp contrast, with wide streets and tall buildings. Residential structures are also different, as most Moslem homes are low and rambling. The faithful Moslem builds his home close to the ground, and an outdoor area facing East is reserved for his daily prayers. It should be noted that the Copts (Christians) are among the oldest inhabitants of this area but were assigned a minority status after the spread of Islamic culture.

We must not assume that a variety of industries and businesses do not exist in North African cities. Fez and Meknes act as collecting and distributing centers for the area over which they have control, and the import-export trade is considerable. Casablanca is, however, the most important seaport and industrial city. Her modern factories produce cement, oil, soap, superphosphates, and other products. Marrakesh is a great inland city where merchants trade at her large market place or participate in the fairs which are held periodically. Marrakesh's leading industries include carpet-making, oil-pressing, leather, silk, and metal work, and butter-making.

Algerian cities exceed Moroccan ones in import-export trade, and much of the mineral and agricultural products of Algeria find their way to France. Algeria is considered a department of metropolitan France, located in Africa, and her inhabitants, as citizens of France, elect representatives for all local and national assemblies including those in Paris.[2] The ports of Orans, Algiers, Bougie, Philippeville, and Bone handle iron ore, phosphorus, salt, wheat, barley, tobacco, olive oil, fruits, vegetables, dates, and wine. Tunis, the site of ancient Carthage, ranks with Kairouan, an old Moslem capital, and Bizerte as one of the leading cities in Tunisia.

Other important cities include Omdurman, the Moslem capital, and Khartoum, the seat of British administration of the Anglo-Egyptian Sudan. Eritrea and Ethiopia have Asmara and Addis Ababa, respectively. The European population differs in the respect that Italians and Britishers predominate.

Libya, an independent kingdom, has two sections, Cyrenaica and Tripolitania. Tripoli is a famous and attractive city in Tripolitania while Benghazi, Tobruk, and Derna are located in Cyrenaica. During the Italian

[1] *Ibid.,* 161–168, ". . . Foreign communities include 60,000 Syrians, 63,000 Jews, 20,-000 Armenians, 69,000 Greeks, 48,000 Italians, 10,000 French, 14,000 British, and 1,085,-000 Copts."

[2] *United Nations World,* "The Non-French Frenchmen: Ten Million African Algerians," 3 (May, 1949), 27–28.

occupation of Libya, modern buildings, monuments, and roads were built on a large scale in anticipation of a permanent outlet for the surplus population of Italy. The same outlay of money and effort was poured into Eritrea and Ethiopia with the same objective.[1]

West Africa. The second and third urban areas to be considered range from along the west seacoast inland to the fringe of the Sahara Desert. Today these areas include Gambia, Nigeria, the Gold Coast, Liberia, Sierra Leone, and French West Africa.

Historically, area two of West Africa developed first, for cities along the Niger River were the capitals and trade cities of several great Negro Moslem empires and kingdoms.[2] Kano, Timbuktu, Sokoto, Zaria, and Kaduna were important cities before European powers gained control of the area (see Map of African Cities). One of the great empires, Ghana, reached its zenith in 1,000 A.D. The city of Ghana, some 250 miles west of Timbuktu, was the capital. This empire was succeeded by the Mali, often called the Mandingo Empire, the greatest Negro empire the world has known. Some of the chiefs in the Bamoko area today are descendants of the Keita, or ruling family, of that time. The capital, Mali, was abandoned in 1660 when the last Mandingo emperor was forced to flee. Today this ancient city is deserted and barren. To the east lay the Gao, or Songhai empire, with Gao as the seat of administration. In 1591 this empire succumbed to Moorish invasion. For several hundred years other empires rose and fell in this area, with the Mossi empire and Fulani Kingdom lasting for several hundred years.

The disintegration of some of the tribal kingdoms, such as the growing unproductivity of the land near the desert regions, caused tribes to migrate to the seacoast. Europeans early became interested in this area, an interest still reflected in such names as the Gold Coast. By the time of Columbus, they found a new source of income: the slave trade. Although the Europeans themselves stayed in the coastal areas, they obtained many slaves from the inland areas, for some of the coastal tribes themselves soon engaged in slave trade and raiding. This trade continued for almost four centuries, attempts to stop it being unsuccessful until the time of the American Civil War. In some areas the population was almost totally dispersed.[3]

The military conquest of Africa followed close upon the growth of trade, with France taking the lead by occupying the area now known as French West Africa, and Great Britain occupying the intervening areas, including Gambia, the Gold Coast, Sierra Leone, and Nigeria. Within the

---

[1] Stamp, *op. cit.,* 262–269; and Pankhurst, *op. cit.,* the entire volume.

[2] Stamp, *op. cit.,* 271–273.

[3] F. J. Pegler, *West Africa* (London: Methuen and Co., Ltd., 1950), Ch. 3.

last two centuries, the colonial powers consolidated their holdings. Each imposed its own distinct colonial policies, which have affected the urban development of the respective areas. Only Liberia is an independent nation, although it too is the product of foreign settlement. Liberia was formed for the benefit of freed slaves whose descendants, although in the minority, still rule the country.

Many of the cities of West Africa antedate European control.[1] Nigeria has some of the largest cities in tropical Africa, including Kano, Lagos, Abeokuta, and Ibadan. Ibadan, an entirely African city, had a population of several hundred thousand even before the English conquest. These West African cities offer a sharp contrast to the usual features of urbanism, for most of the rural-urban distinctions which may be made elsewhere do not apply.[2] For example: the walled city of Kano, one of the ancient Moslem capitals, is located in the midst of a rich farming section, with a million people living within a radius of 30–40 miles. Around the city there are forty walled towns as well as numerous hamlets, spaced at half-mile intervals. During the harvest season Kano's population increases, as a constant stream of buyers goes in and out of the city's gates. Each day as many as 25,000 people may use Kano's trading facilities.[3]

Moreover, some nine square miles of open land are reserved inside the city walls to provide food in case of siege, or other emergencies. The reservation within cities of space for agriculture is frequent in this area. The distinct sections of cities have their own markets, and their inhabitants usually have similar tribal backgrounds, maintaining their relationships with their rural kin.

Kano is not only a famous trading center, but also the residence of the Emir, whose palace is enclosed within a walled section of the city. Many rural headmen maintain a home within the city, although they are away tending their land part of the year. Cocoa cultivators and others also maintain both rural and urban residences. Contemporary Ibadan has a population of half a million residents, and in 1931 Nigeria had 14 cities with populations ranging from 10,000 to 20,000 and ten others with populations between 20,000 and 50,000.[4] All in all, 14 per cent of Nigeria's population was urban. Two decades later her cities showed sizable population increases (see Table 19).

The relatively high urbanization of Nigeria is in part the result of the high concentration of urbanites among the Yoruba. Approximately 30 per cent of the Yoruba live in Ilorin, Lagos, Abeokta, Ibada, Iwo, Oyo, Og-

[1] Russell and Kniffen, *op. cit.,* 363.

[2] M. Herskovits, *Man and His Works* (New York: Alfred A. Knopf, Inc., 1949), 606.

[3] Stamp, *op. cit.,* 314–318.

[4] Lord W. M. Hailey, *Native Administration in the British African Territories* (London: His Majesty's Stationery Office, 1950), 2, 86.

Ewing Galloway

Top, Freetown, Sierra Leone, British West Africa. A large market near the waterfront, to which small boats bring various kinds of produce and goods. The city, the largest seaport of the western seacoast, is a coaling station and known for its ginger, palm-kernels, gold, and diamonds. Population are descendants of nearly every Negro tribe but have developed into a group known as the Sierra Leoni.

Bottom, Fumban, Cameroons, French West Africa. Palace of the Sultan and administration building in one of France's overseas provinces. Men are at work putting covering to wooden frame of dome-like roof at left.

bomosho, Oshogo, and Ede. Some of these cities were founded by the Yoruba during the eighteenth century.

Two cities, Freetown and Monrovia, located respectively in Sierra Leone and Liberia, have somewhat similar and unusual histories.[1] Freetown was founded in 1787 as a haven for 400 runaway slaves stranded in London, and Negroes rescued from slaveships. The first attempt at settlement failed, but repeated attempts were made to keep the community alive, and by 1794 the city became permanently established. Monrovia was brought into being in 1821, largely through the efforts of the American Coloniza-tion Society, to provide a home for freed American slaves. The number who would leave America in order to brave a new country was small, since the ex-slaves were American-born. By 1847, some 3,000 Americo-Liberians had established themselves sufficiently to organize the state of Liberia, with Monrovia as capital. By 1925 there were some 25,000 Amer-ico-Liberians, half of whom lived in Monrovia. Industrialization of Liberia was accelerated by the granting of large tracts to the Firestone Rubber Company.

In both Sierra Leone and Liberia there is a sharp distinction between the descendants of the slaves, who are largely urban and westernized, and the original inhabitants. The former, although a minority, are much more powerful. This distinction is reflected in the ecological pattern of cities. Monrovia, for instance, has two "native" suburbs, Vai-town and Kru-town, inhabited by members of the Vai and Kru tribes.[2]

There are very few Europeans or other non-Africans who have taken up permanent residence in either French West Africa or the colonies and ter-ritories of Great Britain. For instance:

The non-African population of The Gold Coast numbers 6,723, consisting mainly of Europeans employed in government service, the army, commerce, mining, the timber industry, or missionary work, and of Indian, Syrian, and Lebanese traders. In spite of improved health conditions, there are very few signs that many of them intend to become permanent residents of the country.[3]

Whether Europeans will become more numerous is also dependent on the outcome of the nationalistic forces now at work in Africa. In this re-spect there has been a marked difference among colonial policies. Here, as elsewhere, the French policy has been one of maximum integration into the French nation. This is reflected in the classification of westernized

[1] Stamp, *op. cit.*, 288–297.

[2] K. L. Little, "Social Change and Social Class in the Sierra Leone Protectorate," *American Journal of Sociology*, 54 (July, 1948), 10–21.

[3] Permission granted by United Nations, *Non-Self-Governing Territories* (Lake Success, New York: 1949), 262.

natives as European.[1] Great Britain, on the other hand, long attempted to keep a more rigid distinction between Europeans and natives. However, there has been a sharp reversal in recent years, and the Gold Coast is now governed by a native Prime Minister, with a large measure of autonomy for the local government. In general, legal discrimination among races is disappearing in these areas.

The transition to increase native participation in government has not always been a smooth one. Rather it has been marked by heated charges and counter charges, mass meetings, and strikes—particularly in Nigeria and the Gold Coast—the politically most sophisticated of the British possessions. Although Great Britain retains some controls, the officials elected by the natives are predominantly in power, more so than in any other part of Africa.

After the Second World War, France reorganized her farflung colonies and incorporated them into the French Union. The colonies within French West Africa, except Dahomey, became "territories" within the Federation of French West Africa, with the capital at Dakar. Each territory is administered by a governor, responsible to a high commissioner in Dakar, and a popularly elected Assembly composed of both Africans and Europeans. In addition, elected territorial deputies sit as full-fledged members in the French National Assembly. This attempt at integration of the colonies with France has been most successful in cities, where there has been the greatest amount of cultural contact. Dakar, for instance, has 20,000 white inhabitants.[2] There has been considerable post-war industrial expansion, particularly in oil seed, crushing of peanuts, cement and lime-making, boot and shoe manufacturing, and the development of iron ore and bauxite mines.[3] This has helped make possible joint efforts at modernizing Dakar, Abidjan, and other cities.

It is unsafe to draw too many general conclusions about the cities of West Africa, since different urban conditions prevail, ranging from the walled inland cities to those under European influence and planning. Nevertheless, there are some conditions which do set West Africa apart from the rest of the continent. One is the small number of non-Africans resident in the area. Although there are distinct cultural differences among the tribes, as evidenced by the importance of local, Moslem, and Christian religions, this is at least a preponderantly African area with roughly 95 per cent of the total population indigenous to the area.

At the same time there has been a relatively high diffusion of Western values and ways of life. Social status is to a great extent a matter of the

---

[1] *Ibid.,* 78.
[2] Pegler, *op. cit.,* 25.
[3] Stamp, *op. cit.,* 279–281.

degree of westernization. In fact, in the British areas and especially Free-town, learning to speak English, obtaining an education, and being accepted as "white men" are for many desirable goals. This is true not only for men but also for women, many of whom earn their own money.[1] However, Europeans may claim little credit for financial independence of West African women, because it was part of the African culture at a time when European women had practically no property rights at all.

It is significant that the middle class is almost entirely composed of the indigenous population. There are proportionately more civil servants, judges, lawyers, doctors, and teachers drawn from within the various parts of West Africa than is true for most of the rest of the continent. Unlike many other world areas, retail and wholesale trade is not monopolized by outside groups, as is the case with the Chinese in South Asia, for instance. Nevertheless, it is easy to overestimate the size and power of this new middle class.[2] It is still an exceedingly small part of the total population, and one of the main problems here, as in so many other world areas, concerns the impact of further westernization, industrialization, and urbanization in the face of the relative absence of precisely that class which was most closely associated with the development of urbanism in the West.

South Africa. The area of greatest urban expansion in Africa is within the four provinces of the Union of South Africa: Natal, Cape, Transvaal, and Orange Free State. As stated earlier, the urban development of this area is due largely to European efforts. Less than a century ago most of the population were farmers, and the growth of cities and urban population increased after the discovery of diamond fields in 1867 and gold fields in 1884. A brief review of the conditions leading up to this era is helpful in understanding how the urban development in this part of Africa differs from the urban development in other parts of the world.

Population composition and urban distribution. The size of the four major groups, European, Asiatic, Coloured, and Native, has a relationship to the socio-economic status each occupies within the social structure. Also the size of these groups influences the nature of interethnic and interracial relations, whether these are restrictive, relatively free of tension and conflict, or otherwise. The groups will be discussed in the order of the rank accorded them by the census, which reflects the manner in which they are assigned in terms of status, rights, and privileges.

1) European. The early Dutch settlers landed at Cape Town in 1652 and held this city and colony as a strategic berthing point for the vessels of the Dutch East India Company sailing around the Cape of Good Hope on their way to and from Europe and India. The Arab and Portuguese

[1] Little, *op. cit.,* 10, 13–14.
[2] Pegler, *op. cit.,* 147–148.

traders had established a few trading posts along the Cape and at one time settled at Cape Town. However, their activities were superseded by the Dutch and the colony at Cape Town grew to 15,000 persons by 1795.[1] The inhabitants were largely retired employees of the Dutch East India Company; a few pioneer settlers; the servants, mainly Hottentots; and the imported Malay and African slaves. The members of the colony revolted against the Dutch East India Company and placed themselves temporarily under British control between 1795 and 1814. This control became permanent in 1814 when the colony was transferred to Great Britain. Shortly thereafter the Dutch—or Boers, as they came to be known after the revolt —began their Great Trek into the High Veld.[2]

The Boers made their way eastward from the colony in search of rich farmland in the heart of the Veld because of their dislike of British control. Also, the British raised objections against the harsh treatment the Boers imposed on their servants and slaves. The Boers traditionally believed that physical toil was good for the Hottentot servants and the slaves, who were imported in large numbers first from Angola, later from India, Ceylon, and the East Indies. A rigid caste-like social structure had evolved in which the ideology of white supremacy—especially among the Boers—was unyielding. This belief which has never wavered is largely responsible for the interracial tensions in South Africa.

During the early years of the colony prejudice and social distance based on color were largely negligible. It was possible for descendants of slaves to enter the European community following conversion to Christianity and baptism. Gradually, race supplanted the distinction between Christian and non-Christian as a basis for group membership, and the pattern of superordination-subordination crystallized.[3]

The original Dutch colonists were joined in 1683 by French Huguenot settlers, who in time lost their separate identity. British settlers did not arrive in numbers until after 1814. During the nineteenth century British immigration increased, while that from the Netherlands dwindled to a negligible portion of the total immigrants. After the discovery of the diamond and gold fields, a large influx of immigrants from other European countries followed until further immigration was prohibited in 1913.

It should be noted that the influx of Europeans, although curtailed, has not entirely ceased, and the Second World War with its attendant hardships caused many refugees to enter the Union of South Africa until 1948, when the net migration figures showed a temporary decline for 1949 and

[1] Stamp, *op. cit.*, 443–444.

[2] Peattie, *op. cit.*, 22 and Ch. 2.

[3] The author is grateful to Mr. Robert E. T. Roberts for the material on early Dutch colonization and the development of the multi-racial social structure.

1950. The increase of European population from 1904 to 1950 has steadily risen, from 1,116,806 to 2,335,460 in 1946, and to 2,643,187 in 1951. The increase in European population was 9.1 per cent between 1946 to 1951, while that of the Union was 14.2 per cent for the same period.[1]

Thus, the European-white population is heterogeneous, although two main divisions can be made along ethnic lines.[2] According to the census of May 7, 1948, the white population comprised 20.7 per cent of the total. The two main divisions are between those of British birth or descent, and the Boers or Afrikaners of predominantly Dutch ancestry. The latter constituted 55 per cent of the total white population and the former, 35 per cent. The remainder includes Jews, mainly of Central and Eastern European origin (5 per cent), several thousand Germans, and other continental Europeans, who together form another group within the white group. These groups consider South Africa their homeland.

These ethnic divisions have some relationship to socio-economic status because the British predominate in large cities, and the Afrikaners are predominantly rural. It should be noted that there are several hundred thousand Afrikaners, who are "poor whites." They are recent migrants to cities, whose status is being raised by the European population through a monopoly of the skilled occupations at high wages. This practice is directly related to the system of Apartheid, to be discussed later. The English language is used primarily in commercial and industrial transactions, while Afrikaans has been the predominant language used in Parliament and government offices. Moreover, the British own and operate most of the large industrial, commercial, and financial enterprises. The Afrikaners are all native-born, while approximately half of the other Europeans were born in the United Kingdom and Ireland. Most of the whites are fluent in both languages. They tend to ally themselves in two main divisions to form the dominant hierarchy of the social structure.

2) *The Coloured.* The second group are the Coloured, so-called because of their three main genetic mixtures, and who form approximately 8 per cent of the total population. The Coloured are not—with minor exceptions—a product of amalgamation of the Caucasoid and Bantu Natives, but are a separate group established during the first two centuries of the settlement of the Cape Colony consisting of mixed and other colored races. The three main genetic mixtures include descendants of: early European-slave unions, European-Hottentot unions, and Slave-Hottentot unions.[3]

[1] *Statesman's Yearbook,* 1952, 247.

[2] From data supplied by Mr. Robert E. T. Roberts.

[3] Alastair Matheson, "The Cape Coloured People of South Africa" (London: Public Relations Office, South Africa House, 1948), 7; and William M. MacMillan, *The Cape Colour Question* (London: Faber and Gwyer, 1927); Introduction and 28–29.

The slaves were primarily of Malay origin, but some came from the East Indies, Ceylon, and Angola. The Cape Malays are a small Moslem subgroup engaged in fishing and arts and crafts in the vicinity of Cape Town. The few remaining Hottentots and Bushmen, as well as the semi-tribal remnants of the Griquas and Bastaards, are also officially classified as Coloured. It must be remembered that the Boers in their trek to the Veld encountered and fought the Bushmen and all but extinguished them, while the Hottentots were virtually wiped out by disease and hunger before the Dutch settled in Cape Town. These groups have largely merged to form the Colour stratum, and are concentrated in Cape Town and the Western provinces of the Cape of Good Hope. The Coloured, with their centuries of contact with Europeans, are essentially Western in culture and outlook. Many speak both Afrikaans and English.

3) *The Asiatics.* The Asiatics are chiefly of Malaysian stock, although a group of descendants of former indentured Chinese laborers are found in the Johannesburg area. They constitute 2.5 per cent of the total population and are concentrated in Natal where they are numerically equal with the European (10.4 and 10.7 per cent, respectively). The majority, although Union-born, have retained their Hindu or Moslem beliefs and some of their ancestral customs while acquiring much of European culture.

The Indians have risen in the occupational hierarchy. They are no longer indentured laborers on large sugar plantations, as their parents or grandparents were. Today they are mostly skilled laborers, servants, or entrepreneurs in small businesses. Some own small farms, but in general the farming group is restricted in its activities because of the curtailment of land ownership. Others peddle fruits and vegetables. In Natal, however, hotel cooks and waiters and unskilled and semi-skilled laborers are mainly drawn from this group. On the whole, the Indians have attained a higher degree of occupational mobility than either the Coloured or Natives. Many are merchants and businessmen who have acquired considerable wealth.[1] The Indians are subject to laws which regulate their investments, residence, and occupations, and these vary from one part of the Union to the next. The severest legal restrictions are in Natal.[2] Of the Union's eleven largest cities, nine have Indian concentrations varying from 1,114 in Kimberley to 157,292 in Durban (Table 20). The size of the group has some relationship to its treatment. Many Indians have elected to live in Johannesburg, where 16,034 of them were reported in the 1948 census. The latest figures showed an increase of more than 5,000 of them. Capetown and Pretoria had 6,865 and 5,101, respectively in 1948.[3]

[1] Peattie, *op. cit.,* 41–42, 68–70.
[2] *Ibid.,* 70.
[3] *Statesman's Yearbook,* 1949, 1101.

TABLE 20. POPULATION OF MAJOR CITIES BY RACIAL ORIGIN, UNION OF SOUTH AFRICA [1]

City	White	Asiatics	Cape Malaya	Other Coloured	Natives	Total
Johannesburg	359,539	21,576	4,309	33,180	461,410	880,012
Cape Town	111,883	4,188	28,530	77,517	17,667	239,785
Durban	146,805	157,292	694	16,238	142,091	463,120
Pretoria	151,426	5,891	363	5,678	120,824	284,182
Bloemfontein	48,923	3	22	3,797	56,385	109,130
Port Elizabeth	79,509	4,253	2,877	42,565	70,083	199,287
Germiston	72,436	1,838	126	2,238	94,110	169,748
Vereeniging	35,405	767	47	840	59,332	96,391
Kimberley	20,618	1,114	705	13,889	28,373	64,699
Pietermaritzburg	32,623	19,558	121	3,765	36,488	92,555
East London	44,445	1,486	147	5,817	40,820	92,715

[1] *Source:* Union of South Africa Government Information Office; figures forwarded on Sept. 8, 1953.

The majority of the 53,000 Chinese who were imported in 1904 for a 3-year period as indentured laborers for the gold mines, have been repatriated, but a few remain in and around the Johannesburg area. They operate laundries, stores, or truck farms.

4) The Natives. The last but largest group numerically is composed of the Natives, described as "pure blooded aboriginals of the Bantu race," and who constitute 68.7 per cent of the total population. Although a few persons of mixed origin, European-Bantu or Colored-Bantu, are included in the official returns, the Bantus belong to the Negroid race and are the indigenous population of the area.

The Natives belong to a large number of tribes and speak languages of the Bantu linguistic stock. About half of them live in Native areas or reserves where they preserve some of their tribal traditions and have not yet been subjected to the impact of Westernization. Increasing numbers, however, are leaving their villages to work on European-owned farms, in gold mines, or in cities as unskilled laborers. Some have broken tribal ties and become permanent settlers in cities, while others return to the village after the "work period" of several months to years.[1] It cannot be denied that the huge number of natives could provide the labor needed by the mines and other industries. A large number are domestic servants.

Urban growth. Cities increased rapidly after the discovery of diamond and gold mines. Up until 1867 the cities of any importance or size were Cape Town, Port Elizabeth, Pietermaritzburg, and Durban. Because of

[1] J. M. Tinley, *The Native Labor Problem of South Africa* (Chapel Hill: University of North Carolina Press, 1942).

the influx of prospectors and miners to Kimberley during the diamond boom, the city came to be known as the world's diamond center. It has since lost much of its importance and reputation, for some of the mines have closed, and its population has decreased to 64,699.

The discovery of gold had a greater effect upon urban growth than did diamond mining. The entire 70 mile stretch of the reef, lying on either side of Johannesburg, the "Golden City," has developed since 1886. Johannesburg has grown to be the largest city in South Africa, and was the third largest in Africa by 1951. Only Cairo and Alexandria have larger urban populations. East and west of Johannesburg and forming a series of interconnected cities are Springs, Germistown, Benoni, Krugersdorp, Brakpan, and Boksburg.

The most important factor determining the presence or absence of urbanism is the size of European population. Cities, towns, and suburbs having more than 2,000 Europeans are classified as urban. Moreover, there must be "some form of local government" (see Table 3). Since only Europeans are permitted to hold public office, the creation of a municipal government acts as a safeguard where the Native and other non-European groups often exceed the European population (see Table 20).

In 1946, 28 cities with more than 2,000 inhabitants satisfied this definition, as did 18 others having between 2,000 and 5,000 inhabitants. Fourteen others had between 5,000 and 10,000 persons; six, between 10,000 and 20,000; and fifteen, more than 20,000. Among the last group were six metropolitan cities, four of which supported over 100,000 Europeans.[1] There was a total of 81 cities, representing an increase of 27 since 1936.

The growth of cities has paralleled the increase of population for the Union of South Africa. There has been a twofold increase since 1904: from 5,175,824 to 12,646,375 in 1951. The annual rate of increase of Europeans from 1904 to 1946 was 2.6 per cent per year, while that of the other three non-European groups was 2.9 per cent per year.[2] On the other hand, the urban population rose from 36.4 per cent in 1946 to 42.4 per cent in 1951.[3]

In summary, it can be seen that the urban areas are multi-racial in population composition, and that urban development was introduced by European settlers. Unlike North and West Africa the indigenous population had no cities they could call their own. South African cities are European in atmosphere and way of life. The transplantation of a large group of rural persons to cities where the value system, social structure, and mores

[1] Ellen Hellman (ed.), *Handbook on Race Relations in South Africa* (Capetown, London, New York: Oxford University Press, 1949), 24.

[2] Stamp, *op. cit.*, 447

[3] *United Nations Demographic Yearbook*, 1948 and 1952.

A view of Bloemfontein, the "Centre City," capital of the Orange Free State.

are vastly different from tribal life has caused the Natives to exhibit more maladjustments. A consideration is necessary of some of the other factors contributing to the more difficult adjustment of the Natives to urban areas and how these factors may also affect the Coloured and Asiatics. The most troublesome is apartheid.

Apartheid. The most significant factor affecting the settlement and adjustment of the non-European groups in cities is *apartheid.*[1] This policy of maintaining strict racial segregation in cities originated within Transvaal and Orange Free State before the Union of South Africa was created in 1910. It was a continuation of the belief of the early Cape Town colonists that the calling of the Natives was to be servants and slaves. The British, we will recall, had objected to this attitude and this divergence in viewpoint toward other racial groups partly caused the Great Trek and the Boer Wars. Apartheid became legally recognized in 1923 when the Afrikaners and their supporters succeeded in having the Native or Urban Areas Act passed.

This act gave urban administrators definite responsibilities and powers for bringing about residential segregation between Europeans and Na-

[1] Eugene P. Dvorin, *Racial Separation in South Africa* (Chicago: University of Chicago Press, 1952), Chs. 3 and 7.

Union of South Africa Government Information Office

Moletsi location, near Pietersburg, Transvaal. A location is an area of land set aside for the exclusive use of Natives. It may be a heavily populated suburb of a city where Europeans predominate, a tribal village, a collection of huts or houses, or a squatter's community. Transvaal Basutus live in this location. A mud wall encloses the huts.

tives. The law prevents the free influx of Natives into cities and controls their conduct in the Native areas and locations, shanty towns, and compounds. It is also intended to control legally the competition for better residential areas between the "poor whites" and the non-Europeans. The latter groups are taxed heavily to support the segregation system.

The prospect for modifying this policy does not appear likely at this writing, because the 1953 elections have given the Afrikaner Nationalists, headed by Dr. Malan, firmer powers than before.[1] However strict the apartheid policies may be, there is no sign of the urban trend reversing itself, because more Natives are migrating to the city in search of economic opportunities. One of the basic faults in the apartheid theory is that if this practice is enforced as envisioned by Dr. Malan—the Coloured, Asiatics, Natives, and Europeans must develop separately and only by so doing can each race attain its utmost achievements—there would be a shortage of labor in cities, mines, and homes. The Natives are to remain in their rural reserves which will be industrialized. Thus, the Natives will enjoy a higher level of living and the congestions in cities will be reduced. It should be

[1] *Life,* May 4, 1953; 163–4, 166, 168, and 170.

noted that Apartheid is actively supported by the Dutch Reformed
Church, to which the majority of the Afrikaners belong. The church's
leaders are staunch and powerful members of the Nationalist Party, too.
Thus, political issues have unswerving moral backing.

The Coloured are to be disfranchised, thus stamping the mark of "inferior race" on a group which has identified itself with European culture
and industrialization almost from the very beginning of Western influence
in South Africa. In Cape Province where some 813,000 Coloured are
heavily concentrated, they have not been subjected to the severe social,
political, and economic restrictions imposed on the Native. Residential
segregation is not compulsory and although the Coloured may own land,
few do. So long as a Coloured male could read and write and earn a minimum wage of £50 per year, or if he owned property valued at not less
than £75, he could vote.[1]

Outside the Cape, the Coloured are regarded as a part of the Native
population—a fact they very much resent because they also have prejudice
against the Native and Asiatics—and must live in areas especially reserved
for them. Should the Cape Coloured be disfranchized in voting, they will
become more or less an "appendix" of the European population and represent an "intermediate nation" between Natives and Europeans.[2] Other
privileges, such as intermarriage, free use of the municipal transportation
system, and residence in European areas, will be stripped away.

The Indian population is a strong competitor of the European for the
labor and patronage of the Natives.[3] Many Indian shopkeepers undersell
European ones and often have more satisfactory relationships with the
Natives they employ. Under the apartheid system, when enforced, this
economic competition can be controlled, if not eliminated. Steps were
taken to impose restrictions by passing the Asiatic Land Tenure and Indian Representation Act of 1946. Under this land act, definite "unex-
empted" areas in Natal and Transvaal are marked off wherein no Asiatic
is permitted to buy or occupy fixed property without a permit from the
Minister of the Interior. Asiatics may, however, obtain loans on, buy, or
occupy, property in the "exempted" land areas, negotiating with anyone
who wishes to deal with them. The limited franchise the Indians enjoyed
has been curtailed by the Act of 1946, and all Asiatics are completely barred
from Orange Free State, a Boer stronghold. The most drastic policy toward the Indians is "to reduce them to an irreducible minimum." The
repatriation of Indians to the Union of India and Pakistan, or elsewhere, is
the ultimate goal. The fact that 80 per cent of them are urban and Union-

[1] Dvorin, *op. cit.*
[2] *Ibid.*, Ch. 5.
[3] *Ibid.*, Ch. 9.

born and many would be foreigners in India or elsewhere is unimportant.

Within the social hierarchy the Indians form the third horizontal stratum, two rungs below that of the Europeans, one below the Coloured, and one above the Natives.

How the apartheid policies have affected the spatial pattern of cities will be discussed later. Other factors affecting the Natives' adjustment to the urban environment are Pass Laws, labor problems, native taxation, and tribal obligations and detribalization.

Pass laws. During the work day, Natives are permitted to move about within the city in pursuit of their respective occupations or business enterprises if they possess passes.[1] The pass law does not apply equally to Asiatic and Coloured groups.

A pass is purchased within the ward where holders reside and is required before employment is permitted or housing is assigned in the municipally-owned and operated restricted areas, compounds, locations, or the privately owned servants' quarters or penthouses. The pass fee is one of the many categories of taxes imposed upon them. The possession of a pass is one of the methods used for controlling and restricting the movement of the holders. It insures their departures from the European work areas at the end of the work day. Non-possession of a pass is an offense.

One of the greatest sources of tension in urban areas stems from the repeated violations of the pass laws, resulting from the acute housing shortage as well as the inability of the Native newcomers to the city to pay the cost of the pass. Others are denied one when unable to secure work permits. In this way they are encouraged not to stay. However, many with no passes remain, thus adding to the growing list of offenders. Of the 100,000 cases involving non-European offenses tried in Johannesburg's courts, over 50 per cent were for breaches of the pass laws.[2] The mounting defiance of the law by pass holders and concerted efforts to elicit arrests have caused considerable tension within the last few years.

Labor problems. It has generally been conceded by all students of South African urban areas that the recruitment, training, and employment of an adequate labor force to process the mineral and industrial resources present a complicated and perplexing picture. The nature of the multi-racial contacts has produced and aggrevated the problems of a society undergoing a transition to the urban. The retention of demands and obligations related to tribal organization have added others. A multi-racial social system

---

[1] *Handbook on Race Relations in South Africa, op. cit.,* Ch. 12. On page 275, ". . . One of the major difficulties confronting the would-be analyst of the Union's pass laws is the definition of the word 'pass.' Statutes, proclamations, regulations, and by-laws avoid definitions."

[2] John A. Noon, *Labor Problems in Africa* (Philadelphia: University of Pennsylvania Press, 1944), 39.

exists which does not fulfill the desires and goals of the European, Asiatic, Coloured, or the Native populations.[1]

The Natives constitute the largest reserve of manpower required by the various agricultural, mining, and industrial operations of the Union. When agricultural resources were the major means of support of the Native and European groups during the first two centuries of continental development, interracial contacts were minimal, but had assumed the characteristics of superordination-subordination. Interracial friction and tension were not intensified because the relatively large land area was not overcrowded. The ownership of tribal land was acknowledged and Natives had small land plots.

When more manpower was needed than could be drawn from the local area, and indentured workers and slaves could not be imported, a recruiting policy was introduced. An indeterminate work period, ranging from 3 months to several years, places a worker under contract to the employer, and he must leave his family for that period of time. Breaking a work contract is a criminal offense. South African Bantus may work in the Belgian Congo, the able-bodied in Nyasaland may be employed in West Africa, and so on. In fact, Nyasaland had a reserve of 320,000 workers but only 63,000 were absorbed by local enterprises. The remainder were contracted for a two-year period to North and South Rhodesia, the Union of South Africa and elsewhere, during the manpower shortage of the Second World War.[2]

The recruitment policy is recognized generally as being unsatisfactory because annually over 50 per cent of the Natives must be recruited and retrained.[3] The turnover is high, and the composition of the migratory labor force varies from one year to the next. Retraining is necessary if a worker has a period of tribal residence between employments, or he changes to another occupation. Moreover, employers are not willing to assign the skilled occupations to the migrant workers, causing the dissatisfied to go from one type of work to another. Wages are inadequate, housing accommodations are poor, health provisions are meager, and recreation is woefully absent. The migratory workers are generally drawn into the labor force because of the compulsory taxing system, meeting tribal obligations, and earning money to buy Western manufactured products such as bicycles, sewing machines, cloth, shoes, and so on. Earning money to meet tax levies is the strongest force in drawing the male population into the labor force.

Taxation. The foremost reason for the migratory labor situation is the

[1] I. D. MacCrone, *Race Attitudes in South Africa: Historical Experimental and Psychological Studies* (London: Oxford University Press, 1937).

[2] Hailey, *op. cit.*, 14, 78–79.

[3] Noon, *op. cit.*, 134.

compulsory tax imposed upon the Natives in 1925 by the Union of South Africa.[1] Known as "native taxation," every male between 18 and 65 years is required to pay at least these four categories of taxes: (1) the general or poll tax of one pound a year, (2) a local or hut tax of 10s. or more on the occupier, (3) a land tax or a quitrent or squatter's tax, and (4) a provincial hospital tax not exceeding 2s. and 6d. These are in addition to the pass fee. It should be noted that a similar taxing procedure exists in other parts of Africa.

This separate tax system was devised to obtain revenue from persons earning less than £600 per annum and to spread the cost of municipal and state administrative expenses to every able-bodied male.

The tax system has produced some unforeseen problems. Among the most serious is socio-economic discrimination because persons earning less than £600 are Natives. The acceleration of personal disintegration in cities—such as the prevalence of crime, venereal disease, extra-marital unions, and alcoholism—has far greater social implications.[2] An unbalanced sex ratio in both rural and urban areas has also caused greater incidence of social problems. Since 1921 a decided trend has been noted of young wives accompanying their husbands to cities immediately following the rural ceremony.[3] This practice has not been accepted by older women or those who had family obligations in the reserves. In many instances the long periods of enforced separation from husbands—who may have deserted them or formed new alliances—have caused many women to go to cities to find their spouses or earn a living.

In spite of the increased tendency of single and married women to go to cities, the sex ratio in most cities is four males to one female. Cities have an abnormal number of unattached males, many of whom live in "company compounds" in tenement-like structures with few comforts. Compounds are often divided according to tribal affiliations, facilitating the staging of tribal dances as a form of recreation. Since family life is non-existent, the leisure time of these men is often directed toward illicit activities.[4]

Tribal obligations. The various tribes comprising a large part of the African social structure place demands on tribal members. A member has some obligations to his tribe and tribal leader in return for aid, protection, and the working of his land while absent as a migratory worker. If a member ignores these obligations he may lose his land, and his family will become detribalized. He then has neither land nor communal connections, because the owner's right to his land can only be maintained by his return-

---

[1] *Handbook on Race Relations in South Africa, op. cit.,* 294–297.

[2] James G. Leyburn, "Urban Natives in South Africa," *American Sociological Review,* 9 (Oct., 1944), 495–502.

[3] *Handbook on Race Relations in South Africa, op. cit.,* 239–242.

[4] *Ibid.,* 272.

ing to it from time to time.[1] There is an increasing number of detribalized persons who are free from tribal control but have not assimilated enough urban culture to make a good adjustment.

Among certain tribes, but most notably among the Bantu, males often join the labor force to earn sufficient sums to uphold the custom of lobola, or payment of the bride price expected by the future spouse's family.[2] At one time cattle was exclusively used for marriage, death, and fertility rites, but many Natives are giving the equivalent in money, saved from their earnings in cities. Many males who have lost their land and cattle need money as a substitute.

The majority of workers who migrate to cities do so to earn enough to provide food for themselves, their families, and dependents.[3] At the same time they work to meet their tax obligations. This is evidenced by the fact that around 60 per cent of the taxes owed by migratory workers are collected at the place of employment. It can safely be said that the native taxation system has accelerated and extended urbanism and has forced many non-Europeans to adopt urban traits without regard for personal selection or desire. Once the traits are incorporated in their behavior patterns, they are likely to be retained, thus adding to the problem of how to provide for increased wants, meet social obligations, and earn sufficient money to fulfill these demands.

Detribalization. Mention should be made of detribalization and the effect it has upon an increasing number of persons. A detribalized man loses status and role in the group which gives him aid and protection. This affects his family, cutting off kinship relations with others, and will lead to family disorganization.

Since poverty is the primary reason for periodic or prolonged absence from family, tribe, and landplot, detribalization is tantamount to being a social outcast. In many instances, a man goes to the city or from one location to another for so many years that he may not be present when he is declared detribalized. He is unable to help his family adjust to the loss of status. Frequently the wife—after waiting years for her husband's return—goes to the city. Finding her husband in a city is difficult. He may be quartered in a company compound, or may have been sent to another. He may have formed a new union, often with a wife of another detribalized person.

As urbanization has increased, more women have been forced to work in cities, leaving the children behind. Abandoned children are often cared

[1] University of Natal, *The African Factory Worker* (London: Oxford University Press, 1950), 2.

[2] *Ibid.*, 3.

[3] *Ibid.*, 1.

for by relatives and later go to the city to work or to look for parents.

The exact number of detribalized persons is unknown. Detribalization is recognized as one of the major problems associated with industrialization. It is a common form of social and personal disorganization. Since tribal organization is the bond among members, disintegration of the tribe means that its members are increasingly subject to labor recruiting and factors in the process of industrialization (taxes, labor policy, etc.). Detribalized individuals are not given the opportunity to participate in the larger political and social organization of South Africa—they may never be, if Apartheid is maintained.

As a common form of personal disorganization, detribalization has far-reaching consequences, including desertion and non-support of family members, illicit unions, extended unemployment, venereal and other diseases, crime, and juvenile delinquency. Customary institutional controls which regulate social behavior have not been supplanted, since many people do not have normal community life. Many problems could be eliminated if detribalized persons were able to find employment, or were trained for the work the society needs.

Spatial pattern of cities. Whereas in most cities in the United States suburban areas are frequently choice residential sites, inhabited by the better socio-economic classes, the reverse situation is true in many South African cities. The areas some distance from the city are reserved for the Natives. A series of native locations, shanty-towns, compounds, or native villages are located from 4 to 12 miles from the center of the city.[1] Several restricted areas, "Black Belts," and Coloured, and Asiatic quarters, are within the city's boundaries. This type of spatial pattern is found in cities where a sizable non-European group has either temporary or permanent residence. For example, Johannesburg has three restricted Native areas within the city limits and five locations at some distance from the urban fringe.

These restricted areas contrast sharply with the remainder of Johannesburg's physical attractiveness.[2] The American-like business center has sky-scrapers, movies, snack bars, department stores, art galleries, music shops, restaurants, hotels, and other urban institutions. Streets are wide and clean. A good transportation system carries the European population to their places of work and homes. Industrial and commercial establishments are next to the central business district. Beyond this area are the modern apartments and well-constructed homes of many of the 359,539 Europeans,

[1] *Handbook on Race Relations in South Africa,* 254. "In 1946, 89,249 non-Europeans were in locations and 52,879 in Native Areas in Johannesburg.

[2] Union of South Africa State Information Office, *South Africa* (Pretoria: South Africa), 29–36.

Union of South Africa Government Information Office

A "model" Native location at Pietermaritzburg. Note fence enclosing homes on both sides of street.

graded according to socio-economic status. Although the European choice residential sections may be called suburbs, they are actually within the city's confines.

Native areas and locations. The Native areas are separated from those of the Europeans. They may be designated by some physical barrier—a fence with a gate—and placed under the charge of an official. In some cities, a person who wishes to see someone living inside the Native area must show a pass, and this applies to Europeans and other groups. Native areas are the slums of South African cities. Since the enactment of the Native Areas Act—especially where there is considerable hostility between Natives and Europeans—municipal authorities have redeveloped the former Native areas into attractive housing projects for Europeans. The displaced Natives are forced to resettle in locations outside the city limits.

Natives living in areas within and without the city are forbidden to go into the European areas and business district except during working hours or before 9:00 p.m. Most Natives must have passes. Some of the restricted Native districts are extremely overcrowded, have inferior sani-

Union of South Africa Government Information Office

Company compounds, the "area of homeless men" of South African cities, built by mining interests to house the workers recruited for a work period at the mines. These barrack-like structures house thousands of men who are encouraged to remain upon the premises and fraternize with their own tribal members. Groups are transported back and forth from their villages without knowing much of the outside world.

tary facilities, no street lights, no water or sewerage systems, and no recreational space. The streets are unpaved. Many Native-area houses are two-room shacks with dirt floors. Several entire families may share one house, and even take in lodgers.

A few native locations some distance away from the center of the city have three to four-room units built by municipal authorities, but most of these locations have barrack-like block structures with few safeguards for health and welfare. The spread of venereal disease is recognized as being related to the nature of housing, and tuberculosis is one of Africa's major health problems.[1]

The Coloured and Asiatic populations are pressed into any interstices the city has. Few Native or Asiatic persons can own or lease land, so that half or more of these urbanites are renters in municipally constructed and owned property.[2] For example: in the Sophiatown and Martindale,

[1] *Handbook on Race Relations in South Africa*, 254.
[2] *Ibid.*, 255; see also W. J. Browne, "Health as a Factor in African Development," *Phylon*, 14 (Second Quar., 1953), 148–156.

native townships within Johannesburg, less than 600 lots were owned by non-Europeans. About a third were owned by non-residents, mainly Indians, who cannot live there because of restrictions against their living in these areas, but they do derive rentals from the lots. On the other hand, slum-landlordism is not unknown. Rents are excessively high because of the housing shortage and the constant influx of Natives into cities.

Immigrants pouring into the city have used emergency camps which they set up themselves. Moroka Township, near Johannesburg, began as an emergency camp in September, 1945. By August, 1947, the population had swelled to 60,000. Small houses were subsequently built on the 425 acres cleared by the municipal government, but housing needs could not keep pace with population increase. The Morokan squatters had to be evicted and a riot occurred.

Persons who are not required to live in restricted areas or locations are the domestic servants whose quarters are provided by their employers. Others needing residential space often live with the domestics, paying rent, with the consent of the owner. Or the domestics and renters may clandestinely share or rent their quarters with relatives, lodgers, or friends. This came to light when the police conducted a mass pass raid in 1946. Over 13,000 were rounded up in ten days.[1]

In May, 1947, 37,611 non-domestics and 69,000 domestics lived in these servant quarters by possessing licenses issued by the Johannesburg Council. Roughly, some 400,000 mine workers (unattached males) stayed in compounds or dormitories provided by the mining companies. More than a quarter million others lived in restricted areas within the city and a like number in outlying "suburbs." Over 100,000 persons with no housing or lodging accommodations wandered from one place to another, rented small sleeping spaces on a nightly, weekly, or monthly basis, or doubled up with sympathetic relatives or friends.

Some cities have proposed building new Native locations, but the available land is 20 or more miles away from the center of the city. The transportation system may not extend that far and it has been found from a study conducted in Durban that the time it took Native factory workers to travel to and from their work varied from an hour to three and one-half hours. The time was longer if what little transportation they could afford was not in operation.[2] It should be noted that the cost of transportation is high because operators are Europeans. Building costs are high for the same reason.

Segregation in Native and other areas. Within the urban Native Areas and locations are sometimes further divisions. Since members of various

---

[1] *Handbook on Race Relations in South Africa,* 255.
[2] University of Natal, *op. cit.,* 131.

tribes may migrate in a body as a result of signing contracts to work for a company in a given city, specific urban wards are inhabited by Bantu-speaking and other linguistic tribes from various parts of Africa. A linguistic similarity may act as a type of social bond. The need for mutual aid and protection, the performance of rites and ceremonies, and the observance of tribal customs act as binding forces. In the absence of adequate relief and welfare services for migratory workers and settled Natives, tribal members are relied upon during life crises when the immediate family—which has been left in the village—is powerless to help.

Further evidence that the Native Areas are heterogeneous is furnished by the socio-economic status and religious background of the inhabitants. There are segments of migratory and unskilled workers as well as permanently established lawyers, doctors, educators, jurists, factory workers, and domestics. Incomes range from those comparable to European standards to practically nil. The educational level varies from graduates of universities and colleges at home and abroad to the absolutely illiterate. Some have strong tribal ties, but many are detribalized, testifying to the fact that some are new urban immigrants, and others are settlers of many years and generations. Some are Christian converts, but many retain tribal rites and ceremonies. Differences in dress, speech, customs, food habits, and attitudes are common.[1]

The Coloured, as a group, are mainly urban dwellers, but have encountered strong social barriers against their full acceptance into the larger society if they live outside of the Cape. On the whole, they have higher educations, incomes, and occupations than the Natives. Many have risen in the social and occupational hierarchy by becoming professionals or as teachers in Coloured schools.[2] The Coloured group resides separately from the Natives and the Europeans and Asiatics.

Where the Asiatic groups are sufficiently large, there are areas restricted for them. Indians, in turn, are differentiated according to their adherence to the Hindu, Moslem, or other beliefs.[3] Moslem Indians require housing of a special type because their homes and social lives revolve around daily religious observances if the orthodox rituals are maintained. Single story houses with large courtyards facing the open are preferred. Although urban living is undermining religious practices because of the demands of work or business, religious leaders exert strong pressure over their followers.

The cohesiveness of the Moslem Indian community in Johannesburg is being threatened by the invasion and settlement of Natives whose housing

[1] *Handbook on Race Relations in South Africa*, 256.
[2] Matheson, *op. cit.*, 16.
[3] *Handbook on Race Relations in South Africa*, Ch. 24.

needs are so acute they have outbid the rentals the Asiatic tenants can afford. The faithful Moslems who have moved out of the area return for worship at their mosques. Many prefer to remain because the mosques cannot be moved elsewhere.

It should be noted that cities do exist in East Africa, the Belgian Congo, and elsewhere. The scope of this chapter does not include them. It should not be assumed that Nairobi, Mombosa, Leopoldville, and others are not as important as those mentioned. Urban growth in these areas is more recent and there are fewer large cities.

Summary

The impact of urbanization and industrialization upon a tribal organization has had great social effects and created personal and social disorganization that are not found as abundantly where the social structure has evolved into a feudal or semi-feudal type. The transition from the rural-folk society to urban-industrial society proceeds with less disintegration where the local inhabitants are permitted to participate in effecting the change without social, economic, and political restrictions. Where a growing middle class composed of non-Europeans has developed and held a tradition of urban living, such as in West Africa, there is less conflict between the European and indigenous population. The fact that Europeans are "temporary" residents, rather than permanent, makes for better race relations.

The opposite situation is seen in the Union of South Africa where the four major urban groups—European, Coloured, Asiatic and Native—are numerically significant. Restrictive policies are translated into legal measures which are imposed and enforced by the Europeans. Apartheid, or racial segregation, intensifies interracial and interethnic competition for residential space, occupations, and political rights. The population is divided into four distinct social strata. The enlargement of the lower stratum is anticipated, so that in time a small upper stratum of Europeans and a huge lower stratum of all the non-Europeans will evolve. Heterogeneity of population and the size of the various urban groups affect the spatial pattern of cities. Areas within and without the city are designated for the Natives, Coloured, and Asiatics.

In North Africa the heterogeneity of population is reflected in religious affiliations, with quarters for each major faith separated by walls. There are few large cities because of the "lean" environment, lack of water supply, localism, and traditional division of labor. Where Europeanized sections are built adjoining important administrative and religious centers, they likewise form a separate quarter. Large non-industrial cities existed in both North and West Africa before the coming of European colonialism. Conversely, South African cities were primarily built by European settlers, and developed mainly as the result of diamond and gold mining.

DISCUSSION QUESTIONS

1. Why are there varying degrees of urbanization within the African continent?
2. Discuss the heterogeneity of population by comparing the composition of populations of (1) North Africa (2) South Africa.
3. Explain how the labor recruitment policy in South Africa has accelerated urbanism and caused personal disorganization.
4. How does the internal spatial layout of cities differ among American and North African cities? South African?
5. Why does a society with tribal organization experience the impact of urbanism to a greater degree than another form of social organization?
6. How do the cities in French West Africa differ from North Africa?

SUGGESTED PROJECTS

1. Study the role which religion and race play in the spatial pattern of North African cities.
2. Trace the waves of European immigration in South Africa and relate this to the development of a multi-racial social system.
3. Study the various aspects of Apartheid and the methods used for its enforcements.
4. Compare the problems of the Coloured living within and outside the Cape Provinces.

READINGS

Eugene P. Dvorin, *Racial Separation in South Africa.* Chicago: University of Chicago Press, 1952.

Direct quotations from the leaders of the Union of South Africa, Rhodesia, and neighboring areas explaining the philosophy behind Apartheid.

Lord W. M. Hailey, *Native Administration in the British African Territories.* London: His Majesty's Stationery Office, 1950–1951.

A four-volume treatment of East and West Africa under British administration. Detailed accounts of land area, population, racial groups, urban areas, labor force, tribal customs, mineral or agricultural resources, and industrial development.

Ellen Hellman, ed., *Handbook on Race Relations in South Africa,* Capetown, London, New York: Oxford University Press, 1949.

Chapter 11 is devoted to urban areas. The remainder has valuable contributions by competent authorities on housing, health, welfare, population, laws, education, and other topics.

Everett C. Hughes and Helen M. Hughes, *Where Peoples Meet: Ethic and Racial Frontiers*. Glencoe, Ill.: The Free Press, 1952.

A world-wide perspective on race relations. A framework for studying the cultural changes following the contacts of people and the resulting impact on the society and its members.

Herbert Liebesny, *The Government of French North Africa*. Philadelphia: University of Pennsylvania Press, 1950.

A handbook of African problems, dealing specifically with the North African territories under French administration.

Wm. M. MacMillan, *The Cape Coloured Question*. London: Faber and Gwyer, 1927.

A historical and intensive consideration of the various social, economic and political aspects of the interracial marginal man in a part of the Union of South Africa.

Rex Reynolds *Searchlight on South Africa's Native Policy*. South African State Information Office, Pretoria: Government Printing Office, 1947.

A booklet in defense of the Apartheid policy by a South African journalist who has drawn freely upon both official and unofficial sources.

I. Schapera, ed., *Western Civilization and the Natives of South Africa*. London: Geo. Routledge and Sons, Ltd., 1934.

A compilation of articles describing the changes in the tribal organization and culture as affected by westernization and multi-racial contacts. Chapter 11, by a well-known Native leader points out the effects of the segregation system on the Natives.

Horace Miner, *The Primitive City of Timbuctoo*, Princeton: Princeton University Press, 1953.

A city unaffected by longtime Western influence but showing certain urban attributes developed by its own social milieu.

University of Natal Press, *The Durban Housing Survey: A Study of Housing in a Multi-Racial Urban Community, 1952* and *Experiment at Edendale: An Economic Survey of a Peri-Urban Settlement of Africans and Indians in Natal, 1951*.

Two excellent monographs on vital issues written from an objective, sympathetic point of view.

Chapter Seven

The Cities of the United States

T HE GROWTH of cities in the United States has transformed within a relatively short span of time—following the Civil War—a predominantly rural society to one that is generally regarded as the most urban. When the urban growth and development of this country is compared with that of other world regions, one can see that the change has been phenomenal, if not unprecedented, in the history of man. From early colonial times to the present, cities have existed and contributed to the growth of the nation. The slow process of evolution experienced by Europe, during which villages became transformed into tribal centers, later to city-state and feudal towns, and then to primary extraction cities, was greatly accelerated in this country, and at times it was by-passed altogether. The factors associated with urbanization—industrialism, communication and transportation, commerce, population growth and redistribution, and technological innovations—have interacted and influenced the rate of urban growth as well as the percentage of population living under urban conditions.

The urban way of life has become so widely diffused that in many parts of the country there are few clear-cut distinctions between rural and urban areas. This is in marked contrast to most other parts of the world, in which there are pronounced differences between urban and rural ways of life. To the extent that we can speak of an over-all American culture, this has largely become an urban culture.

The growth and development of cities in this country has not been hampered by the type of political and economic influences found in Asia or Africa. In fact, the period of European expansion during the last century which made the most profound changes in the social, political, and economic life of Asia and Africa coincides with the era of rapid urban expansion here. America may be said to contribute a full share when the growth of cities is considered on a world-wide basis. Moreover, America's influence on the urban growth and habit patterns of Asiatic countries during the last fifty years has contributed to the diffusion of urbanism and urbanization. The trend toward providing technical assistance to underdeveloped areas will undoubtedly continue and be a contributing factor in the spread of industrialization and urbanization.

American urban development may be divided into four major periods. The first, from about 1625 to 1850, may be characterized by the rise of commercial cities, located on seacoasts, lakes, and rivers. The second period, between 1850 and 1910, was marked by the growth of primary extraction, railways, and industrial cities, following the development of railroads. The third period, from 1910 to 1940, saw the expansion of cities, and the mounting importance of metropolitan, suburban, and satellite cities. The period since 1940 may be characterized by ever-increasing dominance by and interdependence of metropolitan centers and the growth of airports. Means of communication and transportation have become ever more efficient. In each of these periods, cities have been marked by distinctive physical, social, and population characteristics (Table 21).

TABLE 21. MAJOR PERIODS OF URBAN DEVELOPMENT
IN THE UNITED STATES

Period	Types of Cities	Per Cent Population	Number Cities	Transportation	Ethnic and Racial Groups and Population Movement
1625– 1850	lakeports riverports seaports canal cities	3 to 15.3	6 to 141	riverboats small crafts steamships horse-buggy	North Europeans Africans Located East of Alleghenies and Eastern and Southern seaboard
1850– 1910	as above mining and railroad junction 3 super cities	45.7	2,262	covered wagon railroads street cars as above	North and Eastern Europeans; Asiatics rural-farm movement east-west movement south-west movement
1910– 1940	5 supercities metropolitan growth suburbs satellites	56.5	3,464	railroads interurban and rapid transit buses trucks automobiles airplanes	Eastern and South Europeans; Asiatics rural-farm movement south-north movement east-west movement After 1920, growth of rural-nonfarm areas
1940–	airports increased diversification, metropolitan dominance	64.0	4,284	as above increased use of airplanes helicopters	Redistribution of population from eastern to western and southeastern states Development of southern cities

The Growth of American Cities

The growth of cities and the concentration of population in them reveals the trends accompanying the transformation of a society from rural to urban. In the United States no official census was taken until 1790, almost a century and a half after the first settlement of colonial population along the New England seaboard and a decade and a half after the signing of the Declaration of Independence. However, earlier colonial histories and documents furnish some evidence as to the size of early American towns.[1]

In 1630 New Amsterdam had a population of 300, hardly a city according to modern census definitions. In 60 years its population had grown to 3,000, and the town had some of the attributes associated with urbanism: urban government, luxuries not found in the surrounding hinterland, and a more sophisticated mode of life. At this time only Boston and Philadelphia had larger concentrations of population—7,000 and 4,000 respectively—and the characteristics of town life. Two others, Newport and Charles Town, had 2,600 and 1,100 persons living within their boundaries and were classified as cities by the first official census of 1790. These five cities had about 5 per cent of the country's total population of 206,000 (Table 22).

Very large cities the population of which exceeded the million mark were not known until after 1850 when New York attained this distinction. By 1900 Philadelphia and Chicago joined the rank and only two others, Detroit and Los Angeles, have since been added.

Rate of increase. In 1790, the nation's total urban percentage constituted 3 per cent, and the population was concentrated in a "mere half dozen cities." A subsequent redefinition of the numerical index distinguishing rural from urban residence, established at a minimum of 2,500 population, raised this total to 5.1 per cent.[2] In 1810 urbanites were 7.3 per cent of the country's total population. The proportion was more than doubled, or 15.3 per cent, by 1850. Thirty years later urban dwellers comprised 28.2 per cent of the total population.

Great gains were made by 1890 when more than a third of the people were living in municipalities. Within another three decades, more than one-half of the American people lived in cities. Then, the rate of increase slackened for two decades. The 1930 census revealed that the gains were less than 5 per cent, the smallest in almost a century. However, 56.2 per cent claimed urban places as their residences (Table 22). The returns for 1940 showed almost a stationary urban percentage, 56.5, or a gain of one-

---

[1] Carl Bridenbaugh, *Cities in the Wilderness* (New York: Ronald Press Co., 1938), 6.

[2] National Resources Committee: *Our Cities: Their Role In the National Economy* (Washington, D. C.: United States Government Printing Office, 1937), 1.

TABLE 22. GROWTH OF THE URBAN POPULATION
IN THE UNITED STATES 1790–1950 [1]

Year	Per Cent Urban	Percentage Increase in Per Cent Urban
1790	5.1	—
1800	6.1	19.6
1810	7.3	19.7
1820	7.2	1.4
1830	8.8	22.2
1840	10.8	22.7
1850	15.3	41.7
1860	19.8	29.4
1870	25.7	29.8
1880	28.2	9.7
1890	35.1	24.5
1900	39.7	13.1
1910	45.7	15.1
1920	51.2	12.0
1930	56.2	9.8
1940	56.5	0.5
1946 *	60.0	6.2
1950 †	64.0	19.5

* Estimate.
† United States Bureau of the Census figures.

[1] *Source:* Reproduced from "Projection of Urban Growth and Migration to Cities in the United States" by P. M. Hauser and H. T. Eldridge in *Postwar Problems of Migration.* 1946 Annual Conference of the Milbank Memorial Fund, New York.

half of one per cent, although in absolute numbers the urban population grew. This did not mean the urbanites were going back to farms during the depression of the thirties. Cities were still growing, but at a decreasing rate, and the areas outside the cities' boundaries were attracting more settlers.

The midcentury census took this fact into consideration and redefined the term urban population.[1] Areas supporting more than 2,500 inhabitants —whether the areas were incorporated as cities, boroughs, or villages— were included as well as all incorporated towns of the same size. The only exceptions to the town classification were in New England, New York, and Wisconsin, where towns are considered as minor civil divisions of counties. The populations of densely settled incorporated and unincorporated areas clustering around cities with more than 50,000 inhabitants came within the urban count. In addition, the residents of unincorporated places with 2,500 and more outside any urban fringe were included.

[1] Bureau of the Census, "Population of the United States: Urban and Rural by States, April 1, 1950," Ser. PC–9, No. 3 (June 9, 1952).

The 1950 census treatment of urban population was more realistic in that it disregarded conflicting local definitions of villages, boroughs, or towns. According to the census, a community did not have to be incorporated in order to be classified as urban. Often, persons living in such communities outside the city limits spend more of their waking hours in the main city than they spend in their local communities, and they are really part of the larger socio-economic units.

According to a more inclusive count of urban population, the 1950 total was 64 per cent. Had the 1940 definition been used, 5 per cent fewer persons would have been classified as urban. The actual increase in urban population between 1940 and 1950 was 19.5 per cent, but because the country's total population grew also, the proportional gain was slightly less than 8 per cent.

Number of Cities. Urban growth can be examined in another way. From a "mere half dozen places" in 1625, there were 141 by 1850. The growth of inland cities was accelerated by the building of railroads so that 2,262 centers were scattered throughout the country by 1910. About 500 more cities were founded or reached city status by becoming incorporated between 1910 and 1920; there were 2,262 and 2,723 cities, respectively. The 1930 census listed 3,165 cities and the 1940 returns showed 3,464. The 1950 count recorded 4,284 urban places, or a net increase of 820. Approximately 10 per cent of the 1950 total were unincorporated areas, so that if the 1940 census definition of cities had been used, the net increase during the 1940–1950 decade would be 50 per cent less. More than a third of the unincorporated settlements are found in Massachusetts, California, Maine, and South Carolina.

Periods of Urban Development

Four major periods of urban development can be differentiated for comparative purposes (Table 21). Some idea of the type of cities developing during each period can be seen. The movements of population within the country are correlated with the changes in the modes of transportation.

1625–1850. The first period between 1625 to 1850 was a lengthy one and covered an era preceding the great waves of immigration. The rise of cities was slow, as long as there was an ever-expanding frontier. Rivers, lakes, and the Atlantic seaboard furnished ideal sites for the establishment of commercial centers. During the seventeenth century, trade centers were sparsely dotted along the eastern seaboard from New York to South Carolina. While water transportation enabled direct communication to be maintained, each city sought to gain as complete autonomy as possible. The officials and business leaders of one city vied with those of another in

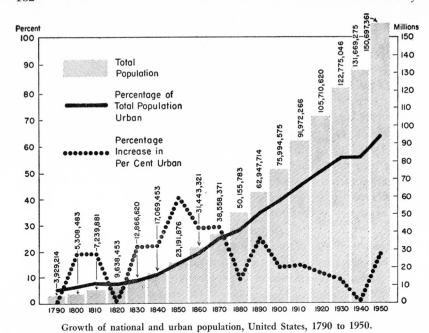

Growth of national and urban population, United States, 1790 to 1950.

exerting control over a wide hinterland and in duplicating sophisticated European town life on American soil.

1) Early towns. The most comprehensive historical records of town life are those of Salem, Massachusetts, which was established in 1628–1630.[1] When land proved scarce, or dissatisfaction with the leadership of those administering the local affairs arose, a group moved elsewhere and founded another town. Salem was said to have taken two years to reach a self-governing stage. First, the General Court of the Colony decreed its legal establishment. Subsequently, the populace petitioned the General Court to become a municipality with an autonomous government.

The early towns were patterned after the old English Manor. The population lived compactly at the center of a chosen site, selected for the purposes of good neighborhood, defense and the best use of the geographical features of the land. The houses and home lots were fenced in and individually owned, while the common fields were outside the town. A surrounding track of absolutely common and undivided land was reserved for pasturage and woodland, administered under communal regulations.

The numerical population of these early towns would not satisfy the modern definitions of a city, but every encouragement was given to promote an increase in numbers as well as to encourage permanent habitation.

[1] See Anne Bush Maclear, *Early New England Towns: A Comparative Study of Their Development* (New York: Columbia University, 1908).

Whenever a group of citizens or families petitioned the General Court for a site to establish a town, a sufficiently long period of time was given to parcel out the land to new residents. The time for attaining the objectives of incorporation frequently had to be extended. Many of these towns became important cities, such as Cambridge, Watertown, Dorchester, Roxbury, and Salem.

2) *Port cities.* The important seaport cities included New Amsterdam (New York), Boston, Newport, Charles Town and Philadelphia. From the standpoint of time, New York is declared to be the first site in the New World deliberately chosen in 1625 by Cryn Fredericksen, an engineer for the Dutch West India Company, for its fine harbor. Boston was selected for similar reasons five years later, while Newport, Rhode Island, was selected in 1639 for a settlement because of an excellent year-round harbor. Charles Town, situated between the Ashley and Cooper Rivers in South Carolina, was chosen thirty-one years later for its command over the exportation of products from the South. It gained commercial importance. A long stretch of wilderness lay between Charles Town and the four northern cities. Philadelphia was founded upon the confluence of two large rivers, the Schuylkill and Delaware, which made it accessible to the sea.[1] Baltimore was settled by 1750 and vied with the others for commercial prominence.

The ethnic composition of the cities varied. English, Dutch, Swedish, and French settlers brought their ingenuity and venturesome spirit into the colonies, erecting houses and government buildings, establishing industries, and promoted commerce. The hinterland, which was extensive and very sparsely settled, offered a sharp contrast to the sophisticated urbanism of these cities. Communication between cities was difficult and slow. Each city maintained its own liberty in settling local affairs.

Commerce and trade with Europe, the Far East, and penetrable parts of the hinterland of the colonies was the main activity of the early seaport cities. Philadelphia and Charles Town served the greatest expanse of territory, much of which was wilderness. Local governments were formed to meet the special needs of the community and to exercise police powers. These governments to a large degree shaped the political institutions found in later American municipalities. By and large, they were English in origin and practice. Gradually, the ties with the mother country became weakened and were finally severed.

The War of 1812 interrupted urban development, with cities suffering a diminished volume of trade. Urban dwellers turned to agricultural pursuits, and cities suffered a loss of population. It should be noted, however, that before 1820 the over-all density of population in the United

[1] Carl Bridenbaugh, *op. cit.,* Chs. 1 and 9.

States was very low. Only 7.2 per cent of the total population resided in the eleven major cities combined.[1] Between 1820 and 1830 urban centers doubled in number, and the percentage of urban populations rose to 8.8. Canals were opened during this period, and the cities bordering rivers and lakes boomed as heavy shipping was facilitated by water transportation.

There was great industrial and commercial growth in New York State after 1825. The opening of the Erie Canal benefited centers along the canal route such as New York City, Buffalo, Rochester, Syracuse, Rome, and Utica. They retained their importance even after the railroads were introduced because they were so located that the railroads touched their boundaries. Many became leading rail centers.[2] Waterways proved inadequate for the transport of goods that required speedy deliveries. Perishable goods demanded rapid transportation, and the construction of railroads was spurred by investors who desired quicker returns. The construction of canals entailed a heavy outlay of capital. Another mode of conveyance had to be used where waterways did not exist, thereby adding to the expense of shipments.

By 1840, the era of heavy railroad construction was fully launched. Many shorter branch routes were also being built. Along the projected lines of rail networks sprang commercial centers, mining camps, junction towns, and industrial cities. Thereafter, markets extended from New York to the Far West.

1850 to 1910. During the decade beginning with 1850 several significant events occurred. One was the discovery of gold. A second was the opening of the trans-Mississippi frontier. There was the unprecedented transformation into cities of forts, mining camps, logging sites, and railroad-repair stations. Territories were organized into states. This period also saw the heaviest immigration from Europe and Asia. Moreover, seaboard cities continued to grow in population and importance and become major railroad terminals.

Once the railway system was extended into the frontier regions—after the middle of the nineteenth century—it paved the way for the settling of population. As an instrument for the rapid dispersion of population, the railroad assisted in connecting the undeveloped frontier with the eastern, southern, and northern states. This helped mold the country into an economic, social, and political unit. When the Golden Spike, connecting the two sections of the transcontinental railroad, was driven into the

---

[1] Adna F. Weber, *The Growth of Cities in the Nineteenth Century: A Study in Statistics* (New York: Columbia University Studies in History, Economics, and Public Law, 1899), Ch. 2.

[2] Eliot Jones and H. B. Vanderblue, *Railroad Cases and Selections* (New York: Macmillan Co., 1935), Chs. 1 and 2.

ground at Promontory Point, Utah in 1869, a new phase of urbanism was at hand.

1) Railroad cities. Outlets for eastern and imported commodities found their way westward and southward, while imports from the Orient moved in the opposite direction. Cities attaining importance included what are now the nation's largest supercities. Others were railroad junctions in their early years and functioned as the repair and supply stations. Important midwestern cities, Chicago, St. Louis, Minneapolis, St. Paul, Omaha, Salt Lake City, and Kansas City, became discharge points for passengers and freight. Permanent branch offices for the various rail systems became an integral part of the city's economic life. Industries and commerce followed, thereby assuring urban survival and prominence, and have outshadowed rail activities.

In 1830, when the railroad construction began, the United States had 39.8 rail miles. By 1890, there were 163,597 miles of railroad. Thereafter, the mileage did not rise as sharply. The United States had 240,156 rail miles in 1950.

Between 1880 and 1890 there was an era of exceptionally rapid expansion of manufacturing and commercial activities. Some economic authorities contend that a period of fifty years is needed for sufficient accumulation of population and wealth to enable a phenomenal growth of industries such as that of the decade 1880–1890. The vast increase in national wealth had its foundations between 1830 and 1880. In the West a trend toward "getting rich quick" was actually realized only after the gold, silver, and other mineral speculations had subsided. A new corporate economic structure was spreading westward, placing western resources under eastern financial control. Population attracted capital and industry, which in turn attracted more population, industry, and capital.

2) A new urbanism. During this period the concentration of wealth in cities became evident. It was also recognized that cities—being the supreme achievement of the new industrialism—had become a controlling factor in national life. Capital, business and financial enterprises, factories, the white-collar middle class, and the wage-earning population were all vital factors linked with urbanism. The city epitomized the center of social and intellectual progress. The steady shift of population from rural to urban centers, together with the huge immigration, created new problems. Among the new demands made by the residents were the installation of better lighting systems, faster communication and transit facilities, greater utilization of the land, and the creation of protective services. Cultural life was introduced. Cities built schools, libraries, art galleries, and museums. Theaters and opera houses drew heavy patronage. Newspapers and periodicals found ready subscribers.

On the other hand, symptoms of urban maladjustments were coming to the fore. Slum conditions were ignored until civic-minded reformers and leaders pointed accusing fingers at common neglect and indifference. The "shame of cities": vice, crime, corruption, and prostitution, had seeped into the new way of life.[1]

Many civic improvements proceeded along health lines. Efforts were directed toward the burial of the surface-draining of streets by installing an underground sewage system. Street cleaning was first introduced in New York by using a corps of white uniformed "angels." The paving of streets was a trial-and-error process. Cobblestones, wood, and granite blocks replaced dirt and gravel roads. Asphalt was imported for use on the wider thoroughfares of many eastern cities. Macadam was less expensive and used on less traveled roadways.

Mechanical inventions appeared and affected the daily habits of urbanites. Philadelphia installed an "el" system. New York's "el" rumbled overhead and the subway, underfoot. Over fifty cities had streetcars. The telephone, when perfected, became indispensable to business transactions. Ten years after the Bell Telephone Company first leased its equipment to subscribers, there were some two hundred and fifty thousand instruments in use. With the expansion of the telegraph and a more expedient postal service, mechanized contacts multiplied.

The automobile had been invented and began to revolutionize the configuration of cities. It gained popularity as a more efficient means of travel than the horse and "bobrail" cars and other types of intra- and inter-urban transportation.

1910 to 1940. The turn of the century brought a period of prosperity and the maturation of western cities. Those located on the Pacific seaboard showed marked and rapid growth. Trade between the two seacoasts, north and south, and foreign countries was facilitated by transcontinental railroads and motor transportation. Air-borne freight and passengers began to compete with the more established modes of travel.

Intracountry migration characterized the population movements to western, northern, and southwestern cities. The movement of southern population supplied much needed labor for factories, farms, and defense industries.

After 1920 large metropolises increased in numbers. When a large center could not cope adequately with its growing population, suburban nuclei mushroomed and clustered around the periphery. Suburbs, incorporated and unincorporated territories, and satellite cities, together with the metropolises created socio-economic units which defied political

---

[1] Arthur Schlesinger, *The Rise of the City, 1879 to 1898* (New York: Macmillan Co., 1933), Ch. 4.

boundaries. For the most part, residents remained within the orbit of the metropolis because of the work and cultural opportunities offered by the large city. They desired the conveniences and services offered such as sanitation, water, shopping, and recreational facilities. The growth of metropolitan cities and districts and rural-nonfarm areas was the significant feature of this period.

1) Metropolitan cities. The growth and increase in number of metropolitan cities, in the main, can be attributed to the role which modern transportation and communication has played in coordinating population and institutions into a functioning whole. The automobile and intra-urban transit enabled residents to live away from their places of work. Interaction is channeled through modern media of communication: the telephone, radio, wire and mail services, and newspapers. The interdependence between the center city and the hinterland was based upon socioeconomic ties.

At the turn of the century, 26 American cities had reached metropolitan status, having a population of 100,000 and more. By 1930 approximately half the population of the United States lived in, or had daily access to, a metropolitan city. Population was moving toward great cities and continued to move for the next two decades. There were 96 and 106 metropolises by 1940 and 1950, respectively. Although the metropolitan cities of 1950 represented but 2.5 per cent of the total number of municipalities, their combined population was half of all the urban residents in the country.[1] The forces underlying greater concentration—transportation and communication—have wrought many changes in the manner of living, thinking, and reaction of the entire country. Big cities set the styles for clothing, house furnishings, architecture, recreation, and entertainment. Opinions and attitudes are colored by "big city folks." The clustering of organizations to meet the needs of the city itself and the hinterland it dominates has accompanied population movements.

2) Metropolitan districts. The metropolis, often called the "central city," exerted dominance that extended beyond its political confines. The inevitable result was the clustering of population and various organizations around or adjacent to its borders. Metropolitan districts, or super-communities, increased as rapidly as metropolitan cities did. In fact, each census has reported more districts than cities. In no other country in the world has such a phenomenon been possible in such a short span of time.

The United States because of its size, wealth, and lack of old-world traditions has been the most fertile spot for metropolitan development.[2]

[1] *Bureau of the Census,* "Population of Urban Places: April 1, 1950," PC–9, No. 8 (Nov. 26, 1952), 1–2. (See Table 1.)

[2] N. S. B. Gras, "Rise of the Metropolitan Community," in E. W. Burgess, (ed.), *The Urban Community* (Chicago: University of Chicago Press, 1926).

Without international boundary lines limiting the hinterland, as in the case of Europe, "economic provinces," or metropolitan districts arose in great numbers. Two primary requisites must be satisfied for the emergence of such districts: the economic development of the hinterland and the rise of business ability and coordination at the center. These groupings were not according to deliberate design and were the result of a drift rather than a definite plan.

At the present time, however, "economic provinces" are being promoted and planned. St. Louis, Cleveland, Chicago, and Los Angeles are excellent illustrations among many. The civic and commercial organizations of these cities advertise regularly in periodicals and newspapers concerning the benefits found in locating in their areas. Such data as the number of railroads and other conveyances entering or leaving the city, the total volume of wholesale and retail business, the kind of industry and commerce, and the opportunities for employment are bait for luring businesses considering relocations or new sites. Workers desiring a change in occupation or residence determine where their skills are best suited. Families seeking cultural advantages take the offerings into consideration.[1]

The Census Bureau since 1910 has had the task of differentiating the "real city" from the political unit. This is largely caused by the fact that the drift of population occurred more rapidly than official definitons could be established. To overcome the difficulty, several definitions of a metropolitan district have attempted to show the functional socio-economic interrelationship between the hinterland and the metropolis. In general, the name of the district bore the name of the central city, or metropolis, although two or more cities could be included.

For two census returns, the population of the metropolis was added to the total number of inhabitants found within a zone of contiguous and adjacent territory not extending beyond a ten-mile limit. Ten years later the ten-mile limit was dispensed with as a criterion and a population density of 150 persons per square mile was substituted. Moreover, the central city needed but 50,000 inhabitants as a minimum, rather than the 200,000 required between 1900–1920.[2] If these two conditions were not met, the district was not considered metropolitan. Therefore, southern and western states had few metropolitan districts. For example, North Carolina ranked seventh among the states in her rate of population growth in 1930 and had five cities which recorded 50,000 inhabitants. None had peripheral

[1] See pamphlet "In the Long Run the Short Haul Pays: The Best Location in the Nation" released by The Cleveland Electric Illuminating Co. Development Department.

[2] United States Bureau of the Census, 1930, *Metropolitan Districts*, pp. 5–6. For 1940 data, see *Population*, I, 11.

clusters of population that showed a density of 150 persons per square mile, the density required for a metropolitan district.

The unprecedented growth of metropolitan districts, from 44 in 1900 to 137 in 1943, gives us another basis for understanding the magnetism which large cities have.[1] Population and organizations are drawn within their dominance. What is more striking is the percentage of people living there. In 1900 about 28 million resided in these areas. Twenty years later 47 million, and within another decade almost one-half the country's population lived in metropolitan districts. Small cities, suburbs, and communities of varying size clustered around the outer fringes of cities, for large cities seldom exist in isolation. In short, the population of these districts grew 200 per cent and that of the United States, 49 per cent during a forty year span.[2] We should remember, however, that the peripheral territories grew at a faster rate than central cities.

The 1950 census enumeration of 168 "standard metropolitan areas" replaced the former procedure of delimiting metropolitan districts according to the old criteria of using county boundary lines instead. A more realistic basis is now possible for obtaining unified areal data, when compiled by federal, state, and local governments as well as private organizations.[3] For the first time also, the concept of "urbanized areas" was introduced, as providing a better separation of urban and rural population in the vicinity of large cities. These changes will be discussed in detail later.

3) *Metropolitan dominance.* Bogue divided central cities into four classes, depending on the size of the city.[4] Type A included central cities containing a million or more inhabitants. Class B cities had 500,000 to 999,-999 persons, while Class C included 250,000 to 499,999. Those having between 100,000 to 249,999 population fell into Class D. This method was used to study the dominance of central cities over their hinterlands. Cities of varying sizes were grouped around the centers selected for analysis. These subdominant hinterland cities varied in aggregation between 2,500 to 50,000 and over. The greater the central city in population and area, the more extensive its dominance. The hinterland cities most accessible and closest to the central city were more subject to the influence of the larger city than those distant, regardless of size of population of the more

---

[1] Abram J. Jaffe, "Population Trends and City Growth," *The Annals of the American Academy of Political and Social Science,* 242 (Nov., 1945), 18–24.

[2] *Ibid.*

[3] Bureau of the Census, "Summary of Characteristics of the Population of Standard Metropolitan Areas: April 1, 1950," Series PC–7, No. 4 (Nov. 20, 1951), 1.

[4] Don J. Bogue, *The Structure of the Metropolitan Community* (Ann Arbor: University of Michigan, 1949), 19–22.

distant cities. Transportation and trade between the outlying cities and the central city followed definite channelized land routes. The movement of people to and from the areas was also patterned in the same manner. More aggregations were apt to form along the routes of transportation than in the in-between areas. The distance over which the central city commanded dominance varied between 25 to 64 miles. Beyond this, the influence of the metropolis was slight.

McKenzie used media of communication for measuring metropolitan dominance and discovered that most subscribers to the central city's newspapers lived within fifty miles.[1] Readers were interested in the metropolis' daily occurrences and also in the merchandise advertised. Shoppers who came to the metropolis were attracted if their shopping could be completed in time for them to return home on the same day. Department stores also found deliveries unprofitable to outlying areas if their vehicles did not complete the journey and return by the end of the working day. Broadcasting stations, included in the study, had most of their listeners living within a fifty-mile radius.

The metropolitan district is a new type of supercommunity. Its socio-economic structure embraces many units which depend upon the center for its finance, recreation, government, education, goods and services, transportation, sanitation, fire protection, and many public utilities. In return, the central city draws its labor supply and consumers from the hinterland. Considerable interdependence results. Each part of the whole may vary in the degree of intercommunity exchange, but the dispersed population requires a variety of needs which only the metropolis can supply.

4) Political complexity. The metropolitan district includes a number of incorporated and unincorporated places, each having separate political jurisdiction. When the 96 districts were ranked in 1930 according to the population of which each type was composed, there were 1,566 separately incorporated municipalities (2,500 and above inhabitants), 677 unincorporated villages (less than 2,500), and over six million in unincorporated territories. These districts cover wholly or in part 250 counties. Twenty-three cut across state boundaries, while four formed parts of three neighboring states.

The larger the district the more incorporated areas it includes. The New York and northeastern New Jersey district exceeded all others with 273 incorporated places in 1930 and a decade later had 291.[2] In addition, 84 townships, 19 counties, and 3 states made up the total of 397 political

[1] R. D. McKenzie, *The Metropolitan Community* (New York: McGraw-Hill Book Co., Inc., 1933).

[2] United States Bureau of the Census, 1940, Vol. II.

subdivisions. Pittsburgh was second with 225 political subdivisions. Cleveland had the smallest number among the nation's ten largest supercommunities. Size, topography, transportation, and the economic structure of the central city are determining factors in the number of incorporated and unincorporated areas found in these districts. Administrative confusion and considerable overlapping of jurisdiction are likely to be present, topics which will be given more consideration in a later chapter.

5) *Rural-nonfarm areas.* Along with the growth in urban population, there has been a great increase in that part of the rural population which does not derive its livelihood from farming. Many of these "rural" inhabitants are by occupation and background actually urbanites who live on the fringes of cities. Under the definition of the metropolitan district used until 1950, this segment of rural non-farm inhabitants could not be classified as urban.

Since 1920, the rural-nonfarm population has exceeded the rural population. Between 1940 and 1946 rural areas suffered an absolute loss of 13 million persons to cities and rural-nonfarm areas.[1] The chief gains accrued to the smallest and newest metropolitan districts. Those having over a million inhabitants attracted either the same or less than the national gain of 7.2 per cent.[2] The two classes of districts which showed an increment above the national population percentage were those which had between 100,000 to 250,000 and 500,000 to 1,000,000 residents.

In 1950, the introduction of the concept of the standard metropolitan area properly identified many more of these urbanites as rural but nonfarm. Consequently, there has been a reduction in the number of people who are rural but nonfarm dwellers as given in the census returns. In 1950, 21 per cent of the population was classified as rural-nonfarm and 15 per cent as rural-farm.[3] The respective rural-nonfarm figures for 1920, 1930, and 1940 were 19, 19.3, and 20.5 per cent. However, these last figures are not strictly comparable to the 1950 data. The decline in the rural-farm population, the remaining segment, can be seen in the change from 1920 to 1950 from 20.7 per cent to 15 per cent, although some of those previously classified as rural-farm were classified as nonfarm in 1950.

1940 to the present. The year 1940 marks the beginning of another period of city growth. Cities in the southern and western United States have grown, while the urban rate of growth in the New England and Middle Atlantic States has decreased. Internal migration has caused a

---

[1] United States Department of Agriculture, *Bulletin No. 7*, SEA series (May 2, 1946).

[2] Amos H. Hawley and Don J. Bogue, "Recent Shifts in Population: The Drift Toward the Metropolitan District, 1930–1940," *The Review of Economic Statistics*, 24 (Aug., 1942), 143–148.

[3] *United States Bureau of the Census*, "General Characteristics of the Population of the United States," Series PC–7, No. 1 (Feb. 25, 1951), 6.

redistribution of population, while high birth rates raised the status of less developed territories and will result in their maturation. A vast movement of population has occurred, and the last ten years has witnessed the greatest dispersion and resettling of persons the country has ever experienced. In addition to the 12 million men in the armed forces by March, 1945, another 15 million civilians migrated to war defense areas or to be near military camps.[1] The heaviest mobility flow was from the South to the North and from the East to the West. Others moved from the North to the Southwest and Southeast. There has been a flow of immigrants from other continents as well.

The Pacific Coast Region has had the greatest growth because of immigration and high birth rates. Many persons moving to California, Oregon, and Washington stayed on after V-J Day; and Nevada and Utah also experienced high increases in new settlers. Utah became an assembling area for heavy machinery, steel manufacturing, and chemical products, whereas her production was formerly geared toward agriculture, light manufacturing, and the smelting of ores.

The southeastern cities attracted textile, chemical, and dye factories, and professional, managerial, clerical, and skilled workers in these fields —some from the northern states—settled in the region. More persons moved in from rural areas to cities within these states. The erection of factories made it possible for many to locate within these states or in adjacent states. For example: North Carolina drew many workers from the states directly south. Other facts which benefited the southern workers and motivated them to remain closer to their home states were the introduction of better wage and hour systems, collective bargaining, increased educational facilities and better social services.

The shift of industry from the eastern seaboard states and congested centers to less industrialized areas of the mountain, southeastern, and southwestern states has continued to the present. In addition to the states mentioned, cities in Arizona, Colorado, Idaho, Montana, Wyoming, and Texas are experiencing a wave of new investments. To a lesser extent those located in Mississippi, Alabama, Kentucky, Tennessee, Louisiana, Oklahoma, and Arkansas are receiving more of the nation's share of industrialization. Therefore, the trend toward raising the income level and wealth of heretofore neglected regions appears to be at hand. To a large extent these manifestations are the results of conscious planning and the advent of the Atomic Age.

Newer modes of transportation—the airplane, helicopter, and jet planes —have reduced distances and may alter the configuration of large cities.

---

[1] War Manpower Commission, *Man Power Statistics*, No. 20 (July, 1945), 9.

Television has also been influential in this respect. Cities with ample room for airport terminals and allied services will rise in importance. Some may supersede centers that depend upon railroads. The use of waterways may again be of greater importance for the transport of heavier and bulkier commodities. There is considerable agitation for the early completion of the St. Lawrence Waterway, for example. Building of a waterway there will cause the railroads to suffer, but the congestion on highways and truck lines will be reduced.

The central city's dominance may extend over wider territories. Helicopters will be able to shuttle between the peripheral and central cities, within cities at different points, and between rural and urban areas. Wider use of the helicopter is already being made. As a taxi service between major and minor air terminals and to suburbs, it has proved successful. Cargo, mail, and perishable items, once carried by motor trucks, are being transferred to helicopters and airplanes.

Some factories will be able to locate nearer raw material sources. Finished products can be distributed quickly by air freight without retarding mass production. Surburban areas may establish industries which will support their populations, thus reducing the heavy flow of traffic and workers into the congested downtown and minor business and shopping districts.

Lower cost is another fact which is mitigating against the older modes of transportation and favoring the new. The difference in cost between railroad and air transportation is rapidly disappearing. In some instances the passenger and freight rates are lower on airplanes. For long distance, uninterrupted transportation, the time-cost-distance factor is favoring the wider use of the airplane and helicopter.

Changing Urban Classifications

The changes in census classifications are not the result of radical and sudden changes in urban characteristics or of the whim of census directors. Rather, they are attempts to present the most realistic and scientifically useful classifications in the face of the constant change in American urban characteristics. The frequency of such changes in the history of the American census reflects both the rapidity of American urban change, and the constant attempts to use classifications which will prove most useful in analyzing census data. Many American cities have mushroomed in recent years, with constant changes within the cities and on their fringes. The main intent of the rural-urban differentiations outlined by the census is to make possible analysis of social groups which

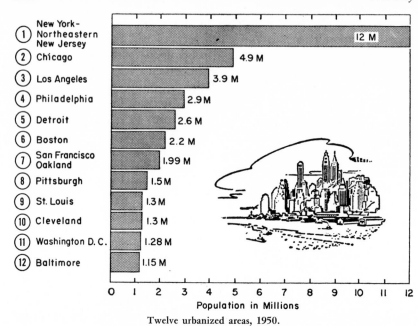

	Population in Millions
① New York-Northeastern New Jersey	12 M
② Chicago	4.9 M
③ Los Angeles	3.9 M
④ Philadelphia	2.9 M
⑤ Detroit	2.6 M
⑥ Boston	2.2 M
⑦ San Francisco Oakland	1.99 M
⑧ Pittsburgh	1.5 M
⑨ St. Louis	1.3 M
⑩ Cleveland	1.3 M
⑪ Washington D. C.	1.28 M
⑫ Baltimore	1.15 M

Population in Millions

Twelve urbanized areas, 1950.

are at least to some degree unlike. Therefore, two new categories—urbanized areas and standard metropolitan areas—were introduced in 1950.[1]

The 1940 population figures for cities having a population of 50,000 or more inhabitants were used as a basis for recording the urbanized areas. A special census was taken to determine how many other cities had reached this size since 1940. Twenty more cities were added later because their population increases were not revealed until the 1950 count was completed. The 157 urbanized areas included 69,249,148 inhabitants, within a total land area of 12,733 square miles.

Since the primary purpose was to include the populations residing at the outer fringes of large cities, several types of contiguous areas—or those already a part of the urbanized area—were included:[2]

1. Incorporated places with 2,500 inhabitants or more.
2. Incorporated places with less than 2,500 inhabitants. In lieu of the required 2,500, a concentration of 100 and more dwelling units, with a density of 500 or more persons per square mile sufficed. This density represents approximately 2,000 persons per square mile, the normal number found to be associated with a closely-spaced street pattern.

[1] Bureau of the Census, "Population and Land Area of Urbanized Areas: Apr. 1, 1950," Series PC–9, No. 4 (Oct. 7, 1952).
[2] *Ibid.*, 2

3. Unincorporated territory with at least 500 dwelling units per square mile.
4. Territory devoted to commercial, industrial, transportational, recreational, and other purposes, funtionally related to the central city.

In short, the city's urban fringe has contiguous to it many areas with a compactness and density of settlement comparable to the occupants of apartment units living on a city street. The population was 5,738 per square mile of land area within all the urbanized areas. The fact that a particular territory is unincorporated does not affect its classification as part of an urbanized area. Incorporation is a local matter which may depend upon the desires of the residents or upon a statute. Industrial, commercial, and other functional areas, dependent upon the larger city, but decentralized, are also included.

In addition, outlying contiguous areas, incorporated or unincorporated, meeting the residential density prerequisites are regarded as part of the urbanized area, as follows:

1. All outlying areas within 1½ miles of the central contiguous urban area, measured along the shortest connecting highway.
2. Any outlying area within 1½ miles of another outlying area, itself within 1½ miles of the central contiguous urban area.

The influence of highways in connecting outlying areas is self-evident. The outlying area most likely to be under the central city's influence is the first type. The second can also be experiencing the same to a lesser degree, but it must be connected to another outlying area within one and one-half miles from the central city.

Any urbanized area may include one or more cities, each of which may serve as a central city, providing it has a minimum of 25,000 inhabitants, and this total amounts to at least two thirds of that of the largest city in the area. Thus, the New York–Northeastern New Jersey urbanized area includes three large cities—New York, Jersey City, and Newark. Each has an urban fringe and outlying areas. Each has more than the 25,000 residents required as the minimum, although two-thirds of the population belongs to New York, the largest center within the urbanized area. The name of each area is identified by the central city, or cities, as for example, the Albany-Troy, urbanized area. Some, such as the Duluth, Minnesota, and Superior, Wisconsin, areas, embrace parts of two states.

Twelve of our largest cities are identified with urbanized areas that include one-fourth of the population of the United States. (See Fig.,

p. 194.) Moreover, the central cities of all of these areas accounted for almost 70 per cent of the total population of the areas.

Standard metropolitan areas. The standard metropolitan area must be distinguished from the urbanized area.[1] The latter is considerably smaller and shows less population than the standard metropolitan area. Both may have the same central city. For instance, Houston is the central city of an urbanized area and of a standard metropolitan area. The central city must have 50,000 inhabitants. However, the standard metropolitan area is defined in terms of one or more contiguous counties. The county was chosen as the constituent unit because it is believed that more kinds of data are compiled or obtained when using the county as a basis rather than minor civil divisions or other types. The exception to this rule is New England where the town rather than the county is generally the geographic unit that is used for statistical compilation. In this region, the areas are defined in terms of contiguous towns or cities.

While the standard metropolitan area has one central city, two or more cities may be found in it, but the next city with 50,000 or more inhabitants must be within a limit of twenty miles. A separate return is not given if the next city has customarily been regarded as a part of the same standard metropolitan area. An example is the St. Paul and Minneapolis area. Parts of several states may be contained within a standard metropolitan area. In general, they are larger in area than the metropolitan districts mentioned above which have now been superseded by the standard metropolitan areas. The data for these two classifications are not comparable.

The special census of the standard metropolitan area determines first, the density of population and the character of the county as a place of work for non-agricultural workers. Second, it seeks to discover to what extent contiguous counties are socially and economically integrated with the central city. The first set of criteria established for the county were as follows:

a. 10,000 non-agricultural workers, or
b. 10 per cent of the non-agricultural workers in the standard metropolitan area, or
c. at least half of its population residing in contiguous minor civil divisions with a population density of 150 or more per square mile.[2]

The second criterion was that the county's non-agricultural workers must constitute at least two-thirds of the total gainfully employed. The evidences required for showing that the county and central city are socially and economically integrated included:

[1] Bureau of the Census "Population of Standard Metropolitan Areas: Apr. 1, 1950," Ser. PC–9, No. 6 (Nov. 24, 1952).
[2] *Ibid.,* 3.

a. 15 per cent or more of the workers residing in the contiguous county work in the county containing the largest city in the standard metropolitan area, or

b. 25 per cent or more of the persons working in the contiguous county reside in the county containing the largest city in the standard metropolitan area, or

c. an average of four or more telephone calls per subscriber per month from the contiguous county to the county containing the largest city in the standard metropolitan area.[1]

As pointed out, the New England areas used contiguous towns or cities as the geographical unit. Therefore, if a population density of 150 or more persons per square mile was present, this was regarded as evidence of social and economic integration. In the case where strong integration was present, but the population density did not exceed 100 or more persons per square mile, the second criterion could be applied.

More than half the population of the United States, or 84,500,680 inhabitants lived in 168 standard metropolitan areas on April 1, 1950. Four-fifths of the country's increase in population between 1940 and 1950 was within these areas. The population grew by 22 per cent, as against 14.5 per cent for the country as a whole. The largest growth was at the outskirts of large cities. The central cities grew by 13.9 per cent, while the outlying parts grew by 35.6 per cent. The increase outside the standard metropolitan areas was 6.1 per cent.[2] Thus, the urbanization of smaller urban and suburban communities adjoining our metropolitan cities is causing the nation's population to become more urbanized.

Significance. More important than the introduction of the two new types of urban classifications is the fact that the characteristics of areas are assuming increasingly definite patterns.

An added significance is that the American urban areal pattern is growing more akin to older societies where urbanization has had a longer history. There, cities have formed themselves into compartment-like entities. A central city is linked to a series of lesser cities; together they function as a social and economic unit. In the United States the mass media of communication form a bond among all urbanites, and facilitate the diffusion of urbanism over a wider area and among a larger number of people. In older societies where the media are less all-pervasive, the individual urban areas stand out more sharply. Thus, urbanization affects the way of life to a lesser degree and may be confined to specific localities.

In light of the projected urban population figures up to the year 2,000, more than three-fourths of the Americans then living may be urban dwell-

[1] *Ibid.*
[2] *Ibid.*, 1.

ers. Depending on different assumptions on future conditions, Hauser's and Eldridge's maximum and medium projections are 90 and 78 per cent respectively.[1] They predict this on the basis of existing trends but caution us to be prepared for a slower rate of growth than that of the past. The leveling of the birth rate plus the fact that there will be relatively less foreign immigration will have some bearing. Nevertheless, urbanized segments of the population will in all probability continue to grow faster than the rural population.[2] Smaller rural families are already in evidence. Yet, an agricultural surplus is accumulating in spite of fewer and fewer farmers. American cities and rural-nonfarm areas are destined to absorb ever greater numbers of the population.

Summary

The growth and numerical increase of cities in the United States have not proceeded at the same rate from early colonial settlement to the present. Four major periods are used as a basis for comparison. The first, 1625 to 1850, had a slow rate of growth, and the cities were mainly located on the eastern seaboard, or near lakes and rivers. The urban institutions founded by early settlers laid the foundation for those arising subsequently in other cities.

The second period extended from 1850 to 1910 when railroad junctions and commercial and mining cities sprang up along the main and arterial routes of railroads. Forty-five per cent of the nation's population was urban. Urbanism as a way of life had become recognized as to its advantages and disadvantages. This period saw the heaviest intercontinental immigration, swelling the population of cities and the territories beyond the trans-Mississippi frontier.

The growth of metropolitan cities and districts characterized the third period, 1910 to 1940. Population was drawn toward large cities and their periphery. Incorporated and unincorporated areas as well as suburbs and satellite cities, clustered around the central city. The automobile, truck, and interurban transit changed the configuration of population and institutional settlement. There were 3,464 cities, 96 metropolitan cities, and 133 metropolitan districts. The urban population was 56.5 per cent, the rural non-farm, 20.5 per cent, and the rural, 23.

The period beginning with 1940 has not ended and is noted for the rise and development of southern and western cities. Moreover, cities with airport facilities will increase in importance, and large cities appear to have

[1] Philip M. Hauser and Hope T. Eldridge, "Projection of Urban Growth and Migration to Cities in the United States," in Milbank Memorial Fund, *Postwar Problems of Migration* (New York: 1947), 159–173.

[2] Jaffe, *op. cit.*, 18.

been growing at a slower rate. Outward movement of population and organizations is more evident. The census redefinition accentuates the increase of cities and number of urbanites. The delineation of 157 urbanized areas affords a better picture of urban and rural residence. The establishment of standard metropolitan areas on a county basis was another change in procedure which was an official recognition of the maturation process of 168 metropolitan areas as to their social and economic integration. The density of population and the percentage of non-agricultural workers are determined for one or more central cities and their outlying areas. By 1950, 64 per cent of the country's population was urban; 21 per cent was rural-nonfarm, and 15, rural. It is probable that the urban configuration here is approaching that of older societies where cities have existed longer, but where they are fewer.

DISCUSSION QUESTIONS

1. How may the Atomic era affect the growth of very large cities?
2. What advantages are gained by establishing standard metropolitan areas on a county basis? Why do some areas include several counties?
3. What was the primary objective of the Census Bureau in defining urbanized areas? Rural-nonfarm areas?
4. How does the metropolitan district differ from the standard metropolitan area?
5. How does the urbanized area differ from the standard metropolitan area?
6. How has the rapid growth of cities affected the census data?
7. What were some of the new technological developments that stimulated urbanization?
8. Is there a probability of river, sea, and lake cities regaining importance?
9. Discuss the various methods used to measure metropolitan dominance.

SUGGESTED PROJECTS

1. Compare the growth of rural-nonfarm population with that of the central city for your metropolitan district for as many decades as statistics are available.
2. Study the physical growth of your city. How has it taken care of population increases?
3. How far does your city have command of its hinterland? Use newspaper circulation, radio wave length, telephone, and television broadcasts, and delivery service of leading stores as measurements.
4. Compare the use of the automobile and similar vehicles to that of the railroad for several decades.
5. Do the same as 4 by comparing the airplane with the automobile.
6. Select an outlying area within 1½ miles from a central city and show its social and economic interrelationships.

7. Compare the density of population of an urban fringe with that of the most congested area of your city.
8. Take one region of the country and compare the growth of cities according to the four major periods outlined.
9. Describe the changes in city living from 1850 to 1950.

READINGS

Don J. Bogue, *The Structure of the Metropolitan Community: A Study of Dominance and Subdominance*. Ann Arbor: University of Michigan Press, 1949.

A comprehensive analysis of the structure of metropolitan communities of varying population size as to their radius of dominance over the hinterland.

Carl Bridenbaugh, *Cities in the Wilderness*. New York: Ronald Press, 1938.

A vivid picture of urban life during the colonial period, portraying the sophistication amidst the primitive conditions of non-developed territories.

Paul K. Hatt and Albert J. Reiss, Jr., eds., *Reader in Urban Sociology*. Glencoe: The Free Press, 1951.

A general reader including specialized topics by authorities in their respective fields.

Ann Bush Maclear, *Early New England Towns: A Comparative Study of Their Development*. New York: Columbia University Press, 1908.

A study of the methods of town organization, early political institutions, and the presence of vested interests.

R. D. McKenzie, *The Metropolitan Community*. New York: McGraw-Hill Co., Inc., 1933.

An analysis of the growth of the metropolitan districts of the United States to 1930.

National Resources Committee, *Our Cities: Their Role in the National Economy*. Washington, D. C.: Government Printing Office, 1937.

The first official publication setting forth the findings of the Committee, showing how cities became the "workshops" of the nation.

George S. Perry, *Cities of America*. New York: McGraw-Hill Book Co., Inc., 1947.

A compilation of studies of leading and distinctive cities, featuring their cultural, social, economic, and political institutions.

Arthur Schlesinger, *The Rise of the City, 1878–1898*. New York: The Macmillan Co., 1933.

A good treatment of a neglected topic, the rise of the American city with its distinct way of life. The social changes that accompany the new urbanism are ably treated.

Adna Ferrin Weber, *The Growth of Cities in the Nineteenth Century: A Study in Statistics*. New York: Columbia University Studies in History, Economics, and Public Law, 1896.

Discusses the cities of the nineteenth century as to location of population, changes in transportation methods, and the documental histories of city formation and growth.

Part Three

The Physical and Population Structure

PROLOGUE   *The chapters in this section deal with three basic aspects of urban development, all of which may be considered as conditions underlying the social organization of cities. Urban ways of life have brought about marked changes and new patterns in population and physical characteristics.*

The interest in urban population composition is a logical consequence of the definition of a city, since we have already seen that the principal characteristics of urbanism are the size, density, and heterogeneity of population. Much of the diversity encountered in urban populations is the result of internal migration, and, in many cases, immigration. The diverse wants and interests of these groups are in turn reflected in demographic differentials. There are perhaps no better indexes of the effects of urbanization and complex social structures than analyses of differences in birth and death rates. Changes in population composition fundamentally alter man's social relationships, as the development of cities indicates. In turn, these new behavior patterns may bring about marked changes in population characteristics.

Other major fields of interest include the distribution of human beings in space, their relationships to their environments, and related patterns of communal organization. Even the casual observer is familiar with the presence of distinct and relatively homogeneous areas within cities. Images of "black belts," factory areas, and wide avenues with wealthy homes come readily to mind. This subsocial ecological base of the city is largely the product of competition for space and subsistence, in conjunction with the interdependence and cooperation based on the division of labor. The ecological organization of cities is a type of dynamic equilibrium, in that it follows predictable patterns, and at the same time is constantly changing. This is the consequence of ecological processes which are constantly in operation.

Both of these major aspects of cities are closely related to the physical structure, which is perhaps the most tangible of all the many urban characteristics. As cities have grown, the amount and complexity of the products of engineering have increased to the extent that some see in urban man but the slave of the technology he has created. Whatever the merits of this argument, the phantom of water shortages, transportation snarls, and other problems at times become a reality. Such crises have drastic and immediate effects on the whole complex pattern of social relationships based on this physical structure.

Chapter Eight

Urban Population Composition

URBAN POPULATION composition is a topic of special interest, since it provides the basis for viewing the heterogeneity and density of population and the degree of interaction between individuals and groups. Various reactions accompany the knowledge relative to the size of population of a given municipality. To many, it is an indication of industrial and commercial prosperity. To others, it signifies crowdedness, slum conditions, or higher crime rates. Still others feel a sense of civic pride, based on the assumption that their city is "best."

Such reactions usually ignore or obscure the significant analyses of population characteristics and their relationship to the city's economic, technological, and social system. (For instance, there are known instances of communities which boast of unusually low death rates, but carefully fail to mention that inhabitants must use a hospital in an adjacent community.) The demographer must take into account the consequences of differences in age, sex, ethnic descent, and social status, to list only a few pertinent variables.

These are distinctions of more than academic interest. The basic phenomena of birth and death are relegated to some of the most intense and divergent human values. Urbanization has brought about many changes in human values. One of the most important has been related to the increased ability of man to control both fertility and mortality. Medical and sanitation advances which accompanied urbanization in the Western world brought about a reduction in mortality and a consequent increase in life expectancy and the size of populations. This change in mortality rates preceded a decrease in fertility, and the resultant unprecedented increase in population led to some of the first serious considerations of population problems. Some men, notably Malthus, foresaw endless cycles of misery as populations outgrew their food supplies.

The advance in the means of controlling fertility came at a time when it seemed to many that a further increase in population might mean calamity. The basic value of survival was weighed against the value of large families. Many other values also entered into the rapid diffusion of the acceptance and use of birth control measures. Urban children became a financial liability rather than an asset. For many, children became a matter of choice rather than an inevitable consequence. Decisions to have children became influenced by factors such as the financial resources available, social expectations as to the proper size of the family, and the desire for luxuries. One outstanding example of the importance of socio-economic factors in determining the birth rate is to be found in the low birth rates of the depression years, followed by the "baby-boom" of the following decade.

This decrease in the birth rate has greatly slowed down the rate of population increase. As a matter of fact, for several decades urban birth rates have fallen below the level required for replacement of existing populations. Cities of Western countries have therefore come to depend on higher rural birth rates and migration to maintain and increase their populations.

The over-all changes described above are of course not equally applicable to all urban populations. One reason for the current concern with population problems in the world's underdeveloped areas arises from our inability to predict whether urbanization elsewhere will have the same ultimate results it has had in the West. There are great demographic differences among the varied sub-groups within Western cities.

Wherever there are significant differences in population characteristics, there are also significant differences in social and cultural characteristics. The seemingly simple statistics which tell us the composition, and the birth and death rates of given groups of people, actually tell us much more. In particular, if we keep in mind the over-all population changes which have accompanied the development of Western cities, they can show the extent to which particular groups have adopted urban ways of life. In this chapter we shall confine most of our attention to the urban population of our own society.

The United States

The 1950 census listed 150,697,361 persons within the boundaries of the United States, representing a gain of almost 20 million since 1940. Fifty years ago the figures stood at 75,995,575, or almost one-half fewer inhabitants. The doubling of population can be attributed to the excess of births over deaths and the influx of young adult immigrants until 1925. The present annual increase is over two and a half million persons. The 1953 total is over 158 million. The center of population is now located in a cornfield near Olney, Illinois. A century ago this midpoint was at the northeast border of West Virginia, just west of the Allegheny Mountains. The westward movement of population has followed industrial and commercial expansion. Both the number and population of cities have increased greatly.

The nation's population can be differentiated in many ways. Primary is the division according to residence: urban, rural-nonfarm, and rural. Characteristics of urban dwellers which are of interest to us are those pertaining to (1) race and nativity, (2) age and sex composition, (3) marital status, (4) birth rates, and (5) mortality rates. Two other aspects, the labor force and religious affiliation, will be discussed in later chapters.

Race and Nativity

The three major races, Caucasoid, Negroid, and Mongoloid, are found in American cities. At times, the category "other," appears in the census returns when special groups have too few members to warrant a separate grouping, or when the group's identity is controversial. Mexicans, Filipinos, and East Indian groups are illustrations. In addition, the nativity of urbanites involves peoples of many national backgrounds, contributing to the heterogeneity of population. For example: within the white group are persons who stem from many countries in Europe, Canada, Mexico, and others. Cities, regardless of where they are located, generally include a high proportion of all racial and ethnic groups.

Caucasoid. The heavy influx of immigrants from Europe until the first quarter of this century has resulted in the settlement in cities of the foreign-born and their descendants. The older immigrants and the native-born make up a relatively high proportion of rural dwellers. In 1940, 8.7 per cent of the population of this nation were classified as foreign-born whites and in 1950, 6.7 per cent.[1] The rural non-farm and rural areas showed declines between the two censuses, from 5.5 to 3.5 and 3.1 to 2.4 per cent, respectively. In other words, a decade ago about one out of every ten Caucasoid persons was foreign-born. The 1950 proportions were smaller, but in absolute numbers the foreign-born Caucasoids still numbered over ten million.[2]

The decrease in the foreign-born Caucasoid population has another significance. In 1940 and 1950, the foreign-born and their second-generation American descendants comprised 31 and 17.5 per cent respectively of the

[1] Bureau of the Census, "General Characteristics of the Population of the United States: April 1, 1950," Series PC–7, No. 1 (Feb. 25, 1951).

[2] George E. Simpson and J. Milton Yinger, *Racial and Cultural Minorities* (New York: Harper & Bros., 1953), Appendix A.

country's total Caucasoid population. This indicates that there is a segment of the population which is subject to the cross-pressures of American and varyingly divergent ethnic patterns, forming what may be considered a "marginal" population. That is, native-borns may be torn between following the cultural patterns of their parents and following those of the American society. Marginal feelings develop when they realize that they do not totally belong to either culture. Ecologically, the results of these pressures are demonstrated by the cultural islands within cities such as, "Little Sicily," "Chinatown," or "Little Poland," which inclue 80 per cent of the foreign-born and their children.

Negroid. The second major racial group is the Negroid. In 1950 the members of this group constituted 9.9 per cent of the nation's population.[1] Since 1940 there was a gain of .1 per cent, as compared to fifty years ago when it was 1.7 per cent. Sixty-eight and one-half per cent of the total Negro population lived in the southern states although they migrated in large numbers during the thirties and the two World Wars. Their intra-country migration to northern, midwestern, western and other cities has resulted in 60 per cent of the group becoming urban by 1950. This is 4 per cent lower than the national urban total.

Where the Negro population is sizable, more native-borns are found. Virtually no foreign-born Negro immigrants have entered the country for over a century. A few immigrants come from within this hemisphere, who constitute less than one-half of one per cent of the total Negro population.

Cities which have had a heavy influx of Negro population are industrially and commercially important such as, New York, Chicago, Detroit, San Francisco, Los Angeles, Cleveland, and others. Rural Negro migrants from the Mississippi Delta farmlands are attracted to large southern cities, Memphis, Little Rock, New Orleans, Houston, and others.[2] Cities in Georgia are preferred by those living within the state. This movement from southern farms to cities is attributed to the decentralization of industries from northern cities and the establishment of new enterprises in the South. It is probable that the rural-urban trend will continue, but Southern cities may attract some who would otherwise turn northward or westward.

Mongoloid and other. The third racial group includes the Japanese, Chinese, Filipinos, and Koreans. Hindus and Polynesians are included under

[1] Bureau of the Census, "General Characteristics of the Population of the United States, Apr. 1, 1950," Ser. PC–7, No. 1 (Feb. 25, 1951). It should be noted that the American definition of a Negro is not strictly a racial definition, since any known Negro ancestry, although it may make a negligible genetic contribution, is sufficient to bring about a classification as a Negro.

[2] A special survey and study made by the *U. S. News and World Report,* June 22, 1951, 50–53.

"other." (See 1st paragraph under Race and Nativity.) Together they constituted less than one-half of one per cent of the total population.

There were 141,768 persons of Japanese ancestry in 1950, 117,629 of Chinese ancestry, and 110,240 of the remaining Mongoloid groups.[1] The Chinese and the Japanese are mainly urban dwellers, with 92 per cent of the Chinese and 71 per cent of the Japanese in cities throughout the country. Until 1942 the Western cities had the largest concentration of these two groups.[2] A redistribution of persons of Japanese ancestry since 1944 has changed the geographic concentration of the group to Des Moines, Chicago, Cleveland, Cincinnati, Washington, Philadelphia, and New York. In both groups the native-born outnumber the foreign-born.

The other Mongoloid groups are found throughout the country. The Koreans have a fair-sized contingent in Chicago, Los Angeles, New York, Denver, and Butte. Some are entrepreneurs in small business, while others are seasonal laborers who return to cities once their farm work is completed. In the Rocky Mountain States the Koreans are employed in the sugar beet fields.

The Filipinos have settlements in cities on the West Coast and in the Rocky Mountain States. Those who are employed by industrial firms are scattered throughout our large metropolitan cities.

The East Indians are negligible in number and are urbanites, engaged in small businesses or professional occupations. Some are employed as farm laborers in Arizona and California.[3]

Age and Sex

Age and sex composition assumes significance when one examines such phenomena as the division of labor, size of labor force, and the consumption of goods and services. Both age and sex classifications are useful to social planners, educators, employers, military authorities, welfare organization, and others. When the age and sex composition of the population is known, the likes, dislikes, interests, activities, attitudes, and adjustments of respective age and sex groups become more meaningful. In recent years there has been a mounting interest in the proportion of the aged in the population.[4]

[1] Bureau of the Census, "General Characteristics of the Population of the United States," Ser. PC–7, No. 1 (Feb. 25, 1951); and *Statistical Abstracts of The United States,* 1953, 38.

[2] Carey McWilliams, *Brothers Under the Skin* (Boston: Little, Brown and Co., 1943), 164–175; Dorothy S. Thomas and Richard S. Nishimoto, *The Spoilage* (Berkeley: University of California Press, 1946).

[3] Gurdial Singh, "East Indians in the United States," *Sociology and Social Research,* 30 (Jan.–Feb., 1946), 213.

[4] Marion B. Smith, "Social Aspects of Sex Distribution of the Age Population," *Social Forces,* 26 (October, 1947), 43–50.

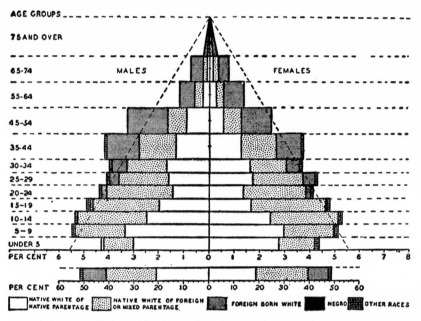

Population pyramid of a middle-class residential area, Calumet Heights in Chicago, Illinois. This chart shows distribution of the population by age, sex, and nativity or color.[1]

Children, persons of working ages, and old people are by no means divided into three equal groups in cities, suburbs, or farms. Each of these residential categories possesses specific age groups resulting from a differential birth or death rate, or from migration. The age compositions of the rural and urban populations have long shown marked differences.

Rural-urban age distribution. In urban centers there had been a decline in the number of children under 15 years of age and older persons above their sixtieth year. The increase in the number of births during the pre-war and post-war years of World War II has temporarily modified the trend. The 1950 census showed a 41 per cent gain for children under 10 years of age and, for those above 60 years, 30 per cent. If the rates are concentrated for those past their sixty-fifth year, the increase is 400 per cent above that at the turn of this century. One group showed a decline, the 10–19-year olds, reflecting the low birth rate that continued through the depression years of the 1930's. In absolute numbers, there is a 2 million drop between 1940 and 1950. Only moderate gains were shown for those between 20–39 years of age.

By 1950, there were over 15 million persons above their sixty-fifth year,

[1] From R. L. Sutherland, J. L. Woodward, and M. L. Maxwell, *Introductory Sociology* (Philadelphia: J. B. Lippincott Company, 1952), 329.

and by 1975, there will be 20 million.[1] The steady increase of this group is more certain than that of those under 15 years of age. The birth rates are apt to fluctuate with socio-economic conditions. In 1900, about 40 per cent of the older people lived in cities, as contrasted to 60 per cent forty years later. Several reasons may be advanced for their continued residence in cities. One major reason is that many own no farms or other property. Many have worked at urban occupations all their lives. Another is that more medical services and welfare assistance are available in cities. Finally, the city offers more opportunities for the use of leisure time. These opportunities include generally available facilities, such as movies, special interest associations, hobby clubs, and social activities specifically designed for this older age group.

Of all men who are 65 and over, 66.3 per cent are married; 23.8 per cent are widowed; 1.7, divorced; and 8.3, bachelors. Of the women of the same age group 36.6 per cent are married; 55.4, widowed; and only 1 per cent are divorced. The unmarried women of advanced age total 8.1 per cent and are but slightly fewer than the males.

Half of the males in this age group are self-employed, whereas only one out of every five in the total male population is self-employed. Perhaps the "economic" old-age factor, as expressed in compulsory or at least expected retirement ages, has caused those who desire to remain financially independent to seek a livelihood in private enterprises.[2] The income for men 65 and over is lower than that of the total male population, however. Many earn less than $1,000 per year, while about a third have absolutely no money income. Another third have annual incomes of less than $500.

In cities, there is a heaping up of population in the adult working age ranges, 20 to 60 years. Taken by age divisions, that of the 30–34 years show the greatest excess. When correlating age with residence, the rural-non-farm areas have slightly more than the average proportion of children under 15 years of age. Families with children move to suburbs and territories adjacent to cities, so as to provide more play space and healthier environment. This means more schools, play equipment, toys, theaters, highways, and playgrounds. Older persons require more books, magazines, radios, television sets, wheelchairs, and institutional care. The nation's economy is being influenced by the changing age composition.

In the urban age groups, 30 to 34 years inclusive, the relative excess of adults can be attributed to two main causes. Opportunities for work in cities are greater and more varied, and also this age range is the period

[1] Findings of Federal Security Agency for the National Conference of the Aging, held in Washington, D. C., August, 1950.

[2] A monograph devoted to the "Social Contribution by the Aging," *The Annals of the American Academy of Political and Social Science*, 279 (Jan., 1952) treats of every aspect pertaining to this group.

of greatest productivity in a person's working life. Assuming that in our society (1) education through high school takes a person into his eighteenth year, (2) several more years are needed to find his place in the occupational hierarchy, and (3) the average working span for most individuals is 35 years, the age bracket 30 to 34 years represents the approaching peak of many occupational careers (other than professional). A gradual recession in working population is noted around the sixtieth year.

Another factor which contributes to the relative excess of urban adults in the 30–34 age groups is the employment of women in industries. Married women, with or without children, who work are most apt to be employed during the years when age, health, and family responsibilities permit. Those with children may find part-time employment and later retire when their children are older or their husbands' financial statuses improve. A great number of single women in these age brackets are employed.

Race and nativity. The foreign-born populations and their children have been known to concentrate in urban centers. This is especially true of the immigrants who arrived later. However, the first- and second-generation Americans who have passed the age of 50 show a greater tendency to settle on farms. Negroes and native whites of native parentage both show a trend toward concentrating in rural-nonfarm territory when they arrive at advanced ages, with the Negroes slightly outranking the whites. Females in both categories show a greater propensity toward such resettlement, but are exceeded by the first generation foreign-born and their descendants in this respect.

Sex Ratio

The sex ratio is another very important aspect of urban population structure.[1] The proportion of males and females has great significance when correlated with birth, death, or marriage rate. The sex ratio affects the types of establishments maintained by a community. Males may be in excess in cities that derive their main activities from primary extractive industries—mining, fishing, and timbering—or from heavy manufacturing—steel, automobiles, cement, and large machinery. Hotels, boarding houses, pool halls, movies, restaurants, dry cleaning and tailoring establishments, and laundries may exist in greater numbers than where families have settled. Where the sex ratio is closer to equal, services are created for women and children: beauty parlors, tea rooms, primary and secondary schools, churches, department stores, and specialty shops are more abundant.

The sex ratio is frequently unbalanced where foreign immigration is

[1] The sex ratio is defined as the number of males per 100 females.

heaviest. Single unmarried males between the ages of 20 and 25 are attracted by the opportunity for greater economic gain, a phenomenon well demonstrated when there was a steady influx of young single men into the country. Until 1930, relatively few women and children entered the country. Thereafter, the increase was attributed to married immigrants sending for their families to join them here. By 1940, the sex ratio for the country stood at 100.7, whereas, ten years earlier it was 102.5. In 1950, the ratio stood at 99. At the turn of the century, the ratio was 106.

Rural-urban distribution. There are marked relationships among residence and sex, nativity, and race.[1] Females are more apt to concentrate in urban areas and males, in rural. This holds true for all races and ethnic groups.

In 1940, the western part of the country retained its traditional pattern of males outnumbering females.[2] For every hundred females, there were 98.5 males in urban areas. The ratio is more significant when broken down into the respective categories of native white, foreign-born, and Negro population in 1940. There were 95.7 native white urban males to every hundred females. The foreign-born urban males exceeded the females by 11 per cent. For every hundred urban Negro females there were 94.4 males.

When the 1940 male and female population of our metropolitan cities is analyzed, it is seen that white females exceeded white males in all but five cities. Marked variations between 31,000 and 4,500 in absolute numbers were shown. Detroit led with the greatest excess of males over females—approximately 31,000—with Gary and San Diego as close seconds—4,600 and 4,500 respectively. Norfolk, Virginia had 3,700 more males and Sacramento, California, 1,500. Several other cities had an excess of males, but the differences were insignificant. If the total urban male and female population used as a basis for analysis includes all races, the excess is greater. Cities engaged in heavy manufacturing, primary extractive industry, and shipping showed the widest variations: Detroit (automobile), Gary (steel), San Diego (shipping and fishing), and Norfolk (shipping). On the other hand, textile milling cities and those offering clerical, sales, and distributing services employ more females. Richmond, Nashville, Knoxville, Dallas, Cambridge, Long Beach, New Orleans, and Charlotte were excellent illustrations; the sex ratio was around 87.

When the sex ratio is analyzed for the 196 centers including counties containing 100,000 or more inhabitants in 1940, only 18 of these had a rise in sex ratio between 1930 and 1940. Only one was constant. In the remainder, the number of males per 100 females was lower than at the beginning

[1] Bureau of Agricultural Economics, *Net Movement Away from Farms in the United States, by Age and Sex, 1940 to 1944,* Bulletin of June 19, 1945.

[2] Bureau of Agricultural Economics, *Farm Population Changes, April 1940 to January 1946,* Bulletin of May 2, 1946

of the previous decade.[1] This is attributed to the fact that there was relatively little foreign immigration.

Negro sex ratio. The ratio of the sexes represents a balancing of the
biological species but differs among racial groups. However, this probably
reflects environmental, rather than genetic differences. The low sex ratio
among Negroes is striking. For the most part, this phenomenon is related
to the low sex ratio at birth, 103 males as compared with 106 among
whites. Higher proportions of masculine stillbirth occur among all preg-
nancies, and the balance is in favor of the females. The higher death rate
among Negro males who survive birth is a second important factor. For
all Negroes, foreign-born as well as native-born, the 1940 ratio was only
95.0. Eliminating the foreign-born, the sex ratio among native Negroes
was slightly lower: 94.9. This group is one not greatly influenced by excessive immigration or emigration.

When comparing urban sex ratios, the white ratio decreased by around
6 per cent, whereas that of the Negro by 2.7 per cent between 1910–1940.
Only in the rural farm territory did the Negro group have a surplus of
male population.

Chinese sex ratio. The ratio of the Mongoloid groups can best be illustrated by that of the Chinese. While it is an accepted fact that during the
early years of the immigration of any ethnic group more single or married
males enter, the restriction of females of the same group results in mounting distortions of the sex ratio. Not only are there more males than females, but there are fewer additions to the group through births. For
example, the Chinese and Japanese populations are smaller today than
when unrestricted immigration took place. This same condition is applicable to all Mongoloid groups, for the primary aim of the Exclusion Acts was
to prevent an increase of population by two methods: (1) restricting the
admission of females except in the admissible classes (wives of merchants,
government officials, travelers, educators, etc.); and (2) discouraging
permanent residence and settlement by forbidding naturalization.[2] A
third method is resorted to by some states (mainly in the western United
States), forbidding intermarriage between Mongoloids and whites. It
should be noted that a small quota of about 100 persons has been established for most Asiatic groups, and the privilege of naturalization has been
extended.

The immigration of Chinese had barely reached its third decade when
the first Exclusion Act was enforced. By 1890 there were 27 Chinese males
to 1 Chinese female. The ratio had been 21 to 1 in the previous decade. The

[1] T. Lynn Smith, *Population Analysis* (New York: McGraw-Hill Book Co., Inc., 1948),
128–129.

[2] Rose Hum Lee, "The Chinese Communities in the Rocky Mountain Region (unpublished Ph.D. dissertation, University of Chicago Libraries, 1947), Ch. 3.

unbalanced sex ratio for the foreign-borns has remained exceedingly high. The closer balance of the last two decades has been attributed to the increase of native-born Chinese women and a decline in the immigration of foreign-born males. In 1940, the sex ratio for the group was almost 3 to 1. With the exception of the Japanese, the other Mongoloid groups are predominantly male and, therefore, have a sex ratio which is comparable to that of the Chinese during the early years of immigration in this country.

The sex ratio has a bearing on the degree and type of personal disorganization found in cities. When the sex ratio is heavily weighed toward the preponderance of male urbanites, there are increases in prostitution, crime, venereal disease, tuberculosis, and illegitimacy. Some Asian and African cities, which have sex ratios as high as 4 to 1, show similar patterns.[1]

Marital Status

Statistics pertaining to the marital status of our population began in 1880. Each subsequent decennial census has classified the marital status of those above fifteen years of age. The younger age ranges are excluded because of the prevailing cultural emphasis upon economic security before undertaking marriage. Many state laws prohibit the marriages of persons below fifteen. It has been customary to use four categories when classifying the population according to marital status: (1) single, (2) married, (3) widowed, and (4) divorced. The Sixteenth Census of the United States (1940) improved the procedure by subdividing the married population into those (1) living with the spouse and (2) living apart. This gave the approximate number of immigrant married men whose wives have remained in the old country. Due to immigration restrictions, an excess of only 103,952 males was shown in 1940, as compared with more than half a million in 1920.

Residence and marital status. There is a very close association between residence and marital status. City, town, village, and farm life vary greatly in their powers to hold or attract single, married, divorced, or widowed persons. Furthermore, the nature of the social and cultural environments prevailing in each of these areas has a bearing upon the choices of mates, and whether marriages will be terminated by death or divorce.

Among all age groups above 15 years, the city contains the highest proportions of spinsters and widows and the lowest of married women. The converse is true of farms, where more women are married. Few remain unmarried or are widowed. It would appear that widowed, divorced,

---

[1] Ching-Yueh Yen, "Crime in Relation to Social Change in China," *American Journal of Sociology*, 40 (1934–1935), 298–308; and *Handbook on Race Relations in South Africa*, *op. cit.*, 272.

or single women migrate from rural areas to urban centers for occupational reasons. If a woman is widowed or single and lives on the farm, there are more opportunities for marriage and remarriage. The excess of rural males is a factor contributing to this condition.

The census returns revealed that native whites of foreign or mixed parentage, although not handicapped like their fathers by an unfavorable sex ratio, seem to have more difficulty finding mates than the foreign-born and native-born of native parentage. The number of bachelors in the "marginal generation" far exceeds that of sons of native parents. The same applied to daughters of foreign or mixed parentage.

When the marital status of the foreign-born parental generation is compared with that of the native-born of foreign or mixed parentage, it is found that the former group finds mates more readily. The reason may be that the foreign-born regard marriage and a family with children as a means of achieving social status. Conversely, their children delay marriage or disregard it entirely to acquire a new occupational, educational, or professional status. This is one indication that the children face a more difficult adjustment in the parents' adopted country.

Widowed. The death of a family member, especially the breadwinner, may completely disintegrate the urban family. The family configuration is altered and a broken family results. Widows are almost one-half as numerous as their unmarried sisters, while there are almost eight single men to every widower. Undoubtedly, the chances for the widower to secure another mate are much greater than for a widow. The higher female life expectancy in this country is a factor making for the relatively large number of widows. In urban centers the average life expectancy of a woman is five years more than a man's, and a greater portion of widows are concentrated there. A second factor is that often woman marry men several years older, and thus chances are greater that the husband will die before the wife. It is estimated that annually about 360,000 wives become widowed, with a corresponding increase in the older age brackets. One fourth of the new widows each year are under 45 years of age.[1]

The Negro population includes an excessively large percentage of widows. In urban territory, as early as age 58, colored widows are as numerous as married women. Higher urban mortality is more evident among Negroes of working ages.[2] This situation does not become parallel among white women until age 67 has been attained. Unfavorable living conditions, lower incomes and thus fewer expenditures for medical services, plus

[1] J. Lotka and L. I. Dublin, *The Money Value of a Man* (New York: Ronald Press Company, 1946), Ch. 3.

[2] Rupert B. Vance, *All These People* (Chapel Hill: University of North Carolina Press, 1945), Ch. 22; also see W. S. Thompson, *Population Problems* (New York: McGraw-Hill Book Company, Inc., 1942), Ch. 9.

the comparative lack of the latter, are contributing factors to the higher Negro death rates, rather than the inability of the race to survive.[1]

Divorced. Divorce is another factor in broken households necessitating many of the same economic, social, emotional, and physiological adjustments brought about by the death of a family member. According to the 1940 census, some 822,600 females and 624,400 males were reported as divorced. The divorced are highly concentrated at the younger ages. One-third of the divorced females are under 35 years of age and another third, 35–44. The divorce families represent 1.6 per cent of the total number of families in this country, but represent 9.3 per cent of the total number of broken families.[2] More females than males are heads of broken families, testifying to the fact that a divorced woman has fewer opportunities for remarriage than the other mate. When the custody of children is awarded the mother, the chances for remarriage are further decreased.

An estimated total of 474,000 divorces were granted in the United States during 1947 as against 610,000 the previous year, an all-time high.[3] The conspicuous rise in the number of divorces in the years following the end of the Second World War has sometimes been attributed to hasty or ill-advised marriages and to unstable conditions associated with the period of national emergency. The decline after 1947 may indicate that the most difficult postwar adjustment period has been passed. Divorce rates, like those of marriage and birth, fluctuate with socio-economic conditions. But the upward trend in divorce rates has been consistent since the turn of this century, and each subsequent year has seen a rate either equal or in excess to that of the previous one. Until 1948 only eight years have shown a decline: 1913, 1918, 1921–22, 1930–32, and 1947.[4] These years were not normal, for either a pre-war, post-war, or depressed economic condition prevailed. In summary, the general upward movement in divorce rates between 1900–1947 culminated in an all time high of 4.3 per 1,000 population in 1946. This was six times the rate of 0.7 recorded at the turn of the century. The 1950 ratio of marriages to divorces was 2.5 per 1,000 population.

Divorces occur more frequently in cities than in rural areas where the mores are more rigid. A second reason for the concentration of divorced persons, especially females, in cities is that if a divorce had been secured in the rural areas, a change of residence may be desirable. Urban areas also offer greater employment opportunities. Of those 15 years of age and over reported as divorced in 1940, cities showed a decidedly higher percentage.

Data on the ten largest cities of the country give additional evidence on

[1] Smith, *op. cit.*, 140–143.

[2] Lotka and Dublin, *op. cit.*, 33.

[3] Federal Security Agency, *United States Summary of Vital Statistics,* 1947, 30, No. 1 (September 15, 1947), 9.

[4] *Ibid.*, 9–10.

the frequency of divorce in cities.[1] A study of the percentage of a state's population residing in a given city and the percentage of the state's divorced population residing in the city shows that the percentage of the state's divorced population 15 years of age and older residing in a given city was significantly higher than that of the state's population of the same age group. The cities studied were Philadelphia, New York, Chicago, Boston, Detroit, Cleveland, Baltimore, Pittsburgh, St. Louis, and Los Angeles. All cities but Philadelphia contained a high percentage of the state's divorced population 15 years of age and older.

When divorce statistics are correlated with the types of occupations customarily associated with urbanism, such as commercial travelers, actors, musicians, physicians, and stenographers, the evidence on higher urban divorce is further substantiated, for these groups have the highest divorce rates. The occupations which necessitate frequent absences from home, business relations with the opposite sex, and minimum control by the community, also have high rates. The groups having the next highest number of divorces include the bankers, plumbers, lawyers, butchers, professors, servants, and merchants. These are mainly urban occupations. Miners, manufacturers, clergymen, carpenters and farmers rank lowest in frequency of divorce.[2]

Birth and Death Rates

The simplest and most common measures of fertility and mortality are the crude birth and death rates.[3] These are defined as the number of births or deaths in a period of time (usually one year) divided by the total size of the population. This figure is multiplied by 1,000, in order to yield a more manageable figure. A crude measure of the rate of population change can be obtained by subtracting the crude death rate from the birth rate.

These rates are usually easiest to obtain, but they are also least reliable in predicting population changes. In order to predict more accurately, one must also take into account other population characteristics. High death rates have a very different meaning in a population with a high proportion of older people—as is the case in Western countries—than in young populations such as characterize the underdeveloped areas. Similarly, birth rates assume more meaning if one takes into account the number of

---

[1] E. W. Burgess and H. J. Locke, *The Family* (New York: American Book Co., 1945), 633–634; also see 2nd edition (1953), 576–577.

[2] See: N. F. Nimkoff, "Occupational Factors and Marriage," *American Journal of Sociology,* 49 (November, 1943), 248–254.

[3] For a presentation of the rates here presented, as well as of other demographic methods, see W. J. Goode and P. K. Hatt, *Methods in Social Research* (New York: McGraw-Hill Book Company, 1952), Ch. 18.

Fertility rates have increased

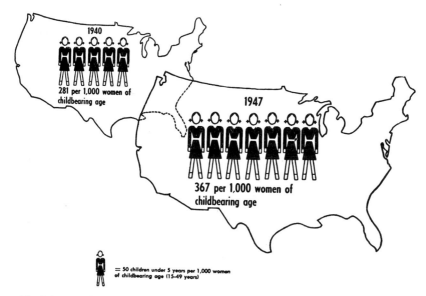

1940

281 per 1,000 women of
childbearing age

1947

367 per 1,000 women of
childbearing age

= 50 children under 5 years per 1,000 women
of childbearing age (15-49 years)

The baby crop has been growing since 1940. By 1947 there were 86 more children per
1,000 women of childbearing age.[1]

women who are of childbearing age. Thus, specific rates may be obtained
by using a more precisely defined population group as a point of reference
for the number of births and deaths. For instance, women of childbearing
age are found in the age group between 15 and 44. The specific birth rate
by age and sex is figured at the number of births per year divided by the
number of women in the population between the ages 15 and 44, multiplied by 100. This analysis can be broken down into smaller age groups
where possible and useful. A similar analysis by age groups can be made
for death rates. Other useful analyses possible include population breakdowns by rural and urban residence, ethnic descent, socio-economic status,
and education, to name a few of those more commonly employed.

One major question about any population is whether or not a given
generation is actually replacing itself. The *gross reproductive rate* is a
measure of the number of daughters born to the women of a generation,
taking account of the age distribution of the mothers. Perfect replacement
would yield a quotient of 1. Any number greater would indicate an in-

[1] From *Children and Youth at the Midcentury—A Chart Book,* prepared by the Midcentury White House Conference on Children and Youth (Raleigh, N. C.: Health Publications Institute, Inc., 1951).

crease, less would indicate a decrease. However, this rate does not take into account the fact that a number of daughters will die before reaching the age of their mothers. The *net reproductive rate* makes an allowance for age-specific mortality, and thus provides a more accurate estimate.

The rates here presented are based on vital statistics reports. Often these are not available or reliable, or not given in sufficiently detailed form for some specific analysis. This is a particularly serious problem for world-wide comparisons, although vital statistics reports are not uniformly reliable even within the United States. Frequently census data may be employed for analogous rates. These are based on comparisons of age groups, *e.g.* children under five years with women of childbearing ages, and reports of deaths to census takers.

It is important to note that all of these rates assume that the conditions under which these rates were derived will obtain in the future. In actuality, change always occurs. Thus a decrease in death rates implies an increase in the net reproductive rate, other things again being equal. Similarly, predictions about the future size of the population made in the thirties were too low since they did not take into account the prosperity of the forties and early fifties. One of the outstanding differentials is between rural and urban birth rates. As the influence of urbanism spreads, lower urban birth rates may lead to populations which are actually decreasing in size.

The predictions made possible by these demographic techniques are of immediate practical significance. Interested users range far beyond the sociologists. They include everyone from obstetricians, school boards, and draft boards to hearing-aid manufacturers, trailer-camp operators, and undertakers.

The crude birth rate reveals fluctuations caused by socio-economic changes. For example: there was a sharp drop after the first year of World War I, 1919, followed by an increase in the next two years. The rate then declined at a relatively rapid rate until 1933, when it reached an all-time low of 16.6.[1] The years of economic recession following the war years affected the rate inversely. Between 1933 and 1940, the rate was irregular.

The gradual upward movement did not become evident until 1941, following the enactment of the Selective Service Act. The rates climbed to 21.5 per 1,000 by 1943, followed by a decline during the next two years, when the separation of family members caused by overseas service was at its height. A sharp rise in rate occurred one year after mobilization. The highest point was reached the ensuing year, or 25.8 per 1,000. Marriages increased after V-J Day in 1945, and were followed by births. Continued high levels of employment also contributed to the upswing.

[1] Federal Security Agency, *op. cit.,* 3.

However, an over-all downward trend in crude birth rates has been present for almost a century. From 36 per 1,000 in 1870, it had fallen to 29 at the turn of the century.[1] A decade later, the rate stood at 25. Just prior to the "war crop" of babies, it was 18 per 1,000.

The inadequacies of the crude birth rate have already been pointed out. Therefore the more refined rates yield more meaningful information.

As can be expected, women in the age groups 15–19 and 20–24 have the highest number of births, and a decline sets in for ages below and above them. The limitation of the size of families in our society is mainly responsible for the upper limit, since it appears that families desiring children have them during the early years of their married life. A study made by the Metropolitan Life Insurance Company revealed that the birth rate is concentrated in the age groups between 22–25 years for mothers and 26–29 for fathers.[2] One-half of the number of babies born a decade ago were to mothers under 25 and to fathers under 29 years. While there was another concentration of births in the next age bracket, 25–29 for mothers and 30–34 for fathers, this is one half as many as for the first group mentioned.

During the Second World War, the babies were born to mothers between 15 to 19 years of age, or a 34.8 per cent increase over 1940.[3] The age of marriage was lower than usual, and many young people started their families immediately. The increase for the groups of mothers between 20–24 and 25–29 rose 16.5 and 9.5 per cent, respectively.

Race, residence, and fertility. A comparison between fertility ratio for the years 1910 to 1940 showed a decline of one-third for the nation as a whole. This phenomenon is sharpest for the largest race and residential class, *i.e.*, the urban white population. It was least pronounced among the non-whites living in urban centers, largely because their rate had fallen earlier to a low level. Furthermore, the rural non-white ratio was characterized by a drop of 29.2 per cent, or below the national average of 33.9. The rural farm non-white group had a fertility rate far above that of any class. This is probably due to the fact that the attitude toward the limitation of families is slower in reaching and being accepted by those living in the remote sections of the South. Lack of education in preventive measures may be an added drawback.[4] On farms, children are yet an economic asset, whereas in cities, it is highly probable that the reverse is true.

The number of white and non-white births in 1947 when related to the respective white and non-white female population aged 15–44 years give

[1] Bureau of the Census, *Statistical Abstract,* 1943, 68.
[2] Lotka and Dublin, *op. cit.,* 31.
[3] Federal Security Agency, *op. cit.,* 4.
[4] For detailed discussion see Vance, *op. cit.,* "The Pattern of High Fertility," Ch. 8, 95–108. Also see Margaret Jarman Haygood, *Mothers of the South* (Chapel Hill: University of North Carolina Press, 1939).

Childbearing has become much safer

But the risk of death for Negro mothers is still 3 times as great as for white mothers

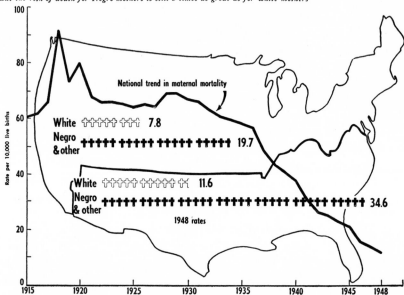

The national trend in maternal mortality has steadily fallen, but the newborn babies of Negro and other groups lost their mothers three times as often as those of the Caucasoid group.[1]

fertility rates of 109.6 per 1,000 for the first group, and 114.2 for the latter. As in previous years, the fertility rates for non-white women under 20 years were much higher than those for the white. However, the white female group between the ages 24–34 had higher rates than non-white. Conversely, the fertility rates for the non-white women, 30–44 years, increased more than for the white. It would appear that in 1947, the group of white mothers had children younger and completed their families earlier than the non-whites. Almost a million families added a second child by 1947, while a million and a half had their first offspring. In no previous year on record have first and second births reached such a high proportion in relation to all births.

For the country as a whole, the net reproduction rate in 1930 was estimated to be 1.11, which may be interpreted to mean a potential increase of 11 per cent a generation. However, by 1933 the rate had fallen to unity. By 1936 the rate was below the replacement level. For the entire urban

[1] From *Children and Youth at the Midcentury—A Chart Book*, prepared by the Midcentury White House Conference on Children and Youth (Raleigh, N. C.: Health Publications Institute, Inc., 1951).

population the net reproduction was .86 which means that reproduction was 14 per cent short of maintenance. For the rural farm and rural-non-farm population of the nation, the rates were 1.32 and 1.59 respectively in 1930. Some of the surplus population migrated to cities.

In 1940, the net reproduction rate for the United States was .96, or .4 per cent below unity. The urban rate was .76, rural-nonfarm, 1.15 and rural farm, 1.36 in 1940. Since birth rates are influenced by socio-economic conditions, the 1940 returns clearly indicated the influence of the depression upon birth rates. If the nation depended wholly on our cities for popula-

TABLE 23. NET REPRODUCTION RATES BY URBAN, RURAL-NONFARM
AND RURAL-FARM RESIDENCE, UNITED STATES, 1930, 1940,
1947, AND 1949 [1]

Year	Total	Urban	Rural-Nonfarm	Rural-Farm
1930	1.11	.86	1.32	1.59
1935–1940	.96	.76	1.15	1.36
1942–1947	1.29	1.08	1.46	1.86
1944–1949	1.38	1.19	1.63	1.81

[1] *Sources: Statistical Abstract of the United States*, 1948, 55; *Statistical Abstract of the United States*, 1952, 43.

tion replacement, a decline of one-fourth of our population in a generation would result. The cities drew population from the villages and farms, which exceeded their quota of birth rates.

The significance of this trend in reproduction becomes more evident when the problem is stated in a different way. For a population to maintain itself at replacement level, 100 newborn girls would in time have 100 daughters and 100 granddaughters. In 1933 the general population of the country had reached this level, but by 1936 the decline in the reproduction rate had begun and has continued through 1940. According to the birth and death rates of 1936, the 100 newborn girls would have had only 95 daughters. By 1940 the birth rates were rising and to the 100 mothers, 102 daughters would have been born. For 1945, the estimated descendants to a like sample of mothers would have been 114 daughters. However, it is well to remember that war brings fluctuations in a trend. These increases may not be permanent indications of a future increase, but in fact, the midcentury net reproduction rate was still above unity.

When populations of American cities have failed to reproduce themselves in the past, immigration came to the rescue. The lower net reproduction rates in cities are partly caused by restrictions against immigration after 1925. Although it appears that the government is considering allowing more immigration, the era of "large waves of immigration" has passed. Thus, cities must continue to look to rural and rural-nonfarm areas for their population replacements or take measures to stimulate self-replacement. Since the rural birth rates have shown a decline, it is expected that rural birth rates will parallel the urban in time. On the other hand, rural-nonfarm birth rates have risen.

It is necessary to make one major qualification about the general trend of American urban net reproduction rates. Table 24 shows the trend of rural and urban net reproduction rates since 1930. It can immediately be seen that there was a sharp increase in the urban net reproduction rates during and after the war years. The general trend is reflected in the rapid growth of the population of the United States, which reached 160 million on August 10, 1953, and which may reach 175 million by the time of the next census in 1960. This is an increase far beyond earlier estimates, and is largely made possible by the fact that urban net reproduction rates currently are above the level needed for replacement. There are some indications that there may have been a change in the American value system in regard to the number of children desired in a family. At least in large parts of the younger middle-class population, three, four, or more children are now the rule rather than the exception. It still remains to be seen whether or not the trend towards larger families is a stable one, but if the present level of living is not seriously curtailed, it is quite possible that earlier pessimistic views of the effects of urbanization on reproductive rates may prove invalid. Currently, there is a net increase of over two million per year, or one every thirteen seconds, a rate not only well above the world rate, but greater than that of India.[1]

Differential fertility based on race and nativity. If the urban population is differentiated on the basis of race and nativity, significant variations in fertility appear. Negro fertility is much lower than is commonly supposed.[2] Some factors have been referred to in earlier pages, *e.g.,* the unbalanced sex ratio and the high mortality rate. The urban Negro's net reproduction rate was slightly lower than that of the white in 1930 and on par with it by 1940. Even in the deep South, which in general had a higher fertility than the North, urban Negroes were reproducing themselves at a rate from 20 to 30 per cent below the rate necessary for replacement.[3] The urban Negro group must depend on rural migrants if it is to replace itself. The immigration of this group is small. In some parts of the country,

[1] "U. S. A.—1975–2000 A.D., Soaring Demands, Shrinking Resources," *Population Bulletin,* 9 (July 1953), 41.

[2] Smith, *op. cit.,* 211–216.

[3] National Resources Committee, *The Problems of a Changing Population* (Washington, D. C.: Government Printing Office, 1938), 134.

the reproduction rate of rural farm Negroes has fallen below the permanent replacement level.[1]

The trend of fertility among the foreign-born population of the country has paralleled that of other groups in that the birth rate has shown a definite lower tendency. In all classes of cities and in rural farm and rural-nonfarm territories, the decline of fertility has been apparent. The differences between the fertility of the native whites and that of the foreign-born, whether for urban or rural divisions, are narrowing. The great majority of the foreign-born persons are urban residents and are, therefore, subject to the social and economic influences which have tended to push the birth rates downward.

Urbanism then, appears to be the principal factor in the falling birth rate and is most marked among the largest race and residential class—the urban white population. Many factors may be included in support of the evidence, but of paramount importance is the cost of rearing children in an urban environment. Also important is the unwillingness of urbanites to forego pleasures and material comforts in favor of children. The individualism of the city person and the diminished control of traditional mores and religious beliefs are other factors. The percentage of childless couples is increasing and is a reminder of the greater freedom which urban women enjoy—of working outside the home and engaging in careers.

Mortality. No one knows the potential life span of the human organism, if illness and risk of accidental death could be discounted. It is quite plausible that some individuals are constitutionally stronger than others, but no limits can be set, and it is difficult to say whether populations taken as a whole show such differentials. Therefore, the most plausible explanation of differences in death rates is that much of the variation must be accounted for by differences in environmental conditions. Longevity is one of the basic values in most cultures, and differences in mortality reflect the way environmental and cultural differences permit the attainment of long life.

In general, American urban areas, except the South, are more favorable, regarding mortality, than rural areas for persons below thirty, and less favorable above this age group. In general, large cities are the most favorable in the lower age group, reflecting improved control of childhood diseases.[2] For the United States and other Western countries, mortality problems have become increasingly problems of adult illness, whereas for

[1] *Ibid.* Also see Smith, *op. cit.,* 216, who writes: "However, in the Delta cotton-plantation sections along the Mississippi River, where such a large share of the state's Negroes are concentrated, the white people who live on farms are reproducing much more rapidly than the Negro."

[2] D. G. Wiehl, "Mortality and Socio-environmental Factors," *Milbank Memorial Fund Quarterly,* 26 (Oct., 1948), 335–365.

Public health measures have almost wiped out some serious communicable diseases

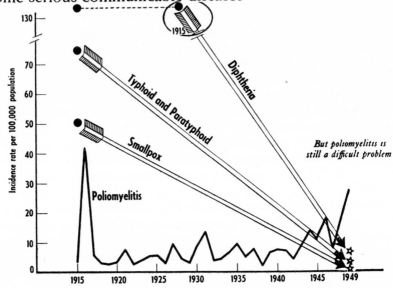

The effect of public health measures upon serious communicable diseases.[1]

underdeveloped areas the problem of infant and child mortality is still paramount.

The downward trend in death rates, both rural and urban, has resulted from the reduction of infant mortality rates and better medical and health services. The crude rate for the United States as a whole was 17.2 in 1900, 14.2 in 1920, and 11.5 by 1933. It was established at 10.8 for 1940 and 10.1 for 1947. In that year, there were 1,445,370 deaths from all causes. This, divided by the total population of the country, as of that date, gives the low rate of 10.1. It is still a moot question as to whether or not this rate can be further reduced. With the aging population and the restriction on immigration, the adult population has moved up the age-ladder to a point where high age-specific mortality rates prevail. Therefore, the over-all rate undoubtedly will increase in the not too distant future.

The infant mortality rate is one of the more significant rates. It is an age-specific rate, computed by comparing the death of infants below one year of age to the total number of births.

There is a close relationship between age and the mortality rate. The

[1] *Children and Youth at the Midcentury—A Chart Book*, prepared by the Midcentury White House Conference on Children and Youth (Raleigh, N. C.: Health Publications Institute, Inc., 1951).

hazards of life are great during infancy, but they decline precipitously to the ages of 10 to 12. The chances of dying during early adolescence are at a minimum, but the age-specific mortality rate begins to rise slowly about halfway through the teens. Thereafter, the trend is ever upward. At 55 or thereabouts, the rise in mortality rates is greatly accelerated.

Sex and mortality rates. Sex is closely linked to age-specific rates. Females of every age group have a lower death rate than the corresponding male groups. Even in the racial groups which show high death rates, the Negro and the Mongoloid, women outlive the men. This is true of urban, rural-nonfarm, and farm territories. It is estimated that on the whole, women live five years longer than men. An even greater difference can be expected for the urban females. It would appear that as women live longer, and this is especially true of married ones, wealth of the group will become more highly concentrated among the females in the older age brackets.

Death by specific causes. In 1947, the United States Bureau of the Census computed mortality rates by chief causes of death. One out of every three deaths was attributed to diseases of the heart.[1] Cancer and other malignant growths were the next great killers. Intracranial lesions of vascular origin were responsible for slightly less than 6 per cent of the fatalities. Nephritis ranked fourth and accounted for about 4 per cent of the total deaths within the course of a year. All four of these are called degenerative diseases and are especially prevalent among older persons. The four together accounted for 56 per cent of all deaths in the country.

Pneumonia and influenza have taken a lower position and are less deadly than even two decades ago, because of advances in controlling and preventing infectious diseases. The same applies to tuberculosis which has taken seventh place. Diabetes, premature birth, and motor-vehicle accidents follow in the order named. These ten leading categories together account for 78 per cent of all deaths in the country.

The above-named causes of death show variations when racial differences are compared. Those which affect the greatest toll among whites are heart disease, cancer, diabetes, and poliomyelitis. On the other hand, the non-whites have a higher proportion of death caused by nephritis, pneumonia, influenza, tuberculosis, premature births, syphilis, diarrhea, and cerebral meningitis. In fact, all childhood diseases, such as whooping cough, measles, rheumatic fever, and dysentery, take proportionally higher tolls of non-whites than whites. This is one indication that the benefits of urbanism have not yet had the same effect on the Negro population as

[1] Theodore D. Woolsey and Iwao M. Moriyama, *Statistical Studies of Heart Diseases, II. Important Factors in Heart Disease Mortality Trends,* Public Health Reports, 63, No. 39 (September 24, 1948), 1247–1273.

they have had on the whites. Not only are the rank orders of mortality causes different for Negroes, showing that the urban reduction of infectious diseases has not had its full impact, but the absolute death rates are also much higher. This applies even for those diseases which have a much lower position in the list of Negro causes of death.

Summary

American cities have been selected by various ethnic and racial groups for their habitats. The foreign-born and their descendants tend to concentrate in cities, while a high proportion of the native-born and their descendants are rural dwellers. Immigrants find wider occupational choices in urban centers. The Negroes constitute less than 10 per cent of the nation's total population and are still mainly in the southern part of the United States. Their migrations to northern, midwestern, and western cities were greatest during the two World Wars and the depression of the thirties. Sixty per cent of them are now urban. The various Mongoloid groups have become urban dwellers and reside in cities where occupational choices favor their settlement.

Urban centers have a deficiency of children under 15 years of age and of people 60 years and above, but have a large adult group between 20 to 60 years. It appears that the older age groups, 60 and above, are increasing in cities because of better health and welfare facilities.

The sex ratio favors males in rural areas, while the converse is true of urban areas. Metropolitan cities which specialize in heavy manufacturing, primary extracting industry, and port activities have an unbalanced sex ratio, whereas textile-milling centers, residential cities, and those engaged in distributive services run largely to females. The Negro sex ratio is unbalanced in favor of the females, due to (1) lower male sex ratio at birth, and (2) the higher death rate of adult male Negroes. Immigration can affect the sex ratio, as demonstrated by the exclusion of the Chinese female; the 1940 ratio was approximately 3 to 1.

The city affects the marital status of its population. More spinsters, widows, and divorced women are found in cities. There has been an increase in the number of widows included in the population as a whole, due to woman's longer span of life and the fact that women marry several years younger than do men. The Negro population includes excessively large percentages of widows in urban centers, and they attain widowhood earlier than white women. Divorced persons find residence in cities preferable to rural non-farm or rural territories. When divorce rates are correlated with urban occupations, the groups having the highest rates are commercial travellers, actors, musicians, physicians, and stenographers.

Birth rates are lower in cities than in rural areas, and the net reproduction rate of cities is inverse to the size of the city's population. If rural and rural-nonfarm territories do not maintain their excessive net reproduction rates, if immigration remains strictly curtailed, and if cities are called upon for population replacement, a decline of urban population will follow. However, if the post-war increase in the urban net reproductive rate is more than temporary, this may not now be a realistic view.

The nation's mortality rates have been considerably lowered due to preventive medicine and reduced infant mortality. The degenerative diseases taking a high toll of lives are: heart, cancer, and malignant tumors, nervous ailments, and nephritis. There is a difference in infant mortality rates by specific causes for the two major races, the white and Negro, since all of the childhood diseases take a proportionally higher toll of non-whites than whites.

DISCUSSION QUESTIONS

1. What social effects may follow if the sex ratio remains unbalanced in large cities? In small cities?
2. What are some of the social effects of an aging population?
3. Why are more old people living in cities than there were 50 years ago?
4. How can race affect the sex distribution of the city's population? Its marital rate?
5. What types of diseases affect urbanites more than rural persons?
6. What measures can be undertaken by the society to stimulate the rearing of larger families in cities?
7. If the rural birth rate falls below the urban, how can cities maintain their population structures?
8. Why do the descendants of the foreign-born show a lower marriage rate?
9. Why do some of the New England states show a higher percentage of foreign-born residents than the Southern states?
10. Why did the urban net reproduction rate fall below unity?

SUGGESTED PROJECTS

1. Study and compare the age structure of your city or local community for the last two census returns. Correlate the changes with nativity, education, and occupation.
2. Study the vital statistics for your city or local community, as to birth and death rates, for a given period and discuss the trends.
3. Write a paper on the social effects of an aging population.
4. Study the changes in the net reproduction rate for the United States for the past fifty years. Compare this with your city.
5. Write a paper on the extent of immigration and emigration into the United States since the turn of this century.

READINGS

E. W. Burgess and H. J. Locke, *The Family*. New York: American Book Co., 1950.
The social effects of mobility on the family is found in Part Four. Chapters on the Negro, rural, and urban family are in Part One.

M. J. Haygood, *Mothers of the South*. Chapel Hill: University of North Carolina Press, 1939.

A research study of the contraceptive and birth habits of a segment of southern mothers.

Bernard de Karpinos, "The Differential True Rates of Growth of the Whole Population of the United States and Their Probable Effects on the General Growth of the Population," *American Journal of Sociology,* Sept. 1938, 258–60.

J. B. Knox, *The People of Tennessee*. Knoxville: University of Tennessee Press, 1949.

A presentation of the social characteristics of the population of Tennessee.

C. A. McMahon, *The People of Atlanta*. Athens: University of Georgia Press, 1950.

A demographic study of the population of the capital city of Georgia.

Carey McWilliams, *Brothers Under the Skin*. Boston: Little, Brown & Co., 1943.

A general discussion of the problems confronting the various minority groups in this country.

Marion B. Smith "Social Aspects of Sex Distribution of the Aged Population," *Social Forces,* 26, Oct. 1947, 43–50.

T. Lynn Smith, *Population Analysis*. New York: McGraw-Hill Book Co., Inc., 1948.

A detailed analysis of the 1940 Census returns of the United States.

Chapter Nine

Ecological Organization

Ｏｎｅ ｏｆ the major fields of urban sociology is concerned with some of the underlying factors that affect the location, size, and integration of communities.[1] The focus of ecology is on the community as an aggregate of individuals or groups within a delimited space and the patterns of interrelations resulting from the adaptation of organisms to their environments. This definition does not especially refer to human communities, and it should be noted that the field of human ecology has largely grown out of the fields of animal and plant ecology. One evidence of this lies in the nature of the concepts employed and the analogies drawn between human and plant and human and animal communities.

Underlying the field of ecology is the Darwinian theory of the struggle for existence among different organisms for limited means of subsistence. At the same time, the very differences among organisms serve as the basis of integration in the community. As organisms become differentiated, they increasingly depend on each other for functions they can no longer perform for themselves. One of the most common misinterpretations of Darwinism has been disregard of these cooperative conditions. Symbiosis is just as important as the struggle for survival which has commonly been stressed.

Human Ecology

Perhaps the major distinction between human and non-human ecology lies in the restriction of human ecology to the study of differences among one given biological species, *homo sapiens.* Animal or plant ecology

[1] For a distinction between society and community, see R. E. Park and E. W. Burgess, *Introduction to the Science of Sociology* (Chicago: University of Chicago Press, 1937), 161–225. On 163, "Community is the term which is applied to societies and social groups where they are considered from the point of the geographic distribution of the individuals and institutions of which they are composed. It follows that every community is a society, but not every society is a community."

stresses the differences among species, although a form of interdependence may result as each specie struggles to survive. In the human ecological
scheme, homogeneous community groups may be regarded as being
analogous to different biological species in the formation of non-human
ecology. Yet we must always keep in mind the extent to which this is an
analogy. Human ecological relationships do not reflect genetic differences
between groups and individuals, but rather the degree to which man can
make adaptations to varying environmental conditions. In the case of
man, the ecological relationships form the base of an extremely complex
social and cultural structure, and it is the ability to create this socio-
cultural organization that makes man unique.

One of the major aspects of the cultural nature of man is technology.
Technology has given man a unique place in the total ecological order.
Man not only reacts to given environments, but is also a creator of environments. Moreover, human ecological patterns and processes largely take
place in environments which are man-made. This factor assumes its
greatest significance in studying man as an urbanite. Students of human
ecology, particularly in the United States, have concentrated on how the
ecological structure affects urban life. Most of our knowledge of human
ecology stems from the study of the internal spatial development and pattern of American cities. The testing of this knowledge and application of
it to cities elsewhere in the world is far from complete. The sparse data we
do have on foreign cities show that we cannot generalize from our findings
without major revision. At the same time, most American sociologists
would agree that the ecological analysis of the city and other social phenomena pertaining to urban life has yielded the best understanding of
the transformation of non-urban societies to the urban.

Natural areas. Cities include many local communities possessing distinct
characteristics. These communities are called "natural areas" to distinguish
them from their politically prescribed boundaries. Natural areas rarely
coincide with the precincts or wards but are characterized by a relatively
homogeneous population when compared to the greater diversity of the
city. Thus, the inhabitants of these local communities have similar socio-
economic or ethnic backgrounds, behavior patterns, values, and sentiments.

Since the term natural areas came into use more than three decades ago,
two definitions have gained acceptance: (1) the generic meaning, as used
by the late Robert E. Park and his associates at the University of Chicago,
and (2) the empirical definition, mainly derived from the testing and
application of the generic usage. Park's definition is as follows:

A region is called a "natural area" because it comes into existence without
design, and performs a function, though the function, as in the case of the

slum, may be contrary to anybody's desire. *It is a natural area because it has a natural history.*[1]

The empirical definition of natural areas is in current use:

Natural areas include all physically distinct territorial units regardless of whether such units were created or conditioned by human activities. Thus, natural areas have been recognized as unit parts of the physical structure of the city. In this sense, the natural area is an area of uniform physical type, bounded by elongated buildings, railroad tracks, arterial thoroughfares, or other similar features.[2]

It can readily be seen that in Park's definition, natural areas are the consequence of the relationship among groups of men.[3] Therefore, a body of customs and traditions and of organized attitudes and sentiments that inhere in these customs are accumulated and transmitted. In Hawley's definition, the physical area is defined and an investigation conducted to determine the characteristics of the population within it. Various indexes, such as median rent, nativity, occupation, education, and others, may be employed for verification.

It may so happen that the natural areas under consideration may have the same physical and social boundaries. "The right side of the tracks" as contrasted with the "wrong side of the tracks" is one example of a coincidence between the two definitions. However, each side of the tracks usually contains several distinct natural areas. These are apparent upon investigation and the degree and kind of interrelationships between each area is uncovered.

Competition for the most favorable location is the force operating to determine the settlement of a given population. In general, the competition is more intense as resources become scarcer. The different communities, in turn, are interdependent as the result of the complex and highly specialized division of labor which characterizes urbanism.

The typical urbanite is subject to many influences beyond those of his local community. The common stimuli provided by the communication media of a mass society are but some of the cross-pressures exerted. Yet the local community plays an extremely important part in shaping the lives of its inhabitants. It is within the confines of the community that much of the socialization and interaction with others occur and recur. Each area has distinct institutional and associational patterns. Frequently, the be-

[1] R. E. Park, *Human Communities* (Glencoe, Ill.: Free Press, 1952), 79 (Italics mine). "Natural" here is used in contrast to planning.

[2] A. H. Hawley, *Human Ecology* (New York: The Ronald Press Co., 1950), 81.

[3] R. E. Park, "The City: Suggestions for the Investigation of Human Behavior in the Urban Environment," *The City* (Chicago: University of Chicago Press, 1925), 113–122.

havior patterns and sentiments of the inhabitants vary extremely from the prevailing cultural norm, as exemplified by the "Bohemian" or "Skid Row" sections of very large cities.

It should not be assumed that the characteristics of given areas of the city remain constant. It has already been mentioned that the ecological organization is the result of various groups and persons seeking to attain a dynamic equilibrium. Cities are societies undergoing constant change, and the ecological processes are the symptoms of adaptations to over-all change. The characteristics of various areas throughout the city are likewise constantly changing as a part of this adaptation. That these transitions are not always without tension and conflict is evidenced by such phenomena as blighted areas and the resistance against the invasion of new inhabitants by the old residents.

Some areas may include stable communities of several generations. This is particularly true of European and other non-American cities. On the other hand, certain areas in American cities may undergo a complete change in one generation. In the latter case, the outward movement of the inhabitants affects the functions of the institutional and organizational patterns of the institutions that remain. For instance, as we shall see in the chapter on religious organization, churches frequently move along with the departed residents and relocate in a new community.

Symbiosis and Commensalism

It should not be inferred that the cooperative and competitive ecological relationships are necessarily conscious so far as their participants are concerned. The two basic ecological relationships, symbiosis and commensalism, have constituent cooperative and competitive elements and underlie human interaction in achieving dynamic equilibrium. However, groups that are ecologically interdependent at times may be in conscious conflict when this equilibrium is disturbed.

Symbiosis is a term used to denote the co-existence and interdependence of unlike groups and persons within a society.[1] This difference results from division of labor and is usually reflected in different functional positions found in a community. All the various groups depend on the same subsistence base and are therefore in competition for the rewards which that base provides. At the same time these groups are interdependent, insofar as one group's existence is related to the next by division of labor.

An example of a symbiotic relationship existing between two groups may be seen in labor-management relations. Although within a complex economic framework such as ours, these are interdependent and could not

[1] For a fuller discussion, see Hawley, *op. cit.,* Chs. 3 and 12.

function without one another, they are still in competition in terms of the rewards afforded by the common base of subsistence.

The term symbiosis has frequently been employed to indicate that a given relationship is mutually beneficial. It would appear to be in direct contrast to parasitism, a condition wherein one organism depends upon another without giving an adequate (or often tangible) return of services. This distinction is frequently difficult to draw, particularly if the over-all ecological intergration of a community or society is under consideration. Many relationships which may appear parasitical from the standpoint of the individuals or groups involved, contribute to the over-all integration of the community. In the final analysis, parasitism is usually a particular type of symbiotic relationship.

Commensalism literally means "to eat at the same table." It is a relationship among individuals or groups which are functionally alike. Whereas symbiosis may be seen as a relationship comparable to a "Gesellschaft" concept, commensalism is closer to a state of "Gemeinschaft," in that it is based on likeness, not diversity. This likeness acts as a social bond promoting collective action at the same time that it provides the basis for competition for attaining the same position. Symbiosis, on the other hand, is present when competition is present in seeking unlike positions. Given an insufficient subsistence base, commensalistic competition may become very severe. One of the functions of the organization of groups which are in a commensalistic relationship is to control this competitive aspect.

Both symbiotic and commensalistic relationships obtain in all communities and each person is drawn into a number of such relationships. However, the relative importance of each of these relationships varies among individuals and groups. Commensalism assumes its greatest significance among homogeneous groups wherein individuals have similar functions. To the extent that differences are emphasized, symbiosis assumes ever greater importance.

The spatial arrangement of populations, organizations, and buildings within cities is to a great extent the consequence of the fundamental ecological relationships of symbiosis and commensalism.

Internal Spatial Pattern

The typical city has a central business district, a manufacturing area, and a residential section. Several theories have been advanced by ecologists as explanations of the internal spatial pattern which has developed, recognizing at all times that the pattern can be disturbed by new land use, changing population structure, and socio-economic factors. By studying the land-use pattern of cities, some generalizations can be made as to the

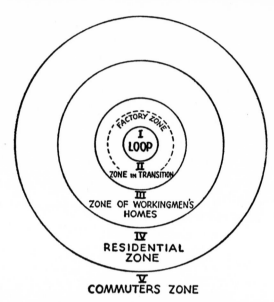

The Concentric Zone diagram of a city.[1]

formation of the ecological structure. The best known theories are the Concentric Zone Theory, the Sector Theory, and the Multi-Nuclear Theory.

Concentric Zone Theory. E. W. Burgess' Concentric Zone Theory is an *ideal abstract,* attempting to conceptualize the city as it grows. Its underlying thesis is that the internal development and expansion of the modern city can best be understood by the study of five concentric zones. Each zone tends to bear characteristics that distinguish it from the others. As population and institutional organizations encroach upon the next zone, settled groups move farther outward. Institutional organizations follow, or may precede population movements.

To interpret the pattern of city growth, Dr. Burgess states:

The typical processes of expansion of the city can best, perhaps, be illustrated by a series of concentric circles, which may be numbered to designate both the successive zones of urban extension and the types of areas differentiated in the process of expansion.

Every community as it grows expands outward from its center. This radial extension from the downtown business district toward the outskirts of the city is due partly to business and industrial pressure and partly to residential pulls. Business and light manufacturing, as they develop, push out from the center of the city and encroach upon residence. At the same time, families are always

[1] Ernest W. Burgess, "The Growth of the City," in Park, Burgess, and McKenzie, *The City* (Chicago: The University of Chicago Press, 1925), 51.

responding to the appeal of more attractive residential districts, further and further removed from the center of the city. . . . The main fact of expansion is the tendency of each inner zone to extend its area by the invasion of the next outer zone.[1]

The zones may be regarded as "ideal types" in that one need not expect that every city will conform exactly to this pattern. Interfering factors, such as peculiarities of topography, zoning ordinances, street plans, or subcenters, may alter this configuration. Chicago, which has frequently been used as an example of Burgess' theory, is prevented by Lake Michigan from assuming the full circular pattern.

The Central Business District. The first or inner zone found in every city is the main business district, the center of transportation and business activity. All streets and both pedestrian and commercial traffic converge at the core of the municipality. Here are found financial, retail, and business districts and the remnants of the wholesale establishments. Large theaters, hotels, office buildings, municipal buildings, downtown churches, and various commercial amusements congregate centrally. Land values are highest and large non-residential structures are erected to house business offices and stores. The district is never devoid of people, for as soon as the workers in skyscrapers turn homeward, the evening crowd of pleasure-seekers swarms into the theaters, restaurants, cafes, and gayly lighted night clubs. Except for transients, few people reside here.

The section within the district which attracts the greatest aggregation of persons is the retail shopping district, where shoppers seek the largest assortment of goods and services. A little beyond this is the financial district which performs specialized functions and need not cater to the convenience of a large number of persons. The wholesale district may lie adjacent to the financial, or it may be nearer the shopping center. Some light manufacturing establishments may also be interspersed among old residences and dilapidated structures. In this country the central business district occupies a relatively small proportion of the entire urban area, but attracts the largest daily influx of population. A large city like Chicago has over 800,000 persons who live within a radius of 80 miles, coming to the downtown area for work, recreation, shopping, or for other reasons.[2]

Zone in Transition. The next zone is a transitional area adjacent to the central business district and is a section which is being invaded by expanding business and light manufacturing. This pressure causes the flight of former residents to more desirable locations in order to escape noise

[1] *The City* by R. E. Park, *et al.,* University of Chicago Press. Copyright by the University of Chicago, 1925, 50.

[2] G. W. Breese, *The Daytime Population of the Central Business District of Chicago with Particular Reference to the Factor of Transportation* (Chicago: University of Chicago Press, 1949), 154–155.

and confusion, and subsequently causes the deterioration of housing. The customary controls of the community have diminished. Being neither a residential nor a business district, the facilities found are inadequate for one type of land use while overabundant for another. For example: if this were a strictly residential district, more playgrounds for children might be present. If it were a business district, playgrounds would be out of character with the neighborhood and would be unnecessary.

The zone of transition was once an area having the finest residences, housing well-to-do and prominent inhabitants. These have moved to newer residential areas such as the periphery, where they have found more suitable sites for constructing new dwellings. Their former palatial homes have been converted into light-housekeeping apartments, cheap hotels, or rooming houses. Rents may be cheap, while land values remain high. Owners are reluctant to improve the property because their ultimate expectation is to realize profit on the value of the land and not the structure above it. This zone typically attracts first-generation immigrants, migrants from rural areas and from other cities. Homeless men and women, social pariahs, and other unconventional individuals drift into this area.

Interspersed among residences are light industries, warehouses, stores, manufacturing plants, gambling houses, vice dens, and saloons. All may exist within the same block. The farther the transition zone stretches, the more dilapidated the district grows. In this area of physical and social disorganization are found the highest incidences of disease, bad housing, and poverty—accounting for the settlement houses, missions, social agencies, and police stations which are scattered throughout the zone.

Zone of Workingmen's Homes. The third is the zone to which more prosperous families and individuals from the zone of transition have moved. Its residents are (1) those who desire to live near but not too close to their work, and (2) those of the second immigrant settlement, or the second generation in this country who have moved from the area of transition. The latter may be the children of immigrants; their parents may have remained in the area with which they are most familiar.

The homes are generally two-flat dwellings of framed construction, with the owner living on the lower floor and the tenant above. If the immigrant parents have moved to Zone III, the father may work in the factory, while the son and daughter typically have jobs in the central business district, attend dance halls and motion pictures in the "bright-light" area, and plan upon marriage to set up homes in Zone IV.[1] Thus a pattern of social mobility has been established which is being emulated by the children. Resi-

[1] E. W. Burgess, "The Value of Sociological Community Studies for the Work of Social Agencies," *Social Forces*, 8 (June, 1930), 483.

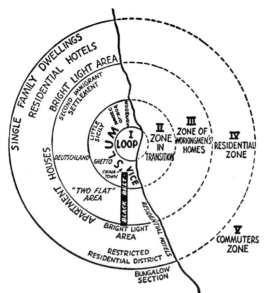

Park, Burgess, McKenzie, *The City,* page 55, by permission
of the University of Chicago Press

The urban areas in Chicago.

dence in Zone III may be regarded as a climb up the social ladder and a
part of the acculturation process. While Zone III falls short of the comforts
and luxuries which are offered in Zone IV or V, that the inhabitants enjoy a better economic status than do residents of Zone II is reflected in the
standard of living.

Zone of Residential Hotels and Apartments. Bordering the area of workingmen's homes is the area of the better residences, inhabited by the
professional people, small businessmen, clerks, salesmen, and business executives. The group is predominantly native white stock of a higher educational level than members of previously discussed zones. Most have had
high school educations, and college training is not uncommon. Women
may outnumber men, as many single business and professional women
reside in Zone IV. A greater degree of community organization is evidenced by women's clubs, churches, parent-teacher associations, teen-age
canteens, nursery schools, etc. All exert some influence over local problems.

Apartments and residential hotels of large and small units abound in
Zone IV, while the more fortunate live in detached houses with yards
and gardens. Home ownership is not typical, however. The "bright-light"
areas offer many amusements and recreational facilities.

This area is noted for its sophistication, *i.e.,* a group of services may be offered to residents under one roof, such as a drug store, beauty parlor, florist shop, gift shop, dry cleaning establishment, and liquor store. Large residential hotels are surrounded by subcenters for shopping and amusement.

Commuters' Zone. At the periphery of the city is the Commuters' Zone, comprising the suburban district and numerous incorporated and unincorporated areas. Rapid transit, railroads, busses, or automobiles connect the outlying areas with the metropolitan center for work, shopping, or entertainment. The residents live in an atmosphere that is the closest to that of the open country, with no sacrifice of urban comforts. Residence in suburban communities implies an economic rating superior to many living elsewhere. Here, most often the mother of the family remains at home, while the husband supports the group. Children of all ages may be found in many homes. Numerous facilities are geared to their welfare. The income of the families may be considerably above the city's median.

The Commuters' Zone arose as a result of the congested conditions of the city as population expanded and city living space became restricted. These urban dwellers, desiring to own their homes, live in a quieter atmosphere, and rear children, have moved to outlying areas. To those who can afford the expense and time to commute, this area proves ideal.

The zones together form the structure of the community. A structure presupposes differentiation, and cohesion is attained through the orderly arrangement of diverse population aggregates. How this came about is related to the ecological processes, the criteria for the dynamic movements of populations and institutional organizations.

Sector Theory. The Sector Theory has as its basic thesis that as a city grows, land close to the center of origin gains in value.[1] When a city is new, utility in land arises when the first buildings are erected, but land values do not increase until population and structures compete for superior locations. At first, even inferior locations may be used because ample room is available for selection. Gradually, land value around the point of origin becomes prohibitive for many activities. The value increases from the center outward, due to the pressure for space at the center and the fact that population and organizations vie for locations near the main axials of transportation.

Where several kinds of businesses compete for land—for example, department stores and hotels for the best downtown sites—land values skyrocket. Once a pattern has been established, adjacent areas along the sector increase in value. Thus, if a sector extending from the center to the periphery is used for low-cost land and housing, persons of low income will settle there. Conversely, if another sector is earmarked as the high-priced land,

[1] R. M. Hurd, *Principles of Land Values* (New York: Record and Guide, 1903 and his 1911 edition).

reserved for a fashionable residential district to accommodate families with high incomes, the entire sector will retain this characteristic. In general, the distribution of land values in cities is due to three causes. The increase in population and wealth causes the relocation and extension of the best residential sections. Changes in transportation such as the installation of surface, elevated, or underground transit, disrupt the internal arrangements of the city. New bridges, turnpikes, tunnels, ferries, and railroad lines bring the same results. Finally, changes in the cultural habits of the population affect land values and initiate population redistribution. For example: second generation Americans may desire to relocate away from the Zone of Transition and select the apartment hotel zone. This would cause a development of that area and redistribute population. Organizations tend to follow, and in time a new type of land use and land value is established.

The theory does not negate the effects of disperson of population upon land values because real estate speculation is often the underlying cause. If a study of land values from the beginning to the present stages of urban development were undertaken, many sectors will reveal a continuous process of evolution.[1] The first stage begins with the land values being comparatively unimportant. Gradually land increases in value and utility, and later decreases in value. This process of birth and decline may be repeated for the same sector.

Hoyt is one of the chief supporters of the Sector Theory. He postulates that urban growth takes place along the main transportation routes or along lines of least resistance to form a star-shaped city. By using empirical methods based on land use and land values, he states that growth along a particular axis usually consists of similar types of land use.[2] The entire city has various sectors radiating from the center. Similar patterns of land use originate near the center and extend toward the periphery. This is especially true of residential areas.

Multi-Nuclear Theory. A third theory is the Multi-Nuclear. In many cities the land-use pattern is built around several nuclei, rather than a single nucleus.[3] These discrete nuclei or centers may date back to the beginning of the municipality. Metropolitan London is a case in point. London and Westminster originated at separate points, separated by open country. One is the center of finance and commerce, the other of political life. In other instances, commercial, industrial, and retail nuclei developed as the

[1] Homer Hoyt, *One Hundred Years of Land Values in Chicago* (Chicago: University of Chicago Press, 1933).

[2] Homer Hoyt, *The Structure and Growth of Residential Neighborhoods in American Cities* (Washington, D. C.: Government Printing Office, 1939).

[3] C. D. Harris and L. Ullman, "The Nature of Cities," *The Annals of the American Academy of Political and Social Science*, 242 (Nov., 1945), 7–17.

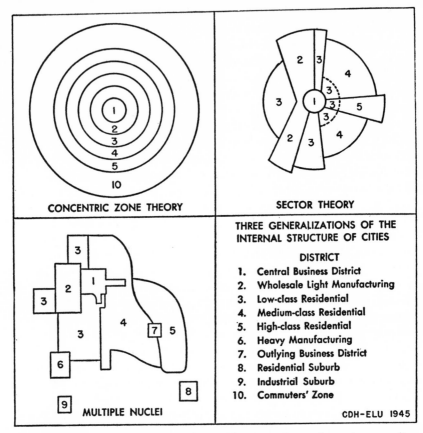

Generalizations of internal structure of cities. The concentric-zone threory is a generaliza-
tion for all cities. The arrangement of the sector theory varies from city to city. The diagram
for multiple nuclei represents one possible pattern among innumerable variations.[1]

growth of the city promoted specialization and decentralization. Most
metropolitan cities in this country follow the second pattern, having
several major and minor nuclei scattered throughout. The rise of separate
and differentiated subcenters reflects a combination of the following four
factors:

1) Certain activities require specialized facilities. The retail district is
located at the point of greatest intra-city accessibility. Likewise, a port
district is nearest the water front. A manufacturing section is located near
the largest grouping of land, water, rail, or air connections and represents
a major nuclear development. The major retail district of any city is
located where intra-city and interurban transits converge.

[1] By permission from the *Annals of the American Academy of Political and Social Science,* 242 (Nov., 1945), 13, in C. D. Harris and E. L. Ullman, "The Nature of Cities."

2) Certain like activities group together because they profit from proximity. For example, in department stores the concentration of potential customers has the opportunity for comparison shopping. Large department stores are usually clustered together. (In China, jade stores occupy one major section, and the same is true of goldsmiths, tinsmiths, and retailers and wholesalers of teak furniture and embroidery.) The only exceptions are service establishments such as grocery stores, dry cleaners, and gasoline stations. These are found in all neighborhoods so as to service customers conveniently and represent minor nuclear developments.

3) Certain unlike activities are detrimental to each other's development. Factories prevent the development of high-class residential sections. Zoning laws are passed and enforced to restrict the establishment of antagonistic activities. Wholesale districts locate where few pedestrians, vehicles, and traffic obstacles are found. Many are located along the belt of railroad trunklines and warehouses.

Criticisms of the theories of urban growth. The very existence of alternative theories, each with supporting evidence, would in itself raise questions as to the ultimate validity of any one theory. The problem is one of adequate description of actual city patterns, and also of adequate accounting for the underlying factors which determine growth patterns.

Much of the validation of the Burgess hypothesis has been in terms of *gradients* of particular phenomena from the center. In terms of this concept, indexes of such phenomena as crime and family disintegration [1] have been observed to vary with the distance from the center. But if these changes are just matters of distance, then the delimitation of zones is arbitrary, and there can be any number of zones. Since Burgess and Hoyt in their formulations see the city divided into homogeneous zones or sectors, with distinct breaks between the natural areas, this would actually seem to be contradictory.[2]

Davie, in a detailed investigation of the characteristics of New Haven [3] found 22 distinct areas. None of the characteristics of these areas fell into a concentric zone pattern. A survey of other studies, and of the zoning maps of twenty American and Canadian cities, led Davie to conclude that the Burgess zonal hypothesis is not universally applicable. He concluded that all cities show:

(1) a central business district, irregular in size but more square or rectangular than circular, (2) commercial land use extending out the radial streets and

[1] Cf. E. R. Mowrer, "The Trend and Ecology of Family Disintegration in Chicago," *American Sociological Review,* 3 (June 1938), 344–353, and C. R. Shaw, "Correlation of Rate of Juvenile Delinquency with Certain Indices of Community Organization and Disorganization," American Sociological Society, *Publications,* 22 (1928), 174–179.

[2] M. A. Alihan, *Social Ecology* (New York: Columbia University Press, 1938), 225.

[3] M. R. Davie, "The Patterns of Urban Growth," in G. P. Murdock (ed.) *Studies in the Science of Society* (New Haven: Yale University Press, 1937).

concentrating at certain strategic points to form sub-centers, (3) industry located near the means of transportation by water or rail, wherever in the city this may be, and it may be anywhere, (4) low-grade housing near the industrial and transportation areas, and (5) second- and first-class housing anywhere else.[1]

Firey, in his study of Boston, also found sharply contrasting areas adjacent to each other. In particular, he found that sentiment and symbolism operated to help certain areas resist the normally expectable inroads of urban growth. The upper-class areas of Beacon Hill and the Commons have kept their residential characteristics as areas with particular symbolic prestige value. Firey further noted that similar pressures also operated in ethnic slum areas.[2] Although the "rational" consideration of better housing for higher income might be expected to be a pressure for outward movement, this does not take into account the social relationships and values which have been established within the area, and which would be disrupted by moving away. Firey found that younger Italians, who had adopted new values were likely to move, but that the older Italians tended to stay in an area which was characterized by markedly different value-systems.

These considerations make it appear that the theories of Burgess and Hoyt must be modified and recognition given to the invalidations. In particular, one should not expect any one of these theories to account for the distribution of all urban phenomena. It is much more likely that certain restricted phenomena would be found to fit best under particular theories. For example, the distribution of wholesale trade might best be described in terms of concentric zones, certain residential areas may assume characteristics of the Sector Theory; whereas some industrial and retail subcenters might be expected to be characteristic of the multiple-nuclear theory. As has been stated in earlier chapters, the spatial patterns of many Asian and African cities differ from the American.

Ecological Processes

The city is conceived of by human ecologists as constantly reaching toward equilibrium, not as a static phenomenon. Five basic processes affect the formation of the spatial pattern. They are concentration, centralization, segregation, invasion, and succession.

Concentration. Concentration is the tendency of human beings and human utilities to mass in areas where nature or man has made conditions

---

[1] *Ibid.*, 159. Permission granted.

[2] W. Firey, "Sentiment and Symbolism as Ecological Variables," *American Sociological Review*, 10 (April 1945), 140–148.

favorable to the satisfaction of sustenance needs.[1] Formerly, the limits of concentration were restricted by the local food supply. Modern industrialism has created new regions of concentrations, the limits of which are determined by their dominance over commerce and industry. Moreover, transportation and communication are vital factors in insuring their strategic importance. Thus, modern concentrations of population and organizations are more dynamic and unpredictable.

Modern concentrations are not the result of natural population increase alone, but represent the shifting of population from one territory to another. A change in population density inevitably affects the spatial distribution of the area. When too great a density occurs, dispersion tends to follow.

Dispersion is the opposite of the process of concentration, since it refers to the loss or outward movement of a population. Dispersion occurs when areas become overcrowded during periods of urban growth, or when resources are inadequate for the population in the given area. Technological changes, or the presence of more attractive work opportunities, may also cause dispersion in one area while concentration occurs in another.

Centralization. Centralization is the clustering of the productive, distributive, and service functions of a city. Although centralization may be at times correlated with concentration, it is a distinct process in that it refers to the clustering not of people but of certain functions. The central business district is the area of highest centralization, while outlying nuclei represent the dispersal of these functions to accommodate the persons who find access to the center of the city difficult or time consuming.

Centralization shows the tendency of human beings to come together at the points where transportation and other facilities converge for specific activities: work, play, business transactions, education, shopping, or cultural entertainment. Queen and Thomas define centralization as the "drawing together of institutions and activities," *i.e.,* the assembling of people to work rather than to reside in a given area.[2] Typically, the downtown or outlying business, manufacturing, or distributive districts nightly are devoid of a large portion of their daytime populations.

In a modern city, the main focal point for centralization is the central business district. Every American city has its Main Street, the area of highest land values, and the locus of transportation and communication. When the central business district has outgrown its capacity to serve a large number of people, and an aggregation of people retards rather than facilitates activity, organizations decentralize, and new centers emerge to

[1] R. D. McKenzie, "The Scope of Human Ecology," in E. W. Burgess (ed.), *The Urban Community* (Chicago: University of Chicago Press, 1926).

[2] S. A. Queen and L. F. Thomas, *The City* (New York: McGraw-Hill Book Co., Inc., 1939), 262.

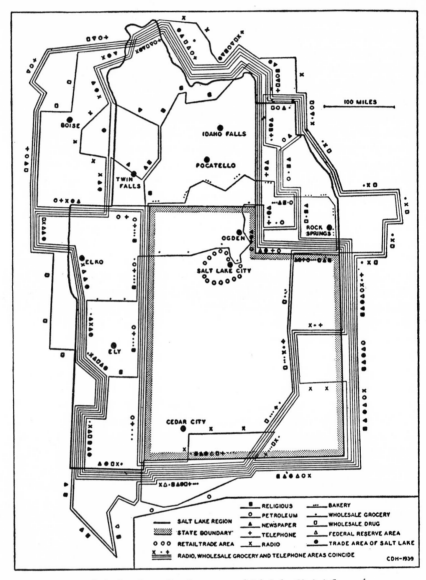

Boundaries based on selected measures of Salt Lake City's influence.[1]

[1] From Chauncy D. Harris, *Salt Lake City: A Regional Capital* (Chicago: University of Chicago Press, 1940), Fig. 10. Used by permission of the author.

satisfy specific interests and activities. These are known as subcenters. The larger the city, the more subnuclear districts are formed, each becoming the retail center of a local community. They draw the appropriate age, sex, cultural, and economic groups.

Centralization and the movement of people. The distribution of retail activities within a city gives an understanding of the function which the central business district plays in relation to the remainder of the community. Residents of a city tend to travel to the central zone to buy certain specialized commodities. The drawing power of this area is indicated by the distances consumers travel to do specialized shopping and has dominance over the entire city and adjacent territories. It is equally probable that subcenters have a similar drawing power, although of a lesser degree. Many persons travel there for their shopping needs. The same applies to neighborhood shopping centers. A study of the shopping habits of approximately 2,000 families living in a middle-class residential district of Seattle disclosed that about 90 per cent purchased their groceries; 50 per cent, their hardware; and 70 per cent, their drugs from the neighborhood stores. Only a small percentage purchased their furniture and clothes locally. For leisure-time activities, a much higher percentage attended local—rather than downtown—establishments, but the opposite was true of the patronage at moving-picture theaters.[1] Standardization of commodities, both in quality and in price, minimizes the element of choice. The result is that all primary standardized services (drug and grocery stores, soft-drink parlors, dry cleaning establishments) are very widely distributed. The more specialized services tend to become more and more highly centralized.

The highly centralized and specialized services bring the largest number of persons to the downtown district. An ebb and flow of population during the different hours of the day furnishes clues as to the types of services needed by the working, the shopping, or the amusement-seeking crowd. These crowds vary in size and intensity, but all move to a focal point for the satisfaction of certain needs or the performance of certain responsibilities and duties. Banks, brokerage houses, legal firms, commission merchants, and wholesalers are quite constantly found near the heart of the city. Some of the light manufacturing industries tend to be drawn toward the center of a city and to remain there after other functions have decentralized to the periphery. Clothing and millinery manufacture and job printing require relatively little ground space per worker. These businesses can operate on small scales, utilize old buildings, be near the retail market and out-of-town buyers, and have access to the source of labor supply.

[1] McKenzie, *op. cit.,* 179.

Time and service, being important, tend to force them to stay close to the central business district.

Decentralization. Decentralization is the term used to characterize the tendency of human beings and organizations to move away from the center of the city and locate on the outskirts. This causes an expansion of the city at the periphery, where land values are lower and space is available. Rapid motor transportation and electric power are accelerating the process, but decentralization is but one phase of the centralization process. The tendency for areas of main centralization to decrease in size while the population increases in number has caused a multiplication of centers, each varying in relative importance. Recentralization occurs at these points.

When referring to population dispersion, a general direction in which persons change their residences is noted. As early as 1899, the tendency was under way for the central zones of cities to decrease in population. The shifts of population may involve (1) considerable milling within a zone, (2) changing residences within a zone, or (3) the invasion of zones distant from the site of former residence. Nor is it uncommon for those at the periphery to relocate within the zone near the central business district. Thus, upon close analysis, both centrifugal and centripetal movements may appear.

Institutional organizations, likewise, show tendencies to decentralize to other zones. Often this precedes population dispersion. The sequence may also be reversed, but decentralization and dispersion are often closely allied in their movements. As population shifts outward, subcenters are formed to serve the needs of the local residents. Specialized religious, commercial, industrial, and recreational organizations may shift to locations more favorable for the type of functions and services they have to perform. If starting anew, they may locate in areas considerably removed from their former sites.

Industrial decentralization. Industrial decentralization occurs in cities where land values are high, transportation facilities become overstrained, and taxes increase. Several other reasons may precipitate the move, *e.g.,* the expansion of an industrial plant requiring larger floor space; utilization of a new form of transportation for raw materials or finished products—a change to the use of trucks instead of railroads—or the removal of the production end of a plant. In the latter case, the control of marketing and purchasing remains at the center zone. The increased use of mechanized methods of communication, telephone, wire, or postal service, forestalls any interruption of the production or the disposal of commodities. New industries, in seeking choice sites, may also locate at the periphery of cities. They may be forced to choose certain sites because the zoning laws forbid the construction of certain types of industrial establishments.

The centrifugal pull is not the same for all types of industry. For example, one of the most comprehensive reports available concerning the century-long movement of industry is to be found in the study of Chicago.[1] The area which is now the central business district was within the city limits in 1850, when the population was 30,000. With the continued expansion of the city the more important manufacturing developments decentralized where the natural advantages, such as rivers, trunk lines of railroads, or the lake front, afforded convenient outlets for raw materials and the marketing of commodities.

Major industrial areas developed in the South Chicago and Calumet Districts. The latter's remarkable growth is indicated by the fact that the commerce of the Calumet River, which had been only one-tenth of that of the Chicago River at the end of the last century, has steadily climbed. Commerce on the Calumet now amounts to five times more than that on the Chicago River. Iron, steel, cement, railroad equipment, beds, chemicals, musical instruments, spirits, oils, and food products are all manufactured in the Calumet District. Another area of rapid industrial expansion is along the northern branch of the Chicago River about three miles from the "Loop." A total of ten important districts of heavy manufacturing exist throughout the city. These centers contain hundreds of industries. The Central Manufacturing District, about five miles north and west of the Loop, has 305 industries. The Clearing Industrial District, ten miles southwest, has over 100 industries. The Healy Industrial District, the Kenwood Manufacturing District, and six others show a similar development.

Heavy manufacturing industries in most cities are more highly decentralized than light manufacturing.[2] One or all of these seven factors may operate as motivating forces in decentralization: (1) comparatively large size of industry; (2) time or service factor unimportant; (3) large ground area per person required; (4) nuisance features frequently present —odors, noise, fire hazards, smoke, etc.; (5) specialized building required; (6) large quantities of fuel or water required; and (7) serious problem of waste disposal. Meat-packing plants, petroleum-refineries, smelteries, automobile manufacturing and assembly plants, sugar-refineries, lumber and flour mills and other industries are often located on the outskirts of many cities in this country.

Commercial decentralization. A second type of decentralization is that of subcenters. The trend toward the creation of these nuclei inside and outside has been pronounced since cities expanded in area and population grew. The volume of trade transacted has mounted annually and sub-

[1] Homer Hoyt, *op. cit.* and Jules Karlin, *Chicago: Backgrounds of Education* (Chicago: Werkman's Book House, 1940), 129–142.

[2] N. P. Gist and L. A. Halbert, *Urban Society* (New York: Thomas Y. Crowell Co., 1948), 122.

centers compete with the central one in this respect. Shoppers are drawn from a wide area and many downtown stores have moved outward.

In general, the location of commercial establishments depends upon the physical site, relation to foreign areas, historical inertia, and internal processes of adjustment.[1] The physical site determines the degree of accessibility of commercial establishments. Subcenters exhibit the same phenomenon as the central shopping center, in that major transportation routes traverse the area or converge at major points. Stores catering to a large clientele locate where population congregates. The commercial establishments must not compete too severely with those in foreign areas, whether adjacent or distant. That is, the presence of like establishments situated too close together would prove disadvantageous for both. A large hardware store may face a loss of customers if a similar one existed within the same district. Inertia is seen when establishments tend to locate in ready-made conditions. The planning and layout of streets, transportation, and public utilities enforce the inertia pattern. Unless a new community is planned, establishments locate where the expense can be reduced to a minimum. Moreover, residents seek familiar locations, thus reinforcing the inertia. Therefore, certain sites are reserved for business, many for residences, and some for parking lots, schools, churches, etc.

Subcenters, scattered throughout the outlying suburban communities and neighborhoods within the city, have mainly retail establishments. A sufficient number of branch wholesale distributors are there to provide goods on short notice. The stores are strung along the important streets, but in a new planned community may form a configuration that occupies a specified area. Subcenters are influenced by the economic status of the surrounding residents. The size and character may differ in various parts of the city. This is more clearly seen in a large metropolitan community. Rolph's study of Baltimore showed that subcenters could be classified into five types.[2]

Type A is capable of meeting the entire needs of the community, is typically located in medium-income neighborhoods where space is at a premium and the shopping area is restricted in size. The diversified services are supplied, but few demands are made for luxury-goods and "high style" clothing. The opposite extreme is characterized by Type E, selling low-cost, standardized goods in smaller quantities, and diversification is not pronounced. The residents are of the lower-income levels, and their tastes and limited purchasing power are reflected by the commercial establishments. Midway between the two extremes are those which have both

[1] J. E. Quinn, *Human Ecology* (New York: Prentice Hall, Inc., 1950), Ch. 5.
[2] *Ibid.*, 81–82.

types of establishments, the diversified and the limited, showing the changing population composition of the neighborhood. In time, an entire community may shift to either the lower-income or the middle-income level. A fourth type is one that is changing from a higher-income level to a medium-income. The centers catering to the higher-income groups have small and undiversified services, as residents make many purchases in the specialized downtown shops. Their patronage in luxury-goods establishments and large department stores supersede that of the neighborhood. Convenient credit transactions and charge accounts facilitate the purchasing of newer merchandise. Close budgeting is not as paramount, and buying items in larger quantities is easier.

Population dispersion. Rapid forms of urban and interurban transit have led to an exodus from the city to the suburbs and created the metropolitan districts. Strings of suburban communities form almost a continuous settlement along a number of radial transportation routes, giving the arrangement the appearance of an organism with great tentacles stretching outward into the open country. The intervening land is built up as more population settles. A suburb or satellite may be annexed by the city if the residents so desire. Sometimes suburban residents are forced to allow annexation in order to insure a continuance of essential utilities and services. Often the necessity to have a sufficient water supply, a good public school system, or police protection has caused annexation.

For more than three decades the rate of population increase of the incorporated and unincorporated areas adjacent and contiguous to central cities has been more rapid than that of the cities themselves. The trend is greatest for areas surrounding metropolitan cities because land area for expansion within the city is limited. This is true of smaller cities on a reduced scale. Beyond the incorporated limits of large or small cities, thousands of persons are literally part and parcel of the main city in all but residence.

Segregation. The word segregation is used with reference to the concentration of specific types of population or institutional organizations within a given area. Social and economic principles operate in forming the ghettos, the hotel or banking districts, and the "Gold Coast." Every area of segregation is the result of selective forces operating to sift persons and institutional organizations. Economic segregation is the primary and most general form of allocation of populations to their respective areas. Other factors such as race, culture, or ethnic origin may operate simultaneously. When organizations congregate and form a segregated group, allied or like services are primary in effecting the formation. That is, Wall Street is close to insurance and commercial brokers, trust companies, and stock exchange. Automobile rows result from like establishments seeking to dominate an area as well as to facilitate comparison shopping. Repeated land use is also associated with segregation.

By far the most common type of human segregation is that of various racial and ethnic groups. In the American urban society, some minority and immigrant groups are found at the points of least resistance, or the low rent areas near the central business district of the city. The immigrants create communities to perpetuate their languages, customs, and cultures. As soon as each group becomes acculturated, it moves outward and a newer immigrant group follows and occupies the area. The larger the city, the more polyglot and heterogeneous are the segregated ethnic communities. Chicago, as an illustration, was once said to be the second most European city in America. Only two cities in Poland had more Poles than Chicago, and but two cities in Ireland had more Irish. Other cities noted for their great ethnic and racial variety are New Bedford, Massachusetts having the largest Portuguese colony (35,000) in this country. New York has the biggest Italian, Jewish, and Negro colonies, while San Francisco is noted for its Chinatown and Little Italy.

Voluntary and involuntary segregation. Immigrants bring with them certain habits, customs, traditions, ideals, interests, and a sense of moral worth which may differ from the prevailing society. Their languages, dress, and social rituals may be strange. By forming groups where the strangeness is minimized and appears natural, the immigrants find protection and aid to meet life's crises in a new environment. Those of European stock find ways and means of escaping the ghetto walls by settling farther and farther away from the colonies of first immigration. Particularly is this true of the children of foreign-born whites who in time find their places in the social and occupational hierarchy of the dominant society. Their segregation, while voluntary in the beginning, may become involuntary after acculturation is achieved. Segregation becomes involuntary when opportunities for breaking down the ghetto walls are restricted by the larger society. Some may return to find expression and to act as go-betweens between the larger society and the ghetto.

However, where racial attributes limit opportunities for a rise in the occupational and social hierarchy, segregation is often involuntary. The desire to escape is hindered by discernible physical attributes, and the possession of a different cultural heritage imposes greater barriers. Chinatowns, Tokyos, and Black Belts do not disappear at the same rate as European ghettos. Often, persons who have encountered repeated rebuffs from the larger society maintain "tourist-attracting" establishments drawing visitors to the ghettos. These also build up their own social hierarchies to designate a social stratification within the group, thereby avoiding competition with members of the dominant society.[1] Restrictive covenants reinforce involuntary segregation, although Supreme Court decisions in 1948 and 1953 have declared such covenants legally unenforceable. In time, the ghettos for persons with racial differences appear "natural," as the habitat of "those who belong there."

Invasion. Invasion occurs when a new type of people, institutional organization, or activity centers in an area previously occupied by a different type, resulting in group displacement or a change in land-use patterns. When new population or organizations penetrate into a segregated area— a universal process in city growth and expansion—a change in the competitive relationship results between the existing population and organizations. In the historic sense, the process of invasion implies the displacement of a higher cultural group by a lower one, and perhaps is a more common process in the local community. The invasion of a higher economic group into a lower economic area is not uncommon. While less frequent, it is a form of population displacement. When the invasion cycle is completed and the complexion of the original neighborhood is altered to the point where it is no longer recognized by its former population, the sociologist calls the result succession.

Invasion may be of two kinds: (1) the movement of one type of population into an area occupied by another type, known as residential invasion, and (2) the movement of commercial or industrial organizations into areas that have previously been used for different purposes, known as institutional invasion. Either may occur without the other, but the two may happen concurrently. Or, industrial invasion may precede residential invasion, and vice versa. If a group of steel manufacturing industries invade a sparsely settled suburb where zoning laws do not prohibit their operation, workers employed by the new enterprise will locate nearby in order to be close to their work. Former residents may move to escape the noise, dirt, soot, and, perhaps, the new residents. In time the community possesses characteristics befitting a steel manufacturing, industrial suburb. The amount of time entailed in the transformation of the community is dependent upon a number of factors such as general resistance or non-resistance of former inhabitants, amount of available housing, and facilities for families. Families may move there, find it undesirable, and leave. A considerable amount of time may elapse between the initial invasion and the end of the cycle.

General movements of people. In almost every city, invasion and displacement of population occur. With the expansion of the central business district, the invasion of light industry into the next zone, and the influx of

---

[1] St. Clair Drake and H. R. Cayton, *Black Metropolis* (New York: Harcourt, Brace and Company, 1945), Chs. 18–23.

workers and transients, the original occupants, overwhelmed by the intrusion of the newcomers and disdaining residence among industrial establishments, begin their movement to areas of greater residential desirability.

In a study of the historical differentiation and succession of land use in Boston, Firey disclosed that the early years of the city's history had but a rudimentary spatial differentiation. The arrival of new and more "class-conscious groups" caused a change in the areas selected for settlement.[1] The presence of the English governor, his officials and assistants, and shrewd entrepreneurs seeking wealth and prominence, began the process of economic and industrial differentiation. A number of fashionable families located near the governor's mansion. Clark's Square became the social center of the city for well-to-do English families. Other prominent families located toward the North End, now Washington and Tremont Streets, and at Pemberton Square. The area below this was said to be "so near the extreme south end of the town as to be socially out of this world."

In the middle of the 1700's, there was a definite shift of the preferred residential district's population from the western to the southern part of the city, where three fashionable dwelling areas were developed. Lower-class residents occupied the back streets and the interstitial or slum areas. After the Revolution the fashionable homes in the North End became deserted when the invasion began by skilled workers and entrepreneurs in small business. Simultaneously an invasion was underway at the water front district. Sailors and transients frequented the "shady" places established for them and drove out all but a few of the substantial families by 1840. Over the course of time, the North End district became a definitely low-class district. When the Irish invaded the area in the 1850's, it became an immigrant community.

Like Boston, other American metropolises have experienced the centrifugal movement of population that is associated with the increase in income and with the assimilation of immigrants into the prevailing culture. Each change means new adjustments for the old and for the invading residents. Cressey used an ingenious method to measure the modification of distance among ethnic and racial groups in Chicago.[2] By computing the median distance from the center of the city of nine specific population groups in 1898 and again in 1930, he compared the extent of the centrifugal movement of each (Table 24). Since it is generally known that North European ethnic groups are more thoroughly assimilated than those from Southern Europe, the distance a given group lived from the

[1] W. Firey, *Land Use in Central Boston* (Cambridge: Harvard University Press, 1947), 42–56.

[2] Paul F. Cressey, "Population Succession in Chicago, 1898–1930," *American Journal of Sociology*, 44 (July, 1938), 59–69.

TABLE 24. MEDIAN DISTANCE IN MILES FROM
THE CENTER OF CITY OF NINE RACIAL OR
NATIONALITY GROUPS IN CHICAGO,
1898 AND 1930 [1]

Racial or Nationality Group	1898	1930
Swedes	3.9	7.0
Old American Stock (white)	4.7	6.6
Irish	3.2	6.4
Germans	3.2	5.7
Czechoslovaks	2.7	5.3
Russians	1.6	4.8
Poles	2.8	4.6
Negroes	2.5	4.5
Italians	1.5	3.3

[1] *Source:* Reproduced with permission from the University of Chicago Press, from Paul F. Cressey, "Population Succession in Chicago, 1898–1930," *American Journal of Sociology,* 44 (July, 1938), 59–69.

center of the city in 1930 was a fairly good index of the degree of the group's assimilation process.

A subsequent study showed that the foreign-born of each group eventually moved radially from the first area of settlement.[1] The groups having the longest settlement went the farthest. Each ten-year period showed an orderly movement of population from the center outward. Between 1930 and 1940, the dislocation was slight because the construction of new homes was infrequent, and the average income was low. The two groups exhibiting the greatest dispersion were the Swedish and Irish, two of the earlier immigrant groups. The persons of German and Austrian descent were approaching the same tendency. The Italians and Russians had less marked dispersion because their settlement came later.

Institutional invasion. Invasion of an area is often more than an influx of individuals or groups. Establishments and organizations catering to the needs of the group follow, and these, in the final analysis, distinguish one community from another. The more divergent the cultural heritage of the group is, the greater the difference in social institutions. A Chinese settlement soon establishes some familial and clan associations for extending aid to the foreign-born aged, ill, and infirm. All persons bearing like surnames can find assistance during a crisis. There are usually language schools and foreign newspapers if the community is sufficiently

[1] R. C. Ford, "Population Succession in Chicago," *American Journal of Sociology,* 56 (Sept., 1950), 156–160.

large to support them. There are general merchandise stores, selling special imported foods, herbs, and paper effigies for religious and Old World festivals. A temple for the inhabitants is usually the first and foremost building to be erected, with the guardian of the temple occupying one of the most revered and respected positions in the community.

Commercial organizations often invade the areas surrounding the central business district in a growing city. Land intended for residential or storage purposes may be put to other uses. In short, as commerce makes further inroads, residents move. Soon commercial activities dominate the area as for example, parking lots. Contributing to the flight of old residents are traffic bottlenecks, high rents, and high taxes.

Factors initiating invasion. The displacement of population in an urban society is complex, but it is reasonable to assume that the struggle for a more advantageous position is a basic factor, although other contributing factors may be equally as effective. Cressey mentions ten possible factors for population invasion: (1) desire for increased social prestige, (2) pressure of wife and children, (3) increased economic resources, (4) desire for better living conditions, (5) activity of real estate agents, (6) desire for home ownership, (7) pressure of vacant homes, (8) changes in transportation facilities, (9) desire to be near one's place of employment or place where employment is sought, and (10) movement of industrial areas.[1]

Another set of factors has been offered by another student of ecology for both population and institutional invasion, and include: (1) change in the size of the population aggregate in the community, (2) change in the racial or ethnic composition of the population, (3) development of a status hierarchy within the minority group, (4) commercial or industrial changes that affect the relative economic status of different groups in the community, (5) residential displacement in other areas, (6) taking over of residential property for business or recreational uses, (7) obsolescence of neighborhoods, (8) establishment of large factories, and (9) the consequent creation of employment in suburban areas.[2]

Successive invasions in a single area. In the Zone in Transition, a continuous succession of ethnic groups may be found. Known as the area of first immigrant settlement, each new ethnic group was segregated into the low-rent areas during the period of adjustment to the new world environment. After each invasion, another group replaces it.

The rate or speed of displacement is by no means uniform in any part of the city, nor is there a set limit to the time involved in the processes of invasion and succession for any given group. The process tends to be ac-

[1] Paul F. Cressey, "The Succession of Cultural Groups in the City of Chicago," (Unpublished Ph.D. dissertation, University of Chicago, 1930).

[2] Harold Gibbard, "Residential Succession, A Study in Human Ecology," (Unpublished Ph.D. dissertation, University of Michigan, 1938).

celerated whenever deep-seated prejudices and hostility are already manifested. Groups possessing readily visible racial characteristics may invoke violent reactions and hasten the ingress and egress of older inhabitants. When they settle in a neighborhood, succession is more rapid than where dissimilar ethnic and cultural traits are the main barriers. In this instance, the cycle is prolonged and resistance may be stubborn.

There is no definite pattern as to where the displaced group resettles. It may be in contiguous territory close to the original site of first settlement, or in a more distant locale. The latter is more common, as the contiguous territory may already be occupied by another group, or groups, and an entirely new site is sought. Students of the city have observed the tendency of certain immigrant and cultural groups to establish second- or third-generation settlements, each spatially removed from the area occupied by the original members of the group. It may be due to their desire to escape the stigma of being considered "foreign." It is evidence of the economic and social differentiation within the group, resulting from occupational and social mobility.

Stages of invasion-succession cycle. Several students of ecology have made attempts to identify the different stages in the invasion-succession cycle. Burgess has listed four stages: the initial movement into the area, the reaction on the part of the occupants, the general influx of newcomers, and the climax or period of complete displacement. McKenzie limits the stages to three: (1) the initial stage, (2) the development or secondary stage, and (3) the climax.[1] Gibbard concluded from his study of Detroit that the invasion cycle had five stages: (1) invasion, (2) resistance, (3) exodus, (4) reintegration of the area, and (5) re-equilibrium.[2] He does point out, however, that not all residential invasions complete the five stages and that his schematic presentation is more ideal than actual. Thus it can be noted that the three aforementioned studies agree on four general points, namely, the initial stage of invasion; reaction and resistance of settled residents against further encroachment; exodus of old residents followed by newcomers; and the climax or succession. It should be noted that in many instances invasion does not gain headway until old residents become panicky, fear a lowering of real estate values, dispose of their property cheaply and quickly, and leave. New buyers, however, may pay considerably higher prices for the same property.

Initial stage. The initial stage is characterized by the movement of a small number of individuals or families into an area. This frequently may pass unnoticed by the original occupants. If the cultural and racial dif-

[1] R. D. McKenzie, "The Ecological Approach to the Study of the Human Community," in *The City* edited by R. E. Park, E. W. Burgess, and R. D. McKenzie (Chicago: University of Chicago Press, 1925), 75.

[2] Gibbard, *op. cit.*, 206–207 and 227.

ferences between the former and new populations are more homogeneous, a considerable penetration may occur before the occupants take steps to show awareness and reaction. Sometimes, the invading new residents take special precautions to conceal their racial or cultural identity, by avoiding social contacts and maintaining social distance. The reaction against them may be postponed. Most invasions start slowly and gain momentum as time passes. A period of ten years may elapse from the date of initial invasion until a proportion of newcomers becomes significant. Gibbard found that in one area of Detroit, ten years elapsed before a nucleus of Negroes became established, while in other areas, only two or three years passed before the racial invasion gathered momentum.

The reaction. A reaction may set in against the newcomers when the original occupants are aware of the invasion. The intensity of the reaction is influenced by a number of contributing factors such as, the prevailing attitude toward the invaders, the cultural or racial characteristics by which the newcomers may be identified, the degree of community or neighborhood solidarity binding the older inhabitants and motivating them toward concerted action, and the extent of home ownership. Home ownership is related to the degree of community solidarity and the interest taken by the residents in the welfare of the community.

An invasion by a population group of a different race from the prevailing residential group brings forth the quickest reaction. Persons with a darker skin will always invoke instantaneous reaction. Gibbard discovered that the old residents of a neighborhood did not oppose the incoming individuals as members of the Jewish, Polish, or Russian groups, but only members of a class economically and socially inferior to their own. Reaction is directed against the incoming groups as "social inferiors."

Various methods may be employed to stem an invasion and to prevent it from gathering momentum. One common device is the neighborhood association, known as "protective," "civic," or "improvement" associations. These have numerous functions, but the outstanding one is directed toward the exclusion of individuals representing unwanted racial, cultural, or economic groups. Property owners form an association and enter into an agreement not to sell or rent to individuals of certain specified groups. Where home ownership exists to a high degree these organizations enforce the agreements more effectively than where a high rate of mobility is present.

When the invasion has proceeded and succession appears as a pronounced threat to existing residents, the protective-civic-improvement associations hold public meetings to develop rapport, *esprit de corps,* reaffirm the purpose of their organizations, and establish policies for counteracting the ingress. At other times, such organizations are formed after an invasion occurs.

The general influx. The third stage of the invasion-succession cycle is reached when the general influx takes place and is accompanied, or possibly preceded, by the rapid abandonment of the area by the original inhabitants. They generally go of their own volition, choosing to live in a different section rather than to remain and have as neighbors persons they dislike or consider inferior. Signs of neglect may be detected, such as the lack of repairs on homes and buildings. The district is no longer regarded as desirable, and the residents fear a loss of prestige or a decline in property values by staying. This hastens the exodus and a type of social void is created. Persons hard-pressed for a place to live may immediately move into the vacated structures which are frequently superior to those left behind. Thus, dispersion may precede the general influx of newcomers.

This stage is equally as characteristic when commercial or industrial invasion is progressing in an area. Inhabitants move to escape the confusion, noise, and change in the environment. The area goes through a transformation and the intervening stage is undesirable for home occupancy. Only those stay who cannot afford to leave.

The climax. The final stage or "climax" comes when complete displacement of the population has resulted. This also affects the institutional organizations of the former community. The buildings are there, but a modification of institutional functions and a conscious attempt to adapt to the new situation is often necessary. A new reorganization of the area is thus brought about. A church may need to modify its services to fit the new group. The school teaches a new group of students. The economic establishments may carry an entirely different line of goods and services.

For example, when the "Tokyos" in western coastal cities were abandoned by the Japanese interned in concentration camps during World War II, these ghettos were invaded by the Negroes attracted there by defense industries. Temples, stores, restaurants, and schools had been vacated. A complete change in the neighborhood followed. Buddhist temples became Baptist churches and so on.

Succession. The concept of succession has reference to the stage which follows the climax. The population composition, organizations, and characteristics of the invaded area are dominated by the new invaders and their cultural traits. Succession is, thus, the end of an invasion cycle and is a recurrent process in city growth. When succession is at hand, the area may continue in a state of disorganization, or it may easily attain equilibrium through effective institutional controls established by the incoming inhabitants.

The advocates of the cyclical theory contend that human beings cannot exist for a long time in a state of disorganization. All efforts are exerted toward reaching and maintaining equilibrium. Disorganization may affect a community in different ways. There may be higher crime rates, personal disorganization, and family tensions, to list a few examples. In time, these unstable conditions tend to be corrected. The cycle may recur, but the periods of equilibrium are longer than those when equilibrium is lacking.

Summary

The ecological organization of the urban society reflects the manner in which competition underlies the spatial distribution of populations and institutional organizations. Each community within the larger society has its typical set of institutions and population composition. A network of interrelationships is created because of interdependence for services, social life, consensus, group values, and labor. Symbiosis is defined as the competition of dissimilar groups for available goods and services of the society. Commensalism is defined as the competitive interaction of like groups.

The internal spatial development and resultant pattern of the city can be viewed in three ways. The Concentric Zone Theory establishes five concentric circles as symbolic of population expansion from the center to the periphery. Changing land use forces the movement outward, with groups constantly invading the next zone. The Sector Theory's main thesis is that the city develops into a star shape. One sector is settled before the next, and one type of land use (residence) influences the total sector. The Multi-Nuclear Theory points to the presence of one site or several sites where the city originated. Many major and minor nuclei develop because of the specialization and decentralization of organizations and the dispersion of population to less congested areas.

Students of human ecology regard the urban center as an entity which is constantly tending to attain and maintain dynamic equilibrium. The five ecological processes, *i.e.,* concentration, centralization, segregation, invasion, and succession, are the "sorters" in sifting, allocating, and assigning individuals and groups to their respective locales, or natural areas. A person's position in the society determines his social relations with (1) members of his own locale, (2) other groups, and (3) the larger society. Ordinarily, man lives in one community. From there he engages in social interaction with others. His social order is superimposed upon the ecological structure.

Concentration is the force which attracts population to a given area and contributes to the growth of the city. Dispersion is the negative aspect; areas may lose population as the population-resource ratio is inversed. Centralization is a phenomenon of control, best illustrated by the main business district, where special services and functions exist. Organizations decentralize, but the control may be retained at the center of dominance. The dispersion of population to outlying areas has caused institutional decentralization so as to better satisfy the needs of the dispersed population. Segregation of population results from the desire for mutual aid and protection by those possessing similar ethnic origin, race, or culture. Organizations segregate when like or allied services function more effectively as a cluster. Invasion is the beginning of a population or institutional movement into an area which eventually results in succession.

DISCUSSION QUESTIONS

1. Give criticisms of the Concentric Zone Theory.
2. Criticize the other two theories.
3. Is there valid evidence of the development of minor nuclei?
4. What types of segregated communities or districts exist in cities?
5. Discuss the McKenzie definition of the five ecological processes.
6. Name examples of commensalism.
7. Name examples of symbiosis.
8. What factors initiate population dispersion? Institutional decentralization?
9. What areas of the city repeatedly experience invasion and succession?
10. Discuss the four stages of the invasion-succession cycle.
11. How does involuntary segregation differ from voluntary segregation?

SUGGESTED PROJECTS

1. Study the invasion and succession cycle of your local community.
2. Observe an area in which the invasion process has reached the protest stage and the methods used for stemming the invaders.
3. Compare the rate of growth of land area for the central business district of your city with that of a subcenter.
4. What types of segregated communities exist in your city? Record the changing population composition and land use.
5. Study the literature on ecology and compare plant ecology with human ecology.
6. Trace the invasion and succession history of an area in your city which is known to have experienced repeated change of population. Where are the original inhabitants?

READINGS

M. A. Alihan, *Social Ecology*. New York: Columbia University Press, 1938.

> Mainly a critique of the theories developed by the human ecologists. Severe criticisms of the Concentric Zone Theory.

E. W. Burgess, "The Value of Sociological Community Studies for the Work of Social Agencies," *Social Forces*, 8 (June, 1930), 481–491. Also, his

"Residential Segregation in American Cities," *Annals of the American Academy of Political and Social Science,* 140 (Nov., 1928), 104–115.

Walter Firey, *Land Use in Central Boston.* Cambridge: Harvard University Press, 1947.

A study of land use in Boston, with emphasis on the impact of cultural values and industrialization upon urban spatial patterns.

A. H. Hawley, *Human Ecology: A Theory of Community Structure.* New York: Ronald Press, 1950.

A thorough treatment of the development of human ecology as compared with other forms.

Homer Hoyt, *The Structure and Growth of Residential Neighborhoods in American Cities.* Washington, D. C.: Government Printing Office, 1939.

A study substantiating the Sector Theory, with detailed maps.

R. M. Hurd, *Principles of City Land Values.* New York: The Record and Guide, 1903 and 1911.

A discussion of land values from the point of origin of any city to its mature state. Factors which influence land values included.

R. E. Park, *Human Communities.* Glencoe, Ill.: The Free Press, 1952.

A collection of the late Dr. Park's major papers on the city and human ecology. Although some of these were pioneering papers, they remain significant and notable for clarity of presentation.

J. E. Quinn, *Human Ecology.* New York: Prentice-Hall, Inc., 1950.

A concisely written volume setting forth the various theories of ecologists and the forces which contribute to the formation of local communities.

Chapter Ten

The World of Artifacts

O UR KNOWLEDGE of many ancient cities and the ways of life of their inhabitants is based almost entirely on the physical remains unearthed by archaeologists. Reconstruction has often been a difficult task, yet the task would appear to be simple compared to the problem facing some future archaeologist studying the remains of a modern city. As urban ways of life have become more complex, there has been a corresponding increase in the complexity of the technology required to maintain a city. At the same time, urbanites have become more and more dependent on the adequate functioning of this technological base.

We usually are not aware of any but the superficial aspects of the physical structure of the city—except in times of a crisis, such as a breakdown in the watermains or the power plant. At the same time, we place a very high value on technology. Progress, at least in the American value system, usually is synonymous with technological achievement. Thus we find that city planning is primarily planning for the development of the physical base. Street systems, transportation terminals and countless other facilities are not only matters of economic determination but of civic pride. Yet, while a beautiful skyline is proudly pointed out, the mass of concrete and steel may conceal an adjacent slum area. The adequacy of a city's technical development depends to a great extent on the earning power and taxation of its citizens. Thus the city as a physical structure reflects its political expression and the socio-economic status of its inhabitants.

Casual observers do not see the numerous pipe lines, wires, cables, and sewers forming an underground network, connecting the city within itself and with the larger world. However, they are conscious of mechanized units unceasingly at work, molding habits, thoughts, and activities of the citizens. These facilities ease the strain and stress of a multitude of persons sharing a given spatial layout. Man is said to be one species needing space to grow and room to spread out. A breadth of territory is required to dis-

263

play his diverse and sundry material accumulations. In cities, the task of the planners is to dovetail neatly the essentials for daily living into an area of land, geographically determined by legislative enactments, to accommodate population, and to furnish room for structures constructed above and beneath the surface. They must also foresee and provide for future population growth and plan sufficient equipment and structures to make the site habitable beyond present needs.

This chapter will be devoted to a consideration of the basic requirements of urbanites which will effect a transition from a rural to an urban way of life. The "shell" of the city would include (1) land—private and public, (2) buildings—residential and non-residential, (3) auxiliary structures or the utility systems consisting of water, sewer, heat and power, (4) fire and police protective apparatus, and (5) streets, transportation arteries and terminals.

Land

The city, with legislatively defined geographical boundaries, includes both public and private land. This is the base upon which residential and non-residential structures are erected. These buildings are of no practical value or use unless linked to the auxiliary structures which provide comforts and the saving of time, essentials for modern living. A house or a government building stands on land, but the structure itself is more or less useless without water, light, and heat. Since all structures cannot be reached without some local transportation, streets are laid to facilitate conveyance of passengers and commodities. To safeguard property and lives, protective equipment is added.

Land use. The number of inhabitants determines the density of settlement in relation to the land area, while the topography shapes the direction and degree of density. Topography in turn affects the land values and land use, the height of buildings, the kind of subdivisions, and the methods of acquisition of real property. In this country, on the whole, little thought has been devoted to a uniform land policy.[1] Whenever land has been acquired by one or more individuals, the dominant trend has been to permit the owner to use the land as he wishes. This has meant the settling of communities by allotting homesteads to those who wanted them. Community subdivisions were in turn subdivided into small lots. These could be sold to private owners, real estate operators, or community development corporations, who could then develop them as their means, taste, and needs dictated, all with a minimum of government interference.

[1] The Twentieth Century Fund, *American Housing: Problems and Prospects* (New York: 1944), Ch. 1.

Overcrowding and slum areas have resulted. The city itself retained a portion of the land for public use for parks, schools, open spaces, streets, and public buildings. These have become inadequate as cities have grown. The community was generally unable to foresee its future needs.

Some parcels of land have yielded maximum returns for private owners because of the competition for available land. Before the present century, land was more abundant and less valuable. The ownership of land is still as paramount a goal for investors as it was decades ago. Due to real estate speculation, faulty titles, and delinquent tax payments, more and more privately owned land is becoming non-productive. Some sites retain a high value by the architectural feat of piling one story above another. Land values are interwoven with structural values. Both are calculated by the extent to which a given population passes or utilizes the site and structure, enhancing its possibilities for attaining a maximum return for the capital invested.

Land values and city growth. Land varies in value throughout the city and increases in real and assessed evaluation as the city matures.[1] The parcels closest to the main business district command the highest prices, while others decrease in value, as affected by accessibility, natural barriers, and transportation. Land values do not grow in haphazard fashion but according to definite alignment with pedestrian and vehicle traffic. A change in transportation routes decreases land values. Other factors, such as sun and shade, density of traffic, noise, hilly inclines, and wide open spaces, also have a bearing.

If the traffic can proceed along a thoroughfare without "detours," land values are stable. Where a street is the axis of the neighborhood, leading to many retail and service stores, land values grow as more people are attracted. If the street leads straight to the heart of the city, values rise accordingly. Transportation routes are often the boundary lines separating one type of socio-economic community from another. They can "hem in" a ghetto or a minor nucleus. Land values may be decidedly lower on the opposite side of the street. Urbanites are quick to change their habits to conform to the focal points of convenience, and they tend to congregate where services are easily obtained. Stores follow the shifting current of travel and rentals rise accordingly.

Land values are further affected by the number of persons seeking services which can be had in a particular location. For example: merchants dealing in women's apparel of different kinds can always afford to pay high rentals, as it has always been known that the fair sex will pay a high price for stylish, seasonal, and unusual merchandise. A larger profit enables merchants to utilize the areas of high rental, an example repeated by the

[1] National Resources Committee, *op. cit.*, 6–7.

specialty shops dealing in women's accessories. They are located near large department stores. The variety stores, dealing in low cost articles, also find locations as close to department stores as possible. They do not advertise but depend upon the large number of shoppers attracted by the department store advertisements. Many shoppers who cannot afford to purchase in the specialty and department stores find substitutes in the variety stores.

Men's shops, on the other hand, usually assemble in a secondary location, often on the sunny or windy side of the street. Men's clothing is more standardized and does not require the same advertising, display space, or featuring of articles before the purchases are made. Shops that require a large floor space at cheaper rentals for their merchandise—the furniture and appliance stores—locate where rent is lower.

In residential areas, the land values are highest where the site is dry, level, and elevated. Hilly and uneven terrain lowers land values. Except in high income residential areas, population tends to cluster within walking distance of the transportation routes. Other factors affecting population distribution are noise, soot and dirt, unpleasant odors, and public utilities.

Residences and Non-residential Structures

Residences. Residences for the city's heterogeneous population are varied in location, design, cost, and comfort.[1] These may be detached, semi-detached, or multi-family dwellings. By a series of processes based upon selection and speculation, dwellings are located where owners find the best values in return for their investments. Ownership and use of property have been regarded as strictly private matters. City authorities, in the main, have maintained a laissez-faire policy concerning improvements, additions, or alterations. Until recently only a minimum amount of control was exercised over residences, resulting partially from the lack of land and rapid population growth. Where restrictions are enforced, it is in response to the recognition that private owners have neglected the interest of the community. Within the last two decades, residences have been built for lower income groups with federal, state, and municipal funds. Slum clearance had to be undertaken by community agencies because owners had been holding on to houses or lots which they hoped to sell at a high profit. Thus, it often happens that the lower income groups live on high-priced land.

The structures in a city are significant indexes of the social and economic status of its inhabitants and the social organization which exists. Buildings, like household goods or office furniture, are determined by the de-

[1] Twentieth Century Fund, *op. cit.*, 26–27.

mands of the consumer, but differ from other forms of consumer's goods in that they have fixed locations.

In residential construction there are at least two general trends that are worthy of special attention. The first is that the availability of residential space has failed to keep abreast with population growth in large cities. The second is the tendency toward multiple dwellings. The first trend is contrary to conditions during the First World War, when the available residential space increased faster than population.[1] The second is related to the rapid increase in the proportion of families housed in apartments. In 257 cities of over 25,000 inhabitants, between 1921 and 1928, the percentage of permits obtained to construct one-family dwellings dropped from 58.3 to 35.2.[2] Multi-family dwellings climbed from 24.4 to 53.7 per cent. In 14 of our largest cities, the permits for multi-family dwellings increased from 34.0 to 64.4 per cent for a similar period.

Skyscraper apartments in large metropolises have broken the residential tradition of the "walk-up" and have changed the manner of urban living. The high land values near the business section prohibit all but the very wealthy or the very poor from living there. This apparent paradox is quite readily explainable.

A very high profit may be obtained by renting ramshackle structures to vast numbers of tenants. Old buildings are frequently subdivided far beyond their original capacity. Since facilities and repairs are kept to the minimum enforced by law, relatively low individual rents yield a profit far beyond most rental returns.

Apartments or hotels near the central business district are desired by business executives, professional groups, and retired persons who prefer to be close to their places of employment or recreation. This type of living makes it possible for a large number of renters to utilize a smaller ground space than if each lived according to the old pattern of land use of a detached home surrounded by a front and back yard. Modern conveniences are supplied to the tenants by a group of services housed under one roof, such as barber shops, beauty parlors, drug stores, restaurants, dry cleaning establishments, cocktail lounges, gift shops, and others. In metropolitan cities, detached homes are declining in number and size, while the multidwellings expand horizontally and vertically.

The American pattern of detached homes is in marked contrast to Western European cities, where there has been a long history of multifamily dwellings.[3] The American trend toward multi-family dwellings

---

[1] McKenzie, *op. cit.*, 216.

[2] U. S. Bureau of Labor Statistics, *Monthly Labor Review*, 31 (April, 1931), 171.

[3] T. Caplow, "Urban Structure in France," *American Sociological Review*, 17 (Oct., 1952), 544–549.

may be seen as an adaptation to an urban way of life, just as the value placed on the detached home and plot of land is largely a carry-over from a rural heritage. Certainly, from a criterion of efficiency of urban organization, the traditional American residential pattern has many disadvantages. The transportation problems of our cities constitute but one consequence of the dispersion of population necessitated by such land-use patterns.

Non-residential structures. Buildings used for factories, offices, warehouses, storage purposes, recreation, hospitals, universities, and churches are non-residential. The extent and types of structures vary with the size of the city and its population. They are predominantly privately owned. The public buildings are financed by the taxpayers, and may include schools, public markets, wharves, warehouses, community centers, beach houses, and museums.

Beginning with the end of the First World War, the trend toward large buildings for non-residential use became popular. For example, office buildings, one of the largest subclasses under this category, tend to tower skyward and are natural structural responses to the operation of economic forces under present conditions of technological improvements. The elevator has made skyscraping heights practical and has added rentable floor space. The traffic carried by elevators grew in volume as the heights of structures and passengers increased. In 1930, the forty-story Equitable Building in New York had 48 passenger elevators, which transported an average of 96,000 persons per day between the hours of 8 A.M. and 6 P.M. Of this total, 12,000 were the workers in the building whose offices occupied 1,220,688 square feet of net rentable space. The remainder of the 96,000 came to transact business within the building. Some 135,000 persons passed daily in and out of its portals.[1]

Towering non-residential structures have spread throughout the country. A group of commercial or professional services can be obtained at the same location. An allied group of services may share a floor or suite of offices, aiding the centralization and segregation processes. For example: insurance offices are housed in the same buildings as brokers and commercial underwriters. Physicians maintain offices where dentists and other specialists rent quarters. Banks, wholesale houses, theaters, hotels, railroad stations, hospitals, schools, and even churches are super-structures. An excellent example of wholesalers and retailers co-operating under one huge roof is the Merchandise Mart in Chicago, the largest commercial structure in the world.

---

[1] For further details see W. C. Clark and J. L. Kingston, *The Sky-Scraper: A Study in the Economic Height of Modern Office Buildings*, American Institute of Steel Construction, 1930.

Auxiliary Structures

Water supply. Of the many functions performed by a city government, none is more important and more generally taken for granted than the provision for an ample supply of pure water. The farm boy who thaws out the frozen handle of a pump in the yard on a winter morning knows that a supply of water does not come without effort. The American city dweller turns on a faucet in the bathroom with never a thought to the engineering skill which has made this comfort possible.

A water system has replaced the private and semi-private wells and springs which served the majority of the inhabitants of this country before the middle of the last century. By 1900, it was unusual to find a city without a central water supply system. In 1951, 74 per cent of all cities with 5,000 and more inhabitants owned and operated their own water systems.[1]

A plentiful supply of water involves three possibilities: (1) the existence of a subterranean water supply extracted by means of wells, (2) the use of nearby surface waters, creeks, lakes, or rivers, with purification and filtration works, and (3) utilizing distant sources of initially better quality conveyed by aqueducts.[2] Each source must be studied as to the amount of water available, possibilities of storage, quality of water, elevation, and resulting costs.

The project may be undertaken by a private water company, under franchise from the city, or the city may construct and operate its own system. As considerable capital is involved, few private concerns can compete with the layout of public funds. The problem of providing sufficient water is by no means a light one. Municipal ownership of the water system began during the nineteenth century. Today, almost all are municipally owned. Several reasons may be advanced for this condition.

One is that the water supply is closely allied with public health and sanitation. To place water distribution under the supervision of a centralized public authority, such as the Department of Public Works, assures regular inspection, tests, and disinfection. Where this is undertaken by a private concern, a municipal agency must supervise it. A second reason for municipal ownership or supervision is that the city itself is the largest individual customer of the water plant. The city needs water to serve parks, fire department, and public buildings, and for street cleaning and sewerage disposal. The city's demands may consume as much as one fourth of the entire daily water supply. An added reason is that water, a

[1] *Municipal Year Book, 1952,* 52.

[2] City of Los Angeles, Board of Water and Power Commissioners, *45th Annual Report,* 1946, 3–20.

prime necessity, should be supplied at cost or as nearly so as possible. A private concern cannot be expected to operate on this basis.

City dwellers demand good water, which means that the water should be free from bacteria, colorless, tasteless, and odorless, neither too hard nor too soft. Chlorination of water is a standard practice for destroying harmful bacteria which may possibly have escaped periodic water inspection. Filtration through mechanical filters is an added safeguard against pollution. In Far Eastern cities, each person or family must take his own precautions or suffer the consequences of typhoid, cholera, or dysentery.

Consumption of water varies with cities. Chicagoans use 292.8 gallons per person annually; New Yorkers, 142.0 gallons; and Philadelphians, 168.0 gallons. In contrast, during the dry season in Hong Kong, water is turned on for but one hour a day. The great number of outlets in every American home, the prevalence of modern bathrooms, as well as large amounts of water utilized for industrial and public purposes, account for the variations. Uncontrolled use of water is rare in Far Eastern cities. Many offices and homes have their own wells and filtration facilities.

The purity of water before it reaches the tap has several important consequences. In particular, it has greatly reduced the likelihood of epidemics, and thus is a major factor in the lowering of the urban death rate. Many industrial operations likewise depend on supplies of pure water.

Where the water supply is insufficient for the growing population and industrial expansion, city officials receive many complaints. Citizens are requested to observe "bathless and shaveless days" and thereby alleviate the shortage. Vigorous efforts are made to spot leaky faucets or penalize wasters. New York City experienced an acute water shortage for several summers. Tucson and Los Angeles are two other municipalities where the growth in population has strained the existing water supply. Large areas of the United States which depend on a subterranean water supply, as is true of many of the Plains states, are faced with a drastic lowering of the water table as demand appears to exceed the supply. In these areas, water has become a dominant political issue. One of the possible consequences is that industries contemplating a selection of new sites would not settle where water is short. The other is that inhabitants may depart and new settlers decide against selecting the city for permanent residence.

Adequate water supplies in suburbs have influenced a large number of suburbanites to live beyond the city limits. The center city is often required to supply water for an entire district at a minimum fee while bearing the cost of water plant and equipment installation. Without a safe and continued flow of water, many cities and outlying areas would become uninhabitable.

Sewers and sewage disposal. A second contribution to urban sanitation and health is the city's disposal of waste through a network of sewers. This responsibility is generally placed under the Department of Engineering or the Department of Public Works. Sewerage systems have become universal in American cities and constitute one of the greatest steps in human history toward controlling innumerable epidemics and diseases. The loss of millions of lives has been averted by the scientific treatment of human excreta, a condition untrue of most non-Western cities. In 1951, 49 per cent of all cities with 5,000 and more inhabitants owned and operated their sewerage treatment plants.[1]

The waste products of a modern city amount annually to thousands of tons. The task of collection, removal, and disposal are assigned to public servants whose responsibility it is to effect prompt service at a minimum cost to taxpayers. Failure to do so would render the city uninhabitable within a short time. In warm weather the menace to health of citizens cannot be minimized. Such accumulations as street waste, garbage, ashes, industrial waste, soot, worn-out articles of human use, discarded clothes, old furniture, papers and magazines, and dilapidated automobiles and machinery must be salvaged or destroyed. Taken as a whole, the amount "wasted" by every member of our population probably exceeds 500 pounds a year. What appears as junk to the average American may be considered usable by persons of another country. The latter, when visiting the United States, are always appalled at the extensiveness of discarded papers, strings, magazines, food, books, and clothing—to mention but a few daily cast-offs.

A corps of 9,000 persons is employed by New York's municipal government to collect and dispose of some thousand tons of daily waste materials coming from homes, businesses, and industrial concerns.[2] Smaller cities may use the scavenger system, whereby firms or junk dealers are licensed by the health department. Others pay a fee for each ton collected and disposed of, according to prearranged contracts.

The innumerable activities of urban people during the course of a day leave the streets, sidewalks, and alleys cluttered with trash and dirt. Parks and other municipal buildings pose a similar problem. The streets are systematically cleaned each night, only to be reheaped the following day. During the winter, snow-removal and coating icy pavements and streets

[1] *Municipal Year Book,* 1952, 52.

[2] The American Public Health Association defines the various kinds of municipal waste by two main categories: organic and inorganic. Organic includes garbage or rejected food waste; night-soil or contents of vaults and cess-pools; sewage, or water-conveyed excreta; and offal, or refuse from slaughter houses and animal substances only. Inorganic includes ashes from household, steam factory; refuse or combustible articles from all sources; also, glass, iron, crockery, house sweepings and everything not included in garbage and ashes; and street sweepings.

with sand or ashes runs into a large sum. The cost is borne by the tax-payers. Efforts are being made to bring court charges against "litterbugs" in some of our cities.

Public Utilities

Public utilities are either private or municipal enterprises providing essential services such as gas, electricity, power, telephone, or transportation. Since it has been recognized that public utilities are natural monopolies and competition could not be relied upon, protective measures against possible abuses were necessary. Public utilities are subject to thorough-going regulation by various agencies of the government and attempts are made to regulate these monopolies. The regulation took two principal forms. One was regulation by means of restrictions imposed in the franchises granted to the public utility companies by laws and ordinances enacted by state legislatures and city councils. The other was regulation by both state and municipal commissions. In the main, the regulations have been taken to insure (1) uniform rates, (2) elimination of competing companies which may endanger continued service, and (3) sufficient capital to provide for expansion and large-scale operation.

Heat, Light, and Power

Among the public utilities supplied by municipalities for the convenience of residents are gas, electricity, and power.

Gas. Gas is said to be the next oldest public utility after water. Where natural gas is found in insufficient quantities to assure a continuous supply, artificial or manufactured gas is used for heat, power, and cooking. The illumination of homes and streets was once done by gas. The widespread adoption of electricity has eliminated this practice. Even though facing serious competition from other forms of heat, gas remains in great demand for heating water and homes, and for refrigeration and industrial processes. In recent years, super gas systems have been installed, strategically located plants serving numerous cities over wide areas. The long-distance transmission of natural gas under high pressure is another development which benefits cities removed from the source of supply.

Nearly 27 cubic miles or almost 4½ trillion cubic feet of natural gas were consumed in the United States in 1948. This quantity of gas, weighing 106 million tons, has about the same heat value as 175 million tons of coal. Despite this record consumption, existing natural reserves would last another 30 years. Discoveries of new fields or extensions of known fields are adding continuously to known reserves. Natural gas is being employed increasingly to replace coal as steam boiler fuel for power generating plants. The production of carbon black for the manufacture of rubber products consumed more natural gas than any other single industrial function. About 37,000 industrial consumers and ten million homes were using natural gas at the end of 1947.[1]

Electricity and power. Electricity was first furnished through a central station in New York City at the beginning of the 1880's. Since that time its consumption has markedly increased. In 1951, 21 per cent of all cities with 5,000 and more inhabitants owned their electric systems.[2] The electric light and power industry has grown to service innumerable industries. Over 70 per cent of the nation's population live in homes illuminated by electricity. The electrification of rural homes followed. In the past the use of electricity grew principally as a matter of convenience, economy, or what we have been educated to consider absolute necessity. In the future, electricity may be utilized to provide more comfort, education, and the elimination of work, whether in home, factory, or office. Many modern homes and offices are electrified throughout.

In metropolitan areas the increased use of electrical power resulted from the electrification of transportation, as in the case of railroad terminals and city approaches. Transportation was electrified partly because of legislative mandate to eliminate smoke, hazards, and other nuisances. Other uses include air conditioning, frozen goods, cooking, heating, electrical appliances, radio, and television.[3] It should be noted that most, if not all, non-Western cities do not have gas systems. Electricity is used to light some sections of the city, and industrial operations depend upon human labor as the major source of power.

Streets and Highways

Many city streets may once have been earthen or cobblestone wagon roads. Previously, they may have been the cowpaths and human roadways traversed by earlier settlers to the center of the community, the market place, and the hub-bub of economic and social life. Now, cement or asphalt hides the former rugged and uneven surfaces. A scheme of street construction has replaced the irregular by-paths and narrow roadways.

The process of centralization in the spatial patterning of modern cities has meant that virtually all urban traffic is directed either toward or away from the main business district. The major transportation routes within

[1] Report of National Industrial Conference Board, 1947.
[2] *Municipal Year Book, 1952,* 52.
[3] M. M. Samuels, "Uses and Sources of Electric Power," in *The Annals of the American Academy of Political and Social Science* (November 1945), 67–78.

Short haul bus loading platform of New York Port Authority's bus terminal at 41st street.

View of railroad yards and New London, Conn., from the Thames River Bridge.

a city stretch outward in a radial fashion from the central core to the periphery. A large portion of passengers and goods is transported along these arterial thoroughfares. The streets become the means of connecting the various parts of the city into a physical whole, as well as reaching out toward the hinterland. To the urbanites who cannot live within walking distance of their work, adequate streets and highways are indispensable. The dispersion of population tends to follow existing transportation routes, as Hoyt emphasizes in his sector theory. However, one must also note the pressures which are exerted to extend facilities to existing areas.

Most municipalities follow the gridiron plan in street layout which, commonly crossing each other at right angles, gives the city a checkerboard appearance. There are advantages and disadvantages to the prevailing practice. While this scheme makes it possible for the city to be divided up into lots of uniform size and facilitates the division of the city into administrative units, it does not permit the free flow of traffic unless it is combined with some other arrangement. In order to gain access to the wider thoroughfares intersecting at major points throughout the city, several streets may converge at a central point. Since speed is an essential characteristic of urbanism, smoothly paved streets are a paramount requisite. With the extensive use of automobiles, trucks, and buses, superhighways are vital for relief of traffic congestion and rapid movement of vehicles.[1]

To facilitate the flow of traffic, protect the highways against improper use, and minimize accidents to pedestrians and travelers, each municipality may exercise its local police power for the regulation of traffic and vehicles. The ever-growing density of traffic and the high speed of modern cars have made this a major responsibility.

As the city itself is not self-sufficient in food, labor, or raw materials, rapid transportation over good streets is needed. By extending avenues of traffic, the area over which the city holds dominance is enlarged. Since the advent of motor trucks, "door-to-door" service has been employed in the transportation of perishable commodities, such as milk, fruits, vegetables, and livestock. Less time is involved in transporting products from the farms to city markets. The time consumed in railroad terminal operations is eliminated. The principal advantages of the motor vehicle are its variety of uses and its removal of the dependence upon schedules and routes of public carriers, railroads, airplanes, and so on. The congestion of traffic as the center of the city is approached has resulted in the construction of new highways which by-pass cities. The limited-access type of highways direct to the hearts of cities are becoming more numerous.

[1] For a thorough treatment see J. Labatut and J. L. Wheaton (eds.), *Highways in Our National Life* (New Haven: Princeton University Press, 1950).

They have developed as a response to the need for eliminating archaic traffic patterns and as the result of the city planning movement.

Superhighways are being constructed in many cities to avoid traffic congestion, loss of time, and accidents. These include streets or thoroughfares located either on the surface of the ground, on a partial or complete elevation, or in a depression. To provide connections with the street systems of the city, there are (except in terminal areas) a limited number of intersections located at important points. They may be separated from thoroughfares by means of viaducts or underpasses having the necessary vamps and driveways. Today, the United States has 3,009,145 miles of highways.

Transportation

Cities, as the loci for industry, commerce, and trade, cannot function without adequate transportation systems. Transportation enables the population to conduct its business, shop, and satisfy the many and diversified needs and demands of modern living. One of the major problems connected with local and inter-city transportation is to provide various kinds of transportation that will serve large masses. Uneven traffic at specific hours of the day may strain the facilities, but a general provision for the diverse types of city movements is important.[1]

The chief daily movements within a city consist of the morning and evening journeys of wage-earners and businessmen between their homes and places of business. Then follow the late morning travelers: the shoppers, mostly women, from residential districts to retail store districts and to downtown recreational attractions. From late afternoon until seven o'clock in the evening, the first group of workers return to their residences. Shortly thereafter, the evening travel to theaters, operas, movies, dance halls, night clubs, and other places of amusements begins. Several hours later, the recreation-seekers trek homeward to begin more or less the same routine the next day. Since the heart of the city has concentration of special services, it acts as a centripetal force attracting the population for specific functions and time periods.

These currents of traffic are the city's life. They enable many people, during business hours, to come into easy contact with others with whom they must communicate. They bring men to material, which is frequently cheaper than bringing material to men. The location of the various routes of travel has a profound influence upon industrial and retail sites, land values, land use, and the ecological distribution of population.

Urban mass transportation can be divided into two main categories.

[1] G. W. Breese, *op. cit.*

There are the conventional surface streetcar and motorbus lines. Larger metropolitan centers frequently have rapid transit systems, such as elevated lines, subways, or special surface rights of way. These are designed for more efficient long distance service with a minimum of interference with and by the typical slow flow of traffic of ordinary urban transportation routes.

Surface transit system. Streetcars and motorbuses have done much to extend the city beyond its periphery. They have connected the hinterland to the city, and together with the railroads have helped to create our metropolitan areas of the last four decades.

Streetcars made their first appearance as horse-drawn railways in 1832. The introduction of the electric streetcar occurred in Richmond, Virginia, in 1887. By 1890 the widespread adoption of electric power was well under way. At the turn of the century most cities of 15,000 or over inhabitants had installed the service. Horse-drawn vehicles and bicycles were replaced by 1910. Cities which did not find it profitable to have their own streetcar systems were serviced by interurban lines passing through them and giving local service.

The introduction of the streetcar represents an important step in the history of American cities. The immediate effect was to relieve population pressure upon the downtown districts. Cities at once began to grow more freely at their peripheries. Streetcar lines were constructed to new subdivisions and stimulated their development.

In the small and moderate-sized cities, all the streetcar lines pass through the downtown district. In larger cities, much of the traffic originates and ends farther out, never reaching the center. Large factory districts away from the downtown district often become terminals of important cross-lines.

The motorbus entered the transportation scene just as the streetcar became popular. Buses have gradually displaced streetcars in smaller cities and have supplemented intraurban and interurban transit systems in larger ones. Motorbuses are used to service suburbs, other sections of cities not populous enough to support streetcar service, and areas where the construction of streetcar tracks would be unprofitable. Also, by running upon streets midway between streetcar lines, they pick up a considerable volume of riders who want quicker and better service. For a city needing additional transportation, the motorbuses provide the answer.

In 1945, there were 1,015 local city bus operators and 420 city-suburban operators. Together they operated approximately 46,000 vehicles conveying almost eight million revenue passengers over 1.5 million bus miles, along 42,943 miles of highway.[1]

[1] National Association of Motor Bus Operators, *Bus Facts,* December 31, 1945.

In Duluth, Minnesota, a tug pushes a loaded ore boat out in St. Louis Bay. Water transportation is valuable for moving heavy commodities.

The clover-leaf intersection of a metropolitan area with automobiles moving in all directions through well-planned overpasses and underpasses.

Rapid transit. The first rapid transit system developed in New York City in 1868. Since then Chicago, Philadelphia, and Boston have adopted both the surface and underground systems. The "el" trains have proven inefficient, cumbersome, and a hinderance to traffic movements, while marring the aesthetic layout of already congested areas. The roaring noise of the elevated travelling past office buildings and homes is an added nuisance. Going underground was the next phase of development which provided rapid transit at all hours. Because private concerns exact profit for the service, operating costs have mounted. The public's demand for cheaper, more efficient and rapid transportation has resulted in municipalities purchasing existing systems and coordinating them under transit authorities.[1] Public ownership of transportation has not been satisfactory, however.

It cannot be denied that merchants' associations and real estate operators with heavy investments have influenced the route of the rapid transit systems. The resulting effects upon land use, land values, and population congestion along major routes of transportation were inevitable. Large department stores in New York, Philadelphia, and Chicago have resisted changes in routes and have directed their efforts toward having substations located where passengers enter or leave directly from their own store entrances. Cities having projected rapid transit systems under consideration are: St. Louis, Los Angeles, Pittsburgh, Detroit, and Cleveland.

Interurban and suburban transportation. Interurban and suburban transit systems developed during the last three decades of this century. These lines usually serve simultaneously several incorporated communities. Suburban lines contributed to the strong decentralized movement of population and industry to suburbs, rural-nonfarm areas, and satellite cities. These handle freight, baggage, mail, and express, in addition to passengers. At the utmost a city and its adjacent suburbs are included on the route of an interurban line. The interurban system carries only passengers and their hand luggage.[2] Because of the rising costs of operation, many single-line interurbans have been discontinued.

The motorbus is a second type of interurban transportation. Many cities are able to exercise a command over surrounding territory by installing a bus service. Some municipalities are located on a transcontinental or branch railway system and yet have no direct shipping contact with nearby places. This is true of cities located west of the Mississippi where the main railway lines run generally east-west. Crosslines are relatively few. Idaho serves as an excellent illustration. Four transcontinental railroads

[1] New York City Transit System, "Public Ownership, Civil Service and Collective Bargaining," *Political Science Quarterly*, 56 (June, 1941).

[2] Stuart Daggett, *Principles of Inland Transportation* (New York: Harper & Bros., 1928), Ch. 5.

traverse the state, but travelers are limited in the direction of their travel. No direct rail route runs north or south. More than half of the state's inhabitants lived in incorporated places, but less than 20 per cent were found in cities having more than 10,000 inhabitants. All cities are widely scattered.[1] Motorbuses fill in the gaps left by the railroads.

In 1939, there were 1,222 intercity motorbus operators manning 12,211 vehicles, a phenomenal growth for a twenty-year period since their installation. By 1945, a greater expansion had occurred; 2,785 intercity motorbus operators conveyed 874,013,000 revenue passengers in 29,000 vehicles over more than one million bus miles, along 371,652 miles of highways.[2] Interurban motorbuses have competed heavily and successfully with railroads, and, according to present indications, more miles will be offered at lower costs.

Transportation terminals. Private corporations and transit authorities provide transportation terminals, whether for passenger and freight loading and discharge, or for the storage of vehicles. Since the city may be served by a network of railroads, each independently owned and operated, freight yards and stations and passenger stations are frequently located in congested central areas. The number of terminals arose from transport agencies competing with each other. Philadelphia's metropolitan area had over 700 railroad freight stations alone. Chicago ranks as the world's rail center; 600 freight trains enter or leave every 24 hours through 255 freight stations. Every 90 seconds, a passenger or freight train enters or leaves the city.

The fact that almost three-fourths of all railway traffic terminates in urban areas, and about 37 per cent of the total railroad freight operating expenses consist of terminal costs, indicates the importance of the terminal problems from the standpoint of national and urban economy.[3] The broad relations between terminals and urban community structure and development have not been fully recognized by transportation companies, shippers, and governmental authorities. One resulting aspect is that they have profoundly influenced the configuration of cities, the trend of population distribution, and the industrial development of urban communities.

Few cities have adequate passenger terminals. In the main, railroad and motorbus stations are located at points accessible to the hotel and shopping districts. Both should be designed and located with reference to the volume and type of business transacted, and to the needs of specific classes of business and industrial enterprises. Large union stations

[1] Thomas C. Donnelly and Arthur N. Holcombe, *Rocky Mountain Politics* (Albuquerque: The University of New Mexico Press, 1940), 174.

[2] National Association of Motor Bus Operators, *op. cit.*, p. 4.

[3] National Resources Committee, *op. cit.*, 62–63.

are being constructed away from the centers of business districts. Union stations are sufficiently accessible to enable quick access to all parts of the city and they facilitate the interchange of passengers between terminals. Where a city has several terminals, the time and cost involved in transferring baggage, passengers, and freight are problems that can be solved partially by coordination and cooperation between transportation companies. In Chicago, the Parmalee Service, operating as an intermediary service between stations, expedites travel and eliminates inconveniences for many travelers.

Motorbus companies typically use buildings located in the business centers or outlying intersections as terminals, with bus loading areas in the rear. This practice is followed in large metropolises as well as small cities. Most city streets are narrow and congested, and the presence of large buses does little to reduce traffic bottlenecks. Where railroads connect with buses, or where both are under one management, better coordination in time schedules and discharge points between motorbus and railroad terminals result. On the whole, cities provide few services for motorbus passengers.

Truck terminals are inadequate, despite the daily growing volume of merchandise entering and leaving the city. Truck terminals should be built near the railroad belt lines, leading to lanes for only truck travel. The loading and unloading of goods can proceed without interruption and would eliminate many accidents. One of the world's most modern and huge freight terminals was erected in Chicago and was in operation by 1951. Merchandise is assembled at maximum speed and carried along overhead conveyors to waiting trucks and trains. Each day 120 boxcars and 275 different fleets of trucks are serviced efficiently by a staff of workers, whose main tasks are clerical and administrative. For short distance hauls within the city, another trucking terminal was constructed.

With the growth of air transportation, 21 per cent of our cities owned and operated their airports while 303 others leased the ground to private operators or governmental agencies.[1]

Protective Apparatus

Fire. For the common protection of urbanites, fire-fighting equipment is not only necessary but vital to public and personal safety. Fires are often disastrous to property and human lives. One of the greatest disasters experienced by a single city was San Francisco which during the nineties suffered a loss of more than 500 million dollars. The Chicago Fire of the seventies still brings forth many comments about the extensive destruc-

[1] *Municipal Year Book*, 1952, 53.

tion. The 1952 losses through fire in the United States amounted to nearly a billion dollars. Industrial losses through fire account for 25 per cent of this amount. Each year the total rises, as population becomes more congested and structures more uninhabitable in many cities. These are direct property losses only. The related costs in fire-fighting, hospitalization, unemployment, production, and business failures are excluded. Nor do the figures disclose the reduction or absolute losses in savings nor the uninsured property and personal goods.

The National Board of Fire Underwriters reported that fires annually destroy some 600,000 buildings throughout the country. Over half this number are homes, apartment buildings, and rooming houses. About 75,000 involve motor vehicles. The known causes are (1) discarded matches, accounting for 30 per cent and (2) misuse of electricity, totaling 11 per cent of all fires. By far the greatest tragedy is the annual loss of 10,000 lives. Two thousand children under five years of age annually are victims of fire. The fire chiefs of 1,720 cities reported over 252,000 residential fires in one year, many of which involved young children.

Municipal fire departments are continually besieged with two major problems: maintaining adequate and scientific apparatus and obtaining trained personnel. The former is dependent upon taxation and citizen's interest, whereas the second is lack of training facilities and careful selection of office-holders. Beginnings are being made in upgrading the efficiency and training of firemen in this country. The University of Southern California enrolled 300 firemen in June, 1951, for a Bachelor of Science degree in Public Administration.[1] In Australia firemen are trained until they have the same efficiency and discipline as a crack military regiment.[2] Fire departments come under the joint supervision of insurance companies, municipal government, and state government. In Italy, fire fighters are pressed into service during any emergency situation, as, for example, a flood or earthquake.

In Far Eastern countries fires are rare because fuel for heating is a luxury few can afford. Houses, mainly brick, are solidly constructed to last several centuries. In the poorer sections, however, where matsheds are erected, fires sweep and destroy many homes before the voluntary fire fighters can control the conflagration. Water is hand drawn from nearby wells while small buckets of water are passed from one person to the next in a futile attempt to quench a burning inferno. Often several hundred matsheds are wiped out at one time.

Police. Police power is the authority to protect the health, safety, comfort, and morals of the population. Police have been empowered by the

[1] *International Fire Fighters,* 34 (June, 1951), 6–8.
[2] *International Fire Fighters,* 32 (Feb., 1949), 3–4.

courts to enforce ordinances related to public nuisances, health, wages, conditions of work, public utilities, and gambling. All mechanized equipment used by the police in carrying out duties of combating crime comes under the category of police power. That is, it is classified as municipal function rather than as material.

In recent decades the equipment required for the apprehension of lawbreakers and the solution of crimes has cost the taxpayers a sizable sum. Police stations are thought of as being of equal importance with fire stations, if not more important. The same attitude applies to the mechanized equipment of the urban police force, the selection and training of personnel, and the adoption of new and efficient techniques.

Physical Equipment and Social Relations

Some generalizations can be made concerning the effect which the city's physical equipment has upon social life. First and foremost is the time factor. Rapid transportation enables the urbanite to gauge distances in terms of minutes rather than miles. During the day many activities are performed with an eye upon the timepiece: conversation, meal-time, relaxation, waiting for goods and services supplied by other urbanites. When a suburbanite or a city dweller changes his place of work, an important consideration is how much time it will take to get there. His satisfaction with the job is often colored by the amount of time consumed in travel. Many recreational or organizational activities are neglected if there are too many miles between home and place of meeting.

Speed is essential to urban fluidity. Time is equated with economic gain or loss. Merchants clock their profits according to the fraction of a minute. Workers are often docked if late to work. Penalties are exacted by deductions from the pay envelope or being discharged. Human beings have value only when they gear their activities to a rigid time schedule.

Another effect of the physical equipment of a city upon social relations is seen in the type of interaction extended from one urbanite to another. Personal relationships often tend to be secondary to time and cost. Loyalty to friends and family suffer in competition with them. Even homemakers, persons with more leisure than wage-earners, succumb to these attitudes and practices. On the other hand, distances will be spanned if a common interest draws people together. In this case, urbanites will travel great distances to maintain friendships.

Under normal conditions, the technological base is taken for granted. After a serious fire or because of unusually severe transport or water supply problems, the cry for reform is loud indeed. Similarly, little control is exercised over land use until the situation has become critical.

Under ordinary circumstances, remedial measures are generally sponsored by only a small segment of the population.

Summary

The physical equipment of cities is evidence that urbanites have effected a transition from a less to a more complex way of life. Such tangibles as land, public and private; buildings, residential and non-residential; and the auxiliary structures consisting of water mains; sewerage disposal systems; utilities plant supplying light, heat, and power; street and transportation systems; and fire-fighting equipment are the basic requirements needed by urban dwellers to live, work and relax within legislatively defined boundaries.

Land, in the main, is privately owned and varies in value throughout the city. Residential land seldom attains as high a value as commercial and industrial parcels. The central business district has the highest land values. There, structural values are correlated with land values, for the two together are in turn linked with population accessibility and maximum use. Public lands are reserved for parks, playgrounds and civic centers, etc., but are often inadequate because of the inability of planners to predict population growth and city expansion.

Both residential and non-residential buildings in metropolitan cities rise to towering heights. They have changed the manner of living and of transacting business since the first decade of this century.

Of the auxiliary structures, none is more important than the water supply, and many cities operate their own systems on a non-profit basis. An adequate sewerage disposal system is correlated with the water supply. These systems are usually publicly owned.

Gas, electricity, and power are furnished to residential and non-residential structures through either private or municipally owned and operated monopolies. The availability of these utilities enables industrial expansion and processing, and also enable the home consumers to make use of labor-saving devices.

Most American cities follow the gridiron plan of rectangular street layouts, thus giving the municipality a checkerboard appearance. Superhighways and highways with limited access are being constructed in some cities to cope with traffic congestion, loss of time, and accidents. Streetcars, motorbuses, rapid transit and private vehicles enable the city to extend its dominance over a wide hinterland, by bringing goods, services, and persons toward the center of the city. Interurban service integrates adjacent and contiguous areas and cities. There is an abundance of poor railroad, bus, and freight terminal facilities in cities. Some reform measures are gaining headway. The erection of freight and passenger terminals in central business districts has influenced land values, land use, population distribution, and the industrial development of municipalities.

The most pronounced effect which the city's physical equipment has upon urban living is seen in the efforts to equate social interaction and other relations with time and cost.

DISCUSSION QUESTIONS

1. What would happen to a modern city if light, heat, and power were suspended for one week?
2. What types of transportation are absolutely essential for urban growth?
3. Has the automobile dispersed population or caused more congestion?
4. Why have cities undertaken to operate public utility systems?
5. What are the advantages of superstructures, whether stores, schools, office buildings, or apartments?
6. How may natural barriers affect land values?
7. What do you understand about the term land-use?
8. How can urban fire hazards be reduced?
9. How has the installation of a modern sewage system affected the health of urbanities?
10. How may the social interaction of individuals and groups be affected by the city's physical equipment?

SUGGESTED PROJECTS

1. Study the reports of cities which suffered from war bombings and see the effect of the destruction of utilities on health and disease.
2. Trace the growth and development of motorbus transportation for your city.
3. Study the transportation system of your city and indicate the changes in city pattern, population distribution, and land values.
4. Study the effect of real estate speculation on land values and land use for your city.
5. Take one essential public utility and show the trend in municipal ownership.
6. Obtain a rating scale issued by the National Board of Fire Underwriters ranking cities according to specified fire equipment. Use this as a comparison for your city and see what measures have been taken to modernize the fire department.
7. Study the growth of mechanized equipment of a modern police department.

READINGS

G. W. Breese, *The Daytime Population of the Central Business District of Chicago: with Special Reference to the Factors of Transportation.* Chicago: University of Chicago Press, 1950.

The census lists only the night population of business districts. This is a study of population movements during the various hours of the day as affected by transportation.

H. W. Gilmore, *Transportation and the Growth of Cities.* Glencoe, Ill.: The Free Press, 1953.

Urban growth as related to the different kinds of transportation.

E. J. Kenealy, *The Cleveland Municipal Light Plant,* 1935 and 1936.

Annual reports of the municipally operated light plant and its achievements.

J. Labatut and J. L. Wheaton, eds., *Highways in Our National Life.* New Haven: Princeton University Press, 1950.

A compilation of articles written by various authorities on the development of highways in the United States.

W. F. Ogburn, "Inventions of Local Transportation and the Patterns of Cities," in *Reader in Urban Sociology* by P. K. Hatt and A. J. Reiss, Jr., eds. Glencoe: The Free Press, 1951, pp. 259–267.

A discussion of the changing patterns of urban configuration and population distribution as new modes of transportation are adopted.

Chapter Eleven

Urban Ghettos

G HETTOS, or segregated communities within cities, have long been a source of interest to sociologists, travelers, writers, and the man in the street.

Ghettos are most numerous where peoples meet for the exchange of goods and services, ideas, and social relations. As a general rule, the larger the city the greater the probability of finding various types of ghettos within its confines. It is rare for a large and important city not to have communities of people who differ in some way from what is considered the prevailing or majority group. Ghettos reflect the heterogeneity of population and the complexity of the internal spatial development and pattern of cities.

Modern urban ghettos differ from the Diaspora of the Jews when they were forced to scatter throughout the ancient Greco-Roman world.[1] Diaspora is a Greek term for a nation, or a part of a nation, separated from its own state or territory, dispersed among other nations and peoples but preserving its national culture, language, religion, race, or territorial identity.

While originally the word "Diaspora" was mainly used to refer to the repeated mass deportation or exile of Jews, it has come to be applied to nationals who have emigrated from their homelands and are politically unprotected by their own governments.[2] The migration of economically depressed groups, the settlement of traders, and the flight of persons from political persecution and their resettlement in another country are included in the broader sense of the term. Instead of diminishing in number, ghettos have increased. The mass movement of people outside their homelands has uprooted many nationals since the Industrial Revolution.[3]

[1] *Encyclopedia of the Social Sciences*, 5, 126–131.

[2] *Ibid.*

[3] Everett C. Hughes and Helen M. Hughes, *Where Peoples Meet: Racial and Ethnic Frontiers* (Glencoe: Free Press, 1952) and Oscar Handlin, *The Uprooted* (Boston: Little, Brown & Co., 1951).

Urban ghettos are as old as city-states. While it cannot be strictly claimed that the Roman and Greek city-states had ghettos, there was nevertheless a clear separation between the plebeians and citizens as to where each group lived and what rights and privileges each enjoyed. To a similar degree ghettos located in various cities of the world tend to symbolize the development and maintenance of a set of interethnic, interfaith, and interracial social relations which do not encompass the total population. They draw attention to groups who differ from the local residents. Depending upon whether the ghettos are in Asia, Africa, Europe, the United States, or elsewhere, similarities and differences in their creation and perpetuation are seen.

Kinds of Ghettos

Historically, ghettos were found where new cultural frontiers were ripe for exploration, leading to economic and political gain.[1] Coastal, commercial, cultural, political, and industrial cities, strategically located at points of access to cultural contacts, offered fertile ground for the formation of ghettos. Or if ghettos did not exist when immigrants landed on foreign soil, the newcomers soon created them. In modern times, ghettos have followed the migration of peoples in search of work. Wherever there is commerce, industrial expansion, raw materials, a natural resource to be tapped, or the need for abundant manpower ghettos may be found. Or ghettos may follow political, military, or welfare activities whereby a small number of persons, representing a strong national power or a technologically advanced nation, takes charge of specific projects. The Point Four Programs are examples. Furthermore, the transplanting of persons as indentured laborers or slaves to another region or continent has contributed to the founding of ghettos as immigrants become settlers in cities after they have made occupational mobility, or been emancipated.

Ghettos may be racially homogeneous but culturally divergent, as seen in those occupied by Americans in Paris, London, Rome, Berlin, and Madrid. Rome's 35,000 foreign residents come from all parts of the world, but the largest ghetto is the American one, where over 3,000 are permanently settled. A like number of Americans are employed by governmental agencies, steamship or airline offices, business corporations, or film companies. Cultural islands inhabited by Britons, Germans, Slavs, Orientals, and others are found.

Although there are no pronounced physical distinctions between the Europeans and Americans, the differences between them in language,

---

[1] Hughes and Hughes, *op. cit.*, Ch. 3.

food habits, standards of living, and folkways act to separate groups. The American community in Paris is sufficiently large to support many "home-side" conveniences, including a pick-up and delivery diaper service, said to be the only one of its kind in Europe.

Many European ghettos result from changes in boundary lines, so that groups within major cities may have Spanish, Greek, Armenian, Polish, Czech, or other origins. At the same time, coastal cities of countries having colonial territories outside of Europe attract settlers from Africa, West Indies, and the Near and Far East.

Liverpool, for example, has migrants from India and several South Pacific countries as well as colonial citizens from Africa, the West Indies, and the Near East.[1] Somalis, Malaysians, Burmese, West Indians, Arabs, East and West Africans, Hindus, and Chinese make up a sizable ghetto in Merseyside, an area comparable to the Zone in Transition in American cities. The majority came as seamen or as workers for war industries. They elected to remain, and many have intermarried with the local population. Unlike immigrants from Ireland, Scotland, and the Isle of Man, the assimilation of the Merseyside settlers poses problems related to racial and religious differences. The same situation applies to French, Spanish, Dutch, and Portuguese cities where non-Europeanized migrants from Far Eastern and African territories have settled.

Ghettos differ in African cities according to their locations. In East African cities many "stranger communities" and "stranger quarters" are at the city's outskirts or in designated areas within the city, resulting from the settlement of Indian and Arab traders and the annual recruitment of African laborers from within the continent. The inhabitants of these "stranger communities" are called "stranger natives" (non-whites), who form suburban communities at the city's outskirts or "stranger quarters" within the cities of Kano, Kaduna, or Zaria.[2] They seem more similar to the Native areas and locations in South African cities. On the other hand, Indians live apart from other religious groups and perpetuate their own culture.

There is little likelihood that the ghetto patterns will change in South African or East African cities because city and town planning authorities have earmarked future Native areas and locations and Asiatic and Coloured areas should the population expand. For example: the town plan as proposed for Lusaka, capital of Northern Rhodesia, completed in 1950 is to be reviewed in five years.[3] No self-contained Native area or township

---

[1] Leo Silberman and Betty Spice, *Colour and Class in Six Liverpool Schools* (Liverpool: University of Liverpool Press, 1950), 7.

[2] Hailey, *op. cit.,* 2, 87.

[3] The Lusaka Management Board, "A Plan for Lusaka, Capital of Northern Rhodesia," April, 1950, 7–8 and 11.

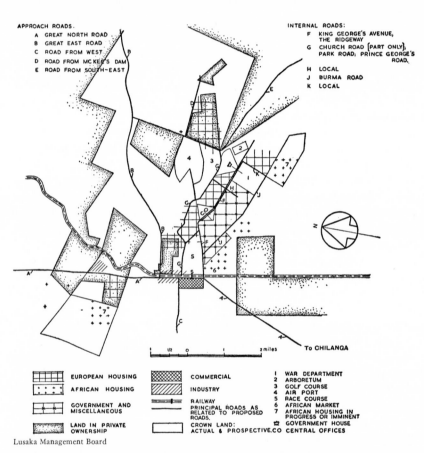

LUSAKA: AS EXISTING 1950

THIS PLAN IS APPROXIMATE ONLY

City plan of Lusáka, Northern Rhodesia, East-Central Africa. Note non-European housing areas at the fringe. Vacant land both inside and outside the city is reserved for a special type of land use, so that segregated Native areas do not encroach upon other areas.

will be allowed to exceed more than 100,000 persons. Five hundred Asiatics are to be permitted to live in the "Inner Town"; in 1950 there were 250 Asiatics there.

In large cities in North Africa ghettos are differentiated by religious affiliation rather than race, when referring to the indigenous population. Walls or some other physical barriers separate quarters with different religious affiliations.

Ghetto formations in cities within the Union of India and Pakistan are based upon caste membership, with religious taboos and observances constituting the barriers between Hindu, Moslem, Christian, Parsis, Sikh, Buddhist, and other believers. Although a division between the Hindu and Moslem populations followed the partition of India, some members of each group remain outside of the prescribed areas of resettlement.[1]

The city of Karachi and the areas surrounding its boundaries has an influx of 815,000 Moslems, while nearly 170,000 Hindus and almost all the Sikhs moved into the Union of India and recreated communities.[2] Most of the Europeans departed. Formerly, each group lived separately because of religious or racial differences. At the present time, religious affiliations constitute the major division between the large Moslem population and the isolated remnants of Hindus and Sikhs face greater segregation than before. On the whole, however, the exchange of the two major religious groups resulted in greater homogeneity.

Two other types of ghettos should be mentioned: those based upon territorial origin and those based upon linguistic similarities. Territorial origin may form the basic social bond between immigrants. Shanghai is a good illustration where Cantonese live apart from Ningponese, Szechuanese, and Hunanese.[3] Ethnic minorities, such as, Manchurians and Mongolians, may again be in different parts of the city.

Where there is such an insufficient number of immigrants that a ghetto cannot be formed on territorial ties, linguistic similarities may be the cohesive force. Persons speaking Bantu form a group and occupy specific wards in South African cities, although they may previously have lived in any of the Union's provinces. Dialects form bonds among peoples of South Asian cities as well.

Ghettos in American cities are so important that they will be discussed in more detail under a separate heading later in this chapter.

[1] Census of Pakistan, 1951, "Population According to Religion," Office of the Census Commissioner, Government of Pakistan, Ministry of Interior, Karachi, Oct., 1951, 34–35.
[2] Census of Pakistan, 1951, "Population According to Religion," Table 6, Census Bulletin No. 2, 34, Statement "K."
[3] See Ch. 4, "North Asian Cities," of this volume.

Characteristics of Ghettos

Several features are characteristic of ghettos during the early and late stages of their formation.[1]

Most ghettos are too small in population to insure the replacement of the group unless more immigrants arrive. Depending upon the nature of the ethnic, religious, and racial interaction between the members of the ghetto and the larger society, the ghetto will disappear if a sufficiently long time elapses between the original settlement of the ghetto and the absorption of the members into the larger society. That is, most ghettos become integrated with the larger social order. This is more often the case when immigrants and the members of the receiving society are ethnically, religiously, and racially homogeneous. Persistence of established ghettos is due largely to the repeated influx of new immigrants or the lack of satisfactory patterns of intergroup accommodation.

An unbalanced sex ratio is another characteristic of ghettos. This mitigates against the survival of ghettos unless new immigrants arrive or more families settle within the ghetto. All first-generation ghettos are predominantly male. The unbalanced sex ratio restricts the selection of mates. Some males may marry native-born women. Should the society regard such unions with disfavor, the offsprings experience a degree of social ostracism, as exemplified by the Eurasians in Asia or the Coloured in Africa. The unfavorable sex balance may cause males to resettle in other ghettos having better sex distributions. This has happened in the United States among Mongoloid groups.[2] Small ghettos peopled by Mongoloids have lost their populations to larger coastal cities located on the Atlantic and Pacific seaboards.

Save for very large ghettos with normal population compositions, most ghettos are too specialized in their institutional framework to provide all the goods and services needed by those living in segregated areas. Few have institutions of higher learning. Many do not have sufficient economic establishments to supply the essentials for everyday living. Food and clothing must be purchased outside, for example, and resold within the ghettos. A degree of reliance upon the larger society is inevitable, and isolation is not as complete as is generally supposed. Isolation is generally restricted to specific areas of social intercourse and hinders continuous interaction, such as membership in clubs, work opportunities, or recreational facilities.

Ghettos are not economically independent. They rely upon the wider

[1] Lee, *op. cit.*, 1–2.
[2] *Ibid.*, 247–248: also see "The Decline of Chinatowns in the United States," *American Journal of Sociology*, 54 (Mar., 1949), 430.

society for the simple reason that most of their residents work outside the community. Since many ghettos resulted from the shortage of manpower or specialized personnel, their existence depends upon the symbiotic relationships developed and maintained with the members of the larger society.

It should be noted that in some societies, African and South Asian in particular, ghettos include more persons than those who set up the pattern of segregation. In the United States we are accustomed to labeling the groups living in ghettos as "minorities," or, if dispersed and regrouped into specific localities by the same term if a retention of cultural, religious, or racial differences is evidenced.[1] Their number is small in comparison to the total society. By implication and factual evidence the majority group is large and more powerful. As the controlling group its language, customs, traditions, and ideologies are normative for the society.

The reverse is true in African and South Asian cities, so that the intergroup relations take on a different character and meaning. The minority (Caucasoids mainly) becomes the group in power by establishing, and often superimposing upon the majority (non-Caucasoid), the patterns of normative behavior. Thus, the majority-minority relations are reversed.[2] Another difference is that the ruled are the original inhabitants, whereas those in power are immigrants. The ruling group is often small but powerful, whereas the majority is frequently without economic and political power.

Whereas in American cities, minorities are often expected to undergo the assimilation process because of the "melting pot" tradition, the opposite is the case of the majority in African and South Asian cities. There assimilation in the strict sense is not the ultimate aim; rather the primary aim is the retention of ghettos.

Ghettos in American Cities

When the United States was experiencing wave after wave of immigration, many ghettos were created at the points of ready access—the areas of transition in major coastal cities. After the transportation lines linked the eastern and western seaboards, other first-generation ghettos were established at major inland cities. Ghettos have often been called "cultural islands" because they represented the addition of self-contained cultural elements to the society. A social bond existed between the immigrants through having common languages, customs, institutional ties, religious

[1] Schermerhorn, *op. cit.,* Ch. 1.
[2] Louis Wirth, "The Problem of Minority Groups," in Ralph Linton (ed.), *The Science of Man in the World Crisis* (New York: Columbia University Press, 1945).

or festive observances, food habits, and the necessity to extend mutual aid and protection to ingroup members living in a new social setting.

It was expected that after undergoing a process of assimilation the foreign-born or their children would break down the invisible ghetto walls that surrounded them and become an integral part of the society's cultural stream. From a historical perspective many ghettos have disappeared where assimilation has proceeded without any major difficulties and ghetto members have effected a degree of social, occupational, and residential mobility.

The fact remains that segregated communities still exist in many cities where the assimilation process has not taken place according to the usual pattern. The "Black Belt" of Chicago, Harlem of New York, the Chinatowns of San Francisco and New York, the Mexican areas of Los Angeles, El Paso, and other Southwestern cities, the Creole communities of New Orleans, Louisiana, and the Puerto Rican settlements in New York are but a few of the many ghettos found in the United States.

Persons who are torn between two cultures because of foreign-born parental pressure and others who have racial or religious differences make up one-third of our total population.[1] Thus, foreign-born status is not the sole criterion for the formation and perpetuation of urban ghettos. As pointed out earlier, 80 per cent of the foreign-born whites and most of their descendants are urbanites. Sixty per cent of the Negroid group are urban and few persons of Mongoloid origin are rural. Ghettos are associated not only with minority status, but they are distinguishable by differences in physiognomy, language, customs, religion, culture-patterns, or any combination of these factors.[2] Often the members of the ghetto are regarded and treated as inherently different and as "not belonging" to the dominant, majority group.

Usually a historical reason provides the basis and rationale for excluding ghetto members from full participation in the dominant group's social life and rights and privileges. The extension of separateness is safeguarded by custom, mores and feelings of pre-eminence. These, in turn, are sanctioned by the society and transmitted from one segment of the society to the next and from one generation to another.

Three historical incidents which caused the creation and retention of urban ghettos are (1) groups transplanted onto American soil, as, for example, the American Negro; (2) migrants accepted for prudential considerations, embracing the European, Ibero-Americans, and Asiatic immigrants; and (3) arbitrary divisions of national boundaries, as experienced by Spanish-Americans.[3] It should be noted that the fourth historical

[1] Simpson and Yinger, *op. cit.,* 721–722.

[2] Schermerhorn, *op. cit.*

[3] *Ibid.,* 7–18.

incident creating minority status is military conquest, and this is best ex-emplified by the status of American Indians. However, they are primarily rural settlers.

By and large the second incident (*i.e.,* immigrants attracted to and per-mitted entry into the country for their roles in furthering the economic expansion of the society) has been most important in the creation and re-tention of ghettos. Since immigrants had diverse backgrounds and often were distinguishable on the basis of physical appearance and apparel, the ghettos identified with these characteristics have not completely disap-peared.

Factors in the growth and decline of ghettos. Few attempts have been made to study the growth, survival, and decline of ghettos. There is a general assumption that native-born inhabitants of the ghettos desire to scale the ghetto walls and often succeed. However, this is not universally true, and the continued existence of these cultural islands is reinforced by renewed waves of immigration, and pressures which prevent many who so desire from leaving the confines of the ghetto.

Ghettos are most prominent in cities which received the first waves of immigrants. However, continued invasion and succession may leave many of these areas with polyglot characteristics, as some of the older genera-tion fail to follow the more general movement while new groups move in, and others remain to exploit the commercial possibilities of ghetto areas. Tourists patronize ghettos as attraction centers, partaking of specialized food served in a novel atmosphere, buying souvenirs, gleaning a glimpse of the unusual, or procuring special items.

Another factor contributing to the survival of ghettos is the redistribu-tion of ethnic or racial population coming from smaller cities or other regions. Isolated members of a minority group may live for years in a small city, move when they become affluent or when they desire greater social and economic opportunities for their children or themselves. But the reverse may also be true. A group that has a huge number in a region may steadily emigrate from the area of settlement in order to gain social and occupational mobility. New ghettos may be created be-cause of population dispersement, as was true of the Japanese group after relocation in the midwestern United States.

"Marooned" families or persons are said to provoke less prejudice and discrimination. The supposition is that they intermingle freely and are wholly accepted by the prevailing society. This may be true when the problem of intermarriage does not become serious. When younger mem-bers of a racial minority group reach marriageable age, the social pressure of the society confronts them. At times parents may be aware of the pres-sures and change residence to spare their children. The move would be toward the cities where more of their group are available for the selection of mates. This phenomenon has been particularly true of the Negro, Mongoloid, and Jewish groups. Small ghettos have declined, but those in large cities have grown and survived.[1] Persons who do not migrate are faced with the possibility of remaining single, or they may permit others to arrange meetings with prospective mates in other cities.

The factors that initiate the decline of ghettos illustrate the symbiotic and commensal relationships they maintain with the larger social order. A ghetto has a dual economic system. One is geared toward supplying the goods and services demanded by its own members, and the other is dependent upon the numerical strength of the group concerned. The ghetto survives as long as the larger society utilizes the services of the ghetto residents and provides employment outside. There are few employment opportunities within the community itself. Many ghetto residents lead dual existences and participate in two social systems. They work away from it but are participants in their own social milieu after work-hours. Economic fluctuations of the larger society affect the ghetto from within and without. Attempts to forestall some of the uncertainties are seen in the Americanization of goods and services, as "attraction baits." In time, the economic establishments attempt to serve the whole city, and transients, rather than the local group. Then the ghetto becomes more like a residential area.

A second factor affecting ghetto decline is the unbalanced sex ratio. As families arrive and children are born into the new society, these families tend to leave the area of first settlement as soon as their social and economic conditions permit. The loss of population and the inability of the group to replace itself with new immigrants has caused many ghettos to decline. The older and single men were left.[2] The unsuccessful ones—this term indicates personal preference in selection of residential site and identifies those who did not find total acceptance within the larger society—find the invisible walls comforting and supportive. Real estate restrictions may be the added reason forcing many to stay and pursue the course of least resistance. Some ghettos of today have remnants of former immigrant groups residing side by side with new arrivals. For example, the Puerto Ricans live among the "unsuccessful" of other migrations: the Irish, Italian, Jewish, or Negro, in the "blighted areas" of Harlem, Bronx, or Brooklyn.[3] Their more fortunate compatriots may live in Central Park West, Riverside Drive, or Washington Heights.

Social and economic change accelerate the decline of ghettos. The widen-

[1] Lee, *op. cit.,* Ch. 8.

[2] Lee, *op. cit.,* Ch. 9.

[3] The Office of Puerto Rico, "The Puerto Ricans of New York City," Washington, D. C.: 1948, 49–50.

ing of occupational opportunities and the relaxing of employment restrictions have made it easier to move out into the larger society. Some do not join this movement because they fear that the barriers may be reerected after a return to normalcy. During the last two world wars, more persons with minority status have experienced occupational mobility than during peacetime. However, they may well be the last to be hired and the first to be fired, especially in the states where no fair-employment-practice legislation exists to safeguard their gains. Depressions can scatter population in search of economic opportunities.

A final cause of the decline of ghettos is the combined force of invasion and succession. The community has definite physical boundaries which mark it off from the surrounding areas. It supports within its confines institutions that meet the needs of the inhabitants. Institutional and population invasion may alter the geographical boundaries and the physical features of the community and result in succession. A community loses its identity when business enterprises invade its environs, causing changing land use and land values. Accompanying this may be a population invasion, when new residents change the population composition and the institutions of the neighborhood. The original group becomes separated, and its identification as a distinct, segregated entity is terminated. The configurations of a community, once altered, seldom again assume their former characteristics.

Where the inhabitants are replaced by others having the same ethnic or racial identity, restrictive covenants may have been the primary factor in enforcing involuntary segregation. The removal of these will cause some expansion into adjacent territories.

In the future, ghettos may be redefined as being the sites of first settlement, selected by rural, intercity, interstate, and intercountry migrants and of immigrants and their descendants. Class and income may be the paramount considerations and race or ethnic origins, incidental. Some large urban ghettos are already showing this type of population composition.

The expressions of prejudice and discrimination extended toward inhabitants of ghettos, especially racial and religious biases, have been the subject of extensive research and action programs. We shall concentrate upon the efforts made by various urban groups toward promoting better human relations.[1] These groups operate upon the proposition that all urbanites should cooperate in performing the functions essential to the society. The greater the cohesiveness of all urbanites, the better the internal solidarity of the city. By and large, the main objective fostered by the groups promoting better human relations involves the removal or reduc-

---

[1] *The Annals of the American Academy of Political and Social Science,* "Controlling Group Prejudice," 244 (Mar., 1946), 117–127.

tion of prejudice and discrimination in housing, education, employment, legislation, vocational guidance, civil rights, recreation, and so on.

Since 1943, 300 urban communities have set up official or unofficial committees for the improvement of intergroup human relations. Thirty-three states have appointed governor's commissions on race relations.[1] Thirty or more municipal committees for "human relations" (or a similar name) have been established through ordinances and are supported by public funds. Full-time staffs are employed who investigate unpleasant incidents reported by citizens and try to bring about adjustment of situations. Thirteen of these municipal committees specify research as one of their important functions.[2] Within a nine-month period in 1949, 149 anti-discrimination bills were introduced in various state legislatures. This trend has continued. On the federal level, several important decisions have been made by the Supreme Court affecting restrictive covenants, employment, education, and civil rights.[3]

Summary

Urban ghettos result from cultural contacts among peoples. Most large cities throughout the world have areas that set off the local inhabitants from immigrants or persons having religious, ethnic, racial, linguistic, or cultural differences. Save for African cities, most ghettos have social rather than physical barriers.

Since the Industrial Revolution there has been a continuous movement of peoples in search of economic opportunity, industrial expansion, a haven from war-torn countries, commerce, or political freedom. Depending upon the type of interethnic, interracial, and interfaith relations developed between the majority-minority groups, ghettos decline or are perpetuated. The countries admitting persons whose backgrounds are more similar to those of the local inhabitants see their ghettos disappear more readily than countries where cultural differences are great.

Ghettos have the following characteristics:

1. They lack political protection of the country of origin.
2. They are too small and specialized to carry on all the usual services and perform the functions required by the ghetto members.
3. They have insufficient population to maintain themselves without new immigration.
4. They have an unbalanced sex ratio in the early stages.
5. They lack economic independence.

[1] *Ibid.*, 106–116.

[2] Schermerhorn, *op. cit.*, 527–529.

[3] American Council on Race Relations, *Supplement to Report 4*, August, 1949.

American ghettos in smaller cities have declined because of four factors:

1. Population or institutional invasion.
2. War or depressions.
3. Lack of immigration.
4. An unbalanced sex ratio.

Two factors make for the survival of ghettos or contribute to the growth of large urban ghettos in the United States: (1) redistribution of population and influx of immigrants, and (2) conversion into "tourist-attracting" areas. It is probable that ghettos of the future will be racially and ethnically mixed and may be based upon economic rather than minority status.

City, state, and federal efforts are being made to promote better human relations in our cities. Voluntary associations at both the local and national level are aiding in reducing prejudice and discrimination.

DISCUSSION QUESTIONS

1. How can a person's physical characteristics retard the assimilation process?
2. What characteristics are common to ghettos?
3. Why do some ghettos persist in spite of the absence of foreign immigration?
4. Compare the different kinds of ghettos found in various parts of the world.
5. How do ghettos of the United States differ from those of South Africa?
6. Why are large cities the points of first settlement of new immigrant groups?

SUGGESTED PROJECTS

1. Study the Puerto Rican and Mexican groups and show how their assimilation may differ from that of the Negro in northern cities.
2. Write a paper on the assimilation process.
3. Study the race relations of Brazil or Hawaii.
4. Study the statutes and federal laws of this country with a view to (1) educational segregation (2) restrictive covenants, or (3) intermarriage.
5. Study the "Black Belt" of a large northern city.

READINGS

Brewton Berry, *Race Relations*. Boston: Houghton, Mifflin Co., 1951.

An approach to race relations according to sociological concepts of interaction.

Carey McWilliams, *A Mask for Privilege: Anti-Semitism in America*. Boston: Little, Brown & Co., 1948.

Showing the patterns of segregation, prejudice, and discrimination toward minorities.

Gunnar Myrdal, *The American Dilemma*. New York: Harper & Bros., 1944.

Two volumes devoted to the development, expression, and extention of prejudicial practices toward the Negro.

R. E. Park, *Race and Culture*. Glencoe, Ill.: The Free Press, 1950.

A compilation of essays on the problem of the social affects of race and culture. A theoretical presentation.

Arnold and Caroline Rose, *America Divided*. New York: Alfred A. Knopf, 1948.

A treatment of minority problems with emphasis on the Negroes.

R. A. Schermerhorn, *These Our People*. Boston: Heath & Co., 1948.

A comprehensive volume on minorities in the United States, with emphasis upon theory, practice, and sentiments.

E. V. Stonequist, *The Marginal Man*. New York: Scribner's, 1937.

A comparison of the marginal man in various cultures and the psychological feelings of marginality.

Louis Wirth, *The Ghetto*. Chicago: University of Chicago Press, 1929.

A natural history approach to the study of the Jewish ghettos, past and present.

Note: The texts on race relations are numerous. Among the new and revised editions are: F. J. Brown and Joseph Roucek, ed., *One America,* New York: Prentice-Hall, 1952; and C. F. Marden, *Minorities in American Society,* New York: American Book Co., 1952.

Part Four

Urban Social Institutions

PROLOGUE *If one examines the culture of any society, one can observe that behavior patterns are largely oriented toward a few basic needs and functions. These recurrent complex behavior patterns revolving around accepted forms of social organization constitute the* institutions *of a society. Thus, institutions are composed of systems of ideal social relations (formal and informal) and systems of social norms or rules which define appropriate behavior for the members of the society.*

This conceptual usage of the word institution *differs from the popular meaning. Institutional behavior in the present sense does not necessarily refer to the actions of the inmate of a hospital or a reformatory as much as to the system wherein this behavior takes place. In the meaning employed here there is a distinction between the institution as referring to an accepted practice and belief, such as religion, and a particular form of institutional organization, such as a church. Both aspects of behavior are interrelated and this fact has often resulted in using the term* institution *when referring to both the accepted behavior patterns and the forms of social organization. The word* family, *for instance, is used to characterize both an accepted practice and a grouping of people constituting a social organization.*

There are a few institutions which are found in almost all societies, since they are concerned with universal human problems. One of these problems is distributing the authority to enforce conformity to social standards, the power which underlies the political *institution. The* economic *institution is based on the production and distribution of goods and services. The problem of regulating sexual relations and the care of offspring underlies the institution of the* family; *and the integration of ethical and supernatural beliefs is within the realm of the* religious *institution. These four types of institutions are frequently referred to as "basic institutions."*

These basic institutions both as to their accepted behavior patterns and forms of social organization are found universally. However, there is great variation in the complexity and rigidity of the form of organization, or institutional structure, and of the system of norms. The institution of the family is universal, but the family as a system of relationships is variable, embracing both monogamous and polygamous forms, for example. Likewise, the sets of standards vary among societies, as may be seen in different regulations of divorce, sexual behavior, and child-rearing practices.

In some of the least complex societies, it is difficult to distinguish among even the basic institutions. As societies become more complex, the institutional structure and functions become more intricate, and the number of distinct institutions increases. In modern Western urban societies, the educational, recreational, and welfare functions have distinct institutional forms.

The word function also has many meanings.[1] As used here, it refers to the relationship of one part of the socio-cultural system to the system as a whole. More precisely, functions are relationships which tend to integrate

---

[1] The discussion of the sociological concept of function on which this presentation is based may be found in Robert Merton's *Social Theory and Social Structure* (Glencoe, Ill.: The Free Press, 1949), Ch. 1.

a society; dysfunctions are relationships which lessen this integration. Relationships which are functional for a society as a whole may be dysfunctional for a sub-group, and a particular relationship may have both functional and dysfunctional elements. Functions (and dysfunctions) may further be classified into manifest and latent functions. Manifest functions are those relationships which are known and intended by members of a society; latent functions are those relationships which are neither known or intended by the members of the society. For example, religious organizations in our society usually have the manifest functions of integrating the community. Frequently, however, they have the latent dysfunction of reinforcing class and ethnic distinctions, a contradiction in functions which is usually not recognized.

The institutional structure in Western urban society is characterized by a great diversity of functions and complex patterns of social organization. The formation of bureaucratic patterns of organization is one of the major characteristics of modern social organization, although bureaucratic patterns have existed in many other societies. Although it has become fashionable to decry all forms of bureaucracy, the formalized sets of relationships which are the essence of bureaucracies still form the most efficient type of institutional organization.

However, the complexity and diversity of needs created in modern urban life has left many needs unfulfilled by the manifest functions of institutional organizations. This leads to the complexity of the latent functions fulfilled by particular organizations. Thus, the political machine is not only concerned with its manifest administrative functions but also with latent functions, such as providing Christmas baskets and obtaining contracts for business firms.

The increasing formalization and specialization of the institutional *structure have one further consequence. To meet specific needs unfulfilled by the institutional structure, there have arisen a great number of associations. Belonging to these organizations is to a varying extent a matter of individual choice. These associations differ in size and purpose, and, at times, attain a complexity of structure and function which gives them many characteristics of an institution.*

Chapter Twelve

Economic Organization

THE CHARACTERISTICS of urbanism in the Western world have largely been a result of the economic changes brought about by industrialization. It is not surprising therefore that the economic institutions and organizations of the West are probably the most complex of all institutional patterns. Some of the implications of the relationship between urbanism and the nature of the economic institution have already been shown, as in the case of the economic factors shaping the ecological and physical structure of the city. Directly or indirectly, aspects of the economic institution will recur frequently throughout this text, as they relate to other phenomena. The occupational structure, one basic reflection of economic organization, will receive special attention in a later chapter. In this chapter, we shall consider two basic aspects of American urban economic organization: industrial structure and the composition of the labor force.

The Industrial Structure

The America of the Revolution was an agrarian country. Most of the framers of the Constitution did not foresee, and many would have been appalled at the thought of, the coming dominance of industry in the United States. Although our basic law often seems maladapted to the needs of an industrial society, it expresses some of the fundamental conditions underlying American industrial development, such as the rights of private property without threat of arbitrary appropriation. The development of industry took place largely with minimal governmental interference, except for protection from external competition.

Factors influencing the location of industry. We have come to identify many regions of the country with concentrations of specific types of industry. Massachusetts and Rhode Island have spinning, weaving, and shoemaking among their leading industries. Connecticut has long been a producer of brass goods, and Pennsylvania is known for carpets. Industrial specialization is in part related to specific natural resources and conditions, but it is also a reflection of the historical period from which certain areas of the country developed. Thus some of the New England States still reflect the industrial structure of earlier days, whereas other areas are characterized by industries which are more recent additions to our over-all industrial structure.

Although investment and other economic factors tend to keep industries in original localities, industries are far from immobile. The accessibility of new raw materials and new markets, changes in transportation and manufacturing methods, and exploitation of natural power have all contributed to a westward movement of industries, parallelling the migration patterns of the population. Since industries find cities their most favorable location, the westward movement of population contributed to the urbanization of the West.

The major factors which govern industrial location in this country may be summarized as follows: (1) nearness to materials, (2) nearness to markets, (3) adequate power, (4) favorable climate, (5) labor supply, (6) investment capital, and (7) momentum of an early start. In South Asian cities, industries are mainly located where colonial powers have control of the area, and raw materials are brought there for processing.

The nearness to materials and markets must be considered not in terms of physical distance alone, but of efficiency of transportation. Cities tend to develop at transportation centers, especially at points where there are breaks in transportation. Chicago, the focus of many rail lines, and a major inland port, airline, and trucking center is perhaps the best example of such a city. These cities tend to include many diverse industries which have little in common except utilization of transportation.

In the early days of industrial development there were considerable advantages to being located near water power.[1] New England cities owed much of their industrial growth to its available water power. Coal and oil have made power available elsewhere. The development of hydroelectric projects has greatly stimulated industrial development in the Pacific Northwest and the Tennessee Valley.

The importance of climate in determining industrial location has been somewhat reduced by technical innovations. For example, air-conditioning has nullified one of the major advantages of locating spinning mills in New England because the proper atmospheric conditions within the plant can be reproduced in the Southern States. And Pacific coast shipbuilders

---

[1] D. S. Kimball and D. S. Kimball, Jr., *Principles of Industrial Organization* (New York: McGraw-Hill Book Co., Inc., 1939), 115–122.

have an advantage over Northeast coast shipbuilders in that their climate makes year-round operations much easier.

Industry depends on an adequate labor supply. The Industrial Revolution was accompanied by a drastic change in agricultural methods. As a result, large numbers of rural unemployed were forced to go to cities in search of employment. This meant that industries had an ample labor force from which to select and to which they could pay low wages. In recent years, the rural-urban drift has diminished to the extent that some cities and their industries are faced with acute labor shortages. These shortages are also most pronounced in industries that depend heavily on skilled labor. Within the United States the rural-urban mobility is greatest in the South, where the cotton picker and other innovations are likely to cause even greater displacement of agricultural workers. As a result industries are moving out of high labor cost areas and into the South, as has been the case with many New England textile plants.

Some industries draw only on particular segments of the labor force. Thus the Berkshire Knitting Mills and the Textile Machine Works operate in the same area because the former depends largely on women, while the latter draws largely on the men in the labor force.

The momentum of an early start is illustrated by various industries. For example, few silverware concerns have ever located outside of the New England states. Other examples include the rubber industry at Akron and automobile manufacturing in Detroit. Cities may develop special facilities, transportation, and a specially trained labor force which may influence late-starters in the same industry to use the same location.

Manufacturing. The period of American industrial expansion may be considered as commencing with the Civil War. Several factors were associated with the rise of large-scale business operations.

One was the Horatio Alger tradition: the idea that a young man working with intensity and persistence would find success inevitable. Coming at a period of population and industrial expansion, the formula worked in many cases, encouraging others to follow the model. Machinery became more complex and efficient, increasing industrial expansion. American wealth, much of which was the result of trading with, but protection against, foreign markets, encouraged native industry. A young and growing population provided an ever-expanding market for basic consumer goods.

The first business combinations characterized by modern business techniques came in 1817: the managerial power to control prices and the amount of production. The marketing of all the finished products was placed in the hands of managerial personnel. Mergers and centralization of production within fewer and fewer corporations became the trend long before the turn of this century.[1] At present there are approximately 300,000 manufacturing establishments in this country. During 1951, private firms invested over two billion dollars in new plants and equipment, an amount exceeded by government investment for defense purposes.

Manufacturing industries are largely located in cities, and, as can be expected, the larger cities have the greater number of individual and plural units. The five supercities outrank all others, with New York claiming the heaviest concentration as the leader in garment, fur, tobacco, and printing industries. Chicago has approximately one-third fewer manufacturing establishments, which is still twice as many as Los Angeles or Philadelphia. Detroit is the fifth in the order of manufacturing supercities.

Although many cities are characterized by one major industry, most cities as they expand take on a more diversified industrial pattern. Older cities on the eastern seaboard have longer industrial histories, and greater concentrations of establishments.

The expansion and urbanization of populations had another important relationship to the nature of industrial development. The development of mass production techniques in most industries greatly facilitated the satisfaction of the needs of a population which could not produce any of these goods for themselves. The food processing industry now exceeds all others in the number of plants, workers, value of products, and inventories, followed by the manufacture of wearing apparel and related products.

Commerce and trade. The growth of manufacturing stimulated and in turn was stimulated by the expansion of commerce. Both wholesale and retail trade have stimulated the growth of cities. The number and proportion of employees in commercial enterprises have constantly increased. This is reflected in the fact that only one-half of a consumer's dollar goes for production costs, the other half covering the cost of marketing. Such services as advertising, insurance, transportation, and selling have become integral parts of the economic organization.[2]

The growth of cities has paralleled the growth of wholesale and retail trade. Transportation facilities are directly connected to those centers where corporations, chain stores, and large-scale financial enterprises and independent businesses concentrate. Metropolitan cities are headquarters for most of the nation's corporate organizations. The automobile has enlarged the average trading area for consumers. Trade that was formerly transacted within a radius of five to six miles has been extended as far as 150 miles. This has resulted in the concentration of major shopping cen-

[1] J. A. Dodd and C. W. Hasek, *Economics: Principles and Applications* (Cincinnati: Southwestern Publishing Co., 1948), Ch. 8.
[2] *Ibid.*, 100–101.

ters in larger cities. Merchandising trade has shifted to cities of between
25,000 to 100,000 inhabitants (Table 25). This is especially noticeable in
the dry goods and wearing apparel. In 1919 there were over 1,000 major
shopping centers in this country, but ten years later the number was reduced to around 700. In 1930 these centers had 7,083 retail chains operating
156,029 stores. Of the chains, 3,177 each operated less than six units or
stores; about 2,000, from 6 to 10 units; over 1,000, from 11 to 25 units;
about 400, from 26 to 50 units; and 337 others more than 50 units. The

TABLE 25. RETAIL TRADE BY CITY SIZE, BUSINESS VOLUME,
AND NUMBER OF EMPLOYEES FOR 1948 [1]

City Size	Number of Stores	Volume Dollar Business (in billions)	Total Employees
500,000 or more inhabitants	328,487	30	1,759,082
250,000 to 499,999	89,186	9	582,168
100,000 to 249,999	126,622	12	730,385
50,000 to 99,999	114,856	10	627,741
25,000 to 49,999	123,133	11	633,974
10,000 to 24,999	174,080	14	768,786
5,000 to 8,999	130,157	9	489,951
2,500 to 4,999	105,947	7	337,629

[1] *Source:* Adapted from United States Census of Business, 1948, Bull. 2-R-5,
5.03 and 5.06.

food stores are the greatest chains, operating the most units. Stores selling
wearing apparel are second. The others in the order of their importance
are the automobile stores and filling stations, general merchandise, furniture and household goods, and restaurants and eating establishments.[1]
Once a city becomes established as a distributing center, new concerns
select it as a point of operation. This trend is pronounced for cities with a
population aggregation of above 250,000. For instance, when an automobile manufacturer installed an assembly plant away from main headquarters, banks, insurance firms, hotels, eating establishments, recreational
facilities, and warehouses followed. New York City leads, Chicago is
second, and Boston third as cities containing head offices of chain store
organizations. Ten others have between three to eight national head offices of chain store organizations, while 15 more have two. Forty have but
one. Thus, 68 cities from the East to the West Coast have 184 head offices of chain store organizations.
Chain stores have shown tremendous growth within the last thirty
years. The growth has been one of constant increase in capital assets and

[1] United States Bureau of the Census, *Census of Distribution:* in the 1930 United States
Summary of Retail Distribution, 5.

in mergers and consolidations. Chain stores serve between 75 and 85 per cent of the nation's urban population. Nearly one-fourth of the units of the three largest food and grocery chains are in cities having less than 10,000 inhabitants. These cater principally to average-income citizens and particularly those living in the most densely populated trading areas. The chain store is one illustration of the application of mass production and distribution practices to retail merchandising. Independent stores have come to rely more and more on catering to specialized wants, carrying smaller but more select stock and items which cannot be profitably produced and distributed in quantity.

The concentration of business. Business enterprises, both manufacturing and commerce, range in size from the corner one-man grocery to General Motors. Businessmen, owners as contrasted to employees, comprise about 8 per cent of the total labor force. Since 1870, however, the proportion of urban businessmen has declined from 17 to 12 per cent.[1] On the surface, this would seem to contradict the belief that business control has become increasingly urban. The important fact to consider is that business has become more and more centralized. In the generation before World War II, the number of manufacturing proprietors decreased by approximately one-third, although the number of manufacturing employees rose by more than one-fourth. Other evidences for the increased centralization of business control are to be found in the number of employees and business volume. "In 1939 one per cent of all the firms in this country—27,-000 giants—engaged over half of all the people working in business. For about thirty years, now, three-fourths of the United States corporations have got only about five per cent of the total corporate income."[2]

Retail stores still include more small businesses, but even here one-fourth of the retail units had 79 per cent of the sales. Furthermore, many independent businessmen, both manufacturers and retailers, although they own their enterprises, through contractual relationships with the "giants" have actually become little more than agents.

This does not stop many from entering business. From 1900 to 1940, almost 16 million new business ventures were launched, for in many instances the initial capital outlay is quite low. However, in the same period, over 14 million businesses failed, showing that small enterprise, which comprised the vast majority of these, is a risky proposition. Dun and Bradstreet's survey of the first six months of 1953, a boom year, shows a monthly failure rate of 700 businesses.[3] The result of this trend has been that the

---

[1] For a fuller presentation, on which this material is based, see C. W. Mills, *White Collar* (New York: Oxford University Press, 1951), Ch. 2.

[2] *Ibid.*, 24.

[3] *U. S. News and World Report,* July 31, 1953, 50–52, "Special Report: Business is Booming—but Failures Rise."

urbanite is decreasingly likely to be an entrepreneur. The typical urbanite has become dependent upon the larger enterprises not only for his goods and services, but for his livelihood.

Finance. The wealth of the country is concentrated in cities. To meet and facilitate the exchange of goods and services required by manufacturing and commerce, great banking systems have developed on a city-wide, county-wide, and state-wide scale. Some are national in scope. California and other states have promulgated laws permitting branch banking, *i.e.,* allowing the establishment and maintenance of branches within the limits of the city where the parent bank is located. Another development of considerable importance was the establishment of chains or groups of banks, bound together by corporate devices for the diverting of banking operations into branches.

At the beginning of the depression over 80 per cent of all the banks were located in cities of less than 10,000 inhabitants. With the mergers resulting from that era, metropolitan banks have grown in assets, clearings, and deposits. The growth of mail-deposits and clearings has widened the radius of banking operations in this country, just as the automobile has enlarged trading areas. Smaller banks find it increasingly difficult to compete against the larger corporations. The once famous "country bank" is rapidly disappearing. Similarly, the small city and county banks located near large commercial centers cannot gain diversification in their operations. Metropolitan banks with large capital and ability to secure trained personnel have the additional advantage of being better able to adjust to the changing industrial and commercial conditions of the country.

In 1930, the United States had over 19,000 banks situated in cities of less than metropolitan size.[1] These constituted four-fifths of the nation's banks, with capital assets of nearly 50 million dollars. Since that time, banking operations have changed. Now, headquarters for chain and parent banks and investment trusts are located in metropolitan centers. Many large banks have substantial control of smaller outlying financial organizations through the acquisition of stock and through affiliated directorates. When a big loan is contemplated and consummated, it may be divided among the banks in the chain. New York conducts the largest volume of banking business in the nation. More financial operations are controlled from this city than from any other. The next important financial center is Chicago, with Detroit ranking third. These cities are largely manufacturing, commercial, and trade centers so that the affiliation between industry and finances is apparent.

In recent years, approximately fifty of the leading insurance companies

[1] G. T. Cartinhous, *Branch, Group, and Chain Banking* (New York: The Macmillan Co., 1931), 1–113.

with head offices in metropolitan cities have engaged in banking operations known as the investment-trust type, a method which limits the investment in one industry or company. The insurance companies have
financed large construction projects, *e.g.,* banks, public utilities, and housing. Investing on a long-time basis, they avoid holdings which might involve responsibility in a particular undertaking and are primarily interested in the investment *per se*. Others in this category are the building
and loan companies, credit unions, sales finance companies, savings bank
and personal finance companies. Security brokers and dealers make loans
to individuals.

Service enterprises. Paralleling the growth of manufacturing and the
distribution of goods is the steady increase of various types of service enterprises. The United States Census of Business classifies services into
seven major groups: personal services, business services, services allied to
transportation, automotive repair services, other repair services, custom industries, and miscellaneous services. Each of these seven classifications is
subdivided into 71 kinds of business undertakings. At the beginning of
World War II, more than 600,000 small individual service enterprises performed 66 per cent of the various services required by individuals and
firms.

Service industries differ from retail trade in two ways. One is that "services" offer activities used primarily by other business organizations rather
than individuals. Some services, however, are entirely for the individual
consumer, who purchases the service as a retail item. The "personal services" are of this nature. There are a few services that are required by both
businesses and individuals, as for example, "automotive repair and other
repair services."

The second difference between the service and retail businesses lies in
the behavior of consumers. The services offered may or may not be utilized by the potential consumers' group. Many urbanites do their own
laundry, radio repairing, and interior decorating. Some business establishments may provide services as an incentive toward patronage. In general,
urbanism is characterized by an increased tendency to depend on others
for services, although cost factors and "do-it-yourself" fads act as checks.

The Labor Force

The labor force represents the portion of the population employed in
the production of goods and services.[1] More precisely, the labor force con-

[1] John Durand, *The Labor Force in the United States, 1890–1960* (New York: Social
Science Research Council, 1946).

One out of five mothers with children
under 18 years of age works outside the home

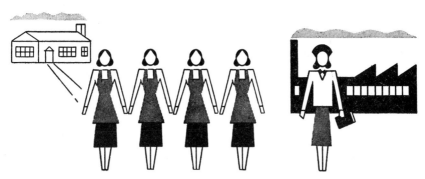

Many mothers with young children work to balance the family budget.[1]

sists of two groups: those working and those seeking work within a specified period. Some may be unemployed when the census is taken but are
not idle through their own volition. On the other hand, not all persons
of working age are permanently employed, regardless of personal or other
reasons. In any community, the population may be reasonably divided into
four major groups: breadwinners, homemakers, students, and miscellaneous unemployed. The last group includes those who are too young or too
old to work, the incapacitated, and those who are able to work but for
some reason remain unemployed.

The size of the labor force is affected by the age composition of the
population. Those above 14 years of age, whether male or female, are potential members of the labor force. In 1951 there were almost 112 million
persons 14 years and over in the United States [2] (Table 26). Persons below
this age are excluded by child labor laws and the fact that compulsory educational requirements restrict the full-time employment of those below sixteen. The labor force has increased in size because of the number of persons reaching adulthood and more older persons experiencing a longer
life span. The estimated 1951 civilian labor force was almost 63 million.
Almost one-half of the potential labor force was unemployed, keeping
house, incapacitated, institutionalized, or did not report. The actual unemployment figure of slightly less than 2,000,000, is extremely low, and

[1] *Children and Youth at the Midcentury—A Chart Book,* prepared by the Midcentury
White House Conference on Children and Youth (Raleigh, N. C.: Health Publications Institute, Inc., 1951).

[2] U. S. Bureau of the Census "Annual Report of the Labor Force, 1951," Series P-50,
No. 40 (May 19, 1952), 2.

TABLE 26. SUMMARY OF EMPLOYMENT STATUS: 1949 AND 1951,
THE UNITED STATES (PERSONS 14 YEARS OF AGE AND OVER) [1]

Employment Status	Annual Average 1951	Annual Average 1949
Non-institutional population 14 years and over	111,924,000	109,623,000
Total labor force, including armed forces	65,832,000	63,571,000
Civilian labor force	62,884,000	62,105,000
Employed	61,005,000	58,709,000
in agriculture	7,054,000	8,026,000
in nonagricultural industries	53,931,000	50,684,000
Unemployed	1,879,000	3,395,000
Not in the labor force	46,092,000	46,051,000

Note: The annual averages presented in this report are averages of the monthly figures obtained from the Census Bureau's Current Population Survey. Since the averages and other figures are based on a sample, they are subject to sampling variability.

[1] *Source:* Bureau of the Census, *Annual Report on the Labor Force,* 1951, Ser. P-50, No. 40 (May 19, 1952), 2, Table A.

includes persons "between jobs." By 1954 the number of unemployed increased to almost four million.

Older cities tend to show a greater increase in the proportion of females in the labor force, which is accounted for in part by the fact that eastern cities have a larger proportion of single women. Areas in which native-born women predominate also tend to show a greater number of women in the labor force. In general, there has been a consistent increase in the number of women in the labor force. The rising trend since the turn of this century is undoubtedly due to (1) economic necessity, (2) the greater number of divorced, widowed, and single women, and (3) social acceptance of women in industries. The number of married women joining the labor force has been equally consistent. Many may be the sole or principal breadwinners.

In many families wives' contributions to family incomes did not make the groups wealthy. Nearly 15,000 families with earning wives were studied before the end of World War II.[1] Almost 3,300 wives were principal earners. In three-fifths of the families the additional income did not raise the annual total earnings above $2,000. In one-eighth, the yearly income was less than $1,000.

In 1950, the annual median income of almost 39 million families was $3,068. The largest single group of nearly four million families earned between $3,000 to $3,499 that year. Ten per cent of the urban and rural-non-farm families earned this amount. On the other hand, 12.9 per cent of the

[1] United States Department of Labor, *Labor Information Bulletin,* Nov., 1944.

urban and rural-nonfarm families earned below $500 that year. Slightly more than a million earned above $10,000. In contrast the groups that were pseudofamilies—unrelated individuals living together as an economic unit—has a median annual income of $2,599. The median annual income for urban and rural-nonfarm families was $3,245.

Both fathers and mothers of 15 per cent of the nation's children were in the labor force. Almost 1.6 million mothers with children of pre-school age worked to raise the level of family living when faced with living costs in 1950. About the same number in each group of mothers with children below the age of junior and senior high schools worked that year.[1]

Far Eastern and American Industrial Structure and Labor Force Differences

When comparing the industrial structure of Far Eastern societies which are becoming urbanized with that of the highly developed one in the United States, several differences are seen.

Primary is the fact that many industries in the Far East operate on a small scale. In most cases the size of the physical plant and the use of mechanical power is minute. China's and Japan's criteria for distinguishing a cottage type industry from a modern factory is the employment of 30 or more persons.[2] In Egypt this number is ten.

Secondly, capitalization is small. In Formosa an enterprise is classified as a factory if it has a paid-up capital of $10,000.

Summary

The economic organization of American cities has shifted from primary extraction to manufacturing industries. The growth of commercial and service enterprises has paralleled the trend. Cities are the workshops of the nation and attract various types of industries because of a ready-made market. Both wholesale and retail establishments are located in cities, with the metropolitan centers having the largest concentration. Financial organizations have located in them and have usurped the role which small banks played before the depression of the thirties. The radius of shopping and banking has been extended by the automobile and mail service. The result has been a decline in the number of shopping centers.

The age, location, and economic base of the city affects the size and character of the labor force. In all cities and industrial areas throughout

[1] Paul C. Glick, "Population Changes: Their Effect on Children and Youth." Paper presented at Midcentury White House Conference on Children and Youth, Washington, D. C., Dec. 4, 1950.

[2] See Chapter 4.

the country, there has been an ever-growing proportion of female employees. As the city's industrial structure matures, there is a tendency toward the consolidation of proprietary and managerial positions, fewer manual and unskilled workers, and a corresponding growth in the number of skilled workers. In contrast, the industrial structure of Far Eastern cities is similar to that of the United States before large-scale organization and production was introduced. The unskilled workers of these cities constitute a large proportion of the labor force.

DISCUSSION QUESTIONS

1. What were the major factors in determining the industrial location in some city in which you are interested?
2. What trends have been present in affecting the gradual shift from extraction to production industries?
3. How have the automobile and mail services affected smaller cities as shopping and financial centers?
4. Discuss the trend of big business.
5. What are chain stores unable to put the neighborhood ones out of business?
6. Why do specialty shops continue in operation?
7. Discuss the role of service enterprises as related to the customer; to the dealer.
8. What factors affect the labor force?
9. Why has there been an increase in female employees?

SUGGESTED PROJECTS

1. Study the growth of retail and manufacturing businesses in the United States since 1800.
2. Compare the changes in the country's labor force from 1870 to the present.
3. Study how the child labor laws have changed the character of the labor force.
4. Study the growth of national corporations and the location of their branch offices in metropolitan cities.

READINGS

Gaines T. Cartinhous, *Branch, Group, and Chain Banking*. New York: The Macmillan Co., 1931.

An account of the intricacies of the banking business.

John Durand, *The Labor Force in the United States, 1890–1960*. New York: Social Science Research Council, 1946.

A comparison of the growth and changes of the nation's labor force. A prediction of its character by 1960.

John P. Nichols, *The Chain Store Tells Its Story*. New York: Institute of Distribution, Inc., 1940.

A readable treatment of the chain store and its growth.

Twentieth Century Fund, *Big Business, Its Growth and Place,* 1937.

A treatment of a controversial topic, taking the position that "big business" is not as big as it seems.

United States Census Bureau. Consult the various volumes for pertinent statistics.

Chapter Thirteen

Political Organization

As SEEN in earlier chapters, the emergence and development of municipal government is often used as an index of urban growth. Some official agencies, such as found within the Federation of Malaya and Union of South Africa, consider this to be the characteristic which distinguishes urban from rural areas. From the earliest cities to the present, political organization as exemplified by that found in urban centers has been a crucial criterion as to whether or not the populace has shifted its local loyalties and ties to a representative form. Modern urban government is complex. In some instances the municipal governments of large cities exert a strong influence over the states or provinces wherein the cities are located.

American Urban Government

American city government has long been a favorite topic of discussion, more likely than not with at least a few overtones of disapproval. At the turn of the century, Lincoln Steffens and his fellow "muckrakers" pointed to the "shame of the cities": abuses by public officials and city bosses who grasped power and wealth at the expense of their constituents. Some reforms have followed, but many hold that the change is far from complete.

A portion of the so-called "abuses" stem from a lag between the growth of cities and municipal services. American cities depend on state legislatures for a definition of governmental powers. Growth and the need for services have frequently gone far beyond the powers granted by legislative enactments. The city problem is often complicated by rural dominance of legislatures and by vested interests. Although the urban householder may be most directly affected by the state of municipal affairs, he is apt to be least interested and active in the political concerns of the city.

Metropolitan areas form another problem, since they frequently encompass parts of more than one state, as in the case of New York City and several Eastern states. They are often composed of a number of distinct political units. Usually cities are underrepresented in state legislatures. Legislatures under the control of rural areas are extremely reluctant to redistrict states in accordance with urban population growth.

City governments operate in a context of constantly increasing functions which the formal political structure frequently cannot or does not satisfy. In this chapter we shall consider some of the patterns of formal political organization and their complex manifest and latent functions.

Municipal Powers and Organization

The city as a municipal corporation is a political body subordinate to state government. As a creation of the state it must meet the following requirements:

(1) It must be an incorporation possessing a charter conveying corporate powers. (2) It must have a corporate name in which all its acts are done, such acts being authenticated by the use of a corporate seal. (3) It must include a body of inhabitants exercising the corporate powers, whether directly or through official agents. (4) It must be an area within which the corporate functions are exercised.

Municipal powers. As a corporation, the municipality has the right to sue and be sued, to possess a seal, and to make and enforce ordinances through designated public officials. However, as a creation of the state, its authority may be enlarged, abridged, or entirely withdrawn at will by the legislature. A great variety of statutory limitations exist, varying from state to state. A case in point is the form of charter a city may adopt, or the method of framing it. In some states, the legislature is forbidden by the constitution to charter cities by special acts; in others, all charters are granted in this manner. Still others prohibit changes in charters unless the citizens consent to them, while some guarantee to the municipal electorates the right to frame their own charters and enforce them without legislative interference.

Other limitations include the amount of indebtedness a city may assume, the control of the police force, and the right of eminent domain. While the last two are not general, the first is universal.

Generally, states grant to cities the power of eminent domain; the right to levy taxes; to own, manage, and sell property; to pass and enforce ordinances; to maintain police power; and the authority to borrow, appropriate, and spend money. Moreover, cities can enter into contracts. No two municipalities have precisely the same set of powers.

Statutes granting municipal powers may be mandatory or permissive. If a statute provided that a city "shall" or "must" perform some act, the power conferred is mandatory. City authorities must exercise it. If a statute provided that a city "may" do something, or that "it shall be lawful," then the power conferred is permissive. The exercise of the power is left to the discretion of the local officials.

Powers granted to the city by the legislature are reflected in the city ordinances, the usual medium through which the municipal authorities put the powers into action.

Charters. City charters may vary with the size of population. The type of charter granted to a first-class city, having a large population, may differ from that granted to a second-class city, having a smaller population. The population basis for classifying cities is arbitrarily established by the state constitution under the assumption that the criteria employed suited cities of more or less the same size. Frequently, no recognition is given to future growth of population or to specific problems, needs, and interests of cities within the group.

To protect cities against overpowering legislatures, the most effective measure devised is that known as the "home-rule charter" system. Missouri appears to have been the first to give this provision in 1875 to cities of over 100,000 inhabitants. This enabled them to frame and enact their own charters. The voters of the city may elect a charter board of thirteen members, either to frame a new city charter or to revise an old one.

Forms of Municipal Government

Municipal governments have undergone changes since the founding of cities. The colonists modeled their city governments after those in England. Other forms followed when voters became dissatisfied with existing types. Cities were regarded as extensions of the state. No provision had been made for cities when the federal government came into existence, so that states framed constitutions minimizing the importance of local governments. No single factor is responsible for faulty government, but often explanations can be found: (1) in the lack of flexibility in structure because of strict adherence to traditional forms of local government, (2) with regard to incompetent and, at times, corrupt officials who failed to achieve the end for which structure provided the means, and (3) in the indifference of the electorate in demanding reforms commensurate with changing conditions.

As cities multiplied in number and importance, states increased their functions by removing restrictions contained in their constitutions. Other forms of local government, the commission and the city manager, were created as a solution.

Mayor-council form. The traditional form of municipal government in the United States is the mayor-council form. Almost 1,400 municipalities having more than 5,000 inhabitants use this type (Table 27).[1] The executive and legislative officials are elected by the people. Powers of the two groups are kept separate to balance and offset each other, thus forestalling arbitrary and oppressive governmental action. This thesis of the separation and balance of power underlies both the strong-mayor and weak-council or the weak-mayor strong-council forms of municipal government.

The weak-mayor, strong-council form. This plan was established to guard carefully against the strong executive. The mayor functions as the chief executive of the city but has few real powers. He makes a few important appointments which usually have to be ratified by the city council before they become effective. In most cities, the mayor is granted the power to veto legislation passed by the city council, but the council can override the veto. Thus, the control of the administration is shared by the mayor and the council alike.

This plan is unpopular because the power of the mayor is so restricted that he cannot be held responsible for any phase of the government's activities. Should the mayor attempt to overcome this limitation and gain more power, he must win the council members over to his general views. However, this results in political manipulation and favoritism. By promoting a strong political party organization, coordination between the executive and legislative bodies results in a fusion of powers.

The strong-mayor plan. This plan seeks to remedy some of the severe defects of the weak-mayor plan while retaining the general mayor-council form. New York, Chicago, Boston, Detroit, and Los Angeles possess this type of government.

The mayor is given almost complete control of the city's administration. He appoints and removes most of the department heads, approves or vetoes legislation passed by the council, and exercises considerable control over the city budget. The council is usually elected by wards while the total electorate chooses the mayor, the judges and clerks of the municipal court, perhaps the board of education, and others. Since the number of elected officials varies in cities, the precise size of the ballot is indefinite.

The main advantage of the plan is the concentration of executive authority in the hands of the mayor. Thus, he can be charged with abuse of power when he shifts his responsibility to others, just as he wins praise as an effective administrator by conscientiously overseeing the affairs of

[1] *The Municipal Year Book*, 1951, 39.

TABLE 27. THE GOVERNMENT OF AMERICAN CITIES BY SIZE OF POPULATION, 1950 [1]

Population Group	Total Number Cities	Mayor Council		Commissioner		Manager	
		Number	Per Cent	Number	Per Cent	Number	Per Cent
Over 500,000 excludes Washington, D. C.	17	15	88.2	1	5.9	1	5.9
250,000 to 500,000	21	7	33.3	7	33.3	7	33.3
100,000 to 250,000	67	29	43.3	17	25.4	21	31.3
50,000 to 100,000	125	47	37.6	30	24.0	48	38.4
25,000 to 50,000	243	112	46.1	51	21.0	80	32.9
10,000 to 25,000	754	401	53.2	125	16.6	228	30.2
5,000 to 10,000	1,091	778	71.0	105	9.6	208	19.1
All cities over 5,000	2,318	1,389	59.9	336	14.5	593	25.6

[1] Source: By permission from The Municipal Year Book, 1951, 39 (Table 1), of the International City Managers' Association, Chicago, Ill.

the municipality. He can be held responsible for the powers given him by the electorate. The short ballot is another good feature of the strong-mayor plan.

One of the disadvantages is that the electorate does not always select the best official for the position. The strong-mayor plan has not eliminated graft and favoritism. A strong mayor often controls the party responsible for his election and maintains this power beyond the expiration of his term. Defeat of the machine is difficult and members of the electorate may find themselves saddled with an incompetent and dishonest executive.

A second disadvantage of the strong-mayor plan is that the separation of powers between the council and mayor does not always exist. Where a party machine has been entrenched, the council is often pressed to carry out the policies of the mayor rather than to check his power. The result is that legislative and executive powers are fused.

The final drawback to the strong-mayor plan is that conflicts between the mayor and the council may develop. Although the councilmen know that policy-making and the execution of the ordinances passed are their functions and administration belongs to the mayor, they may resent the latter's control over the administration. When borderline cases arise over which each side believes it has jurisdiction, there is a test of power. Both councilmen and mayor want to take credit for solving important problems. This way they attempt to insure re-election.

New York is an example of a city with a strong-mayor government. The mayor has strong, centralized powers. He appoints nearly all the department heads, with or without the council's approval. His veto power is great, as is his control over the budget. He grants franchises for municipal utilities.

Philadelphia is an illustration of the combined strong-mayor and strong-council plan. The mayor is not without authority, but he is greatly restricted in his appointments of department heads and members of boards and commissions. They must be approved by the council. The electorate selects eleven important administrative offices. The council may completely ignore the budget proposed by the mayor and substitute its own.

Commission form. The first departure from the traditional mayor-council form of city government was the commission form. This type negated the time-honored theories of the separation of the administrative and legislative powers. The commission form is based on the theory that the principle of division of powers has no place in business administration. Since the work of city authorities is business, not government, all legislative and administrative authority should be fused and concentrated within one agency.

The commission form of local government first appeared in Galveston,

Texas in 1901, when a critical situation faced the residents of the city after a tidal wave swept in from the Gulf. About one-third of the city was destroyed. Municipal authorities were faced with the problem of reconstruction. Since the old, corrupt, and inefficient government was literally swept away, and the city's finances were in a depleted state, the main real estate owners requested the legislature to place the city under receivership in order to avoid financial ruin. They also requested that the powers formerly vested in the mayor, aldermen, and other auxiliary organs of city government be delegated to five commission men. The legislature acted accordingly. At a popular election held every two years, five commissioners are elected. One man is chosen mayor-president. He presides at all of the commission's meetings but otherwise has no special powers. Other cities may have seven commissioners elected for four years. The variations of the commission form of city government are best illustrated by the Galveston and Des Moines plans.

Galveston and Des Moines plans. In the first, known as the Galveston Plan, the commissioners themselves are not expected to be experts responsible for the actual operating of any of the administrative departments. Elected officials are given the power to hire and discharge heads of departments appointed by commissioners. The commissioners formulate policies and are responsible to the people for the actions of the department heads in regard to accounts and finance, public safety, public affairs and health, streets and public improvements, and parks and public property.

The second plan, more frequently adopted, is known as the Des Moines Plan. Each commissioner actually heads one of the departments and holds a full-time position with salary. In the Des Moines Plan, the government is divided into five general departments. The mayor is superintendent of the public affairs department. A commissioner-at-large is elected to act as superintendent of each of the departments and, as the executive officer, is responsible for its proper operation. The five officials comprise a city council managing the affairs of the city, much as a board of directors manages the affairs of a large corporation. The officials are vested with all save judicial powers. Districts, wards, and party lines are abolished in the popular election of officials. Such subordinate officials as the chief of police, city clerk, city engineer, city treasurer, and city auditor are appointed by the council and may be discharged at will. Each department has several subsidiary organs within it. For instance, the Department of Public Affairs includes the legal department, the municipal court, city clerk's office, and municipal garage. All the subordinate positions within the departments, except common laborers and private secretaries, are selected through civil service examinations.

In 1950 approximately 15 per cent of all cities were organized according to the commission form (see Table 27). This form never held much appeal for large metropolitan cities. Only one city of more than 500,000 used it. Most cities adopting it had a range of population between 5,000 to 25,-000. Denver, for example, relinquished the plan in 1916; Lynn and Salem in Massachusetts did likewise. Large cities operating under the commission form include Newark, New Orleans, Portland (Oregon), St. Paul, Omaha, Birmingham, and Memphis.

The commission form of local government concentrates the responsibility for efficient government in a group of five or seven commissioners. These commissioners cannot shift the responsibility elsewhere, since no council exists to bear the brunt. To the commissioners goes credit for accomplishments and criticisms of what remains undone or that which has been improperly executed. Friction between the legislative and executive officials is eliminated, however.

Another feature of the commission plan is its simplicity.[1] The average citizen can understand the machinery of local administration. The short ballot enables the voters to examine, more vigorously, the qualifications of the candidates. The resulting economy in salaries, elections, and operating expenses should not be underestimated. Galveston, on the brink of bankruptcy when the new form was initiated, saved one million dollars in less than five years.

The disadvantages of the commission form are several. One stems from the concentration of powers in the group of men who combine legislative and administrative duties. This group may not be sufficiently large to perform all the needed functions. When power is not concentrated, commissioners may "pass the buck." They may act as one or as several separate units. Rivalry between commissioners is not uncommon. "Log-rolling" is practiced. The department receiving the largest appropriation can demonstrate "more" improvements while the unpopular commissioner is punished. Public interest suffers indirectly.

A serious weakness, apparently difficult to overcome, is that commissioners are often amateurs in the field of government and may not have the knowledge and skill for administering the departments which they head. Personal popularity often supersedes competence. In Topeka, Kansas, the water commissioner was a barber by trade; the public-works commissioner, a newspaper reporter; and the street commissioner, a housemover.

The city-manager form. The third and final form of city government is the city-manager type, known also as the council-manager or the commission-manager. Staunton, Virginia, is generally accredited with initiat-

---

[1] D. G. Bishop and E. D. Starratt, *The Structure of Local Government* (Washington, D. C.: The National Council for the Social Studies, 1945), 27.

ing the city-manager form in 1908 in order to strengthen a tottering mayor-council government. The mayor and bicameral council passed an ordinance authorizing the employment of a general manager. They delegated to him the authority to direct all administrative affairs when the officials could no longer cope with the inefficiency of council committees in handling municipal problems. Lockport, New York, and Sumter, South Carolina, followed the experiment. Dayton, in 1914, was the first large city to test the new form and her experience removed any doubts of impracticability and unworkable administrative problems.

By 1920, 227 cities had adopted the city-manager form. The depression of the thirties slowed the rate of adoptions. By 1952, over 1,000 cities used this form, whereas in 1951, only 593 cities had this form of government.[1] Cities with 10,000 to 25,000 inhabitants find it most suitable. Only one municipality with a population of more than 500,000 uses the plan. All but six states have statutes permitting its adoption.[2]

The city-manager form of local government is based on the theory that private business enterprise functions most efficiently and economically when administered by a capable executive. He carries out the policies determined by a board of officers. The two functions, policy-making and policy-executing, can be separated but coordinated when a third person, the liaison, administers the execution of policies. An analogous practice is found in various school, park, and health boards which for years have been entrusting the administration of their affairs to appointed superintendents, directors, or managers.

The acceptance of the city-manager plan was furthered by the recognition that growing functions and services in cities paralleled the increases in population and the physical sizes of municipalities. A capable administrator appointed by the council to run an economical and well-coordinated government gained public favor. By the application of the manager's specialized knowledge and techniques to such procedures as a modern budgetary control system, centralized purchasing, internal auditing, and proper personnel selection, an integrated organization should result.[3]

General description of the city-manager form. The city-manager form provides for an elective council which appoints the manager. Councils in the city-manager cities are generally smaller than those of the mayor-council form. Elected by the people, the council is directly responsible to them. As the policy-determining agency of the city, it has two main functions: (1) to pass ordinances, and (2) to select and supervise the city manager.

[1] *The Municipal Year Book,* 1952, 1.

[2] C. M. Kneier, *City Government in the United States* (New York: Harper & Bros., 1947), 309.

[3] Clarence E. Ridley and Orin F. Nolting, *The City-Manager Profession.* (Chicago: The University of Chicago Press, 1934), 10–12.

In most cities the office of mayor is retained. As the presiding official, the mayor has no important powers as a member of the council. He is the ceremonial head of the government. The city manager, on the other hand, manages the affairs of the municipality.

The council holds the key to the success or failure of the manager plan, for much depends upon its judgment in selecting, cooperating with, and working with the manager. The elected councilmen have been of a higher caliber. The council can devote more attention to general policies and programs, instead of wasting it on minor and routinized matters. All the administrative departments are responsible to the manager. The short ballot is used.

Advantages and disadvantages of the city-manager form. The primary advantage of the city-manager form is its businesslike character. The voters correspond to the stockholders of a corporation, the city council to the board of directors or trustees, and the city manager, to the general manager who is employed to manage the corporation. Modeled from a type of organization with which the electorate is familiar, it has been termed "the best type of local government devised." [1]

The greatest advantage of the city-manager form is that trained administrators are drafted for urban management. Many public servants in other forms of government lack training in public administration.

A third argument in favor of the city-manager form is that it rids the city administration of the influence of partisan politics. The city manager is not under the pressure of groups seeking favors for the "machine." In fact, a political machine finds sterile ground under this plan. Many cities have adopted this form of government to free themselves from a corrupt government.

Impartial selection of civil servants is an additional advantage. The merit system can function without political pressure. The more qualified his subordinates, the more superior the work of the city manager becomes. He cannot afford to jeopardize his own position by selecting incompetent persons. Civil servants are freed from campaign assessments and political activity. Payrolls are difficult to pad. City managers have effected savings by (1) eliminating waste in materials and supplies; (2) reducing city indebtedness by retiring bonds when mature and meeting interest payments; (3) lowering the tax rate by initiating a sounder financial program; and (4) promoting long-range health, safety, and educational measures.

A decided advantage is the democratic relationship existing between the governed and the governing. In other forms of municipal government, public officials have an obligation to the electorate but many fail to render

[1] Bishop and Starratt, *op. cit.*, 33.

periodic reports of their activities. Mayors seldom make reports; city managers, however, can and do. Since this is one criterion of satisfactory service, the issuance of good reports has become a matter of professional pride.

By far the most constant complaint is that the benefits are temporary. The city-manager government becomes increasingly like the old one abandoned in its favor. Civic pride and ardor for reform subside after the initial pitch of enthusiasm has passed. Another complaint is that a good city manager is induced to leave one position for another with higher salary, and successive managers are chosen from local residents. Not a few states specify that a non-voter cannot accept the position of city manager, thereby paving the return for partisan politics. Confidence in the plan is shaken and then abandoned.

Where abandonments occur, faulty city charters and bad governmental practices usually have worked in a combination that could not be overcome by change. The city-manager form of government is blamed, whereas the basic reasons for the failure have not been attacked. From 1908 to April, 1947, only 29 cities abandoned the plan. Among them were Cleveland and Akron, Ohio; Trenton, New Jersey; Fall River, Massachusetts; Tampa, Florida; and Binghamton, New York. In an analysis of the 25 cases of abandonment up to 1940, Bromage gave the following as main reasons: (1) defective charters, (2) economic recessions when voters showed their resentment against taxes by changing the form of government, and (3) strong organization and effective work by political interests to overthrow this form while citizens did not exert sufficient effort to maintain it.[1] This study indicated that citizens in these cities did not give this form a fair trial.

Cities with a population totaling 500,000 or more have not adopted this form. The main reasons appear to be (1) a firmly entrenched political party machine and (2) the complexity of metropolitan government. In 1950, 25.6 per cent of all cities above 5,000 population used this form of government (see Table 27).

Metropolitan Governments

A metropolitan area embraces varied and manifold political units but is often regarded as a social and economic unit. It is a physical unit larger than the political confines of the central city. Politically, however, a metropolitan area is not a single unit. The central city and the many incorporated and unincorporated territories are each organized into distinct governmental entities.

[1] A. W. Bromage, *Manager Plan Abandonments* (New York: National Municipal League, 1940).

Until now our discussion has been confined to the political organization of cities wherein the political boundaries divide one entity from the next. For the past four decades a new political problem has defied easy solution: how to amalgamate the manifold political units, achieve efficient municipal administration, and retain the functions required by the growing population of metropolitan areas.

Confusion arises when population and institutional organizations depart from the central city, locate in satellite and suburban communities, and become independent political units but remain dependent upon the larger for all but political protection. This is not as troublesome as the trend toward creating many coterminous districts and governments within the area to cope with expanding functions and services demanded by the total unit. The interdependence of the periphery and the central city becomes accentuated. Central cities have been unable to annex sufficient territory to embrace the influx of population and to stem the mushroom growth clustering their boundaries. Peripheral units have grown at a greater rate than the central cities, and very large metropolitan cities appear to have attained maximum areal growth; but the welfare of the smaller political units cannot be ignored.

Within the metropolitan area several coterminous governments may coexist. For example, a county government performs some of the same functions and services as the municipality. The state government extends its influence and control over the municipality and the county. Recently the federal government has been invading the city's confines to render services and to levy taxes.

Without a doubt, the most detrimental effect these governments have upon urbanites is the excessive taxation which is levied to provide for the overlapping services. The larger the city, the more tax-levying and tax-collecting bodies and special districts there are. When these fail to cope with the growing number of functions or social problems, special authorities or districts are created. Urbanites are becoming increasingly aware of housing authorities, port authorities, transit authorities, and other such agencies. These are not as widespread as the creation of special districts to furnish water, heat, light, and power, transportation, sewage disposal, and health inspection to suburbs and outlying areas.

In some instances a municipality's regulatory powers may invade other states. For example, Chicago authorities inspect milk at the dairies located in five neighboring states. This takes inspectors into areas supplying the city's milk supply and requiring food and sanitation standards set by Chicago's agencies. On the other hand, a state statute may compel a city to enlarge its utility services outside its boundaries but limits the city's power to regulate rates. Water rates provide a good illustration. Thus, the larger city actually bears the expense of construction without being able to charge a rate which is sufficient to compensate for this expenditure. In turn, the outlying areas may sell at a profit the utilities extended from the central city. In this manner they bolster their financial status and use the profit for other civic improvements. New York and Chicago are two examples of cities required by law to furnish utilities to certain suburban municipalities but are unable to establish rates that compensate for the increased expenditure.

Special metropolitan authorities and districts. The features which distinguish special metropolitan authorities from other units of government functioning in the area must be recognized to understand the complexity of metropolitan government. Metropolitan authorities and districts are established through legislative acts or by constitutional amendments. They exercise jurisdiction over some specified function or functions of local government. A sanitary district is an excellent illustration. It includes the entire city and other outlying sanitary districts, incorporated or defined by law as a district.

These districts do not coincide with existing political boundaries. They are supported by funds raised within the district. The more districts, the more tax-levying and tax-collecting bodies abound. Finally, these districts are distinct from federal, state, county, or special authorities having charge of administrative or improvement activities which have no special reference to a metropolitan area. A case in point is the Miami Conservancy Commission which is a special authority related to topography and not metropolitan conditions.

These special authorities or districts are established for the purpose of handling particular problems of metropolitan scope. A single agency is needed to perform the service which cannot be provided for by other methods. They may also serve as a channel for equalizing the tax burden required to support a particular function which takes in a territory larger than the existing units. Or they restrict the taxing area to include only those people immediately benefiting by the function. In many instances the desire to evade the existing tax or debt limits of a municipality prompts the creation of an authority. On the other hand, they do solve a problem in local administration, coping with wider services and functions without necessarily altering the structure of local government.

On the whole, little resistance is manifested against the establishment of metropolitan authorities or districts because the machine politicians of the area see the possibility of more jobs to be allocated to their party members. Little or no opposition is forthcoming from suburban politicians. The pressure to be annexed to the central city in order to enjoy better utility, health, and transit facilities is removed. Of interest are the conclusions of a study of suburbanites fringing Milwaukee. They stated that their flight to the periphery was directly associated with the amount of urban conveniences the central city supplied.[1]

Over thirty large special districts are to be found in the nation's most densely populated supercities and their environs. These deal with the problems of sewage, recreation, water supply and distribution, bridges, highways, transit, parks, ports, housing, mosquito abatement, forest preserves, police power, fire protection, and public health. In addition, small special districts have been organized in unincorporated territory to supply these same services, including several small suburban municipalities within their jurisdiction. For example, in 1943, the nine counties around San Francisco contained 168 special districts of the following types: two irrigation; nine cemetery, one drainage; fifty-one fire; two high school library; fifty-one lighting; nine mosquito abatement; one police protection; eighteen sanitary; three sewer maintenance, fifteen water, five utility; and one water-conservation.

Districts may cross state lines; an interstate compact was signed by Pennsylvania and New Jersey relative to the building of bridges in the Philadelphia metropolitan area. New York, New Jersey, and Connecticut have similar arrangements for sanitation in the New York area. However, more interstate compacts have not been used for the solution of metropolitan problems because of state jealousies and special interests. From a long-range point of view, special districts and authorities increase the confusion between independent and semi-independent governmental units.

County governments. Every metropolitan area is related to a county government which is traditionally a rural government. Urban conditions do not require its jurisdiction, but the tradition of retaining the county government is firmly rooted. The political boundaries of the city may be contained in one or more counties, while the entire metropolitan area may contain many county governments. Chicago's metropolitan area includes Cook County and fourteen others.[2] Metropolitan officials must work through them. Designed primarily for dealing with rural problems, legislative and executive authority are fused in a county board or its equivalent while an array of officials cause overlapping jurisdiction. Some state statutes provide for additional officials as the population grows. A host

---

[1] Richard Dewey, "Peripheral Expansion in Milwaukee County," *American Journal of Sociology,* 54 (Sept., 1948), 118–125. On page 124, "Certain services and utilities are essential to the way of life which urban Americans have come to know, even in suburban America. . . . When asked to evaluate a list of services, a majority checked: transportation, utilities, water, sidewalks, and to-the-door mail service."

[2] Charles E. Merriam, Spencer D. Parratt, and Albert Lepawsky, *The Government of the Metropolitan Region of Chicago* (Chicago: University of Chicago Press, 1933), Ch. 5.

of other administrative and judicial instrumentalities duplicate the functions of municipal, state, and federal agencies in such local matters as public welfare, judicial and law enforcement, highway construction, education, and review of tax assessments.[1]

Other governments. Mention should be made of two other types of governments operating within the political boundaries of cities, *i.e.,* township and federal. The township governments are retained out of tradition because of the success that New England self-government enjoyed in colonial America. Township boundaries are not abolished when a municipality adds more territory, thereby causing a division of many municipalities into two or more parts. No legal provisions have been enacted to provide for township adaptations to changing community interests or jurisdictions. No matter how disadvantageously a township is situated in relation to the general community, it retains its historical identity, goes through the motions of holding meetings and electing its officials.

The federal government, by using the state as an intermediate agency for promoting welfare activities, cannot avoid concerning itself with the administrative and fiscal adequacy of local governmental units. Congress utilizes the subsidy system for carrying out functions related to general welfare. It executes them in cooperation with state and local governments. The county, as the agent of the state, is selected as the administrative unit for the promotion of public health and assistance. Yet, metropolitan cities are often used for dispensing federal grants-in-aid when applied to Social Security, public works, relief programs, and housing. Of long standing is the extension of federal regulatory control over the conditions of rapid interurban transit. More recently it has stipulated the type of radio and television programs broadcasted from urban stations. Credit control affords another illustration.

Recommended solutions. One of the most frequently advocated solutions for efficient municipal government is the consolidation of city and county, but this may not be feasible for the majority of our metropolitan areas because not one of the seventeen most populous metropolitan areas is contained in a single county. Another solution might be the annexation of sister municipalities fringing the periphery, thus eliminating lesser governmental units. This proposal met with resistance from suburban areas who see no advantage in being absorbed. The fear of heavy taxation has acted as a great deterrent.

A long-range solution has been recommended: that of merging special authorities with city or county. Where special ones (such as the school

[1] For a complete tabulation, see the Census report, *County Boards and Commissions.* The Bureau of Census has issued another report, *Governmental Units in the United States,* 1942, listing special units of government.

and park districts) are coterminous with the central city, they can be integrated. For example, within fifty miles of downtown Chicago—in the states of Illinois, Indiana, and Wisconsin—there were 1,268 special districts, 11 sanitary districts, 978 school districts, 70 park districts, four forest preserve districts, 190 drainage districts, four mosquito-abatement districts, and one public health district in 1932.[1] The number of special districts was reduced to 1,247 two years later by the consolidation of 22 park districts into the Chicago Park District.[2] Obviously, more consolidation is possible. Between 1942–1951 one third of the total number of school districts had been consolidated but there was a 43 per cent increase in special districts for the same period.

Another school of thought has advocated the reorganization of the county to coincide with the physical boundaries of the metropolitan area and the reassignment to the county of the functions which traditionally belonged to it. It could absorb those connected with planning, granting franchises, ownership and operation of utilities, and creating special taxing districts for the purpose of supplying any work, utility, or service. By the amalgamation of units an over-all metropolitan entity would carry out the functions pertaining to the entire area.

A more startling suggestion has been that proposed by Detroit, Chicago, and New York: setting up the metropolitan area as a separate state of the Union, known as the city-state. The chief advantage would be elimination of friction with state government. The plan would place metropolitan cities and areas in direct relationship with the federal government. Objections raised by state officials were loud and widespread.

This plan has been adopted in China. About a dozen large municipalities are autonomous and responsible to the central rather than the provincial government. When representatives are elected to the national legislature, cities send theirs in proportion to their population. Urban problems and interests are considered at the top level of the society. Mayors of cities are appointed by the national government rather than elected. They rank above the governor in many instances. For example, the former mayors of Shanghai and Nanking were prominent national and international figures.

No wholesale attempts are being made here toward adopting any of the suggested reforms. Pittsburgh, New York, and Philadelphia have made some headway in integrations. Metropolitan Pittsburgh is the result of the fusion of the county and city governments as related to specific function, thus avoiding overlapping. The metropolitan government is

---

[1] Merriam, Parratt, and Lepawsky, *op. cit.,* 9, Table 3.
[2] Victor Jones, *Metropolitan Government* (Chicago: University of Chicago Press, 1942), 136.

more important than that of the county or city. New York has consolidated five boroughs into one unit under one mayor. The respective boroughs are allotted the functions they can best perform or which by nature of their expediency necessitates this action. During the middle of the last century the Pennsylvania legislature took steps to place the county in a secondary position, subordinate to Philadelphia's city government. St. Louis and Baltimore have a somewhat similar setup.

The most common method for effecting consolidation is for a city to annex the outlying areas. This has occurred in most countries where cities have grown in size and population. New York and Los Angeles are two examples of increased territorial expansion since their incorporation. The need for an adequate water supply was the primary factor in bringing smaller units under the city's jurisdiction. Los Angeles grew enormously after a 250-mile aqueduct was built to the Owens River. Scores of suburban cities were forced to be annexed in order to have a sufficient supply of water. Further consolidations will be made with the twelve cities that joined with Los Angeles in constructing the Colorado River aqueduct.

The Political Machine and Its Latent Functions

To this point we have been mainly concerned with the manifest functions of the formal political organization. But we have already noted many cases in which the governmental structure seems inadequate to the needs of the population. The political machine arose in response to the needs of large segments of the population as well as for party efficiency. It is customary to deride political machines for their graft, corruption, and inefficiency. However, if viewed from the standpoint of those it serves, the political machine may be seen as an efficient and often beneficial organization. As Merton points out, it is easy to let moral judgment obscure the actual functions of the machine.[1] What appears dysfunctional as viewed from a certain set of norms may be highly functional from others.

One of the major functions of the machine is to fill in the impersonal structure of government with more effective personal relationships. For many, impersonal social services, no matter how well organized, do not have the same appeal as the ward-heeler's personal touch. The "deprived classes" are in many instances better served by the machine than by official bodies.

Each of the two major parties has built effective machines for cornering the votes of the electorate, with carefully organized hierarchies from boss to precinct captain and committeeman. Huge sums of money are spent

[1] See Merton, *op. cit.*, 70–71.

during each election, and the whole city is honeycombed with political workers. Their duties are to secure the votes of those who live in the wards and precincts, the smallest political units of the city.

Organization is the key word of urban politics. Kent, who studied the structure and function in most American cities, stated that there are about 250,000 precinct executives in this country.[1] As the "grass root" link to the total structure, the local committeeman is most important in persuading voters and in granting favors in return for votes. Immediately above him in the political pyramid is the ward committeeman, usually a former precinct captain who has been awarded the higher office because of his success at the precinct level.[2] He supervises and oversees all the precinct workers under his command. At the apex is the boss, a powerful personality who often possesses a mixture of traits that defies easy analysis. Such famous and infamous party bosses as Tom Pendergast of Kansas City, "Big Tim" Sullivan of the Bowery, "Duke" Edwin H. Vare of Philadelphia, and "Big Bill" Thompson of Chicago are names and figureheads known to many as symbolizing political power, wealth, and status.[3]

As can be expected the party machine functions more effectively in metropolitan cities. Where more foreign-borns and persons of low income live, the party workers find more opportunities to be helpful. Some of the services dispensed at the local levels include finding jobs for the unemployed; providing food, clothing, and fuel to needy families; and assisting individuals in securing citizenship papers. Settling personal and marital discord; securing loans, relief, pensions, or other benefits from social agencies; "fixing" tax reductions and parking violation; and raising bond for bail are others. The more gratuitous services they give, the more certain the votes will be forthcoming at election time.

We have already seen some of the welfare functions of the machine. Other groups are also finding the machine useful. Businesses, both big and small, are frequently well served by political machines. The "fix" is often more efficient, from the standpoint of the businessman, than above-board enterprise. Thus, the machine controls competition without "official interference," and such services as transportation and utilities are the most obvious examples.

The political machine and the rackets are frequently linked. One important factor pointed out by Merton is the opportunity for social mobility furnished by these two organizations. "Politics and the rackets have furnished an important means of social mobility for individuals, who, be-

[1] Frank R. Kent, *The Great Game of Politics* (New York: Doubleday, Page & Co., 1928).

[2] Harold F. Gosnell, *Machine Politics: Chicago Model* (Chicago: University of Chicago Press, 1937).

[3] J. T. Slater, *Boss Rule* (New York: McGraw-Hill Book Co., Inc., 1935).

cause of ethnic background and low class position, are blocked from advancement in the 'respectable' channels." [1] Disregarding the moral and legal aspects of this problem, the rewards for advancement are not notably different for "legitimate" and "illegitimate" activities. The rackets, again ignoring moral considerations, furnish goods and services as functions of laws of supply and demand which are not economically distinguishable from legal business activities. Political machines are extremely useful in protecting such "business" activities as gambling and prostitution. It is interesting to note that there are an estimated 500,000 prostitutes in the United States as compared with 200,000 doctors and 200,000 nurses. [2]

Political corruption. Various forms of corrupt practice have been unearthed, most of them commonplace, but newer and more extensive involvement of governmental officials came to light during the Kefauver investigations. Indeed, a whole network of relationships, from the federal down to the local level, was uncovered. Law-enforcement agents were shown to be regulating illicit activities rather than suppressing them.

Padding the city payroll is widely practiced. Names of fictitious office holders or relatives of key officials are listed. They draw a salary although not actually performing any public duties. The money is pocketed by office holders as "extra" compensation for duties to the party. The demise of an official does not necessarily end the payment of his salary. "Kickbacks" for getting a job are not uncommon.

Another method to defraud taxpayers is to divert public funds to firms who have helped the existing party gain power. Contracts, franchises, and purchase orders are awarded to firms and individuals having "inside pull." For years Chicago purchased coal from a high-paid official, who made substantial profits from his coal transactions. The city of Chicago was his biggest buyer.

Highway construction is another avenue of graft. A contractor in the "Windy City" testified before the city council, when summoned to explain his unique business methods, that he possessed no "equipment" whatsoever for asphalting highways. He had been awarded several sizable contracts for building and keeping the highways in order. He never satisfactorily explained how the "work" was accomplished, although he offered a set of account books as evidence.

Purchasing tax-delinquent parcels of land when projected highways or housing sites are selected and "profiting from inside information" is another form of political abuse. Holding companies are formed to "corner" large blocks of real estate and resell to the city at a substantial profit.

Bribes and cut-backs to officials are difficult to prove but become the

[1] *Ibid.*, 77.
[2] *Ibid.*, 78.

subject of periodic investigations when the practice runs out-of-hand. Where gambling and vice are "wide-open" in a city, protection is guaranteed by law enforcement and city officials. The recent Kefauver Commission's investigation is attempting to "break" the national network of gambling, bribes, peddling of narcotics, and homicides. Gangland methods are forced upon non-compliers.[1] Secret societies are suspected of being the power behind the network of illegal activities, crime, and corruption. All large cities in the nation are involved and form a "ring" of interconnections. "Capone" activities survive under different names, usually masked by more genteel business fronts.

Implications for reform. Some of the points made should not be construed as an argument against reform. Rather, if reform is desired, it would appear crucial to take into account the latent functions of the machine. A reform movement which does not examine the manifold functional relationships involved, and consequently does little to satisfy or control the needs involved, has very little chance of success.

Summary

Municipal administration in the United States has lagged behind the growing functions and services demanded by urbanites. Several "lags" are noted. One is that state constitutions have few provisions for municipal growth and fail to enact enabling legislation with sufficient speed to overcome earlier deficiencies. A second is attitudinal resistance toward any change, thereby reinforcing the tradition that the local government is an "arm" of the state. Only such powers and functions as the latter deem necessary are granted to cities. A third is rooted in the indifference of the citizenry. Finally there is the failure to integrate large metropolitan areas which embrace many coterminous, underlying, and overlapping governmental units with the nation's political development.

States vary in the type of charters granted cities. Since 1900 some statutes have been liberalized, permitting the choice of several forms of local government: (1) the mayor-council, (2) the commission, and (3) the city-manager. A change in the structure of local government was one method of attaining better and sounder administration. Most cities use the mayor-council form.

Since 1910, the metropolitan area has increased in national importance. To cope with problems related to health, welfare, education, taxation, parks, and utilities, special districts or authorities were created through legislation. Instead of systematically planning for the expansion of services to suit population growth, cities have created more and more special dis-

[1] W. F. Whyte, *Street Corner Society* (Chicago: University of Chicago Press, 1943), Ch. 4.

tricts and authorities. These may exercise jurisdiction over a substantial part of the metropolitan area, a small portion of it, or the entirety. Over thirty of these are to be found in the nation's most densely populated supercities and their environs. They coexist with lesser government units, village, township, and county.

Suggested solutions for making more efficient the multitude of large and small governmental units within metropolitan districts include: (1) the fusion of city and county governments; (2) merging of special authorities with city or county; (3) reorganization of the county to embrace the entire metropolitan area; (4) establishment of a city-state; and (5) annexation of contiguous territory.

The political machine performs many functions left unfulfilled by formal government. Not only does it provide the "personal touch" but it also serves the welfare needs of minority groups and the business interests, shady or otherwise, of allied groups.

The weaknesses of urban political organization center around several areas: graft, corrupt administration, inefficiency, unethical diversion of public funds to private enterprises, and unjust promotion and demotion. These are some of the dysfunctions of urban government seen in the party machine and its well-organized hierarchy.

DISCUSSION QUESTIONS

1. What tangible evidence do we have that municipal administration is efficient or inefficient?
2. What new statutes have been enacted in your state to liberalize powers for local government?
3. Name six advantages for the city-manager form of government as contrasted to the mayor-council form.
4. Are there various forms of municipal government in your state?
5. Are party machines losing control in metropolitan cities?
6. Of the several suggestions offered for the elimination of overlapping metropolitan governments, which is the most feasible? Which appear the least satisfactory?
7. Why do suburban areas resist annexation?
8. Explain the growing functions of city governments.
9. Explain the latent functions connected with the party machine.

SUGGESTED PROJECTS

1. Study the growth of machine politics and account for the various functions it performs at the grass root level.
2. Study the personalities of "party bosses" and explain their success in metropolitan areas.

3. Compare the constitutional changes of your state with those of Ohio as they relate to "home rule."
4. Study the growth of special districts and authorities in the nation's thirty largest metropolitan areas.
5. Compare the city-manager government of Cincinnati, Ohio, with that of Kansas City, Kansas, during the Pendergast rule.
6. Prepare a reform program which takes into account the latent functions of political machines.

READINGS

F. L. Bird, *A Study of the Port of New York Authority*. New York: Dun and Bradstreet, 1949.

A comprehensive account of the functions and operation of the New York Port Authority.

D. G. Bishop and E. E. Starratt, *The Structure of Local Government*. Washington, D. C.: The National Council for the Social Studies, 1945.

Compares the structure of the mayor-council, commission, and city-manager forms of urban government. Gives the advantages and disadvantages of all types.

Victor Jones, *Metropolitan Government*. Chicago: University of Chicago Press, 1942.

A study of the role of metropolitan governments as to their functions and complexity.

F. R. Kent, *The Great Game of Politics*. New York: Doubleday & Co., 1928.

A study of the hierarchy of the political machine and the special services dispensed at the grass roots.

C. E. Merriam, S. D. Parratt, and A. Lepawsky, *The Government of the Metropolitan Region of Chicago*. Chicago: University of Chicago Press, 1933.

A research report on the "governments" within governments of the Chicago metropolitan region.

J. T. Salter, *Boss Rule: Portraits in City Politics*. New York: McGraw-Hill Book Co., Inc., 1935.

A graphic description of famous and infamous city bosses.

Lincoln Steffens, *The Autobiography of Lincoln Steffens*. New York: Harcourt, Brace and Co., 1931.

An exposé of "the shame of cities" and the role which Lincoln Steffens played in arousing public opinion.

Urban Government, Supplementary Report of the Urbanism Committee to the National Resources Committee, Government Printing Office, 1939.

E. W. Weidner, *The American County, Patchwork of Boards.* New York: National Municipal League, 1940.

A treatment of a complex subject, the county boards and their hindrance of effective urban administration.

Chapter Fourteen

Religious Organization

IT IS "common knowledge" that city-dwellers are not religious and that church-going and church membership are primarily rural virtues. Like much that is claimed to be common knowledge, this statement is far from substantiation by the facts, should we use the size of urban church membership, that is, belonging to a church, as a criterion. Urban churches may have larger memberships but they are frequently confronted with the problems of irregular church-going and changing attitudes and beliefs.

One of the principal results of urbanization has been secularization of life. Whereas religion in a folk society is usually intricately interwoven with all behavior, urban religion tends to separate itself from every-day affairs. Religious concerns, both in belief and ritual, are restricted to specific places and situations. As is the case of most urban institutions, religion becomes increasingly complex in its organization. At the same time, the nature of religious beliefs and practices varies according to a particular faith, denomination, social status, ethnic or racial group, and geographical location. Indeed, religious behavior and organization are as heterogeneous as the urban population they spring from.

Many Americans have departed from the Puritan custom of reserving the Sabbath as the day of rest and prayer. The automobile has helped to destroy the pleasure taboos. Sunday outings have become an almost universal urban practice. Where "Blue-Sundays" are enforced, an exodus of pleasure-seekers during the week-end counteracts legal bans on certain forms of entertainment or even work. The urbanite can turn the radio dial and tune in sermons delivered by preachers of national and international fame. Men, women, and children can attend "church" in their homes, informally attired as they lounge in favorite chairs, or be otherwise occupied with other activities. In brief, Sunday has become a more secularized day.

It should be reiterated here that the church is the main source of diffusion of urbanism in so-called backward areas and has played an important role in creating a group of adherents and supporters of western values and behavior patterns.

Major Denominations and Faiths

It is extremely difficult to present an accurate account of American church membership and religious belief. The decennial census contains inadequate information on religious affiliation; and the Census of Religious Bodies, since it samples organizations rather than individuals, is subject to error. Some churches, such as the Roman Catholic Church, usually consider anyone baptized a member of the Church, regardless of subsequent attendance. Other churches count only actual members of congregations, omitting children who have not been formally admitted. Besides variations in definition of church members, one may assume a general tendency toward overenumeration within the definition. Finally, membership is not identical with religious belief. For instance, mobile urbanites often do not renew membership when they settle in new communities, whereas others maintain church memberships without participation or belief.

American city churches include all major denominations and faiths. In 1936, some 199,302 churches and synagogues existed in the United States as against 232,154 during the previous decade.[1] The largest gains were made since 1940, and by 1951, there were 284,592 houses of worship, according to the *Yearbook of American Churches* and the Statistical Abstract of the United States. Approximately one-third of the nation's total were urban churches. While the rural churches are larger in absolute numbers, their average attendance is smaller. As the size of the city's population increases, the average total membership mounts. Major metropolises, such as New York, Chicago, Cleveland, Detroit, Boston, and Philadelphia, showed an average membership of over 1,100 members for each church.

In a 1948 report the *Christian Herald* listed the nation's total Protestant membership at 45,000,000 including four major groups: Baptist, Methodist, Lutheran, and Presbyterian. By 1951, the membership had risen to 52,000,-000 for these denominations. In turn, each denomination was subdivided, with the Lutheran having 13 subgroups; Baptist 12; Presbyterian (including reformed churches) 7; and Methodist 5. Five other denominations, the Episcopal, Disciples, Congregational, Evangelical, United Brethren,

[1] United States Bureau of the Census, *Religious Bodies in the United States, 1936* (1941), 19.

and Church of Christ, claimed over 6 million members. Together they comprised 90 per cent of the country's total Protestant membership. The 181 smaller denominations and sects divided the remaining worshippers between them. The Roman Catholic is the largest in the non-Protestant group, with about 29 million members, or 20 per cent of the nation. Nearly 2 million, representing about 40 per cent of the Jewish population, are members of the Orthodox, Conservative, and Reformed Synagogues.[1] Some 250,000 are "seatholders" (purchasers for admission on "Holy Days") and may be said to be "partly active." According to 1953 figures, there was a total of 88,673,005 church members of all faiths.

Not all denominations are equally represented in the city. On the one hand, the more formal and "non-fundamentalist" denominations tend to be urban. Thus Congregationalists, Episcopalians, Lutherans, Presbyterians, and Unitarians are primarily urban, as are the northern Methodists and Baptists. On the other hand, certain segments of the urban population have reacted to the formality of these urban denominations. Thus many of the more evangelical sects and other groups which have tried to reinstitute more personalized beliefs and practices, are also predominantly urban.

More than one-half of the country's population are church members, but not all are active participants.[2] Nonmembers are not necessarily disbelievers, however. How to induce more active participation in church activities remains one of the primary problems confronting religious leadership of every faith. The American Baptist convention made a survey of its membership of 1,600,000 during 1949 and 1950. It was found that 38 per cent never attended church, 42 per cent "more or less regularly," and 20 per cent "only a few times a year." Slightly more than half its membership contributed to the budget of their 7000 local churches. Various Rabbis reported that, except for High Holy Days, the average attendance seldom exceeded ten per cent of the synagogue membership. A study of a "Southern parish" showed that although residents of the territorial units covered by the parish listed themselves as Catholics, a house-to-house census and survey disclosed that many were "dormant," and more were actually "non-Catholic" by reason of having given up Church affiliations.[3] The highest attendance at masses was on Easter Sunday. The author concluded that the urban environment and secularization presented many personal and institutional "blocks" to spiritual values. The

---

[1] *American Jewish Yearbook*, 52 (1951), 86.

[2] *Annals of the American Academy of Political and Social Science*, "Organized Religion," 256 (Mar., 1948), 25–35.

[3] Joseph H. Fichter, *Southern Parish: Dynamics of a City Church* (Chicago: University of Chicago Press, 1951); also see his "The Profile of Catholic Religious Life," *American Journal of Sociology*, 58 (Sept., 1952), 145–150.

parish leaders must understand the social and institutional patterns operating in the parish in order to raise the level of religious participation.

Aspects of Urban Religion

Other aspects of organized religion include specialization, cooperation, and stratification. The church of a given city changes as the city matures.[1] The "first" church is usually a community church, serving all of its residents. When 5000 inhabitants are settled, local neighborhood churches develop, often under the direct sponsorship of the original church. In time, the latter may decline in influence and prestige while the newer church grows powerful and strong. The most notable changes occur when the city reaches 50,000 population. Specialization and social stratification of membership set in.

Specialization. The modern church conducts many specialized functions and services that earlier ones had no need to undertake: *e.g.,* recreational and social activities. Large urban churches show an increasing tendency toward a fine division of labor brought about by specialization in services and activities. A trained group worker may be in charge of the physical education program or a professional social worker may supervise the welfare activities. Bureaucratic administration, large capital holdings, and heavy overhead expenditures almost place such churches in the category of pseudo-business organizations. Even sermons are specialized; topics are selected to suit the composition of the congregation. Small discussion groups may analyze and put the message into social action.

Cooperation. Cooperation in urban churches has resulted from a recognition that accommodation can be achieved between divergent faiths and denominations through tolerance and understanding. Competition, rivalry, and conflict have gradually decreased owing partly to the concerted effort of religious leaders to stress common goals rather than doctrinal differences. A policy toward combating prejudice and discrimination between races and faiths has been stressed at the interdenominational level. Church federations; interracial, interfaith, and interchurch rallies; interdenominational agreements; and ministerial associations have promoted more cooperation.

Duplication of work in a given location has often been avoided by interdenominational agreement. A new church may not be established in an area where the existing one has difficulty retaining its membership.

The most conspicuous trend of organized religion is toward unity. Reexamination of the intellectual foundations of religious belief has raised

[1] Murray H. Leiffer, *City and Church in Transition* (Chicago: Willet, Clark & Co., 1938).

new issues unrelated to the old divisions.[1] Cooperation has brought new understanding. Since the beginning of the twentieth century, the Federal Council of Churches of Christ in America and the International Council of Religious Education have brought together many of the significant Protestant agencies and persuaded them to work toward unity. Mergers of several related denominations have been accomplished, reducing inter-denominational rivalry and conflict. Since the end of the Second World War, a World Council of Churches has been formed whose goal is toward wider unity. As can be expected, there is much to be done before the ideal is achieved.

Stratification. Church membership tends to reflect the social and economic status of the congregation. Although there is no clearly defined national pattern of social classes, and the most accurate studies of social classes have been confined to the community level, the relation of religion to socio-economic status is *suggested* by four polls taken between 1945–1946 and analyzed by the Department of Research and Education of the Federal Council of Churches. These findings were compared with an earlier one taken by the Office of Public Opinion Research at Princeton University.[2]

Despite the absence of conclusive evidence that church membership intensifies and reaffirms socio-economic status, it is generally accepted that religious behavior varies with economic levels of the population. The reason is that almost from the very beginning of organized religion in this country Protestantism has tended to be associated with the higher socio-economic stratum. As late as 1880 the country was predominantly Protestant and church membership in this faith had been considerably broadened during the great revivals of this century to include the rural population, the Negroes, and the middle and upper classes of new cities. On the other hand, after 1880, the Roman Catholic Church increased its strength among urban industrial workers, many of whom immigrated from Ireland and Southern Europe. These two broad trends more or less correlate with the present-day socio-economic status of the respective faiths and denominations.

Table 28 shows the per cent distribution of religious bodies between 1945–1947 according to the upper, middle, and lower classes. Eight groups constituted the sample: six of the larger Protestant denominations, the Catholic, and the Jewish. For the upper class, the Episcopalian and Congregational denominations had the largest percentage (24) of membership. Jewish and Presbyterian followed with 22 per cent each. The two having the lowest percentage were the Lutheran with 11, and the Catholic,

[1] *Annals of the American Academy of Political and Social Science*, 256 (Mar., 1948), 23–24.
[2] *Ibid.*, 84–91.

TABLE 28. CLASS COMPOSITION OF RELIGIOUS
BODIES, 1945–1946 [1]

| | *Per Cent Distribution* | | |
Body	*Upper Class*	*Middle Class*	*Lower Class*
Entire Sample	13	31	56
Catholic	9	25	66
Jewish	22	32	46
Methodist	13	35	52
Baptist	8	24	68
Presbyterian	22	40	38
Lutheran	11	36	53
Episcopalian	24	34	42
Congregational	24	43	33

Note: Derived from a breakdown of four polls taken by the American Institute of Public Opinion covering approximately 12,000 cases. Each poll covered a "voting sample" of approximately 3,000 cases.

[1] *Source:* With permission from L. Pope, "Religion and the Class Structure," *The Annals of the American Academy of Political and Social Science,* 256 (Mar., 1948), 86.

with 9. The percentage for the entire sample of approximately 12,000 cases was 13.

The middle class comprised 31 per cent of the entire sample. However, several groups showed greater middle-class participation. The Congregational ranked first with 43 per cent, while the Presbyterian had 40. In fact, all but two were higher than the sample's average of 31 per cent. The Catholic faith showed 25 per cent and the Baptist, 24. Of the lower class, the percentage for the entire sample was 56. Six were below this figure. The Catholic faith had 66 per cent and the Baptist, 68. The denomination having the lowest percentage was the Congregational, or 33.

All major religious bodies in the United States are reported to draw far higher percentage of their members from the lower class than they did before World War II. There remains a significant difference between the Catholic constituency and all others save the Baptist, which parallels it almost precisely in stratification. Distribution of the Jewish group is very much like that of the Episcopalian; the majority of the members of both still come from the middle and upper classes. This is even more characteristic of the Presbyterians and the Congregationalists.

When religious affiliation is correlated with occupation, the entire sample showed the following tendencies: 19 per cent were business and professional workers; 20 per cent white collar occupations; 44 per cent urban manual workers, and 17 per cent farmers.[1] The groups having the highest number of business and professional workers were the Jewish, Presbyterian, Episcopalian, and Congregational. The Jewish group had more "white-collar" occupations than the rest, followed by the Presbyterian, Episcopalian, and Catholic groups. Catholics and Baptists had the highest number of urban manual workers. The Lutherans ranked third, and the remaining five were all below the percentage of the total sample. The Lutheran, Methodist, and Baptist groups have many members engaged in farming.

When these same eight groups were broken down to show the religious adherents' educational levels, 11 per cent were college graduates, 48 per cent high school or more, and 52 per cent less than high school. The groups showing a high percentage of membership with less than high school education were the Catholic, Baptist, and Lutheran. The Congregational, Episcopalian, Presbyterian, Jewish, and Methodist had a large percentage who completed high school. The Presbyterian and Episcopalian denominations had the greatest number of college graduates, followed by the Congregationalists and Jewish groups. The Methodist had 12 per cent or slightly more than the average for the whole sample.

Ethnic Churches

Ethnic groups which once maintained their own parish-like churches find that the services and functions which appealed to the first-generation, foreign-born elements no longer suffice for the English-speaking native-born group. These churches often experience great difficulty in meeting financial obligations and in attracting a non-foreign language speaking group to attend their services. Economic weaknesses face the diminishing old-timers; but the church, the symbol of ties to the "old country," declines at a slow rate because of the group's cohesion, financial sacrifices, and rigid theology. These churches often survive in areas where other churches have succumbed to population or institutional invasion and succession. The English-speaking group may shift its membership to other urban churches as acculturation proceeds. In emulation of the members of the dominant society, the native-born seek to enhance their social prestige by joining recognized "respectable" institutions. Ethnic city churches which still retain their religious identity include the Bulgarian, Greek, Roumanian, Russian, Serbian, Syrian Antiochian, and Ukrainian.[2] Only the Russian Orthodox and Scandinavian Lutheran denominations have a significant number of rural churches.

[1] *Ibid.*, 87.
[2] Bureau of the Census, *Religious Bodies, Selected Statistics,* 1936, 20–21.

Ethnic churches are said by Warner and Srole to be a religious system organized as a sub-system within the national social system.[1] That is, the body of control officers and the priesthood were recruited from the "old country." The "old world" religious leaders and system acted as media of self-control. The group's identity was preserved while the members adjusted themselves to the prevailing social system. In time, the group's expectations changed. A gradual conformity to the standards and mores of the new environment follows, although the old-world name of the church may be retained. The more the group's beliefs and ritualistic practices diverge from the prevailing social system, the longer the old church's subsystem will be retained. The location, whether urban or rural, is also a contributing factor. Urban ethnic churches undergo quicker accommodation.

Where racial differences are intertwined with ritualistic and religious beliefs, such as manifested by the Oriental Buddhist churches (sometimes called Temples), a homogeneous congregation is attracted. Some 73,000 Buddhists worship in this country, mainly in urban areas. During the early stage, the church was completely foreign in character. The hybrid stage comes when two distinct and separate services are conducted. One is for the American-born, English-speaking group, while the other is for the foreign-born, foreign-language group. The same priest may conduct both services, but he must be bilingual and know two cultures. His behavior toward the orthodox group is attuned to the customs and ceremonies exhibited by the foreign-born members. More bowing, ritualistic offerings, and longer services are expected. Buddhist churches have spread throughout the eastern and middle-western cities. Formerly, they were localized in the Rocky Mountain and coastal areas. A few Caucasian converts mix with the English-speaking congregation. Cooperation with the churches of the larger community is stressed.

Urban Influences and the Church

The church in urban centers is continuously confronted with cultural conflicts, social change, and a high rate of social and physical mobility. Heterogeneity of population, as well as the presence of many faiths and divergent religious practices, beliefs, and attitudes, leave an imprint upon religious organization. Adaptation to a changing environment is experienced by virtually all urban churches. A study of the life cycle of religious organizations would reveal a series of adaptations each has faced, as well as provide an answer to the solutions adopted. Two major influences, in-

---

[1] W. Lloyd Warner and Leo Srole, *The Social Systems of American Ethnic Groups* (New Haven: Yale University Press, 1946), Ch. 7.

vasion and succession and changing attitudes, beliefs, and practices, confront all established churches. What are the most common methods used in seeking adaptations when faced with population or institutional invasion? What evidence can be offered for the changing attitudes, beliefs, and practices?

Invasion and succession. Invasion is one major influence which often causes the relocation of a church. Invasion undergoes four stages: initial stage, reaction, general influx, and climax. During the time that invasion is in operation, the population and established institutional organizations of an area are experiencing confusion and uncertainty. There is an influx and outflow of residents, thus affecting the membership of organizations as well as altering customary behavior patterns. The configuration of the invaded and decentralized areas is disrupted until equilibrium results. The church, however, is one institutional organization which attempts to cling tenaciously to the old site and is often the last to give way to the incoming population and organizations. The egress of former members of the congregation may precede the abandonment of the physical structure and removal of the internal organization to a new location. The ebbing church organization may make valiant attempts to adjust to the new situation. In the main, three courses are open to a church facing invasion and succession.

The primary and foremost adaptation is for the church to follow the congregation it has served and re-establish itself. If it is a downtown church, the initial move may be into the adjacent zone. It may repeat this process several times during its institutional life, finally locating far from its first site. A church which seeks to serve the descendants of the first congregation is apt to adopt this pattern. Douglass, in studying the life cycle of one thousand Protestant churches, disclosed that this is not uncommon.[1] For example, a Protestant church in St. Louis has already experienced three removals. The first move in 1850 was a distance of four city blocks. Four years later, the church moved twelve blocks; twenty-two years later it moved two and one-half miles.

The second method of adaptation is to remain at its present site. A concerted attempt may be made to retain its former congregation by stressing sentimental ties and religious and theological tenets, depending heavily on publicity to maintain cohesion and loyalty. At the same time, there may be efforts to serve the area's new population. A whole-hearted attempt may be made to change church policy, activities, and forms of worship. But since a considerable share of the church's financial support may still come from the older members, their wishes and demands may block radical changes.

[1] H. Paul Douglass, *One Thousand City Churches* (New York: Harper & Brothers, 1926).

The third method is for the church to remain and attempt to attract a new constituency. The original congregation may or may not return, but the new group's demands and wishes are given preference. Thus, a new type of membership is housed within the old building. A new minister may be called to preach a new type of sermon. Different hymns and religious practices follow. New functions may be added. The church begins a new cycle. This policy is adopted when there is recognition that the departed members of the congregation may be so widely scattered that the pursuit of old church followers is futile.

It should be noted that religious organizations are less likely to disappear than, say, economic ones, because they (the former) have a protected position by reason of their having a greater degree of belief and faith in their creation and continuance. Moreover, they are generally more resistant to social change and are more apt to relocate elsewhere without altering their structure or functions.

Attitudes, beliefs, and practices. Other important influences affecting urban churches center around their membership's changing attitudes, practices, and beliefs. While these are intangible items to measure, recent surveys and studies have disclosed some salient facts. In the main, these pertain to the Protestant denominations.

Hornell Hart's study of religious publications from 1919 to 1941 showed a decline in religious articles in popular publications.[1] The discussion of religious topics in magazines decreased by an average rate of 2.5 per cent between 1931 and 1941. Those articles pertaining to traditional and institutional features, such as "The Church," "Church Unity," "Theology," "Future Life," "Missions," etc., were less popular than those related to ethical and spiritual life, such as "War and Christianity," "Christian Ethics," and "Prayer." The depression brought about an eight-fold increase in the discussion of the role of the church in promoting peace of mind.

When a major crisis faces the nation, people seek the guidance of the church to a greater extent than when conditions are normal. Since 1941 there has been an increase in the production of the devotional type of books designed to meet the spiritual needs of the average person. Old stand-bys, books on daily Bible readings and sermons of popular preachers bound in volumes, were in great demand. Fear and insecurity caused many to seek religion as a source of comfort. Many religious leaders were sought for their role as helpers rather than as emphasizers of doctrinal controversies.

Some of the practices of traditional religion have been on the wane for a considerable period of time, such as: the family going to church together, group reading of the Bible, and saying grace at mealtime. A decline in

[1] Hornell Hart, "Religion," *American Journal of Sociology*, 47 (May, 1942), 888–897.

these practices is more evident in native-born children and urban families. A study made in connection with *Recent Social Trends* showed that 40 per cent of urban children studied attended church with their families.[1] Ten per cent read the Bible with the family unit, while thirty per cent said grace at mealtime. These practices have probably remained unchanged. Kincheloe's study pointed to a decline in the number of young adults attending churches.[2] The percentage of church members 14 years of age in newer and more rapidly growing cities is less than one-seventh of the total population. In older cities, the percentage is higher.

Many persons attend church services without becoming members of the organization. This leads to irregular attendance and remaining on the fringe of an organization with no permanent affiliation. On the whole, Catholic churches do not lose as many members by changing attitudes, beliefs, and practices as do Protestant churches. A recent Catholic national survey showed that 18 per cent remained away from church services altogether.

Middletown and Elmtown

Two community studies, Middletown and Elmtown, reveal the relation of religion to social position. Lynd's study of Middletown, a medium-sized Indiana city, concluded that religious attitudes showed greater resistance to change when compared to changes in (1) getting a living, (2) making a home, (3) training the young, (4) using leisure time, and (5) engaging in community activities.[3] While Middletownites indicated a high degree of belief in the supremacy of Christianity, the Bible, God, and in existence after death, church-going habits revealed an entirely different picture. More believed in the doctrines than took an active part in church activities. The working-class families of Middletown showed a stronger belief in religion than the businessmen's families. For reasons of policy, the latter belonged to a church but showed less concern with religious doctrine. Parents declared that they did not know what religious beliefs to teach their young, and showed feelings of guilt and uneasiness in their replies.

In restudying Middletown some years later, the Lynds discovered that the inhabitants were confused concerning the functions of organized religion. The depression had acutely shaken the faith of many believers, and

[1] *Recent Social Trends in the United States* (New York: McGraw-Hill Book Co., 1937), 1012–1032.

[2] S. C. Kincheloe, *The American City and Its Church* (New York: Friendship Press, Inc., 1938), 91–92.

[3] Robert S. and Helen M. Lynd, *Middletown* (New York: Harcourt, Brace and Co., 1929), 497.

the clergy avoided current controversial issues. The latter either relied heavily upon old theological terminology or were silent. They talked in such generalities that their positions became ambiguous and confusing to their followers. Issues arousing bitter dissension—labor organization, social planning in the interest of the masses, the redistribution of wealth, birth control, politics, wage scales, and social insurance—were sidetracked. As a result, the clergy were portrayed as "harried, overworked, and perplexed." [1]

Hollingshead's recent study of Elmtown, a middle-western city, listed ten organized churches, nine Protestant and one Catholic.[2] The prestige structure portrayed the cultural characteristics of five classes as to religious attitudes, beliefs, and practices.

Class I families, the uppers, all retained membership in the Federated Church. However, service attendance is not markedly frequent or regular. They do contribute freely to the church treasury, and may spend heavily on improvements. The age groups which participate most in church affairs are the elderly and the 5–12 year olds.

Class II can be characterized as the upper-middle. Almost every family was church-affiliated and active in one way or another in church work. The women of this class headed the Women's Christian Temperance Union, the three church societies, and the civic organizations for intercommunity improvement. Predominantly Protestant, they could be relied upon for lay-leadership in church affairs. Approximately one-half of the adults attended church regularly. If married, the couple participated jointly whenever possible. Men were more lax in attendance, but rationalized their absence, although seldom admitting that they had no interest in religious services. They contributed to church finances and made no objections if wives attended.

Class III, the lower-middle group, exhibited stronger class feelings than the rest. Since approximately two families out of three traced their ancestry to a European country, religious affiliations showed their ethnic backgrounds. Large numbers of this group belonged to Catholic and Lutheran churches. The Federated and Methodist churches were preferred by the more established members of the group, while a few belonged to the Baptist. Membership in the Free Methodist, Pentecostal, and Church of God was avoided for prestige reasons. In comparison to other classes, church attendance by both sexes was greatest and appeared to confer a kind of moral respectability desired by this stratum. Women of this group were very active in church guilds, study groups, missionary societies,

---

[1] Robert S. and Helen M. Lynd, *Middletown in Transition* (New York: Harcourt, Brace and Co., 1937), 312; Ch. 8 deals with religion.

[2] A. B. Hollingshead, *Elmtown's Youth* (New York: John Wiley and Sons, Inc., 1945), Ch. 5.

and welfare organizations. Moreover, church committee membership was largely drawn from this group. They cooperated with those belonging to the next higher social stratum in managing church affairs. A person of this class who resigned from church membership suffered wide condemnation. Members of this group are extremely anxious to reinforce their social position by church attendance and work in charitable organizations.

Class IV families comprised the upper-lower stratum. Coming from varied denominational and ethnic backgrounds, their religious practices fluctuated from strict avoidance to enthusiastic zeal. Some families claimed to have had neither the financial means nor the time to support the churches, while others were hostile toward religion. Some had no local church affiliations whatsoever, while others attended faithfully. Members of this class did not have the same proportion of church workers and leaders.

Class V, the lower-lower stratum, were often recipients of the local charity dispensed by the three upper strata. Religious ties were either tenuous or nonexistent. About three-fourths of such families claimed religious connections "in spirit" only. Active church participation was infrequent and strong hostility was expressed by some toward religious personnel and churchgoers. Many declared that they were unwelcome, which, indeed, they were. When members of Class V met as "church workers" they held meetings in abandoned stores, lofts, and private homes of the Pentecoastal, Pilgrim Holiness, and Church of God sects. Women of this class were more ardent and emotional worshippers than the men.

The foregoing substantiates the tentative conclusions of the Department of Research and Education of the Federal Council of Churches. In a very general sense, churches are often associated with the middle classes and socio-economic differences have a bearing on church affiliations and participation.

Types of City Churches

To date, no satisfactory and adequate classification for the numerous types of Protestant and Catholic city churches has been developed, although there is general recognition that church organization and behavior patterns of church members vary according to the community wherein the church is located. Moreover, no systematic classification is available for the Catholic or other faiths excepting in a general way. Seven types (mainly Protestant) have been delineated by Kincheloe and Douglass, establishing certain characteristics that reflect their adaptation to their environment and church congregations.[1] Thus, both external and internal

[1] Kincheloe, *op. cit.*, and Douglass, *op. cit.*

influences interact to produce these characteristics and these influences are
more pronounced in large cities.

Downtown churches. The downtown church, situated in the center of
the main business district, administers to a widespread congregation scattered throughout the city and its environs as well as to the transient "hotel
population." Often called the "metropolitan" church, it holds a position of
religious dominance, although few members live close by. Urbanites, accustomed to using downtown facilities for work, recreation, and other
interests, regard a Sunday trip downtown to attend church service as a
matter of routine. Instead of a neighborhood relation based upon physical
proximity, a new and distinctly urbanized human association is substituted.

Such a church, related to the city as a whole, becomes virtually independent of the social conditions prevailing in its immediate vicinity. Sermons and forms of worship are adapted to the heterogeneous membership; programs are broad, timely, and specialized. The composition and
size of the congregation may vary from week to week. Great reliance is
placed upon newspaper and radio publicity as media for gaining repeated
attendance. Considerable effort is directed toward selecting renowned religious leaders as speakers, themselves leaders of other large city churches.
Good music is another drawing card. Excellent examples are the Central
Church of Chicago, the Sunday Evening Club, and the Temple, all located in office-like buildings in the downtown business center.

Several other characteristics distinguish the downtown church from
other types in the city. Efficient management and administration may
cause social distance between the church leaders and the membership.
Customary church socials, missionary societies, and Bible study groups
may be lacking. The church's financial status is modest because the
wealthy religious churchgoers reside elsewhere. Moreover, the church
building's appearance might resemble the office buildings that surround
it, devoid of the shrubbery and well-kept lawns of residential neighborhoods.

The inner-city church. Another type of downtown religious organization, located near the fringe of the business area and bordering the area of
transition, is the inner-city church. Once situated in an exclusive residential area, racial, ethnic, commercial, or industrial invasion has threatened
its life cycle. The church decided to remain in its old site and cater to
a young adult city-wide population. An entirely new congregation has
been recruited and a new staff of religious workers has been employed to
meet the needs of the young adults attending Sunday school, morning or
evening services. A well-planned program includes forums, summer
camps, physical education, religious education, and young people's clubs.

Evening activities attract young people from downtown professional and business organizations. Having few local ties, their leisure activities are satisfied by the church where they can establish social contacts. Moreover, the church's emphasis is on non-commercial recreation.

Although located near the area of transition, the church does not necessarily concern itself with the problems of the neighborhood. Its emphasis is upon "internal adaptation." Efficiently administered to cater to a scattered adult population, a change in the group's composition does not affect the range of activities. Trained personnel conduct the various programs and accept long or short-time participants as a phase of urban mobility. Assistant minister(s), a gymnasium superintendent, a director of girl's work, a director of boy's work, a social service worker, "church visitors," and a large clerical staff, together with the high educated minister, may constitute the internal organization. Even musicians and choir members may be paid. A large operating budget is a prerequisite.

Institutional church and neighborhood house. In some cities the institutional church and neighborhood house, under the auspices and control of a given denomination or faith, has almost completely adopted the methods and spirit of the social settlement house. Others utilize the methods of the latter but have a primary aim in view: that of bringing people into a definite commitment with an established church. This objective is needed in our society where the ethnic church fails to meet the needs of native-borns and the fact that church membership varies with socio-economic status. Moreover, persons who have not acquired the prevailing religious behavior patterns find the institutional church and neighborhood house as a source of education.

However, the financial status of these church organizations are often precarious because contributors to a general city fund (community fund, for example) do not favor the use of neighborhood houses for religious services. Many of these churches are forced to rely upon the parent denomination for a large portion of their support. More than sixty neighborhood houses are maintained by the Presbyterian denomination, and about forty by the Northern Baptists. The exact number maintained by other denominations and faiths are unknown. All are located in northern industrial centers and they have attempted to cope with the economic, social, and personal problems of their members.

Neighborhood houses fulfill several functions. They become the centers of acquaintances and understanding. They help to create a united community, despite the differences in race, religion, and ethnic background. Through group work and personal contacts, many persons learn the American way of group participation. Programs for the various age groups are offered. By means of speakers, forums, classes, and discussion materials, the problems related to the city, the nation, or the world are treated. Attention is devoted to the special needs of the community wherein the institution is located. Concerted social action may follow.

Other functions provided by the neighborhood houses include vocational guidance; infant welfare and clinical services for the community; adult and pre-school education; and community programs. In times of economic recession, they initiate tax-supported relief. Frequently they act as sources of referrals to community agencies specializing on a given phase of welfare, such as free hospitalization, old age assistance, aid to dependent children, and domestic problems. They have helped to lower the juvenile delinquency rate by providing leadership and supervision through wholesome recreation.

Rooming-house church. The church in the rooming-house area survives with difficulty. Situated in the area of transition, with an extremely high rate of residential mobility, the church struggles to sustain membership. Residents of the area often desire anonymity and purposely avoid contact with the socially accepted members of the society who want to make or keep them "good." Many inhabitants have psychological, emotional, and vocational needs which can only be solved by personal counseling and guidance. Unfortunately, the religious leaders sent to the rooming-house church area are often unequipped for such services. Young, low paid, and inexperienced workers with a "missionary" viewpoint are often attracted. Although the parent denomination (of which the rooming-house church is a part and finds its support from this source) recognize the needs of the residents of the area, there are few attempts to provide trained social workers and adequate facilities for long-range programs. Even the equipment for wholesome recreation may be lacking.

The area of transition is where many new immigrants to cities find their first moorings, and their needs for the stabilizing influences of the church are greater than for other urbanites. Many young people coming to the city do not find personal invitations from church leaders. Lack of interest on the part of established religious organizations contributes to the rise of many sects which will be discussed later.

Industrial area church. The historic Protestant church, with its traditional form of worship, has experienced difficulty in retaining its identity in industrial areas. As indicated earlier, the influx of immigrants with Catholic beliefs and practices after 1880 resulted in a differentiation of religious organization and behavior patterns to result. The industrial area church of a Protestant denomination is faced with a small number of the British-American elements in the community and so must be strategically located to draw upon the latter group.

Programs geared to the special interests of all age groups must be adopted in order to achieve a community-church spirit and an attitude of exclusiveness. While the range of activities may be broad, frugality and simplicity are traits that appeal to the worshipers. At the same time, church services must be conducted in a traditional and ritualistic setting.

A final characteristic of the church in the industrial area is that the minister and employed staff may be paid low salaries, but appreciation of their worth is often expressed by small gifts from the congregation. Moreover, the religious leaders are more intimately associated with the families of the area, and there is considerable reliance upon their guidance and counsel.

Apartment-house area church. The church in the apartment area attracts individuals and families whose behavior patterns often parallel those living in the area of transition, in that residential mobility contributes to the struggle which the church has to contend with in maintaining membership. In other respects the apartment-house church differs from the rooming-house church. The members of the former have higher educational, economic, and social status; many single professional and business men and women and families live in this high-rental zone of the city. The physical plant of the apartment-house church as well as the church personnel are frequently excellent. Many churches in this area of the city have developed ingenious techniques for disseminating information and publicity about their programs, forums, sermons, and musical offerings. Many churches are well equipped to offer fellowship to those who wish it, and staff members make follow-up calls to newcomers in the area. In this manner they successfully recruit membership to fill in the gap left by those moving out of the area. Some of the apartment-house churches lose annually from one-fourth to one-third of their old members through residential and occupational changes.

Suburban church. There are many types of suburban churches. Taken as a whole, they are well staffed and well equipped. The church building is frequently pretentious and elaborately furnished. There is considerably more family participation in church activities than in many other areas of the city. Some suburban pulpits are filled by outstanding ministers with long years of experience and training. If the suburban church is located in a wealthy suburb (as compared with those built by real estate or industrial corporations for families in the middle-income ranges), conventional Protestant sermons, music, and ritual are in evidence. Perhaps the greatest difference between the wealthy suburban and other types of outlying churches is that many church members are leaders of important organizations in the city to which the suburb is symbiotically attached. Moreover, these leaders frequently promote projects to provide financial assistance to needy persons belonging to the same denomination.

Store-front church. We have seen that the nature of organized religion frequently does not fulfill the needs of the diverse socio-economic groups of the city. The phenomenon of religious sects, of which the store-front church and mission provide excellent illustrations, stem in part from the failure of established churches to satisfy the emotional and spiritual needs of a large number of urbanites. The total number of sects, cults, missions, and store-front churches in the United States is unknown. That they are an urban phenomenon is generally recognized.

A store-front church may begin its life cycle as a protest against a parent denomination, frequently in an attempt to return to a fundamentalistic approach. The ultimate aim is to nurture the small "protest" nucleus into a full-fledged, socially accepted congregation. This objective is seldom realized because the lack of financial backing, trained personnel, and sustained membership contribute to their disappearance. In fact, the term "fly-by-night" church is often used when referring to the new church organization. Moreover, personality clashes between religious leaders and members or between members themselves have often resulted in the dissolution of the organization.

The store-front church fulfills several functions for its members. Primary is the fact that there is more personal contact between religious leaders and members. Not infrequently, primary terms, such as "brother" or "sister" are used and to urbanites who may not have family ties this display of familiarity is meaningful. Secondly, urbanites who need emotional release are able to do so at church meetings. Ample opportunity is provided for "confessions," uninhibited responses, and "amens." Thirdly, the members need not fear to appear in church without their "Sunday best." Fourthly, the store-front church provides an avenue of leadership and status for a segment of the urban population which cannot be found elsewhere. The "Reverend" may be a janitor during the week, but on Sunday he is an exalted member of a cohesive in-group. Indeed, he may contribute a portion of his earnings toward the expense of maintaining the store-front church. Fifthly, this type of church fills a gap in the religious organization of the city in areas undergoing transition from one type of land use to the next. Lastly, it does not adhere closely to socio-economic, ethnic, or racial lines. It is perhaps significant that store-front churches are more frequently found in racial ghettos, low-income areas, and areas of homeless men.

The Negro Church

About five-sevenths of the total Negro population in the United States are members of churches, a considerably larger proportion than is recorded for the country's white population.[1] Almost 6.5 million Negro church members belong to the Baptist denomination and 1.7 million to the Methodist. Within the church hierarchy are 35 all-Negro church bodies, claiming almost 9 million members. Racially mixed denominations claim less than 1 million followers, while over 300,000 belong to the Catholic faith. The growth of Negro urban churches has resulted from the migration of Negro worshipers to 25 northern and 13 southern cities. The Negro church is one organization which has largely resulted from the leadership within the group.

The church as the center of Negro social organization has fulfilled several functions. The church enables worshipers of a different racial background to belong to an established organization whose behavior patterns and values are accepted by the larger society. The nature of religious practice and belief with its emotional overtones enhances the morale of the members of a subordinate racial group. The worshiper finds understanding and rapport amidst familiar surroundings and faces. He can rise, temporarily, above some of the handicaps encountered in daily living. The congenial informality of the church offers fellowship and personal recognition. Furthermore, opportunities for leadership are found in religious organizations which may be denied in the economic and political realm. Finally, the church ministers to the various social and economic groupings within the Negro population through differentiation in rituals and belief.[2] It should be noted that the members of this group are apt to change churches as they attain greater economic and social status as those of other groups in the population.

Upper-class behavior. The most important elements of the Negro upper-class population are not to be found in church activities. Those who attend church regularly are inclined to devote themselves to the ritualistic or deliberative type of activity. Generally speaking, upper-class behavior calls for self-control. Thus, church membership, without active and regular participation in church activities, is not uncommon. The Negro upper-class belongs largely to the Episcopalian, Presbyterian, or Congregational denominations. A rise in the social scale calls for a change in membership. The Episcopalian is regarded as the "high" church, a rating which stems from the fact that the denomination is a branch of the Church of England, and early American settlers imported it. Upper-class Negro families may join the denomination to reinforce class status.

Middle-class behavior. The Negro upper-middle class shows the greatest variety in church attendance and in associational interests. Members of

---

[1] *Negro Handbook*, 1946–47, 153–159.

[2] Vattel Daniel, "Ritual and Stratification in Chicago Negro Churches," *American Sociological Review*, 7 (June, 1942), 352–361.

the middle class emulate the ritual and ceremony of the upper-class churches, but they attend services more faithfully. While many attend for spiritual uplift, some may attend for status reasons, others for business contacts, and still others for sociability.

The Negro lower-middle class is a strong supporter of the semi-demonstrative or store-front churches, but those who can do so join the larger churches for prestige. Others, who are less well-off, are able to join the smaller Baptist and Methodist churches.

Lower-class behavior. Large numbers of the Negro lower class are affiliated with the Baptist, Pentecostal, and Spiritual congregations. Most of these religious groups are sects or store-front churches and are characterized by religious fervour. These churches are usually housed in an abandoned store-room or former business locations. However, they serve a great purpose—that of initiating the newly arrived rural migrants into city life. The informal and unembellished patterns of worship and religious instruction have been little affected by the influences of a more complex structure and culture. The rural church—its organization and procedures —tends to be preserved, and a greater adherence to fundamental religious beliefs and opinions is retained.

St. Clair Drake reports in his study of Chicago's "Bronzeville" that nearly 500 Negro religious organizations, claiming at least 200,000 members and distributed over 30 denominations, exist.[1] In the main, the worshipers identify themselves with "race" churches, and about 10 per cent of the churches in "Bronzeville" are small, store-front or house churches with an average membership of fewer than 25 persons.

Summary

Urban influences, environmental and attitudinal, have caused the churches to seek various adaptations in order to survive. Protestant churches lose more members because of changing attitudes, beliefs, and practices than do the Catholic churches. Church membership does not necessarily correlate with church attendance. Religious behavior and attendance seem to fluctuate with the socio-economic conditions of the country. City churches attract better-trained and better-paid clergy.

Urban churches exhibit tendencies toward specialization, cooperation, and stratification. In order to attract and cater to a heterogeneous population; forms of worship, sermons, and rituals may become specialized. Often, the church serves as the social center of the community.

Studies of Middletown and Elmtown revealed significant class differ-

[1] Drake and Cayton, *op. cit.,* 412–429.

ences in religious attendance, beliefs, and attitudes. The lower-middle stratum in Elmtown is the most "moral" and conservative. The church attendance of the lower-middle class is higher than that of either of the two upper or of the lower classes. Religious organizations decline in influence at both extreme ends of the social scale, among the most privileged and among the most disadvantaged. In this very general sense, the churches are associated with the middle class. Middletown's way of life showed religious beliefs to be the most difficult to change as contrasted to earning a living, rearing children, or other phases of life. There were more people who professed Christian beliefs than there were church members.

Ethnic churches experience difficulty in retaining their membership as the English-speaking group grows larger. Those which can be identified with the more recent immigrant groups still retain their original names. Financial difficulties add to their problems.

When churches are faced with either population or institutional invasion, they seek one of three forms of adaptation in order to survive. One is to move with the original congregation. Another is to remain in the old site and depend heavily upon communicating literature to strengthen the loyalty and participation of old members. Little attention is paid to the surrounding neighborhood or its problems. A third method of adaptation is to remain in the area undergoing invasion and succession, adopt a different policy, initiate other forms of worship, and employ new personnel.

Types of city churches include the downtown, the inner-city, the institutional churches and neighborhood house, the rooming-house, the industrial area, the apartment-house, and the suburban. Each possesses salient characteristics. The composition of membership varies according to the environment in which the church seeks to render service. The most regular churches are found in suburbs. Store-front churches, sects, and cults tend to grow and die in short time-spans due to financial shortages, personality clashes, and fluctuating memberships. Their life cycles are short, but they appear to satisfy emotional and spiritual needs when more orthodox churches fail.

Urban Negro churches perform several functions for their members. They enable worshipers of a different racial background to belong to an established organization whose behavior patterns and values are accepted by the larger society. The church enhances the morale of the members of a minority group. Opportunities for leadership are more abundant than in other organizations. The various social classes within the Negro population can be differentiated by membership in deliberate, semi-demonstrative, or demonstrative churches.

DISCUSSION QUESTIONS

1. What has caused the change in religious attitudes, beliefs, and practices among urbanites?
2. Why were lower class families less inclined toward church attendance in Elmtown?
3. What various types of city churches have been found by Douglass and Kincheloe?
4. What needs does the Negro church fulfill? Are there differences in social class and religious behavior?
5. What functions do the "store-front" churches perform?
6. Discuss the role and problems of the ethnic churches.
7. How do churches intensify social stratification?
8. Explain how church attendance may vary with socio-economic times.
9. How have urban churches shown cooperation?

SUGGESTED PROJECTS

1. Study the functions of a "rescue mission" or "store-front church" and its membership and leadership.
2. Compare the rise and development of the Negro church in northern and southern cities.
3. Make a comparative study of the various types of churches of your city as they relate to the zonal pattern.
4. Make a study of a given ethnic church and show how the organization attempts to survive as its members become native-born and English-speaking.
5. Do the same as 4, but study the problems of the members when the foreign-born and native-born groups are equally strong numerically.
6. Study the church-going habits and attitudes of the American middle class.

READINGS

Annals of the American Academy of Political and Social Science, 256, March 1948.

>An issue devoted to organized religion and religious behavior in the United States.

Vettel Daniel, "Ritual and Stratification in Chicago Negro Churches," *American Sociological Review*, 7, June 1942, 353–361.

H. Paul Douglass, *One Thousand City Churches*. New York: Harper & Bros., 1926.

>A detailed survey of city churches and their adaptations to changing urban conditions.

C. Luther Fry, *Recent Social Trends in the United States*. New York: Mc-Graw-Hill Book Co., Inc., 1933.

> The chapter on religious trends shows the changing behavior patterns of urban family in church attendance, etc.

A. B. Hollingshead, *Elmtown's Youth*. New York: John Wiley & Sons, Inc., 1949, Ch. 3.

> A comparison of the religious behavior of the five major social classes in a midwestern city.

Samuel C. Kincheloe, *The American City and Its Churches*. New York: Friendship Press, Inc., 1938.

> A treatment of different types of urban churches.

Kenneth Miller, *Man and God In the City*. New York: Friendship Press, 1954.

> A discussion of urban behavior, church-going habits, and different kinds of churches.

W. Lloyd Warner and Leo Srole, *The Social Systems of American Ethnic Groups*. New Haven: Yale University Press, 1946, Ch. 7.

> The ethnic church's role in social control.

Chapter Fifteen

The Urban Family

T HE AMERICAN urban family has fallen into a recognized institutional organization, a pattern distinguishable from the traditional family of our rural heritage. The urban family is characterized by smaller size, changed functions, and distinct modes of interaction among its members.

Reactions to these changes in organization and behavior patterns are not always favorable.[1] The growing independence and freedom of women have contributed to the family's difficulties. Other critics believe that the increasing number of childless couples makes home ties less binding. Many say that urban living is to blame for the breakdown of traditional family relationships. On the other hand, defenders of the urban family contend that these conditions are symptoms of the urban family undergoing adjustments and adaptations to rapid social change and the development of new social norms.[2]

Despite much speculation as to final effects, there is little doubt that urban influences have affected the family as an institution. By considering some pertinent aspects of the American urban family, we shall gain insight of the various changes it has undergone. At the same time, we should recognize that *urban family* is a general term. Urban families differ according to socio-economic status, ethnic origin, nativity, and religion —to name a few distinctions.[3] Families which have recently settled in cities and had formerly lived in rural areas may undergo a process of assimilation to the same degree as immigrant families. Therefore, in comparing parts of the city, one may see similarities and differences. Generally speaking, however, the urban family has come to mean the institution

---

[1] C. C. Zimmerman, *Family and Civilization* (New York: Harper & Bros., 1947), 760–767.

[2] Ruth S. Cavan, *The American Family* (New York: Thomas Y. Crowell Co., 1953), Ch. 1.

[3] Burgess and Locke, *op. cit.*, Ch. 4; and E. R. Mowrer, *The Family* (Chicago: University of Chicago Press, 1932), 187.

identified with the Protestant, Caucasoid, American middle class. Family members of this class have had at least high school education. The family head is usually employed at work above skilled labor. This emphasis is due largely to the greater amount of research and empirical evidence obtained for this class group. The findings, although applicable in a large part to all American families, are, nevertheless, more valid for the broad middle class.

The Changing Environment

In the past, traditional family institutions were associated with a rural setting, where the family members worked together at a common enterprise. Industrialization is one of the great forces which effected the social change out of which grew the urban family. Mechanization of farming and change from handicrafts to production of goods by machines contributed to city-ward migration. Working methods changed as production units were enlarged. The employer used to know his hired men and co-workers as friends, neighbors, or kin. Today many executives in large business corporations find it impossible to know more than a few of their employees, who may number several thousands. When more than one member of the family works, the places of employment may be separate, and their associates may belong to different groups or sections of the city. Each member of the family specializes. Different hours of work may interfere with primary contacts in the home.

The decline if not the loss of some of the factors making for familism and the ascendancy of individualism is another major change experienced by the urban family in Western societies. Familism as a concept implies that the welfare of the family is more important than the individual's and that the latter functions for the group. Its aims and purposes are identical with his. A high degree of family stability results in the willingness of the family members to stay together in spite of difficulties. When decisions are made concerning common expenditure, common activities, and common goals, the decision favors the group. Conversely, in the Western urban family, each member is inclined to regard his earnings as his own, pursues his own occupational, educational, and recreational interests, and is less likely to feel that the continuation of the family line and tradition is vital. Moreover, few urban families can claim that several generations have lived and grown up under the same roof. It is not uncommon for parents to be in one area while children live where their work takes them. The modern family has been decentralized geographically as well as socially.

The urban family has had to adjust its way of life to suit the tempo of life found in cities. Rapid means of transportation and communication have made urbanites scurry from one activity to another. Most activities are outside the home, resulting in increased physical and ideational mobility. Children and parents are subjected to more complex ideas, values, and modes of behavior. Informal social controls, exerted by neighborly gossip, primary face-to-face contacts, and community leaders have declined to a large degree. Moreover, the family's integration and interaction suffers as the result of competing activities found outside of the home.

All of these changes do not cause the urban family to be less important; rather, they illustrate the adaptations which have been made to suit a new and demanding environment.[1] The fact that the marriage rates have not materially slackened despite the more difficult adjustments required of individuals is in itself significant. The family, as an institution, is as important as it ever was in training the young, in fostering and developing the emotional and affectional patterns of its members, and in cultural transmission.

It should be noted that whereas most major institutional organizations have grown in complexity and that functions have increased through the impact of urbanization, the reverse is true of the family. The family has shrunk in size and lost control of some of its traditional functions as urbanization increased. These aspects will be further explained in the following pages.

Size of the Urban Family

Early American Colonial families were considerably larger than those of today, and parents were often said to be "blessed with a store of children."[2] Children were an economic asset which enhanced the parents' status. The father played a strict role as breadwinner, disciplinarian, and social head of the family. The careers of the mothers centered around the household: caring for the home, husband, children, and kin. Children were expected to be obedient and respectful to parents and elders. A well-behaved and well-regulated family was highly commended by the community and especially by the church authorities. The behavior of the group was governed by traditions, mores, and religious rituals.

As cities grew, a gradual change in the size of the family as well as living habits occurred. The decrease in the number of children per family and the increase of childless couples constitute a major trend accompanying urbanization. In an earlier chapter we learned that the birth rate of

[1] E. W. Burgess and Paul Wallin, *Engagement and Marriage* (Philadelphia: J. B. Lippincott Co., 1953), Ch. 19.

[2] For a discussion of the Colonial family see A. W. Calhoun, *A Social History of the American Family,* I (Cleveland: Arthur H. Clark Co., 1917); and E. S. Morgan, *The Puritan Family* (Boston: Trustees of the Public Library, 1944).

Most children are in low and moderate income families

Out of every 100 children: Are in families with incomes (1948):

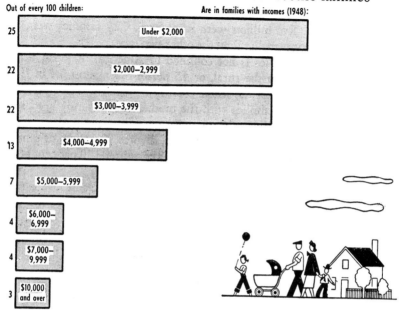

25	Under $2,000
22	$2,000–2,999
22	$3,000–3,999
13	$4,000–4,999
7	$5,000–5,999
4	$6,000–6,999
4	$7,000–9,999
3	$10,000 and over

Family income and number of children: three children out of every hundred are in families with over $10,000 annual income as compared with 25 out of every hundred in those earning below $2,000.[1]

cities dropped below the net reproduction rate, and replenishment of population came from rural families. The mid-century census showed a higher rate because of the increased births preceding and following the Second World War. Parents of the present generation are said to be aware of the drawbacks in rearing a small family, especially a single child. An interest in larger families may be revived.

Whether large families are becoming more common and the trend which began a decade or so ago will continue is a debatable point. American birth rates seem to fluctuate with socio-economic conditions. Other factors, such as a large adult childbearing group by 1960 and 1970 and a continued high standard of living, may cause the absolute increase in population to remain high for several decades.[2] It is estimated that 75 per

[1] *Children and Youth at the Midcentury—A Chart Book*, prepared by the Midcentury White House Conference on Children and Youth (Raleigh, N. C.: Health Publications Institute, 1951).

[2] W. F. Ogburn and M. F. Nimkoff, *Sociology* (Boston: Houghton, Mifflin Co., 1950), 335–337; and J. S. Davis, "Fifty Million More Americans," *Foreign Affairs*, 28 (Apr., 1950), 412–426.

cent of the American families with two children are now adding a third child to the family circle; and the remaining percentage, a fourth or fifth child. In 1950, 27 million families lived in cities. About 7 million were rural-nonfarm and five million were rural-farm. City families were approximately .5 persons smaller than the other two types.

Smaller families in cities is not confined to America. In Japan urban families are smaller than the rural, or 4.5 persons as against 5.4 in 1950. The over-all family size for the whole country of Japan was five persons.[1]

In the United States families with the mother as the family head supporting one or more children were twice as numerous in cities as on farms. More broken homes caused by death, divorce, desertion, or separation are found in cities. In 1950 these families constituted 10 per cent of all families.[2]

The over-all picture of the size of the American families in 1950 is seen in Table 29. Almost a third of the total number of families were two-per-

TABLE 29. SIZE OF AMERICAN
FAMILIES, 1950 [1]

Number of persons	Per Cent
2	32.9
3	25.1
4	20.7
5	11.1
6	5.4
7 or more	4.9
Total	100.0

[1] *Source:* Statistical Abstract of the United States, 1952, 46.

son units, 25 per cent consisted of three persons, while 20 per cent had four members. Families with five and more persons made up 20 per cent of the total number of family units. Stated in another way, all but 20 per cent of our families, regardless of their residence, fell within the category of small families. It should be noted that two-person families may be childless couples or a head of the family with one offspring, and that three-person units may contain two family heads and one child or one head and two children, and so on. Assuming that within the five-person families there are two family heads and three children, these units constituted but 11 per cent of the total families in the nation. Families with more than four children totaled slightly more than 10 per cent.

[1] Office of the Prime Minister of Japan, *op. cit.,* Bull. 52, Sec. 3.
[2] *Statistical Abstract of the United States, 1952,* 16 and 46.

Of course, the capacity for producing offspring has not been curtailed because of the environment. Lack of children is caused by new practices and attitudes which are so widespread in this country that a brief consideration of them is timely.

Control of family size. One of the major factors associated with the small urban family can be directly correlated with the extensive use of contraceptives. One sure method to gauge the extent to which contraceptive devices are employed is to study the mounting sums of money spent on contraceptive preparations and devices, a sum exceeding that spent on jewelry. Another method is to trace the growth of noncommercial birth-control clinics. From one such center started in 1923 by Margaret Sanger, the Planned Parenthood Federation reported that 39 states and the District of Columbia in 1949 had 552 clinics.[1] Moreover, Margaret Sanger's trips to Far Eastern cities, at the invitation of leading women's organizations during the 1920's and 1950's, have resulted in birth control clinics being established in Japanese and East Indian cities.

A change in the public attitude sanctioning the limitation of family size was a natural outgrowth of population shift to urban centers. The enactment of laws against child labor may have had some direct bearing. The emancipation of women and the weakening of religious controls furthered the practice of disseminating birth-control information to married persons. In fact, a recent public opinion poll favored giving this information to the unmarried in this country.[2] Moreover, there has been a gradual decline of legal restrictions against disseminating birth-control information. One of the most important factors favoring the small family is the psychological and social acceptance of the concept of the "proper rearing of children," stressing quality rather than quantity.[3] This belief is firmly rooted in the middle- and upper-class families of the nation. Large families are regarded as dissipating the material and social advantages which should be equally shared by each member of the group.

One social effect of the decrease in family size is that parents are freed at an earlier age from the responsibility of rearing young children. Between 1900 and 1930 unbroken families with wives under 45 years and which had either no children or no grown children living at home, increased three per cent. In 1948, two-thirds of these families had no adult relatives eighteen years or over living with them, other than the head or his wife. Nearly one-half had no sons or daughters under 18 years of age at home.[4]

Parents no longer look to their children as the sole source of emotional

[1] *New York Times*, Sept. 11, 1950, 25.
[2] *Public Opinion Quarterly*, 11, 1947, 278.
[3] W. S. Thompson, *Population Problems*, 185 and 367–371.
[4] Ogburn and Nimkoff, *op. cit.*, 474.

satisfaction and do not rely as much upon them for financial support in later years. Parents are expected to regain their "lost youth" when children leave home. Many join organizations, travel, buy luxury items, move to smaller quarters, or settle in warmer climates. Many participants in spectator sports, concerts, and charity events are older or childless couples. Adult education courses are frequently geared toward this group who are anxious to keep abreast of the times in order to understand the problems faced by the younger generation. Many others volunteer their services to religious, welfare, and other agencies.

General Effects of Urbanization

The urban family has experienced environmental changes which alter its life and habits. Foremost in our consideration is the decline in neighborliness resulting from the impersonal nature of urban living and the greater degree of residential mobility found in cities. A family may reside next door to another for years, seldom visiting or even speaking. Amenities, if exchanged, are frequently in the hall when passing. People who live at the same address may not know businesses or family backgrounds. If one visits friends, he may go out of his neighborhood or community and fraternize with those whose interests are more akin to his own.

In neighborhoods with many children, the mothers and children are more friendly. This may be caused by the need of each unit to support and utilize the services offered by the neighborhood's institutional organizations, rather than because of the desire for genuine friendship. Moreover, the diminished size of the urban family forces children to seek associates for play and recreation, thus inducing mothers to become acquainted. Where families own detached homes in residential districts, and the area is not separated by apartments, the families are more congenial and take a more active interest in community affairs.

Using several criteria to measure the degree of participation in neighborhood activities, McClenahan's study showed that length of residence influenced the probabilities of wider acquaintance and continued contacts.[1] Home ownership was more significant in promoting interest in the kind of neighbors, adequacy of local institutions, and neighborhood well-being. Home ownership also fostered continued social contacts and increased acquaintance with others in the area. Other factors having some bearing in participation in local neighborhood activities included the presence or absence of children, common adult interest in recreation, occupation, or hobby, and a friendly approach to others.

[1] B. A. McClenahan, *The Changing Urban Neighborhood* (Los Angeles: University of Southern California, 1929).

These local community participation patterns applied to native-white, middle-class, residential neighborhoods. Where the social milieu is oriented around ethnic or racial ties, the patterns of social contacts differed. The residents were likely to form an integrated social world within the community. An example is the "Black Belt" of some of our cities.

Multi-dwellings. The trend toward multi-dwellings was well advanced by the second decade of this century, and apartment living became necessary as land values rose and space diminished with the increase of urban population. In order to obtain a fair return on the investment placed on high-value land and construction, owners reduced the size of living units to make rentals low. The shrinking size of the urban family was also instrumental in hastening the trend. In former years, walk-up apartments and family duplexes were common. Now, those serviced by elevators are increasing in number. Not only have dwellings towered to skyscraping heights, but every inch of available ground space is utilized.

Small efficiency apartments are increasing. Large apartments of six to eight rooms are becoming more rare in metropolitan cities, while rents have climbed out of proportion to the space utilized. Four decades ago, almost 50 per cent of apartments were fairly large. Today, these are subdivided into several tiny cubicles. One of the first rooms to be sacrificed was the guest room. Later, the dining room was omitted and the arrangement of a flat board between two benches was substituted and called the "dining nook." Kitchen-dining room or living-dining room combinations are hailed as "step-savers." The most "compact" apartments use one room as combination living-dining-bedroom. The bed is hidden behind double doors disguised by full-length mirrors or fine panelling. Even the bathroom can be reduced in size through the substitution of shower for tub. Correspondent to these reductions in living quarters is the growth of tourist homes, motels, hotels, cocktail lounges, and eating establishments for the accommodation of guests.

Cubicle-living has served to heighten the lack of privacy between members of the family. Where young children are confined to small quarters, parents are forced to use the room as the nursery and playroom or turn the children loose on the sidewalks or narrow streets. The increase in traffic hazards has made for serious restrictions on play and added to parent-child tension. Playgrounds and recreational facilities have not grown at the same pace as the number of dwelling units.

In 1930, one urban family out of every eight lived in an apartment house. In 1945, five out of every ten families shared a dwelling with one or more families. In contrast, single dwellings have multiplied in suburbs, satellites, and territories contiguous to the city. The largest proportion of single-family houses built since 1925 has been in cities having between 25,-

000 to 50,000 residents. Los Angeles seems to be the only large city of the nation's biggest ten that has built single homes in excess of the other metropolitan cities.[1] At the other extreme is New York where the land is so costly and so limited in extent that the only answer to expansion has been in construction of high buildings.

Home ownership. The trend toward multi-dwellings and the high cost of home construction within the city proper has reduced the extent of home ownership among urbanites. However, the ownership of a home is still a symbol of achievement in our society. Other factors being equal, owning a home represents thrift, planning, stability, and success. Once families owned their homes and children grew into adulthood in the community of their birth. This tendency is less apparent today because of urban conditions.

The desire to own homes has not diminished, but many families prefer renting rather than being tied financially to one locality. The probabilities of neighborhoods changing in population and institutional characteristics are greater and cause some families to prefer renting their quarters. Frequently, a change in work forces a move within a city or to another city or state. In these instances, home ownership is an encumbrance. Moreover, fluctuating tax rates cause many families to avoid the uncertain financial burden attached to the annual upkeep of homes.

The national trend of home ownership from 1890 to 1945 has been generally upward because of the great gains made in the construction of rural-nonfarm homes.[2] In the fastest growing cities of 25,000 to one million inhabitants, home ownership has climbed, while in cities above this population total, there is a drop. This is due to the shift of population to rural-nonfarm areas and the need to build housing to accommodate the newcomers.

Another study also showed that we are a nation of home-owners, though perhaps more in terms of values than in actuality.[3] Between 1890 and April, 1947, a 16 per cent increase in the proportion of owner-to-total occupied home units was evident. Most of the gains were not within the city's political confines and the professionals, clerical and sales workers, proprietors, and the managers do not show as high a percentage of ownership as do the semi-skilled and skilled workers. Many of the latter are foreign-born, whose desire for security, status, and stability may motivate them to ownership. They may be those who do not have the attributes or

[1] U. S. Department of Labor, Bureau of Labor Statistics, *Building Construction*, 1940, Bull. 693, 12.

[2] H. M. Muller, *Urban Home Ownership* (Philadelphia: University of Pennsylvania, 1947), Ch. 1.

[3] Lillian Cohen, "Family Characteristics of Home Owners," *American Journal of Sociology*, 55 (May, 1950), 565–571.

inclinations to "climb." A home compensates for the many expenditures which are essential for social and occupational mobility.

Native-white families in 22 of the largest metropolitan districts include a larger tenant group than the foreign-born home-owners's group. Some of the highest rents are paid by the proprietors, managers, officials, and upper-class native-white families. Maintaining a standard-of-living and "keeping up with the Jones's" are more pronouncedly exhibited by members of these groups. On the other hand, home ownership is greater among minority groups because the crowded living conditions, rent exploitations, run-down neighborhoods, and a more limited rental market force renters who can afford to purchase homes to do so.

Other social characteristics of home ownership may be seen. As male heads of families grow older, the percentage of owners become larger. More home-owners than renters have growing children. More show successful marital adjustment than those who rent living quarters. Purchasing a home seems to be an integrating factor in marriage and may also be indicative of the willingness to assume the responsibilities of family life.

Family Income and Expenditures

The urban family has lost its economic self-sufficiency and is dependent upon the earning capacity of one or more of its members to purchase the necessities of life. Food, shelter, and clothing are daily requirements, while other items may be added as the income warrants. By examining the income and expenditures of various income groups, we see the effect which economic fluctuations have upon urban families.

In 1945, a year of prosperity, nearly half of the city families of two or more persons reported annual incomes between $1,500 and $3,500.[1] Thirteen per cent earned less than $1,500, while the remaining 38 per cent had incomes above $3,500. The median annual income for this family size was approximately $3,000. This figure may represent the combined earnings of one, two, or more members of the familial unit. Families have had to spend unusually large parts of their incomes for food, or 32 per cent for two or more persons. At the higher income levels, food took one-fourth of the annual income. Rising costs threaten families of low incomes with deficient diet, because less can be spent on meat, milk, vegetables, and fruits. Spot studies made by the Bureau of Human Nutrition and Home Economics in a county in Georgia and one in Ohio concluded that many low-income families had poor diets.

Housing is another important item that requires an outlay of cash.

[1] U. S. Department of Agriculture, *How Families Use Their Incomes,* Miscellaneous Publication, No. 653.

Most large families have lower incomes than small families

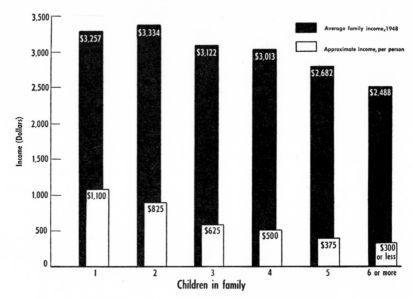

Income per person decreases as families grow larger.[1]

When heat, light, and furnishings for the home are included, the annual expenditures are proportionately greater for the low income than for the high. Many of the low-income groups pay $25 monthly rentals and live in quarters having no heating and sanitation facilities. The lower-income families have little choice of desirable quarters. Poor housing can lead to health problems, thus indirectly raising the rental costs and directly reducing the expenditures on other essentials.

Clothing expenditures are affected by many factors: the family income, place of residence, age, and the size and composition of the family. In general, the greater the influence of urbanism, the larger the outlay of cash for clothing. For both husbands and wives, the spending rose markedly as a shift was made from farm to small city, or from a small city to a large one. If there are children, the expenditures mount as the children grow older. Parents reduce their clothing purchases to accommodate the children whose needs change with age. If the mother remains at home, she cuts

[1] *Children and Youth at the Midcentury—A Chart Book,* prepared by the Midcentury White House Conference on Children and Youth (Raleigh, N. C.: Health Publications Institute, Inc., 1951).

down her share. The median-income family of 1945 spent 13 per cent of its annual income on clothing.[1]

Other items include medical care, transportation, gifts, and taxes. Proportionally more is spent on each item as the annual income goes over $1,500. Low-income families cannot afford serious illnesses. They may go years without any untoward incidents. When illness does occur, going into debt or relying upon agency assistance are probable results. The median-income urban family earning $3,000 annually spent 5 per cent of the total earnings for medical services. About 10 per cent went for transportation, personal care, recreation, tobacco, reading matter, formal education, and miscellaneous.[2] Gifts and contributions took 4 per cent and the cost of operating automobiles showed a similar figure.

Similar items of expenditure may appear on the family budget for the various income levels of the urban family, but more is spent by the higher income groups for variety, quality, and taste. Rising prices, steady employment, illness, and personal preferences alter budgetary outlays so that each family spends on that which it deems most important.

The urban family has lost its economic self-sufficiency because of its great dependence upon cash to purchase daily items. Being unable to produce the variety of goods and services required by the members of the group, steady employment is vital, since expenditures for food, shelter, clothing, and miscellaneous items continue to be necessary regardless of circumstances. Many families are unable to save something of their current earning for a "rainy day."

In metropolitan areas a higher proportion of married women work than in smaller cities. Fewer of those living in rural-nonfarm territories are employed. The differential is partly due to the greater employment opportunities found in larger cities. Employment is also more pronounced when no young children are in the home, yet the wives of the poorest families with children are most likely to be in the labor force. It would appear that the primary determinant whether married women work or not is the economic status of the family, rather than the presence or absence of children.

Changes in Family Functions

The American urban family as a social unit has experienced a reduction in functions as well as in size.[3] The smaller unit, however, is unable to

---

[1] U. S. Department of Agriculture, *op. cit.*
[2] U. S. Bureau of Labor Statistics.
[3] Burgess and Locke, *op. cit.*, 501–510.

undertake some of the functions the Puritan family maintained when a large group of persons, often of several generations, lived together. Some of the functions which have been transferred outside of the home to other organizations came as the result of urbanization and industrialization.

Various tasks once connected with housekeeping and personal services are no longer performed in the home. Making of candles; the growing, spinning, and dyeing of flax for weaving into cloth and fashionable garments; and the preparation of food for the table were once done within the home. The women of the household provided them as a matter of course. Today, many ready-made items are substituted and preferred. Shops specializing in supplying these items have steadily multiplied.

Another function which the family today has come to share with other institutions is the protection and care of children. When mothers did not have outside employment, day-nurseries, nursery schools, kindergartens, and camps were unheard of. Baby-sitters were the grandmothers, relatives, or the hired girl. Children at an early age now come under the care and guidance of teachers, camp counselors, recreational directors, and group leaders whose training fits them to be "substitute parents." When parents fail in their roles and their care or discipline prove inadequate, private schools, foster homes, orphanages, or the detention or correctional institutions may provide temporary or long-time care. An entire set of laws pertains to the "rights of children" as a protection against irresponsible, cruel, or ineffective parents. Relatives do not assume the care of as many neglected and orphaned children as was once the custom. Specialized schools and therapeutic centers have arisen for the care and retraining of "problem children."

Education of the children is mainly in the hands of public schools, supplemented by parochial and a few private schools. The parents' role in teaching their offspring the three "R's" is a supplementary one. Not only do schools furnish information and skills which are often far beyond the abilities of the parents to give—but schools are also valued for furnishing the wide number and range of social contacts which characterize urban life. Whereas at one time the family heads taught their offspring the skills needed for adulthood (*i.e.,* housekeeping for daughters and occupations for sons), vocational and professional schools now assume this role.

The father of the family is no longer the religious leader that he once was. The Puritan father was required by the church to gather all the family members living within his household and read the Bible together. Daily prayers and the reading and discussion of religious literature were part of daily living. Today, parents exercise freedom in adhering to, or omitting, religious practices for themselves and their children.

Formerly, there was a great deal of family visiting, including picnics, festivals, and family reunions. Christenings, funerals, marriages, and birthdays were family get-togethers, occasions which afforded the relatives the opportunity of experiencing and reaffirming solidarity and cohesion. Today, commercial recreation has superseded family gatherings while smaller living quarters mitigate against large-group entertaining. Moreover, family members find and pursue their own interests outside of the family circle. At a very early age, children associate with peers of their own age and sex and it is not uncommon for families to plan their get-togethers with a separation of interests in mind. The installation of television sets may bring some of the family recreation back into the home, although preoccupation with the television screen may not motivate primary group interaction.

The growing population of oldsters has brought to a head the problems of how to provide for the welfare of aging persons who no longer are productive but have contributed to the welfare of the society during their active and able years. Many could not save sufficiently to guarantee an income during the nonproductive period. The small family is not the best means of "social security." The burden of raising a family and caring for older parents and relatives has proved difficult for the productive adult population of the society. Thus another function has been transferred, and a system of social security was adopted to spread the cost.

Another function which is seldom mentioned is the parents' role in supervising and controlling the courtship and approval of the mates selected by their children. While many writers claim that there was great freedom in the selection of mates in a frontier society and that romanticism has always been accepted as a value, parental consent to the courtship, engagement, and marriage of a prospective mate was fairly general until the turn of this century. Today, chaperones are considered "Victorian." Dating has become an accepted practice. Whereas at one time parents decided when and where young people could go out together, today children make the decisions themselves and may or may not inform their parents as to whom they date or where they are spending their time. The loss of the function of discipline and control of growing children is perhaps one of the greatest changes experienced by the American family which has caused the most discussion and, at times, serious consequences, should deviant behavior develop.

The functions which the urban family has retained are (1) providing affection, (2) development of personality, and (3) cultural transmission and socialization. No other institution has been able to replace the family in performing these functions. The process of socialization begins with the family and its role in channelizing emotions, attitudes, values, and behavior patterns remains. Although schools, churches, and other institutional organizations also undertake cultural transmission and socialization, the family's part in implanting and supplementing the larger society's cultural norms and expectations during infancy should not be overlooked. Indeed, in a rapidly changing society the family's role in performing the three functions mentioned are of supreme importance.

Summary

The American urban family is characterized by smaller size than the earlier rural family, by changed functions, and by different patterns of interaction among its members. Although there is considerable disagreement as to the good and bad features of urbanism upon family members and family relationships, there is general acceptance that the urban family as an institution differs from the traditional family of our rural heritage in form of organization as well as in behavior patterns.

One of the general effects of urbanization on the family is the decline of neighborliness and the degree of neighborhood and community contacts. The family's living quarters have shrunk in size and fewer urban families own their homes. On the other hand, home ownership has increased among rural-nonfarm families. The loss of economic self-sufficiency has resulted in more women working outside the home. Lower-income mothers of young children are more frequently employed. Proportionately more married women work in metropolitan cities than in smaller cities.

The changing environment and the smaller family have caused some of the historical functions of the family to be transferred to other institutions and affected the nature of intrafamily interaction and relationships. The important functions retained include affection, personality development, and cultural transmission and socialization.

DISCUSSION QUESTIONS

1. In what ways can additions to income be made for families in cities earning less than the median income?
2. Will more leisure-time activities revert to the home because of television?
3. What advantages can the urban family of today claim as compared to the colonial families? To the families at the turn of this century?
4. Will the development of small, self-contained communities within large metropolises reduce the social distance of urbanites?
5. What are the advantages or disadvantages of home ownership?
6. What functions have been transferred from the home?
7. What functions have been retained by the urban family?

SUGGESTED PROJECTS

1. Prepare a paper showing the changing size of the American urban family for the past century.
2. Study the median annual incomes for urban families for several decades and relate this to economic changes.
3. Draw up a series of questions which would test "social distance" in cities and obtain the results from a field study.
4. Compare the home-ownership of immigrants against native-born citizens. Include the non-whites in the study.
5. Write a critical analysis of the theories advanced by the authorities who foresee the eventual disintegration of the family as an institution.
6. Study the changing roles of husband and wife as they are affected by the urban environment.

READINGS

R. N. Anshen, ed. *The Family: Its Functions and Destiny.* New York: Harper & Bros., 1949.

A series of articles comparing the family in various societies.

H. S. Bossard, *The Sociology of Child Development.* New York: Harper, 1948.

Excellent material on the changing urban family.

A. W. Calhoun, *A Social History of the American Family.* Cleveland: The Arthur and Grove Co., 1917.

A descriptive account of the Colonial family in its social setting.

John Sirjamai, *The American Family In the Twentieth Century,* Cambridge: Harvard University Press, 1953.

A comprehensive study of the American family of this century; clearly written and provocative.

C. C. Zimmerman, *Family and Civilization,* New York: Harper & Bros., 1947.

A volume predicting the eventual disintegration of the modern family and the fall of Western civilization.

P. K. Whelpton and C. V. Kiser, *Social and Psychological Factors Affecting Fertility,* Milbank Memorial Fund, 1951.

A monograph dealing with the "hidden" factors affecting fertility in a midwestern metropolis.

Chapter Sixteen

Voluntary Associations

O<small>NE OF</small> the major characteristics of an urbanized, complex society is the number of alternative positions which an individual may hold, and over which he has some measure of control. Many of these alternative positions are with voluntary associations, groups in which membership is at least to some degree a matter of choice, and of which the city affords an incredible diversity. Some voluntary associations, such as church or labor groups, may function primarily to implement institutional organizations. But, as institutions are characterized by more and more complex and specialized organizations, they fail to meet many of the needs of urbanites. A large number of voluntary associations assume institutional characteristics themselves, whereas others are much more limited in scope and membership, with little to distinguish them from more informal social groupings, such as cliques.

Although the term *voluntary association* would imply that the individual had complete freedom of choice of belonging, this is not necessarily the case. Social pressures do operate to force membership on the one hand, and to deny it, on the other. The country club which some feel obliged to join just to maintain social position or business contacts may deny membership to others because of their social or ethnic backgrounds. A man does not have to work in a given factory, but refusing to work there may involve his livelihood. He may not want to join the union to get employment, but he may have to do so as a matter of expediency. A choice may still remain, and to this extent the association is "voluntary," but in social reality some choices involve serious social and economic sacrifices.

Associations

An association is a voluntary group of people organized to pursue a common interest. The group is recognized as such even though the personnel may undergo change. As long as the interests persist and are to some extent met, they are the bond holding the group together. Voluntary associations vary in size, depending in large measure on the scope of the interest. These organizations may range anywhere from a half-dozen to a half-million or more members, although many of the larger groups are broken down into sub-groups in order to facilitate more effective interaction among members. Some, however, involve no face-to-face relationships at all, such as some hobby groups communicating through the mails.

Voluntary associations also differ in the intricacy of organization and the intensity and scope of the control of behavior they exercise over their members. Labor unions may exercise a strong control over their memberships within a limited range of interests, yet the country club member, too, is subject to controls of a more subtle sort, for frequently this type of association carries with it an extremely wide variety of subtle controls, from manners to clothes, from politics to social beliefs.

Some voluntary associations are primarily composites of cliques, and are at times almost indistinguishable from them, as in the case of many social clubs.

Cliques are less definitely organized than associations. They permit more intimate and continuous primary face-to-face contacts. The membership is sufficiently small to enable each to be known to the others. People are addressed by Christian names or nicknames. Rules and regulations are arrived at by informal discussion and agreement, but are binding upon the individual as long as he remains a part of the group. When referred to by an outsider, no specific name may be accorded the group. The activity itself may provide the term of reference. The "gang," the "bridge crowd," the "fast set," or the "Jones crowd," are examples. Membership in a clique is a surer sign of belonging than membership in the association, for generally "birds of a feather flock together."

Historical development. Associations flourish and multiply where the population is large and heterogeneous. Small communities having but a few hundred inhabitants would be faced with the problem of duplication of membership and the limitation of recruits. Associations began in this country before the Civil War, coinciding with the growth of canal cities around the 1820's. They were so numerous and diversified that a visitor, De Tocqueville, wrote about them after a stay in the United States.[1] He pointed out that where the French government or a man of noble rank undertook a new project, here an association would certainly be formed to spearhead it. Americans of all ages, all conditions, and all dispositions

[1] Alex de Tocqueville, *Democracy in America* (Cambridge: Sever and Francis, 1862), I, 216 and II, 123; also see "The Function of Associations in American Life" in H. H. Gerth and C. W. Mills, from *Max Weber: Essays in Sociology* (New York: Oxford University Press, 1946).

were constantly founding associations. Indeed, he declared, a society is organized to inculcate some truth or to foster some new feeling.

The growth of associations was greatest during the latter part of the nineteenth century. Thousands of new ones appeared, and it was a rare citizen who did not become affiliated with four or five organizations. The depression of the thirties struck a heavy blow at a large number of associations because financially hard-pressed individuals withdrew their memberships. Purely social clubs suffered more than the professional or occupational associations.

Associations may be local, regional, or national. To gather the membership together, conventions are periodically called. America is the land of conventions. Baltimore, Chicago, Cleveland, Denver, New York, Los Angeles, New Orleans, Philadelphia, and San Francisco have reputations as convention cities. Houston, Cincinnati, and Atlanta are gaining fame for the same purpose. In 1952 Chicago had almost a thousand conventions. Some 1,400 hotels alone took in more than $3.5 million, while the remainder of the $10 million spent by 40,000 conventioneers at the two national Democratic and Republican conventions was divided among 2,200 restaurants, numerous recreational and entertainment places, and stores. About $1.2 million was spent for food and about the same for all forms of recreation and entertainment.

Many persons regard the prevalence of voluntary associations as symbols of a democratic way of life. As the population grows, separated by geographic distance, and as face-to-face contacts are limited, associations provide the media whereby groups and individuals articulate their desires, hopes, and fears. Persons having similar needs are able to meet and seek means to solve their problems.

Small vs. large city. Associations were first organized in large urban centers and later spread to the smaller cities. Some have penetrated rural areas and are filling a need for organized activities. On the other hand, Four H Clubs and Farm Bureau originated in rural areas. Specialized associations tend to remain concentrated in metropolises. The Bar Association and the bankers' clubs are excellent illustrations. Conversely, the Elk's organization and Young People's Christian Endeavor Leagues are more developed in smaller cities. The Business and Professional Women's Club faces less competition in smaller centers because career women from various fields belong to it. In large municipalities, separate associations representing each field are organized.

There are three times more associations found in cities with 6,000 inhabitants than where the population is 2,000. The smaller population makes it easier for an association to be organized around multi-functions. A city of 17,000 may have about 85 associations, whereas a municipality of 42,000 inhabitants would have about 450.[1] It should be noted that fewer associations exist in cities of the same sizes in other parts of the world.

Income and associations. The general level of income has a bearing on the number of associations in a community. Money is a restricting factor while time is another determining factor. In a study of Westchester County, New York, half the women were shown to be without club membership, and in a neighboring poorer suburb, over three-fourths joined no clubs whatsoever because of the lack of funds and time.[2] In the poorer suburb, women were employed outside the home, while in the first instance, the family budget may not permit both spouses to join clubs. When money was allotted for this expenditure, the breadwinner of the family used club membership for furthering his work, contacts, and prestige. Southern states have fewer associations in general than other sections of the country. The chief associations of the laboring groups are trade unions and fraternal societies. Professional persons join more organizations than do the laboring men.

Urban Environment and Associations

As we have seen, the city is fertile ground for the formation and increase of associations. The need for specialization and delegation of authority where large numbers must cooperate for accomplishing common goals and interests is effected through associations. Moreover, associations increase the efficiency of a given institutional organization and link similar or diverse institutions together in a network. For example, the noonday businessmen's luncheon clubs bring together owners and operators of small businesses, large corporation executives, and junior executives. Since each group has problems related to its kind of work or enterprise, meeting together in a social atmosphere facilitates exchange of ideas and cognizance of one another's problems. When a common problem touches the group, representatives can be chosen to cope with it. Moreover, concerted expression carries more weight and influence.

The sheer size of urban population, its proximity, diversity, and easy contact makes the city the perfect setting for voluntary associations. No matter what a person's hobby, vocation, religion, ethnic background, age, sex, race, political affiliation, or value system, he can find others with like interests or beliefs. As a result nearly every kind of group acquires a voluntaristic character.

Voluntary associations have replaced or supplemented neighborhoods as

[1] Ogburn and Nimkoff, *op. cit.,* 364–367.
[2] G. Lundberg, M. Komarovsky, and A. McInery, *Leisure: A Suburban Study* (New York: Columbia University Press, 1934).

social units in cities. They may actually overshadow the family in their appeal and binding force. What urban newspapers print as news is often an account of the activities, opinions, and attitudes of the members of important associations. Associational activities round out the social life of the urbanite and lift him out of his immediate environment. He becomes important and accepted as a member of the larger society.

Life Cycle of Associations

As organized groups, associations have fairly definite schemes of arrangement. Organized because of common interests, they supplement formalized institutional hierarchies in promoting effective interaction.

Aid to institutions. Many associations are created to aid institutions by making members become a vital part of the social organization. The greater the gap between the purposes of an institution and its ability to accomplish these objectives, the longer the association's life cycle. For example, the Child Welfare League helps schools, families, churches, and medical institutions to attain objectives. Such an association has a longer life cycle than the local bowling club or cycling foursome. Similarly, Rotary Clubs, Better Business Bureaus, and trade unions are more permanent, attract wider membership, and are better organized than those devoted to the adoption and pursuit of fads and fashions. When the membership is convinced that the group is vital to society, or can reform a segment of it, the life cycle of the association is extended. But, while some have added new functions from time to time as new demands arose, others have done the exact opposite.

Enlarged functions. Many associations continue to survive although the original purpose for which they were organized has changed. As an adaptive process, an enlarged set of functions has recruited wider support, or a single function has brought the same results. An excellent illustration is the Parent-Teachers' Association. Originally, these two important groups believed that a closer relationship between them was vital in effecting better adjustment of children studying in educational institutions. Problems affecting pre-college pupils could be mutually explored and handled. The community organizations affecting the welfare of the students were invited to cooperate. Today, many undertake specific community projects: improving the library facilities, playgrounds, health services, etc.

Clashes of Personality. Clashes of personality frequently cause associational decline, spurring the creation of new associations. In an institutional organization, clashes of this nature do not alter the entire structure, which is inflexible. Personnel may change but only for that part of the organization affected. In associations, however, a conflict between the members and officials, or between opposing camps within the membership, creates a schism. Officials may be overanxious to enhance their authority or overstep it. Their interests may be at variance with the membership's. Differences in policy matters may split the group's cohesion, and a lack of common understanding is revealed.

Social change. Changing social conditions affect associations more drastically than institutional organizations. Leisure-time groups suffer losses of membership during wartime or periods of economic recession. Technological changes produce the same results. On the other hand, other types may come into importance during periods of emergency and have life cycles limited to the emergency period, as, for example, the United Service Organizations and American Women's Volunteer Service. They may be revived, if needed. War brought about the neighborhood protective associations and entertainment committees for servicemen. Soon after a return to normalcy, the activities were either curtailed or abandoned.

Invasion and succession. Invasion and succession can end the activities of an association by scattering the membership and altering the configuration of a community. Associations may terminate their existence, as have ethnic associations. When a neighborhood is invaded by persons belonging to other social classes, ethnic backgrounds, or occupations, new associations arise.

Poor organization. Other reasons for associational decline may include poor organization, disinterested membership, or duplication of effort. Faulty organization can cause a waste of energy. Disinterested membership may be directly related to faulty organization, and duplication of effort may be due to the same cause.

In general, the mortality rate of associations is high. Annually, countless associations spontaneously begin and die before the common purpose, organizational procedure, and acceptance of officers are carried through. Many decline because there is no real purpose to the organization.

Classification of Associations

The kinds of associations that abound in this country defy the imagination and effort to enumerate them systematically.[1] In general, they may be broadly classified as: (1) social, (2) recreational, (3) cultural, (4) familial, (5) educational, (6) racial, (7) ethnic, (8) religious, (9) economic, (10) political, (11) occupational, or (12) organized for certain age groups or specifically for men or women. Each differentiation could be subdivided and any classificatory system is unsatisfactory. For example, the Ladies' Aid Society is a Protestant service organization for women members of

[1] R. M. MacIver, *Society* (New York: Farrar & Rinehart, Inc., 1937), Ch. 13.

any given church. It may simultaneously be the missionary society, the local Red Cross chapter, or the group raising money for decorating the church quarters. Placing the Ladies' Aid Society under the category of either the religious, sex, welfare, or social would not be incorrect.

Major categories. Any classification of associations is inadequate because of overlapping interests and functions. Changing membership, policy, and interests further complicate the delineation. Only a suggestive and partial list can be offered:

Economic	Industrial, financial, and agricultural organizations, protective and insurance societies, better business bureaus, manufacturers' associations, real estate boards, loan associations, association of wholesalers, etc.
Vocational and Professional	Medical societies, craft unions, engineering societies, research institutes, garment workers' union, labor unions, clerical unions, and organizations for diamond cutters, jewelers, bus drivers, etc.
Educational	Teachers groups, study clubs, literary societies, parent-teachers' associations, poetry clubs, book-review clubs, professors' associations, alumni associations, aid to handicapped, vocational rehabilitation, adult education, etc.
Political	Political parties, political clubs, committees, lobbies, propagandist groups, association of city, state, county, or federal employees, League of Women Voters, or groups promoting independent tickets and candidates, etc.
Civic and Welfare	City clubs; better housing and neighborhood conservation committees; combating disease, etc.; reform or philanthropic groups; women's clubs; consumers' organizations; prevention of juvenile delinquency, crime, suicide, or other social problems.
Social	Country clubs, cliques, fraternities, sororities, lodges, secret societies, dessert clubs, card clubs, etc.
Religious	Ministerial alliances, interracial church groups, young people's religious associations, ladies' aid societies, missionary societies, married couples' socials, interfaith committees, etc.
Health and Recreation	Sports, games, dancing, gymnastics, and other exercise groups for diversion and amusement, Judo societies, fencing clubs, nudist colonies, hiking clubs, anglers clubs, etc.

Ethnic	Columbia Society, Swedish-American Society, German Club, Zionist clubs, etc.
Racial	Association for the Advancement of Colored People, Japanese-American Citizenship Alliance, Chinese Benevolent Association, etc.
Class	Junior League, Daughters of the American Revolution, Saddle and Cycle Club, Cotillion Committee, Debutante Clubs, etc.
Age (limited to age periods of relatively short range)	School and college societies, debating societies, Boy Scouts, Girl Scouts, junior women's clubs, Junior Chamber of Commerce, or Oldsters Club.
Sex	American Association of University Women, Chamber of Commerce, Rotary Club, Zonta, Veterans of Foreign Wars, and Nurses' Associations.
Anti-Social	Criminal or delinquent gangs, underworld organizations, gambling clubs, etc.

It would be obvious from the foregoing that urban population is, indeed, heterogeneous. The composition of population according to age, sex, occupation, or common interest is sufficiently diversified to enable simultaneous membership in several associations. Joining is one of the social pressures exerted upon urbanites and assumes the criterion of "social maturity." A prospective employee is often requested to list his membership in some form of collective group affiliation other than his primary group. A man who has wide contacts is preferred on the theory that his ability to adjust to various groups indicates better personal and vocational adjustment. Co-workers having diverse backgrounds and interests come from various sections of the city, and his acceptance of co-workers is a prerequisite to efficiency and cooperation.

A person may become a member of an association without actually knowing all the members. A national organization can never marshal its entire membership at one time. Representatives are selected and delegated the task of speaking for the entire association at local, regional, or national meetings. The absent members consider themselves a vital part of the association by periodically voting by mail. Officers are elected and important policies are decided in this manner. Even local chapters may follow this pattern.

The Function of Associations in Society

Associations do perform specific functions for the society. Several can be used as illustrations.[1]

[1] C. R. Henderson, "The Place and Function of Voluntary Associations," *American Journal of Sociology,* I, 1895–1896, 327–334.

Division of labor. The existence of associations calls attention to the division of labor. In a simple society, division of labor is regulated by custom. In modern, urbanized society, every occupation, profession, or service has its specialized branches which are all interdependent. When a given occupation has sufficient numbers, the workers organize to protect their interests.

Each time that a new type of work is created, an association appears to perpetuate the advantages accrued and to attain more. For example, the Association of Secretaries is striving to attain professional status by (1) setting up standards, (2) forbidding the use of the term "secretary" by typists, bookkeepers, file clerks, switchboard operators, etc., (3) requiring a certificate of graduation from a recognized school offering secretarial training, and (4) establishing a wage scale. Members of the Association of Secretaries believe that the public needs to be educated about their special type of service.

Socio-economic stratification. Another function may be to reinforce the various socio-economic strata in the society.[1] Organizations admitting members of a given social stratum complement the stratification and perpetuate it. While it is theoretically true that parents and their children may belong to organizations of their choice, the younger generation is often directed by the parents in its social life. Parents belonging to exclusive country clubs make certain that their children belong to them or other associations of the same status. Moreover, we have already seen how socio-economic status affects associational membership and that lack of money limits participation in associations.

Racial groupings. Racial lines are accentuated by associations. Many associations are in existence because of the group's need for self-expression and advancement, a situation more true for racial minorities than the dominant group. Issues concerning the minorities are discussed and solved. The same applies to ethnic group associations, such as the Puerto Rican and Mexican organizations. In general, however, racial associations persist longer than those with ethnic differences, although some of the latter may in time become "social" groups.

Associations and attitudes. In a complex urban society, the individual may derive or modify some of his attitudes and beliefs from the specific groups to which he belongs. In this respect, associations become *reference groups* for the individual, in that attitudes and beliefs upheld by the associations may be sufficiently strong to change some of the individual's behavior patterns.[2] Or he may belong to different associations that support

[1] M. S. Minnus, "Cleavage in Women's Organizations: A Reflection of the Social Structure of a City," *American Sociological Review*, 18 (Feb., 1953), 47–53.

[2] For a discussion of the significance of reference groups see R. K. Merton and A. S. Kitt, "Contributions to the Theory of Reference Group Behavior," in R. K. Merton and

two different and opposite attitudes and beliefs. One example is the problem of an individual who belongs simultaneously to a union which strongly opposes racial discrimination and to a club which equally strongly supports discriminatory measures. This type of ambivalence is one of the distinguishing characteristics of urban societies, in that urbanites are faced with alternate choices, and they must continuously try to reconcile these divergencies.

Socialization. Associations permit socialization on an informal basis and satisfy the gregariousness of the members. Many members join because they wish to be entertained. Many associational programs are intended to provide light entertainment, fill leisure-time, and give opportunities for wider acquaintance in a society where primary contacts are extended or nonexistent. The program chairman of an association is often more important than the president, because upon him falls the responsibility of keeping the members satisfied. A fraternity or sorority provides continuing social life for its members and devotes considerable time and effort to recruiting members. Exchange of social affairs and dates with other fraternities or sororities brings some social security for the in-group members. Non-members are not assured of the same regularity of social life or prestige as members.

Pressure groups. Associations often become pressure groups when their interests are threatened. They act to enforce the wishes of the membership.[1] During the period when a problem confronts the association, the representatives have a greater degree of control over the actions of the members. Political parties, trade or labor unions, and, at times, vocational groups are often labeled "pressure groups," even though no pressing issues are at hand demanding a united front. At times these groups make their opinions and wishes felt throughout the society by "pressure politics" or by lobbying.

All pressure groups seek specific gains for their members and personnel may be employed for this objective. Thus, they wield an influence which is greater than their actual numbers, because they exert pressure on the public to take sides with whatever gains they may be seeking. For example, the American Federation of Labor, the Congress of Industrial Organization, and independent unions claim 16 million members, or roughly a fifth of the nation's gainfully employed, but the gains they attain often benefit less organized groups. Moreover, other groups use their tactics, such as strikes, boycotts, and collective bargaining.

P. F. Lazarsfeld, eds., *Studies in the Scope and Method of "The American Soldier"* (Glencoe, Ill.: The Free Press, 1950), 40–105.

[1] Herbert Goldhamer, "Voluntary Associations in the United States," in *The Study of Contemporary Society* (10th ed., University of Chicago Bookstore, Sept., 1942).

Adaptation to anomie. One of the characteristics of modern urban life is the state of *anomie*. This is a state in which there no longer appears to be any clear definitions of how to act, but rather insecurity, tension, and loneliness.[1] It is a consequence of the multiplicity of ways of life and expectation of behavior characterizing urban life. Individuals join an association, or several of them, as a way out of anomie. Even political clubs have to be social in nature by providing parties and outings. A type of fellowship develops at such get-togethers and the group that sponsors such activities becomes more important to the individual.

Associations in "Yankee City"

The investigation of "Yankee City" by Warner and Lunt yielded much information on the characteristics of associations in a medium-sized New England city.[2] The range of associations and the total membership of each social class received great emphasis in the research in order to arrive at an idea of the status positions of the participants. Warner and Lunt found 357 associations among a population of 14,000. Many persons had several affiliations, while others had none. In general, the members of the upper two strata belonged to more associations than the lower groups.

Associations confined to one social class, although restricted, were more numerous than those drawing members from all six social classes. For example, the "Yankee City" American Legion and the Boy Scout Troop had city-wide membership, cutting across class lines. A variety of ethnic groups was represented and cooperated on common projects. A united front was displayed on national holidays and in parades.

As the class rank rose, the proportion of the members joining associations rose. A differential of one per cent characterized the associational membership between the upper-upper and lower-upper strata. The "joiners" of the upper-middle class dropped to 64 per cent, but this was still ten per cent higher than the association members of the lower-middle. Associations were joined by 39 per cent of the upper-lower stratum. The lower-lower class had 22 per cent membership in associations. In absolute numbers, however, the lower-middle had the largest memberships because the lower-middle class was one of the two largest groups within the city. (The other was the upper-lower.) In short, proportionately fewer persons of the lower strata had associational affiliations. Money, time, and interest are factors affecting membership in local or national organizations.

[1] See E. Durkheim, *Suicide,* tr. by J. A. Spalding and G. Simpson (Glencoe, Ill.: The Free Press, 1951), particularly Bk. 2, Ch. 5, and Bk. 3.

[2] W. L. Warner and P. S. Lunt, *The Social Life of a Modern Community* (New Haven: Yale University Press, 1941), Ch. 16.

Men and women were not equal in their inclinations to join associations. Men joined more frequently than did women. But, when divided into their respective class ranks, women of the upper-classes held more memberships in organizations than did their spouses. This was a reflection of their greater leisure and the social pressure of the society expecting the more privileged to use their time profitably. Many women belonged to welfare and philanthropic organizations or met with committees aiming for community betterment.

Ethnic associations attracted male membership. If the percentage of foreign-born population was large, the sex divisions were more rigid. For the wives and other members of the family, a separate organization was formed, a type of satellite association annexed to the parent organization. The two associations met separately and on special occasions combined their activities.

Altogether, 22,063 cliques were identified. These informal associations were not organized according to a formal set of rules, as was the case of the formal associations. Methods of initiation or resignation and extent of obligations and privileges were not prescribed. Rather, informal behavior and intimate interaction were characteristic of the activities of the clique. Being accepted by a clique was important in "Yankee City" social circles, because cliques provided greater opportunities for social mobility than did formal associations.

No specific names needed to be used when referring to the in-group members. They belonged and the out-group referred to them as the "Jones crowd," the Country Club set, or the "best families." Members addressed each other by their first names and social solidarity was achieved by intimate sharing of experiences. Cliques were graded according to age, sex, and class. The upper-upper class members had the greatest number of cliques. The socially ambitious members of the lower strata strove to be invited and included in the social life of the upper-class cliques.

Summary

The number of associations increased greatly in the United States after the 1820's, particularly in large cities. Associations were organized to pursue any number of a wide range of common interests found in urban areas where the population is heterogeneous. Membership may be determined by such factors as age, sex, occupation, religion, race, class, or political interests. Associations vary in size of membership and may be local, regional, or national in scope. Cliques are less formally organized and they provide more intimate contacts among members of the in-group and greater opportunities for social mobility than associations.

The life cycles of associations are affected by (1) interests and purposes, (2) functions, (3) personalities, (4) social change, and (5) type of organization.

Associations perform specific functions in society. They reflect the divisions of labor and reinforce socio-economic differentiations. The racial and ethnic composition of the population is frequently accentuated by exclusive associations. Associations may integrate the society by providing the basis for informal contacts and concerted action may follow. They satisfy the gregariousness of the members. They may act as pressure groups expressing the wishes of the members and forcing these wishes upon society in general. For some persons, they become reference groups or sources of correct social behavior. Some associations become extremely complex and assume many of the characteristics of institutions, whereas others are almost indistinguishable from cliques.

DISCUSSION QUESTIONS

1. How may the size of the cities affect the number of associations?
2. What are the rules and regulations commonly used for controlling associational behavior?
3. How does social control operate in cliques?
4. How do associations integrate other groups which would otherwise be excluded from effective participation in the society?
5. What are the common causes for the disintegration of associations?
6. How can associations and cliques reflect the socio-economic groupings of a community or city?
7. How do associations show the increase of specialization in modern society?
8. Why are classifications of associations inadequate in explaining their aims and memberships?

SUGGESTED PROJECTS

1. Study the literature on voluntary associations according to class membership and compare the degree of participation.
2. Study the role of the clique in exerting pressure on the behavior of the members.
3. Study the growth and decline of ethnic associations in a large city.
4. Study the role which racial associations play in a large city.
5. Study a pressure group's method for achieving gains for its members.

READINGS

F. Bushee, "Social Organization in a Small City," *American Journal of Sociology*, 51, Nov., 1945, 217–226.

Floyd Dotson, "Voluntary Associations of Urban Dwellers," *American Sociological Review,* 16, Oct., 1951, 687–693.

E. C. Hughes, *French Canada in Transition.* Chicago: University of Chicago Press, 1943.

Chapter 13 analyzes the voluntary associations in sorting and mobilizing people for action and sociability.

Mirra Komarovsky, "The Voluntary Association of Urban Dwellers," *American Sociological Review,* 11, Dec., 1946, 686–698.

R. M. MacIver, *Society.* New York: Farrar and Rinehart, Inc., 1937, Ch. 13. Also see 1949 edition.

A treatment of associations and their major types.

W. F. Ogburn and M. F. Nimkoff, *Sociology.* New York: Houghton Mifflin Co., 1950, Ch. 18.

Author's study of associations according to the size of cities.

David Riesman, *Individualism Reconsidered.* Glencoe: The Free Press, 1954, esp. 232–241 and 266–270.

A series of essays evaluating changes in our society and how these affect behavior patterns. Individuals are not as individualistic as is commonly believed.

Alexis de Tocqueville, *Democracy in America.* Cambridge: Sever and Francis, 1862, I and II.

Compares the formation of European and American associations.

W. L. Warner and P. S. Lunt, *The Social Life of a Modern Community.* New Haven: Yale University Press, 1941.

A study of the associational and clique affiliations of community according to class membership.

Part Five

Urban Ways of Life

PROLOGUE *Urban ways of behavior are as complex and many-sided as the city itself and are best seen from several different approaches. Studying social differentiation of individuals is one approach and analysis of the influence of mass media on human behavior and conduct is another. The manner in which social contacts are cultivated during leisure time reflects the diversity of activities found in an urban setting. The presence of various personality types in cities has provided a rewarding study of the impact of urbanization on behavior patterns.*

The urban stratification system can be viewed from two standpoints, i.e., from the economic order and the social order. Because social differentiation is often related to occupational rating, the economic hierarchy shows important correlations with social rank. The status system based on honors and prestige, rather than material rewards, is related to the social order. Community studies have used both objective and subjective criteria in analyzing class membership. Persons with physical visibility or minority status are evaluated within their own social systems and by the larger society. Through these various approaches the heterogeneous urban populations are stratified into a pattern of social arrangement.

The term mass media includes newspapers, books, periodicals, radio, movies, television, and other means of communication reaching large numbers of people. Mass media have replaced many primary contacts and the introduction and adoption of each type of medium has brought about modification in human behavior. In modern urbanized society mass culture has developed a set of behavior patterns which are fairly uniform for the society as a whole. These behavior patterns conflict with the elements of traditional culture transmitted by the family and other institutional organizations. With the city covering an extensive land area and comprised of various local communities, a major means of contact between residents of the city proper and people residing in surrounding areas is through the local community papers and weeklies. In many ways newspapers and other media provide a sense of community which might well be termed a pseudo-Gemeinschaft. *The Negro and immigrant presses function as media of interaction and education for racial and ethnic groups.*

Leisure-time activities have shifted from within the small, intimate group to entertainment on a large, impersonal scale. Urban living, with its greater tensions and strains, seems to require the constant addition of novel forms of entertainment. Commercial, quasi-commercial, public, private, and illegal types of entertainment may each be differentiated into many sub-categories. Participation in various leisure-time activities can be related to corresponding socio-economic strata.

Certain changes in personal behavior patterns are a distinct result of urbanization. Cities attract people because they afford different ways of life, and within the city people can find others who act like them and accept them as equals. Many social types have come to be identified with specific natural areas of the city. Local sentiments and traditions influence their life organizations, while the roles they play have value to these natural areas and the larger society.

Chapter Seventeen

Urban Stratification

W E HAVE already observed some of the phenomena related to social stratification, such as the relationship of birth and death rates, ecological patterns, and institutional functions, to socio-economic status. Every known society has some basis (although imperfect) for dividing and ranking people within the general social system. There are relative high and low positions, and the people within a stratum may show differences when compared with the next in goods and services or prestige and status. These differences constitute some of the bases of social differentiation.

However, the chief criteria of such differentiation vary to a great extent. Considerations of age, sex, kinship, and race are of importance to any society. Particularly in small and less complex societies, these factors are often the principal bases of determining social differences. It is in the larger and more complex societies that differentiation in terms of an evaluative ranking of social position—not primarily based on these four criteria —becomes more and more important.

The Nature of Stratification in a Mass Society

In contemporary Western societies, characterized by the intricate social relationships engendered by urbanism and the occupational diversity, social stratification has become the most significant basis of social differentiation. At the same time, the bases of stratification have become exceedingly complex and, at times, arbitrary because the growth of cities brought changes in the social structure, and great masses of people did not know where they belonged. For many purposes it has been convenient to present simplified models of American stratification patterns with "layer-cake" models, picturing three classes: lower, middle, and upper, with subdivisions within each class. Many criticisms have been aimed at this scheme because some critics question the existence of clear-cut class distinctions in our society. They point out that there is no strong class-consciousness among the general population, which is not the case in European societies, where an urban society evolved from a feudal social order. Others claim that there are several overlapping stratification systems.

What makes social stratification difficult to pin down in our society is that the analysis of class divisions and the ranking of an individual's position in the social system began in academic circles. There have been attempts to give the essential characteristics of the open class, estate, and caste systems. The average American is only vaguely aware of class differences. Although studies have been made to find the common denominators that set one social class apart from another, answers given by the man in the street are sufficiently varied to arouse suspicion as to the validity of some of the research findings. Moreover, researchers themselves disagree on what criteria, whether income, occupations, family background, feelings of belongingness to a given social class, or class culture should be used as objective indexes of measurement. Thus, there could be different meanings to the question, "What social class do you belong to?" The mere fact that a large number approached reported "middle class" may not indicate a realistic self-rating, because many persons may have assigned themselves to a class they hoped to belong to eventually or a class to which they had formerly belonged.

For the urban sociologist, the most important consideration for studying social differentiation is to help synthesize the social realities that pertain to the urban social structure and its institutions.

Two of the institutional systems which are of greatest importance to Western society are, in Weber's formulation, that related to the *economic order* and that pertaining to the *social order*.[1] Economic stratification may be defined in terms of varying "life chances": the possibilities of persons born in certain groups to acquire economic wealth. Weber defines classes, then, as groups that obtain varying shares of the products of the economic system. It is possible, though, to extend the "life chances" concept to include the acquisition of things other than economic, since property is not the only unequally distributed value in society. The "social" order is based on such non-economic factors as "honor," "esteem," and perhaps "talents" that have little direct monetary value. Class members constitute status groups within the social order and are characterized by their behavior: patterns of consumption, the way they think politically, their attitudes and social behavior, and, in general, their styles of life.[2] Persons within any particular status group think and act in ways that distinguish that group

[1] Paul K. Hatt, "Stratification in Mass Society," *American Sociological Review*, 15 (April, 1950), 216–222.

[2] Oliver C. Cox, "Max Weber on Social Stratification: A Critique," *American Sociological Review*, 15 (April, 1950), 225–226.

from the others, and persons within any single group associate with one another on an equal basis, ranking non-members as being either inferior or superior in social hierarchy.

There is a definite distinction between these two orders (*i.e.,* economic and social), and the relative placement of individuals may differ depending on which dimension is used. It should be noted, though, that in any society that places strong emphasis on economic acquisition, there is a high but not perfect correlation between the two stratification orders.

In addition to the institutional orders mentioned it is necessary to consider how the people of a community analyze prestige ratings and assign positions to members within the community. The work of Lloyd Warner and his associates made use of such an approach in studying urban communities in various parts of the country, although some sociologists claim that Warner's studies were centered in more or less "static" communities, where class lines were perhaps more clearly delineated than in other American areas.[1] We have already mentioned that the general features of urbanism have transcended most local communities, imposing a mass pattern of urban traits on society in general. The extension of urban traits has helped create a mass and fairly fluid society and has had its impact in patterns of social stratification, with the hierarchy of prestige (as it pertains to urban occupations) carried into other areas. So there is a mass societal as well as local frame of reference within which social stratification may be studied.

Within one or more of the orders mentioned above, the general empirical investigations of stratification may be made from two different approaches. The first attempts to find one or more indexes, objectively measurable, which show high correlation with all the orders of stratification. Among the most measurable of these indexes are occupation, income, education, and value or rent of home. Among the more subjective but still measurable factors are political attitudes, social behavior, group mores, and others, all of which have a relation to social class. The second method may be described as an attempt to measure all the different aspects of stratification rather than the selection of a few indexes. This method is based on the assumption that the quantified measurements of all aspects may be added up to form a sum total indicative of an individual's specific position in the hierarchy of class, power, and prestige. The work of Davis has followed this tack, examining social differentiation within a system of statuses and roles.[2]

Status is here defined as a system of differential expectations and evalua-

[1] W. L. Warner and P. S. Lunt, *op. cit.;* and W. L. Warner, *American Life: Dream and Reality* (Chicago: University of Chicago Press, 1953), Chs. 2 and 3.

[2] Kingsley Davis, *Human Society* (New York: The Macmillan Company, 1949), 91–96.

tions of social functions. In simpler language, society expects certain things from certain functions (*e.g.,* ditch-digging, research, merchandising, teaching), and statuses vary according to the "value" (in the eyes of . society) of these functions. These assigned values in turn determine social positions and give *prestige* to those holding them. At the same time, individuals are rated on the way they actually perform these roles, which may be termed the *esteem* given that person. For instance, a political office may offer prestige to the person holding it, but how he is esteemed depends on his performance in carrying out the expected social role associated with the position. The final estimate of the status of any person, then, would be based on the prestige associated with his function and his behavior within that function. The problem associated with this refined mode of analysis is this: in complex urban society, how is one to measure, add, and properly weigh the large number of functions held by an individual, who may simultaneously be grocer, father, church member, and member of several voluntary associations, each with its own particular role?

It is not feasible to discuss in detail all the facets of urban stratification. Two illustrations of the different approaches to the analysis of urban status systems have been selected as particularly significant examples. The ethnic and racial aspects of stratification are presented to show how restrictions may be imposed upon members of minority groups and the manner in which they influence the status hierarchy.

Occupation

Occupation is perhaps the best single index of urban stratification. This should not be surprising since an increasingly complex division of labor is one of the major characteristics of urbanism. By and large, personal qualities or esteem factors are less important in urban status evaluations than in smaller communities, so that status characteristics assume greater significance. Of all possible statuses in a society, occupation is one of the most readily seen. Likewise, occupation is significant, since it involves some of the most important functions in an industrial society.

The classification employed in Table 30 may be seen to correspond roughly to the social prestige of the occupations listed, although each category covers a wide range of prestige positions. For example, doctors, dieticians, and accountants are subsumed under the professional category. However, the basis of the classification is the similarity of the actual work performed and the training required to enter a given profession. Even within the ten-year period shown, there is a definite increase in the various urban occupations. The proportion of the labor force with the greatest increases include the professional, clerical, craftsmen, and operative cate-

TABLE 30. MAJOR OCCUPATION GROUP OF EMPLOYED PERSONS,
UNITED STATES, 1950 AND 1940, AND 57 MOST POPULOUS
STANDARD METROPOLITAN AREAS, 1950 [1]

	United States, Per Cent		57 Standard Metropolitan Areas,* 1950, Per Cent	
Occupations	1950	1940	Median	Range
Total employed, all occupations	100	100	100	100–100
Professional, technical, and kindred workers	9	8	10	6–15
Managers, officials, and proprietors, including farm	17	20	10	8–15
Clerical and kindred workers	12	10	15	9–27
Sales workers	7	7	8	6–11
Craftsmen, foremen, and kindred workers	14	11	16	12–20
Operatives and kindred workers	20	18	21	10–44
Private household workers	3	5	2	1–6
Service workers, except private household	7	7	9	5–14
Laborers, except mine	11	14	7	4–12
Occupation not reported	1	1	1	1–2

* The 57 standard metropolitan areas are those which in 1940 had populations of 250,000 or more.

[1] With permission from S. A. Queen and D. B. Carpenter, *The American City* (New York: The McGraw-Hill Book Co., Inc., 1953), Table 28, 211.

gories. The percentage of laborers and private household workers showed a decline.

If we look at the characteristics of the labor force over a longer period of time, the change in the occupational structure becomes even more apparent. The traditional image of the American middle-class is one of small-business entrepreneurs, a stable group of self-employed, property-owning businessmen. In the early nineteenth century, this group constituted a majority of the population. By 1870, it comprised about one-third of the labor force; now this group composes only one-fifth of it. As the old middle classes have declined, a new salaried middle class, the white-collar group, has assumed increasing importance.[1] In other words, ownership of property has become less significant in the classification of the majority of Americans. The majority of the Americans are now employees rather than employers or self-employed.[2]

The new white-collar group is fairly heterogeneous, and the great bulk

[1] C. W. Mills, *op. cit.*, 63.
[2] *Ibid.*, 65.

of the employees are of the lower middle-income brackets. However, this new group's occupations range from the top to almost the bottom of the occupational hierarchy of modern society. If we were to formulate a picture of the place of the white-collar groups within the social structure, the employees would form a new pyramid within the old pyramid of society at large, rather than comprise a horizontal layer. Since 1900 there has been a relatively sharp decline of sales people and a steady rise of office workers. Today the three largest occupational groups in the white-collar segment are school teachers, sales people in and out of stores, and assorted office workers. More than half the members of the middle class are white-collar workers. The new middle class increased from 15 to 56 per cent between 1870 to 1940. In contrast, the old middle class declined from 85 to 44 per cent (Table 31).

This change is also reflected in the proportion of workers in industry. There has been a decline in the number of workers engaged in the extraction of natural resources and production of commodities, while the number employed in servicing, distributing, and coordinating activities has risen. By 1940 only 11 per cent of the white-collar workers were found in

TABLE 31. THE LABOR FORCE BY CLASS, THE
UNITED STATES, 1870–1940 [1]

| | Per Cent | |
The Labor Force	*1870*	*1940*
Old Middle Class	33	20
New Middle Class	6	25
Wage-workers	61	35
Total	100	100

| | Per Cent | |
The Middle Classes	*1870*	*1940*
Old Middle Class	85	44
Farmer	62	23
Businessmen	21	19
Free Professionals	2	2
New Middle Class	15	56
Managers	2	6
Salaried Professionals	4	14
Salespeople	7	14
Office Workers	2	22
Total	100	100

[1] *Source:* From *White Collar*, by C. Wright Mills. Copyright 1951 by Oxford University Press, Inc., 63 and 65.

industries primarily involved in the production of commodities, as against 32 per cent in service industries, 44 per cent in distribution, and 60 per cent in coordination. These trends are directly related to three major causes: (1) increased productivity of machinery used in manufacturing, (2) the magnification of distribution, and (3) increased scale of coordination.[1]

An examination of the change in the occupational structure of Chicago and Philadelphia from 1910 to 1940 shows that these metropolises reflected national changes, although these large urban centers showed less drastic change than the nation as a whole.[2] The largest proportionate increase was in typically urban occupations, particularly the professional and semi-professional group. In Philadelphia and in the nation as a whole the second largest increases were in clerical and sales workers and the like, whereas in Chicago, the number of service workers showed greater increase. Craftsmen, foremen, and machine operators and the like also showed proportionate increases. The other occupational groups all showed a relative decline. In general, the occupational changes were less pronounced in Philadelphia than in Chicago. Since Chicago is a much younger city, it is probable that as Chicago becomes more stable in its population growth, it will also become more stable in its occupational structure.

The prestige of occupations. The foregoing material has shown some of the characteristics of the American urban occupational structure in terms of the actual make-up of the labor force. These are essentially objectively measurable characteristics, but they do not yield the answer to one vital question: Do the members of the American society themselves see occupational differences as a system of stratification, and, if so, what are the actual values they place on these occupations?

The most comprehensive investigation of the prestige of occupations in the United States was undertaken on the basis of a 1946 nation-wide survey, in which respondents were asked to rate each of 90 occupations.[3] As a result, a set of nearly consistent ratings was obtained, covering the entire possible range of evaluations. The highest ratings were accorded to the positions of Supreme Court Justice, physician, and state governor, while nonfarm labor positions were rated lowest (Table 32).

Although there were some regional differences and differences in size of communities, the ratings were fairly consistent. The Midwest tended to rate all positions lower, and ratings also decreased with size of com-

---

[1] *Ibid.*, 66.

[2] Eleanor Bernet "Changes in the Occupational Structure of the Labor Force in Chicago, Philadelphia, and the United States, 1910 and 1940," in Paul K. Hatt and A. J. Reiss, Jr., *Reader in Urban Sociology* (Glencoe: Free Press, 1951), 326–343.

[3] C. C. North and Paul K. Hatt, "Jobs and Occupations: A Popular Evaluation," in L. Wilson and W. L. Kolb, *Sociological Analysis* (New York: Harcourt, Brace & Co., 1949), 464–474.

TABLE 32. PRESTIGE OF OCCUPATIONAL GROUPS,
THE UNITED STATES [1]

Classification	Number of Occupations	Average Score †
Government officials *	8	90.8
Professional and semi-professional workers	30	80.6
Proprietors, managers, and officials (except farm)	11	74.9
Clerical, sales, and kindred workers	6	68.2
Craftsmen, foremen, and kindred workers	7	68.0
Farmers and farm managers	3	61.3
Protective service workers	3	58.0
Operatives and kindred workers	8	52.8
Farm laborers	1	50.0
Service workers (except domestic and protective)	7	46.7
Laborers (except farm workers)	6	45.8

* The census classifies some of these officials as professional and others as managerial.
† Possible range: 20–100.

[1] *Source:* With permission from C. C. North and Paul K. Hatt, "Jobs and Occupations: A Popular Evaluation," in L. Wilson and W. L. Kolb, *Sociological Analysis* (New York: Harcourt, Brace & Co., Inc., 1949), 467.

munity. Metropolitan residents gave higher ratings to such occupations as artist and musician in symphony orchestra, and to communication and scientific occupations. The "urbane" character of the Northeast is perhaps the reason for relatively higher ratings of court judges, psychologists, sociologists, economists, and bartenders.

When asked to name the one main characteristic of a job giving it "excellent standing," respondents listed most frequently high pay, service to humanity, cost of preparation for it in money and effort, and social prestige. It is interesting to note that inhabitants of large cities placed highest emphasis on social prestige. Income appeared more important to the lower-income respondent.

Although a consistent series of rankings had already been obtained, subsequent analysis showed many dissimilar occupations had identical prestige ratings. Airline pilots, artists, and sociologists were rated alike. It was found that the occupations rated could be placed in a number of categories of similar occupations, or situses.[1] Prestige ratings within each situs were much more consistent, so that it would appear that individuals tend to rate occupations according to what they think another occupation is like. These persons who participated in the rating would rank airline pilots

[1] Paul K. Hatt, "Occupation and Social Stratification," *American Journal of Sociology,* 55 (May, 1950), 533–543.

with radar engineers, or another related occupation, rather than in terms of specific occupations.

Although the precise formulation of these situses is tentative, since only a limited list of occupations were employed in the study, the distinction between situs and status may prove useful for future studies. If people actually do relate themselves to certain occupational groups, there could be good evidence for the existence of a number of status hierarchies which in themselves are differentially evaluated. Individuals might actually move both within and between status hierarchies, each of which might have different consequences for their way of life.

New occupations and new ways of life. The occupational shift to ever greater proportions of white-collar employees has had a drastic effect on American urban ways of life. Many urbanites must "sell" their personalities as well as goods or services. The salesman must at all costs keep up appearances, and professionals must be concerned with a constant fight for position.

Although for Americans the word bureaucracy has sinister implications, more urbanites are actually becoming members of bureaucratic organizations, because more and more business operations are concerned with organizational coordination. A large segment of the urban population has been caught up in impersonal and routinized work patterns on the one hand, and almost desperate striving for better social positions on the other.

The Community Reputational Approach

If one were to ask a student in a sociology class if social classes existed in America it is more than likely that the answer would not be negative. Asked to name them, he would probably give the six classes, upper and lower-upper, upper- and lower-middle, and upper- and lower-lower. Such an answer would reflect the influence of the popularization of Warner's work in the field of stratification. As has already been mentioned, this work has up to now been based largely on a number of studies of small cities. The largest community studied, "Yankee City," has about 17,000 residents, and the other communities are much smaller. Nevertheless, the claim has been made that these communities are typical of the American stratification system.

Although a series of indexes has subsequently been developed, the definition of classes rests primarily on the placement of members of the community by other members of the same community.[1] This placement is in

[1] For a fuller discussion see W. L. Warner, M. Meeker, and K. Eells, *Social Class in America* (Chicago: Science Research Associates, 1949).

terms of relative ranking on the basis of such criteria as known friendship patterns (cliques), and "status reputation." On the basis of a number of interviews obtained from reputable old residents of the community, the number of classes is determined. The usual pattern has been one of the six classes mentioned above. In the case of Jonesville, a community of 6,000, no differentiations could be found within the upper class.[1]

Hollingshead, studying the same community, found that each class differed in its participation in community life.[2] Class II (31 families) was found to identify itself with Class I (4 families), although half had only recently achieved this status, and considered themselves superior to the rest of the community. Class III (158 families) was the most mobile, many of whom had risen from Class IV (312 families) who in turn disapproved of their striving. Class V (230 families) was generally avoided as the "scum" of the city and was for the most part outside of community social life. Whereas the superior position of Class I was based on inheritance, Class II was identified on the basis of such factors as, occupation, education, income, and social influence. Class IV was respectable but was expected to follow the leadership of others. By and large, each class had a distinct subculture.

This type of pattern has been found in many similar communities. However, one of the basic problems in study of stratification has remained: the lack of any substantial basis for intercommunity comparison. Warner has developed a set of indexes: occupation, source of income, house type, and dwelling areas. Taken together these show a correlation of .872 with community reputation. Even more interesting is the correlation of occupation alone, .91, which again shows the significance of occupation in the American status system.[3] Whereas each community study usually still represents only the actual community studied, these indexes are applicable in the larger society.

It is claimed that all the classes are clearly distinguishable and are true classes rather than status groups. However, there is evidence within the data gathered in these community studies that this is not really the case.[4] The classes at the extremes of the status range are quite stable, but those between are characterized by variability in placement and marked histories of mobility. In the case of the largest class, the upper-lower, there is particular doubt as to the existence of any distinct class. Thus, it appears that

---

[1] W. L. Warner and Associates, *Democracy in Jonesville, op. cit.*

[2] A. B. Hollingshead, "Selected Characteristics of Classes in a Middle Western Community," *American Sociological Review,* 12 (Aug., 1947), 385–395.

[3] W. L. Warner *et al., Social Class in America, op. cit.,* 168.

[4] For a searching critique, see H. W. Pfautz and O. D. Duncan, "A Critical Evaluation of Warner's Work in Community Stratification," *American Sociological Review,* 15 (Apr., 1950), 205–215.

the American urban stratification system is characterized by gradations, rather than distinct classes.

Mobility

In sociological usage, mobility has referred to two types of changes in the status of an individual. Horizontal mobility refers to a change in residence, vertical mobility to a change in social status.[1] At first glance, these two types of mobility would appear to have little in common. If, however, we consider the implication that one type of movement has for the other, we see that horizontal and vertical mobility are related.

Both horizontal and vertical mobility increased as Western nations became urbanized. It has already been noted that one way for a medieval serf to change his status was to migrate to the city and thus become a free man, with a chance for upward social mobility. Migration makes it possible for an individual to break his old patterns of social relationships and adapt to new status positions with less interference from the past. Thus, the great amount of horizontal mobility characteristic of modern urban societies facilitates vertical mobility.

It is also necessary to distinguish between social mobility on the part of an individual and a general change in the social structure. One of the characteristics of the American status system has been the raising of whole occupational groups in prestige and in life chances. The nursing profession is a good case in point, developing from a more or less routinized bedside care of patients to one of professional rating. Persons engaged in more routinized work are now classified as "nurses' aides." These upgradings to a great extent reflect the changes in economic requirements for particular occupations and the trend toward greater specialization. When upgradings occur, the individual's social status is raised, but his position relative to his associates remains more or less constant.

One of the greatest conflicts in the American value system is between the belief that each individual should have an equal chance to make his way in the world and the belief that the offspring should get the benefits of their parents' position. These forces have tended to make America neither a wholly open nor a wholly closed society. One of the questions most frequently raised is whether or not class lines in America are becoming more rigid. The work of Warner and other students using his approach maintains that definite classes do exist in America, but that the lines of demarcation are blurred.

One major investigation of occupational mobility in an American city showed that no categorical statement could be made on over-all changes in

[1] Pitirim Sorokin, *Social Mobility* (New York: Harper & Bros., 1927), 494.

mobility.[1] The mobility rates for Indianapolis for a period of time around 1910 and 1949 showed that in both periods mobility rates were lower than would have been the case if no barriers to mobility existed, but that, nevertheless, substantial mobility was possible. At the later date, there was increased mobility in the professional occupations and decreased mobility in the semiprofessional, business, and clerical occupations. However, if one considers the origin of those who changed status, the extreme status positions—*i.e.,* professional and semiprofessional on the one hand, and unskilled and farming on the other—these were more likely to be entered by workers who originally held positions not far removed in the status hierarchy.

If one considers status stability rather than mobility, it becomes apparent that most sons are quite likely to enter their fathers' occupations. It is generally true of our society that status stability tends to exceed mobility.[2] Occupational inheritance is smallest in clerical and semiskilled occupations—the occupations which are at the middle of the prestige hierarchy. This appears to reflect the fact that these occupations are neither extremely attractive—thus tending to promote occupational stability—nor are they marked by serious handicaps to mobility, such as limited educational opportunity. It has long been one of the American cultural beliefs that anyone who wanted to get ahead could do so. However, upward mobility usually requires training, and there is ample evidence that educational opportunity is decidedly smaller for individuals of lower status, compared to those of higher status with equal intelligence.[3]

Although there has been no gross over-all change in American mobility rates, there have been changes in some of the channels of mobility. Education has become increasingly important, whereas some of the other channels, such as working one's way up in the place of employment, have become more difficult. Working one's way up is difficult because of the increased routinization of many occupations, which prevents the individual from gaining any knowledge at work outside of his own limited job.[4]

For some members of the American society, "getting ahead in the world" is no longer a strong motivating factor. This is true of many at the lower end of the status hierarchy, and of those barred from advancement by ethnic discrimination.[5] There is an increasing belief that upward mo-

[1] N. Rogoff, "Recent Trends in Urban Occupational Mobility," in Hatt and Reiss, *op. cit.,* 406–420.

[2] This has been found in many other studies, in particular cf. North and Hatt, *op. cit.*

[3] E. Sibley, "Some Demographic Clues to Stratification," *American Sociological Review,* 7 (June, 1942), 322–325.

[4] W. L. Warner and J. O. Low, *The Social System of the Modern Factory* (New Haven: Yale University Press, 1947), Ch. 9.

[5] A. Davis, "The Motivation of the Underprivileged Worker," in W. F. Whyte (ed.), *Industry and Society* (New York: McGraw-Hill Book Co., Inc., 1946).

bility is not the reward of effort but a matter of luck. This is, indeed, a far cry from the legend of Horatio Alger, but it also reflects the unprecedented status range which characterizes modern American cities.

The anonymity and horizontal mobility of urban life which have facilitated upward social mobility for many people also make it possible for others to descend the social ladder. It is much easier to disappear in urban settings and thus avoid relationships from previous status positions. The extreme illustrations are the Skid Row inhabitants. However, most mobility does appear to be directed upward,[1] particularly since there is still an expansion of opportunities in the urban occupations affording prestige.

Ethnic and Racial Aspects of Stratification

A sizable part of the American urban population is at least in part differentiated from the status hierarchy on the basis of ethnic background. For some, this may mean only partial exclusion. Jews are admitted in restricted numbers to the professions through the operation of school quotas. In business, they have been often restricted themselves to certain fields. Socially they may meet varying forms of discrimination. Nevertheless, Jews are by and large part of the status hierarchy, and many of the successful may transcend social and occupational limitations. Similarly, other ethnic groups have also found restrictions, often encountering greater obstacles to mobility and lack of employment opportunities. Yet, under specific conditions individuals may become accepted in the class-status order.

The one sizable group which is largely excluded from social acceptance within the prevalent status order is the Negro population, which has many aspects of a racial caste.[2] Within the Negro group a stratification order has developed which resembles that of the rest of American society. However, the urban Negro largely depends on white employers, and his employment opportunities are limited, although the "job ceiling" is gradually becoming more flexible.[3] As a result, the occupational distribution for the Negro population shows many more Negroes in what to the white population are low-prestige occupations, and proportionately fewer in middle- and upper-class occupations.[4] One consequence of this is that within the Negro social hierarchy almost all white-collar occupations have relatively

[1] C. McGuire, "Social Stratification and Mobility Patterns," *American Sociological Review,* 15 (Apr., 1950), 195–204.

[2] Gunnar Myrdal, *An American Dilemma: The Negro Problem and Modern Democracy* (New York: Harper & Bros., 1944), 674–675.

[3] Drake and Cayton, *op. cit.,* 326.

[4] M. C. Hill and B. C. McCall, "Social Stratification in 'Georgia Town,'" *American Sociological Review,* 15 (Dec., 1950), 721–729.

higher prestige. Many occupations which are valued at some distance from the top in the white hierarchy comprise the Negro upper class.[1]

Two of the major channels for mobility in the Negro status hierarchy have been civil service positions—since in most of them discrimination is illegal—and businesses primarily serving the Negro population. Negro insurance companies, funeral homes, and beauty shops are examples; the ministry has a greater representation of Negroes than any other profession. The number of Negro teachers, lawyers, physicians, dentists, social workers, and journalists is increasing. The May, 1954, Supreme Court decision, declaring segregated education as illegal, will open more opportunities for an enlarged professional group. There will be more Negro teachers, superintendents of schools, psychologists, school nurses, and so on. It is expected that this decision will pave the way for the end of other segregation patterns, especially in housing and employment. As is the case of other minority groups, illegal activities furnish means of mobility for some.

A number of community studies using the Warner approach has been made in the South which stress the caste-like characteristics of Negro stratification. One such study by Hill and McCall found that the white lower class in the community was actually disproportionately small, since the large Negro lower-class filled nearly all the lower-class occupations.[2] However, the strict applicability of the concept of "caste" to the Negro appears questionable. As the Negro becomes more urban and job opportunities increase, it is likely that greater integration with the over-all status hierarchy will take place, and that the increase of comparable status positions will gradually follow the change in Negro-white relations.

Summary

American urban stratification may be seen in several contexts. It is a function both of community and general social values. With increasing urbanization, prestige values based on position tend more and more to eclipse esteem evaluations, based on personal acquaintance. Stratification also depends on institutional systems, of which the economic and social orders are of particular significance.

It is possible to approximate the status hierarchies through the use of indexes. The index of occupation appears to be the most useful. The occupational characteristics of the labor force have changed drastically in the last eighty years. The property-holders and self-employed have decreased

---

[1] E. F. Frazier, *The Negro in the United States* (New York: The Macmillan Co., 1949), 291.

[2] Hill and McCall, *op. cit.*, 726.

in importance, while urban occupations have expanded. Particularly significant of the change is the growth of a new employee middle class which staffs bureaucracies and sales forces.

Smaller communities may be studied in terms of ratings of individuals who are acquainted with each other. Thus a measure of the status system is obtained by taking into account a number of values.

Although there have been some changes in mobility patterns, there has been no distinct change in over-all mobility rates. Although occupational inheritance or stability is pronounced, mobility is characteristic of most segments of the American population, particularly those in intermediate positions in the American status system.

The restrictions placed upon ethnic groups are not as rigid as those experienced by the Negro population, although the "job ceiling" is gradually becoming more flexible. There is a stratification order resembling that of the rest of the American society, but occupations which in the white population have low-prestige ratings are ranked higher by Negroes.

DISCUSSION QUESTIONS

1. Why is it more accurate for an urban-industrial society to be characterized by a number of stratification systems than simply one, using age, sex, or kinship?
2. What are the essential differences between Weber's economic and social orders?
3. Of what value are community studies? Prestige ratings and status?
4. Why is occupation the best single index of urban stratification?
5. What results did the investigation of prestige of occupations reveal?
6. In what two ways may mobility be experienced by an individual?
7. What is meant by status stability?
8. Discuss the restrictions experienced by ethnic and racial groups when attempting mobility.

SUGGESTED PROJECTS

1. Compare the findings of the community reputation approaches with Weber's economic and social orders.
2. Discuss the role of income and education in American stratification.
3. Discuss the areas of conflict in the American class system.
4. Trace the changes between the old and new middle classes.
5. Analyze the role of class differences in American politics.
6. How realistic is the "American Dream"?

READINGS

Reinhard Bendix and S. M. Lipset, *Class, Status and Power: A Reader in Social Stratification*. Glencoe: Free Press, 1953.

Covers a wide range of topics: theories of class structure, status and power relations, differential class behavior, social mobility in the United States. Also an analysis of comparative social structures.

Oliver C. Cox, *Caste, Class, and Race: A Study in Social Dynamics*. New York: Doubleday & Co., 1948.

A provocative comparison of three much-abused concepts: caste, class, and race.

Allison Davis and Burleigh and M. Gardner, *Deep South*. Chicago: University of Chicago Press, 1941.

A study of the class system of "Old City," a bi-racial society.

J. W. McConnell, *Evolution of Social Classes*. Washington, D. C.: American Council on Public Affairs, 1942.

How social classes evolved from the past to the present.

C. C. North, *Social Differentiation*. Chapel Hill: University of North Carolina Press, 1926.

The population of a society may be differentiated by sex, age, race, class, or economic status.

Pitirim Sorokin, *Social Mobility*. New York: Harper & Bros., 1927.

The concept of social mobility is studied as to its vertical, horizontal, and other aspects.

W. L. Warner, M. Meeker, and K. Eells, *Social Class in America: A Manual of Procedure for the Measure of Social Structure*. Chicago: Science Research Association, 1949.

This establishes the objective and subjective criteria for (the Index of Status Characteristics and Evaluative Participation) for measuring class membership.

Chapter Eighteen

Media of Communication

THE DEVELOPMENT and perfection of methods of communication other than by word of mouth and the use of ideographic symbols mark one of the important achievements associated with urbanism. A more detailed recording of the accomplishments of mankind through the ages followed the creation of a system of writing, enabling us to reconstruct the life and thought of previous generations. We have seen in earlier chapters that the differential between the educational levels of the rural and urban population is a frequently used index of the degree of urbanization a society has reached.

If the size of a literate group in less urbanized areas were known, we would have a fair picture of the class status of the urban population. In such areas, education is often correlated with class status, and in some instances, as in colonial territories, with racial background. At the same time, we would know what persons were subjected to the stimuli of modern media of communication and how responsive they are to public opinion, fads, and fashions, changing values, and behavior patterns. The impact of westernization is more likely to be diffused among the educated group because there is a common talking point between this segment of the population and urbanites elsewhere.

Modern media of communication have contributed to the development of a general pattern of urban life, because they have enabled more persons living geographically distant to intercommunicate and exchange ideas. The fact that urbanites live in areas more extensive than most persons can traverse in a day, and in which events occur more frequently than they can keep track of, has caused them to rely upon mass media for social communication. Thousands, if not millions, are simultaneously reached and influenced at one time.

Media of lasting impact on personal behavior include books; periodicals; special interest publications catering to various occupational, sex, age, religious, racial, and class groups; and community newspapers. The size of each reading group and the manner in which the public is divided into respective "audiences" based on common interest, are results of urbanization. These subdivisions emphasize the heterogeneity of urban population and indicate the growth of a mass culture which has been accepted and integrated into behavior patterns of urbanites.

Societies with relatively little urbanization have newspapers, periodicals, books, and, perhaps, radio and television, but the small and select literate public does not warrant a wide range of material to be disseminated. The "audience" however, may be larger than the literate segment of the population as information is disseminated through face-to-face contacts and intergroup communication. For example, one person reads, interprets, and evaluates the news for a number of listeners. Thus, modern media become the "talking point" for wider group interaction.

As more and more persons respond to the stimuli of mass media and their values and attitudes become modified, the greater the probabilities of a mass culture emerging and superceding the traditional culture: its mores, rituals, customs, and behavior patterns. In time, rural persons removed from the mass media and their stimuli retain and transmit the traditional culture, while urbanites adopt the mass culture. Urbanites are more likely to accept new ideas, ideologies, fads and fashions. When mass culture predominates, as in the United States, the traditional culture is considerably weakened, but is still present. The permanent institutional organizations, schools, churches, and families impart and diffuse the traditional culture. Because art objects and art forms (books, movies, home furnishings, drama and so on) are made and transmitted through mass production and media, and because they are designed to sell to the mass consumer, the United States is perhaps the first society in which artistic criteria are primarily determined by mass taste. Mass taste is not always based on ethical standards, as exemplified by some of the comics sold to young children. Thus quantity of sales, not quality of form or ethical norms, becomes important to publishers, writers, producers, actors, and so on, if they are to survive financially, if not artistically. The dichotomy of artistic standards into what is popular (and hence "salable") and what is "good" by the standards of the "enlightened" few, has helped create a sort of intellectual stratification into "highbrow," "middlebrow," and "lowbrow."

But more important than the gap between public and esoteric taste is the influence of mass media on personality formation and behavior patterns. Much space will be given in this chapter to the influence of the urban press, which helped to create the mass behavior patterns found here and elsewhere for which radio, movies, and television were later slanted.

Mass Culture

Our urbanism is characterized by the development of a mass culture and the collective action of large aggregates of people. Although members of American society are loosely organized for the most part and remain anonymous to one another, they still share and participate in a mass culture.[1] They accept and adopt new behavior and thought patterns disseminated by mass media, and up to a point the diversity of ethnic, religious, social classes, and racial background become obscured. Regional differences are less pronounced because the networks of modern communication reach farms, suburbs, cities, states, and regions alike. What was formerly a fairly stable society, rooted to mores and traditional social expectations, is being replaced by a society whose members are more and more inclined to adopt fads and fashions. Housewives on the farm and in the city use the same recipe printed in the women's section of the newspaper or magazines. Each housewife, though miles away and unknown to the other may be learning the same ideas on home decoration, childrearing, budgeting, personal beautification, or how women in other societies manage their homes and social obligations.

The adoption of rapidly changing behavior patterns increased as the society became more urbanized, and the development of a mass culture has resulted within the short span of a hundred years. Americans have developed some basic traits distinguishing them from the urbanites of other societies and are often characterized by foreign visitors as "always on the go," impatient with cumbersome details, secularized, and economically individualistic. An American abroad is recognized by his enthusiasm, free spending, and an insistence on luxuries.

One pronounced social effect our mass media have produced is ideational mobility, or the desire to keep constantly abreast with changing ideas. Most Americans fear to be labeled old-fashioned. Another is the creation of a gap between generations. Persons born before the turn of this century cling more closely to the mores and traditional culture. Their children, by contrast, have more readily adopted many of the elements of mass culture. The grandchildren find both older generations out-of-date. This trend is likely to continue, although considerable criticism has been aimed at the impact which mass media have made on the young during their impressionable and formative years. Despite the development of mass culture, elements of the traditional culture remain as do those of diverse subcultures. Perma-

[1] J. W. Bennett and M. M. Tumin, *Social Life* (New York: A. A. Knopf, Inc., 1948), Chs. 30 and 31.

nent social organizations often use the media of communication to reinforce basic ideological patterns, and vice versa.

As a contrast, less urbanized areas do not exhibit the same degree of ideational mobility, and there is a real distinction between rural and urban modes of life. A village but a short distance from the city may have a different dialect, and its members may dress differently. Age-old folklore, mores, and tradition are the unifying elements of the village culture, and it is more difficult to arouse collective action. The same villagers who move to cities soon learn to view the world with a different perspective. They feel the pressures of public opinion and are exposed to diverse behavior patterns and the impact of new ideas and values. This impact is often seen when their occupational statuses are jeopardized and political events threaten their security. The boycotts, strikes, riots, and protest demonstrations flaring up in many parts of the Far and Near East and Africa are staged by urban mobs with comparatively little experience in other forms of collective action. A modification of behavior patterns has resulted, and the process of assimilation in an urban culture is underway. The more rapidly the villagers learn to understand the relationship between changing events and personal needs, the more frequently they will adapt to new stimuli.

Urban Press

Broadly speaking, the urban press includes (1) daily newspapers, (2) special interest journals, and (3) magazines. There are types of reading matter dealing with the particular personal interests of each segment of the reading public. By far the most important medium of appeal is the daily newspaper, which is read by millions. Information concerning events happening in any part of the city or world is available very soon after the events occur. Every city in the nation has at least one daily paper, and metropolises usually support several competing papers. The urban press has been defined as "the establishment which undertakes to convey news and opinion to the general public through regular periodical outpourings of the printing press."[1] It is "a department store in print," with something for everyone. Its functions from past to present have changed, however.

Changing functions. The early urban press began as an adjunct of parliamentary government. At the time of the Revolutionary War, editors established themselves in the public view as spokesmen for the people against unfair governmental practices. News gathering and release was a recognized public service, and the Constitution of the United States made specific provisions guaranteeing the press freedom from political interfer-

[1] *Encyclopedia of the Social Sciences,* 12 (1934), 325–44.

ence. Use of the mails was granted for newspaper distribution to insure freedom of circulation. It was assumed that newspapers would use these privileges to convey the tidings of events of public importance.

Other functions of the newspaper arose to suit the demands of the times. The newspaper became a vehicle of popular features in addition to its role as a conveyer of news. James Gordon Bennett took advantage of the concessions granted publishers to release news in the form of human interest stories. More people bought and read daily papers as a pleasurable pastime. "Human interest" became the criterion of good copy. Sales mounted as a sign that people had become tired of "the dull business air of the large morning papers"[1] and that they approved of the more lively character of the new papers. The editor, while not a salesman, had to become aware of the market for his stories. He had to know what stories held human interest and would sell more papers. Political situations have always been of vital interest to the American public—and to this day occupy a great deal of newspaper space—but the fortunes or misfortunes of popular personalities often get bolder headlines and more space. A good illustration is the Godfrey–La Rosa "humility" incident, which was featured on the front page of leading newspapers while the Trieste affair, an international event which could affect the lives of millions outside of the territory, was relegated to the second page. Moreover, the former incident became the "talking point" among urbanites whose lives are socially and spatially distant from one another as they met in offices, social gatherings, and public places. Initiating social intercourse among diverse people is a function of today's newspaper.

Another function is to reaffirm the liberal or conservative points of view found in a given segment of the reading public. In order to promote circulation, the management of a newspaper outlines its editorial policy and consistently adheres to it. Editorials are written from the point of view of this policy. The public which agrees with this policy is expected to buy the paper, and often supporters of other views buy it to read diverse opinions. Where only one paper is published in a city, readers purchase the paper for other features: comic strips, pictorial layouts, advertisements, or reports of social activities.

When newspapers were independently owned, managed, and distributed, strong opinions were reflected in the editorials. Many editors were crusaders who took emphatic and courageous stands. Readers were guided by the papers in making decisions. However, the Horace Greeleys, Charles Danas, and William Allen Whites have disappeared, and the era of personalized journalism is no more. The depression of the 1930's dealt a heavy

[1] H. M. Hughes, "The Lindbergh Case: A Study of Human Interest and Politics," *American Journal of Sociology*, 45 (Nov., 1937), 12–23.

blow at small independent dailies. Mounting production costs, labor problems, and competition worked further hardships. Mergers and chain newspaper combines have separated personal opinion from institutional policy.[1] Editorials are becoming more and more colored by the viewpoints of chain-owners, leading stockholders, or advertisers. However, when the general public is confused by changing events, such as war, exposures of dishonesty and graft, or shortage of teachers and elementary schools, the newspapers often supply the facts and act as "advisers."

Through advertisements in newspapers buyers and sellers are brought together. The larger the paper's circulation, the more advertising space costs. The price paid for the paper at the newsstands barely covers the expenses connected with distribution, handling, and labor. Since the end of the last century, featured writers and editors have sold stories and articles to leading newspaper chains and syndicates. Their columns increase sales and attract followers of leading journalists in the fields of radio, current events, sports, theater, books, finance, styles, and humor. Editors assume no responsibility for the views expressed but regard them as aspects of specialization.[2]

The New York *Times,* St. Louis *Post-Dispatch,* and *Christian Science Monitor,* a trio whose tone and layouts retain individuality, remain national rather than local papers. They also strive to provide something for everybody but they do so more impartially than their competitors.

In studying the urban press as a "social instrument," Lee declared that as the society changed and became more urbanized, the press had to adapt to the new social setting or be superseded.[3] The newspaper "supplements and partially supplants more primitive means of transmission in response to the peculiar need of urban civilization." The press had to change its method of news-gathering, format, style and tone of writing to increase its circulation. The major point is that urban institutions, of which the press is one of the most important contemporary types, must be sensitive to the changing environment and make changes within themselves.

Evening newspapers are more popular than morning ones in most cities. Most readers have time after the working day to enjoy their papers. Evening editions have a total circulation of around 35 million, and morning papers, 20 million. At present the total daily newspaper circulation is around 55 million copies. A drop of about 2 million is recorded for Sunday. Once there was a fear that the movies, radio, and television would drive the newspapers out of existence. This fear has since been proved

[1] O. G. Villard, *The Disappearing Daily* (New York: Alfred A. Knopf, Inc., 1944), 1–3.

[2] H. E. Barnes and O. M. Ruedi, *The American Way of Life* (New York: Prentice-Hall, Inc., 1950), 514–518.

[3] A. M. Lee, *The Daily Newspaper in America* (New York: The Macmillan Company, 1937), 3–6.

groundless. Leading newspapers broadcast their headlines daily over large networks, thereby stimulating sales. Television has made it possible for readers to see and hear leading commentators, analysts, and persons in the news. Telecast services can bring events right into the home as soon as they happen.

Chain newspapers. For some decades newspapers have been labeled big business. Small independent papers cannot complete with chain owner-ship or national syndicates in circulation, advertising, and specialization. The number of daily papers reached its peak in 1917, when more than 2,500 were published. Consolidations, mergers, and bankruptcies reduced the number to 1,877 in 1940. Stated in another way, three decades ago over 42 per cent of America's cities had competing dailies, but by 1950 only 6.8 per cent of all cities had dailies under more than one ownership. This trend has also affected large cities. In 25 of our largest cities, seven inde-pendent papers suspended publication between 1946 and 1951. A few pa-pers which have been "interred in the graveyard of the daily press" include the Philadelphia *Record*, Seattle *Star*, New York's *PM*, Minneapolis *Times*, Oakland *Post-Enquirer*, St. Louis *Star-Times*, and New York *Sun*.[1]

Although there are fewer independent newspapers in the country, al-most one-half the newspaper readers purchase their papers from chain owners. These same owners directly control 56.4 per cent of the morning papers and 40.4 per cent of the evening issues. Thus, readers are buying and reading more and more papers from fewer enterprises. The Scripps-Howard, Gannet, Hearst, and McCormick chains are among the most prominent. These chains own from three to as many as 25 papers in dif-ferent cities.

The increase of chain newspapers reflect the tendency of urban business enterprises to grow in size and scope. In this respect chain ownership of newspapers is not in itself unusual. What is more important is the impact of this trend on the reading public and the role of chain newspapers in molding public opinion and influencing behavior patterns.

The chain newspapers set the tone on socio-economic and socio-political issues for small and large urban dailies. By dominating the news-gathering and news-releasing sources, the chains can select, edit, and disseminate news which is considered acceptable to their subscribers and advertisers. They can suppress news which may be really important, too. They may present a united front, thus giving them great power over various political, civic, or international issues. Since many chains supply news to small pa-pers without facilities for news-gathering and personnel to write featured articles, their influence in molding public opinion is far-reaching.

[1] A. M. Lee, "The Pall of Orthodoxy," *Nation* (Aug. 11, 1951), 110–111.

Since newspaper owners are interested in wide circulation and profit-making and the accurate portrayal of events may take secondary place, newspapers print news which has mass appeal and stimulates mass reaction. Some personal story or current incident is deliberately selected to be the "talking point" of the day.[1] Year in and year out this pattern is repeated, and readers become so conditioned to bold headlines and a definite format of the front page that they equate "no news" with the inability of the daily issue of the paper to arouse their reactions. Newspapers not only "sell" news, but sometimes "create" it.

Sensationalism often revolves around human interest: unusual, strange, bizarre, humorous, tragic, and scandalous human situations. When the source of interest centers on lost children, romance, royalty, murder, or phenomenal and unusual success, readers' emotions are stirred. Mass behavior may become extremely random as in the case of lost, kidnaped, or abused children. Readers are often sufficiently excited and aroused to join in the hunt for lost or kidnaped children or to pressure civil authorities to punish sadistic adults when young children are known to suffer abuse. Many readers identify themselves with the suffering parents and keep up with the tragic event by following newspaper reports. These same readers may be typical urbanites insofar as they do not concern themselves with the welfare of neighborhood children who may lack play space, who study in overcrowded classrooms, or who live in rundown apartments.

Other types of human interest material published in newspapers include the notification of baptisms, births, deaths, engagements, or marriages. Considerable space is devoted to the activities of prominent, wealthy, or successful persons. The newspapers would not be complete without tales of murder, deserted wives, the good loser, the juvenile delinquent, and the victims of fraud, robbery, and physical violence.[2] People gossip about and discuss these accounts and speak of "newspaper personalities" by name and deed. This is often seen when readers discuss international figures whose activities are described by a reporter on the scene. American readers are conditioned to such stereotype terms as "the fainting prime minister," or "the sobbing prime minister," when referring to Mossadegh of the Middle East. Most readers are more concerned with his wearing apparel, pajamas, at public gatherings than what the direct result of his decision on the world's oil supply will be. Few readers bother to interpret the news they read or to see the event in the social context in which it occurs. Such behavior may appear strange to us, although normal in the society to which the person belongs. As a medium for initiating "small talk," the daily newspaper has replaced the small-town back-fence gossip about

[1] Hughes, *op. cit.*
[2] *Encyclopedia of Social Sciences*, 6, 459–461.

neighbors between neighbors. Sophisticated urbanites may gossip about persons in the news living thousands of miles away.

Chain newspapers have contributed to the development of mass taste since their advertisements reach a larger buying public. Not only do they influence merchandising, but also the popularity and profit of movies, operatic ventures, photography, musical selections, and art. The criterion for a successful product or event is the number of items sold to the masses.

There are several good features which chain newspapers have over small papers. More important international and national news can be brought to the readers, thus broadening their social horizons. Many chains employ competent correspondents who report "hot" news from the source. They can provide a larger paper at cheaper cost. Lastly, they can reduce sectionalism and prejudice.

Tabloids and Periodicals

Tabloids and periodicals are two other media which reflect the influence of the urban environment upon behavior patterns as well as the development of reading taste according to socio-economic levels.

Tabloids. The picture or tabloid newspaper developed as a result of the speed of modern living and the desire of readers to get news quickly and simply. The magazine-size newspaper is more convenient to carry and read in crowded subways, buses, and streetcars. While some maintain a high standard, many tabloids have a reputation for unreliability. At best, news dissemination is cut to a minimum. A boldface caption in large type replaces lengthy explanation, and there are many pictures. In the face of the complex nature of events in a complex urban world, the tabloid is an outstanding illustration of the value placed on simplification, and often gross oversimplification.

Periodicals. Some 18,500 periodicals are published in the United States, about 3,500 of which are issued monthly and some 1,400 weekly. The circulation of many nationally known periodicals is in the multimillions. Several important trends in the changing urban press may also be observed in the periodical field. With the decline of personalized journalism and the change in the editorial policy of most newspapers, nationally read periodicals of a serious nature have taken on the function of effectively guiding public opinion on leading issues. A wider range of opinion can be found within the field of periodicals than in the urban newspaper.

The periodical field has also adopted the practice initiated by the urban press, of recognizing the changing reading habits of urban people. More and more digests are published, condensing the current news and describing personalities in brief and concise form. Pocket editions are popular because of the variety of subjects treated. Many pictorial magazines, with virtually no heavy reading, have increased in circulation.

Another trend is in the introduction of "class" magazines, catering to a given socio-economic group, of which high-priced women's fashion magazines are excellent illustrations. Home decorations is another area where this trend is reflected. Other magazines cater to specific age and sex groups together with socio-economic differentiation. Finally, a countless variety of "self-help" magazines have a wide market. Perhaps as a protest against mass production of articles and against the urge that many urbanites have to show their creativity, magazines specializing in handicraft have great appeal. Many give instructions on carpentry, gardening, sewing, and the like. There are many periodicals which deal with techniques for the attainment of better interpersonal relationships—rearing children, being companionable to family members, becoming better citizens, and so on.

The magazine audience. That a large segment of the American public prefers less serious reading has significant sociological implications.[1] It is often assumed by students of sociology and those with a college education that with increased literacy among the country's general population, more and more persons should be concerned with local, national, and international affairs. The literate group of our population also assumes that others share their propensity to avoid "soap operas" and can detect the bias in news content. Such a situation was not revealed in a study of Sandusky, Ohio: reading as well as radio-listening varied according to socio-economic and educational levels. Thirty-five per cent of the lowest socio-economic group of Sandusky, Ohio, reported that they did not read magazines of the conventional type, as contrasted to 7 per cent of the highest status group. Another group in the same study was asked how many books they had read; 82 per cent of the lowest socio-economic level reported less than one book a month, while 59 per cent of the highest group had read the same amount.

What is more revealing is the kind of material the persons in the lower economic group read. We learn from the accumulation of data on reading and radio listening habits that there is a consistent tendency on the part of the lower economic group to be less inclined toward serious reading or listening. The members of this group are not drawn to subjects the applicability of which to personal life is not immediately foreseen. Nor are they particularly interested in materials that provide a basis for evaluating more fully the world about them. However, many are eager to learn ways and means of becoming richer. A nation-wide survey of women magazine

[1] Genevieve Knupfer, "Portrait of the Underdog," in Reinhard Bendix and S. M. Lipset, *Class, Status, and Power: A Reader on Social Stratification* (Glencoe, Ill.: The Free Press, 1953), 258–259.

readers showed that more of higher socio-economic status read *Time Magazine* than *True Confessions,* while the reverse applied to women of low socio-economic status. For the latter, fiction had more appeal than public affairs.

More time is spent by women of the lower economic levels on escape materials stressing the out-of-the-ordinary emotional situations involving love and romance, adventure and excitement, and superhuman feats. The modern versions of Cinderella, Prince Charming, Robin Hood, and Sir Galahad provide the readers with personal gratification and an escape from their customary life routines.

Materials that belong in this category of escapism are the detective stories, true love tales and personal confessions "never before told," *Police Gazette,* and a host of others. The escape type of materials has a large reading public among children. Comic books, bearing such titles as *Superman, Miss Universe, Wonder Woman,* are sold by the millions to children. The pictorial versions of popular movie heroes involved in various adventures stir the imagination of many boys and girls and indirectly influence the type of games they play.

The Urban Weekly

Two major types of papers can be classified as urban weeklies, the suburban press and the community paper.[1] Both possess characteristics in common, *i.e.,* small circulation, weekly distribution, a small staff of workers, and minimum financial assets. Since city-wide papers often minimize local-area events and personalities, the urban weeklies developed in response to changing conditions. Each serves to strengthen the social solidarity of the local area. As marshalling forces, they surpass the city-wide dailies when local issues are involved.

The suburban press. The suburban weekly is a new form of journalism, growing along with the automobile era and the multiplication of suburbs. With the decline of personalized journalism and the control of urban dailies by big corporations, editors desiring journalism as a profession founded suburban and community papers.[2]

The weeklies are extremely diversified in content, style, and editorial policy for they must adapt to the community's expectations and orientations in order to survive. The local residents can step into the editor's office and express their opinions on editorial policies or enlist the editor's support on local issues. News pertaining to the home, education, schools,

[1] M. Janowitz, "The Imagery of the Urban Community Press" in Hatt and Reiss, *op. cit.,* 532–541.
[2] M. V. Cosse, *The Suburban Weekly* (New York: Columbia University Press, 1928).

church, recreation, and social activities of persons and clubs attract local interest. The suburban papers serve as important channels for merchandising goods and exchanging services between large industries and local residents. Of utmost importance is the objective, constructive interpretation of current happenings and issues as they affect the local community. Mr. "Suburbanite" gets his national and international news from the city paper, but depends upon his local paper to find out why and how he would be affected if the local political scene changed.

One of the primary functions of the editor of the suburban paper is to make his readers "community conscious." He takes a stand on local issues. He joins the active civic and social groups, thus maintaining good relationships with local residents. In many instances, he manages, edits, and solicits advertisements and subscriptions for his paper. He is an integrating force within the community.

Community papers. Large metropolitan cities are subdivided into local communities, often embracing wider areas and containing larger populations than suburbs.[1] These communities arise through the growth of new subdivisions, or the annexation of villages, unincorporated and incorporated areas, and former suburbs to the larger city over a period of time. The names of the former locales may be retained, symbolizing the retention of local sentiments, cohesion, and orientation. As a functioning part of the larger city, these communities exist symbiotically tied to the larger cities. Since the local community may provide all the necessary services for daily living—save, in some cases, employment—the residents spend a great portion of their time within the community and identify with it. The regular urban dailies supply the municipal, state, national, or international news. Local papers emphasize community affairs, and local readers can identify, either vicariously or actually, with local personalities, issues, and activities. As an integrating social force the community papers influence the imagery of local residents.

Imagery of community newspaper readership. A study was undertaken of three communities, representing the lower, upper-lower, and lower-middle class in Chicago.[2] Readers from among the 82 weekly community newspapers published in 1950 with a combined circulation of a million copies were selected to learn what attitudes and conceptions they had toward their papers.

First, the readers regarded their community newspapers as auxiliary and not competing sources of news. Most of the persons interviewed were

[1] For example, Chicago has 75 local communities, and almost all of them have a community paper.

[2] M. Janowitz, *The Urban Community Press: An Empirical Study of Metropolitan Integration* (Glencoe, Ill.: The Free Press, 1952), Hatt and Reiss, *op. cit.*

satisfied with the emphasis on, and coverage of, local affairs. This was verified by analysis of the news content of a three-month sample of the 1949 editions of local-area papers. Three-fourths of the space was devoted to community affairs; about 15 per cent was given to city-wide news, and the remainder to state, national, international, and miscellaneous items. The local papers held great meaning for local readers because it was through this medium that they learned to know their communities.

A second finding was that the readers did not generally perceive the community press as being commercialized. They did not object to local advertisements, nor did they believe that the papers exerted influential and powerful pressure in business circles. On the contrary, readers believed that the advertisements aided in daily living and that the papers' primary contributions were in promoting community spirit.

Also the readers did not believe that the papers were political or partisan, even though the readers knew or read of their papers sponsoring and endorsing candidates for given elections. On the contrary, more readers believed the papers worked to obtain better community facilities.

Finally, the readers generally saw the papers as a means for extending their personal and social contacts because of editorial emphasis on the activities of voluntary associations, and local personalities. Women, more than men, received more satisfaction from reading social and personal news. Persons who had lived in the area longest and had had wider contacts showed more interest in these items. On the other hand, many readers regarded the local papers as a source of "substitute gratification," mentioning the fact that "anyone who wants to" can get mentioned in the columns or have his picture printed. These readers expressed dissatisfaction with the city-wide practice of slighting local-area news excepting on designated days of the week. To the local readers the community newspapers were not only more personal but more democratic in tone.

It should be noted that urban weeklies are experiencing the same difficulties as daily newspapers in meeting rising costs, and there is a tendency for syndicates and corporations to own and manage several community papers.

The Negro Press

Another noteworthy phase of urban journalism in this country is the growth and importance of the Negro press. The first *Freedom Journal* was founded in 1827 as an organization championing the abolition of slavery. The Negro press has been an advocate of human rights. Traditionally, it has been regarded as a "special pleader" for liberty, equality, and justice. The tone and contents have won it the label of the "fighting press." First and foremost, the Negro press is interested in the advancement of the Negro group.[1]

During the Civil War, a number of papers mushroomed into existence, but many of them were fly-by-night ventures which did not survive for lack of finances and trained personnel. Moreover, they were not free to express the thoughts of enslaved Negroes, and it was not until the members of the Negro group settled in northern cities that the press gained momentum. Today, about 200 weekly and semi-weekly Negro newspapers are published, in addition to some 100 monthly, bimonthly, and quarterly magazines and bulletins. The twenty large regional and national papers carry local and national advertising and news items, while the so-called "middle-class papers," which depend upon local subscribers, have a limited circulation of around 5,000. The large weekly press has a total circulation of about 1.5 million, while periodicals and magazines have a half million.

The circulation of any given paper is not an accurate measurement of the wide influence the Negro press has upon the members of the in-group. Papers are passed from one person, family, store, church, lodge, or club to another, and the Negro press is the greatest single power welding the Negro group together. The contents of the newspapers and periodicals are read aloud in informal gatherings and passed by word of mouth among those who do not read or cannot afford a subscription. This method of creating solidarity through personal dissemination of important issues also exists in South African cities among the Bantus. The Bantu press is said to be one of the forces promoting boycotts, strikes, and protest movements.[2]

The largest weekly Negro papers are the Pittsburgh *Courier*, the *Afro-American*, the Chicago *Defender*, and the *Journal and Guide*. The two outstanding papers published in New York are the Amsterdam *Press* and People's *Voice*. The midwestern papers are the Kansas City *Call*, Ohio State *News*, Cleveland *Call and Post*, and St. Louis *Argus*.[3] The most fearless editorials are published in the North, as expected, where circulation and news coverage is greater than in the South. At present, the western part of the country is seeing a growth and development of the Negro press because of the influx of subscribers. Already 18 papers have been founded.

Functions of the Negro press. One of the paramount functions of the Negro press is to maintain communication between the members of the Negro group. Even though the Negro population is scattered, the press

[1] Myrdal, *op. cit.*, Vol. 2, Ch. 42.
[2] *Handbook on Race Relations in South Africa*, Ch. 20, "The Non-European Press."
[3] *The Negro Handbook*, 1949, 281.

creates communities of interest centering around local, state, regional, national, or international events or issues.

A second function is education of the group as to health, franchise, civil rights, and the need for literacy. Others stress the necessity to assume civic responsibility or the need to improve professional standards and competence. Associational activities occupy a large portion of space because large urban dailies do not always accord recognition to them.

A third function of the Negro press is to publicize the successful personalities of the group. Profiles of leaders in business, art, music, sports, churches, and society are popular. Those who desire success find inspiration and encouragement.

The Immigrant Press

The immigrant press prints the foreign-language papers. Its growth coincided with the growth of cities in the United States but has diminished in numbers as new immigrants were restricted after World War I. The natural course of assimilation has reduced the number of foreign-language readers. However, close to a thousand foreign-language papers, magazines, periodicals, and associational organs are read daily, weekly, or monthly by 8 million subscribers. The numbers of people reached may be more extensive because many associations, lodges, and community centers are regular subscribers.

The foreign-language press dates back to the third decade of the seventeenth century, when Benjamin Franklin published the first foreign-language paper (it was in German). After this venture in 1732, other German-language papers followed, chiefly religious in tone.[1] Toward the end of the century, French language papers appeared in leading American cities. In fact, many such papers were published until the First World War. A wave of public sentiment forced the decline of circulation and the bankruptcy of publishing plants, with the German papers suffering the highest mortality. New York, Cincinnati, Buffalo, Chicago, and St. Louis were headquarters for various foreign-language papers during the height of immigration. Practically every sizable group settling here has brought its press with it, or established one soon after arrival.

The Scandinavian press sprang up in the midwest around 1870, and the Chinese, on the West Coast at about the same time. Today, the largest concentration of foreign-language papers is in New York City. German, Yiddish, Italian, Arabic, Bohemian, and Greek papers are located there and have some of the largest circulations. Chicago has the largest number of Russian and Polish papers.

[1] F. L. Mott, *American Journalism* (New York: The Macmillan Co., 1945).

Functions of the immigrant press. Why should the immigrant press continue to exist long after the immigrants themselves have accepted American culture? Its functions may provide an insight into the role that the foreign-language press plays for a segment of the population.

Primary is the fact that the foreign-language papers afford the new citizens a "window" through which they can view and understand the immediate environment.[1] Many attitudes, values, and behavior patterns are puzzling, and perhaps seem strange and even hostile. These can be explained and understood when presented in a familiar language. In time the immigrant incorporates new behavior patterns into his own. Problems affecting the group are accorded space and interpretation. As the English language becomes the medium of communication, the foreign-language paper is discarded or read as a supplement to the regular ones.

Another important reason for the existence of the immigrant press is that the larger urban dailies seldom give much space and recognition to the associational activities of the immigrant group. Hence, the press serves as a medium of information and notification as to immigrant group activities. When necessary, it can draw members together for concerted action.

Although immigrants have left their ancestral homes, they nevertheless desire to learn about happenings there. The foreign-language press prints political, economic, and religious news that enables the immigrants to keep up with old world news. When there is a catastrophe, the newspapers make appeals for funds. A country that is striving for freedom or liberation from domination spurs subscribers to buy papers published in the language of the original homeland. For instance, there is a growing number of subscribers to Yiddish- and Polish-language papers here because of the emotional stirrings created by recent political events in Israel and Poland.

A final function is that of having the native-born children of foreign-born parents retain a knowledge of the language of their parents. However, the young Americans find the urban dailies and magazines more appealing. The immigrant press has difficulty in maintaining a sizable circulation as the foreign-language readers decline in numbers. Some must resort to printing a large section in English for the sole purpose of attracting subscribers among the native-born. The newspaper becomes a "hybrid" instrument to forestall the eventual suspension of publication. Usually, sports news, dances and activities of clubs, and the leaders of the younger group are printed in English.[2] On the whole, the immigrant press has been harassed by lack of adequate finances and trained personnel. For these reasons, it has never become big business. Like the Negro press, however, the

---

[1] R. E. Park, *The Immigrant Press and Its Control* (New York: Harper & Bros., 1922).

[2] Consult copies of *The Chinese Press* printed in San Francisco, Cal.

existence of the immigrant press reflects the heterogeneity of urban population and the nucleation of subgroups.

Other Media

The telegraph, telephone, radio, television, and moving pictures are other important media of mass communication. All have served to heighten ideational mobility, while at the same time creating more secondary contacts. In cities, it is possible for business firms to have a "telephone acquaintance" with clients and associates in branch offices without ever knowing what they look like. Without telegraph and telephone services, the economic functions of the nation would be seriously crippled. These instruments enable the location of executive offices far from factories and break down the isolation between the various areas of the nation. Economy of time and cost have stimulated the adoption and development of greater improvements.

Radio. The radio is enormously popular as an advertising medium and the daily radio listening public is between 50 and 80 millions. About 114 million radio sets are in use. Some time during the day radio sets are turned on in three out of every four homes. The most popular listening hours are between 7:00 and 10:00 P.M. As a contrast, there are about 10 million radio sets in South America and the same number in other parts of North America, excluding the United States. Europe has 67 million sets, while Asia has 14 million. Africa has 3 million radios, or a million and a half fewer than Australia. In short, the United States has half of the world's radios.

Radio audiences, like newspaper readers, differ according to socio-economic status. A radio listening survey here showed that 73 per cent of the higher socio-economic status group listened to classical music, as compared to only 57 per cent of the lower socio-economic group. The Buffalo survey confirmed the same tendency when classifying listeners of educational programs, serious dramatizations, and public affairs. A study of the most popular programs in a midwestern town indicated that the greatest following was among the lower socio-economic group in regard to broadcasts featuring comedy and variety, sports, serial stories, and religious and service programs.[1]

In order to determine the size and composition of the radio audience and the effects of serial and educational programs upon behavior and reactions of listeners, a preliminary intensive interview of 100 women was conducted. The purpose was to see if daytime radio listening by women had any relationship to psychological gratification. Three major types of gratifi-

[1] Bendix and Lipset, *op. cit.,* 259.

cation were experienced by these women listening to serials. Some enjoyed them merely because they gave emotional release, "the chance to cry," the enjoyment in experiencing the "surprises, happy or sad," and the opportunity for expressing aggressiveness by those burdened with their own problems. The latter group said that "it made them feel better to know that other people have troubles, too." [1]

In contrast are those who found compensation listening to the sorrows portrayed by the serial characters, while others felt superior in knowing that the characters were not "real life." There is little doubt that many serials provide a channel for those wishing to escape from their own sorrows, disappointments, and failures by hearing the radio characters successfully overcoming their daily handicaps. Women who were inclined to worry more than the average, regardless of educational level, listened more frequently to serials.

Many listeners felt that they received advice from the programs that instruct them about how to behave in given situations. The Iowa survey embraced 2,500 listeners, 41 per cent of whom claimed they were helped by educational programs, and 28 per cent replied that they were not helped. The remainder gave a variety of answers: "they did not know," "never thought of it that way," or were noncommittal. The less formal education a woman had, the more she was likely to consider programs "explaining things" as helpful. The programs enabled listeners to advise others by referring to the radio sources. Thus, people could give advice without taking responsibility should the suggestions work out adversely, or the result fall short of expectations. [2]

These findings point to the great social responsibility facing the radio writers engaged in devising serials and educational programs. While a large proportion of the listeners tune in the radio to be entertained, and writers of programs aim for entertainment rather than education, there is little doubt that the objectives of the writers and listeners do not coincide. Radio and television can be used to promote greater awareness of social problems, public affairs, and other topics, and will reach a large segment of the population. [3]

Like the urban press, the radio plays a great role in the spreading of cultures, and its influence has permeated the remote areas of the world where programs are beamed from stations in this country. Some of the effects of radio have been the increase of public education, mass entertainment, and propaganda. Personalities are glamorized whose ways of behaving are imitated by many listeners. Events of local areas, regions, nations,

[1] Theodore M. Newcomb, E. L. Hartley, and others, *Readings in Social Psychology* (New York: Henry Holt & Co., 1947), 561–566, from Herta Herzog, "Psychological Gratification in Daytime Radio Listening."

[2] *Ibid.*, 562–565.

[3] *Ibid.*, 565–566.

and the world are brought into nearly every household in the land. Although there has been considerable disagreement as to the good and bad effects of radio, there is no denying that it has provided some forms of inexpensive and informal recreation and education that other media and forms of leisure-time activities do not include. Perhaps the groups who have benefited the most are invalids and others unable to have normal social intercourse because of various reasons.

The influence of radio on public opinion is tremendous and has not yet been fully recognized. It is probably more powerful than the written page, because the human voice has greater power to sway emotions, and under proper conditions the radio can unite the thoughts of many citizens on a national issue. The fireside chats of the late President Roosevelt had this effect. The excited voice of the news commentator covering a rescue or human interest story brings the drama of life into the home.

The radio, like the urban press, can create stereotype situations and reactions. Listeners follow the programs that satisfy their impulses and desires. Soap operas, sensational news releases, and murder mysteries are broadcasted regularly. Roundtable discussions, information on technological advances, world affairs, and symphonic music are brought within the hearing of millions. Like the urban press, radio has something for every type of listener, and the beneficial social effects are mixed with the less desirable.

Television. An important new medium is television, invented in 1926 and introduced on a commercial scale when the World's Fair opened in Chicago. The various programs are still in the exploratory stage, but there are indications that this newer instrument will eclipse radio, press, wireless, and other media in impact and scope. Television may bring about great changes in behavior patterns, attitudes, and beliefs. Since the end of World War II, television has come into its own, and when color television is perfected, another step in its widespread adoption and use in homes and elsewhere is assured. At the end of 1946 some 50,000 sets were in use, and two years later, over a million sets. By 1952 one-third of the nation's homes had installed television and an additional million sets are in use elsewhere. It is estimated that 1,000 new sets are added daily, a spectacular growth caused by increased output and lowered costs. Television now reaches more than 60 per cent of the population, most of which is urban.

The social impact of television may be even greater than that of radio because visual appeal can be very effectively exploited. It has been claimed for television that it brings the "truth" directly into the home. The claim that the camera "does not lie" was analyzed by a study of MacArthur Day in Chicago,[1] an event observed by millions of spectators and video viewers.

[1] Kurt Lang and G. E. Lang, "The Unique Perspective of Television," *American Sociological Review*, 18 (Feb., 1953), 3–12.

It was discovered that the assumed reportorial accuracy was far from an actuality. The scope of the camera necessitates selection. The unseen part of the subject remains open to suggestion and inference. Attempts at filling the gaps are made by the commentators on the scene. Television cameramen are interested in good shots, while the commentators are inclined to bias their reactions and the behavior of the crowd. However, in the study of MacArthur Day the viewers at home had a much more comprehensive picture of a continuous event, while the spectators lining the streets to greet the general caught only a part of the total spectacle. More disappointments were noted among the spectators in the streets than those at home or viewers from high buildings. Television commentators and cameramen created the impression that the spectacle and crowds were greater than they actually were. Indirectly, this tone was repeated in the press and in radio broadcasts, pointing to the probable misconceptions which may be televised and reinforced. In brief, television is attempting to conform to the viewers' expectations in order to assure steady interest. This is a social responsibility facing the telecasters when selecting materials.

Sociologists are divided in their opinions on the social effects of television. Some believe that one of the beneficial results is the return of recreation to the home, while others wonder if preoccupation with television makes for less intimate family interaction. More believe that family conflicts may develop as the result of differences of opinion over what programs to see. Disruption of home routine by television has created some criticism. Television has changed some self-entertaining habits in the home.

Summary

The urban environment is too vast for important daily events to be disseminated by word of mouth or face-to-face interaction. Modern media of communication developed in response to changing social conditions, functioning effectively to bring urbanites living spatially apart into communities of interest. Groups sharing like objectives are brought together for concerted action.

The various media have influenced the development of mass culture and in highly urbanized societies supersede and weaken the stable culture. Uniformity of dress, language, new behavior patterns, tastes, and values are found as a result of mass media, while in less urbanized areas, mores, traditions, and customs of the stable culture predominate. To counteract the adverse social effects of mass media, permanent social organizations are using these media to reinforce stable cultural elements. Subcultural elements are yet found in the American society, and older generations are less inclined to adopt new fads and fashions. The diffusion of urban traits into rural areas has resulted in narrowing the gap between urban and rural ways of life. The gap remains wide in other than American societies.

The urban press is the most important medium of communication. A variety of material is included (1) daily newspapers, (2) special interest organs, (3) periodicals, (4) sensationalized features, and (5) community papers. Large cities offer a wide variety of newspapers, but they all may be owned and operated by one management or by a chain. The trend is toward more mergers, resulting in the standardization of content, news gathering, release, and distribution. Circulation has climbed, although the number of independent papers has decreased.

The Negro press is a growing institution and is the greatest single force uniting the members of the group. From a crusading, race-conscious organ, it has become an educational medium. The Negro press is seeking to improve race relations.

The immigrant press has existed longer than the Negro press but has dwindled in importance as native-borns increased. However, the persistence of immigrant papers is due to the role they play in holding the members of a subculture together and aiding in the assimilation process.

Other media, radio and television, have contributed to ideational mobility and influenced the acceptance and adoption of new behavior patterns. Like the urban press, their audiences are heterogeneous and specialized, reflecting the expression of diverse interests related to social, racial, educational, religious, occupational, and political backgrounds. While these media are primarily regarded as providing entertainment, rather than education, many listeners and viewers use them as sources of instruction and are unaware of the discrepancy between these two approaches. The audiences of the lower socio-economic level avoid more frequently than the higher socio-economic level radio programs and reading materials of a serious nature.

DISCUSSION QUESTIONS

1. What shades of opinion are reflected in the papers sold in your city?
2. How can a newspaper reader distinguish between propaganda and fact?
3. To what extent do the editorial columns reflect the true views of the editor?
4. Can several newspapers operate profitably in your city?
5. Do neighborhood or community papers provide a good clue to the social relations of the area?
6. Are communities of interest reflected in the subscription to special papers, *i.e.,* labor, religious education, racial, ethnic, etc.?
7. What groups read periodicals, and how do the readers differ?

8. What are the social effects of the radio? Of television?
9. What functions are performed by the Negro press?
10. What functions are performed by the immigrant press?

SUGGESTED PROJECTS

1. Compare the growth of the tabloids with that of the urban weeklies.
2. Analyze the news coverage of a community or suburban weekly as to (1) local news, (2) city-wide news, and (3) others.
3. Study the changing functions of the urban daily press as an institution.
4. Compare the growth of the Negro press with that of the immigrant press, or the growth of the South African native press with that of the Negro press in America.
5. Study the class stratification of periodicals.
6. Study the impact upon young children of (1) radio, and (2) television.

READINGS

M. V. Coose, *The Suburban Weekly*. New York: Columbia University Press, 1938.

The growth of urban weeklies as an integrating force in the local community.

A. M. Lee, *The Daily Newspaper in America*. New York: The Macmillan Co., 1937.

The changing institutional functions of the urban dailies and the tendency toward big business. Also later edition.

P. F. Lazarfeld and P. L. Kendall, *Radio Listening in America*. New York: Prentice-Hall, Inc., 1948.

The listening habits and preferences of radio audiences.

V. V. Oak, *The Negro Press*. Yellow Springs: Antioch Press, 1948.

A historical treatment of the Negro press and its emphasis from its founding to the present.

R. E. Park, *The Immigrant Press and Its Control*. New York: Harper & Bros., 1922.

The organization and social significance of the foreign-language press.

O. G. Villard, *The Disappearing Daily*. New York: Alfred A. Knopf, Inc., 1944.

The decline of independent dailies and the increase of specialization, standardization, and corporation control of once competing papers.

Chapter Nineteen

Leisure-time Activities

Increased leisure is a result of mechanization and urbanization, and a variety of leisure-time activities has accompanied the growth of cities. One of the main distinctions between the agricultural and nonagricultural portion of the population—dating back to the era of ancient cities—has been the comparative leisure enjoyed by the latter. Leisure early became identified with social and occupational status, and the amount of time which was devoted to the pursuit of leisure was significant of wealth. The upper class, or those who wished to be part of it, therefore, promoted public events so as to be seen and envied, or they patronized the arts, music, poetry, drama, literature, and other sedentary amusement. The lower socio-economic groups had few moments of leisure.

As an increasing number of urbanites were freed from food-growing, and a higher division of labor developed, more persons could engage in the pursuit of leisure. A variety of activities has developed that encompasses the diverse incomes and interests of urban people. The rise of commercial entertainment has replaced the activities formerly organized by kings, nobles, or persons delegated this responsibility. New and spectacular forms of entertainment designed to attract a given segment of the urban public have superseded private and tax-supported forms of recreation and entertainment. The shortening of the workday and workweek has permitted the average urbanite to have a block of time which can be devoted to leisure-time activities. Although there are activities which symbolize class status, such as yachting, polo, horseback riding, or vacations abroad, the distinctions are not as definite as they once were.

The term leisure refers to activities which are not linked with obligations and duties. Each society has rules and regulations governing the performance of gainful employment, but when workers are not so occupied, they are free to engage in and select leisure-time activities of various types. These activities have a dual purpose. They provide relaxation and pleas-

435

ure, and they increase social interaction with other individuals or groups.

Leisure-time pursuits include all forms of recreation. The terms have different connotations, but they are not as implicit as they once were. Recreation refers to physical activities wherein the participant seeks to rebuild his mental and muscular system through some refreshing and stimulating form of activity. Many Americans indulge in mass recreation as spectators, rather than as active participants. There are a hundred times more television-viewers or radio-listeners of sports and music than there are athletes or musicians.

Amusement refers to relatively unorganized forms of leisure-time activities in which every participant and performer finds pleasure in invoking fun and humor. Parlor games are good illustrations. However, when amusements became organized and commercialized, the term entertainment is used. Today, the primary purpose of the entertainment business is to amuse individuals and groups by featuring talented and highly paid performers and to stage mass productions accommodating thousands.

For our purposes leisure-time activities include all forms of amusement which are not directly related to the fulfillment of work obligations and duties. Several major categories of such activities are treated in the following sections to show the diversification and selection offered to urbanites. The growth of occupations in the leisure-time field is an established trend, and the influence which entertainers have made in promoting fads and fashions and changing behavior patterns are other topics of consideration. The relationship between socio-economic status and leisure-time pursuits has sociological significance.

Urban Environment and Leisure

Since increased leisure is directly related to the growth of cities, what specific conditions produced the change? During the last century some major changes have followed increased urbanization and industrialization, and they have affected the young and old, men and women.

All gainfully employed persons in the United States have benefited from the reduction of working time. Fifty years ago, the 60-hour workweek was general, whereas today the 40-hour week is the standard. Many business organizations operate on a five-day basis, and the long week end and the evening hours provide more opportunities for leisure-time activities. Legal restrictions on child labor have resulted in many activities being planned for the young up to their late teens. Urban children have many after-school hours for recreation and play. The education for the use of leisure time is a part of every school curriculum. The growth of an older population group has also affected recreation and entertainment trends. Programs and clubs for older people are increasing and are suited to physical and emotional needs. The introduction and adoption of more adult education programs, occupational therapy, hobby clubs, and discussion groups are directly related to the changing age composition of the population.

Another condition creating more leisure is the mechanization of industry and the resultant rise in output of goods and services in a shorter period of time. Mass-production techniques have contributed to the shorter workday and workweek. Technological changes and unemployment have caused many workers to be idle for extended periods, and leisure-time activities fill the gap. During the depression of the thirties, considerable attention was devoted by the United States government to promoting inexpensive pursuits and instructing many to find outlets for their creativity through the arts and crafts. These activities are open to workers facing temporary lay-offs for one reason or another.

The higher standard of living which workers enjoy has made it possible for them to set aside sums of money for leisure-time activities. The growth of commercial and quasi-commercial recreation and entertainment is directly related to the higher wage scale and the fact that most workers have vacations with pay. This has indirectly increased the amount of national income spent on traveling and motoring facilities. "Package vacations," planned cruises, and tours with accommodations and meals, to local and foreign places are an interesting development. This trend has indirectly influenced dressing habits—sport clothes for men, women, and children.

Urban living conditions demand a greater amount of rest and relaxation from the routinized, often monotonous tasks performed indoors under artificial surroundings. Routine, repetition, pressure to "get ahead," and the noise and din of the city produce nervous tensions. Leisure-time activities are needed to offset them.

Other conditions affecting leisure are related to the increased freedom of women and the relaxation of religious objections to recreation. In former times women were confined to the home, and housework consumed a large portion of the day. With the widespread use of mechanical devices, housework has lost much of its drudgery. The growth of leisure-time activities for women has followed. This affected women more than men, and, on the whole, the former have more leisure.

The demand for more varied forms of recreation and entertainment has also resulted in more leisure-time activities. Commercial, private, and public organizations have devoted more funds and attention to promoting activities.

General Categories of Leisure-Time Activities

Several general categories of leisure-time activities are found in the United States, the society which has made the greatest number of changes in the modes of spending leisure-time.[1]

Commercial. Most popular and widespread are the commercial forms of leisure, provided by movies, night clubs, concerts, theaters, sports, and others. These forms of mass recreation attract large audiences and the bigger the reputation of the star performer and supporting performers, the higher the price of admission. A huge audience signifies the popularity and appeal of the activity. The exclusive spots and expensive attractions draw the wealthier clientele, but they alone cannot carry the expense of staging the modern forms of organized leisure. At best, exclusiveness is confined to purchasing the entire performance or the house for one or more evenings.

Spectator sports. One of the outstanding developments in American recreation in the twentieth century has been the extensive commercialization of spectator sports. Millions attend the big league games while the baseball season is at its height. More tune in or see them on the radio and television. A large following is attracted to hockey, ice follies, boxing, wrestling, and tennis, golf, and bowling matches. "Thrill" amusements, auto racing, horse and greyhound racing, and stunt flying, are very popular. Women are among some of the most ardent "thrill" fans, and many follow wrestling and boxing matches with regularity.

Entertainers in spectator sports and amusements. A distinction should be made between those who are the spectators, the participant-observers paying a price for the feature, and those who work to provide various forms of entertainment. Corresponding to the growth of spectator sports has been the increasing number of professional performers specializing in all major sports and entertainment. Their salaries are paid out of gate or box office receipts, or they may be sponsored by a leading corporation. Leading stars often earn higher salaries than corporation presidents, lawyers, and other professionals. A leading crooner's annual income may exceed that of the President of the United States. Radio and stage stars rival television personalities in commanding top salaries from several media. Competition between national producers undoubtedly boosts the incomes of popular idols.

Fans adore their favorites, and the box office receipts furnish testimony to the wide appeal of famous actors and actresses. Their private lives are

[1] For a discussion of leisure-time activities in this and other countries, see Martin H. Neumeyer and Esther S. Neumeyer, *Leisure and Recreation* (New York: A. S. Barnes & Co., 1949), Chs. 2, 3, and 4.

subjected to the "gold fish bowl" treatment, and the myths and legends about their private and public lives often form topics of heated conversation. These myths and legends may be consciously created by publicity agents. Leading entertainers set fashions in clothing and home furnishings and advertise countless varieties of products. Vast numbers of everyday items win distinction and acceptance because of the bewitching endorsement and testimonial of famous people. To many young adults, these idols personify the ultimate in ideational and social mobility, and many seek to emulate them. Youngsters are directly or indirectly affected, for they wear the clothes, play with the toys, and eat cereals endorsed by stars of their age groups. Older people can now imitate "glamorous" grandmothers or grandfathers.

Quasi-commercial. The multiplication of voluntary associations, institutional organizations, and secondary groups in urban society has stimulated quasi-commercial activities.[1] The essential difference between quasi-commercial and the strictly commercial forms is that the quasi-commercials are not operated solely for profit on an organized day-to-day business basis. The purposes or projects of a given association, organization, club, or social group may be the *raison d'etre* for benefit events. Tickets are sold to the members, the public, and interested supporters of the cause. The price paid for the entertainment is supposed to cover the expenses incurred and net a profit for the attainment of specific goals. Any profit made is spent through the customary commercial channels. An exchange of goods and services is implied in the appeal for public and membership support. Merchants may contribute to enlarge the proceeds but may become the indirect beneficiaries when the profit is spent. For example, a fashion show to raise funds for a children's hospital treating cardiac cases would involve new equipment from local merchants.

The media of communication lend their services by according recognition to the leading personalities promoting the event. The affairs sponsored by the upper-class members command the society page and testify to the fact that the "haves" do not ignore the plight of the "have-nots." The participation of the upper class in these socially sanctioned undertakings is an obligation to class membership and signifies that the members are performing useful public service. This brings public approval and nullifies the popular conception that members of the upper class live useless and wasteful lives.[2]

Whereas commercial entertainment activities give status and mobility to star performers, quasi-commercial activities often reaffirm the status of

[1] Gist and Halbert, *op. cit.*, 436.
[2] H. S. Bossard and Eleanor S. Boll, "Rites of Passage—A Contemporary Study," *Social Forces* (Mar., 1948), 247–255.

the sponsors and supporters. Many such events are oriented around class participation and sponsorship, for the members of the middle class are equally prone to undertake them. "Little theater" groups are an example.

Private. Most of the private leisure-time activities involve cliques and personal friends. The prime objective is to mix socially with congenial companions, whenever the members of the group agree. A few persons or couples may informally get together and share mutual interests: bridge, gossiping, hiking, and so on. Before the rise of commercial recreation, almost all entertainment was private. In rural and rural-nonfarm areas private leisure-time activities are more common than they are in cities.

In Hollingshead's study, it was found that 120 recreational cliques existed in "Elmtown," ranging from two to seven members for each. The modal membership was four persons for both the boys' and girls' cliques.[1] Group ties were strongly associated with an adolescent's position in the class structure and his high school grade. When class lines were crossed, as in the case of a third of the adolescents, the adjacent class was involved. Persons too remote in the class hierarchy were seldom involved, as in private activities one's best friends were selected on the basis of mutual interests and social considerations.

Public. Some type of public recreation has always existed in this country, as, for example, national parks and vacation areas, but municipal public facilities for leisure-time activity did not become organized until 1906. At that time the municipal playground movement began. The concept of community recreation has since become an accepted phase of community organization.[2] The provision for more forms of tax-supported municipal recreation is increasing as more children grow up in cities, and overcrowded living quarters limit space for their daily activities. The building of parks and playgrounds hardly keeps abreast of the growing population.

During the summer months, many municipalities operate swimming pools, day camps, supervised playgrounds, picnic grounds, and amateur theaters. Other cities maintain year-round activities by instituting community centers, museums, and libraries.

Illegal. Despite the curbs on illegal forms of recreation, many persons persist in supporting all types offered. Handbooks and "policy rackets" flourish on an extensive scale in large cities, and they are tightly structured and interwoven with the political and business life of these municipalities. The Kefauver investigation revealed the magnitude of these operations which appeal to rich and poor alike. Cities have a ready-made consumer

[1] Hollingshead, *op. cit.* Ch. 9.
[2] George D. Butler, *Introduction to Community Recreation,* 2nd ed. (New York: McGraw-Hill Book Co. Inc., 1949), 59.

base, and illegal forms of recreation are difficult to suppress. Fabulous sums are spent annually in gambling for "easy money" or for the thrill of taking a chance.

Despite statutes prohibiting all forms of gambling, these activities persist because raffles, lotteries, roulette, and bingo are frequently used for raising funds. Churches, hospitals, clubs, schools, and fraternal organizations are permitted by statute to use these devices for "worthy causes," but many commercial "clubs" abuse the privilege. Enforcement of the gambling laws is generally recognized as difficult because such organizations are technically within the law.[1]

Many games of chance circumvent the law by offering prizes in money or merchandise, so that pinball machines, dice games, and slot machines are frequently found in taverns, night clubs, private clubs, pool halls, and waiting rooms. Most states have required the destruction of slot and pinball machines.[2] The yearly gross intake from slot machines alone was around $2 billion, while about $4 million was spent for "protection." Four million more dollars were spent by manufacturers and distributors of slot machines for supporting a corps of lobbyists, lawyers, and public relations personnel.

Another common form of illegal recreation is betting on sport or other events, horse racing, elections, and professional football, basketball, hockey games, and so on. Prize fights are tame without some element of betting on the winner. The fact that direct telephone or wire services are established in cities for placing and following the bets made on commercial recreation and entertainment increases the excitement and attracts more players.

The "numbers" game, often known as "lottery" or "policy," is the most widely played game in the country's large metropolitan cities. Between one and three million dollars are annually spent by the rich and poor alike, although the players in the lower economic brackets are the most numerous.[3] Since a chance can be bought for as little as ten cents, and twenty-five cents is the most common amount spent by the lower-income groups, it is a "poor man's game of chance." The big operators in metropolitan cities have grown wealthy and some "king" sellers of policy slips may do as much as $50,000 worth of business a week.

Bingo drawings are considered "small-time" amusement by public authorities and are seldom supervised. Children often engage in bingo or keeno games along with their elders, thereby developing an interest in

---

[1] *The Annals of the American Academy of Political and Social Science,* "Gambling," 269 (Mar., 1950), 1–8.
[2] *Ibid.,* 27.
[3] *Ibid.,* 39–45.

and attraction for other gambling games.[1] They can come to regard "beating the law" as a part of the total game of chance. Indeed, many parents speculate regularly on stocks and bonds, which may be looked upon as a legalized form of chance. All forms of speculation have an underlying, powerful appeal: to win money by easy methods. The increase of one's capital often brings admiration, publicity, and recognition. It is estimated that fifty million adults—mainly urbanites—gamble regularly and if occasional gamblers were counted, this number would be double.[2]

Brightly colored punchboards displayed in restaurants and elsewhere attract 15 million adults who pay small change to win various kinds of merchandise worth considerably less than the total intake. How many children spend their pennies in neighborhood stores hoping to win candy, dolls, or toys will never be determined.

Professional types of gambling. Spectators need to be distinguished from those who perform, finance, promote, or organize amusements. Like distinctions must be made in games of chance. The regular players consist of one group, while the other group is made up of professionals who manipulate the games of chance. Their aids, assistant operators and the vast number of auxiliary helpers, whether private or public, should be included.

Outstanding personality types connected with the myriad of illegal games include the professional gamblers, the "bankers" (owners or operators of casinos), operators, confidence men, cardsharps, crapshooters, runners, bookmakers, markers, etc. These are urban occupations supported by public demand. Gambling establishments frequently employ strong-arm men, bouncers, gangsters, and other "shady" characters to enforce rules or protect customers. These professional gambling groups influence the selection and election of public officials. Gradually, but surely, they corrupt city, state, and Federal government agencies.[3] The underworld wields great influence in legislation, moreover.

In this social milieu thrive the harlot, the pimp, the pickpocket, the safecracker, the "stickup man," the blackmailer, the extortionist, the labor racketeer, the municipal "fixer," the "shakedown copper," and other criminals. These are social types peculiar to cities. It is interesting that professionals connected with some illegal forms of entertainment are subject to tax laws. When they are prosecuted they are charged with skillful evasion of income tax, not gambling. However, new legislation is being enacted to control these activities by requiring a license. This turn in events grew out of the Kefauver investigations.

[1] *Ibid.*, 73–74.
[2] *Ibid.*, 77–80.
[3] *Ibid.*, 114–133.

The Movies

The most common form of commercial recreation is the cinema. Primarily an urban vehicle of entertainment, it has enjoyed wide popularity since 1895, the date of the first introduction of the moving pictures to the American public. Their impact upon the youth and adults has been a controversial topic, for a weekly audience of approximately 100 million comes under the direct or indirect influence of movies.[1] This figure does not include those who feel the impact of movies through educational media in schools, organizations, homes, and other places.

The movies in urban life. There are specific reasons for the large scale development of motion picture theaters and theater chains in cities. The small space required and the relatively low cost of operation make them ideal for crowded communities where buildings on small lots are available for theaters. Downtown theaters reach magnificent and splendid proportions, but neighborhood theaters are frequently converted from small stores.

One-third of the movie-goers are minors. The movie theater has become the meeting place for many movie fans, and keeping up with the movies is a habit. The movies appeal especially to the population between 14 and 45 years of age, a group representing the bulk of the nation's urbanites.[2] However, many younger minors are initiated into the movie habit by their parents. Mothers send their children to the movies and feel at ease, knowing that youngsters, held by a strong fascination, will remain there until brought home. The lack of playground space is a major reason for many patronizing the movies as a form of recreation.

The tension of city life and the need for escape, together with the varied working shifts of city dwellers, give the movies added appeal. At almost any hour of the day, movies are open. Workers can drop in after work and relax for a few hours. Movie producers aim to please the citizens earning over $1,500 annually, residing in a city with over 50,000 inhabitants. This group represents the "average man," but women, in the final analysis, determine the success or failure of a given picture.[3] The greatest majority of fan club members, readers of movie magazines, and writers of fan letters are women.

Movies which are most successful in large metropolises do not hold the

---

[1] *The Annals of the American Academy of Political and Social Science,* "The Motion Picture Industry," 254 (Nov., 1947), 18–19.
[2] M. F. Thorp, *America At the Movies* (New Haven: Yale University Press, 1939), 15.
[3] *Ibid.,* 4–10.

same appeal for audiences in smaller cities. The spectacular productions with their exotic, elaborate, and splendid staging and costuming, are financial losses in small communities. The same situation applies to the unusual and unexpected themes, as, for example, gruesome murders, questionable morals, and racial tensions. In large cities, the more bizarre and controversial pictures draw large audiences seeking novel experiences through vicarious participation. An analysis of the movies showed that 69 per cent of them were staged in wealthy or ultra-wealthy locales. Modern or middle-class settings were used in 25 per cent, as contrasted to 4 per cent in poor surroundings. When this is correlated with the fact that the movies are geared to the "average man's pocketbook," the role they play as media of escape becomes more meaningful and poignant. The remoteness of the actual lives of spectators from those of the cinema stars is unmistakable. No solutions are offered as to how the audience may achieve the same ideals or goals, but that many imitate the behavior patterns of entertainers that are readily copied should not be overlooked.

Social effects of movies. One of the significant social effects of the cinema is its impact on fashions and fads and the shift in the leadership of new styles and innovations from the upper class to popular entertainers within the last four decades. This change has also been seen in home furnishings and other durable goods. What the leading stars wear, use, or endorse has a decided influence on the nation's consumption patterns, and a popular hero or heroine has often started a fad. Moreover, stars influence children in the use of certain articles. For example, toy items based on the "Snow White" movies netted two million dollars.[1] Promotion of these articles is often done through the movie screen, and manufacturers and distributors spend 67 million dollars annually on this form of advertising.

The most pronounced social effects of the movies are their oversimplification and romanticizing of real life situations. The undue emphasis upon premarital romantic love is one phase that cannot be denied. The trials, achievements, or desires of older persons are not often dealt with. Moviegoers identify themselves with parts the actors are portraying. One of the greatest appeals the movies has is that each member of the audience shares with many others the same emotions in a hushed and subdued atmosphere. The motion picture is a type of entertainment which especially attracts the single and the lonely.

Movies are apt to repeat trite and worn-out themes, and in this respect they follow a device adopted by the daily newspaper, of emphasizing the unusual, bizarre, and sensational. Like newspapers, they devote considerable attention to "shady" activities, while unintentionally they may be glamorizing the role of the "reformed hero or heroine." This portrayal of

[1] *The Film Daily Year Book,* 1937, 9.

"getting away with it" has had far-reaching consequences, and many civic leaders and parents attribute the increase of unlawful activities of young teenagers and adults to the movies. One author states that a segment of our basic values is vividly portrayed, glorified, and magnified, at the expense of a total range of values.[1] Children, who comprise over one-third of the audiences, are the most impressionable age group. They are likely to imitate what they see in pictures. Fear of the ill-effects movies have upon children led to censorship. Many studies show that the behavior patterns of modern American youth have been influenced by unrealistic movie norms and values.

Movies influence the behavior of young urban adults in other countries and especially the Far East, where urbanization and Westernization is increasing. The greatest impact is on interpersonal relations, such as the individual selection of mates rather than courtship under parental control. The influence on wedding attire is equally great. Modern Chinese women, for example, prefer Western wedding gowns, bouquets, veils, and high-heeled slippers, often minutely copied from movie magazines. The elaborate eighteen-course wedding feasts are old-fashioned, and receptions where tea is served with cream and sugar and rich French pastries are substituted. The bridal-red sedan chair has given way to the auto. The groom's attire is also Western: the lapel flower, silk hat, and cutaway coat. The fact that the average American does not make such elaborate arrangements is not understood, because, as said earlier, movies generally portray the life of the upper socio-economic levels.

Good aspects should not be overlooked. When used as an educational medium, movies can produce a change in attitude toward minorities and stimulate an interest in fair play, cleanliness, courtesy, and healthy morals. They can produce a desire to travel and promote better international relations through an understanding of the life and thought of various social classes and their subclasses.

Since the end of the Second World War, more producers in this country are staging realistic themes dealing with the adjustment problems of veterans, the lot of the racial "line-crosser," the treatment and recovery of emotionally or mentally disturbed patients, and the effects of prejudice and discrimination on helpless victims.

Despite the criticisms leveled at the movies, it remains the most popular form of entertainment attended by the whole family. Discriminating parents often select the movies recommended by reliable magazines to which they subscribe, or they cooperate with other parents in the community toward arranging special programs for the appropriate age level. This move-

[1] Hortense Powdermaker, *Hollywood: The Dream Factory* (New York: Little Brown & Co., 1950).

ment is taking hold in many cities, and special features for children are shown in neighborhood theaters.

In summary, the popularity of the movies will continue so long as urban conditions reduce the number of face-to-face contacts that lead to impersonality and loneliness for many persons. Modern man is often lonely and desperately in need of personal relationships. By going to the movies he has the illusion of close, intimate, personal contact with exciting and beautiful people. He knows their names, what they wear, eat, and say, and they talk directly to him. His loneliness is briefly assuaged.

Leisure-time and Income

The question arises as to how a person's socio-economic status is related to leisure-time activities. Given such constant factors as the shorter working day, the wide range of activities from which to make a selection, and the right of the poor and rich alike to engage in and enjoy leisure, what other factors may exist? Why do some groups fail to participate in the available facilities?

Lundberg's study. In a study of leisure of 520,947 inhabitants of Westchester County, New York, Lundberg listed 63 golf courses, 24 boat and yacht clubs, 7 polo clubs, 6 symphonic orchestral groups, and 54 "modest" movie theaters. The community public facilities included 10 bathing beaches, 2 airports, 130 tennis courts, 27 libraries, a county-operated amusement park, "Playland," and 17,273 acres of parks.[1] One out of every five owned a car, but many commuted to work and to satisfy other pursuits in New York City.

Despite the imposing list of facilities, less than half of the county's population belonged to a club or any other form of voluntary association. Lundberg attributed this to the fact that four-fifths of the gainfully employed had annual incomes below $3,500. Since club membership as well as leisure-time activities required money, those with incomes below this amount could not afford to belong or expend their earnings for other than absolute necessities. The fact that the study was made during the last depression showed the tendencies of many "joiners" to drop associational and recreational memberships when faced with reduced incomes. The author pointed out that many of these activities symbolized the competitive striving for status which many persons in modern life exhibit through joining, or trying to join, the "right" organizations. Membership was not as important as the impression the "joiners" made upon others with whom they came into contact.[2] He concluded that organization is a prerequisite

[1] Lundberg, *et al., op. cit.,* 53–85.
[2] *Ibid.,* 90.

for the satisfactory utilization of leisure, and many activities must be supported by a large membership.

Urbanites and suburbanites all face the loss of a portion of their actual leisure-time because of the distances they must travel between the place of work and the home. In determining the standard allowance for leisure in an industrialized civilization, an estimated 85 days was the annual maximum.[1]

The average daily reading time of the Westchesterians was 57 minutes. Women—with more leisure-time than the men—read more, visited, and did club work. When not working, the men showed tendencies toward active sports, golf, hunting, and fishing. Many patronized commercial entertainments or listened to the radio.

Komarovsky's study. Another study worth noting is that of Komarovsky, which attempted to determine the patterns of participation in organized group activities for 2,223 adults of New York City.[2] Focusing on such factors as social class, education, income, nativity, sex, occupation, and religion, the degree of organized group affiliations was correlated. Komarovsky's basic assumption is that the average urbanite has generally become divorced from his primary, neighborhood, and community groups. The city-dweller is regarded as living with one group, playing with a second, praying with a third, and working with a fourth. More affiliations may group him with a fifth or sixth connected with political or associational interests.

Questionnaires were mailed to respondents in various occupational groups. Some worked with the Metropolitan Life Insurance Company, Macy's Department Store, two hospitals, several factories, and business organizations. Teachers, nurses, physicians, engineers, business executives, sales personnel of both sexes, semi-skilled and skilled workers, and others were reached. Their incomes ranged from $2,000 to $15,000 per year. The sample also included unskilled workers whose annual income was between $1,000 to $3,000. Each of the groups selected included married and unmarried persons, and members of the Protestant, Catholic, and Jewish faiths. The educational attainment varied from elementary school through doctoral degrees.

The extent of voluntary associational participation was shown for the various economic and occupation groups as follows:

1. Of the unskilled workers (dishwashers, laundry workers, packers, etc.), 32 per cent belonged, as against 68 who had no other affiliation save the church.

[1] *Ibid.*

[2] Mirra Komarovsky, "The Voluntary Associations of Urban Dwellers," *American Sociological Review*, 11 (Dec., 1946), 686–698.

2. Of the semi-skilled and skilled workers (printers, clothing workers, drivers for milk distributing companies, etc.), 44 per cent belonged. One group's returns showed a high degree of organization; many members were foreign-born males, employees of a clothing concern, who frequently belonged to a Landsmanshaften, a fraternal order for mutual-aid, in addition to union membership.
3. Of the white-collar workers, 47 per cent joined voluntary associations.
4. Of the business men's group, 67 per cent of those earning below $3,000 annually had one or more affiliations. When earning above this annual income, the affiliations rose accordingly.
5. Of the professionals, 68 per cent of those earning below $3,000 annually had one or more affiliations, but when the income exceeded this, 84 per cent showed greater participation in voluntary associations. The latter group was the most highly organized.

When the sample was broken down to determine the pattern of organizational affiliations for the two sexes, the males were more highly organized and joined more groups than the opposite sex. In the lower economic classes, organized group life is largely carried on by the males, while in the upper classes the activities are more evenly divided between the sexes. For example, only 9 per cent of the unskilled female workers had organized group affiliations, as contrasted to 25 for the skilled, 37 for the white-collared, 44 for the business woman, 61 for the nurses, 71 for the professional earning under $3,000 yearly, and 88 for those earning between $3,000–$5,000. When the annual income exceeded $5,000, 100 per cent partook in organized group affiliations.

Komarvosky further compared her findings with the study made of Westchester County (in which she assisted), which showed that the typical wife of the man earning less than $5,000 yearly had joined two voluntary associations. The husband, however, had membership in one more voluntary association than she had. If the annual income exceeded $10,000, each spouse held three associational memberships. These findings disclosed that segments of our population are cut off from channels of power, information, growth, and a sense of participation in purposive social action because of financial status. Groups that have the greatest need to be included are those who can least afford to support voluntary associational activities. Social relations are thus circumscribed for those earning below $3,000 a year. The only exceptions are the professionals who join organizations because of social expectations and the need to have their proficiency recognized. A significant conclusion reached is that not all urbanites are "joiners."

Working-class families. Since most of the studies on membership in voluntary associations are concentrated upon the middle and upper classes, what groups do the working-class families join? Dotson's study of 50 lower-income families of New Haven showed that researchers had overlooked the instances of informal social participation within the family and kin groups in cities.[1] These activities are not borne out by associational records, since the entertainment is done privately, and such data can only be obtained through interviews. He discovered that three-fifths of the men and four-fifths of the women and children did not have formal associational membership. Even if they joined organizations, their attendance was erratic, and their most active participation was in athletic and church groups.

Dotson found that two-fifths of the husbands and wives interviewed had no intimate friends outside of their own families and relatives, and much of their social life revolved around their various kin groups. Some were very active in clique groups formed before or after marriage, and the friendships continued for many years. The frequent pastime was visiting each other's homes and playing cards. However, the author warns that these findings may not be substantiated by a sample of single persons or for families living in a city younger than New Haven. New Haven's sample was unique in the respect that the persons interviewed had lived many years there, and that married couples had adult sisters, brothers, other relations and childhood friends in the same city. On the other hand, a South Dakota town study showed that friendship contacts among the lower socio-economic groups are apt to be confined to a narrower area. Twenty-seven per cent of this group exchanged visits with friends outside of their immediate neighborhood while 90 per cent of the higher socio-economic group did.[2]

Too Much Leisure?

As all the foregoing has shown, the modern urbanite has an unprecedented array of opportunities for utilizing an unprecedented amount of leisure time. Yet an apparently paradoxical statement is more and more frequently heard, "I can't think of a thing to do." Part of this problem is undoubtedly related to the actual cost of leisure-time activities. On the other hand, it appears that for many the very diversity of possible activity makes a choice difficult. For them, too many things to do becomes the equivalent of nothing to do. Also, the new thrill, which many urbanites must have at all costs, becomes harder and harder to attain. So, in the midst of plenty, comes the ever greater threat of boredom. Just as leisure as a

---

[1] Floyd Dotson, "Patterns of Voluntary Association Among Urban Working-Class Families," *American Sociological Review*, 16 (Oct., 1951), 687–693.

[2] Bendix and Lipset, *op. cit.*, 258.

distinctive phase of human existence is largely a product of urbanism, so boredom has become a major problem of the modern urbanite.

Much of this is attributable to the passive character of so many modern activities which emphasize spectatorship rather than participation. Alarmists bemoan the death of creativity in urban life. They say that leisure time is spent in vicarious enjoyment of the work of others. Yet, the picture is not wholly black. One can also point to the growth of "do-it-yourself" activities, the rise of amateur music and art, sports, and other more creative or self-expressive leisure-time activities. But these are largely characteristic only of segments of the urban population.

One of the major urban educational problems has become education for the use of leisure, for boredom is perhaps one of the most disintegrative of all urban social characteristics. It seems that boredom and the unwise use of leisure-time has accompanied the rise of juvenile delinquency of the 8–18-year-olds in our cities since 1948.

In spite of all the possibilities for leisure-time activity, many urbanites find leisure a problem rather than a means of recreation. One of the major urban problems, therefore, has come to be one of learning how to utilize leisure time. With the prospects of even greater leisure with a shorter workday and workweek—when and if new sources of energy, such as atomic power, are adopted—there may need to be even greater emphasis as to how to use constructively the extra leisure time.

Summary

City-dwellers enjoy a definite block of leisure-time because of the modernization of industry, shorter working hours, and the rising standard of living.

Significant trends in leisure-time pursuits are traceable to the turn of this century. The increase in spectator's sports, where huge audiences participate simultaneously, is notable. The growth of commercial and spectator sports has resulted in the increase of a body of personnel who work to entertain the public. Some of the highest paid salaries in the country are earned by star performers, promoters, public relations staff, and special writers and editors in the entertainment world. The impact of entertainers upon the society is upon the (1) segmentation and overemphasis of given values at the expense of a total range, (2) initiation of fads and fashions, (3) modes of life and manners, and (4) ideational mobility.

Quasi-commercial activities have paralleled the growth of voluntary associations and organizations which promote projects requiring the support of (1) their membership, (2) the public, and (3) sponsors. These reinforce the status of the participants and sponsors, whereas the spectator sports influence others to strive for social and occupational mobility. The profits derived from the projects are spent through the ordinary commercial channels for the purchase of goods and services needed by institutional organizations or social groups. The upper-class members sponsor many "causes" to counteract the common conception that they live useless and wasteful lives.

Private forms of recreations have declined with the growth of commercial recreation, but their persistence and extent is not accurately known because of the absence of recorded data. The formation of cliques and informal visiting of friends and relatives applies to all social classes, but these two activities are more frequently the major forms of recreation among families of lower economic status. Both Lundberg and Komarovsky's studies showed a relationship between income, occupation, and the degree of formal, organized group affiliations.

Municipal public recreation and amusement have become extensive since the playground movement began half a century ago. Municipal projects vary according to size of city and interest of officials. Cities may have playgrounds, picnic grounds, camping sites, community centers, parks, or other special facilities.

Illegal games have reached tremendous proportions insofar as the number of regular participants and the money they spend are concerned. These games of chance are difficult to suppress because many of them are used to promote "worthy causes." Millions of dollars are spent annually to protect gambling establishments, while large sums are used to employ lobbyists, lawyers, and public relations personnel, all with the aim of providing urbanites with opportunities to win "easy money."

One of the problems growing out of increased leisure is how to use it without direction and how to overcome boredom. Despite the wide choice of leisure-time activities, many urbanites lack the education for the use of their moments of leisure.

DISCUSSION QUESTIONS

1. What evidence do we have that recreation and entertainment are big business?
2. Enlarge upon the list of types of occupations in the entertainment world.
3. What urban conditions influenced the growth of the various types of leisure-time activities?
4. What quasi-commercial activities are prominently publicized in your city?
5. Discuss the positive social effects of the movies.
6. Discuss the negative social effects of the movies.
7. What type of private activities are available for those who do not engage in the commercialized forms of entertainment?

8. What types of public recreational facilities are promoted by your municipality?
9. In the future, will more or less leisure be available?
10. Discuss the growth of illegal forms of recreation.

SUGGESTED PROJECTS

1. Compare the use of leisure-time of your grandparents' and parents' generations and that of your own.
2. Study the popular forms of commerical recreation and determine the socioeconomic status of the participants.
3. Write a paper on the findings of the Kefauver investigations.
4. Study the effect of the movies upon young children's behavior.
5. Study the interrelationship of fads and fashions and the entertainment industry.
6. Study the growth of public recreation for cities.
7. Trace the development of recreation and organizations for older people.

READINGS

The Annals of the American Academy of Political and Social Sciences, "Gambling," 269, May, 1950.

Herbert Blumer, *Movies and Conduct.* Chicago: University of Chicago Press, 1933.

A study of adolescents movie-going habits and the influence of the cinema on behavior patterns.

G. A. Lundberg, *et al., Leisure: A Suburban Study.* New York: Columbia University Press, 1934.

A study of Westchester County's residents' leisure-time participation.

H. D. Mayer and C. K. Brightbill, *Community Recreation.* New York: D. C. Heath & Co., 1948.

The growth of the community recreation movement.

Martin H. and Esther S. Neumeyer, *Leisure and Recreation.* New York: A. S. Barnes & Co., 1949.

The theory and development of leisure; includes various forms of recreation found throughout the world.

Hortense Powdermaker, *Hollywood: The Dream Factory.* New York: Little, Brown & Co., 1950.

An anthropologist looks at Hollywood and its impact on young adults.

Chapter Twenty

Urban Personality and Social Types

T HE CENTRAL emphasis in this chapter is on the special aspects of the total range of behavior patterns exhibited by urbanites after being subjected to the urban environment. Given the fact that more and more persons are growing up or living in cities, the effects of urbanization on personal behavior can be isolated and contrasted with the effects upon rural persons.

As urbanization increased, the socialization process changed, resulting in modified behavior patterns. At the same time, social contacts differ in content, if not in form, so that a greater degree of impersonalness, social distance, and anonymity has resulted. The premium on time has reduced face-to-face contacts, while the division of labor and social class differences often separate persons working within a given organization and living in the same community or city. The reduction of social contacts and ideational mobility have increased the feelings of insecurity of many urbanites.

Some of the personality traits found in urbanites are directly related to the division of labor and the degree to which persons in a given occupation strive to live up to the social expectations contained in the work situation. Many successful professional and business people carry these behavior patterns into their families and social life. Persons are cultivated because of their "connections" or a vacation spot is selected where "shop talk" can be had with others sharing similar interests.

Large cities are known for the variety of social types, or persons with distinct life organizations, who reflect the varying behavior patterns identified with diverse socio-economic, racial, and ethnic backgrounds. Social types are distinguishable from the members of their own group and the people in the general population. "Skid Row" types as well as upper- and middle-class types are the products of the urban environment.

Students of sociology, and to some extent the public at large, are aware

453

of the social effects of cultural impact upon an individual's personality formation. His personality, from the sociological viewpoint, is the result of cultural experiences which define and routinize his activities.[1] Attitudes, ideas, beliefs, customs, and all the components of social behavior are transmitted through social interaction. The individual learns, internalizes, and integrates these behavior patterns into his life organization. The socialization process is continuous and dynamic, and modification of behavior patterns is constant.

While there may be disagreements among various disciplines as to which factors are most important in forming personality patterns (biological basis or original nature; individual differences in social experience; psychogenic traits; or cultural conditioning), all agree that personality is a complex phenomenon. All agree that many component elements interact and constitute what is known as personality, and that they are influenced by group interaction. Personality then is the sum total of an individual's physical, social, and psychological traits, integrated and unified into a working whole.[2]

Certain behavior patterns are sufficiently prevalent to be regarded as directly attributed to and resulting from the impact of urbanization. The term "urban impress" as here used is an aspect of the general phase of cultural conditioning. The end process is more readily observable when the personality traits of urban and rural persons are compared. The urban impress affects the social and psychological make-up, the reaction patterns, and the life scheme of urbanites and influences the social relations between individuals and groups. Common traits associated with urban impress include anonymity, social distance, ideational mobility, feelings of insecurity, and speed.

Anonymity. The very nature of city life, with its heterogeneous mixture of people of all social classes, races, creeds, occupations, and ethnic origins, contributes to the sense of anonymity. Anonymity is the loss of identity in a city teeming with millions. Many urbanites live in a social void, or vacuum, in which institutional norms are not effective in controlling or regulating their social behavior. Although they are aware of the existence of many institutional organizations and many people around them, they do not feel a sense of belongingness to any one group or community. Socially, they are poor in the midst of plenty.

---

[1] Burgess and Locke, *op. cit.,* Chs. 7 and 8.

[2] Department of Sociology, *Methods of Personality Study: A Symposium,* University of Chicago, 1946, "Introduction" by Dr. E. W. Burgess: "Biology deals with constitutional aspects of personality; psychology with individual differences; psychiatry with psychogenic characteristics and processes; cultural anthropology with personality as the subjective aspect of culture; and sociology with the socially defined attributes of personality, such as status and role."

Anonymity is furthered by the fact that different interests separate one person from the next, and even those having daily contacts with members of a group do not know them intimately. Seldom seen in all social situations, only the segment of the total personality is known. An excellent illustration of the concept of anonymity is the case of the trusted community leader who is suddenly arrested for the misappropriation of funds. His reputation as a good father and provider, church-goer and trustee of the church, and respected employer had never before been sullied. This man had successfully hidden his "double life" from his family, and the exposure was as surprising to them as to the general community. Living a dual existence is easier in cities, where family origin, social background, and group affiliations are imperfectly known.

Anonymity is at the same time a cause as well as an effect of personal behavior. Many urbanites seek to remain anonymous, while others want to be more intimate and sociable with others. Persons possessing divergent schemes of life seek to remain anonymous, but when their desires and aspirations are blocked they have difficulty in finding some intimate friend to whom they can unburden their anxieties and frustrations. The higher rate of suicides in cities has been attributed to the fact that some urbanites experiencing disillusion and disappointment are faced with the knowledge that "no one cares." Other factors contributing to higher suicide rates in cities are the impersonality of urbanites, weakening of institutional controls, and financial setbacks.[1]

Moreover, many social activities in cities are conducted on a large scale, thus reducing the opportunities for intimate, continuous social contacts. However, many urbanites join activities without wishing to be involved in more than the specific purpose at hand.

Extreme cases of anonymity are the "forgotten men and women" found in vice and rooming house areas and the "Skid Rows" of cities. The true identities of these residents are often obscure or unknown. Having withdrawn from active participation in the normal social system, they represent only a collection of inhabitants with various and obscure socio-economic, racial, religious, ideological, and educational backgrounds. For the most part they live outside the pale of regulated monogamous living, and they do not necessarily join organizations or uphold prevailing norms. Said Cohen in her study of three rooming-house sections of Los Angeles and of Hollywood, California:[2]

[1] Ruth S. Cavan, *Suicide* (Chicago: University of Chicago Press, 1928), 81, shows that rates vary from one section of the city to the next, with the highest rates in areas of transition. For a thorough discussion of suicide in various societies, see E. Durkheim, *Suicide, op. cit.*

[2] Lillian Cohen, "Los Angeles Rooming-house Kaleidoscope," *American Sociological Review*, 16 (June, 1951), 316–326. Reprinted by permission.

These human fringes highlight the special character of modern society; the anonymity and impersonality of urban living, and its resultant egocentricity and personal disorganization; the efficiency of our competitive economic system and the poverty of its human by-products.

The collection of individuals in her study resided in the rooming-house areas in downtown Los Angeles and Hollywood. The latter had actors, writers, immoral women, self-sacrificing parents, waiters, chefs, bartenders, clerical workers, and professionals. Many of the service workers regarded their occupations as temporary stepping stones to professional careers. Many of them were reaching for goals and values they believed the movie industry offered but blamed "imponderable environmental obstacles" for their failures. In addition, there were many others who had grown old and disillusioned in their attempts to surmount these obstacles, but whose mental conceptions of themselves revolved around being big actors, writers, or directors. A great many dreamed of becoming successful once more. These are the "casts-offs" in viciously competitive Hollywood, clinging tenaciously to their goals and values and waiting for the "break" when all will be well.

The rooming-house areas of American cities are mainly in the areas of transition, close to central business districts. Within these areas are the other extremes of behavior patterns and socio-economic status, attributes of the "Gold Coasters." [1] These people live in the highest rent areas of the city but are socially distant to the inhabitants of nearby slums.

Social distance. City people live physically close, but are socially distant. [2] Social distance is directly related to anonymity as well as the fact that social interaction is often based on specific interests, rather than geographical location. Social distance is equated with impersonality and contributes to the development of stereotyping and categorical conclusions about social situations, individuals, and groups. Prejudicial and discriminatory actions may follow. A kind of social cleavage divides persons and groups because of the absence of an interacting medium drawing persons together. The apartment dweller is a good case in point. He lives at the same address with perhaps hundreds of neighbors, but he has rarely, if ever, spent time with them. Urbanites are nigh-dwellers, not neighbors.

Social distance functions as an artificial social barrier. When prolonged, groups develop antipathies toward other groups without factual reasons. The cleavage existing between social classes, races, and occupational groups calls for many coordinating agencies to work for and maintain harmony

[1] H. W. Zorbaugh, *The Gold Coast and the Slum* (Chicago: University of Chicago Press, 1929).

[2] R. E. Park, "The Concept of Social Distance," *Sociology and Social Research*, 8 (May–June, 1924), 339–344.

between them. In truth, one half of the urban population does not know how the other half lives. If this much were known in a metropolis, social distance would be consideraly reduced.

Social distance is considerably heightened by the multiplication of mechanized contacts found in cities. The telephone, telegraph, radio, newspaper, and typewriter have made it possible to "keep people at a distance" and contact them when some utilitarian transaction arises. People become the means to an end, and those persons who can assist in the accomplishment of specific aims are temporarily sought and cultivated. Once these aims are achieved, some time may elapse before contacts are resumed; in some cases they are never resumed. Therefore, the forms of social interaction are present, but the content (sentiment, loyalty, and reciprocity) of social contacts is superficial and fleeting.[1] At times, even family members are treated in this manner. A casual invitation to "get together" or "hope we see each other very soon" is not taken at face value unless a specific time and place are set.

Ideational mobility. The increase in mechanized and secondary contacts give rise to ideational mobility. Ideational mobility is the extent and degree to which a person, family, or group is influenced by current trends in thought and values.[2] Modern media of communication, radio, movies, and newspapers, play a large part in stimulating ideational mobility. This means that the larger world, with its extensive range of attitudes, ideas, and values, has invaded personal life and thought, and lifted a man, women, or child outside of his local area and culture. As the world becomes ever-larger and ever-changing, new schemes of behavior may be learned which are not sanctioned by the family, school, and church.

Ideational mobility brings about observable changes in personal behavior. The individualization of interests, secularization of ideas and values, sophistication, and disregard for customary social controls are more probable. A marked increase in individuality has followed, and persons seek contact with others who will accept their schemes of life. Moreover, children may live in one world and parents in another. Educators do not always understand the students who come under their guidance. Church leaders are said to be "backward," while the business men accuse the labor groups of being disinterested in management problems, or vice versa. Ideational mobility affects imagery, sensitivity, and impulse, so that each group may not understand the other's wishes and motives. In turn, this heightens social distance.

---

[1] Georg Simmel, "The Metropolis and Mental Life," in *The Sociology of Georg Simmel,* trans. by Kurt H. Wolff (Glencoe, Ill.: The Free Press, 1950).
[2] Burgess and Locke, *op. cit.,* 492–495.

Residential mobility may cause ideational mobility, for a different social environment often requires a change in habit patterns. As more and more persons move from one neighborhood to the next, or from one city, county, or state to another, the increase in ideational mobility follows. These persons are being subjected to more intense physical, social, and mental stimuli, while at the same time they attempt to meet the problems of adjustment in a new environment.

Insecurity. Feelings of insecurity in cities stem largely from the fleeting nature of social contacts and the dependency upon many others for various needs. These feelings range from vague anxieties to deep-seated fears encountered in general and specific situations. Older persons experience financial and emotional insecurities when non-productive. Productive young adults may not find the right type of work after years of preparation. Or they may have difficulty in finding a satisfying social life because work and play activities take place within two separate spheres. Others may feel a sense of personal unworthiness because their accomplishments seem to lack glamor and importance. These manifestations of insecurity could be elaborated upon. The greater incidence of personality distortions and emotional problems in cities substantiate the presence of greater feelings of insecurity and their resulting effects.

Some authorities claim that these feelings of insecurity can be detected in young children living in cities, and various studies have been conducted to test this proposition. In studying the personality adjustment between farm, small town, and city children, Mangus found that farm and small town children had a higher level of personal and social adjustment than the latter.[1] Big-city children were less self-reliant, had a smaller sense of personal worth, and had feelings of non-belongingness to others. They had greater withdrawal tendencies and more symptoms of anxiety. Their social skills were less developed, thus causing them to be poorly adjusted in school and community relations.

Stott's and the White House Conference's studies concluded the opposite: city children were better adjusted, more independent, and more resourceful. They concluded that city children showed more independence when making decisions regarding personal problems and resolving difficulties. They were more rational in their thinking (*i.e.,* free from irrational and emotionalized associations), and had more social training in the development of leadership. Moreover, these two studies showed that the general level of family relationships was higher in urban areas. Parents had more time to devote to the children and this directly contributed to the general higher degree of personality adjustment of urban children. It

[1] A. R. Mangus, "Personality Adjustment of Rural and Urban Children," *American Sociological Review,* 13 (Oct., 1948), 566–575.

should be noted that the conclusions between the Mangus' and these two studies vary because the criteria selected for measurement are not exactly comparable.

However, these studies do show that a stable home and community life are conducive to better emotional adjustment. The family's and community's efforts to provide a consistent set of informal and formal controls based upon a general agreement on morality and values had a great influence. Parents and community leaders who understood the nature of city life, with its divergent social and moral codes, heterogeneous population, range of secondary contacts, and the greater degree of physical and social stimuli, helped to reduce some of the feelings of insecurity experienced by city children.

Speed. Perhaps the most common trait found in all urbanites is haste. As an outgrowth of greater efficiency and large-scale operations, transactions are geared toward punctuality and precision. Time has become equated with money lost or gained, so that city people are bound to be pushed by demands on their time.[1] Urbanites speed from one place to another; a minute's delay may make them miss the bus, street car, or train. They are "docked" on payday if they come late to work. Even when engaging in leisure-time activities, their eyes are on the clock. Meetings are held according to a prescribed agenda that fits a set number of minutes, else the membership fidgets and becomes bored. Busy managers sandwich in meetings or discussions with their noontime meal. Many executives eat lunch at their desks, all the while giving dictation, answering or making telephone calls, or reviewing reports of sub-department heads.

Genuine relaxation is seldom possible for many urbanites. A vacation means changing the scene of operation rather than leaving work behind. Many persons fly to and from a vacation without actually seeing or enjoying the new surroundings. Departure is timed to the end of a working day or workweek. People rush to the train, airplane, or automobile to get out of the city, only to rush back in the opposite direction at the end of the "break."

Distances within cities are measured by numbers of minutes or hours, rather than in terms of miles. Cooking a meal at home is undertaken with the idea that so many minutes are required in the operation, rather than what may be the most nourishing or wholesome. Children learn to hurry at an early age: getting to school on time, being dismissed on the minute, and heading home on a vehicle that leaves precisely on the dot. They rush out to play and run home to dinner. In spite of the many time-saving gadgets and devices invented to leave more and more minutes free from some drudgery or operation, the urban day is still too short.

[1] Simmel, *op. cit.*

Personality and Division of Labor

Within every reader's experience is the ability to name some personality characteristics and attitudes belonging to doctors, lawyers, salesmen, or entertainers. At one time, the classification of personality differences was based on what society considered "good" or "bad," as possessed by the minister, teacher, housewife, or father when contrasted to those of the sinners, criminals, ne'er-do-wells, or paupers. With the increased division of labor and the constant addition of new urban occupations and professions, the arbitrary assignment of behavior patterns and social expectations contained in each type of work becomes more difficult. It is generally recognized that a particular type of work may develop personality characteristics that act as a sort of badge. In each type of work are social expectations, sanctioned by society, which channel, routinize, and define the social behavior of the workers in specific groups and social situations.[1] These expectations are acted out when performing duties and obligations in connection with the work situation. They pattern relations between individuals and groups. A worker leaving one kind of work and entering another would have to unlearn some of the old set of social expectations and adopt a new set. Correct role-playing brings status and recognition and the enjoyment of certain rights and privileges.

In a broad sense, each type of occupation has a history, and an office, or title, is given to the work performed. A teacher's title carries with it the common and collective expectations of the holder having a definite amount of formal training, the ability to deal with the problems of young charges, and the aptitude to teach the social heritage and values of the community and society. The longer an urban occupation has been in existence, the greater the expectations and the more rigid the requirements are for entrance into the field of work. This is especially true of established professions such as medicine, law, and theology. Moreover, the group belonging to a given profession has developed a body of sentiments, attitudes, ethics, and policy which any new applicant must learn, accept, and practice before becoming a "regular" or one of the group.[2]

In cities where specialization and competition interact to force concentration upon one's chosen work, as well as the pressure to become an "expert" in the field or in one subdivision of it, a worker may overplay his role. "Shop talk" is commonly heard at social gatherings. At times, the language for communicating the work interest to another worker is un-

[1] Walter Coutu, "Role-Playing vs. Role-Taking: An Appeal for Clarification," *American Sociological Review*, 16 (Apr., 1951), 180–187.
[2] E. C. Hughes, "Personality Types and the Division of Labor," *American Journal of Sociology*, 33 (Mar., 1928), 754–768.

intelligible to those who do not engage in the same type of occupation. Cities abound with specialists whose language, sentiments, and attitudes are not understood by another group.

Moreover, the premium placed upon keeping abreast with the new practices and techniques of any occupation or profession influences the cultivation of friends, pursuit of leisure-time activities, and the selection of reading matter. Membership in formal associations is expected of professionals seeking recognition in their field. Making contacts is so important that many business and professional men exploit their leisure to make contacts.[1] The pressure upon the semiskilled, skilled, and unskilled take a different form; they may join associations for collective bargaining rather than learning about changing functions or techniques.

Although one's workday is short as compared to the whole day, strict adherence to work-roles are expected of those wishing to retain their statuses. This leaves an imprint upon personality to a degree that can be detected. It is only when a new occupation or profession is in the process of "becoming" that the worker is free from a well-defined set of ethics and rigid role-playing. For example, the jokes about the psychiatrist stem largely from the fact that the medical profession thought of them as outsiders for a long time because untrained "quacks" took liberties with psychoanalytic techniques, and the trained psychiatrist could not be distinguished from the untrained. As the profession took steps to standardize training requirements, the members of the profession gained status. In the process some distinguishing characteristics (especially language) came to be attributed to psychiatrists.

Social Types

The sociologist has been interested in discovering social types in cities because this approach provides a basis for studying various kinds and groups of people found in cities. This technique gives insight into the impact of the urban environment on life organization. Studies pertaining to the social types of a given area or community in the city have been undertaken to evaluate the roles which these persons played within the locality. The findings reveal that social types developed as the result of social interaction, competition, accommodation, and selective segregation. These aspects of social behavior are commonly found in cities.[2] For example, the hobo is a social type found in a specific area of the city. He can be studied and data obtained about his life organization. His attitudes, his own and

[1] David Riesman, N. Glazer, and R. Denney, *The Lonely Crowd: A Study of the Changing American Character* (New Haven: Yale University Press, 1950), Ch. 7.

[2] H. W. Zorbaugh, "The Dweller in Furnished Rooms: An Urban Type," in E. W. Burgess, *The Urban Community, op. cit.,* 98–106.

the group's conception of his role, and the social situation which produced him have become known. No single factor is responsible for the development of this social type, but the data obtained from these studies showed that a series of interrelated events contributed to this phenomenon. A better understanding of human nature has followed, and this has made it possible to classify various other social types found within the general society.

A classification of social types is useful in two ways.[1] First, it refers to a social function which is important to the group and indicates the valuation which the group places on the persons who perform that function. Good illustrations are the "financial tycoon" and the "debutante," both typifying success and achievement to the members of their groups and performing a function that the group values. Moreover, it reveals the structure of the group and the nature of its relations with outside groups. Second, it enables persons who are designated as social types to be analyzed. They are often sensitive to the general conception of their roles, and intensive study can reveal the direction of their habits and interests, or the characteristic "run of attention." Their personal traits tend to become fixed and persist in spite of a change in environment.

For example, *The Ghetto* presents several Jewish types. One of the differences between Jews and non-Jews is, perhaps, the persistence of a set of cultural traits relating to religious rituals.[2] They are fairly uniform throughout the world wherever the members of the group have settled. If rituals are strictly observed, the participants' social, psychological, and economic activities are influenced. To understand how several Jewish types have developed, one would need to know how their religious practices pervaded their life organization.

Wirth found several Jewish types within the larger group. The "Mensch" (literally "human being") represents a type who has status but has achieved financial success without sacrificing his identity as a Jew. On the other hand, the "Allrightnick" has experienced similar attainment but has cast aside most of the cultural traits of his group. At the other extreme is the "Schlemiel," equally capable of personifying the commercial spirit, but is sometimes quite shiftless and helpless. He fails in everything he undertakes and the group has good-naturedly nicknamed him. In America, the "Luftmensch" (literally "cur man") is identified with the hobo because of his just-getting-by philosophy. Vocational types centering around the synagogue include the rabbi, the teacher, the "Chazan" (cantor) and the "Shochet" (slaughter). More types are mentioned which show that the persistence of a social type depends upon a favorable set of attitudes and

[1] Department of Sociology, The University of Chicago, *Methods of Personality Study: A Symposium, op. cit.,* 85–96.

[2] Louis Wirth, *The Ghetto* (Chicago: The University of Chicago Press, 1928), Chs. 5, 6, 12.

habits being retained by the members of the group toward a given type. For example, the "Yeshiba Bochar" (Talmudical student) and the "Melammed" (rabbinical teacher) exist as types only if a community prizes them. The members of the community support them financially and accord them admiration and status.

Another sociological study of note is *The Hobo*.[1] Five types are found in the area of homeless men: the "seasonal worker," the "hobo," "tramp," "homeguard," and "bum." The essential difference between them is that the "seasonal worker" is one who likes adventure, goes far away to a job, returns to the city, and spends all that he has saved. The "hobo" travels and works occasionally and his hang-out is the jungles and railroad yards of cities. The "tramp" wanders but does not work at all; he lives off of others by begging. The "homeguard" works occasionally but does not wander away from the city. He will take day-by-day employment but never a steady job. The "bum" does not work or wander.

Strong's study of the social types of a Negro community is good illustration of the way the data can be used.[2] By describing such types as the "striver," the "race man," the "Uncle Tom," "mammy," etc., we know something about the character of Negro-white relations. By knowing the "run of attention" of the "race man" (who may be the leader of the community) we understand the ambivalent attitudes he has toward both groups. In short, the methods used have been important as another approach to the study of the city and in enabling one to describe empirically different social types.

Social class status is reflected in social types. The "debutante," the "playboy," the "wealthy philanthropist," the "board member," "society matron," and the "dowager" are upper-class types. The "club woman," "promoter," "news reporter," "realtor," "high-power executive," "salesgirl," "waitress," "precinct captain," and "political boss" show the range of types within the middle-class. Deviants of the underworld society are known by the titles of "gangster," "gun-moll," "fixer," "gambler," "runner," and so on. The pimp and the prostitute have a "run of attention" that sets them apart. Large cities have more types than small centers. Extremes within the types are definitely big-city phenomena.

A final question should be raised. What tangible evidence is there that an industrialized and urbanized society like ours has produced specific changes in life organization? That is, can the processes relating to these changes be empirically and descriptively verified? What conclusions can be drawn when earlier generations of Americans are compared with the

[1] Nels Anderson, *The Hobo, the Sociology of the Homeless Man* (Chicago: University of Chicago Press, 1923), 87–95.

[2] Samuel M. Strong, "Social Types in the Negro Community in Chicago," unpublished Ph.D. dissertation, University of Chicago Libraries, 1940,

present, especially in large cities? Riesman has suggested the hypothesis that three prevailing social types have evolved because of changes in population and technology. They are the (1) tradition-directed, (2) inner-directed, and (3) other-directed.[1] His main area of concentration is upon the changing social character as distinguished from the total personality. Social character is composed of the patterned uniformities of learned responses that distinguish men of different regions, eras, and groups. The processes which produced these changes are related to and brought about by two correlates, population and technology. Resultant variations are revealed by comparing ancient and modern societies, when traced to the socializing process related to inculcating conformity.

The tradition-directed person is best illustrated by the immigrant from Europe or Mexico. He is a product of a clearly defined social order wherein the individual's conformity patterns are dictated to a very large degree by power relations among the various age and sex groups. Age-old institutional controls regulate behavior according to accepted norms, and the individual learns to adapt to the society through standard social situations rather than upon being inventive or individualistic. Such a society has a high-growth potential in population, with the natural rate of increase (the balance between birth and death rates) fluctuating within narrow limits. India, China, Egypt, and parts of Central and South America are good illustrations. Industrialization is relatively absent and the population-land-food ratio is precarious. To mitigate the social effects of individual disorganization caused by famines, diseases, or floods, a stable and unchanging social structure, together with a strong web of values, offers stability to those faced with social disorganization.

The inner-directed type of person is the product of a transitional phase of population growth, appearing midway between the tradition-directed and a highly urbanized, or outer-directed, society. Such a social order emerged in the Western world during the Renaissance and Reformation eras, when scientific and medical advances changed the character of population growth. Better methods of agriculture and greater industrialization followed. A new social organization developed, promoting exploration, colonization, and imperialism. More opportunities were available for personal mobility, and adventurous persons were encouraged to exploit and settle new lands. Changes in the social environment caused a weakening of traditional controls. Moreover, persons who settled outside the homeland were confronted with more choices in patterns of living as well as needing to adjust to new social relations. Gradually, the members of the society managed to live socially without strict adherence to tradition-direction.

Traditional conformities were replaced by inner-directed controls. These

[1] Riesman *et al., op. cit.,* Ch. 1.

controls were implanted in infancy by elders and were aimed toward a wide choice of goals, such as money, possessions, power, knowledge, fame, and so on. With the increased choice of alternatives offered by a changing social order, the inner-directed person strove to reconcile his own personal goals with those wanted by the society. His efforts were constantly directed toward maintaining the "right" way of living, working, playing, and child-rearing. The Puritan is one outstanding example of this personality type.

The other-directed person hardly thinks of himself as an individual; he lives in an era during which the world has shrunk in size. His own society has become highly centralized and bureaucraticized. Population has declined to the point where material wants and leisure are abundant. Indeed, a surplus of goods and services is great enough to be "wasted." A large portion of the population—the old, young, and some of the better-off economically—can be supported by the productive persons in the various "service industries."

Urbanization, according to Riesman, has contributed to the increase of other-directed types, especially among the younger members of the urban middle class of large cities. Their social character is greatly influenced by mass media. Moreover, their contemporaries, rather than elders or traditions, are the source of direction for social behavior. Their behavior patterns are shaped by their peers, who may be personal acquaintances, or by the glamorized personalities heard and seen through mass media. Although these patterns are internalized early in life, the other-directed types still depend upon external guidance throughout their lives. This reliance upon other-direction brings about an exceptional sensitivity to the actions and wishes of others. Therefore, the other-directed social type may not have any deep feelings of belongingness to any specific locality.

Summary

Specific behavior patterns are formed in urbanites as a result of the urban environment. These patterns interact with personality formation. Among the more prevalent attitudinal and social traits exhibited by urbanites are anonymity, social distance, ideational mobility, feelings of insecurity, and speed.

Division of labor and constant addition of new urban occupations and professions has caused the strict playing of roles according to social expectations. Only when a new type of work is in the process of becoming established can the worker be free from the traditions, code of ethics, and regulations governing his conduct. Specialization and competition have caused many workers to carry their work-roles outside of the work situation, influencing their leisure-time and social contacts. Strict role-playing affects personality traits but can lead to greater status, rights, and privileges.

Social types furnish data for the study of various kinds and groups of people in cities. A classification of social types according to specific areas or socio-economic groups was devised and has made it possible to evaluate the social roles within a given area, community, or group. Moreover, the nature of the group's relations with other groups became known. The series of interrelated events which produced a social type were revealed.

Riesman's three major social types, related to changes in population and technology, correspond to the social structure of the society. The tradition-directed types belong to a society where age-old institutional controls regulate behavior according to accepted norms. The inner-directed types developed after the social order changed as a result of exploration and colonization. Inner-controls replaced traditional controls as more persons in the society were offered a wide range of socially accepted goals, and these goals became the direction motivating personal conformity. The outer-directed types are found among the urban middle class of large cities, and their behavior patterns are learned from peer groups or personalities seen or heard over mass media.

DISCUSSION QUESTIONS

1. Show how urban impress affects the social and psychological makeup of urbanites.
2. Discuss some examples of anonymity from your experience.
3. How may social distance lead to stereotyping?
4. Discuss the relationship between ideational mobility and insecurity.
5. Will the atomic age affect the swift tempo of urban living?
6. How do social expectations influence the personality of a ward politician? Of a nurse? Of a minister?
7. Name some other social types found in cities according to the various zones. Do the same with Riesman's hypothesis.

SUGGESTED PROJECTS

1. Study the social types discussed in the literature on immigrants.
2. Select one sub-cultural group or race and learn how the social types provide clues to the nature of human relations.
3. Select for study one well-established profession and try to reach some conclusions concerning the role of the professional man in modern society.
4. Do the same as three but select a social deviate.
5. Study the genesis, development, and transmission of social expectations.
6. Study the contributions made by the classification of social types as another approach to the study of the city.

READINGS

Paul G. Cressey, *The Taxi-Dance Hall.* Chicago: The University of Chicago Press, 1932.

A study of personalities of taxi-dancers and the patrons of taxi-dance halls.

M. Donovan, *The Saleslady.* Chicago: The University of Chicago Press, 1939.

The life organization of a worker in the "new middle class."

W. I. Thomas and F. Znaniecki, *The Polish Peasant in Europe and America.* New York: Alfred A. Knopf, 1918–20, 1927. See Vol. 2.

An intensive study of immigrant types.

David Riesman, Nathan Glazer, and Revel Denney, *The Lonely Crowd: A Study of Changing American Character.* New Haven: Yale University Press, 1950.

Traces the changes in American character as affected by population and technology, thus affecting social character. Three major social types are revealed.

Georg Simmel, "The Metropolis and Mental Life," in *The Sociology of Georg Simmel,* translated by Kurt H. Wolff. Glencoe, Ill.: The Free Press, 1950.

A description of the utilitarian nature of the metropolis as it affects social contacts.

University of Chicago, Department of Sociology, *Methods of Personality Study: A Symposium.* Chicago: University of Chicago Press, 1946.

Part Six

Urban Social Problems

PROLOGUE   *The chapters in this section are selected to illustrate the prevalence of certain types of social and personal disorganization and their interrelationship to social problems. We are all familiar with such problems as congestion, crime, housing, unemployment, divorce, juvenile delinquency, and so on. These are mainly urban problems resulting from the process of a society changing from the rural to urban way of life. Our concern is with not only the appearance and increase of these urban problems but the effect these have upon the individual and the society.*

It is necessary to recognize that all societies are constantly changing and that change brings dislocation within, and at times a disintegration of, social systems. This dislocation of social systems in turn affects the customary behavior patterns, values, attitudes, beliefs, and mores of the members of the society because social systems are primarily a cause *of social behavior as well as a* result *of interwoven patterns of social relationships. The simplest illustration is the family, the smallest social system, the breakdown of which has often resulted in personal disorganization. Therefore, it is often possible to trace personal disorganization to social disorganization. Personal disorganization results from the disruption of group consensus and the weakening of social norms and values which normally control personal or group behavior patterns. In a sense, personal disorganization symbolizes the inadequacy of traditional behavior patterns to meet new social demands. This inadequacy represents a failure of the socialization process.*

Symptoms resulting from the breakdown in social and personal organization are called social problems. Crime, divorce, and other types of problems are the end results of the disorganization process and, if sufficiently widespread, may cause further social and personal disorganization. Hence, the members of the society who are concerned with the consequences of the disorganizing process devise ways and means of solving and preventing these problems. In the final analysis, social problems are socially defined and reflect the attempt of society to bring divergent behavior in line with socially approved norms.

Social disorganization may be viewed from several approaches. Among the most well known is the "cultural lag" theory which sees a disproportionate rate of social change taking place between the material and nonmaterial parts of culture. This "lag" between the fast (material) and slow-moving (nonmaterial) parts of the culture causes social disorganization and the greater the gap between these two parts, the greater the rate of social disorganization. Personal disorganization and the manifestations of social problems which follow social disorganization are identified as having some causal relationship to the "lag." Moreover, a series of interrelated factors may be identified as contributing to the disorganizing process.

Another approach sees social disorganization and its attendant consequences, social problems, as stemming from four main sources. Primary are those that are related to some unfavorable aspect of the physical environment, such as natural barriers, geological formations, floods, droughts, and pests. The next set arises from defects in the composition of the population: unfavorable tendencies in the rate of growth, distorted geographical distribution, high mortality rates, unbalanced sex ratio, and so on. The third source is faulty and disruptive social arrangements, pertaining to the failure in social organization, social control, or intergroup relations. Stated in another way these problems relate to faulty social systems, and include institutional crises, race tensions and conflicts, and juvenile delinquency. The last set follows the clash between various classes or subgroups within the society over divergent ideals or social values, generally in conflict with those held by the majority group or those upheld by the prevailing social system.

When social problems appear they are discerned and so defined by the perception of many groups within the society. The social situation giving rise to social problems is recognized as needing redefinition or the social system concerned needs reorganization. A social problem has the following elements: (1) a situation capable of measurement, (2) a value believed to be threatened, and (3) a realization that the situation and the values may be reconciled by group action.[1]

The following chapters deal with urban phenomena of interstitial or blighted areas, housing problems, and personal and social disorganization. Blighted areas arising from urban expansion are found in varying degrees in different parts of the city. Housing problems are caused by a series of interrelated factors, of which land-use patterns, delinquent taxation, faulty titles, and mobility of population are but a few. Personal and social disorganization may have definite ecological patterns in American cities. Where possible, a comparison of these problems with those of other cities is made.

[1] Francis E. Merrill, "The Study of Social Problems," *American Sociological Review*, 13 (June, 1948), 251.

Limited space forbids including all the social problems found in urban societies, although there is general recognition that urbanization and industrialization have brought about an increasing number of such problems. Throughout the preceding chapters mention was made of those that fit the context, as gambling, graft, unbalanced sex ratio, inefficient municipal administration, and institutional crises.

Chapter Twenty-one

Interstitial or Blighted Areas

T HE GROWTH and development of interstitial areas, more commonly known as disorganized, slum, or blighted areas, was once accepted as a natural outcome of urban expansion. These problems have not been considered "inevitable" since the turn of this century, following the disclosure by journalists, social workers, and civic-minded leaders that conditions found in the tenement sections of New York, Chicago, and other metropolises were affecting the health, social relations, and behavior patterns of the residents as well as others living outside of the areas.

Their rise and persistence is recognized as being related to many complex factors, changing land values, slum landlordism, population dispersion, industrial decentralization, invasion and succession, and others. At the same time, there is greater awareness of the different types of interstitial areas, the functions they perform for certain groups in the society, and the social effects upon individuals and society.

The phenomenon of blighted areas has had compelling interest to students and researchers alike. The use of the terms "interstitial," "blight," and "slum" has largely resulted from the process of cross-perception at work among various members of the society and the concerted efforts made to cope with the interrelated factors causing their emergence and continuance.

Interstice is a geographical term used to indicate any abrupt break, crevice, or change in the topography of the land surface brought about by erosions, floods, earthquakes, sinking of land surface, or other geological formations. Few cities are built on so perfect a site that no evidence of geological distortions are evident. Cities have been built on the sides of mountains, on top of mountain passes, in deep valleys, and near swamps, deserts, plateaus, or rivers. Within the city's confines may be natural barriers: lakes, rivers, hills, gullies, and depressions. The founders of cities selected areas for settlement that best lent themselves to easy control and development, while satisfying the greatest number of timely advantages for population and institutional organizations. As cities expanded and population increased, the less favorable sites were utilized.

The city's layout took into account the natural terrain, while the population was distributed and buildings arranged to circumvent the natural geographical distortions. Interstitial areas were avoided because they showed a tendency to magnetize the "discards" of nature and man: leaves, branches, trees, roots, rocks, sand, and other forms of organic and inorganic wastes. In time, persons selected these areas for settlement, and frequently their habit patterns were in contrast to those of the prevailing inhabitants. Interstitial areas came to have both physical and social characteristics setting them apart; as, for example, thieves'-hideouts on the sandy banks of the river. The term came to mean a "geographical and social interstitial area in the city, pertaining to spaces that intervene between one thing and another. There are also fissures and breaks in the structure of the social organization." [1]

As the symptoms of community disintegration and personal disorganization became associated with particular urban sections, the term "disorganized areas" came into use when referring to slums, vice areas, ganglands, road-house belts, and, often, ghettos. The latter has the characteristics of deteriorating neighborhoods, shifting populations, and distorted sex ratios. But frequently it is cohesive and integrated, as, for example, the areas of immigrant settlement or communities inhabited by Mongoloid members. Disorganized areas and slums came to be used interchangeably; but the latter refers more to a greater-than-usual degree of deteriorated surroundings, implying a lower socio-economic status of its inhabitants. In the correct use of the term, "disorganized areas" contain inhabitants whose behavior patterns and value systems are distinguishable from those of the general population, although a high degree of physical deterioration may be present.

As civic leaders sought to re-establish social equilibrium in these areas, they recognized that deteriorated environment plus the breakdown of social organization can affect adjacent areas. The term "blighted area" came into use, suggesting that this type of area has some of the characteristics of a disease, and the unaffected part of the city may in time become infected.[2] However, as a disease it can be cured or prevented. The symptoms of personal disorganization can be reduced if not entirely eliminated. And as the members of the society attempted to isolate the various factors

---

[1] F. M. Thrasher, *The Gang: A Study of 1313 Gangs in Chicago* (Chicago: University of Chicago Press, 1927), passim; and Karlin, *op. cit.,* 170–171.

[2] Los Angeles, California City Planning Commission, *Blight: The Problem, The Remedy,* 1948, 1.

associated with slum areas, the older term, "interstitial," gave way to "blighted area." In African cities, slums are the Native areas and locations created by segregation practices.

Characteristics of Blighted Areas

The phenomenon of blight is manifested by a wide variety of conditions, *i.e.,* physical, environmental, economic, and social factors. It is not necessarily confined to residential and densely populated areas; it may be present in commercial, industrial, and even in undeveloped vacant areas. The physical and environmental characteristics include the following, either alone or in combination: [1]

1) Poorly constructed or designed buildings.
2) Inadequate ventilation, light, and sanitation.
3) Insufficient open spaces and recreational facilities.
4) High density of population.
5) Overcrowding of dwelling units.
6) Obsolescence and disrepair of structures.
7) Faulty subdivision design of the land, usually evidenced by an inadequate street pattern, lack of open spaces and essential utilities, and danger of water submersion.
8) All other factors which cause the structure to be unfit or unsafe to occupy for residential, commercial, industrial, or other purposes. The existence of them is conducive to ill health, transmission of disease, infant mortality, delinquency, and crime.

These social factors are present either singly or in combination:

1) Breakdown of community organization.
2) Ineffective formal and informal controls which educational, religious, penal, governmental, familial, and recreational institutions attempt to establish and maintain.
3) Absence of voluntary associations for the informal control of the inhabitants according to age, sex, occupation, race, ethnicity, or other common interests. More far reaching is the lack of the will and desire to organize spontaneous groups.
4) The extension of controls from outside the area as a means toward effecting community consciousness and cohesion. These well-meaning attempts are generally spotty and often failures because the inhabitants do not always understand and appreciate the motivations of nonresidents.

[1] *Ibid.*

5) High indexes of personal disorganization: juvenile delinquency, prostitution, illegitimacy, crime, suicide, tuberculosis, venereal disease,
desertions, broken homes, alcoholism, etc.

Miscellaneous factors may include the following:

1) No over-all land-use policy.
2) Real estate speculation.
3) Unclear land titles or delinquent parcels of land and buildings.
4) Invasion and succession.
5) Changing land values.
6) Faulty lay-out of transportation arteries.
7) Restrictive covenants or other agreements.

From the sociological point of view, the social and ecological factors are
as significant as the resulting social problems that follow the disintegration
of community and institutional controls. Restrictive agreements and invasion and succession affect intergroup relations, which, in turn, may cause
more disorganization and further social problems.

The cost of blight. It is difficult to impress the problems of blighted areas
on the average citizen unless he is given concrete facts upon which to base
action. Such studies may have two approaches, one related to the monetary
cost and the other to social cost. Numerous studies have been made showing the cost of blight in terms of higher taxation as well as the increasing
rates of personal disorganization. Both types are useful in combating
blight.

The Federal Works Agency made a study of blighted areas in various
cities throughout the nation, disclosing some significant facts. Slum and
blighted districts comprised about 20 per cent of all the metropolitan residential areas, and they accounted for 33 per cent of the total population.
In addition, 45 per cent of the major crimes, 55 per cent of the juvenile
delinquency, and 50 per cent of all arrests made by the police were recorded in these areas. The greatest incidence of tuberculosis and disease
occurred there, or 60 and 50 per cent respectively. Fire hazards were greater
than in other parts of the city, for 35 per cent of all fires resulted from
blighted conditions.[1]

The report further revealed that only 6 per cent of the real property
revenues were obtained from the blighted areas. Nevertheless, a large portion of the cities' revenues were invested in attempting to stem the spread
and perpetuation of blighted conditions. The cost of redevelopment and
efforts to reduce disease and other problems was heavily subsidized by
other more productive areas. About 45 per cent of the cost of city services

[1] *Ibid.,* 1.

Poor housing means poor chances for children
A comparison of 4 slum areas and 4 good areas in Chicago shows these conditions:

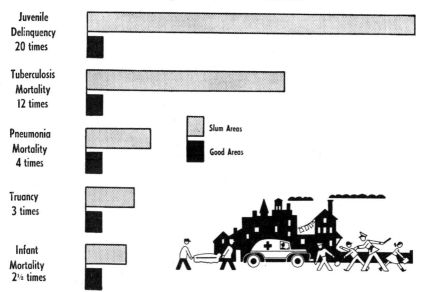

The social cost of poor housing is 2 to 20 times higher in slum areas, depending upon the index used.[1]

went to these areas, which means that the rest of the city received a disproportionately smaller share.

Los Angeles study. The Los Angeles City Planning Commission undertook a comparative study of a blighted area in Boyle Heights and an unblighted one in the West Adams District.[2] Whereas the annual per capita real property tax revenue derived from the former was $4.25, that of the West Adams District was $11.30. Fire, police, health, and recreational service cost $7.00 per capita as against $3.67. An estimated annual subsidization of almost $300,000 was made to the Boyle Heights area alone, an amount woefully inadequate in terms of the real needs. Were there no budgetary limitations, the amount expended should have been five-fold.

Los Angeles had more than 20 square miles of blighted residential areas located near the center of the city, affecting a total population of 375,000. Moreover, certain sections of the San Fernando Valley and the far western part of the city had scattered blighted districts. By contrast, it has less than

[1] *Children and Youth at the Midcentury—A Chart Book,* prepared by the Midcentury White House Conference on Children and Youth (Raleigh, N. C.: Health Publications Institute, Inc., 1951).

[2] *Ibid.,* 4.

older cities. Chicago, the second largest city in this country and the fourth largest in the world, has 15,000 acres of blighted and near-blighted territory.[1] A conservative estimate placed the annual loss in taxes at 15 million dollars on property valuations totaling 500 million. The greatest stretch of deterioration is near the heart of the city.

It should be noted that tax loss is not directly related to the inhabitants of the blighted areas, for few are property owners. Slum landlordism, mentioned earlier, operates in a vicious circle.[2] Landlords maintain social distance with the inhabitants of blighted areas but may be active in slum-clearance programs (at the same time that they are delinquent in tax payments), upholding the high rentals charged slum-dwellers. They may permit the property to deteriorate during a period of changing land values and population shifts, with a view toward finding a buyer who will absorb the taxes owed to the city. Or the property is permitted to deteriorate to force a revaluation, and repairs are neglected during the reassessment. The consequence of such practices may result in increased fire hazards, congestion, and higher incidence of tuberculosis, illness, and death.

Major Types

Several types of blighted areas exist in American cities, depending upon the size, population composition, and the length of time the city has been established, and on the rate of peripheral expansion. A study of the major types will reveal their location, the essential characteristics of each, and the factors contributing to their perpetuation.

Slums. By far the most common type of interstitial area is the slum, located near or in the Zone in Transition and between the borderline of the business and residential districts. The area was once residential. The encroachment of businesses or light-manufacturing houses from the center of the city initiated the flight of former residents. Those who could not afford the more desirable locations remained and mixed with the in-migrants possessing lower incomes. The physical deterioration of the area is the main characteristic that sets it apart.

Slums may be found elsewhere within the city and need not be concentrated in the Zone in Transition. They appear where a break from one type of land use to another is in process. If a residential district is being transformed into an industrial one, slum conditions exist until one dominant type of activity takes over. Moreover, they develop wherever major transportation routes cut through the city from the center to the periphery.

[1] The Metropolitan Housing Council, "Reclaiming Chicago's Blighted Areas."

[2] National Committee on Segregation in the Nation's Capital, "Segregation in Washington," Chs. 5 and 6.

Large cities with heavy transportation arteries radiating outward from the downtown district produce blight when the main thoroughfares become centers of population aggregation. The tendency is for overuse of land on the streets nearest to the transportation system. Major intersections and nuclei become blighted. Elevated and surface transit lines attract establishments to service travelers and commuters, thereby making the section unfit for purely residential sites. Both residents and small businesses compete for space. Railroad tracks cause a similar phenomenon. Laid when the city was in its infancy, no provisions were made to take care of future land-use needs. Wherever the tracks cut through commercial or residential areas, blight follows. "Hobo jungles" and ganglands are often found there.

Unplanned population growth and urban expansion are responsible for more slums. Areas which should be reserved for industries are not zoned. When in need of larger land areas and forced to relocate, industries may utilize vacant sites adjacent to choice residential areas. Their nearness causes residents to move, and the process of deterioration repeats itself.

Lastly, the rectangular gridiron layout of city streets, having no centers, gardens, or other points of interest, produces confusion in land use and land values.[1] The layout becomes impractical when population and facilities increase, since there are no horizontal or vertical limits at which either should stop. Older European cities were built around centers, *e.g.,* a cathedral, public garden, or civic building. Streets leading to them were built according to the cul-de-sac or circular pattern, thus constricting the unimaginative clustering of people and buildings. Archaic street designing contributed to the growth of many interstitial areas.

In the United States there was no dearth of land when cities were growing. Wastefulness was condoned and many deserted pockets of unused land resulted, causing the scattered settlement of people and facilities. The Zone in Transition shows the highest number of slums because the tendency was to build up the land closest to the site of historical origin. As the city expanded outward at a time when land was not at a premium, the need to redevelop deteriorated sections was not paramount. "Eating out the heart of cities" became a repeated process until city officials and merchants realized the loss of income through taxation and purchases. They also became concerned with the rising incidence of personal and social maladjustments that affected the city as a whole.

Immigrant colonies. The constant influx of migrants into the city has kept alive the ghettos of some large cities. Mainly located in the section adjacent to the downtown business center, they are easily accessible to newcomers. Subjected to wave after wave of invasion and succession, the en-

[1] Patrick Geddes, *Cities in Evolution* (New York: Oxford University Press, 1950), 170–171.

vironment has acquired a delapidated appearance. A mixture of residences, industries, and businesses may be found there. Some ghettos do not exhibit community disorganization but mainly physical deterioration.

Roadhouse belts. The urban fringe which defines the legal limit of the city has a ragged, uneven appearance and a clustering of dissimilar activities. Interspersed among farm lands are undeveloped subdivisions, scattered estates and detached homes, gas stations, and stalls for the sale of farm products, pottery, gardening equipment, antiques, and handwoven rugs. Cemeteries and pockets of wasteland may break the landscape. In sharp contrast are clusters of cocktail bars, dancing pavilions, amusement centers, golf links, motels, tourist camps, and gambling establishments. Because of mixed land use as well as few community controls, the area has many characteristics of the blighted area.[1] The term rurban (rural-urban condensed) suggests that the area is not strictly farm land and yet has many urban characteristics.

Although the rurban fringe is relatively accessible to the center of the city, it does not have the economic requirements of a community—an adequate tax base, nor reasonable fire protection, health, and sanitation. This area is seldom included in over-all city planning or redevelopment, so that it remains blighted and marginal. When urbanites move outward, they often resettle in rural-nonfarm areas rather than at the city limits. This is another reason for the rurban fringe being neglected in city-wide planning.

With the building of highways and the extensive use of automobiles and interurban transportation, roadhouse belts have appeared both at major intersections and secluded spots, catering to a segment of the pleasure hunting crowd. Patrons seeking novel entertainment, good food, and various forms of illicit or legitimate amusements find the roadhouse belt a source of satisfaction. Far removed from the centers of population, these establishments are relatively free from law-enforcement agencies and other public supervision. Thus, ample opportunities are present for conducting the type of enterprises which attract patrons from a wide area. Calumet City, Illinois, is close enough to the Indiana-Illinois state lines to sport a "Rialto" District. Stickney, an independent minor civil division wedged between two sections of Chicago's western city limits, operates honky-tonks, taxi-dance halls, cocktail lounges, casinos, and floor shows on a night-to-morning basis. Steubenville, Ohio, thrives because of a Pennsylvania "blue law." Some establishments are "fronts" for prostitution and gangster activities. Personalities of the underworld mix with regular patrons, who are mainly from the better residential areas of the city.

Respectable patrons are attracted to roadhouse belts because there they

[1] Walter Firey, "Ecological Considerations in Planning for Rurban Fringes," *American Sociological Review*, 11 (Aug., 1946), 411–421.

are temporarily freed from the watchful eyes of their social group. They may behave as their impulses dictate. Anonymity is assured while they have a "good time." The salient point about the existence of roadhouses and vice areas is that they can survive only if supported by a satisfied and recurrent clientele. "Closings," when they occur, are usually temporary because of the "protection" accorded them by law enforcement officials in return for monetary considerations.

Vice areas. Vice areas illustrate the coexistence of respectable and non-respectable activities in the social milieu. These districts are accessible to many who seek deviant social outlets. The presence of vice, *i.e.,* commercialized prostitution, is most marked in areas of highest residential mobility, rapid population changes, and a disproportionate sex ratio. The absence of normal home life for many is a contributing factor.

Suppression of prostitution has driven this form of vice undercover, so that the old-time red-light districts are not always exhibited as a segregated grouping of houses. However, various shops or hotels may act as "fronts" for the promotion of the trade, and "call girls" or "pick ups" go there frequently to make contacts. Persons residing outside the area are as apt to perpetuate vice as the residents within it. Prostitution, too, is frequently a source of "added income" to public officials, and a sum is paid to them for "protection." Other factors contribute to the persistence of vice areas, of course. There is little community life and no organized efforts are exerted to expose or close resorts catering to prostitution. Economic factors play their share. Owners of the buildings used for this purpose are interested not in the tenants but in high rents. It is generally known that houses of prostitution pay higher-than-average rentals as a form of protection and guarantee of non-interference by owners. In some instances, owners belong to high-income brackets and live in the better residential sections of the city. Since agents or realtors handle the financial details, the absentee owners need not be concerned with the morals of the tenants.[1]

Vice areas attract persons whose social behavior deviates from the prevailing members of the society. The professional criminals, or near-criminals, may be found there. Drug addicts and alcoholics gravitate toward these districts. In brief, the indexes used to determine the distribution of vice throughout the city include one or more of the following: burlesque shows, rescue missions, crime, narcotics, alcoholism and other major social problems, disproportion of sexes, and absence of community organization.

"Skid Row." Areas of homeless men, or "skid rows," develop in every large city to accommodate hobos, tramps, bums, and homeless males and females. Frequently demoralized and possessing different schemes of life, they find refuge among their own kind and those who make up the under-

[1] R. E. L. Faris, *Social Disorganization* (New York: The Ronald Press Co., 1948), Ch. 7.

world. The prostitute, dope addict, alcoholic, dice girl, panhandler, pimp, thief, gangster, or jack-roller may be among their friends. Characteristic of the area are cheap lodging houses, rescue missions, "slave market" employment agencies, pawnshops, second-hand clothing shops, and flophouses. The "hobohemia" boasts a "bright-light district" of burlesque shows, strip-tease joints, cocktail bars, and liquor stores. Barber "colleges" operated and often owned by women barbers are not uncommon fronts for houses of prostitution.[1]

Cities located where transportation breaks attract migrants and homeless persons. Chicago is said to have a steady population of 30,000 in the "Skid Row" district skirting the business district. Many are seasonal laborers. Others pride themselves on "getting by" through jack-rolling, gambling, taking day work, or "scrubbing" for their meals. Their large aggregation makes it possible to support goods and services desired by the group, *i.e.,* meals, lodging, social service, employment bureaus, entertainment, second hand shops, and gambling. Kansas City, Omaha, Denver, St. Louis, New York, and other metropolises, where transportation arteries converge, become the temporary "home" of wanderers in search of work. According to Anderson, the problem of migrants is as modern as technological change.[2]

Remedial Measures

Slum clearance is one of the remedial measures adopted for the correction and prevention of some of the social disorganization and social problems associated with blighted areas. However, remedial measures are ineffective without ordinances, which must be enforced after their enactment. Moreover, ordinances do not function effectively unless there is community awareness of what is being remedied and how. It has become evident to many urbanites seeking to remove all slums that the very nature of urban expansion and the constant shifts of population as well as the general clearance and rebuilding of deteriorated property built many decades ago presents many problems to clear and rebuild every slum. The entire city cannot be rebuilt, nor can the taxpayers bear the burden of continuous slum clearance and rebuilding programs. Furthermore, there is also a serious question as to whether the city's problems would be solved by more and more such programs and if all the incidences of personal disorganization would thus disappear.[3] From the preceding paragraphs we

[1] Nels Anderson, *op. cit.*

[2] Nels Anderson, *Men on the Move,* Chicago: University of Chicago Press, 1940, Pt. 2.

[3] J. P. Dean, "The Myths of Housing Reform," *American Sociological Review,* 14 (Apr., 1949), 281–288.

State of New York, Division of Housing, Martha Holmes, photographer

Leisure-time activities before slum clearance.

State of New York, Division of Housing, Martha Holmes, photographer

Supervised constructive activities in the same areas after redevelopment.

learn that some well-to-do citizens may contribute to slum conditions, just as they may support and be supported by the income from the services offered by vice areas.

Therefore, a practical, in-between type of remedial measure has been adopted in many cities to preserve "middle-age areas" as well as rehabitate slum areas by block conservation. Slum clearance and redevelopment is a slow and expensive method, and one of the greatest criticisms against it is that in the interim many persons are displaced from homes, although sad and delapidated, and may be in a worse plight than ever. An immediate program to reduce on a wide scale the glaring health, fire, and safety hazards found in slum areas was devised by Baltimore, Maryland.[1]

The Baltimore Plan. The Baltimore Plan combines conservation with concerted action. The plan proceeded on the rightful assumption that every city has ordinances relating to health, fire, and building requirements that are not being met in slum districts. Violation of such ordinances constituted a criminal offense.

Baltimore officials undertook a block-by-block enforcement drive to compel the slum landlords to comply with minimum housing standards. Furthermore, the tenants were required to do their share by obeying health and sanitary laws. This dual attack was necessary because landlords of delapidated houses often claim that tenants, not owners, create slum conditions. After a year and a half of slow but steady effort, Block Number One testified to the fact that remarkable results could be achieved. Blocks of houses now surround a paved and sunny courtyard where children play on swings and other equipment donated by a civic organization. This area was once a pile of debris and garbage. Every dwelling is rid of rats, windowless rooms, bad stairs and flooring, cracking walls, and fallen ceilings. Each unit was repaired to comply with the minimum health and safety standards.

The cost to Baltimore was slight: a salaried inspection staff and occasionally the necessary court action.

The main expenses incurred by the transformation were borne by the property owners. Increased rentals now repay them for the alterations because tenants are willing to pay extra rent for improved quarters.

Before the plan could be put into effect, a city-wide educational program was jointly waged by many civic and municipal bodies. The municipal "family"—the health, police, and building departments—instructed their inspectors to list and enforce illegal conditions found in the 62 houses located on Block One. Court action faced landlords and tenants alike if existing defects went uncorrected within a specified time. The first notices

---

[1] J. E. Nordskog, E. C. McDonagh, and M. J. Vincent, *Analyzing Social Problems* (New York: Dryden Press, 1950), 652–657.

were almost totally disregarded. By degrees, the landlords and tenants discovered that these notices were not passing fancies. Many paid heavy fines.

To cope with evasions, delays in hearings, "influence," and other obstacles, a Housing Court was created in 1947. This agency speeded hearings. A separate magistrate, familiar with housing, health, and fire violations, presided. Sixteen policemen were delegated to become a special housing-sanitation squad. Within eighteen months some 2,300 cases were satisfactorily disposed of. Many cases can now be taken care of by the special squad without court hearings, for the landlords and tenants have learned to heed their warnings and make restitution. More gratifying than this is the fact that many landlords and tenants cooperated in rehabilitating conditions before the inspectors arrived.

The educational program waged along with slum clearance has taught the Baltimoreans that taxpayers, as a group, underwrote the investment of property owners in slum areas. Forty per cent of their large city budget had gone toward the support of the central district alone, which occupied but 10 per cent of the city's total land surface. Property assessments and tax collections dropped as conditions worsened. Each year taxpayers expended 14 million dollars more than was collected for protective and other services.

Summary

The genesis, development, and prolonged manifestation of interstitial areas illustrates the process of social disorganization and the resultant social effects connected with a social problem. The term "interstitial area" has undergone several changes in meanings owing to the recognition of the multiple factors causing their growth. Through concerted action, social reorganization through remedial measures is undertaken by various groups whose cross-perception defined disorganized, slum, or blighted areas as a social problem. Their basic attempts center around preventing the "blight" to encroach on adjacent areas and to reduce fire, health, and safety hazards.

The major types of interstitial areas include slums, immigrant and racial colonies, roadhouse belts, vice areas, and "skid rows." They may be located where major routes of transportation converge or traverse, at the urban fringe, in the Zones in Transition, near vacant lands, and even small areas within the better residential sections. Major factors causing their growth include: changing land values and land use, invasion and succession, the magnetizing of persons who have a life scheme and conduct divergent from the prevailing social norm, disproportionate sex ratio, breakdown in community and institutional controls, public demand for "escape diversions," and public indifference. The social effects vary from personal and social disorganization to severe drainage of public funds for protective services and subsidization.

The Baltimore Plan is an illustration of conservation rather than slum clearance and redevelopment, undertaken by the joint sponsorship of civic and municipal agencies.

DISCUSSION QUESTIONS

1. Explain the different characteristics of each type of interstitial or blighted area.
2. What are the major factors causing their growth?
3. To what extent are they the result of landlord indifference?
4. Why were slum areas not declared social problems when they first developed?
5. Explain how these areas are related to the process of urban expansion.
6. Why is concerted action needed to eliminate or redevelop these areas?
7. Distinguish between the long-time and immediate plans for slum clearance, according to the Baltimore Plan.

SUGGESTED PROJECTS

1. Compare the Baltimore Plan with the redevelopment projects undertaken for your city and indicate the different results.
2. Study the legislation enacted by your state for slum clearance and redevelopment and relate this to the municipal ordinances of your city.
3. Compare the Gold Coast and slum according to first-hand observation and analysis or from a library study.
4. Study the leading redevelopment programs and compare them with those that combine conservation with redevelopment.
5. Study the history of the area of your city known to have the highest rate of social disorganization.
6. List all the interstitial areas for your city and study the factors leading to their existence.

READINGS

Mabel A. Elliott and Francis E. Merrill, *Social Disorganization*. New York: Harper & Bros., 1941.

A comprehensive treatment of the nature of social organization and disorganization included in Part One.

Robert E. L. Faris, *Social Disorganization*. New York: Ronald Press, 1948.

A sociological text dealing with personal and social disorganization.

J. E. Nordskog, E. C. McDonagh, and M. J. Vincent, *Analyzing Social Problems*. New York: Dryden Press, 1950.

A collection of readings on various kinds of social problems.

A. M. and E. B. Lee, *Social Problems in America*. New York: Henry Holt & Co., Inc., 1949.

A book dealing with the social problems mainly found in urban America.

Robert A. Walker, *The Planning Function in Urban Government*. Chicago: University of Chicago Press, 1950.

The transition from voluntary citizenship planning to urban planning as a municipal function. A comprehensive statement of the findings of the Urbanism Committee of the National Resources Committee as to the steps needed to abolish slums.

Harvey Zorbaugh, *The Gold Coast and the Slum*. Chicago: University of Chicago Press, 1929.

A graphic comparison of two adjacent areas in Chicago, as to life schemes and conduct.

Chapter Twenty-two

Housing Problems

Housing is a primary requirement for healthful living and as a base of operation for many human activities. Shelter and food are matters of great concern to many urbanites who do not have ancestral homes and farm lands to meet these needs but must depend upon their availability in a competitive market. There is no food shortage in this country, but a housing shortage has existed since World War I, when cities experienced an influx of defense workers and civilians following servicemen from one camp to another. From the first few chapters of this text we learned that housing problems are found in other cities of the world and are not unique in our society.

Although the displacement of population in this country during the First World War was not as great as during World War II, the shortage of houses and the general deterioration of older units became recognized as an added problem. Cities organized housing committees to cope with the shortage, but these were generally powerless to correct the situation. Many were volunteer committees with no legislative authority, and many disbanded as soon as the First War ended. However, it can safely be said that war, a type of social disorganization affecting the masses, highlighted a need which perhaps would have been permitted to be neglected for a time if many cities had not simultaneously been faced with solving the problem, even if temporarily.

Until the depression of the thirties very little effort was made to build public housing; it was the belief of many citizens that private industry could erect sufficient units at a cost which the average person can afford. Between World War I and the introduction of public housing, more units had become uninhabitable while more people moved to cities. Moreover, the public at large realized that housing costs had risen to the point where a large segment of the lower socio-economic groups could not hope to save sufficiently to become home-owners. The available units were ab-

A view of the Wald Area, a section of the New York slums, before redevelopment began.

The same area today.

sorbed by the higher-income brackets. Thus, another type of social disorganization, depression, brought our housing problems into greater focus
and revealed the series of interrelated factors contributing to housing.
Since that time the country at large has become "housing minded" as the
Second World War furthered the trend, and although both public and
private housing projects have been initiated, the problems of adequate
and good housing have not been entirely removed.

We shall examine the following related topics and see what factors have
contributed to the housing problem. A consideration of the housing characteristics in 1950 will give us some indication of the concrete steps taken
since World War I and their relationship to various regions of the country.

Housing Characteristics of the United States

The country's midcentury housing census showed that of the 48,750,000
dwelling units, 86 per cent were in urban and rural-nonfarm areas. When
these units were proportioned according to urban, rural-nonfarm, and rural
areas, the percentages were 64, 22, and 14, respectively.[1] In other words, the
percentage of population and housing in each type of area was about equal.
It would seem then that the ratio of population and dwelling units were
matched. When taken for the nation as a whole, this would seem the case.
When these statistics are analyzed on a standard metropolitan area or
regional basis, the ratio is not as equal.

Out of a total of 168 standard metropolitan areas, 57 were selected for
intensive study.[2] In 1947 the census bureau estimated that 2.4 million
families were living with other primary units and that 10 per cent of all
married couples in the metropolitan areas shared their living quarters or
lived with others. The shortage was heaviest in areas attracting the largest
influx of new migrants: San Francisco–Oakland; Washington, D. C.; Los
Angeles; Portland; San Antonio; and Norfolk–Portsmouth–Newport
News.[3] The 1950 census showed that 57 metropolitan areas contained
about 43 per cent of all the dwelling units and that new units had
not kept abreast with population growth. The percentage increase of
households ranged from 34 to 61 per cent and, in general, the dwelling
units had shrunk in size, with the smallest median number of rooms in the
South and West.

Furthermore, in 42 of the 57 metropolitan areas, there were more owners

[1] Bureau of the Census, "Housing Characteristics of the United States," Ser. HC-5, No. 1
(Feb. 17, 1951).

[2] Bureau of the Census, "Summary of Housing Characteristics for Selected Standard Metropolitan Areas, April 1, 1950," Ser. HC-5, No. 4 (Nov. 30, 1951), 1–2.

[3] Bureau of the Census, "Population Characteristics of Metropolitan Districts: April,
1947," Ser. P-21, No. 35 (Aug., 1947).

than renters, as compared with only 6 such areas in 1940. At the same time, the median size of the household varied from 2.5 to 3.4 persons, with households containing 2 or 3 persons most numerous. There was less crowding on a per room basis because the percentage of 1-person occupants of dwelling units rose from 6 to as high as 16 per cent in some areas. However, this made for fewer dwelling units for larger households, which increased from 5 per cent in some areas to 15 in others. Indirectly this resulted in overcrowding in many units.

When housing was studied on a regional basis, the northeast, north central, southern, and western regions showed 16, 18, 27, and 41 per cent respective increases.[1] The northeast had one-third of the nation's urban population in 1950, a gain of 25.5 per cent between the two decades, but had a 16 per cent increase of dwelling units. The south had about half of the northeastern urban total and exceeded the latter by 11 per cent in new units. It should be noted that more multi-dwelling units were added in the regions of higher urban concentrations than in the areas showing greater urbanization since the Second World War, the west and south.

It was concluded that although the total number of dwelling units had risen by 23 per cent between 1940 and 1950, a higher proportion resulted from the conversion of single-dwellings into two or more units than through new construction. Some non-residential structures had been converted into residential use. A very significant trend is thus revealed. There were more owner-occupied units by 1950, this being the greatest shift since 1890. Home ownership, especially in rural-nonfarm areas rose 54 per cent between decades, with many owners living in their own homes and in many instances renting out some of the premises. Others invested in rental property to a greater extent than in 1940.

Renters, however, paid higher rent for smaller quarters than a decade ago. This was owing to the relatively few available premises, since only 1.6 per cent of all dwelling units were vacant, offered for rent or sale, or available for occupancy. On the whole, urbanites enjoyed improved sanitary facilities by 1950. Despite this improvement, 7 million homes lacked running water, of which half were in cities.[2]

Major Factors Affecting Housing

To gain a comprehensive view of the housing problem, the major factors affecting it will be discussed. As a multi-dimensional problem, any or all of the following may be applicable to any given locality.[3]

[1] Bureau of the Census, "Housing Characteristics by Regions, April 1, 1950," Ser. PC-7, No. 3 (Apr. 30, 1950).

[2] Bureau of the Census, Ser. HC-5, No. 1, *op.* cit.

[3] Twentieth Century Fund, American Housing, *op. cit.,* Ch. 12.

Housing Policy. One of the primary obstacles to adequate housing is the lack of an over-all policy as to (1) who should build houses (private or public agencies) and (2) the lack of a municipal policy. Those who do not favor the intervention of public or municipal agencies in the field of traditionally private enterprise regard all attempts of the former to ease housing shortages as "socializing" the industry. The realtors and the building trade prefer future owners to contract with them for their housing needs. Moreover, owning a home has been traditionally regarded as a symbol of achievement and success. Those who are "nonsuccessful," so to speak, should not have homes constructed for them.

Opponents of this latter view consider the expenditure of public funds as "paternalism." Indirectly this would encourage lazy habits and foster the widespread tendency to shift this responsibility to the resourceful and enterprising. It would be comparable, they argue, to a redistribution of wealth, with those in the lower-income brackets benefitting without due exertion. Housing construction and the sale of land should remain in the hands of private industry. Therefore, the opposition of pressure groups have been sufficient to deter the enactment of a clear-cut over-all policy.

Land-use policies. Until three decades ago, this country had not experienced a dearth of land nor felt the necessity to create land-use policies. The fact that farmland was once given free to those who homesteaded has obscured the land problem of cities. Moreover, there was at one time more unused land around cities that could be annexed. Thus, land area has shrunk in proportion to urban population; and even though there is cheap land in cities, these areas are frequently inaccessible by cheap transportation.

The practice of designating land use for specific purposes was not enforced until about the end of the First World War. Commercial, industrial, and residential structures were built wherever the owner desired, and a laissez-faire policy prevailed. This policy also applied to arteries of transportation and terminals. The tendency has been to overcrowd already crowded sections that have good transportation and conveniences, while large tracts of land remain undeveloped because their value is based on commercial rather than residential use. The inequalities of land values affect those in the lower and middle-income brackets. Land values have climbed in most cities to unprecedented heights, while the earning power of many citizens has not kept abreast with the trend.

Poor layout of cities and badly planned streets inhibit effective land use. A great many municipalities have grown without planning or control. A typical subdivision was laid out according to the gridiron plan, with streets forming blocks of approximately 600 × 250 feet.[1] This layout is wasteful

[1] *Ibid.*, 19–20.

in that considerable area is designated for front and back streets, alleys, and arteries of transportation. Lots were shaped accordingly and are now unsuited to modern automobile traffic. Many streets have become traffic hazards since the tremendous increase in trucks and automobiles. The present land-use practice is suited to an era when it was the custom for front porches to face the street. The out-house had to be some distance away from the street, and to hide this now outmoded edifice, backyards faced backyards.

Excessive subdividing has added to the land shortage. Many owners discovered that the down payment on lots was the least of the expenses. Assessments for utilities, taxes, mortgage payments, and interests have tied many parcels which cannot be sold because of faulty titles. Therefore, it is not an uncommon sight to find many vacant lots near to other structures. A survey revealed that in 57 cities, tax delinquencies on vacant lots alone were highest on all forms of real estate. Many lots were in ten-year arrears. Scattered parcels do not attract investors seeking large tracts for multi-dwellings, nor can they be used or purchased by small builders until the delinquencies are cleared.

Housing industry and practices. The housing industry itself is not geared toward the production of low-cost units. Each group participating in the total building process specializes in one type of work, and each group clings to its independent operations, usually defined in terms of union jurisdiction. The building industry can truthfully be said to be in the craft stage. Some 30,000 parts of varying size, design, and production go into the construction of an average-size home.[1] Each group exacts its price for the products supplied, so that the builder cannot always be certain of delivery, ultimate cost, and timing. Since each group engaged in construction is organized to protect its respective interests, no foreseeable reforms are seen in transforming the housing industry to suit the era of multi-dwellings, standardized equipment, and a mass housing market.

Manufacturers of building equipment often join with the building trades in preventing the adoption of new production methods, installations, and materials. It has not been uncommon for them to bar the enactment of performance codes, permitting the use of new materials as they appear on the market, as a practical substitute for outmoded specification codes. In some cities, the pressure they exert is sufficiently great to prevent the erection of prefabricated units in new subdivisions, thus keeping the cost of homes high. Rural and suburban territories have benefited from the erection of more prefabricated homes as a result.

Home financing. Many home owners do not have the required funds to

[1] R. U. Ratcliff, *Urban Land Economics* (New York: McGraw-Hill Book Co., Inc., 1949), Chs. 7 and 8.

purchase or build a home outright. Loans are obtained from investment or loan companies, banks, or private investors. In general, the prospective owner has reasonable expectation of meeting his obligations, and the usual method is to pay a fairly standard interest and a stipulated sum each month toward the repayment of the borrowed capital. However, many prospective owners have experienced difficulties in dealing with unscrupulous lenders or have lost their equity when unable to meet the terms of the contractual agreement. During the economic recession of the thirties, many mortgages remained unpaid, and foreclosures followed. Investors seldom can effect a quick resale of real property; for this reason, interest rates and payments are seldom advantageous to the buyer. The risk is borne by the borrower, whether he defaults or the investment agency goes bankrupt.

The present trend of increased taxes on real property, the major source of revenue for municipal governments, has worked a hardship on home-owners. Revaluations are seldom undertaken if property depreciates, land values change, or the municipal indebtedness is reduced. Hence, the home-owner faces additional financial problems. Owning a home becomes a burden rather than a saving in such instances. Not infrequently, taxation is raised because of financial needs of the city which have no relation to housing or land needs. For example, if the municipal treasury faces a deficit because of many delinquent tax parcels, the regular paying owners may be charged more than their share to insure replenishment. It is not uncommon for taxpayers with political influence to get their taxes reduced while honest taxpayers cannot.

Mobility. Occupational and residential mobility have directly affected the state of urban homes. In areas of high residential mobility, renters depreciate property and permit it to deteriorate without regard for the cost of repairs and loss to the owner. Overuse of property and rapid tenant turnover have caused deterioration of otherwise good real estate. Invasion and succession have added to the problem. Neighborhoods with substantial homes undergo conversions to accommodate the new occupants. Mobility and changing neighborhoods decrease home ownership, which, in turn, depreciates property. Persons having few community ties are not concerned with the upkeep of property. In addition, owners of property in areas that experience successive turnover of tenants are more interested in profit than upkeep of the property itself. They reason that persons who cannot own homes will "put up with anything." Slums and blighted conditions withdraw many otherwise inhabitable units off the housing market.

Taxation. The flight of urban residents to suburbs, satellite cities, and territories contiguous and adjacent to large cities has caused a serious problem: how to find sufficient funds to maintain and provide for all the services required by those who remain. Persons with greater ability to pay taxes may move where land values and tax assessments are lower. The large city is often required by legislation to furnish water, police, education, sanitary, and other facilities at nominal cost to outlying areas, thus causing a higher per capita cost to overburdened local taxpayers. No large city today is solvent because expenditures exceed revenues.[1]

The Census Bureau in 1949 studied the record-breaking budgets of 37 of our large cities having more than 250,000 inhabitants. It found that they spent 3 billion dollars more than the previous year. New York, the heaviest spender, had a budget outlay of more than a billion and a quarter dollars. Chicago came next, with almost 186 million. Moreover, their current operation expenditures had increased 7.2 per cent since 1948. Public safety accounted for the largest outlay of funds, followed by school expenditures. Public welfare exceeded the amounts spent for health and hospital services. Expenditures for sanitation and health took fifth and sixth place.

The gross indebtedness of these large cities was 6 billion dollars, or 200 million more than 1948. The largest municipal debts were recorded for New York, Philadelphia, Detroit, and Los Angeles. In short, real property and personal taxes, major sources of revenues, fail to keep abreast of expenditures. A rigorous search for additional tax sources continues but is unable to offset the rising cost of services required by urbanites.[2] During periods of economic recession, property tax delinquencies greatly complicate a city's financial problems. It is not uncommon for a city to go bankrupt. One direct consequence of municipal deficits is for city officials to rely more and more upon the state for cutbacks or grants-in-aid.[3] Should subsidization from the state be insufficient, cities turn to the Federal government for funds. Whichever financial course the city officials take, they do so with the awareness that more pressures and interference in local affairs from higher official bodies are inevitable. Untapped sources for raising local revenues are almost non-existent, and the debts owed by all cities reached $18,830,000,000 in 1951.[4]

Restrictive covenants. Considerable mention has been made of the problem of segregation in the chapter on human ecology. Involuntary segregation is often enforced by the use of restrictive covenants, thus intensifying the housing problem for the racial and ethnic minorities. Although the enforcement of them has been declared unconstitutional by the Supreme Court of the United States, racial minorities have difficulties in finding suitable housing. Retention and use of these covenants by real estate

---

[1] R. W. Lindholm, *Public Finance and Fiscal Policy* (New York: Pitman Publishing Corp., 1950), 413–415.

[2] A. M. Hillhouse and M. Magelssen, *Where Cities Get Their Money* (Chicago: Municipal Finance Officers Assn., 1945).

[3] See "A National Municipal Policy," *Public Management*, Jan. 1949, 2–5.

[4] *Municipal Year Book, 1952*, 3–4.

agencies or private owners are often difficult to prove. The expense involved in litigation attempting to show their enforcement is an added problem.

Restrictive covenants also work a hardship on middle-income groups. Some areas of the city are reserved for the erection of residences which exceed the amount middle-income groups can afford. An agreement exists between property-owners to uphold the type of neighborhood established according to socio-economic status.

Zoning regulations. Until after the First World War, no strict enforcement of zoning laws was undertaken by municipal authorities. Many existing ordinances are outmoded, and new ones are not being enacted with sufficient speed to suit growing cities. Areas once designated for industries may be kept as such, although residential land is more needed; or vice versa. In some cities, areas are zoned for a given type of structure, and although the neighborhood has changed, the ordinances remain unchanged. For example, in a former single-home large residential area in Chicago, an orphanage was ordered by the court to relocate during a severe housing shortage, even though the house it occupied (14 rooms and 5 bathrooms) was too large for a small modern family. This house remained untenanted for many years.

More land at cheaper prices would be available for housing if unused industrial and commercial sites could be redesignated for homes. Efforts to change the regulation require the concerted effort of a group of prospective owners or a development company. One individual finds the cost of litigation prohibitive. Moreover, zoning boards are frequently unmindful of the needs of one person, whereas group pressure spurs them to action.

Housing inspection. Most cities have too few building inspectors to report building violations, reconversions, fire hazards, and faulty constructions. Homes long overused, unhealthful to the occupants, and in serious need of major repairs are not condemned or demolished in the interest of public safety. Conservation of homes would add to the number of dwelling units, as well as reduce the cost of subsidization which is expended on combating veneral disease, tuberculosis, crime, and the protection of property.

Although most cities have inspection ordinances, inspectors are overworked and have no time to make systematic checks on buildings under their jurisdiction. More time is spent on inspecting new buildings to see if the building codes are observed. Follow-up checks are not executed. Citizens, whose duty it is to report building violations, are often indifferent.

Building codes. When cities were new, municipal building codes were drafted to specify materials to be used in the construction of buildings of various types. In the main, building codes have remained unchanged, although new materials are constantly being manufactured. The average citizen is unaware of the pressures exerted by the manufacturers and sellers of certain materials to have their products used in lieu of others that may cost less.

In order to modernize building codes to suit new production methods, specification codes should be substituted.[1] Permission should be granted to builders to use newer and less expensive materials if they are found after proper demonstration to be as effective as older types. Liberalizing building codes would permit the installation of more standardized and efficient fixtures in new buildings. A good illustration is the prohibition of prefabricated homes within city limits because of existing codes and the pressures exerted by housing contractors and labor unions. However, prefabricated homes are permitted in rural-nonfarm areas, and there has been a 6 per cent increase of them since 1951.

Real estate speculation. No one can travel through urban areas undergoing development, or about to be developed, without failing to be impressed by the frequency of premature subdivisions and nebulous communities being promoted by real estate and home building agencies. In many instances street improvements, sidewalks, and other conveniences are often missing; street names on posts may be the only evidence of a future community. A shed with the agency's name in large letters on a big sign is certain to be seen. Or a model house and a great number of widely separated homes may be there. The fact that the proposed new community did not materialize may be owing to overspeculation and the failure of lot owners to finance home building.

This practice of overspeculation on real estate exists in all the cities of the nation. A study of this situation by a national agency resulted in the proposal that cities adopt measures to restrict misuse of land within their boundaries in order to accommodate the increase of urban population. The agency also proposed that the city oversee or regulate the examination of title, the sale and transfer of real estate, and the financing of new construction. Moreover, the city should revert to the housing market delinquent parcels of land or real estate which have been deeded to it (or the county, if this agency has this responsibility). These measures would reduce real estate speculation and return many delinquent parcels into income-producing units.

Community facilities. Many communities fail to provide adequate facilities to stimulate the erection of future homes. Many fail to provide sufficient facilities to insure retention of settled residents. The decentralization

---

[1] Urbanism Committee, National Resources Committee, *Urban Planning and Land Policies* (Washington, D. C.: Government Printing Office, 1939), Vol. 2, Pt. 3.

trend in many cities is directly related to the inadequacy of schools, playgrounds, parks, fire prevention, and parking facilities. The flight of residents to outlying areas has contributed to the decline of once well-preserved neighborhoods. And, many home-owners have moved because of other environmental nuisances, such as smoke, soot, noise, and cluttered streets.

Middle-income needs. Since the depression of the thirties, housing projects have been built for the low-income groups by Federal, state, or municipal funds. Although the number of units constructed are inadequate for all who need better homes, the practice of building public housing for the low-income segment of the population is no longer as rigidly opposed as it once was. The upper-income brackets have no housing problem to speak of. The middle-income groups, consisting of the white-collar and professionals whose incomes range between $4,000 to $6,000 a year, are faced with a shortage of housing. Neither public nor private projects have been built to accommodate this large group of renters, which at one time constituted a larger proportion of home-owners of the country. They are often unable to afford homes erected by private builders because of the rising cost of living and uncertain tax assessments and upkeep. Moreover, they may earn too much to be eligible for public housing projects. Moving to the suburbs has provided a solution for those who have saved enough to make the required down payment. Many families in this income bracket, however, are unable to find reasonably priced homes because builders have not concentrated on their needs.

The increase of cooperative apartments has been a partial answer to middle-income needs. Many, however, can afford neither the initial capital outlay nor the regular monthly assessments, which in some instances are higher than rent. A solution might be for some agency or corporation to build them homes or cooperative apartments and retire the outlay of capital in the form of rent.

Solutions

Several solutions have been made to cope with the housing problem in our cities. Thirty states now have legislation enabling slum clearance and urban redevelopment. Both types of statutes are essential if cities are to benefit from the Housing Act of 1949.[1] Briefly, this act authorized the erection of 810,000 public housing units for a six-year period terminating in 1955. Moreover, it provided for a billion dollars in loans and $500 million in grants for urban redevelopment. Before any project is permitted, com-

[1] See *The American City*, Aug., 1949, and Sept., 1949 issues.

munity studies and planning must be undertaken and submitted for approval. Several cities have taken advantage of it.

Other Federal efforts include public housing projects built under the Works Project Administration. The Federal Housing Administration, its successor, established a system of insuring home mortgages. The Home Loan Bank system buys mortgages from building and loan organizations, insuring their deposits and buying their stock.[1] Veterans' housing and loans have aided another group in owning homes. The public housing program added nearly a quarter of a million low-rental dwelling units and some 50,000 war housing units. In the process, approximately 114,000 substandard structures were eliminated, with 82 per cent of them completely demolished and rebuilt. Improvements in health and social welfare, *i.e.,* the reduction of infant mortality, tuberculosis, communicable diseases, home accidents, fires, and juvenile delinquency, constituted the greatest gains.[2]

Municipal efforts are largely concentrated within the 450 large centers which have active housing committees and authorities. Some are responsible to the city council and others to the special district of which they are an integral part, as, for example, a metropolitan housing authority. Many are fortunate to have the active cooperation of business, banking, industrial, and professional leadership. New York, one of the leaders in this field, has the most advanced legislation. "Mixed housing," or the unbiased selection of tenants on the basis of need and not racial background, was stipulated by statute where public funds were used.

Private enterprise has entered the field of low cost housing in an effort to fulfill a public need. In addition to the architects, constructors, and investors promoting projects, insurance companies are also engaged in erecting housing of various types to suit various income levels.[3] They believe that by so doing they are aiding some of their 75 million policyholders who need homes, at the same time promoting the health and welfare of American families. Their projects began soon after the First World War when they participated in limited dividend housing. Since 1938 they have undertaken to construct, own, operate, and rent units in various cities which have redevelopment programs embracing large tracts of delinquent tax land or large undeveloped areas to accommodate sizable buildings.

[1] Charles Abrams, *A Housing Program for America* (New York: League for Industrial Democracy, 1946) and Federal Home Loan Bank Board, "Home Financing in Relation to Business Fluctuations," April, 1938.

[2] Naomi Barer, "A Note on Tuberculosis Among Residents of a Housing Project," *Public Housing,* Aug., 1945, 133 and her "Delinquency Before, After, Admission to New Haven Housing Development, *Journal of Housing,* Dec. 1945—Jan. 1946, 27.

[3] Otto L. Nelson, Jr., "The Life Insurance Company in the Housing Field," Apr. 22, 1948 address at Annual Meeting, Metropolitan Housing Council of Chicago.

Examples of large housing developments erected by private builders as a direct equity investment include Arlington Heights, Illinois; Lake Meadows, in Chicago, a New York Life Insurance Company project with 2,000 apartments;[1] and the Parkchester group in New York, by the Metropolitan Life Insurance Company. Over 100,000 persons are living in various life insurance housing sites, and additional units are being planned for a similar number.

Industrial projects should not be overlooked, as, for example, those of Hershey, Pennsylvania, and Jamestown, New York. Employers built homes and sold or rented them to their employees at considerable saving. They operated on the theory that labor turnover is lessened when employees find good and satisfactory living accommodations.

Summary

While the country's midcentury housing picture is brighter than a decade ago, one-third of the population is still ill-housed. The housing problem is more acute in metropolitan areas that attracted new migrants during World War II than in small cities. New construction was greater in the southern and western cities than in New England, which has a higher concentration of urban population.

The following major factors affect housing: (1) no over-all national or municipal housing policy, (2) land-use practices, (3) state and condition of housing industry and practices, (4) home-financing methods, (5) mobility, (6) restrictive covenants, (7) zoning, (8) housing inspection, (9) building codes, (10) real estate speculation, (11) community facilities, (12) taxation, and (13) middle-income needs.

Solutions have come from several major sources. Public funds have provided the greatest bulk of low-rental units for low-income families and for veterans' housing. Municipal efforts are mainly confined to larger cities, where special housing committees or authorities have made considerable headway toward the systematic redevelopment of neighborhoods. Private efforts on a wide scale have come from major insurance companies, directly interested in an equity investment, and from building and real estate companies.

DISCUSSION QUESTIONS

1. What improvements have been reported by the census bureau for the country's housing since 1940?
2. Why has housing construction lagged behind population growth?

[1] Chicago Land Clearance Commission Report, 1951, 4–11.

3. What are the basic controversies between the supporters and opponents of public-financed housing?
4. Why is the building trade unequipped to undertake mass housing?
5. What role do investment companies play in creating the housing shortage?
6. Why does one authority speak of the middle income groups as being neglected in housing construction?
7. To what extent are housing problems related to zoning, faulty titles, and lack of cheap land?

SUGGESTED PROJECTS

1. Study the ordinances and the enforcement procedures of the Pittsburgh Housing Authority.
2. Make a historical analysis of New York State's housing statutes and compare them with those of your state.
3. Trace the growth and changes in congressional acts relating to public housing.
4. Study the activities of a large metropolitan housing authority.
5. Study the growth or decline of home ownership in selected cities and, if possible, correlate this with family income and occupation.
6. Compare the housing problem and solutions of Sweden and the United States (or England and the United States).

READINGS

Charles Abrams, *The Future of Housing.* New York: Harper & Bros., 1946.

A statement of current problems of housing and proposals for solutions.

Marquis W. Childs, *Sweden, The Middle Way.* New Haven: Yale University Press, 1936.

An account of the policies and methods for coping with the housing needs of Sweden.

Miles L. Colean, *American Housing.* New York: The Twentieth Century Fund, 1944.

A volume on the factual findings of the problems and prospects of American housing. A set of recommendations included.

Elizabeth Denby, *Europe Rehoused.* New York: W. W. Norton & Co., Inc., 1938.

A survey of the rebuilding of homes in major European cities after the First World War.

Frederick Gutheim, *Houses for Family Living.* New York: The Women's Foundation, 1948.

An analysis of the uses made of homes by family members.

National Resources Committee, *Urban Planning and Land Policies*. Washington, D. C.: Government Printing Office, 1939.

Case studies of communities developed by industrial, governmental, and real estate agencies. Analyses and conclusions of each.

National Housing Agency, *Hearings before the Subcommittee on Housing and Urban Redevelopment of the Special Committee on Post-War Economic Policy and Planning,* Pt. 6, "Housing and Urban Redevelopment." Washington, D. C., USGPO, 1945.

Defines the postwar national housing and urban development policies.

Chapter Twenty-three

Personal and Social Disorganization

O UR ATTENTION has frequently been drawn to the incidents of disorganization in urban life. As a phase of social evolution, social disorganization and personal disorganization appear in some form of maladjustment. These may develop and become specific social problems. Certain areas of the city are more disorganized than others and the residents show more symptoms of personal disorganization. However, these manifestations of social maladjustment are multidimensional and do not necessarily have a cause-and-effect relationship. By studying various theories and researches concerning the genesis and development of the more common types of maladjustments, we gain insight into their social effects upon persons, groups, and society. In the main, the examples selected stem from those conflicts arising from divergent ideals and social values that differ from the norms prevailing in the larger social system.

Process of Disorganization

In personal disorganization, a breakdown of group consensus and social norms which normally control a person's or group's behavior patterns is present. It is the reverse of the process of social organization, a cohesive and binding force, strengthening the person's or group's conception of the position or status occupied within the society. Effective social organization gives added weight to the values, norms, and behavior patterns taught and transmitted by the society. Through social interaction they are sanctioned as forms of social control. When these are no longer effective, social disorganization has developed, which, in turn, can contribute to personal disorganization.

Some time elapses before the divergent standards and norms manifest themselves. Symptoms of maladjustment may be found among a large

503

number of persons belonging to one group or they may be scattered throughout the society. In totality, however, they may be sufficiently large in numbers to constitute a threat to the values and norms. Often personal disorganization follows the disintegration, disorganization, or crisis experienced by the total society. What has happened is that the impact of social disorganization has accelerated the personal disorganizing process. For example, war, prolonged economic recession, or vast migration is often accompanied by rising incidents of desertion, divorce, illegitimacy, crime, and venereal disease. Even during normal periods, some forms of personal disintegration or disorganization are present in a society. It is a matter of degree and varies according to the definition accorded to divergent behavior by the society. At one time, few crimes were attributed to women because there was general belief that their "gentle natures" harbored no criminal tendencies. Today, the increase in crime rates to some degree is related to the greater freedom experienced by women and the realization that criminal behavior is not innate but acquired through the socialization process and in this sense may be considered for some as a part of normal behavior patterns.

Confusion is a marked indication of disorganization. Whether personal or social disorganization is involved, the process begins with the inability to find satisfactory solutions to problems at hand. Tension, anxiety, and conflict interact, accumulate, and dominate the normal course of activities. Symptoms of maladjustment and disorganization are the end result of unsolved tensions and the inability to find satisfactory solutions. Dynamic urban society presents more tensions, anxieties, and conflicts related to employment, interpersonal relations, status, and norms than do static and more stable societies, where events change less rapidly and centuries-old social institutions clarify and reinforce the individual's identity.

Causes for personal disorganization. Personal disorganization may stem from the conflict arising when social expectations do not meet personal expectations. Social expectations are the organized forms of accepted behavior patterns transmitted by the group. These are learned by the members of the society through the normal course of socialization, but they may be at variance with what the person himself wishes.

The inability to resolve two sets of expectations, personal and social, may bring on fears, anxieties, tensions, and conflicts.[1] This is largely due to the failure of the socialization process to provide solutions to overpowering and oppressive problems. An excellent case in point: social expectations in our society are that men exceed women in economic, artistic,

[1] For a thorough, scholarly discussion of "The Sociology of Personal Disorders," cf. S. Kirson Weinberg, *Society and Personality Disorders* (New York: Prentice-Hall, Inc., 1952), Ch. 1.

and literary spheres. So-called supremacy in these areas assures a man retention of his status, but he must continuously demonstrate superiority since there is a growing acceptance of women in all fields of human endeavor. A man is still expected to be the major breadwinner, even though his spouse may be willing to share expenses and responsibilities, and no desire to usurp the husband's role is involved. Women, on the other hand, are expected to marry and achieve success in their traditional social role, as wife-mother, despite society's applause when they achieve vocational eminence. This leads to status dilemma and wondering which roles are more important. The multiplicity of roles is a pronounced feature of urban life.

Playing too many conflicting social roles, each with its set of expectations, may become overtaxing. In a rapidly changing society, new roles are constantly being created which have no established norms upon which individuals may rely. New expectations have not been organized and transmitted, leaving the persons filling such roles with a sense of frustration and anxiety. Or, the society has a preconceived set of expectations, borrowed from a role similar but not identical, to which they expect the "new role-holders" to exhibit. For example: few laymen know the difference between a clinical psychologist and a psychoanalyst. Thus, the gap between personal and social expectations may be the underlying source of tensions and conflicts. Some other causes of conflicts and tensions contributing to personal disorganization include: loss of status, marital unhappiness, sex problems, distorted parent-child relationships, and financial losses.

Ecological Distribution of Disorganization

Certain sections of the city have higher incidences of social and personal disorganization than others. The underlying approach to the study of the relationship between human ecology and specific cultural areas, or natural areas, is that both normal and pathological aspects of human behavior are found there. Where the pathological aspects, as defined by the prevailing society, influence and distort the social relations and behavior patterns of the residents of the area, social and personal disorganization has developed. If the city were intensively studied according to the presence of various types of disorganization, the rate of pathological behavior would vary from the center to the periphery. Each area would have its specific types and rates, therefore. The more common incidences of disorganization as they relate to given local areas are listed in the following pages.

Juvenile delinquency. Shaw and McKay, two outstanding scholars, undertook to discover the relationship between natural areas and juvenile delinquency.[1] Their major hypothesis is that the distribution of juvenile delinquents in space and time follows the pattern of the physical structure and the social organization of the American city. If the trend in city growth is expansion from the center to the periphery, two consequences are shown: (1) physical deterioration of residences will be highest around the central business district, lowest at the outskirts, and intermediate in between; (2) social disorganization will correspondingly be greatest in the central zone, least at the outer zone, and moderate in the middle zone.

Applying this thesis to twenty selected cities, they found a high degree of uniformity in delinquency rates from one year to the next, according to the zonal pattern of American municipalities. Juvenile delinquency is shown to be highly correlated with a number of presumably separate factors: population change, poverty and dependency, percentage of Negro and foreign-born population, adult crime, health conditions, poor housing, mental disorders, and differences in social values.[2]

Gangs often commit delinquent acts. Ganglands are located in areas with high juvenile delinquency rates. Shaw found 1,313 gangs located in the interstitial areas forming a semi-circle around Chicago's loop.[3] Other boys and girls often get into trouble when associating with members of gangs. Delinquent activities may lead to adult criminal tendencies, for these younger people are often initiated into another social system. Used as decoys and accomplices by adult criminals, seeing and coveting the rewards gained by the older members, and disregarding institutional controls, delinquents may grow up with another set of social expectations that carry over into adult life.

Prior to the Second World War, about one per cent of the nation's children passed through the juvenile court each year, or between 170,000 to 200,000.[4] The rate increased during the war, but varied by states and counties. Between 1940 and 1943 various juvenile courts reported the greatest increase, but by 1946 a decrease in the total number of cases was recorded by the United States Children's Bureau.[5] The chief offenses causing boys to be referred to juvenile courts are stealing, acts of carelessness or mischief, and traffic violations.[6] Girls were referred on charges of being un-

---

[1] Clifford R. Shaw and Henry D. McKay, *Juvenile Delinquency and Urban Areas*, (Chicago: University of Chicago Press, 1942).

[2] "Social Factors in Juvenile Delinquency," *Report on the Causes of Crime*, National Commission on Law Observance and Enforcement, 13, Vol. 2 (1931).

[3] Thrasher, *op. cit.*

[4] M. H. Neumeyer, *Juvenile Delinquency in Modern Society* (New York: D. Van Nostrand Co., Inc., 1949).

[5] *Juvenile Court Statistics, 1944 and 1946.* Supplement to *The Child*, 2 (Nov., 1946), 11.

[6] This was found to be applicable to juvenile delinquents of Chinese ancestry. See Rose Hum Lee, "The Delinquent, Neglected, and Dependent Chinese Boys and Girls of the San Francisco Bay Region," *Journal of Social Psychology*, 36 (1952), 15–34.

governable, running away, and engaging in sex offenses. These charges accounted for nearly 6 out of 10 referrals to juvenile courts.[1] Thus, not only does the frequency of personal disorganization rise during a period of social crisis, but the types of delinquency may be correlated.[2]

Some studies warn against accepting statistics as the sole criterion for measuring the extent and trend of juvenile delinquency, for a myriad of subtle factors may be involved. Other viewpoints concerning the rising incidences cite the failure of personal and social controls,[3] and the conflict of values.[4] The problem of juvenile delinquency and its control occupied the attention of the Gluecks, who devised a set of selective factors to be used as items in establishing prediction tables.[5] The increase of juvenile delinquency by 30 per cent and especially among the young teeners since 1948 has caused considerable consternation among national and local leaders. There is an increase of delinquents in the middle-class and high income suburban areas of cities and it is estimated that around a million children get into trouble with the law at the present time. All, however, may not be committed to the juvenile court but are released if the authorities are satisfied that a warning is enough. Of those committed, crime is the major type of deviancy. Two out of every three crimes are attributed to juveniles under 18.

What causes alarm is that many of the delinquents do not lack good home environments, playgrounds or leisure-time activities, or finances; and parents (especially mothers) devote more-than-average attention to rearing children in comparison with the lower income areas of the city. At one time, it was thought that juvenile delinquency was associated with poverty, broken homes, and bad company. The behavior pattern was associated with low income and slum areas. That it should affect the upper income families—the members of which regard themselves as the upholders of the norms and values of the American society—is causing reconsideration of many of the heretofore known factors related to the development of juvenile delinquency. In fact, the new delinquents are more vicious.

The most serious manifestations of this "new" delinquency are vandalism, group conflicts, traffic violations, thefts, murders, and sex deviancies.

[1] "Understanding Juvenile Delinquency," Children's Bureau Publication, 300 (1943) and "Controlling Juvenile Delinquency," same Bureau, (1943), 301.

[2] *Annals of the American Academy of Political and Social Science,* "Juvenile Delinquency," 261 (Jan., 1949), 10–20.

[3] Albert J. Reiss, Jr., "Delinquency as the Failure of Personal and Social Controls," *American Sociological Review,* 16 (Apr., 1951), 196–208.

[4] Milton L. Barron, "Juvenile Delinquency and American Values," *American Sociological Review,* 16 (Apr., 1951), 208–216; and Sol Kobrin, "The Conflict of Values in Delinquency Areas," same journal, 16 (Oct., 1951), 653–662.

[5] Sheldon and Eleanor Glueck, *Unraveling Juvenile Delinquency,* (New York: Commonwealth Fund, 1950). See criticisms of research in the *American Sociological Journal,* 57 (Sept., 1951), 107–120.

Crime. The seriousness of the rising incidence of crime is shown in the annual reports of the Federal Bureau of Investigation, compiled from the summaries submitted by urban police departments.[1] An increase of criminal cases by 6.4 per cent for the first six months of 1952 and projected for the rest of the year on the basis of previous comparisons brought the estimated total to over 2 million. Within an average day, one larceny was committed every 26 seconds, an automobile theft every 2.45 minutes, and an aggravated assault every 6.23 minutes. Two rape cases occurred hourly. Every 4.6 minutes, a murder, manslaughter, or assault-to-kill case took place. From 1951 to 1952 robberies jumped 13.8 per cent, burglaries 8.7 per cent, car thefts 8.8 per cent, and all other types of theft 4.8 per cent. Negligent manslaughter, mostly traffic incidents leading to death, rose 7.7 per cent. In Chicago alone, these deaths increased 18 per cent within a year's time; murders within city boundaries showed a 10.2 per cent increase. According to the latest reports, the rates of all types of crime are rising.

An interesting comparison to the United States crime picture is that reported by the Chief of Police of Oslo, Norway. In 1952 not a single murder was committed in that city of 417,288 inhabitants. Serious thefts dropped to 1,878 cases that year as compared with 2,058 the previous year.[2]

Organized crime is often linked with juvenile delinquency, especially where males are involved. Older juvenile delinquents often cooperate with older and experienced criminals. Organized crime is present when a group of persons within one or more communities combine for the avowed purpose of engaging in criminal activities. Often a hierarchy is built up and may be a part of a network operating throughout the state, nation, or world. The pattern of organized crime is feudal in character. Its hierarchy is held together by authoritarian leaders, intense personal loyalties, the criminal code of ethics, and self-protection from the law.[3] Alliances and agreements with rival gangster chiefs are not uncommon.

Smaller gangs may be integrated with larger ones for gang warfare, killings, and actual compromises. Leaders may be interested in several kinds of criminal operations: liquor, narcotics, lottery, prostitution, receiving stolen goods, organized illicit gambling, and rackets of various types. They aim to carve out their own underworld empire, similar to those of business barons of the economic and financial world. These "top men" are often immune to legal punishment and imprisonment because of their alliance with politics. Some control the city's political machine. Indeed, Al Capone's empire became more powerful than Chicago's political ma-

[1] Report dated Sept. 22, 1952.

[2] Reported in Jan. 1, 1953 issues of Chicago *Tribune*.

[3] E. W. Burgess, *The Illinois Crime Survey,* The Illinois Association for Criminal Justice, Chicago, 1926, 1004.

chine. New "empires" have been revealed by the Kefauver investigations. Their networks are spread throughout large American and foreign cities. This is especially true of drug and diamond smuggling.

One commentary on the "success story" of gangsters is that when the "top man" does climb in the hierarchy, it has the ironical earmarks of the Horatio Alger myth. A slum boy, unaccustomed to power, status, and luxury, can climb to an underworld pinnacle in a relatively short time. Publicity as to his success and power is not lacking, and within his own group he symbolizes status and wealth. Newspapers, films, radio, and television often distort and glamorize gangsters' activities and achievements. According to the stereotype, a successful gangster lives in palatial luxury. He indulges in expensive vacations and elaborate entertainments, while men and women of influence and rank fraternize with him. His children can attend the nicest schools, either within or without the country. Distorted publicity of this sort subverts traditional attitudes toward achievement.

White-collar crime. Large American cities are fruitful ground for many forms of white-collar crime. The exact extent of white-collar crime is unknown, for such activities are not always recorded nor even normally included within the scope of socially defined criminality.[1] Many crimes are committed by persons of respectability and high social status in the course of business operations and occupations. Misrepresentation is one of the more common forms and has increased as modern business methods have become more competitive, impersonal, and rapid. Deliberate falsification of facts is difficult to prove because of the many salesmen, advertising agents, brokers, and middlemen intervening between the seller and the purchaser. Misrepresentation includes, for example, false labeling and the adulteration of commodities. It was discovered by the Federal Trade Commission in examination of several hundred current advertisements in periodicals and radio in 1935 that 10 per cent were misleading. Through rigid supervision, this percentage was reduced to 7 in 1941. This figure pertained to drugs, foods, cosmetics, specialty and novelty goods.

One of the primary reasons why laws have been ineffective in combating white-collar crime is because the purchaser has little motivation to initiate prosecution. Since the amount involved is minor, costly legal action is unjustified. Secondly, the law of fraud is limited in its power to establish proof of intent and proof of damage. Many cases are dismissed and misrepresenters are seldom convicted. Thirdly, manufacturers and dealers of a given product are well organized; when investigations prove their claims to be false, their national associations exert pressure on the parties concerned to avoid further complications.

[1] E. H. Sutherland, *White Collar Crime* (New York: Dryden Press, 1949), 9 and 111.

White-collar crime is crime that actually breaks existing laws, but its extent is not popularly known because knowledge of it seldom goes beyond the occupation within which it occurs. Fee-splitting among doctors is illegal in many states, for instance, but in the case of flagrant violations, the practitioner is more often punished by the national professional association of doctors than by the law. Embezzlement and fraud within banks and corporations, when detected, are hushed up whenever possible. Among other white-collar crimes are income-tax falsification, smuggling by tourists, falsification of financial records, and a host of other dishonest practices that include bribery, collusion, false advertising, short-weighting, misuse of company funds and so on. The criminologist is interested in white-collar crime because its pervasiveness in a money-market-machine economy, such as that of the United States, seems to refute the assumption that crime in general is more closely associated with poverty and the lower socio-economic groups. Such assumptions often resulted from analyses of prison populations and court records. Many white-collar criminals are brought to justice in civil suits rather than criminal trial, and are more likely to be treated with more leniency owing to the social status of the defendant. Yet in the United States more than a hundred times as much money is illegally obtained annually through embezzlement and fraud than is taken through robbery and burglary. The urban sociologist is interested in white-collar crime not because it is strictly an urban social phenomena, but because it appears to thrive more in the individualistic, changing, competitive social climate of the city.

Ecological distribution. Several studies based on criminal records have been made to show the relationship of residential areas and crime. Where the upper and middle classes live, the residents are relatively free from crime. The lower classes show higher incidents due to adverse environmental and social conditions such as accidents, disease, unemployment, family difficulties, and living among the underworld traditions and institutions. In Warner's study of a modern New England community, the upper-upper and lower-upper classes accounted for less than 1 per cent of all arrests; the upper-middle and lower-middle, 10 per cent; and the upper-lower and lower-lower, almost 90 per cent.[1] Moreover, the arrests of the two upper subclasses were for driving and parking violations and other petty complaints.

Hollingshead's study of Elmtown over a seven-year period showed that parents of the two upper classes had no criminal records.[2] The two middle-class groups had .4 and 13.8 per cent respectively. The mothers of the adolescents studied had no records or convictions. Conversely,

[1] Warner and Srole, *op. cit.*
[2] Hollingshead, *op. cit.*

46 per cent of the fathers and 8 per cent of the mothers belonging to the lowest class had been convicted one or more times in local courts for drunkenness, disorderly conduct, sex offenses, neglect of families, and other crimes. The higher incidences, however, can be due to the law officers being more inclined to make arrests there and because the members of this class do not have much influence with the law and have little legal advice.

The two upper classes engaged more in white-collar crime and black-marketing, which are not defined by society as problems. Sutherland's studies showed that "sharp practices" such as manipulation of stocks, payments of money or merchandise to obtain contracts, favors, legislation, embezzlement, and tax frauds, cost the public even more than rackets. Several million dollars are annually embezzled by respectable members of the community, and blackmarketing was extensively practiced during the war. The wartime hoarding of tires, steel, sugar, food, meat, and butter for profit existed to a larger degree among high-income levels.[1]

Size of city and crime. The Uniform Crime Reports showed that the criminal elements of the population are more active and more concentrated in metropolises having more than 100,000 inhabitants.[2] Cities on the whole have higher rates than rural areas. Between 1946 and 1947, rural rates increased twice as rapidly as the urban but were still lower when the two kinds of residences were compared. For the first six months of 1950, rural crime rates rose 7.4 per cent and urban, 1.9 as against the same period of the previous year. Law enforcement authorities of 1,662 cities (total population 60 million) and an equal number of sheriffs, village officers, and state police covering a population of 36 million reported increases in rape, aggravated assault, burglaries, and larceny. Rural areas had a greater percentage increase in offenses involving murder, non-negligent manslaughter, and robbery.

Crime in other countries. In any society, the presence of crime is not unusual, but the prevalence of a specific type is often related to changing social conditions.

Recent reports from "Greater Stockholm," a metropolitan area with almost a million population, indicated a serious upsurge in some types of crime. Safecracking and burglary rose from 16,000 cases in 1937 to 54,000 in 1950 and 65,000 in 1951. Embezzlements showed an increase also.

In China, the type of crimes commonly found in big seaport cities are thefts of property, kidnaping, drug addiction, and prostitution.[3] Of interest is the tie-up between males and females in the kidnaping of a father

[1] Sutherland, *op. cit.*, 117.

[2] *Uniform Crime Reports,* Annual Bulletin, 58, No. 2 (1947), 79 and 106.

[3] Ching-Yueh Yen, "Crime in Relation to Social Change in China," *American Journal of Sociology,* 40 (1934–35), 301.

or son of wealthy households. A woman accomplice enters the home as a servant, learns the routine of the household, and disappears after the victim has been spirited away. The police are seldom notified and the kidnapers collect heavy ransom. A cultural custom enters into the practice. Because of the necessity for the male to continue the family line and perform ancestral rites, the money is paid. If a female member of the same household were kidnaped, the ransom would not necessarily be paid.

A notable increase in female crimes has followed the breakdown of family control and the growing independence of women.[1] Widows and single women going to cities to find employment may be disappointed in their attempts, and may engage in crime or prostitution. Dealers in white-slave trade, claiming to be agents for urban factories, often go to the rural areas for fresh recruits. They contract with the woman's family for her work period, agreeing to remit a sum of money to the family. More is remitted if she comes under the "carry rice" system (*i.e.,* if she provides her own room and board), and less if the room and board is paid by the agent while she is making an adjustment to urban life. However, once the victim is in the agent's care, her destination may be a brothel.

In traditional China, theft, mistreatment of the husband's parents, murder, and adultery were regarded as female crimes. On the whole, few were committed because of the strict control exercised by the family. Most crimes involving women have appeared since 1931.

Mental disorders. Faris and Dunham employed the ecological approach to the study of urban mental disorders, with special reference to Chicago.[2] By plotting on a map the spatial distribution of several thousand patients before their admission to several Chicago mental hospitals, the researchers were able to correlate the type of mental disorders with other symptoms of personal and social disorganization. They found that the rate for certain types progressively decreased in frequency from the center to the peripheral areas of the city.

Insanity was highest in the area immediately adjacent to the central business district. When correlated with other personal and social disorders, the same distributive pattern was revealed. Schizophrenia tended to concentrate in the Zone in Transition near the center of the city, while manic-depressive cases showed a reverse pattern. They developed more frequently in the higher economic and cultural sections.[3] The etiology, or the physical bases, as well as the social factors causing the development of the various types, may have some bearing; or they may be more difficult to detect

[1] Cheng Ch'eng-K'un, "The Chinese Large Family System and Its Disorganization," *Social Forces,* 17 (1939), 538–545.

[2] Robert E. L. Faris and H. Warren Dunham, *Mental Disorders in Urban Areas* (Chicago: University of Chicago Press, 1939).

[3] *Ibid.,* Chs. 3 and 4.

as in the case of manic-depressive psychoses. Schizophrenia may be precipitated by the absence of essential intimate primary contacts, thus leaving the afflicted person virtually anonymous, brooding in psychological isolation.[1] The factors causing manic-depressive psychotic behavior are less clear.

The study further showed that other forms of psychoses which have a clearer organic foundation followed the general pattern of decreasing from the center to the periphery. For example, alcoholic psychoses had distributions similar to schizophrenia, with the highest rates in the Zone in Transition. Psychoses resulting from syphilis were concentrated in the areas of rooming houses, homeless men, and commercial vice, where the probabilities of venereal infection are greatest. It should be noted that this was a pioneer study and did not have the benefit of later and more definitive data.

There is general interest in the problem of mental disorders because of its effect on the afflicted person, the cost to society in treatment, the shortage of facilities, and the growing recognition that more persons may have the illness as the result of increased urbanization. The United States Surgeon General's office estimated in July, 1948, that about $\frac{1}{17}$th of the nation's people suffered from some form of acute mental disorders. In the future, this percentage may rise to one out of every ten. At present there are facilities to care for 600,000 of the more serious cases, or about 60 per cent of the total group so affected. Studies are being made to furnish more data for the development of an effective program of treatment and prevention.

Family disorganization and zonal patterns. Family disorganization has a dual significance, and what affects it may be symptomatic for two types of disorganization, personal and social. The presence or absence of social problems in the family is reflected by the general society. Some factors associated with family disorganization are desertion, non-support, crime, alcoholism, severe religious differences, temperamental incompatibility, and emotional instability.

The incidence of divorce has frequently been used as an index of family disorganization. As seen in earlier chapters, divorces have increased consistently within the past century. Highest divorce rates came after the end of World War II, when one divorce occurred out of every three marriages. The present rate is one out of every four.

The divorce rates, as given by official agencies, do not provide sufficient breakdowns as to the variations in the rates found in particular sections of the city. A general over-all figure is used for the ratio of marriages to

---

[1] Robert E. L. Faris, "Cultural Isolation and the Schizophrenic Personality," *American Journal of Sociology*, 40 (Sept., 1934), 155–169.

The divorce rate has been climbing for years

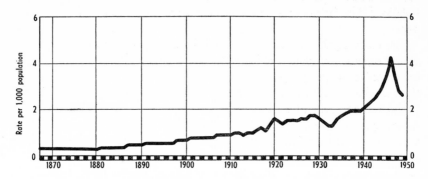

However, the number of divorces has decreased since the all-time high in 1946

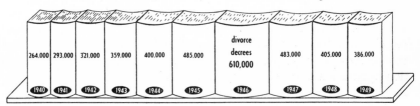

| 264,000 | 293,000 | 321,000 | 359,000 | 400,000 | 485,000 | divorce decrees 610,000 | 483,000 | 405,000 | 386,000 |
| 1940 | 1941 | 1942 | 1943 | 1944 | 1945 | 1946 | 1947 | 1948 | 1949 |

The divorce rate, 1867 through 1949—showing its climb over the decades and the total number of divorces each year, 1940 through 1949. The highest number of divorces were recorded for 1946, immediately after World War II.[1]

divorces for a given year. Moreover, divorce represents the end result of family disorganization, and many of the events leading to this final legal action are unknown. In the same way we have inadequate knowledge of the extent of separations and desertions. These behavior patterns occur with sufficient frequency to challenge students of the family to do research on these manifestations and to correlate them with various social factors, such as, religion, education, income, and so on. Few studies, however, have been done on the exact rates of divorce, desertion, and other forms of family disorganization in a given area of a city.

One of the few studies attempting to relate the patterns of family disorganization to the major areas of the city was done by Mowrer.[2] The underlying thesis of this study is that the disorganized family may be considered as a manifestation of the culture pattern prevailing in a par-

[1] *Children and Youth at the Midcentury—A Chart Book,* prepared by the Midcentury White House Conference on Children and Youth (Raleigh, N. C.: Health Publications Institute, Inc., 1951).

[2] Ernest R. Mowrer, *Family Disorganization* (Chicago: University of Chicago Press, 1927) 110.

ticular area of the city. Family life in cities tends to assume certain characteristics that roughly correspond to the various zones of the city. Each of these general zones in turn derive their family patterns from the population composition, according to race, ethnic, religious, or economic background.

Zones may be subdivided into other natural areas of family stability or instability. For example, it would be wrong to suppose that no stable family life exists in the rooming-house area or the racial ghettos. In fact, a recent study of selected rooming-house areas of Los Angeles showed some families with a high degree of stability.[1] The generalized types of family areas found in Mowrer's study of Chicago are as follows:[2]

1) The *non-family area,* located in the business district of the city, includes the predominantly male sections of "Skid Row," factory areas, and wholesale establishments. Broadly speaking, no family life existed and hence no family disorganization.

2) The *emancipated-family area* comprises the district of rooming houses, kitchenette apartments, and apartment hotels. This is a relatively childless area. The interests of both wife and husband center outside the home. Family disorganization is manifested by a high divorce rate.

3) The *paternal-family areas* are those occupied by foreign-born workers, immigrant colonies, and tenement-dwellers. Family disorganization takes the form of desertion. Two reasons may be given for this behavior: religious convictions of a large number and ignorance or unacceptance of divorce procedures. Divorce rates are therefore virtually nonexistent, but the poor man's divorce, or desertion, is high.

4) The *equalitarian-family areas* are inhabited by many professional men and women, business executives, and families with upper-middle status. Both spouses may work and share responsibilities. Families have few children. Many are childless couples. When divorce is resorted to, either spouse may initiate the suit. The divorce rate here is not as high as in area two.

5) The *suburban areas* have the most stable family life, where mother is more apt to play her traditional role as wife-mother. Children are more frequent. The mother participates in local civic affairs, while the father commutes daily to the center of the big city. While divorce is not infrequent, desertion is practically unknown. The divorce rates are lowest here.

Family disorganization is the end result of a series of interrelated and interactive events. Whether the initial cause be labeled (crime or nonsupport, etc.) the disorganizing process has fairly definite stages. There is a breakdown of consensus, followed by periodic expressions of conflicts

[1] Lillian Cohen, *op. cit.*
[2] Ernest R. Mowrer, *The Family* (Chicago: The University of Chicago Press, 1932).

and tensions through quarrels and interruptions of family routine and goals. The residue of hostility interferes with intimate interaction, leading to greater conflicts and tensions. The more heated and frequent these periods of conflicts and tensions become, the sooner the family disintegration occurs. What the society sees is the last phase, desertion or divorce. However, the attitudes toward keeping the family united as a group or permitting it to disintegrate may be affected by the norms of the community in which the family resides.

Alcoholism. There are many types of drinking patterns, as revealed by the Yale Center of Alcohol Studies.[1] There are many drinking patterns but no specific "alcoholic personality." Alcoholism is both a determinant and a product of social disorganization, and almost always a symptom of personal disorganization. The pathological drinker is a person whose use of alcoholic beverages interferes repeatedly with his health and personal relations and materially reduces his efficiency and dependability in life situations. Associated with the condition is a state of tension, the origin of which may be psychological, physiological, or social, or a blending of all three. Alcohol is resorted to for the relief of this discomfort. Not all pathological drinkers are habitual drinkers.

It has long been contended by many students and observers of alcoholism that "Skid Rows" and zone in transition abound with addictive alcoholics. Straus and McCarthy found in the study of 444 males in New York's Bowery district that 43 per cent were classified as "uncontrolled" drinkers (drinking to the limit at every opportunity); 28 per cent, heavy drinkers (some control); 17 per cent, moderate though steady drinkers; and 11 per cent, nondrinkers. Of the nondrinkers, 37 out of the 47 had used alcoholic beverages in the past.

Evidence showed that pathological drinking is characteristic of a majority of the so-called homeless males, but that a substantial portion are not addictive drinkers. These persons are more concerned with obtaining some degree of relief or escape from discomfort as often as possible and who wish to maintain this relief as long as possible. They adapt their drinking practices to different pay periods and to variations in their living conditions.

A study of the New Haven area suggested that a shift from an irregular to a steady drinking pattern with advancing age was a likely sequence.[2] Some of the older men in discussing the history of their drinking behavior disclosed this change was generally associated with a more routinized existence.

[1] Robert Straus and Raymond G. McCarthy, "Nonaddictive Pathological Drinking Patterns of Homeless Men," *Quarterly Journal of Studies of Alcohol,* 12 (Dec. 1951), 601–611.

[2] Robert Straus, "Alcohol and the Homeless Man," *Quarterly Journal of Studies of Alcohol,* 7 (1946), 360–404.

In both studies there is considerable evidence of early family disorganization or broken homes. Fully half the men lost one or both parents before they were 20 years of age. Many had no marital or religious ties; many had no close personal associations. In general, all were unsocialized in the sense that they never had opportunities for acquiring many of the basic techniques for getting along and adjusting in society. They had resorted to a way of life that minimized personal responsibilities and had come to rely on institutionalized existence (shelter homes, lodging houses, hotels). Their basic necessities are provided in a routinized manner. A fairly constant use of alcohol was part of the routine adjustment to life at this level.

Some sources claim that women are becoming more addicted to excessive drinking; others say the young generation is showing the same tendency. It is estimated that 65 per cent of all adults drink, but that many do so for sociability or because it is consumed as a part of food. In some homes, young people begin earlier because their parents permit it or it is in the home as a part of the general items. Families with higher income status who use alcoholic beverages in or out of the home for entertainment initiate their children to the use of it earlier, but this does not imply excess.

Groups and individuals that for social reasons consume alcoholic beverages as a part of their daily or periodic routine have few so-called problem drinkers. Alcoholic beverages are consumed and thought of as food or related to some social, cultural, or religious ritual. Italians, French, Jews, and Chinese are cases in point.

In the United States, Negroes and Irish ethnic groups in large urban areas were found to have the highest proportions of alcoholic psychoses. Groups such as the Jewish that have a strong in-group solidarity or where the primary group relations act as a binding force in social interaction have fewer cases of pathological drinking. However, it appears that the drinking habits of the members of these groups vary as their general life patterns vary. That is, as members become more emancipated or rise in social status, drinking patterns change.[1] Thus, it is unsafe to generalize on the total drinking population of the country as a whole or of a given group until more data is obtained for each.

Other problems. Illegitimacy, drug addiction, and prostitution can be cited as other manifestations of personal disorganization. Space forbids a thorough treatment of each, but brief mention is necessary.

Illegitimacy in the United States is considered a social problem because of its connection with other vices, because it is often symptomatic of the end process of personal disorganization, and because it is a serious threat

---

[1] From data collected by the author on the drinking attitudes and habits of foreign-born and native-born Chinese in this country.

to the patriarchal, monogamic family system.[1] The prolonged support and care of the child, its legal status, and the social stigma vent upon child and mother add to the complexity of the problem. At times, adultery may be committed by both spouses, thus increasing the number of illegitimate children as well as the incidence of extramarital relations. The true extent of this practice is unknown, but reported annual cases in the United States are said to be in excess of 100,000.

Prostitution is disapproved of in most Western societies, although many others sanction it as a type of occupation for women. The reasons given by women who engage in it are complex.[2] Some women prefer prostitution to other forms of employment; others have been driven to a "life of sin"; more have drifted into it as the result of a series of adverse or adventurous circumstances. Prostitution, if unregulated, is considered a threat to the family system and as undermining the moral values of the whole society. All societies, however, believe in the control of sex drives, and in most societies prostitution symbolizes sexual excess. The resulting social effects—indifference to the welfare of the family, excess spending, or venereal infection—have widespread disapproval.

Drug addiction carries social stigma because of its debilitating effects, but it is a habit acquired through group influence. In time, there is disregard for normal social activities. The persons resorting to harmful depressants eventually injure and destroy their control over physical and social activities.[3] The drug problem is gaining considerable attention in this country because of the growing number of addicts, especially among young teen-age groups. New York recently reported an eightfold increase of arrests over the preceding year. Other large cities have had similar experiences, and considerable attention is being devoted to understanding the relationship of the drug problem to other forms of organized crime.

Summary

Personal and social disorganization results from the breakdown of group consensus and controls and the inability to solve the problems at hand. Personal and social disorganization are often interrelated because one affects the other. Social problems follow and are symptomatic of the disintegrating and disorganizing process. These problems take various forms, such as crime, drug addiction, illegitimacy, alcoholism, juvenile delinquency, and prostitution, to name a few. The causes bringing them to a head are varied and complex. In the main, they reflect an accumula-

[1] Consult Burgess and Locke, *op. cit.,* or any textbook on the family.

[2] W. C. Reckless, "A Sociologist Looks at Prostitution," *Federal Probation,* 7, 13; also see his *Vice in Chicago* (Chicago: University of Chicago Press, 1933).

[3] A. R. Lindesmith, *Opiate Addiction* (Bloomington, Indiana: Principia Press, 1947).

tive process which becomes more intense and frequent as the crisis appears. Fears, anxieties, conflicts, and tensions are present. Urban living, with its heavy demands upon the individual, intensifies them. The extent of family disorganization is often considered a good gauge of personal and social disorganization.

During periods of social crisis, such as wars and depressions, experienced by the whole population, the disorganization process is accelerated, and more manifestations of maladjustments are revealed. These symptoms are regarded as problems when the actions go counter to the basic moral and value systems of the society. Society believes it has provided sufficient controls and incentives to make it possible for all persons to adjust. When disorganization increases, there is an awareness that specific areas of needs are unmet. However, in the normal process of social development, some symptoms of maladjustment, whether personal or social, are found.

Various studies show an interrelationship among juvenile delinquency, white-collar crime, family disorganization, and specific types of mental disorders, and the natural areas of the city and the socio-economic status of the inhabitants.

DISCUSSION QUESTIONS

1. Discuss the process of personal or social disorganization.
2. What basic moral or social values are endangered by crime?
3. Why is "white collar crime" neglected as a phase of disorganization?
4. Why is family disorganization a good illustration of the interrelationship of personal and social disorganization?
5. Why has drug addiction increased? Why has more attention been paid to it within the last two years?
6. Explain the statement: The vices are bound to organize crime.
7. What areas of the city show the highest incidence of juvenile delinquency?
8. What value does the ecological distribution of disorganization have for sociological studies?
9. What is the distinction between the pathological drinker and the addictive drinker?

SUGGESTED PROJECTS

1. Take Shaw and McKay's thesis for the study of juvenile delinquency in twenty urban areas and compare the findings with juvenile delinquency rates in your city.
2. Study the literature on the approaches of various authors to analysis of the disorganization process.

3. Take any one of the symptoms of disorganization mentioned in this chapter (or one of your own choice) and compare its extent and meaning in a society other than ours.

4. Study the social effects of depression or war upon any one of the symptoms of disorganization.

5. Study the changing attitudes toward any of the symptoms of maladjustment described in this chapter (or one of your choice).

READINGS

Emile Durkheim, *Suicide*. Glencoe, Ill.: The Free Press, 1950.

One of the earlier studies of suicide showing cultural, religious, and other influences.

Robert E. L. Faris and H. Warren Dunham, *Mental Disorders in Urban Areas*. Chicago: University of Chicago Press, 1942.

An ecological study of schizophrenia and other psychoses.

Walter C. Reckless, *The Crime Problem*. New York: Appleton-Century-Crofts Co., Inc., 1950.

The common types of crime and treatment of offenders.

Clifford R. Shaw and Henry D. McKay, *Juvenile Delinquency in Urban Areas*. Chicago: University of Chicago Press, 1942.

The ecological distribution of juvenile delinquency in selected cities.

E. H. Sutherland, *White Collar Crime*. New York: Dryden Press, 1949.

An exposure of criminal activities in "respectable" businesses and occupations.

S. Kirson Weinberg, *Society and Personality Disorders*. New York: Prentice-Hall, Inc., 1952.

An integrated analysis of disordered behavior from social-psychological and sociological viewpoints.

Part Seven

Urban Planning and Future Trends

PROLOGUE *The first of the chapters in this section takes into consideration some of the measures adopted by various societies to overcome the pressing defects connected with urban growth and expansion.*

Urban planning is a phase of community organization, directed toward some expressed purposes and goals. Planning is predicated on the assumption that man's past experience gives him the insight and foresight to prevent various aspects of disintegration (and hence social problems) by taking deliberate action. As cities grew in land area and population, their configuration and spatial patterns in many instances, and more especially in this country, were determined more by haphazard circumstance than by orderly design. Planning is a social and collective process guided by the systematic charting of goals as defined by citizens, planning agencies, institutional organizations, and voluntary associations. The municipal, state, or national governments frequently must enact the necessary legal measures, provide the funds (or permit private sources to do so), and authorize personnel to execute the planning procedures.

In many cities planning has been added to the growing list of municipal

522

functions, and planning commissions are a part of the municipal government. In some societies planning comes under the supervision of a national division of the government. Planning agencies are created to meet the larger needs and goals of cities and to overcome to some degree the diversified interests of various segments of the urban population. Planning has largely been concerned with the physical aspects of cities, but school, health, recreation, transportation, and other needs are frequently included.

The final chapter, on future trends, points to some of the effects the Atomic Age may have on our way of life. Some of these changes are already with us, while others are in the blueprint stage and are receiving considerable discussion. A new era of urbanism has begun. From all indications it will surpass former eras in its impact on mankind.

Chapter Twenty-four

Planning and Model Communities

U RBAN PLANNING is a social process involving a series of progressive steps either to redevelop deteriorated sections of the city, build new communities according to established policies or goals, or provide plans for future areal and population expansion.

In some American cities voluntary committees work together to define the scope of planning and the policies to be adopted and executed. In others, this is done by a group of planning experts as a part of regular municipal functions and with citizen cooperation. A third group of cities may use experts and citizens in an advisory capacity.

In some countries urban planning is often a part of national policy, and uniform laws and practices are enforced. Many northern European countries became interested in urban planning at the turn of this century. In some areas slum conditions had existed for over a century before any effort was made to remove them. Limited land area had made it necessary for careful plans to be drafted and approved before any execution of plans was undertaken.

In relatively underdeveloped areas, city planning, when undertaken, is directly in the hands of governmental officials, for several reasons. The population, on the whole, is often unable to cope with the magnitude of its needs. Urban planning necessitates an overhaul of the total social and physical environment, since much of the rudimentary equipment (*e.g.,* water, electricity, and streets) is lacking. The philosophy of planning is essentially paternalistic, and the outlay of capital for improving urban conditions must come from a central source, often the national treasury. The poverty of the average urbanite and his preoccupation with obtaining the scarce daily necessities of life are of more immediate concern to him. Indeed, the concept of planning is not understood by the common man in underdeveloped countries.

Carl Byoir & Associates, Inc.

Levittown, Pennsylvania, a complete pre-planned modern community with 16,000 homes, and with schools, churches, a shopping center, playgrounds, and facilities to accommodate its residents. When this plan is completed by the end of 1954, Levittown is expected to rank as the tenth largest city in the state of Pennsylvania.

Successful planning takes into consideration the needs of the whole city, the whole country, and all its related aspects: transportation, land use, recreational facilities, physical equipment, and others. Model communities point to the practical aspects of pre-planning—research that precedes the execution of plans or segments of them. An appraisal of the advantages and criticisms levied against planning will give us some basis for evaluating the effectiveness of our urban planning programs. We must not assume that urban planning *per se* will automatically eliminate all of the problems found in cities, nor that new ones will not develop.

History of Planning

Urban planning dates back to the earliest cities, when ancient capitals were built according to a plan designed in most cases to satisfy the power and vanity of a ruler. Large groups of workers were recruited for the various tasks, and frequently the end result was one of esthetic, if not functional, triumph. Planning, therefore, is not "new."

More recently the heavy influx of population to defense areas in this country and in Europe brought the problem of city planning to a head. The shortage of housing following the bombing of cities in Europe made it imperative that urban redevelopment be undertaken by governmental agencies. Many authorities interested in planning realized that cities established after the Industrial Revolution had expanded in population and land area faster than was true of older cities. Moreover, little consideration had been given to the interrelationship between the various communities and neighborhoods within cities so that they might be coordinated into an integrated whole.[1] Therefore, industrial or business sections were often themselves fairly complete and integrated but not necessarily related efficiently or effectively to the rest of the city and its environs. The steady decline of the volume of retail business in most of America's downtown metropolitan centers is an excellent illustration.

A related factor contributing to the disharmonious growth and expansion of cities was the adoption of the gridiron plan, which does not allow for "breaks" in radial expansion, except at major and minor transportation converging points. In most of the older European and Far Eastern cities, urban development focused on many subcenters, cathedrals or temples, parks, historical sites, or groups of prominent public buildings. These were strategically located throughout the city and became the sites on which population and institutional organizations clustered. Moreover, many older cities were constricted by a wall, contributing to orderly growth and expansion within the city's confines.

Abercrombie contends that natural growth, or laissez-faire development, dominated the pattern of modern urban expansion and that the radial or gridiron plan of development followed.[2] Controlled or planned growth of cities often resembled a spider-web formation, final configuration of which was shapely and organized. For example, the rurban fringe is even, not ragged. The major transportation arteries go outward from the center like the spokes of the wheel, while the areas around the center and between the spokes form a definite concentric pattern. On the other hand, unplanned modern cities do not follow the ideal, planned, radial expansion scheme. The spokes of the wheel are the uneven transportation arteries which in practice follow population and industrial expansion. Overuse of land has caused deterioration, decentralization, and invasion and succession which, in turn, has "eaten out the heart of cities."

[1] Patrick Abercrombie, *Town and Country Planning* (London: Oxford University Press, 1944), Ch. 1.
[2] *Ibid.,* 13–14.

LUSAKA: PLAN AS PROPOSED

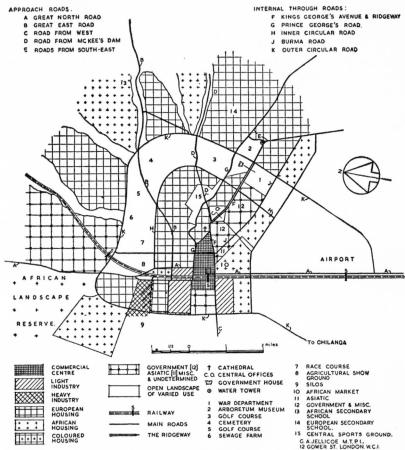

APPROACH ROADS.
A GREAT NORTH ROAD
B GREAT EAST ROAD
C ROAD FROM WEST
D ROAD FROM MC KEE'S DAM
E ROADS FROM SOUTH-EAST

INTERNAL THROUGH ROADS:
F KINGS GEORGE'S AVENUE & RIDGEWAY
G PRINCE GEORGE'S ROAD.
H INNER CIRCULAR ROAD
J BURMA ROAD
K OUTER CIRCULAR ROAD

AIRPORT

AFRICAN

LANDSCAPE

RESERVE.

To CHILANGA

2 miles

	COMMERCIAL CENTRE			GOVERNMENT (12) ASIATIC (11) MISC. & UNDETERMINED	† CATHEDRAL	7 RACE COURSE
	LIGHT INDUSTRY			OPEN LANDSCAPE OF VARIED USE	C.O. CENTRAL OFFICES	8 AGRICULTURAL SHOW GROUND
	HEAVY INDUSTRY				▭ GOVERNMENT HOUSE	9 SILOS
	EUROPEAN HOUSING			RAILWAY	⊚ WATER TOWER	10 AFRICAN MARKET
	AFRICAN HOUSING			MAIN ROADS	1 WAR DEPARTMENT	11 ASIATIC
	COLOURED HOUSING			THE RIDGEWAY	2 ARBORETUM MUSEUM	12 GOVERNMENT & MISC.

1 WAR DEPARTMENT
2 ARBORETUM MUSEUM
3 GOLF COURSE
4 CEMETERY
5 GOLF COURSE
6 SEWAGE FARM

7 RACE COURSE
8 AGRICULTURAL SHOW GROUND
9 SILOS
10 AFRICAN MARKET
11 ASIATIC
12 GOVERNMENT & MISC.
13 AFRICAN SECONDARY SCHOOL
14 EUROPEAN SECONDARY SCHOOL.
15 CENTRAL SPORTS GROUND.

G. A. JELLICOE M.T.P.I.
12 GOWER ST. LONDON. W.C.I.

Lusaka Management Board

Proposed development plan of Lusaka, Northern Rhodesia, to cope with the "absorbing problems attached to planning a multi-racial society." Planning here consists of establishing boundary lines for residential areas; transportation to accommodate "Europeans by private cars and natives primarily by foot, but an increasing number by cycle"; and to meet "the biological need to create for the European a landscape as stimulating and vivid as that of his native land and thus avoid boredom, and within this framework, for the native something of his own background of sky and forest and thus avoid unsettlement."

Cities having the spider-web formation include Paris, Vienna, and Berlin. Washington, D. C.'s older section is so constructed, but the newer section has the gridiron plan and large tracts of unused land.

Planning in Selected Countries

A comparison of the methods adopted by various countries will show how planning differs, even though the goals and objectives may be similar.[1]

England, Wales, Scotland. Perhaps one of the first countries to revitalize municipal planning was England; in 1907 legislation was enacted toward this end. Wales and Scotland followed suit. Country and town planning powers in England and Wales are vested in the Minister of Town and Country Planning, and, in Scotland, in the Secretary of State. A separate Ministry for England and Wales was established in 1943, taking over the powers previously held by the Ministry of Health and later by the Ministry of Works. In Scotland, the Secretary of State acts through the Department of Health.

Two Town and Country Planning Acts were passed in August, 1947 and applied throughout England and Wales. These acts greatly strengthened the powers of central and local authorities in controlling the redevelopment of each country according to a set of master plans. All proposed plans must be approved and coordinated with those of the whole country. Eight sites were selected for the building of new cities, varying in size to accommodate between 10,000 to 60,000 inhabitants. Six are intended for the rehousing of Londonites who have suffered from overcrowdedness resulting from the destruction of homesites through bombing, deterioration, and population increase. The other sites are to be used in relocating families living in substandard structures in Durham's mining areas.

The United States. The urban planning movement in this country began around the time of the First World War.[2] Cities appointed voluntary planning commissions to cope with housing congestion in defense areas, but a major portion of their efforts was spent in enacting and enforcing zoning laws, rather than in city planning. (It must be recognized that many professional and lay citizens confuse zoning with planning.) By and large, the services of the members constituting the planning commissions were well meaning but spasmodic, characterized more by zeal than by professional knowledge.

After a time municipal officials and some citizens realized their misconception: that a city becomes beautiful or well laid out because of zoning

[1] Unless specified, data in this section was taken from United Nations, *Housing and Town and Country Planning* (Lake Success: April, 1949), Bulletin 2.

[2] Federal Housing Administration, *Handbook on Urban Redevelopment for Cities in the United States* (Washington, D. C.: United States Government Printing Office, 1941).

enforcement. The "heart" of many cities was blighted and needed either redevelopment or demolition. Volunteer commissions could not undertake the task, and the employment of professionally trained personnel, the creation of municipal planning agencies, and the inclusion of a specified sum for planning within the municipal budget began. Voluntary citizen groups were used in projects, whose primary concern was seeing that the needs of a given community were translated into realization through the professional planners.

To guarantee the existence and continuance of municipal planning agencies or commissions, ordinances were enacted specifying city planning as another municipal function. Altogether about a thousand official and unofficial planning commissions or agencies were established by 1948 and listed by the International City Manager's Association.[1] The planning data of 889 cities have been compiled, although not all submit up-to-date annual reports. Of this total in 1952, 848 cities had active planning functions; 721 of them had an official planning commission or agency. Unofficial planning groups operated in 35 cities and 92 had no official or unofficial committee, commission, or agency. Six members constituted the average official or unofficial planning agency or commission.[2]

Planning functions have been seriously hampered by the smallness of annual appropriations. Almost a fifth of the municipal agencies or commissions received annually the woefully inadequate sum of one thousand dollars. A full-time planning director was employed by 158 cities, while many used the services of the city engineer, city manager, or other officials. About 170 cities had one or more full-time employees. Many cities of more than 10,000 inhabitants have appropriated no funds for planning.[3] To date, much of the planning has been done by professional city-planning consultants and landscape architects. The more realistic commissions do not simply beautify the environment but tackle city-wide problems related to traffic, zoning, subdivision control, water supply, schools, libraries, industrial growth, and population composition and movements.

Large metropolises have undertaken planning as an integral part of their functions. Their planning commissions not only set up intra-city plans but included as well the interrelationship with the hinterlands and regional environs. New York City began thirty years ago to draw up the most extensive regional survey of its kind. The results are contained in eight volumes known as the *Regional Plan of New York and Its Environs,* covering such topics as "Major Economic Factors in Metropolitan Growth and Arrangement," "Population, Land Values, and Government," "High-

[1] *Municipal Year Book, 1949,* 123–124.
[2] *Municipal Year Book, 1952,* 275.
[3] *Ibid.,* 276

way Traffic," "Transit and Transportation," "Public Recreation," "Buildings—Their Uses and the Spaces about Them," "Neighborhood and Community Planning," and "Physical Conditions and Public Services." Two summary volumes describing and illustrating the plan complete the study.[1] From internal municipal planning, large cities are broadening their objectives to include their relationship to the county, the region, the state, and the nation.[2]

Union of India. One major fact stands out in India's planning efforts since the beginning of the Second World War.[3] The rate of population increase has greatly exceeded the housing accommodations and other facilities in crowded industrial cities. Even the rural areas are failing in this respect, with 87 per cent of the village population affected. Overcrowding is greatest in cities, however, where building regulations are not strictly enforced. Neither the adequacy of the water supply nor the existing minimal amount of sanitary facilities are regularly inspected. Violations are not corrected, although the powers of enforcement are granted to municipal authorities. Moreover, the Health Department has no legal powers to inspect existing dwellings and cannot condemn those which are unfit for inhabitation. As a result, workers attracted to war and peacetime industries in Calcutta, Madras, Bombay, Cawnpore, and other cities can do little about alleviating overcrowded and unsanitary conditions. Thousands are virtually homeless.

Several industrial firms have attempted to solve some of the problems for their employees. A few cities have made headway with slum clearance and redevelopment. Regardless of how rapidly these new projects are planned and put into action, they do not keep pace with the annual increase of 5 million persons. The situation is worsened by recent social changes which are gradually disintegrating the caste and family systems. More migrants are turning cityward, which, in turn, aggrevates the situation.

A proposal has been made to alleviate some of the new problems facing the central government. Various provincial governments are being encouraged to cooperate with their respective local agencies and authorities in undertaking town and village planning. The central government is to act in a coordinating capacity, helping with the establishment of provincial

[1] For a critical summary see Lewis Mumford, "The Plan of New York," *New Republic,* 71 (June 15 and 22, 1932), 121–126, 146–154; and the July 6, 1932 issue of the same magazine, in defense of the plan by Thomas Adams. Also consult R. L. Duffus, *Mastering a Metropolis* (New York: Harper & Bros., 1930) and Regional Plan Association, *From Plan to Reality* (New York: The Association, 1933 and 1937).

[2] Robert A. Walker, *The Planning Function in Urban Government* (Chicago: University of Chicago Press, 1950), 122–128.

[3] United Nations, *op. cit.,* 22–26, adopted from the *Report of the Health Survey and Development Committee* (Delhi and Calcutta: Government of India Press, 1946).

Ministries of Housing and Town and Village Planning. Unless the various levels are coordinated, the central government will find its task insurmountable.

Implementation of planning measures. Most countries which have planning schemes find that they must enact other legal measures to implement their existing laws and to effect coordination between various governmental levels.[1] Most laws were passed when the local areas did not have present-day complicated needs, and no provision had been made for a general coordinating agency. One of the needed measures was the right to assemble small parcels of land into larger tracts; another, to prevent unwholesome interference from vested interests. Provision for the training of town planning experts and research personnel are other needs.

Germany and Italy had monetary problems and had to decide which of the war torn sections should be rebuilt first and according to what design. Some of these obstacles have been overcome, but many cities still show the ravages of war.

In the United States where urban planning takes place under more normal conditions, some concrete steps have been devised for successful drafting and execution of plans, as we shall see in the following pages.

Planning: Aims and Steps

Planning is a social and collective process which requires consensus as the basis for reaching goals.[2] City planning therefore involves a conscientious exercise of powers delegated to municipal authorities. The primary objective of the planning agency is to develop a master design for the entire city and as many sectional plans as are needed. Good city planning embraces present and future needs of the municipality, emphasizing common welfare and utilization of the best means in obtaining it. Effective planning requires serious deliberation and an interchange of ideas among all concerned. Years of effort may be required before the ultimate objectives are reached.

The city as a whole should be intensively studied, as should its relationship to the county, state, region, and nation.[3] Important facts must be gathered at the outset. Strategic or large-scale social planning geared to a master plan and design should be differentiated from piecemeal or practical planning. This latter type is concerned with sectional or correctional redevelopment, resulting from pressures exerted by vested interest groups.

---

[1] International Congress for Housing and Town Planning, *The Implementation of Planning Measures* (Amsterdam: 1950).

[2] Arthur Hillman, *Community Organization and Planning* (New York: The Macmillan Co., 1950), Chs. 1 and 4.

[3] Arthur Hillman and Robert J. Casey, *Tomorrow's Chicago* (Chicago: University of Chicago Press, 1953), especially Part 3.

There is little attempt to visualize distribution of industrial, residential, or commercial areas in regard to the future.

Steps in planning. Nine steps have been suggested to achieve good urban planning.[1]

1) Gathering of data pertaining to the forces that brought the city into being, what has kept it alive, and what its future growth may be. Its location, natural resources, transportation facilities, markets, terminals, and the extent of its dominance over the hinterland should be taken into consideration.

2) Compilation and analysis of the composition of the population. Inhabitants are then differentiated as to their social characteristics, ethnic, religious, racial, occupational, or other backgrounds. Age and sex distribution and prevailing birth and death trends should be considered. These facts enable the planners to know what facilities must be provided.

3) A study should be made of ecological distribution of population and how well needs of the inhabitants are satisfied within their natural areas.

4) A map should be made showing existing land-use patterns. The amount of municipal services and facilities and their adequacy or inadequacy should be considered in regard to each area.

5) Special attention should be paid to all requirements of each economic or ethnic group. A census of dwellings would give a clearer picture of what is needed.

6) Analyzation should be made of the location of passenger and freight terminals and whether or not loading and unloading interferes with traffic. Parking problems and the existing types of transportation should be part of this study.

7) The forces and factors that influence population distribution and dispersion and commercial and industrial decentralization should be appraised in regard to present and future trends.

8) Special problems confronting the particular city should be studied: lack of necessary legislation, financial problems, citizenship inertia, and so on.

9) The objectives set forth in the master plan should be carried out in conjunction with various government or private agencies. An educational program outlining plans is important to their successful execution.

Execution of Plans

Several cities have put their plans into execution after the gathering of basic data. Syracuse, New York, Chicago, and Letchworth, England, are examples.

A preliminary study was made of Syracuse, New York, located in Onon-

[1] Guy Greer, *Your City Tomorrow* (New York: The Macmillan Co., 1947), 66–69.

daga County, showing its relationship to surrounding areas. The population had increased in the usual ways, and growth trends were similar to those of the whole country. Other social characteristics of the population included: a growing proportion of the older age ranges, a decline of foreign-born heads of families, and an increase of small families with native-born parents. The occupational distribution showed mainly semi-skilled, skilled, semi-professional, and professional groups.

Although the population of Syracuse had increased, there was a noticeable tendency on the part of older residents to move toward suburban districts. One of the major needs was to coordinate the fringe areas with the central city. Syracuse had difficulties in persuading the state legislature to enlarge municipal powers in overhauling the tax structure or to float bonds to make necessary improvements. On the basis of the study it was recommended that Syracuse combine with other communities in the adjacent area and vote for removal of legal barriers.

The Chicago Plan Commission was created by an ordinance passed on July 12, 1939.[1] After World War II its aims were to map out a comprehensive plan for the orderly development, integration, and improvement of the city of Chicago. The plan was submitted to the City Council for adoption after the necessary research was made by a group of 29 experts. The execution of long range plans was left to the departments and agencies of the city government.

By 1945 the city council had received and partially adopted (1) the master plan of residential land use, (2) the plans for the subdividing and standards set up for the development of new neighborhoods, and (3) the proposed expressway development program. During 1944 the Plan Commission had studied various city departments and agencies which handled public works construction and how they might cooperate in the execution of the plan. Some of the express highways are already under way and nearing completion.

In conjunction with the Chicago Land Clearance Commission two studies were made on redevelopment possibilities.[2] One dealt with the ten square miles of Chicago's most severely blighted areas and the other, a 117 acre site of the Near Northwest Side Redevelopment Council. Both sites are under redevelopment as a result of the studies. An aim of both commissions is to reactivate "dead" subdivisions—uncertain as to title, tax delinquent, etc.—as a means for checking the flight of people and organizations to suburban areas. That is, many parcels of land would be returned to active use.

In England there is an attempt to retain some of the rural atmosphere

[1] 1944 Report of Chicago Plan Commission, *City Planning for Chicago*.
[2] 1950 and 1951 Reports of Chicago Land Clearance Commission.

in new urban centers. Many garden cities, replicas of Letchworth and Welwyn, the original garden cities, are surrounded at the periphery by a wide belt of green shrubbery.[1] The idea is to forestall the eventual appearance of the uneven and ragged urban fringe which is often associated with unplanned radial expansion. The green belt replaces the wide boulevards or thick walls of former eras and constricts and controls internal growth. World War II interrupted the building of these cities, but the idea is being incorporated in new planned centers.

The green belt idea was adopted by America when planning new suburbs during the mid-thirties. There are green belt cities in Maryland and Wisconsin. The main difference between green belt cities and the garden cities of England is that the latter are planned for long-range growth, whereas most of the American communities reached completion very quickly. England's new cities are designed to include commerce, industry, and farming, while at the same time being desirable places of settlement. The American counterparts are extensions of large cities and are mainly residential in nature. The residents commute to work elsewhere and return at night.

In England, the new cities assembled a sufficiently large acreage to provide for future growth. Letchworth has not yet reached its maximum population of 35,000, the size which was considered right when the area was reserved for the city. Approximately half of the acreage was reserved for farms near to the green belt, while the inner portions were zoned for residential, commercial, and public uses. The city can be economically and industrially self-sufficient.

Letchworth and Welwyn, the true garden cities, are especially created with the work-resident relationships envisioned by their planners.[2] Considerable forethought was devoted to the municipal acquisition of the desired land. Street planning and zoning enforcements were established before any construction was permitted. Buildings for each type of land use were charted. Industrial areas are not permitted to encroach upon sections reserved for residential or public structures. None can extend beyond the point where farmland is reserved for the growth of the food supply for the inhabitants.

Appraisal of Results

The Urbanism Committee of the National Resources Committee of the United States analyzed the benefits accruing from the case study of 144

[1] Ebenezer Howard, *Garden Cities of Tomorrow*, new edition edited by F. J. Osborn, (London: Faber and Faber, 1945); and F. J. Osborn, *Green-Belt Cities: The British Contribution*, (London: Faber and Faber, 1946).

[2] Abercrombie, *op. cit.*, 85, 113–118, 177–178.

Heliopolis, modern suburb six miles from the heart of Cairo, Egypt, retains Arabesque architecture amid many modern conveniences.

Krutown, suburb of Liberia, West Africa, has a mixture of modern and local architecture and conveniences.

planned communities.[1] Before 1916 the majority of them were built by (1) industry, (2) philanthropic organizations, (3) government agencies, and (4) real estate enterprises. Within the past two decades public funds have built some model communities.

Major industries established communities with a profit motive in mind. They were concerned with ready access to a stable labor supply, raw materials, and markets. Of the seventy-seven such communities studied, eighteen were built by textile industries, eleven by coal-mining companies, nine by steel industries, eight by pulp and paper industries, and the remainder by other manufacturing enterprises. Cities built by industries accounted for nearly 60 per cent of the planned communities scattered throughout the country and Canada.

These have grown into stable and solid communities because the industries themselves are prosperous and have provided the means of livelihood for the inhabitants. Outstanding examples of such undertakings include Hershey, Pennsylvania (chocolate), Alcoa, Tennessee (aluminum manufacturing), Kohler, Wisconsin (plumbing fixtures and pumps), Kincaid, Illinois (coal mining), Peacedale, Rhode Island (textiles), and Espanola, Ontario (paper and pulp).

Government agencies built communities for wartime industries or peacetime public works. Several shipbuilding communities, *i.e.* Brooklawn, New Jersey; Mare Island, California; and Cradock, Virginia are cases. Those for power, reclamation, and demonstration projects are Boulder City, Nevada; Norris, Tennessee; and Greenbelt, Maryland.

Philanthropic organizations have entered the field with the idea of helping certain income or occupational groups in finding a better social and healthful environment in which to live, rear children, and maintain wholesome community activities. Low cost community building and subsequent upkeep of facilities are reflected in Radburn, New Jersey; Mariemont, Ohio; and Forest Hills Gardens, New York, built for middle-income families and located in or near large metropolises.

Communities developed by real estate enterprises are the most extensive and varied. Some have achieved national fame, as, for example, Coral Gables, Florida; Garden City, New York; River Oaks of Houston, Texas; and St. Francis Woods, California.

On the basis of the study, it was concluded that planned communities are comparatively free from overcrowding of buildings and population, when contrasted to unplanned ones. Furthermore, their inhabitants enjoyed greater convenience and safety and a more healthful and attractive environment. There were more community facilities. The planning of streets and motorways reduced noise, accidents, and tensions. Some of the

[1] For a complete list, see Urbanism Committee, *op. cit.,* Section 2.

land area was reserved for green lawns, trees, and parks, and the shopping areas were concentrated and separated from residential and public structures.

There is an unusually high degree of social cohesion and morale found in these communities. There was greater social interaction and concern for maintaining the community's existence, striving for improvements, and more readiness in solving problems of interest to all the inhabitants. Many of the ills associated with unplanned urban living, *i.e.,* disease, personal disorganization, and breakdown of consensus and community norms, were relatively absent.

Criticisms. Despite the clear demonstration of the gains made by planned communities, there are severe critics of such undertakings. A consideration of them is necessary to give us a rounded picture of what planning has or has not accomplished.

One of the most severe criticisms against planning is that the city becomes interested and involved in real estate operations. Despite the best cautions taken, some officials will engage in real estate manipulations and profit from inside information. The critics cite many instances when city officials or their friends have profited by buying property along proposed express highway routes or slum clearance sites and reselling it to the city under a private corporation.

They have also been critical of the lay-out and environmental design of planned communities. The critics decry the tendency to favor one income, occupational, or racial group at the expense of the rest of the citizenry, many of whom are in need of better accommodations and pleasant surroundings, but who are denied the privilege of living in these communities. Critics declare that the extra taxation levied for the construction and support of these projects is undemocratic and arbitrary. Moreover, they contend that planned communities are esthetic rather than practical and that most of the plans were approved by citizens and planners with little regard for cost, need, or habits of future occupants. For example, in a large suburban Virginia housing development two families were evicted because they sat on the front rather than the back lawn, thus marring the scenery. In another, a blind veteran of World War II was denied an apartment because he had a seeing-eye dog, and the operators of the Farlington project refused to waive the "no pets" rule.[1] Considerable criticism has been levied against the method of selection of tenants and home-owners by laying down autocratic and arbitrary regulations. A complaint often heard is that most planned communities occupy more land area than is warranted, and if one of the primary reasons for planning and redevelopment is to accom-

[1] *Sun Times,* Sept. 5, 1953.

modate more population in a limited geographical location, the purpose is defeated.

Another point made by the critics is that in a rapidly changing society where sudden technological inventions occur, the best blueprints are outmoded in a short time. No agency or person is able to predict, for example, the social effects of the atomic or hydrogen bomb on cities. It has already been conceded that our building codes are unsuited to this new era, and that attention should be devoted to finding new housing materials and construction methods. No agency has been able to predict or control population movements, nor can anyone prevent the decline of industrial communities faced with technological adjustment.

The most general criticism revolves around the basic issue: should private or public interests build cities and plan new communities? Traditionally, private interests dominated, and the critics believe that a departure from this trend will eventually lead to a pattern contrary to democratic ideals.

However, many critics are not aware of the fact that some problems are too large in scope and objectives for the average urbanite to undertake, and that municipal leadership and powers are needed to cope with them.[1] A good share of the criticism is due to the lack of understanding as to the real purpose and function of planning.

Summary

Planning city growth and expansion is not a new concept, but many persons who oppose its inclusion within the municipal government as an added function have not been adequately informed of its scope and importance. More countries are interested in urban planning than is generally known.

Since effective planning results from consensus among citizens, professionals, laymen, and municipal officials, it is a social and collective process. A conscious exercise of municipal powers toward the development of an over-all plan and needed sectional plans forms the basis of preplanning and future execution of them. Nine basic steps are involved in the successful execution of plans and objectives. New legal measures are often required to implement existing plans.

An appraisal of the results accruing from 144 planned communities in the United States and Canada revealed that (1) they are relatively free from overcrowding of buildings and population, (2) their inhabitants

[1] The Bureau of Urban Research, *Urban Planning and Public Opinion* (Princeton: Princeton University Press, Sept., 1942), No. 1.

enjoy greater convenience, greater safety, and a more healthful and attractive environment, (3) there is an unusually high degree of social cohesion and interaction within the communities. Without a doubt the greatest asset is in the saving of human lives.

Criticisms of planning occur in four areas: (1) municipal interference in real estate operations, (2) over-esthetic emphasis upon environment, (3) undemocratic segregation of income and ethnic groups, and (4) unpredictability of population and urban growth in a highly advanced technological society.

DISCUSSION QUESTIONS

1. Discuss the history of city planning and cite examples of planned cities built before the Industrial Revolution.
2. Why did most western societies become interested in urban planning during and after World War I?
3. What is the spider's web urban expansion like, and why has it produced more orderly growth of cities?
4. What defects are attributed to the gridiron plan of urban growth?
5. Why is it necessary to make plans for internal city growth in relationship to the county, the state, or the nation?
6. What are some of the basic steps in the planning process?
7. What type of legal measures had to be passed to implement planning in many countries?
8. Discuss the benefits accruing from the study of the Urbanism Committee in regard to planned communities.
9. Discuss the major criticisms against planning.

SUGGESTED PROJECTS

1. Take the list of 144 communities analyzed by the Urbanism Committees and write a paper on their methods of study.
2. Study the literature on England's "Garden Cities" and the "Green Belt" cities of the United States and compare their layouts, philosophies underlying the execution of policy, and their population composition.
3. Study the major achievements of the City Planning Commission of your city or a large metropolis in your state.
4. Study the planning problems of a non-Western society.

READINGS

Patrick Abercrombie, *Town and Country Planning*. London: Oxford University Press, 1944.

A small volume tracing the process of planning as against laissez-faire found in many countries of the world.

Charles K. Agle, *An Approach to Urban Planning*. Princeton: Princeton University Press, 1953.

A thorough and well-considered study of city-planning by a leading expert.

Annals of the American Academy of Political and Social Science, "The Impact of Atomic Energy," 290 (Nov. 1, 1953), esp. 66–76.

Robert L. Dickinson, *City Region and Regionalism*. New York: Oxford University Press, 1947.

A study of urban regional development and its application to various world areas.

Arthur Hillman, *Community Organization and Planning*. New York: The Macmillan Co., 1950.

A thorough treatment of the role of community organization and planning in its theoretical and practical application.

Arthur Hillman and Robert J. Casey, *Tomorrow's Chicago*. Chicago: University of Chicago Press, 1953.

A popular and well-illustrated presentation of the metropolitan plans and objectives for Chicago's future.

Urbanism Committee, *Urban Planning and Land Policies*. Washington, D. C.: Government Printing Office, 1939.

A survey of the land use patterns and urban planning for 144 industrial, philanthropic, real estate, and government communities. A good section on conclusions and recommendations.

United Nations, *Housing and Town and Country Planning*. Lake Success: April 1949, Bulletin 2.

A brief statement of accomplishments and plans for various countries. A good treatment of the needs of so-called "undeveloped areas" in the tropics.

Chapter Twenty-five

Future Trends and Objectives

SINCE THE invention of the atomic and hydrogen bombs there has been considerable speculation concerning the future of our cities. Much prophecy has been indulged in by official and lay sources. It is interesting to note that the pessimistic predictions are gradually subsiding, while plans for improving and rebuilding cities continue. This chapter will attempt to *summarize* the foreseeable trends as the facts point to them after the midcentury.

The topics of urban composition and size of city, transportation, and other changes and their probable effects on the mode of living will be discussed. While in no sense advocating what "ought to be," the last section, "Objectives," classifies the values and goals often expressed and held by a large segment of the population which, in the final analysis, holds the key to the attainment of goals. The study of urbanism and urbanization is a means to an end: an approach to, and an understanding of, the dynamic nature of social change, the processes involved and the interrelationship with the future.

Population Composition and Size of City

One of the significant trends is the continued increase of urban population in absolute numbers—if not in percentage—as the result of the general increase of population of the country as a whole. The upsurge of births since 1940 has upset all previous predictions of the probable decline of both urban and national population. The latest census prediction for 1975 is 221 million Americans. Schools will have 48 per cent more children than now, if the present birth trends continue, and every year nearly three million more people will be added to the population.[1]

A postwar projection—based on the assumption of mixed economic con-

[1] *U. S. News and World Report,* Sept. 11, 1953, 18–19.

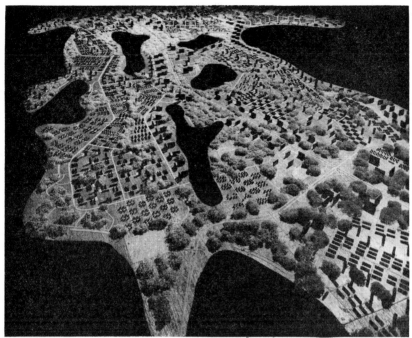

Hedrich-Blessing

Detailed close-up of proposed "lake city" development, a "dream island," to be built on Lake Michigan in Chicago's south side. Note the lagoons, expressways, parks, tall apartment buildings, and individual homes of future "Lake Islands."

ditions—forecasts the following urban increases for each decade through the year 2,000: 10.8 per cent, 1950–1960; 9.4 per cent, 1960–1970; 7.7 per cent, 1970–1980; 5.5 per cent, 1980–1990; and 4.2 per cent, 1990–2000.[1] This means there will be an absolute increase of urban population during each decade, and the midcentury proportion of 64 per cent of the country's total may not rise to any great extent. However, the increase of rural-non-farm population is expected to continue in both absolute numbers and percentage, and the rural population may decline by five per cent. Outlying areas of large cities will see the greatest growth of population.

In an earlier chapter there was mention of the higher percentage of older persons living in cities since 1930. This trend is expected to continue. By 1975 there will be an increase of 52 per cent. More and more persons are born, grow up, and spend their entire existences under urban conditions. For many, going back to the farm at the time of retirement is as improbable as migrating to a foreign country and resettling. While no statistics are available as to the return of population from suburbs and rural-

[1] Hauser and Eldridge, *op. cit.*, 158–173.

nonfarm areas to the central city, there are some indications that the up-keep of homes and grounds—both in terms of physical labor and mone-tary considerations—are burdensome to persons with grown children living away from home. Some of these couples have moved back into the city where more activities are geared toward the older age ranges.

As one author puts it: The old will stay in the city while their children raise their grandchildren outside of the city limits.[1] With the continued tendency of industry to decentralize to areas where more space and cheaper land are available for plant construction, more persons of working ages will be closer to their work by living outside the confines of the city. A disproportionate sex ratio, together with an aging population and differ-ential marital status, will be more of an urban phenomenon than it is to-day. Women are outliving men by five years, on the average, so that the proportion of females to males may become still greater and widows still more numerous than widowers. Also, there is likely to be an increase in the number of unmarried persons remaining in cities until a change of status is made.

The conditions described above will require a change in some of the facilities the city provides: medical and welfare services for the older age ranges and more recreational and housing facilities to suit non-family units or childless couples.[2] More emphasis may be placed on commercial enter-tainment and cultural activities, such as concerts, art exhibits, reading ma-terials, and sedentary leisure-time pursuits.

The multi-dwellings of today, so unsuited to families with young chil-dren, will be in greater demand as the old population groups seek more comforts and services supplied at the places of residence. Childless couples and couples who have reared their children and moved back into the city may likewise be tenants. Indirectly, this will reduce the congestion in cities. Thus, one of the fears of the Atomic Age—that cities will be more overcrowded, and more congested and unsafe—may be unfounded because of the ecological processes in operation.

The aging population of cities may also be accompanied by changing consumer's habits and taste, so that industries, business establishments, and service industries catering to the working-age groups and to young chil-dren will be more and more inclined to decentralize to new areas. Such items as luxury goods and food packaged in smaller quantities will still be found in cities.

So far our discussion has been confined to the city and the rural-nonfarm areas. Another trend of population redistribution has been taking place in

[1] Churchill, *op. cit.*, 131–132.

[2] New York's future public housing projects require at least 5 per cent of the dwelling units be set aside for the aging, with special facilities to reduce accidents. A separate wing is set aside; cf. *New York State Builds Lives and Homes*, 1952, 47–50.

the southern and western states, where new cities are growing at a rapid rate. Industrial decentralization away from congested cities has been encouraged by high-level policy makers since the beginning of World War II.[1] Munitions plants were advised to spread out instead of concentrating in half a dozen areas along the Pacific seaboard. Steel plants, machine-tool industries, automobile assembly plants, and chemical industries are gradually dispersing. This will indirectly affect the population composition of cities in the Rocky Mountain, southern, and western regions. Also, in regions where industries are being relocated, there are conscious attempts to control the size of population, limiting cities to no more than 50,000 inhabitants. Whether this is feasible or not remains to be demonstrated.

It has been suggested that as major industries disperse and select new sites, controlling the size of a city be a matter of conscious planning. To furnish some basis for the control of city size, use can be made of findings that an industry employing a thousand workers requires 7,000 more persons to supply the community needs. If the optimum population of the city is to remain around 50,000, industries that employ 7,000 workers would bring the total population within this range. This city size is believed to be large enough to satisfy the daily cultural and social needs of the residents.[2]

With the growth of planned communities in outlying areas and our knowledge of population trends, controlling the size of urban centers and location of facilities is not as difficult as might be thought. For example, Park Forest, Illinois, a planned city 35 miles from Chicago, was built to accommodate 30,000 inhabitants and to meet the needs of military personnel, junior business executives, and professionals, all of whom are required to move frequently. The builders of Park Forest realized that few desirable homes in congenial residential neighborhoods were available on a one-year lease basis, and that subletting was not always satisfactory to lessee or landlord.

A group of rental dwellings and apartments were built for these persons being promoted to better positions or transferred from one city to another, or who moved to permanent homes in other residential suburbs. Later, houses were added for permanent owners, and each area was designated for a specific purpose: schools, shopping centers, and so forth. A parking area for 3,500 cars surrounds the main shopping district. The houses were built around a semi-circle enabling residents to come into closer contact; each circle of families is expected to make its own rules governing noise, nuisance, and abuse of property.

---

[1] "National Security Factors in Industrial Locations," National Security Resources Board, Washington, D. C., Document 66 (July, 1948), 4.

[2] *Ibid.*

One of the significant and unintended consequences of the community's growth is that the permanent residents (especially the women) have become so content with their surroundings that they rarely go outside the community. Another consequence is the development of neighborhood patterns which segregate residents into local areas. However, when an issue confronts the entire community, residents express their opinions. For example: residents voted to invite downtown stores to locate in the shopping center, and the store receiving the highest number of votes was selected.

An example of a big city meeting its population trends is New York, which anticipates an addition of one million families by 1970, many of whom are expected to settle in outlying communities within a radius of 30 to 40 miles of Manhattan. Plans have been made to guide the growth of these centers so that they conform to the safety requirements of atomic defense. Additional transportation and community facilities are being extended to these areas. It should be noted that New York City and the state of New York were among the first to undertake community redevelopment, slum clearance, and urban planning, and have set the precedent for many such programs in this country.

Transportation

There are several new trends in modes of transportation and internal city transportation facilities which should accommodate the increase of traffic. In former times a change in the mode of transportation affected the spatial pattern of cities, and the adoption of the automobile extended the radius of dominance of the metropolitan centers. Although city planning has been concentrated upon slum clearance and redevelopment, the integration of plans for better traffic facilities with these programs has accompanied the changes made in and around these areas. Attention is centered upon accommodation of the automobile rather than street cars and railway terminals. Wider use of air transportation will probably bring other alterations to city patterns.

Within less than three decades after air transportation was introduced in this country, over 25 million persons, mainly urbanites, made scheduled intercity flights.[1] In 1951 intercity passenger miles for rail, Pullman, and air trunk lines were almost identical. There is also the likelihood that air freight may exceed former methods of transportation, especially for perishable items. Whereas at one time there was considerable discussion of union stations, today more attention is directed to ever-growing airports at the city's outskirts and branch airports close to the downtown business

[1] Air Transport Association of America "Air Transport Facts and Figures," 1952, 4 and 5.

district. Should the latter increase, large tracts of land must be assembled which in turn will affect the spatial patterns of cities.

The use of the helicopter as a mode of transportation will make further changes.[1] Helicopter fields will be needed in the same manner that parking lots are today in most cities. Use of the helicopter has been introduced for transporting mail from the main post office to suburban areas or to outlying airports. Within two and a half years after this service was inaugurated in Chicago more than seven million pieces of mail were handled. Other major cities have either adopted this practice, or propose to do so in the near future, and it is expected that overnight first-class mail service throughout the nation will follow. Closer communication between cities will widen markets and the exchange of goods and services.

The use of the helicopter as a taxi and feeder service may bring a wider dispersion of population and organizations. In some cities passengers from suburban areas now use this service to major airports. Extensions of helicopter service between cities within a region are also being introduced, thus promoting regional development.

What the jet planes will do to cities is not clear, but commercial flights between London and South African and Asian cities began two years ago. The planes travel at a speed of eight miles a minute, and fly eight miles high. It requires only 36 hours to fly from London to Tokyo, with stops at Beirut, Karachi, Calcutta, Rangoon, Bangkok, and Manila. By 1956 jet plane flights between Europe and North American cities will be regularly scheduled; the "trial flight" between London and Rio de Janeiro took place on September 15, 1953. Since jet plane commercial flights are not profitable for distances under a thousand miles, widely scattered cities will be linked together, while cities closer together will be serviced by the aircraft now in use. A social significance of this is the greater impact of Westernization on cities in underdeveloped areas which will result in a different pattern of intercity relationships. Another social significance is that jet airfields require more land area for take-offs and landings and will affect land-use patterns. This condition is being reported by Johannesburg.

Transportation facilities within the city are undergoing rapid changes in many parts of the country. Streets are being widened for express highways and traffic diverted along one-way lanes. Nineteen million more cars are on the road than a decade ago, and more are expected as population increases. There are 44 per cent more passenger cars and 78 per cent more trucks than a decade ago. Nearly 60 per cent of all automobile mileage is used in cities or between cities and the rural-nonfarm areas by urbanites going to and from work, since public transportation facilities have not kept

[1] G. L. Wilson and L. A. Bryan, *Air Transportation* (New York: Prentice-Hall, Inc., 1949), 43–44, 532–533.

abreast with population dispersion and industrial decentralization to out-lying urban fringes.

It should be noted that changes in transportation facilities within and without cities are being encouraged during the atomic era as an important civilian defense measure. Better highways will help in the rapid evacuation of population to less congested areas. Should this precaution be unnecessary, additional facilities will speed the movement of vehicles which is keeping abreast with population growth. Considerable attention is being devoted to the construction of a better coordinated system of national highways which will link all cities into a network.[1]

Trends in Other Fields

Other changes in urban living are being seen. Advances in medicine will further lengthen the life span. As cities combat smoke and soot, respiratory disease will lessen. Considerable attention has been paid to smoke elimination and control, with outstanding success in Pittsburgh, St. Louis, and Los Angeles. Most large cities require electric or diesel railway engines in order to reduce the smoke and soot menace in the interest of health. With the wider use of air-conditioning, solar and radiant heating, and the increased electrification of homes and non-residential structures—trends well under-way—cleaner cities should result. There may be even greater improvements when atomic energy is adopted.

The rising incidence of emotional and mental diseases is of great concern to everyone. Better methods for diagnosis and treatment are being applied, and more programs and research directed toward the goal of mental and emotional health. The current researches and programs concerned with interpersonal and intergroup tensions and problems are gaining wider acceptance and practice.

Although interracial problems have not been solved, and there is some discrimination in employment, housing, civil rights, and education, a survey of seventeen major cities conducted by the American Civil Liberties Union concluded that more opportunities are being accorded persons with minority status.

One of the most heartening trends is that more and more urbanites are inquiring into the nature of the urban environment. The understanding of what constitutes the city and the impact of this understanding on social behavior is not confined to the classroom. It touches the life of everyone, and this recognition has created more discussions among laymen about cities and their complexity. As more and more persons attempt to formu-

[1] See Public Law 350.

late their thoughts and observations and try to solve some of their problems, changes are inevitable.

Objectives

Several objectives are listed below—not necessarily in order of their importance—pointing to what could bring about better urban conditions. Based on a survey of the literature, workshops, programs, and associations working for the improvement of cities, these objectives represent to a large degree the values and goals of many urbanites and some problem areas which have been neglected or ignored.[1]

1) Better coordination among mayors and officials of cities. More cooperation in solving common problems of cities should be attempted. Periodic meetings of metropolitan city mayors have taken place, but these meetings should become routine.

2) Better coordination among municipal, suburban, and state officials. This would eliminate many misunderstandings on the introduction, enactment, and enforcement of new legislation.

3) Elimination of politics in municipal affairs. Far too often, legislators from smaller cities or rural territories—for political reasons only—block legislation which is vital to the city. There are growing disclosures of connections among crime, graft, and politics. Trained personnel, selected through a sound civil service system, would do much toward removing cumbersome and inefficient municipal administration. Competent personnel is especially needed in large metropolitan cities throughout the country.

4) A bureau of municipal research, staffed with competent, non-political personnel, should become an integral part of the city government. The aim of such a bureau would be directed toward seeking solutions of specific problems facing the city. For example, decisions related to the adoption of newer types of housing materials or the inadequate functioning of a given department within the government should be delegated to the bureau of municipal research. Some cities have appointed small "Hoover Commissions" for the latter purpose, but their work is often inadequate because of the political nature of the appointments. The gathering and supplementation of basic data required by all other governmental units should be part of the bureau's functions. Thus it would become a central point for municipal integration.

5) One of the problems growing out of increased services required by urbanites is the inability of cities to raise sufficient revenues. Cities borrow

[1] See Greer, *op. cit.*, 130; *Journal of American Institute of Planners, op. cit.*, 103–108; and *Survey Graphic* (Apr., 1944), 204–205.

money without regard for sound fiscal policy.[1] Therefore, few cities are solvent, and during periods of economic recession, some have gone into bankruptcy. Personnel trained in economics and finance should tackle these problems, or experts should be employed when needed. The common practice is to propose increasingly larger annual budgets without first knowing how revenues may be obtained or how debts may be reduced. Conversely, taxpayers do not always pay lower taxes when the city does have a surplus of funds.

6) There is real need for better methods and agencies for the protection of citizens, and there is general dissatisfaction with the inadequate personnel and the manner in which law-breakers are penalized. The same situation applies to those needing municipal care and treatment. For example, police departments should undertake more training programs and prepare new personnel for effective public service.[2] Traffic courts presided over by a special judge should handle traffic violations. Domestic relations courts should have social workers and counsellors in addition to judges trained in family and child welfare. Juvenile delinquent cases should be handled by experienced social case workers and probation officers, and judges skilled in the handling of young people should be selected. Correction, mental, and all tax-supported institutions should be improved and better managed. More facilities should be provided for any type of illness or disease that comes under municipal responsibility.

7) A better check on intercity migration is a public service that could lead to a decrease in the incidence of personal frustrations and, perhaps, disorganization. This may be accomplished by cities forwarding reliable data on their job opportunities, so that some attempts can be made to guide seasonal, inexperienced, and unemployed workers to job opportunities. Mere rumors of work have caused many persons to travel great distances, become stranded, and become liabilities to the receiving city.

We have already noted the phenomenon of seasonal workers in the "Skid Row" areas of large cities, but few urbanites are aware of the families that "follow the sun," moving from one city to another in search of work. Many children do not stay long enough in one city to attend school. Some become the future inhabitants of "Skid Row."

8) The inclusion of sociologists and social scientists in municipal and related agencies that deal with social and personal problems such as, penal and crime commissions and institutions, housing, city-planning, research, and policy-making. When social scientists go out of their roles as scientists to apply their knowledge to social problems, they are armed with the interrelated theories and facts of their field. Applied social science is predi-

---

[1] Hillhouse and Magelssen, *op. cit.*, and Lindholm, *op. cit.*, 413–415.
[2] Chicago Commission on Human Relations, *Five-Year Report, 1947–1951*, 21–22.

cated on the principle that better predictions of the outcome of social situations are possible and more social problems reduced, if not totally eliminated, by the application of its theories.

9) The development of the hydrogen bomb and the possible total destruction of important cities has brought to the fore the problem of civilian protection during wartime. Urbanites are looking to Federal and municipal authorities for safety measures commensurate with the power and force of the new bomb.

Such plans as these are, of course, beyond the working sphere of the social scientist. Social scientists are citizens, too, and as such may express their opinions. Also, one of the *raisons d'etre* of science is its use in pursuit of the goals of mankind. Science cannot determine what these goals should be. However, scientific knowledge of urbanism and urbanization is invaluable in helping us attain the kind of cities and city life which we desire.

Index

Abercrombie, Patrick, 525, 533, 538
Abrams, Charles, 499, 501
Accidents, fire, 281–283
Adams, Thomas, 529
Africa, 138–176
  European influences, 138–139
  major cities, 141–142
  major urban areas, 139, 141–143
  map of major urban areas, 139
  Central Africa, (*See* Belgian Congo), 174
  East Africa (*Also see* Urban ghettos, Planning and model communities)
    Lusaka, Uganda, 289–290
    map of Lusaka, 290
    proposed city plan of Lusaka, 526
  North Africa, 143–151
    Alexandria, 142, 144, 146
    Algeria, 142, 143, 150
    Anglo-Egyptian Sudan, 140, 142, 150
    bazaars, 145, 149
    Cairo, 141, 142, 144, 146, 149–150
    Caliph of Morocco, 146
    Casablanca, 142, 144, 146, 150
    Egypt, 143, 144, 149
    Ethiopia, 142, 143, 144, 149, 151
    ethnic division of labor, 144–146, 149–150
    "Europeanized" indigenous population, 143
    Europeans in, 143, 146, 147, 150–151
    Fez, 142, 144, 145, 146, 147–149, 150
    former invasions into, 143
    Jews in, 143, 145, 146, 147, 149
    major cities, 142 (*See* cities mentioned by name)
    millet system, 145
    minorities in, 143, 145, 147, 149, 150
    modern European influence in, 141, 143–144, 150
    Morocco, 142–143, 144, 146, 147, 149
    Moslems in, 143, 146, 149–150
    number of cities, 144
    population of area, 143–144
    Rabat, 142, 145, 146
    spatial pattern of cities, 145, 146–150
    Sultan of Morocco, 146
    town and city differentiation, 145–146
    Tunis, 142, 144, 145, 146, 148
    Tunisia, 142, 143, 147, 148

Africa—(*Continued*)
  South Africa, 156–174
    Afrikaners (Boers), 158
    apartheid, 162–165
    Asiatics in, 159–160, 171–172, 173
    Bantu, 158, 160, 173, 426
    Bantu Press, 426
    Chinese in, 159, 160
    Coloured in, 158–159, 164, 171–172, 173
    definition of city, 37, 161
    detribalization, 160, 167, 168–169, 173
    Dutch in, 156–157
    European population, 158, 160, 161
    Indians in, 159, 164–165, 172, 173–174
    Jews in, 158
    Johannesburg, 141, 142, 159, 160, 161, 165, 169, 172
    labor problems, 165–166
    major cities, 142, 160, 161
    Malan, Dr. Daniel F., 163
    multi-racial social structure, 156, 158, 165–166
    Native areas and locations, 163, 165, 170–173
    Native compounds, 163, 165, 167, 172
    Native migratory workers, 160, 166, 172
    Native reserves, 163
    Natives in, 160, 166, 167, 172
    Natives in cities, 160, 163, 170–172
    number of cities, 169
    other Europeans, 158
    pass laws, 165, 170
    population composition and urban distribution, 156–160
    "poor whites," 158, 163
    racial tensions, 156–157, 159, 162–169, 172
    segregation and spatial patterns of cities, 169–174
    segregation in native and other areas, 172–174
    slums, 170–174
    taxation, 163, 166–167
    tribal obligations, 165, 167–168
    urban growth, 141, 142, 160–162
    urban population, 37, 161
    women in cities, 167, 168–169

Africa—(*Continued*)
  West Africa, 151–156
    British influence, 151–152
    "Europeanized natives," 154, 155–156
    Europeans in, 154–155
    French influence, 151–152, 154–155
    Freetown, 142, 153, 154
    Gold Coast, 140, 142, 151, 154, 155
    Ibadan, 142, 152, 154
    indigenous middle class, 154
    Kano, 142, 152
    Liberia, 152, 154
    major cities, 142, 152–154
    major urban areas, 139, 141, 151
    Monrovia, 154
    Native cities, 151, 152
    Negro kingdoms, 151
    Nigeria, 142, 151, 152, 155
    Sierra Leone, 151, 154
    slave trade, 151
    Yoruba in cities, 152, 154
Afrikaners (Boers), (*See* S. Africa), 158
Agle, C. K., 539
Airplane (*See* Transportation)
Alexandria (*Also see* N. Africa), 142, 144,
  146
Algeria (*Also see* N. Africa), 142, 143, 150
Alihan, M. A., 243, 261
Allbright, W. A., 138
American Council on Race Relations, 298
Ancient cities
  Africa, 138, 144
  Alexandria, 142, 144, 146
  Babylon, 22, 23
  Baghdad, 138
  Carthage, 23, 150
  China, 40–44, 58, 61–63
  India, Union of, 40, 96–98
  Memphis, 20–21, 42, 97
  Near East, 20–23
  Nippur, 21, 22, 138
  Thebes, 20–21, 42, 97
  Troy, 28
Anderson, Nels, 463, 482
Anglo-Egyptian Sudan (*See* N. Africa), 140,
  142, 150
Anomie (*Also see* Suicide *and* Voluntary
  associations), 390, 455
Anonymity, 454–456
Anshen, R. N., 379
Area of Transition (*See* Zone of Transition,
  Ecological organization; Interstitial or
  Blighted areas)
Asia (*Also see* N. *and* S. Asian cities)
  definition of Asian cities, 37, 72, 79, 88,
    116, 117, 120, 131

Asia—(*Continued*)
  excavations in ancient cities of China, 41;
    in India, Union of, 41
  map of Asian cities, 43
Associations (*See* Voluntary associations)
Atomic age
  decentralization of industries, 192, 542–
    543
  effect on cities, 192–193, 522, 540, 546,
    547
  leisure-time activities, 450
Australia, 132–134
  major cities of, 133
  Melbourne, 133
  size of urban population, 133
  Sydney, 133
  urban problems, 134
Auxiliary structures (*See* World of artifacts),
  269–272
Ayers, W., 66

Baltimore Plan (*Also see* Interstitial *or*
  Blighted areas), 484–485
Bangkok (*Also see* Thailand), 116, 117, 118
Bantu (*Also see* S. Africa), 158, 160, 173,
  426
Baptist church, 342, 343, 345–347, 360
Barer, Naomi, 499
Barnes, H. E., 418
Barron, Milton L., 507
Behavior patterns (*Also see* Personality traits,
  Voluntary associations, *and* Urban
  ways of life)
  life organization and, 463–464
  mass media and, 10–12, 444–446, 457,
    465
  of social types, 461–463
  traditional culture and, 12–13, 414, 415–
    416
  urban impact on personality, 453–454
Belgian Congo (*Also see* Central Africa),
  174
Benares (*See* India, Union of)
Bendix, Reinhard, 412, 429
Benedict, Ruth, 72, 91
Bennett, J. W., 415
Bernert, Eleanor, 403
Berry, Brewton, 299
Bird, F. L., 339
Birla, G. O., 105
Birth rate, United States, 218–225
Bishop, D. G., 325, 327, 339
Black Belts (*See* Ecological organization,
  Urban ghettos)
Blighted areas (*Also see* Interstitial areas),
  473–485
  characteristics of, 475–476

Blighted areas—(*Continued*)
cost of, 476–478
definition of interstitial, 473–475
immigrant colonies, 479–480
inhabitants of, 478–480, 481–482
location of, 474
Los Angeles Study, 477–478
remedial measures, 483–485
roadhouse belts, 480–481
Skid Row, 481–482
slums, 478–479
vice areas, 481
Blofield, John, 54
Blumer, Herbert, 452
Blunt, E. A. H., 111
Bogue, Don J., 189, 191, 200
Boll, Eleanor, 439
Bombay (*Also see* India, Union of), 90, 104, 105, 108, 112
Bossard, H. S., 439
Bossard, James, 379
Bourg (*See* Medieval city: China, Europe)
China, 45–47
Europe
decline of, 29–31
as defense city, 27–28
spatial pattern of, 28
Bowden, Witt, 32, 33, 36
Braidwood, Lydia, 22
Breese, G. W., 237, 276, 286
Bridenbaugh, Carl, 179, 183, 200
Brightbill, C. K., 452
Bromage, Arthur W., 328
Brown, F. J., 300
Browne, W. J., 171
Bryan, L. A., 545
Buck, J. L., 47
Buddhism
in Burma, 94
in China, 46
in India, Union of, 98, 107
in Japan, 43
in United States, 348
Bureau of Urban Research, 537
Burgess, E. W., 218, 230, 231, 236, 238, 261, 364, 366, 375, 454, 457, 508, 517
Burma, 94–96
Burmese in industries, 95–96
Chinese in, 95
control of industries, 95–96
Europeans in, 95
Indians in, 95
Mandalay, 94
present industrial development, 96
size of urban population, 95
Butler, Geo. D., 440

Cairo (*Also see* Africa *and* Egypt), 141, 142, 144, 146, 149–150
division of labor, 150
spatial pattern of, 149–150
suburb of, 534
Calcutta (*Also see* India, Union of), 90, 105
Calhoun, A. W., 366, 379
Caplow, T., 267
Carpenter, D. B., 401
Carr-Saunders, A. M., 36
Cartinhous, Gaines T., 311, 316
Casablanca (*Also see* N. Africa), 142, 144, 146, 150
Casey, Robert J., 530, 539
Caste (*See* India, Union of), 111–112
Catholic church (*Also see* Religious organization), 342, 343, 345–347
Cavan, Ruth S., 455
Cayton, H. R., 253, 360, 409
Central business district
banking in, 237
daytime population, 247
different location of, 237
function of, 245
as retail center, 237
Centralization (*Also see* Ecological organization), 245–248
Ceylon, 132
Chang, Kai-Ngau, 53
Chen Ta, 36, 65, 66
Chen, Theo. H. E., 67
Cheng, Ch'eng-Kun, 512
Chicago
Black Belt, 294
Concentric Zone Theory, as applied to, 236–240
crime, 508, 509
delinquency in, 506
divorce, 218
family disorganization in, 513–515
gangland, 506
Gold Coast and the slum, 456
Housing Authority, 500
industrial districts, 249, 308
insanity, 512–513
land values, 249
machine politics in, 335, 336, 509
mayors of, 321
mental disorders in, 512–513
metropolitan area of, 331, 333, 342
metropolitan government of, 321, 495
occupational structure of, 403
overlapping government units in, 329, 333
Plan Commission, 531–532
population succession in, 255
Skid Row, 455, 482

Chicago—(*Continued*)
  transit system, 279
  vice in, 517
Children
  Children's Bureau publications, 507
  church-going habits of, 351
  effects of mass media on, 415, 423, 433,
    444–446
  personality development of, 458–459
  in urban family, 366–370
  with working mothers, 375
Childs, Marquis W., 501
China, 42–72
  ancient cities, 40–44
  Arabs in, 48, 49
  British merchants in Canton, 49–50
  Buddhism in, 46; influence on spatial pat-
    tern of cities, 63–64
  Canton, 48, 49–52, 53, 58, 59, 63; map of,
    51
  Chungking, 54, 55, 59
  Confucius (ethical system), 45–46; in-
    fluence on family, 63; on social and oc-
    cupational mobility, 45, 64–65; social
    structure, 45–46, 64–65; spatial pattern
    of cities, 51, 63
  Dairen, 52, 54, 58
  defense cities, 45–47
  ecological organization, 58–64
  Eurasians, 59–60
  extraterritoriality, 50–52
  foreign concessions (*See* extraterritoriality)
  Ghettos, 59
  Harbin, 54, 60, 66
  Hong Kong, 53, 54, 55, 58, 59, 66
  hsiens (counties), 57–58
  industrial development, 52
  inland cities, 53, 54, 58; ecological or-
    ganization of, 63–64
  Japanese in, 53, 60
  Macao, 66; Eurasians in, 59–60; Portu-
    guese in, 49, 54, 60
  Marco Polo, 49
  market centers, 57
  medieval cities, 58; ecological organiza-
    tion of, 61–63
  modern cities, 52–55, 58; ecological or-
    ganization of, 58–61; influence of west-
    ernization, 52
  Mongolia, cities of, 57–58
  municipal government (special municipal-
    ities), 54; other political units, 57–58
  Nanking, 44–45, 58
  non-industrial factors promoting urban
    growth, 69–72
  number of cities, 55–57; table of cities,
    56

China—(*Continued*)
  occupations in Shanghai, 66
  Opium War, 50, 53
  Overseas Chinese population, 67 (*Also see*
    Chinese in S. African, S. Asian, and
    U. S. cities)
  Peking, 45, 54, 55, 58
  "People's Government," 45, 54–55
  periods of urban growth, 42–55
  Sampan population, 62–63, 70
  Shanghai, 52, 53, 54, 58, 59, 61, 66
  Sinkiang, cities of, 55, 57–58
  size of urban population 55; table of, 57
  slums, 62–63
  social and occupational structure, 64–69
  Sun Yat-sen, Dr., 44
  Taoism (ethical system), 45–46; influence
    on spatial pattern, 46, 54
  temples, 63–64
  Tibet, 53, 55
  Tientsin, 52, 54, 58
  transportation, 53, 62–63
  unpaid family workers, 70–71
  Western influence, 42, 45, 46, 48–55, 58–
    59, 64–65, 69–71
Chinese-Americans, 209, 214–215
Chinese in (*Also see* Overseas Chinese popu-
    lation, China) Burma, 95; Indochina,
    113, 114–116; Indonesia, 127; Malay
    States, 121–123; Philippines, 130, 131–
    132; Thailand, 116, 119–120; South
    Africa, 159, 160; United States, 209,
    214–215
Churches (*See* Religious organization)
Churchill, Henry S., 41, 97, 542
City, definition of
  Australia, 132
  Belgium, 37
  Canada, 37
  Columbia, 37
  Denmark, 37
  Formosa, 88
  France, 37
  India, Union of, 37, 72
  Ireland, 37
  Japan, 72, 79
  Malay States, 37, 120
  Mexico, 37
  New Zealand, 37, 134
  Panama, 37
  Philippines, 131
  Portugal, 37
  South Africa, Union of, 37, 161
  Sweden, 37
  Thailand, 116, 117
  United Kingdom, 37
  United States, 37, 179

Cities of the United States (*See* United States, cities of), 177–199

City-manager government (*Also see* Political organization), 322, 325–328

City-planning (*Also see* Planning and model communities), 523–526

City-states, 20–26

Civil defense, 543, 549

Clark, W. C., 268

Classification of cities, 14

Cliques (*See* Voluntary associations *and* Leisure-time activities)

Cohen, Lillian, 372, 455, 514

Colean, Miles L., 501

Colonial policies (*Also see* African cities), 143–144

Commensalism (*See* Ecological organization)

Commerce and trade (*Also see* Economic organization), 308–310

Commercial recreation (*Also see* Leisure-time activities), 438–439

Commonwealth v. *Moir*, 1901, 26

Community as distinguished from society, 231 fn.

Community papers (*Also see* Media of communication), 424–425

Company towns (*Also see* Planning and model communities), 535

Concentration (*Also see* Ecological organization), 244–245

Concentric Zone Theory (*Also see* Ecological organization), 236–240
   central business district, 237; Commuters' Zone, 240; contributions and criticisms of, 243–244; gradients, 223; Zone in Transition, 237–238; Zone of Workingmen's Homes, 238–239; Zone of Residential Hotels and Apartments, 239–240

Confucius, Confucianism (*See* China)

Congregation (*See* Religious organization)

Coon, Carleton S., 144, 147

Cooper-Cole, Fay, 118

Coose, M. V., 423

Cotterill, H. B., 26

Coulanges, Numa Dennis Fustel de, 24

Coutu, Walter, 460

Cox, Oliver, 398, 412

Creel, Herrlee G., 41, 44, 46

Cressey, Geo. B., 113, 136

Cressey, Paul F., 254, 256

Cressey, Paul G., 467

Crime (*Also see* Disorganization, personal and social *and* Social problems)
   adult, 508–509
   in Africa, 160, 167
   in China, 511–512

Crime—(*Continued*)
   ecological distribution of, 510–511
   in Norway, 508
   in Stockholm, 511
   juvenile, 507
   increase of, 508–509
   women in, 504, 511–512
   white-collar, 509–510

Crow, Carl, 92

Cuaston, E. C. N., 75

Cultural islands (*See* Ecological organization *and* Urban ghettos)

Daggett, Stuart, 279

Daniel, Vattel, 359, 362

Davie, M. R., 243

Davis, A., 408, 412

Davis, J. S., 387

Davis, Kingsley, 41, 97, 100, 103, 107, 111, 112, 399

Dean, J. P., 482

Decentralization (*Also see* Ecological organization), 248–251

Decker, Clarence, 91

Delinquent taxes (*Also see* Housing problems), 478, 493

Denby, Elizabeth, 501

Denney, R., 461, 467

Des Moines, Iowa (*See* Des Moines plan, Political organization), 324–325

Dewey, Richard, 331

Dickinson, Robt. L., 539

Disorganization, personal and social (*Also see* Crime *and* Social problems)
   alcoholism, 515–517
   crime in China, 511–512
   crime in Norway, 508
   crime in Stockholm, 511
   common sources of, 503–505; 518–519
   detribalization, 160, 167, 168–169, 173
   divorce, 512–516
   drug addiction, 518
   ecological distribution of crime, 505–506, 507, 510–511
   family disorganization and zonal patterns, 513–516
   illegitimacy, 517
   juvenile delinquency, 505–509
   mental disorders, 512–513
   political corruption and graft, 336–337, 508–509
   process of disorganization, 503–505
   prostitution, 517–518
   size of city and crime, 511
   suicide, 455
   white-collar crime, 509–510

Dodd, J. A., 308
Donnelly, Thos. C., 280
Donovan, M., 467
Dotson, Floyd, 393, 449
Douglass, H. Paul, 349, 353, 362
Drake, St. Clair, 253, 360, 409
Dublin, L. I., 216, 217, 221
DuBois, Cora, 137
Duffus, R. L., 529
Duncan, O. D., 406
Dunham, H. Warren, 512, 520
Durand, John, 312, 316
Durkheim, E., 390, 455, 519
Dvorin, Eugene P., 162, 164, 175

East Africa (*See* Africa)
Eckstein, Gustave, 76
Ecological aspects of social disorders (*See* Disorganization, personal and social)
Ecological organization (*Also see* Spatial patterns of cities), 231–261
  commensalism, 234–235
  commercial decentralization, 249–250
  Commuters' Zone, 240
  central business district, 237
  centralization, 245–247; and movement of people, 247–248
  concentration, 244–245
  Concentric Zone theory, 236–240
  criticisms of theories of urban growth, 240–241
  decentralization, 248–251
  ecological processes, 244–260
  ethnic groups' dispersion, Chicago, 254–255
  factors initiating invasion, 256
  human ecology, 231–232
  industrial decentralization, 248–249
  internal spatial pattern, 235–244
  invasion, 235–254; institutional, 255–256
  invasion-succession and community configuration, 297
  multi-nuclear theory, 241–243
  natural areas, 232–234
  other variables influencing invasion-succession, 254–255
  population dispersion, 251
  sector theory, 240–241
  segregation, 251–252
  stages of invasion-succession, 257–260
  succession, 259–260
  successive invasions in a single area, 256
  symbiosis, 234–235
  voluntary and involuntary segregation, 252–253
  Zone in Transition, 237–230

Ecological organization—(*Continued*)
  Zone of Residential Hotels and Apartments, 239–240
  Zone of Workingmen's Homes, 238–239
Economic Organization (*Also see* Urban stratification), 305–316
  chain stores, 308–310
  commerce and trade, 308–310
  concentration of business, 310–311
  factors influencing location of industry, 305–307
  Far Eastern-American difference, 315
  finance, 311–312
  industrial structure, 305–312
  investments, life insurance companies, 311–312
  labor force, 312–315
  manufacturing industries, 307–308
  occupational structure, 400–403
  retail trade by city size, 309
  service industries, 312
  size of labor force, 313–314
  women in labor force, 315, 375
Eells, E., 405, 412
Egypt (*See* N. Africa)
Eldridge, Hope T., 180, 198, 541
Elliott, Mabel A., 486
Elmtown (*Also see* Religious organization), 352–353
Embree, John F., 72, 91
Episcopal city (*See* Medieval cities)
Ericksen, Gordon, 40
Ethiopia (*Also see* N. Africa), 142, 143, 144, 149, 151
Ethnic churches (*Also see* Religious organization), 347–348
Eurasians (*Also see* Métis)
  in Hong Kong, 59–60
  in Indochina, 115
  in Indonesia, 127–128, 129–130
  in Malay States, 125
European-built cities in non-Western regions (*See* Africa and Asia)

Fads and fashions (*See* Media of communication)
Faris, Robert E. L., 481, 486, 512, 513, 520
Farrar, Ekvall, 53
Fei, Hsiao-tung, 65, 70
Fertility (*See* Urban population composition)
Fez (*Also see* N. Africa), 142, 144, 145, 146, 147–149, 150
Fichter, Jos. F., 343
Finance, Municipal
  concentration of financial organizations, 311–312
  indebtedness, 319, 494–495

Finance, Municipal—(*Continued*)
new sources of revenue, 329, 330, 495, 547–548
Firey, W., 244, 254, 262, 480
Ford, R. C., 255
Foreign-born (*Also see* United States, Urban population composition), 207–209
Forman, Harrison, 52, 53
Formosa (*Also see* Taiwan), 86–89
Frazier, E. F., 410
Freeman, Otis W., 127, 128, 131, 134, 137
Freetown (*Also see* West Africa), 142, 153. 154
Fried, Morton H., 68
Frost, John, 40
Fry, C. Luther, 363
Future trends and objectives, 540–549
better protective services, 548
Bureau of Municipal Research, 547
civilian defense, 543, 544
co-ordination between officials, 547
future urban population, 540–541
industrial decentralization, 543
intercity migration data, 548
jet-plane intercity relationships, 545
objectives, 547–549
population composition and size of city, 540–544
social scientists' role in municipal affairs, 548–549
transportation changes, 544–546
trends in other fields, 546–547

Galveston, Texas (*See* Galveston Plan, Political organization), 342–345
Gambling (*Also see* Leisure-time activities), 440–442
Gao, Huei-shung, 50
Garden cities, 533
Gardner, B., 412
Gardner, M., 412
Geddes, Patrick, 40, 479
Gemeinschaft, 5, 235, 396
Gesellschaft, 5, 235
Ghettos (*See* Black Belts; Native areas and locations in S. Africa; Natural areas; Urban ghettos)
Gibbard, Harold, 256, 257
Giese, J., 30
Gilmore, H. W., 286
Gist, N. P., 34, 249, 439
Glazer, N., 461, 467
Glick, Paul C., 315
Glueck, Eleanor, 507
Glueck, Sheldon, 507
Gold Coast (*Also see* W. Africa), 142, 151, 154, 155

Goldhamer, Herbert, 389
Goode, W. J., 218
Goodrich, L. C., 48
Gosnell, Harold F., 335
Gould, Randall, 54
Grajdanzev, Andrew J., 84
Gras, N. S. B., 40, 187
Grattan, Hardey C., 137
Greeks (*See* Ancient cities)
Greenbelt cities (*See* Planning and model communities)
Greer, Guy, 531, 574
Gridiron street plan (*See* World of artifacts *and* Planning and model communities)
Gutheim, Frederick, 501

Hagood, Margaret J., 221, 230
Hailey, Lord W. M., 152, 166, 175, 289
Halbert, L. A., 249, 439
Handlin, Oscar, 287
Hanse League (*See* Medieval cities)
Harris, C. D., 241, 242, 246
Hart, Hornell, 350
Hartley, E. L., 430
Hasek, C. W., 308
Hatt, P. K., 200, 218, 398, 403, 404
Hauser, Ernest O., 52
Hauser, Philip M., 180, 198, 541
Hawley, A. H., 191, 233, 234, 262
Hayden, Jos. R., 131, 132
Hellman, Ellen, 161, 175
Henderson, C. R., 381
Herskovits, M., 152
Herzog, Herta, 430
Heterogeneity (*Also see* Urban population composition), 205–229
in defining the city, 7–8
Hill, M. C., 409
Hillhouse, A. M., 495, 548
Hillman, Arthur, 530, 539
Holcombe, Arthur H., 280
Hollingshead, A. B., 352, 363, 440, 510
Homeless men, areas of (*Also see* Interstitial *and* Blighted areas), 454, 481–482
alcoholism in, 516
anonymity in, 455–456
hobos, 463; hobo jungles, 463–479
location of, 463, 516
social types, 463, 481–482
Home ownership (*Also see* Urban family *and* Housing problems)
by ethnic background, 372–373
increase of, 372
marital status and, 373
taxation and, 372
Horizontal mobility (*See* Urban stratification)

Horner, Francis J., 74
Hourani, A. H., 145
Housing problems, 488–501
  building codes, 496–497
  community facilities, 497–498
  cooperative housing, 498
  extent of problem, 488–491
  factors contributing to, 491–498
  federal efforts, 499
  home financing, 493–494
  Housing Act, 1949, 498
  housing characteristics of United States,
    490–491
  housing industry and practices, 493
  housing inspection, 496
  industrial projects, 500
  insurance company projects, 499–500
  land-use policies, 492–493
  middle-income needs, 498
  mobility, 494–495
  municipal efforts, 499
  private enterprise and housing, 499–500
  real estate speculation, 497
  remedial measures, 499–500
  restrictive covenants, 495–496
  taxation, 495
  zoning regulations, 496
Howard, Ebenezer, 533
Hoyt, Homer, 241, 249, 262
Hughes, E. C., 176, 287, 288, 393, 460
Hughes, H. M., 176, 287, 288, 417, 420
Hunter, A. C., 50
Hurd, R. M., 240, 262
Hutton, J. H., 111
Hyderabad (*See* Pakistan)

Ibadan (*See* W. Africa)
Immigrant (*See* Urban population composi-
  tion; foreign-born)
Immigrant Press (*See* Media of communi-
  cation)
India, Union of, 96–112
  Benares, 98
  Bombay, 90, 104, 105, 108, 112
  Calcutta, 90, 105
  caste and urban environment, 111–112
  caste and urban residence, 106–108
  census definition of city, 100
  Christians, 107, 108
  future urbanization, 104–106
  growth of urban population, 100, 101,
    103–104
  Hindus, 98, 107
  Indians in Burma, 95–96; in China, 59;
    in Indonesia, 127–128; Malay States,
    123; in S. Africa, 159, 164–165, 172,
    173–174; in Thailand, 116

India, Union of—(*Continued*)
  industrial future, 104–106
  Jains, 107, 108
  Jews, 107, 108
  male–female urban residence, 108–111
  Mohen-jo-daro excavations, 96
  Moslems, 98, 107
  natural resources, 105
  New Delhi, 98
  number and location of cities, 100–104
  Parsi, 107, 108
  partition, 101, 103–104
  post-British cities, 99–101
  pre-British cities, 97–99
  religious cities, 98
  Sikhs, 107
  size of urban population, 100
  Untouchables, 112
Indochina, 112–116
  Caucasoids in, 112, 113, 114
  Chinese in, 113, 114–116
  industrial development, 113–114
  major cities, 113
  Métis, 115
  social and occupational structure, 114–116
  social organization of Chinese in, 114–
    115
  urban population, 112
Indonesia, 127–130
  Eurasians and social structure, 127, 129–
    130
  major cities of, 128–129
  population composition, 127
  relationship to The Netherlands, 127,
    129–130
  urban population, 128
Industrialization, as criteria for urban
    growth, 3–4
Industries (*Also see* Ecological *and* Economic
    organization)
  centralization of, 247
  concentration of, 245, 306, 308, 310
  cottage type, 315
  decentralization of, 248–249, 543
  momentum of early start, 307–308
Interstitial areas (*Also see* Blighted areas),
    473–487
Invasion and succession (*Also see* Ecological
    organization, Interstitial *and* Blighted
    areas, Urban ghettos)
  and blight, 476
  and ghetto decline, 297
  factors initiating, 256–257
  kinds of invasion, 253–256
  stages of cycle, 257–260
  urban churches and, 349–350
Issawi, C., 21, 149

Jaffe, Abram J., 189, 198
Janowitz, M., 423–424
Janse, A. R. T., 137
Japan, 72–86
  Buddhism, 73
  commerce and trade, 74–75, 80
  control of family size, 369
  cultural centers, 73, 79–80
  definition of city "shi," 72
  factors promoting urban growth, 75–76,
    77
  factory workers, 83
  feudalism, 73–75
  industrial growth, 75–76, 79
  industrial and occupational structure, 81–
    84
  Japanese in Korea, 75, 76, 77
  Kobe, 73, 80
  males and labor force, 81–84
  major industries, 76, 79–81
  major urban industries, 83
  major urban occupations, 82
  Nagasaki, 74, 80
  Nara, 73
  number of cities, 77–79
  Osaka, 74, 77, 80
  periods of urban growth, 72–79
  sex ratio, 79
  Shoguns, Shogunate, 73–74
  size of urban family, 368
  size of urban population, 72
  Tokyo, 73, 74, 77, 79–80
  type of cities, 79–81
  women in labor force, 82–83
  Yokohama, 75, 79–80
  Zaibaitsu, 75, 76
Japanese-Americans, 209, 259
Jefferson, Mark, 34, 141
Jews
  in India, Union of, 107, 108
  in N. Africa, 143, 145, 146, 147, 149
  in S. Africa, 158
  in United States, 296, 343, 346, 347, 409
Johannesburg (*Also see* S. Africa), 141, 142,
    159, 160, 161, 165, 169, 172
Jones, A. H. M., 23
Jones, Elliot, 184
Jones, Victor, 333, 339
Juvenile delinquency (*Also see* Disorganiza-
    tion, personal and social; Crime)
  ecological distribution of, 505–506, 507
  Juvenile court statistics, 506–507
  recent trends in, 507, 508
  Shaw's Study, 505–506
  socio-economic factors, 506, 507
  value conflicts, 507

Kano (*Also see* W. Africa), 142, 152
Karachi (*Also see* Pakistan), 103, 104, 106
Karlin, Jules, 249
Karpinos, Bernard de, 230
Karpovich, Michael, 32, 33, 36
Kendall, P. L., 434
Kenealy, E. J., 286
Kennedy, Raymond, 140, 143
Kent, Frank R., 335, 339
Keyes, F., 47, 55, 57
Kimball, Dexter S., 306
Kimball, Dexter S., Jr., 306
Kincheloe, S. C., 351, 353, 363
King, F. H., 47
Kingston, J. L., 268
Kirby, Stuart, 54
Kiser, C. V., 379
Kitt, A. S., 388
Kneedler, G. M., 14
Knier, Charles M., 326
Kniffen, Fred B., 53, 70, 73, 75, 87, 152
Knox, J. B., 230
Knupfer, Genevieve, 422
Kobe, 73, 80
Kobrin, Sol, 507
Kolb, W. L., 403
Komarovsky, Mirra, 383, 393, 446
Korea, 84–86
  factors affecting urbanization, 85–86
  Japanese in, 84, 85
  N. Korean cities, 84–85
  occupations of Japanese, 86, 87
  occupations of Koreans, 86, 87
  Seoul, 84, 85
  size of urban population, 84
  S. Korean cities, 85
Kroef, J. M. van der, 129
Kwong, Ed. Y. K., 45

Labatut, J., 48, 275, 286
Labor force, size of in
  Burma, 95
  Formosa, 89
  Japan, 82
  Korea, 87
  Malay States, 125
  United States, 312–315
Labor unions (*See* Voluntary associations)
Land use (*See* Ecological organization,
    Housing problems, Interstitial *and*
    Blighted areas, World of artifacts)
Land values (*See* Ecological organization,
    Housing problems, Interstitial *and*
    Blighted areas, World of artifacts)
Lane, W. J., 48
Lang, G. E., 431
Lang, Kurt, 431

Lasker, Bruno, 95
Latourette, K., 45
Lazarsfeld, P. F., 389, 434
Lee, A. M., 418, 419, 434, 487
Lee, E. B., 487
Lee, Rose Hum, 70, 202, 295, 506
Lee, Shu-ching, 72
Leiffer, Murray H., 344
Leisure-time activities, 435–451
    commercial forms, 438–439
    effect of movies on children, 443, 444–445, 446
    entertainers in, 438–439
    gambling and political corruption, 440, 442
    illegal, 440–443
    income and, 446–449
    movies, 443–446
    occupations and, 447–449
    "policy" games as, 441
    private, 440, 448–449
    professional types of gambling, 442
    public, 440
    quasi-commercial, 439–440
    social effect of movies, 444–446
    spectator sports and amusements, 438–439
    too much leisure? 449–450
    urban environment and, 436–442
Lepawsky, 331, 333, 339
Leybun, James, 166
Liang Yuan, 44, 45, 48, 56, 57, 73
Liberia (*Also see* W. Africa), 152, 154
Liebesny, Herbert, 176
Life insurance companies (*Also see* Ecological organization *and* Housing problems)
    in housing, 499, 500
    investments by, 311–312
Lindesmith, A. R., 518
Lindholm, R. W., 495
Lingnam Social Research Institute (*See* Sampan population, China)
Linton, Ralph, 140
Lipset, S. M., 412, 422, 429
Little, K. L., 154, 156
Liverpool, England (*See* Merseyside, Urban ghettos)
Locke, H. J., 230, 364, 375, 454, 457, 517
London Colonial Office, 33
Lory, Hillis, 76
Los Angeles, California; study of blight, 477–478
Lotka, J., 216, 217, 221
Low, J. O., 408
Lundberg, G., 383, 446, 452
Lusaka, Uganda (*See* E. Africa)

Lutheran church (*See* Religious organization)
Lynd, Helen M., 351, 352
Lynd, Robert S., 351, 352

McCall, B. C., 409
McCarthy, Raymond G., 515
McClenahan, B. A., 370
McConnell, J. W., 412
MacCrone, I. D., 166
McCune, Geo. M., 84, 86, 87, 91
McDonagh, E. C., 484, 487
McGuire, C., 409
McInery, A., 383
MacIver, R. M., 385, 393
McKay, H. D., 506, 520
McKenzie, R. D., 190, 200, 245, 247, 257, 267
MacLear, Anne B., 182, 200
McMahon, C. A., 230
MacMillan, W. M., 158, 176
MacNair, H. F., 42, 45, 46, 91
McWilliams, Carey, 209, 230, 299
Magelssen, M., 495, 548
Malay States, 120–127
    Caucasoids in, 125
    Chinese in, 121–123
    Eurasians in, 125–126
    factors retarding industrialization, 126–127
    Indians in, 123
    major cities, 121, 122
    Malaysians, 123–125
    occupations of Malaysians, Chinese, Indians, Europeans, Eurasians, 121–126
    urban population, 120–121
Mandalay (*Also see* Burma), 94
Mangus, A. R., 458
Manila (*Also see* Philippines), 131
Manufacturing industries (*Also see* Economic organization), 307–308
Marden, C. F., 300
Martin, Edwin M., 91
Mass production (*Also see* Economic organization), 307–308
Matheson, Alastair, 158, 173
Maxwell, M. L., 210
Mayer, K. B., 36, 452
Media of communication, 413–433
    Bantu Press, 426
    chain newspapers, 419–421
    community papers, 421–425
    effect on behavior patterns, 10–12, 444–446, 457, 465
    effect on children, 415, 423, 443, 444–446

Media of communication—(*Continued*)
  effect on other societies, 10–12, 416, 429, 445
  functions of Negro press, 426–427
  functions of newspapers, 416–419
  human interest, 417
  imagery of community newspaper readership, 424–425
  immigrant press, 427–429
  magazine audience, 422–423
  mass culture, 10–12, 415–516
  movies, 443–446
  Negro press, 425–427
  newspaper circulation, 418–420
  radio, 429–431; listening behavior, 429–431
  suburban press, 423–424
  tabloids and periodicals, 421–423
  television, 431–432
  traditional culture, 10–13, 414, 415–416
Medieval cities (Episcopal cities, Bourgs, Commerce and trade cities), 27–31
Meeker, M., 405, 412
Melbourne (*Also see* Australia), 133
Merriam, C. E., 331, 333, 339
Merrill, Francis E., 471, 486
Merseyside, Liverpool (*Also see* Urban ghettos), 289
Merton, R. K., 302, 334
Methodist denomination (*See* Religious organization)
Métis (*Also see* Eurasians), 115
Metropolitan cities
  Africa, 142
  Asia, 55, 56, 77, 78, 79, 84, 88, 103, 104
  Europe, 31–39
  Oceania, 128, 129
  United States, 177–201
  in world, 34
Metropolitan districts, 187–196
  census definition, 188–189, 193–197
  metropolitan dominance, 189–190, 193
  metropolitan governments, 328–334
  political complexity, 190–191, 328–334
  significance of census classifications, 197–198
  standard metropolitan areas, 196–197
  urbanized areas, 194–196
Metropolitan government, 328–334
  Chicago, 329–330, 331, 333
  complexity of, 328–330
  London, 35
  New York, 331, 333–334
  overlapping jurisdiction, 331–332
  Philadelphia, 331, 333–334
  Pittsburgh, 333–334
  remedies for, 332–334

Metropolitan government—(*Continued*)
  San Francisco, 331
  United States, 328–336
Middle class (*See* Urban stratification *and* Medieval cities)
Middletown (*See* Religious organization)
Miller, Kenneth, 363
Mills, C. W., 310, 401, 402
Miner, Horace, 176
Minnus, Mhyra S., 388
Mobility (*Also see* Urban stratification and Housing problems), 407–409, 494–495
Model communities (*Also see* Planning and model communities), 523–539
Modern warfare and population dispersion, 10, 36, 55, 77, 84, 95, 157–158, 166, 186, 192
Monrovia (*See* W. Africa)
Morgan, E. S., 366
Moriyama, Iwao M., 227
Morocco (*See* N. Africa)
Moslems in
  E. Africa, 289–291
  India, Union of, 98, 291
  N. Africa, 143, 146, 147, 149, 150
  Pakistan, 107, 291
  Thailand, 116
  S. Africa, 159, 173, 174
  W. Africa, 154
Mott, F. L., 427
Movies (*Also see* Leisure-time activities), 443–446
Mowrer, E. R., 243, 513, 514
Mukerji, Dhurjate, 137
Muller, H. M., 327
Multi-dwellings (*Also see* Housing problems, Urban family, World of artifacts), 265–268, 371–372, 491
Multi-nuclear theory (*Also see* Ecological organization), 241–243
  criticisms of, 244
  factors influencing major and minor nuclei, 242–243
  general description of, 241–242
Mumford, Louis, 40, 529
Munger, E. S., 140
Munro, W. B., 23, 26
Municipal budgets (*See* Finance, municipal)
Municipal government
  city-states, 24–25, 26
  China, 51, 57, 333
  London, 35, 37
  Philippines, 131
  Thailand, 116–118
  United States, 318–328
Myrdal, Gunnar, 300, 409, 426

Nagasaki (*Also see* Japan), 74, 80

Nara (*Also see* Japan), 73

National Committee on Segregation in the Nation's capital, 478

Native cities (*See* N. and W. African *and* N. and S. Asian cities)

Nativity (*See* Urban population composition)

Natural areas (*Also see* Ecological organization *and* Urban ghettos)
  definition of, 232–233
  indexes, 233
  nature of, 233–234

Negro
  alcoholism, 517
  in Black Belt, 294, 295, 371
  churches, 358–360
  fertility, 208, 224–225
  mortality, 277–278
  press, 425–427, 433
  occupations of, 408, 409–410
  restrictive covenants, 253
  segregation of, 252
  sex ratio, 213, 214
  social types, 463
  widows, 216

Neighborhood
  decline of neighborliness, 366, 370, 371–372, 456
  local communities, 232–234
  neighborhood houses, 355–356

Nelson, M. Frederick, 84

Nelson, Otto L., 499

Net reproduction rate, United States, 220, 222–225

Neumeyer, E. S., 438, 452

Neumeyer, Martin H., 438, 452, 506

Newcomb, Theo. M., 430

New Delhi (*See* India, Union of)

Newspapers (*See* Media of communication)

New York, N. Y.
  as headquarters of national organizations, 308–309
  metropolitan government of, 331–333
  seaport, 179, 183
  study of, and environs, 528–529
  transit system, 279

New Zealand, 134–135
  major cities of, 135
  urban industries, 134
  urban population, 134

Nichols, John P., 317

Nigeria (*Also see* W. Africa), 142, 151, 152, 155

Nimkoff, M. F., 218, 367, 369, 379, 383, 393

Nippur (*See* Ancient cities)

Nishimoto, Richard S., 209

Nitobe, Inazo, 75

Nolting, Orin F., 326

Non-industrial factors and city growth
  China, 51–52, 61–62, 69–72
  Indochina, 113–114
  Korea, 85–86
  Malay States, 126, 127

Noon, J. A., 165, 166

Nordskog, J. E., 484, 487

Norins, Martin N., 55

North, C. C., 403, 412

Oak, V. V., 434

Objectives of future cities (*See* Future trends and objectives)

Occupational structure
  Burma, 95
  Chicago, 403
  China, 64–68
  India, Union of, 108–110
  Indochina, 114–116
  Japan, 81–84
  Korea, 86–87
  Malay States, 121–126
  Middle Ages, Europe, 29–30
  Pakistan, 108–110
  Philadelphia, 403
  Thailand, 119
  United States, 400–403

Occupations (*Also see* Economic organization *and* Urban stratification)
  age of city and, 403
  changing nature of, 404
  ethnic and racial difference in, 409–410
  labor force and, 312–315
  mobility and, 407–409
  prestige of, 403–405
  urban personality and, 460–461

Ogburn, W. F., 286, 367, 369, 383, 393

O'Malley, L. S. S., 111

Optimum size of cities (*See* Future trends and objectives)

Osaka (*Also see* Japan), 74, 77, 80

Osborn, F. J., 533

Pakistan, 96–112
  caste and urban environment, 111–112
  East Pakistan, 105, 106
  future urbanization, 104–106
  Hindus in, 107
  Hyderabad, 103
  industrialization, 106
  Karachi, 103, 104, 106
  number and location of cities, 103–104
  partition, 101, 103–104

Pakistan—(*Continued*)
size of urban population, 100–101, 103–104
Unobad, 106
urban residence and religious affiliations, 103, 107
West Pakistan, 105, 106, 107
Palm, Franklin C., 29
Pankhurst, Sylvia, 143
Park, R. E., 231, 233, 237, 262, 300, 428, 434, 456
Parratt, Spencer D. 331, 333, 339
Peattie, Roderick, 141, 157, 159
Pegler, F. J., 151, 155, 156
Periodicals (*Also see* Media of communication), 421–423
Periods of urban growth
China, 42–55
India, Union of, 96–101
Japan, 72–79
United States, 178, 181–193
Perry, Geo. S., 200
Personality traits (*Also see* Media of communication; Disorganization, personal and social; Urban personality *and* Social types; *and* World of artifacts)
anonymity, 454–456
anxiety, 458
conflict of roles, 504–505
effect of mass media, 413–414
ideational mobility, 457–458
occupational influences, 460–461
physical equipment and social relations, 283
social distance, 456–457
speed, 283, 459
Pfautz, H. W., 406
Philippines, 130–132
Chinese in, 130, 131–132
major cities, 131
Manila, 131
municipal areas and barrios, 131
urban population, 130
Pirenne, Henri, 27, 28, 29, 40
Pithawalla, Maneck B., 105
Planning and model communities, 523–539
aims and steps in planning, 530–531
ancient, 524–525
criticisms of, 536–537, 538
execution of plans, 531–533
favorable aspects of, 533–536, 537–538
garden cities, 533
Great Britain, 527, 532–533
Greenbelt cities, 533
in India, Union of, 529–530
laissez-faire, 525–527
metropolitan planning, 528–529

Planning and model communities—(*Continued*)
modern planned communities, 543–544
municipal government function, 530–532
preplanning, 525–527
private planning, 535
regional, 530–532
spider-web formation, 525–527
steps in, 521
United States, 527–529, 533
Police protection (*Also see* World of artifacts), 282, 283
Political organization, 318–338
advantages-disadvantages, city-manager government, 327–328
advantages-disadvantages, commission government, 325
advantages-disadvantages, mayor-council government, 321, 323
city charters, 320
city-manager, 322, 323–328
commission, 322, 323–325
county governments, 331–332
Des Moines Plan, 324–325
forms of municipal government, 320–328
Galveston Plan, 324–325
Los Angeles metropolitan government, 334
mayor-council, 321–323
municipal powers, 319–320
other governments, 332
overlapping governments, 328–331
political corruption, 336–337
political machines and latent functions, 334–337
reforms, 337
strong-mayor, 321–323
Politics (*See* Political organization)
Population composition of cities (*Also see* Urban population composition)
Australia, 132
Burma, 95
China, 55, 56, 57, 62, 66
Indochina, 113, 115
Indonesia, 128
Japan, 72, 73, 77, 79, 82, 83, 90
Korea, 87, 90
Malay States, 121 123
New Zealand, 135
North Africa, 143, 145, 149
Philippines, 131, 132
South Africa, 156, 159, 162, 172
Taiwan, 88, 90
Thailand, 117
United States, 205–230
West Africa, 152
Powdermaker, Hortense, 445, 452

Presbyterian church (*See* Religious organization)

Professions (*Also see* Urban stratification), 401–404

Protective apparatus (*Also see* World of artifacts), 281–283

Public management of utilities and transportation, 269, 272–273, 279

Public utilities (*Also see* World of artifacts), 272–273

Purcell, Victor, 121

Queen, S. A., 245, 401

Quinn, J. E., 250, 262

Rabat (*Also see* N. Africa), 142, 145, 146

Ratcliff, Richard U., 493

Reckless, Walter C., 517, 520

Reever, W. D., 116, 119

Reimer, Svend, 30

Reischauer, Edwin O., 91

Reiss, Albert J., Jr., 200, 507

Religious organization, 341–361
    apartment-house area church, 357
    attitudes, beliefs, and practices, 350–351
    Buddhists in United States, 348
    Catholics, 342, 343, 345–347
    class composition of religious bodies, 1945–1946, 346
    cooperation, 344–345
    downtown churches, 354
    education and, 347
    Elmtown's, 352–353
    ethnic churches, 347–348
    family influence and church practices, 350–353
    industrial area church, 356–357
    inner-city church, 354–355
    institutional church and neighborhood house, 355–356
    invasion and succession and, 349–350
    Jewish, 343, 345, 347
    major faiths and denominations, 342–344
    Middletown in, 351–352
    Negro church, 358–360
    occupations and, 345–347, 351
    Protestants, 342–343, 345–347
    rooming-house church, 356
    size of Negro church population, 358–359
    size of urban religious population, 342–343
    specialization, 344
    stratification, 345–347
    store-front church, 358
    suburban church, 357
    type of city churches, 353–358
    urban influence and the church, 341–342, 348–357

Religious organization and changing values in non-western societies, 12–13, 65, 120, 342

Residential and non-residential structures (*See* World of artifacts)

Restrictive covenants (*See* Ecological organization, Housing problems, Interstitial *and* Blighted areas, Urban ghettos)

Retail trade (*Also see* Economic organization), 308–310

Reynolds, Rex, 176

Ridley, Clarence E., 326

Riencourt, Amaury de, 53

Riesman, David, 393, 461, 464, 467

Riggs, R. B., 68

Roberts, Robert E. T., 139, 158

Rogoff, N., 408

Rooming-house area studies, 445–446

Rose, Arnold, 300

Rose, Caroline, 300

Rosinger, L. K., 42, 91, 95, 105, 106, 114, 120, 127

Roucek, Jos., 300

Ruedi, O. M., 418

Rural-folk societies, 5–6, 138–139

Rural-nonfarm areas (*Also see* Cities of the United States), 191
    fertility rates in, 222–223
    home ownership in, 491
    race and nativity and, 207

Rurban fringe (*Also see* Interstitial *or* Blighted areas), 480–481

Russell, Richard J., 53, 70, 73, 75, 87, 153

Russia, 53, 55 105

Salter, J. T., 339

Samuels, M. M., 273

Satellite cities, 178, 186–187

Schapera, I., 176

Schechtman, Jos. B., 103

Schermerhorn, R. A., 144, 293, 295, 298, 300

Schlesinger, Arthur M., 186, 201

Schwartz, Benjamin I., 54

Sector theory (*Also see* Ecological organization), 240–241
    criticisms of, 244
    factors promoting radial expansion, 240–241
    residential areas and, 241

Segregation (*Also see* Ecological organization)
    definition of, 251–252
    in Asian cities, 49–52, 53, 59–61, 107, 113, 115, 291
    in East Africa, 289–290, 526

Segregation—(*Continued*)
in North Africa, 146–150, 291
restrictive covenants and, 253, 495–496
in South Africa, 169–174, 291
urban ghettos and, 287–299
voluntary and involuntary, 252–253
Seoul (*See* Korea)
Service industries (*See* Economic organization *and* Urban stratification), 312, 402–403, 404
Sewers and sewerage disposal (*Also see* World of artifacts), 270–272
Sex ratio; cities of
Australia, 132
India, Union of, 109
Japan, 79
United States, 212–215
Sharma, Tulsi R., 105
Shaw, Clifford R., 243, 506, 520
Shen, T. H., 70
Shih, Kuo-heng, 70, 92
Shrine cities, 17, 21–22, 44, 48
Shryock, J. K., 46
Siam (*See* Thailand), 116–120
Sibley, E., 408
Sierra Leone (*See* West Africa)
Silberman, Leo, 289
Simmel, Geo., 457, 459, 467
Simpson, Geo., E., 207, 294
Singh, Gurdial, 209
Sirjamai, John, 379
Skid Row (*See* Areas of Homeless Men, Crime, Vice, Zone of transition, Ecological organization)
Skinner, G. W., 115, 121, 137
Slater, Gilbert, 97
Slater, J. T., 335
Slums (*See* Interstitial *or* Blighted areas), 478–479
clearance of, 482
cost of blight, 476–478
location of, 478–479
of other regions, 62–63, 170–172
redevelopment of, 482–485
Smith, Marion B., 209, 230
Smith, T. E., 120, 121, 122, 123, 124, 126
Smith, T. Lynn, 214, 217, 224, 225, 230
Social distance, 126, 456–457
Social institutions, 301–380
as behavior patterns, 301–302
functions of, 302–303
latent functions of, 334–336
major types of, 305–380
manifest functions of, 303
as organization structure, 301, 302

Social mobility (*Also see* Mobility *and* Urban stratification), 407–409
Social participation (*Also see* Voluntary associations), 380–392
Social problems (*Also see* Interstitial *and* blighted areas; Housing problems; *and* Disorganization, personal and social), 503–519
adult crime, 508–509
alcoholism, 515–517
common sources of, 503–505, 518, 519
crime in China, 511–512; in Norway, 508; in Stockholm, 511
defining, 469–472, 503–505, 518–519
detribalization, 160, 167, 168–169, 173
divorce, 512–516
drug addiction, 518
ecological distribution of crime, 505–506, 507, 510–511
family disorganization and zonal patterns, 513–516
housing, 488–501
illegitimacy, 517
interstitial or blighted area, 473–485
juvenile delinquency, 505–507, 508, 509
mental disorders, 512–513
political corruption and graft, 336–337, 508–509
prostitution, 517–518
size of city and crime, 511
suicide, 455
white-collar crime, 509–510
Social status (*Also see* Status; Urban stratification), 397, 398, 399–400, 407–410
Social stratification (*Also see* Urban stratification), 397–411
Social structure
China, 64–68
Indochina, 114–116
Malay States, 121–126
South Africa, 156–160
United States, 401–403
Social types, 461–465
ethnic, 462–463
hobo, 461–462, 463
in recreation, 438–439
inner-directed person, 464, 466
middle-class, 463
other-directed person, 464, 465, 466
professional gambling, 440–442, 463
racial, 463
tradition-directed, 464, 466
underworld, 463
upper-class, 463
usefulness of, 462, 466
Sorokin, Pitirim, 407, 412
South Africa (*Also see* Africa), 156–174

South Asia (*Also see* Burma, Ceylon, Indo-
china, Indonesia, Malay States, Pakistan,
Philippines, Union of India), 93–132
Sovani, N. V., 105
Spatial pattern of cities
American, 235–244
Canton, 51
Chinese, 50–52, 58–64
Lusaka, Uganda, 290, 526
North African, 146–150
Salt Lake, 246
South African, 169–174
Spice, Betty, 289
Srole, Leo, 363, 510
Stamp, L. Dudley, 141, 142, 146, 151, 152,
154, 155, 157, 161
Standard metropolitan areas (*Also see* Met-
ropolitan districts), 196–198
definition of, 196–197
population increase in, 198
Starratt, D., 325, 329
Steffens, Lincoln, 339
Stonequist, E. V., 300
Stott, Leland H., 458
Straus, Robert, 515, 516
Streets, layout of (*See* World of artifacts)
Strong, Samuel S., 463
Suburban press (*Also see* Media of com-
munication), 423–424
Suburbs (*See* Metropolitan districts, Stand-
ard metropolitan areas, *and* Planning
and model communities)
Succession (*See* Invasion and succession)
Suicide (*See* Anomie; Disorganization, per-
sonal and social; *and* Social problems)
Sultan of Malay States, 120
Sultan of Morocco, 146
Sutherland, E. H., 210, 509, 511, **520**
Sydney, Australia, 133
Symbiosis (*Also see* Ecological organiza-
tion), 234–235

Taiwan (Formosa), 86–89
development of industries, 89
major cities, 88
major occupations, 89
size of urban population, 88
United States' influence, 89
Taoism (*See* China)
Tauber, Irene B., 71
Thailand (Siam), 116–120
Bangkok, 116, 117, 118
Chinese in, 116, 119–120
Indians and Malaysians in, 116
major cities, 118–119
municipal government, 116–117
pile villages, 118

Thailand—(*Continued*)
social and occupational structure, 119–
120
western influence in, 120
Thomas, Dorothy S., 209
Thomas, L. F., 245
Thomas, Lowell, Jr., 53
Thomas, W. I., 467
Thompson, Virginia, 113, 114, 118, 120,
122, 123, 125, 137
Thompson, Warren S., 75, 84, 85, 105, 216,
369
Thorp, F., 442
Thrasher, F. M., 474
Tinley, J. M., 160
Tocqueville, Alexis de, 381, 393
Tokyo (*See* Japan)
Tong, Hollington K., 54
Tourist camps and motels (*See* Rurban
fringe)
Transportation
airplane, 178, 193, 275, 544
automobile, 545
city growth and, 181, 184–185, 186, 192–
193, 241, 275
cost and time factors, 275
effect on city patterns, 274, 275
future trends, 544
helicopters, 545
highways, 275, 276, 546
interurban transit, 279–280
jet planes, 545
land values and, 265
motorbuses, 277, 279, 281
population movements and, 265
railroad, 178, 185–186
rapid transit, 279, 545–546
slum areas and, 479, 482
street cars, 277
terminals, 280, 281
traffic problems, 275
trucks, 275, 545
Tumin, M. M., 415
Tunis, Tunisia (*See* North Africa)

Ullman, L., 241, 242
Union of India (*See* India, Union of)
Union of South Africa (*See* South Africa)
United States, cities of, 177–199
airports, 178, 193
census definition, 37, 179, 180, 188–189;
194–197
changing urban classifications, 193–197
coastal cities, 178, 179, 183–184
dispersion of industries, 192
early towns, 182
economic provinces, 188

United States, cities of—(*Continued*)
  incorporated and unincorporated areas, 190–191
  increase of urban population, 178, 179, 180
  metropolitan cities, 178, 187
  metropolitan districts, 178, 187–189, 190
  metropolitan dominance, 189–190
  metropolitan political complexity, 190–191, 328–334
  municipal government, 183, 318–328
  major periods of urban development, 178 (table)
  new urbanism, railroad era, 183–184
  number of cities, 178, 181
  periods of urban development, 181–193
  railroad cities, 178, 185–186
  rate of increase, 179–180
  rural-nonfarm areas, 191; population, 190, 207, 223, 225
  rural population, 191, 198, 199, 223, 225
  satellite cities, 178
  slums, 186
  size of urban population, 178, 180
  Southern cities, 192
  standard metropolitan areas, 196–197
  suburbs, 193
  transportation and urban growth, 181, 184–185, 186, 192–193, 279–280
  urbanized areas, 194–196
Urban decline
  Africa, 144, 151
  Ancient cities, 23
  China, 41, 42, 44–45
  city-states, 26
  India, Union of, 41, 96, 97–98, 155
  Indochina, 113
Urban family, 364–378
  changing environment and, 365–366
  control of family size, 369–370
  criticisms against, 364
  functions retained by, 377–378
  general effects of urbanization on, 370–373
  home ownership, 372–373
  income and expenditures, 373–375
  loss of family functions, 375–377
  mothers employed, 375
  multi-dwellings and family interaction, 371–372
  size of urban family, Japan, 368; United States, 366–369
Urban ghettos (*Also see* Natural areas; Native areas and locations, South Africa), 287–298
  Africa, 289–291
  Asia, 291

Urban ghettos—(*Continued*)
  change in boundary lines and, 289
  characteristics of, 288, 292–293
  culturally divergent, 288–289
  diaspora, meaning of, 287–288
  Europe, 288–289
  factors promoting growth and decline of, 295–299
  future of, 297
  immigrants and, 295
  invasion, succession, and decline, 297
  Jewish, 287
  language, 291
  race relations and, 297, 298
  racial, 289
  religious, 291
  United States, 293–299
Urbanism
  definition of, 7
  new behavior patterns and (*See* Part V)
Urbanization
  definition of, 7
  factors promoting, 3, 4
  Westernization and, 6, 7, 9–10, 14–15
Urbanized areas (*Also see* United States, cities of), 194–196
  definition of, 194–195
Urban personality (*See* Personality traits *and* Social types)
Urban population composition, in the United States (*Also see* Population composition of cities), 205–230
  age and sex, 209–212
  age distribution, 210–212
  birth rates, 218–225
  Caucasoid, 207–208
  crude death rate, 228
  death by specific causes, 227–228
  divorce, 217–218
  differential fertility based on race-nativity, 224
  foreign-born, 207–208, 212
  marginal generation, 208, 212, 216
  marital status, 215–218
  Mongoloid and others, 208–209, 214–215
  mortality rates, 225–228; and race, 228
  native-born, 207
  Negroid, 208, 212, 214
  race and nativity, 207–209, 212
  race, residence, and fertility, 221–224
  rural-nonfarm, 191, 207, 223, 225
  rural population, 191, 198–199, 207, 223, 225
  sex ratio, 212–215
  widowed, 216–217
Urban stratification, 397–411
  caste-like, 410

Urban stratification—(*Continued*)
  community reputation approach, 405–407
  Davis's social order, 399–400
  ethnic and racial aspects of, 409–410
  nature of mass stratification, 397–400
  "new and old middle-class," 401–403
  new occupations and, 405
  occupational structure, Chicago and Phil-
    adelphia, 403
  occupational structure, United States, 401
  occupations and, 400–405
  prestige of occupations and, 403–405
  situs groups, 404
  Weber's economic order and, 398–399
Urban ways of life, 3, 7–15, 395–396
Urban weekly (*See* Media of communication)
Usher, Abbott P., 32, 33, 36

Vance, Rupert, 216, 221
Vanderblue, H. B., 184
Villard, O. G., 418, 434
Vincent, M. J., 484, 487
Voluntary associations, 380–392
  anomie and, 390
  city size and, 382–383
  class membership and, 388, 390
  classification of, 385–387
  cliques, 381, 391
  division of labor and, 388
  ethnic, 391
  function of, 387–389
  historical development, 381–383
  life cycle of, 384–385
  pressure groups as, 389
  racial groupings and, 388
  reference groups and, 388
  socialization and, 389
  urban environment and, 383–384
  "Yankee City," 390–391

Wales, Nym, 66
Walker, Robert A., 487, 529
Wallin, Paul, 366
Warner, W. Lloyd, 348, 363, 390, 393, 399,
  408, 412, 510
Water supply (*See* World of artifacts)
Weber, Adna F., 184, 201
Weidner, E. W., 340
Weinberg, S. K., 504, 520
Wells, H. G., 23
Werner, E. T. C., 50
West Africa (*See* Africa)
Western cities (*See* Western European cities
  and Cities of the United States)
Wheaton, J. L., 275, 286
Whelpton, P. K., 379

White, Anne T., 28
Wholesale trade and enterprises (*Also see*
  Economic organization), 308–310
Whyte, W. F., 337
Wiehl, D. G., 225
Weischhoff, H. A., 140
Willoughby, W. W., 52
Wilson, G. L., 545
Wilson, L., 403
Winfield, G. F., 47
Winstedt, R., 121
Wirth, Louis, 7, 293, 300, 462
Wolff, Kurt H., 457
Women in labor force
  Japan, 81–83
  India, Union of, 108–111
  Malay States, 122, 123–125
  United States, 211–212, 315, 375
Woodward, J. L., 210
Woolsey, Theo. D., 227
World of artifacts, (*Also see* Transporta-
  tion), 263–285
  auxiliary structures, 269–272
  electricity and power, 273
  fire protection, 281–282
  gas, 272–273
  highways, 275–276
  interurban transit, 279–280
  land, 264–266
  land use and behavior patterns, 283–284
  land values and city growth, 265–266
  motorbuses, 277, 279, 281
  multi-dwellings, 266–267
  nonresidential structures, 268
  police protection apparatus, 282, 283
  public utilities, 272–273
  rapid transit, 279
  residential structures, 267–269
  sewers and sewerage disposal, 270–272
  street cars, 277
  terminals, 280–281
  water supply, 269–270
Wu, Pak Si, 42
Wyatt, Woodrow, 96, 114, 119, 120, 125,
  129

Yen, Ching-Yueh, 215, 519
Yinger, J. Milton, 207, 294
Yokohama (*See* Japan)

Zaibaitsu (*See* Japan)
Zimmerman, C. C., 364, 379
Znaniecki, F., 467
Zoning (*Also see* Housing problems), 496,
  527–528
Zorbaugh, H. W., 456, 461, 487

Date Due